Creating Nonfiction

Creating Nonfiction
A Guide and Anthology

Becky Bradway
Wilkes University

Doug Hesse
University of Denver

Bedford/St. Martin's

Boston ◆ *New York*

For Bedford/St. Martin's

Senior Developmental Editor: John Sullivan
Project Editor: Peter Jacoby
Production Supervisor: Jennifer Peterson
Marketing Manager: Molly Parke
Art Director: Anna Palchik
Text Design: Joan O'Connor
Copy Editor: Elizabeth Gardner
Indexer: Kirsten Kite
Cover Design: Donna Lee Dennison
Photo Research: Rachel Youdelman
On the cover: To Jewishness, 2004, by Pelle Cass. Courtesy of the artist. Photographer Pelle Cass (pellecass.com) inscribed the poem "To Jewishness" by New York School poet Kenneth Koch (1925–2002) onto a cup and saucer to make this photograph. Inspired by Koch's innovative poetry, Cass says his aim was to "incorporate a poem into a photograph in a non-clichéd way and to make a work of art that is, all at once, a piece of writing, a sculpture, a drawing, and a photograph."
Composition: Macmillan Publishing Solutions
Printing and Binding: Haddon Craftsmen, Inc., an RR Donnelley & Sons Company

President: Joan E. Feinberg
Editorial Director: Denise B. Wydra
Editor in Chief: Karen S. Henry
Director of Marketing: Karen R. Soeltz
Director of Editing, Design, and Production: Marcia Cohen
Assistant Director of Editing, Design, and Production: Elise S. Kaiser
Managing Editor: Shuli Traub

Library of Congress Control Number: 2008939083

For information, write: Bedford/St. Martin's, 75 Arlington Street, Boston, MA 02116   (617-399-4000)

ISBN-10: 0-312-44706-X
ISBN-13: 978-0-312-44706-9

Acknowledgments

This book is dedicated to David Foster Wallace,
a teacher whose belief in the purpose and
value of every word changed us all.

Preface

From composition and creative writing programs to literature and journalism departments, the demand for courses in creative nonfiction has been on the rise. It is emerging as one of the most important contemporary genres, one that captures the imagination and commitment of student writers. In fusing the conventions of reportage with the aesthetics of literature and the passion for self-expression, it confederates the genres variously known as literary nonfiction, creative nonfiction, literary journalism, or even plain old nonfiction, in all their varieties: essay, place writing, memoir, and so on. *Creating Nonfiction* gathers what we've found most useful over the many years that we've written and taught the genre. It brings together a guide that explains how to read and write creative nonfiction, an anthology that represents the range and variety of contemporary creative nonfiction, and a full complement of additional materials that will encourage and stimulate novice writers. This book, then, serves writers and readers—writing and reading of course entwined—but mostly writers, reflected in our title choice of the verbal, "creating." We've intended it for courses in creative nonfiction, creative writing, advanced writing, prose writing across genres, first year writing, and other courses whose teachers take seriously the art and craft of writing for serious readers, readers who want both to think and to be enlivened. It's also here to serve readers and writers from beyond the university—those who want to write memoirs, travelogues, new journalism, and other creative forms—and those who love to read.

The Guide

The first half of the book is a guide in three parts ("Meanings," "Craft," and "Research") and is devoted to helping students understand and analyze the inner workings of creative nonfiction. We start in part 1, "Meanings," with two chapters that first define creative nonfiction and then exemplify its many traditions. As we note in the first chapter, almost every attempt to define the genre founders at the start, at the very problem of something being "non." So multiple are the subgenres, forms, and kinds of creative nonfiction that to catalog them is to catch the sea in a sieve. Still, we've found that beginning writers, especially, want to understand these distinctions, along with matters like the hazy line between fact and fiction and the ethics of creating nonfiction. That's reasonable. Too, we believe that understanding some traditions and threads actually helps writers; getting the lay of different lands suggests the kinds of crops and buildings that have traditionally worked well there. However, we intend our definitions and kinds to be generative and enabling, not constrictive or disciplining. Better than anyone, we can contest our choices and count exceptions to our categories.

In part 2, "Craft," we turn to chapters on form, description, dialogue, and style. Creative nonfiction includes many techniques to help readers to see situations as fully as the writer does: many are drawn from practices in fiction writing and differ both from those used in traditional academic papers and from purely expressive modes of personal exploration. (While self-discovery may be an important aspect of creative nonfiction writing, fostering it is not the specific aim of this book.) We discuss techniques of style, dramatic organization, and point of view; the relationships among scene, summary, reflection, plotting, pacing, and so on. We illustrate techniques with essay excerpts to explain the ways that writers explore an idea, create a scene, reveal an individual's personality (including her or his own), explore a personal epiphany, and/or make a point. Writers learn not from convenient generic platitudes but, rather, from advice grounded in authors' actual practices. We've distilled such advice into chapters on various facets of planning, shaping, revising, and burnishing creative nonfiction.

We offer no algorithmic gimmicks for writing effective creative nonfiction; we avoid foolish advice that guarantees brilliance. At the same time, creative nonfiction is neither inscrutable nor mysterious. There are tools and tricks of the practice, things that artists and artisans can helpfully show apprentices. Actively understanding technique begins to split the practice of writing from the act of reading. Our approach, then, has been to write as writers to other writers, staying within the bounds of what is helpful and true to the art, craft, and artifacts of creative nonfiction, being as full and clear as space and sensibility permit. We conclude part 2 with a chapter on revision, addressing the practices of professional writers, primarily to emphasize that revision is not (only) a classroom exercise; and we include work from two authors featured in the anthology, Leila Philip and Paul Lisicky, who were kind—and courageous—enough to allow us to reprint drafts of their writing alongside final versions.

One key to reading and writing creative nonfiction is to understand the writer's choice and use of source materials. The final section of the guide, then, is part 3, "Research." Creative nonfiction writers use three main types of sources, almost always in various combinations and proportions. *Memory or lived experience* is simply life as the writer has lived it, without a specific design that those experiences should become materials for writing. *Investigation or intentional observation* purposefully gathers materials for an intended writing project, through such means as interviews, planned experiences, or directed observations. *Readings or research* may furnish materials at the outset of writing or later in the process, by design or by opportunity. The point in discussing these source materials is not to establish boundaries or modes. Indeed, it is the interplay among them that often matters most. Writers who are sensitive to their possibilities have a greater range. The chapters on using writing sources and interviewing illustrate some of these possibilities by discussing excerpts from several works. The final chapter includes exercises that can be used by teachers in the classrooms or by writers working on their own.

The Anthology

The largest part of this book comprises over fifty works of creative nonfiction, arranged alphabetically so as not to impose artificial constraints or orderings. (Alternative contents, by topic, subgenre, and techniques and strategies, are found on page xxiii.) Tempting though a historical tour might have been, we focused on nonfiction as it's being created and published today, by new and established writers. Any anthologists that aspire to guide writers through a new terrain have the responsibility to do so helpfully and sensitively, with respect and care for how the literary land lies.

We made our selections with the following factors in mind:

- *The current and potential importance of the writer.* We include a mixture of very familiar, even canonical writers (such as Annie Dillard and Edward Hoagland) and the best emerging ones (Touré, for instance).

- *The relevance to undergraduate students.* We chose pieces that interest students while challenging them in terms of style, content, and/or construction.

- *The representation of various kinds of Americans (and a few non-Americans).* We've considered race; class; age; gender; personal style; religion; familial, cultural, and geographic origin; and viewpoint.

- *The representation of different types of subjects and approaches.* We chose a spectrum of types, from personal memoir to literary journalism to social commentary to satire, and have included a number of graphic works. We tried to achieve a balance of these types, so that the book would not consist predominantly of memoir. Similarly, we selected a wide range of topics, from Kim Barnes describing the danger and excitement of fighting wildfires in Montana to Guy Delisle, in an excerpt from his graphic novel *Pyongyang*, writing about North Korea.

- *The applicability of the piece to various kinds of writing assignments.* We want this to be as useful a classroom text as possible. We chose teachable texts.

- *The uniqueness of the essay to this anthology.* For the most part, we have not repeated essays published in other creative nonfiction textbooks. Instead, we include fresh, adventurous selections; in one such piece, an excerpt from his book *Candyfreak*, Steve Almond parlays a quirky obsession with confections into a sensitive description of obscure candy and its makers.

We have included editorial apparatus with the readings in the anthology. A photo of each author helps readers get some sense of the writer, and each piece is preceded by a short biographical sketch and a brief introduction placing it in context.

The Interviews

We feel that writers' viewpoints are essential, and our belief is reflected in the twenty-two interviews that Becky conducted with some of the writers featured here, who were extremely generous and generative in their insights. These interviews immediately follow each interviewee's reading selection. With the exception of the Norman Mailer interview, all others—with writers as varied as Rick Moody, Sheryl St. Germain, Gerald Early, Maxine Hong Kingston, and David Foster Wallace—are original to this book and reveal, better than mere description, the thinking and writing practices of working authors. We have selected the interview format over the long craft essay because of its easy reference potential. The spontaneity afforded by the format provides some off-the-cuff honesty on the part of the writers. They also serve to exemplify some of the points made in chapter 9 on interviewing.

Ultimately, we trust writers and teachers to use this book in ways that fit their own needs and experiences. The chapters can be assigned to emphasize style, research, or genre, and appropriate selections from the anthology can be paired to match that emphasis. We've made the richest (and most interesting) book we could, a book of writers and writing, for writers.

Acknowledgments

We appreciate the writers and teachers who reviewed the manuscript in its early versions, including Thomas Amorose, Seattle Pacific University; Rebecca Blevins Faery, Massachusetts Institute of Technology; Michael Martone, University of Alabama; Kirsti Sandy, Keene State College; Valerie

Smith, Quinnipiac University; Jennifer Spinner, Saint Joseph's University; and Jennifer Whetham, Green River Community College. We are also extremely grateful to those writers and reviewers who chose to remain anonymous.

The Bedford/St. Martin's folks have warranted their impeccable professional reputations and then some. We especially thank editor extraordinaire Nancy Perry, for years of wisdom and caring for writing, and B/SM president Joan Feinberg for decisive guidance from atop. Marketing specialist Jimmy Fleming joined many thoughtful, formative conversations. John Sullivan had a nuanced, smart editorial hand and showed patience far beyond what we deserved. His dedication to this book is deeply appreciated. Editorial assistant Alicia Young helped with innumerable details, and image researcher Rachel Youdelman tracked down author photos. Shuli Traub and Peter Jacoby expertly guided us through production. Deeper in our backgrounds are writers and teachers who helped us inform our best thoughts about creative nonfiction: for Doug, Carl Klaus, David Hamilton, Paul Diehl, Susan Lohafer, and David Foster Wallace; for Becky, J. Michael Lennon, Charles Harris, Stephen Koch, and David Foster Wallace. We also thank Lesley Paige Osburn, novelist and student journalist, for her assistance on biographies and especially on writing exercises. She brought a college student's critical eye to the proceedings and told us what beginning writers *really* wanted to know. Becky also thanks her creative nonfiction students at Wilkes University's MFA in Creative Writing Program and at Denver University for giving their feedback as the book's (usually willing) guinea pigs. It's their insight that makes teaching worth doing. The stupid thoughts belong to us.

Above all else, we appreciate the writers who let us publish their work and who let us phone them, e-mail them, postcard them, buttonhole them. Thank you.

Becky Bradway and Doug Hesse
Denver, June 2008

Contents

10 Ideas for Writing 134

Part Four: Anthology 155

Steve Almond, from *Candyfreak* 157
"I hoped to seek out other purebred candyfreaks, men and women who still made bars the old way, in small factories, and who did so not primarily for profit but out of an authentic passion for candy bars."
    Interview with Steve Almond 169

Margaret Atwood, *A Path Taken, with All the Certainty of Youth* 171
"If I had suspected anything about the role I would be expected to fulfill, not just as a writer, but as a female writer—how irrevocably doomed!—I would have flung my leaky blue blob-making ballpoint pen across the room."

Tara Bahrampour, *Persia on the Pacific* 174
"Los Angeles and Iran lie at opposite ends of the world, but for the past twenty-five years—ever since the first Iranians fleeing the revolution established an exile outpost in L.A.—the two places have been closely linked."
    Interview with Tara Bahrampour 185

Kim Barnes, *The Ashes of August* 188
"Born and raised within a fifty-mile radius of where I now live, I have memories of late summer that are infused with fire."
    Interview with Kim Barnes 202

Gabrielle Bell, from *Lucky* [Graphic Memoir] 206
"In order to sustain us through mind-numbing jobs, it is necessary to tell ourselves lies, and mine is that if only I was surrounded by France, I would no longer feel perpetually ill at ease."
    Interview with Gabrielle Bell 215

Sven Birkerts, *Reflections of a Nonpolitical Man; or, Why I Can't in Good Conscience Write about Noam Chomsky* 217
"I faced the difficult fact: I will do nothing overt to further causes I believe in—I will do nothing *political*."

Chester Brown, from *Louis Riel* [Graphic Biography] 224
"Why have I been brought here? I'm not crazy! I'm a prophet! I must free my people!"

toes. . . . It's an effort, I'm guessing, to let him know, if it weren't already obvious, that as much as I want to carry on our parents' legacy, he and I will also be doing some *experimenting*."

"But if I expect pessimism to work, then I'm being optimistic. Which is bad. Isn't it?"

"Of course, the rock paintings are not just pointer signs. They hold far more significance. They refer to a spiritual geography, and are meant to provide teaching and dream guides to generations of Anishinaabeg."

"Catherine. She's my one and only sibling. . . . We were just beginning to hammer out the new terms of our relationship when my marriage went into a skid."

"The administration of Marion, as well as the Bureau of Prisons, maintains that the population of USP-Marion, being radically different from all other prison populations, merits such radical conditions as total lockdown and justifies the forty thousand dollars per year per man that it costs to maintain those conditions."

"Our town was then a kind of modern frontier village, insular and close, full of purpose and people pulling together, like immigrants to a new land."

"In a circus you didn't have to—weren't supposed to—avert your eyes, and that may have been its ultimate kick."

"Eric Robert Rudolph will be formally charged in October for the Northside clinic bombing. Some Bible-based Christians believe that any business offering to stop the human organism's growth in the womb deals in murder, and that whoever kills a man or woman working there saves lives."

"Judging from the reams of odd theories sent daily to science journals, universities, and researchers, science cranks are more prolific than ever."

"Homelessness as a significant problem occurs in countries stricken by war, famine, plague, and natural disaster. And here, in the USA. Why are we not carrying on with ourselves, our neighbors, and the people who represent us the conversation that begins with the question, *What on earth is wrong with us?*"

"As they watched for the next wave, the boys turned toward the ocean. . . . When a good wave arrived, they turned, faced shore, and came shooting in, some taking the wave to the right and some to the left, their bodies fishlike, one arm out in front, the hand and fingers pointed before them, like a swordfish's beak."

"Our freedom as a later generation of Indians has also meant a freedom from Gandhi worship."

"And I see now his faith in his God was learning to winter-out those Pennsylvania winters and those hard communions. But if those communions were difficult, were they empty? . . . Was my father wasting his time? Was he wasting his life?"

"I did not want to civilize war by glorifying it or by forgetting the sacrifices involved."

"Things are happening inside my head. One minute I work on a new song, which I'm planning to send to the producers of *The Partridge Family*, the next I think about the street names in Cambridge Park, a development under construction near our house in Cherry Hill. Everyone who knows me knows that I want to be a builder, a famous builder, like Bill Levitt, when I'm older."

"There was always art in a criminal act—no crime could ever be as automatic as a production process—but graffiti writers were opposite to criminals, since they were living through the stages of the crime in order to commit an artistic act."

"With a patience that rivals Job's, the migrant gathers information, plans, packs, says good-bye to her family, then strikes out. It is not Disneyland she hopes for, but dignity."
"Empty plastic water jugs, a backpack, a baby bottle, soap, Colgate toothpaste, a hairbrush, a sardine can, a sock, and used AeroMéxico tickets."

Alternative Contents

By Topic

Coming of Age

The Culture of Place

Entertainment and Sport

Ethics

Home

Identity

Nature and Science

Race, Society, and Politics

Relationships

By Subgenre

The Essay

Graphic Works

Literary Journalism

Lyric and Reflective Essays

Memoir

By Techniques and Strategies

Describing Events

Explaining a Position

Exploring Cultural Significance

Profiling People and Place

Recalling the Past

Representing Culture and World

Representing Self

PART **1**

Meanings

CHAPTER 1

Defining Creative Nonfiction

Defining something by what it's not is both unsatisfying and perilous. Hundreds of writers and scholars have made this point about the kinds of writing featured in this book. We'll agree that creative nonfiction is an inadequate term for fact-based writing with literary qualities, yet we use it anyway, for reasons we'll explain. We can say that creative nonfiction is supposed to be true (although what "true" means is not at all clear and "facts" can often not be verified). It is what fiction isn't, except very often it reads like a story. It isn't journalism, except when it is (and is then called "new journalism," or "the new new journalism," or "literary journalism"). The writer usually appears as "I," with a strong personal presence (although there are some pieces in which the writer is absent as a character). We can say that creative nonfiction is prose (except when it's mixed with graphics). Nearly every supposition about creative nonfiction can be countered with an example in which it is just not so. Complicating definitions further is the welter of subgenres crowding beneath the creative nonfiction umbrella, diverse in length, topic, approach, and purpose.

> "One unarguable characteristic of creative nonfiction is a strong authorial voice and style."

One unarguable characteristic of creative nonfiction is a strong authorial voice and style. Even if the writer doesn't make a personal appearance, we can tell that a distinct individual has produced those words—and that he or she is yelling or whispering. Unlike types of writing that aspire to objectivity, concealing that a person produced them, works of creative nonfiction wear their making and makers on their sleeves. Still, we assume their writers are making every attempt to tell the truth. It is prose with a narrative

3

trajectory of some kind, writing with a teller. It is prose in which how something is said is as compelling as *what* is said.

Nobody much likes the term *creative nonfiction*. The challenges are many:

- Doesn't all nonfiction require the writer to be creative? Isn't everyone creative?
- What is creative as opposed to uncreative, anyway?
- Why don't they just call it a memoir (or essay or article or history or prose poem or new journalism or whatever it is)?
- Why don't they come up with a better term? What about literary nonfiction? Fictional nonfiction? Nonboring nonfiction?

Oh, people have tried to devise that alternative label. Most of the terms are just too specific; they don't encompass creative nonfiction's many subgenres or take into account the pieces that cross several subgenres. The term *literary nonfiction* is sometimes used interchangeably with creative nonfiction, but it just hasn't stuck. This is mainly because universities with creative writing programs have adopted "creative nonfiction" as a course of study or major emphasis. The more people study creative nonfiction in college, the more standard becomes the use of the term.

Literary nonfiction is actually a more accurate term, since it does connote all of the stylistic and aesthetic elements that make creative nonfiction what it is. The term creative nonfiction, on the other hand, implies that thin line between fact and fiction. If newspaper journalism is too creative, for instance, we assume that it's taking liberties with the facts. "Creative" admits to a bit of open-endedness in the requirement that the writer hew to "just the facts."

A Visit to the Bookstore

A slew of subgenres come together to make up that big hodgepodge that is creative nonfiction. Memoir, personal essay, narrative journalism, the poetic or lyric essay, travel and adventure essays, literary journals, nature and environment writing, profiles, the nonfiction novel, cultural critiques, and even some reviews all come under its heading. Yet much creative nonfiction falls under more than one of these subcategories. Go into your standard bookstore and you rarely find a section expressly for creative nonfiction. These books are scattered all over the store, by subject; they're found under sociology, architecture, travel, political science, and on and on—and often they don't quite belong there. A memoir about a child who travels widely across several continents might end up in travel, biography, African American studies, essay—who knows? Although a book may be less "about" New Zealand and more about the people the writer meets there, it may well be found among the travel guides. In most stores, and in most libraries, there is no simple creative nonfiction place where readers can find the book. The venerable *New York Times Book Review* divides its reviews simply into "fiction" or "nonfiction."

One way to see what is and what isn't creative nonfiction is to wander around that bookstore. Let's say we go in looking for Frank Conroy's memoir, *Stop-Time*. *Stop-Time* is the story of Conroy's childhood and is widely admired for the beauty of the writing and the honesty of the story. (An excerpt from this book is on page 241.) The book's jacket subtitles it "The Classic Memoir of Adolescence." You might find *Stop-Time* in the literature section (if there is one)—or in the essay section (if there is one). But it may well turn up in the biography section, along with all of the movie stars' and politicians' bios, most of which are not creative nonfiction. Memoirs are often sorted in with biographies, which are usually written by historians or journalists. Most biographies don't include either the writer's direct presence or reflections by the writer. They focus less on creating an aesthetically lively artifact than on presenting information. Their main goal is not to move or change readers but to inform them in a way their writers will hope make money.

Stop-Time, on the other hand, is clearly told as a story with dramatic ups and downs and includes the author's feelings and insights. The book moves, often, very close to the perspective of a twelve-year-old—Conroy lets us see his world through the eyes of the child he once was:

> The crowd was silent, watching me. I took a deep breath and threw, following the fall of the yo-yo with my eyes, turning slightly, matador-fashion, as it passed me. My finger caught the string, the yo-yo came up and over, and missed. Without pausing I threw again. "Second time," I yelled, so there would be no misunderstanding. The circle had been too big. This time I made it small, sacrificing beauty for security. The yo-yo fell where it belonged and spun for a moment. (A moment I don't rush, my arms widespread, my eyes locked on the spinning toy. The Trick! There it is, brief and magic, right before your eyes! My hands are frozen in the middle of a deaf-and-dumb sentence, holding the whole airy, tenuous statement aloft for everyone to see.) With a quick snap I broke up the trick and made my catch.

This piece clearly attempts to capture the emotion of a moment in time. It features a child's game. It doesn't want to convince us that the yo-yo is a worthwhile toy, or tell us the history of yo-yos, or give us the physics of a yo-yo's spin. Certainly there is nonfiction that does just that. From this one paragraph of Conroy's, we get the sense that this piece is a story, a narrative. If we didn't know better, we might think it was fiction, but since this book labels itself a memoir, we must assume that what Conroy is telling us is fundamentally true.

Here's another example. Wandering down the Travel aisle, we come across the book *The Global Soul* by Pico Iyer. Iyer, who was raised in India, educated in Britain, and now lives in Japan, often writes of the way the world is becoming a single global nation. Because he often writes about being in transit, with pieces set in different countries, his books nearly always get filed under Travel. Yet Iyer's books will never tell you which hotel has the best rates or which highway has the least traffic, even though they are probably perched right beside the travel guides.

How can you tell this without reading the whole book? Flip to nearly any page of *The Global Soul* and you'll be greeted by an "I." (And it *is* a kind of greeting, creating a sense that the writer trusts the reader enough to reveal himself.) Glancing through the book, you'll see that along with its reflections, there are plenty of facts: the airport in L.A. has its own $10-million office, Toronto is the most multicultural city in the world, and in 1930, Atlanta was the second-largest city in the world in terms of office space. You won't see facts like these in *Stop-Time*, yet both are works of creative nonfiction. While Iyer imparts all manner of random information, the book is not mainly about the facts, and people don't read it for the facts alone. They read it to enjoy good stories set in all kinds of places, or because they like the cleverness of the book's structure, or because of the writer's background and sense of humor. But someone who wanted to find out the best museum in Atlanta would probably not pick up Iyer's book—it would just be too opinionated, stylistic, scattered, and personal.

Finally, you might be looking for a collection of essays by novelist Leslie Marmon Silko. (Her essay "Uncle Tony's Goat" is found on page 666.) Her book *Yellow Woman and a Beauty of the Spirit* focuses upon various aspects of contemporary Native American life and mythology. It also includes a number of pieces about environmental catastrophe. Where in the bookstore might you find it?

Logically, *Yellow Woman* would be found in the essays section—but this is rather unlikely. It will probably turn up in the sociology, social issues, or Native American sections. It may even be shelved beside Silko's novels in Fiction. If you were a casual browser, Silko's book might easily be overlooked.

What Creative Nonfiction Is Probably Not

So now that we've acknowledged the lack of consensus about what creative nonfiction is and where it belongs, we can move on to what it isn't. It isn't traditional newspaper journalism, or logical argument, or academic examination, or a business report. A creative nonfiction writer doesn't aim necessarily to persuade or inform the reader but to move her. The goal isn't to relay facts in an objective tone—precisely the opposite. People read creative nonfiction not because they have to but because they want to. They read it not to exhume information or ideas (although they may well) but rather for the quality of the reading experience itself.

Despite the use of poetic lyricism and fictional scene, creative nonfiction is not a fabrication, a

"A creative nonfiction writer doesn't aim necessarily to persuade or inform the reader but to move her."

fiction. It is supposed to be true to the author's best ability. The story and people in creative nonfiction are based upon actual events, people, and information. The complications of relaying the truth and working through the black, white, and grey areas of "fact" haunt us (and taunt us). When a writer decides what "truth" is, he is going through a very personal process of intuition and evaluation. Since a written work is not reality itself, and since art requires imagination, how does a writer tell a true story in an artful, honest manner? There is no simple answer to this riddle.

Creative nonfiction makes no pretense of objectivity; the writer admits that she is coming from her own point of view. Writers want to bring readers into their worlds. Even when we want to repulse readers, we still want them to pay attention. While the distance between reader and writer is narrowed in the moments of reading, this doesn't necessarily mean that the writer is revealing details of her own personal life. The nitty-gritty of the writer's life may not enter into the piece at all. The writer's *persona* is there, though—we are aware of this person, this voice. The voice and style are what make a piece personal—not the confession of intimate knowledge or experience. In creative nonfiction that voice is never neutral, as it is supposed to be in journalistic or business writing. The language that projects the writer's voice is inventive and stylistic, sometimes lyrical, sometimes conversational, occasionally elegant. That voice can be engaging, abrasive, hesitant, cranky, philosophical—but it is not invisible. The voice reminds us that there is not only a human behind this work, but a specific (and, we hope, interesting) flawed human, at that.

Creative nonfiction even allows for literary license: reconstructing scenes and dialogue, even reporting what a subject is—or might be—thinking. The ultimate question might be: Why does this form even exist? Why not just write fiction? Or journalism?

It exists because it has to. Creative nonfiction is more than just "using the real names." It allows the writer to do things that can't be done in either fiction or journalism—it breaks through walls on all sides.

The diarist and scholar of the essay Carl Klaus has observed that the essay has a dual nature: it is a story of events that is also a story of the writer's mental journey. Creative nonfiction usually displays a kind of self-consciousness—a need to comment on the process of writing "reality" and a need to examine the writer's own position in and upon the events. This compulsive drive toward honesty is understood only by the individual writer; he may simply need to tell the story in that way, finding fiction too masked and too defined by its own genre conventions.

Creative nonfiction writers usually feel the need to explore an idea in a direct and complex way—in a manner that doesn't generally take place in the always-show-never-tell environment of fiction and that is usually too limited by the space and authorial restrictions of journalism. Virginia Woolf said that this "fierce attachment to an idea" is the essay's "backbone." For many writers, chasing an idea is compelled by a need to right a wrong, to reform. "When I sit down to write a book," George Orwell said, "I do not say to myself, 'I am going to produce a work of art.' I write it because there is some lie that I want to expose, some fact to which I want to draw attention, and my initial concern is to get a hearing." Creative nonfiction nearly always pleads for understanding, whether it be of a social problem or something as seemingly mundane as the isolation of childhood.

Lawrence Weschler, a complex and unusual essayist, explained why he writes creative nonfiction:

> The part of my sensibility which I demonstrate in nonfiction makes fiction an impossible mode for me. That's because to me the world is already filled to bursting with interconnections, interrelationships, consequences, and consequences of consequences. The world as it is is overdetermined: the web of all those interrelationships is dense to the point of saturation. That's what my reporting becomes about: taking any single knot and worrying out the threads, tracing the interconnections, following the mesh through into the wide, outlying mesh, establishing the proper analogies, ferreting out the false strands. If I were somehow to be forced to write a fiction about, say, a make-believe Caribbean island, I wouldn't know where to put it, because the Caribbean as it is is already full—there's no room in it for any fictional islands. Dropping one in there would provoke a tidal wave, and all other places would be swept away.

As for the option of writing journalism instead—well, that's not an option. "Essays belong to the animal kingdom," said Edward Hoagland, "with a surface that generates sparks, like a coat of fur, compared with the flat, conventional cotton of the magazine article writer, who works in the vegetable kingdom, instead." The forms are entirely different, as this book will, we hope, make clear.

Creative nonfiction allows for a certain looseness of exploration. Some writers (like both of us) are attracted to creative nonfiction for its very lack of definition. Over 250 years ago Samuel Johnson defined the essay as "a loose sally of the mind; an irregular indigested piece; not a regular and orderly composition." This very irregularity is what makes creative nonfiction so much fun to write, if the writer is comfortable with that openness.

Creative Nonfiction Referenced in This Chapter

Conroy, Frank. *Stop-Time*. New York: Penguin, 1977.

Hoagland, Edward. "What I Think, What I Am." In *Modern American Prose: Fifteen Writers + 15*, 3rd ed., edited by John Clifford and Robert DiYanni. New York: McGraw-Hill, 1993.

Iyer, Pico. *The Global Soul: Jet Lag, Shopping Malls, and the Search for Home*. New York: Vintage, 2001.

Silko, Leslie Marmon. *Yellow Woman and a Beauty of the Spirit*. New York: Simon & Schuster, 1997.

Weschler, Lawrence. "In Lieu of a Preface: Why I Can't Write Fiction." In *Vermeer in Bosnia*: *Selected Writings*. New York: Vintage, 2005.

Woolf, Virginia. "The Modern Essay." In *The Common Reader*, First Series. San Diego and; New York: Harvest Books, 1984. First published 1925 by Harcourt.

Works about Writing and Literature

Johnson, Samuel. *A Dictionary of the English Language*. London, 1755.

Klaus, Carl, Chris Anderson, and Rebecca Blevins Faery. *In Depth: Essayists for Our Time*. Fort Worth: Harcourt Brace Jovanovich, 1993.

Orwell, George. "Why I Write." In *Why I Write*. New York: Penguin Books, 2005.

CHAPTER 2

The Plentiful Permutations of Creative Nonfiction

Creative nonfiction hosts seemingly endless genres. It's tempting to say that naming and defining all of these categories is irrelevant. While most creative nonfiction doesn't fit easily into any single subcategory, we seem to want labels anyway, perhaps to reduce confusion for readers and booksellers and academicians. More importantly, we think that understanding different subgenres of creative nonfiction can help writers recognize their options. So a bit of history and explanation of common genres are in order.

A Scant History

It's nearly impossible to mark the origin of creative nonfiction, even keeping only to the Western tradition. Plato's *Dialogues*, with their scenes and re-created conversations, for example, are hardly straightforward nonfictional treatises. Practically and conventionally, though, the sixteenth century is a useful starting place. In 1580 Michel de Montaigne published his *Essais* (literally, "tries"), relatively short works that combine autobiography, opinion, and information on topics ranging from smells to cannibals, in a style more associative than formally logical. Thus the origins of the essay are a far cry from the stuffy school genre commonly conjured by the term today. Some twenty years later, Francis Bacon called his own aphoristic and freeflowing works essays, too, though they lacked Montaigne's autobiographical presence. While scattered books—Jeremy Taylor's 1650 *Holy Living*, Thomas Browne's 1658 *Urne Burial*, Abraham Crowley's 1667

Essays (which intermixed poetry and prose)—represent early forays into creative nonfiction, the rise of periodical publications at the end of the seventeenth and beginning of the eighteenth centuries most directly energized these genres.

Prominent among them are Joseph Addison and Richard Steele's *Tatler* and *Spectator*, twice-weekly publications published from 1709 to 1712 that had brief essays, character sketches, and short fictions, sometimes contributed by writers like Jonathan Swift. Benjamin Franklin emulated these publications in many of his own essays (even including one on farts) and wrote a famous *Autobiography*.

It took early-nineteenth-century Romanticism, which celebrated individuals' experiences and direct encounters with natural phenomena, to generate more recognizably contemporary creative nonfiction forms. Periodicals remained vital to essayists like Charles Lamb (a contemplative and confessional personal essayist), William Hazlitt (a critic and sometime journalist), and Thomas De Quincey (whose works include the 1821 *Confessions of an English Opium Eater*). Mary Russell Mitford's sketches of English village life, first published in *The Ladies Magazine* in 1819 and later collected as *Our Village*, represent an early tradition of nature writing most famously exemplified by Henry David Thoreau's *Walden*. Mark Twain's raucous *Roughing It* and *Innocents Abroad* demonstrate a vibrant tradition of literary travel writing.

Essayists like Virginia Woolf traveled more the terrain of books and ideas, though Woolf's volumes of *A Common Reader* include lyrical and personal nonfiction, too, such as her much anthologized "The Death of a Moth." Other mid-twentieth-century periodical writers like E. B. White used personal experiences (in White's case, of life in New York City and on a farm on the Maine coast) to frame observations on contemporary life. These appeared primarily in magazines like *Harper's* and *The New Yorker*, which continue to provide prominent venues for creative nonfiction, along with scores of literary magazines (think of *The Georgia Review* or the *Missouri Review*) and book presses, large and small.

Mainstream periodicals, of course, feature "news" and "articles" as well as the kinds of "features" that encompass creative nonfiction. In the last half of the twentieth century, a journalistic tradition arose to complement the "objective" stance of traditional reportage. In this "new journalism" (from authors as diverse as Hunter S. Thompson in *Rolling Stone*, Tom Wolfe in the *New York World Tribune*, and Joan Didion in *Esquire* and *Travel and Leisure*), the author's personality and perspectives are as much the focus as the people or events being profiled.

Magazines haven't been the only scene for this type of creative nonfiction. George Orwell's book *The Road to Wigan Pier* (1937) is an example of aesthetic first-person immersion journalism; it describes Orwell living three months among working-class families in northern England. In like fashion, John McPhee spent months aboard a merchant marine vessel to write *Looking for a Ship* (1990), and Jennifer Price explored cookbooks, films, and the Mall of America to write *Flight Maps: Adventures with Nature in Modern America* (1999).

Nowadays, all kinds of publishers have embraced creative nonfiction, and so have all manner of writers—this writing moving from sideline tributary to main channel. Annie Dillard's "Author's Note" in *Teaching a Stone to Talk* (1982) now seems almost quaint. Dillard observed that

> "Nowadays, all kinds of publishers have embraced creative nonfiction."

> some of these have not been published before; others such as "Living Like Weasels" and "The Deer at Providencia," were published obscurely. At any rate, this is not a collection of occasional pieces, such as a writer brings out to supplement his real work; instead this is my real work, such as it is.

As essayists, as journalists, as *writers,* people who are creating nonfiction continue to find expectant readers for their work, for reasons perhaps enmeshed at some level with wide interests in reality television—which is scarcely real, after all. In the current scene, as has been true for the past century, creative nonfiction writers can successfully publish both essays and book-length work. Michael Pollan, for example, published two of the four pieces in *The Botany of Desire* (2001) in the *New York Times Magazine* before developing the larger book. Writers who identify topics as plain as potatoes (one of Pollan's chapters) or lofty as astronauts (the subject of Tom Wolfe's *The Right Stuff*, 1980) and who can write about them with style and personality will be able to choose from many of creative nonfiction's many tributaries: the essay, the memoir, travel writing, journalism, and others.

Memoir

When many people think of creative nonfiction, what usually pops into their heads is one subgenre: memoir. Memoir writers re-create their pasts. What this means varies tremendously based upon the writer's style, position in life, purpose for writing the book, and age. A memoir doesn't necessarily cover the entire span of a life; most explore only a brief period or flash between one time and another, past to present and back. Autobiographies aspire to a bigger sweep, encompassing the entirety of a life with the goal of a fairly complete picture. While some memoirs have as their purpose explaining the whys and hows of the writer's personal life, many use the memoir as a way to explore a particular subject or idea.

Memoirs are rarely overviews of "she was born, she lived, she died." The most popular memoirs usually tell about "how I became notorious/ powerful" and "these are the movie stars/artists/politicians I met." These sorts of popular memoirs are usually read not for their literary value but for their gossip quotient. Most of them aren't really creative nonfiction because they don't use inventive language and style, don't have a voice, and are often written by cowriters or ghostwriters.

These memoirs give memoir a bad name.

Good memoirs attempt to give form to the formless, to bring coherence to the random, meaningless details of a life. Some of the best are stories of childhood. We've mentioned Frank Conroy's *Stop-Time* in chapter 1. Another example is Paul Lisicky's essay "New World," found on page 509. Lisicky's piece reflects a kind of universal discomfort that nearly everyone has experienced as a child. If the label didn't tell you it was creative nonfiction, you might think that it was a short story. It uses vivid descriptions, dialogue, and the interior perceptions of a young child. The piece goes further than just saying "this happened to me"; it demonstrates the inability to understand the actions of mysterious adults and the resulting insecurity.

Some memoirs serve in some measure to examine culture. An example of this is Tara Bahrampour's book *To See and See Again* (1999), which explores her childhood as an Iranian American. (An essay by Tara Bahrampour, "Persia on the Pacific," can be found on page 174.) Her use of scene, emotion, and a child's perception place it in the realm of the literary memoir, taking it far from the territory of sociology:

> "The news, the news!" Baba clicked the buttons on the motel TV, frowning at the lag time before the picture bloomed over the screen. All at once, Peter Jennings' face appeared and his voice blasted painfully down onto our beds.
>
> "We're not deaf," I said, peeling the tissue off my grilled cheese sandwich, feigning indifference.
>
> "Shhhhh!" Baba answered.
>
> We watched the whole broadcast turned up high. During the ads, Baba frantically flipped through the other channels, trying to find Tehran, as if any second the revolution might be over and we could go back home, if only we didn't miss the news segment that told us so.

To See and See Again is driven not by a sense of "I'm going to tell you everything about myself" but by the author's desire for people to understand the identity conflicts experienced by all immigrants, by Iranian Americans, and, finally, by herself.

Dave Eggers's *A Heartbreaking Work of Staggering Genius* (2001, excerpted on page 342) is a literary memoir that has had a sustained popularity. There are a couple of reasons: it tells the rather sad story of a teenager who raises his younger brother after his parents' deaths, and it is written in an entertaining way. It is, above all, quirky, melding scenes, asides, lists, pop culture references, digressions, drawings, and pretty much everything else into one five-hundred-page package. It was written when Eggers was twenty-nine. *Heartbreaking* is less a personal sorting-out than a conglomeration of ideas, stories, and images intended to engage readers. It has little of the personal reflection that characterizes, say, a private diary.

About those diaries.

A diary is another permutation of memoir. Most diaries are unrevised and spontaneous writing, usually covering day-to-day events in the writer's life. Most personal diaries are published because of the writer's notoriety or death, or because of a specific historical value. A rare few are published because they are beautifully written and uncommonly revealing, as with the diaries of Anaïs Nin. Often journals are excerpted and used in the context of a longer piece, as when a writer quotes from her own or someone else's journal. (Robin Hemley's 1998 book *Nola*, for one, uses passages from his schizophrenic sister's journals, as well as his own.) Here we're clearly speaking of printed diaries, not the ubiquitous blog. More on those shortly.

A different kind of diary is Karen Tei Yamashita's *Circle K Cycles* (2001; a chapter is on page 779). It's a chronological account of events, poems, recipes, and musings, all of them carefully revised. In this case, "diary" is less a personal, confessional account than a kind of collection of events from a particular time in the writer's life, recounted in a *seemingly* free-form and random way. Another example of this type of diary is graphic writer Julie Doucet's *My New York Diary* (1999)—a book that is certainly no casual construction, given its detailed illustrations, but which does tell a revealing story of Doucet's time in New York City.

Today most public diaries aren't found on the bookstore shelves, but on the Internet. Blogs require no editor—just a bunch of peers and strangers willing to click the link. Personal blogs serve both as confessional diaries and as mass mailings. But most of them aren't interesting enough to sustain preservation in books. The exception is that rare well-written blog composed by someone caught in a historical moment, such as the Iraqi blogger Salam Pax, whose blog entries were published by Grove Press, or exceptional authors such as Andrew Sullivan and S. L. Wisenberg, whose online columns are often expanded into fully developed essays for book publication. (Wisenberg's essay "Holocaust Girls/Lemon" appears on page 774.)

"A good literary memoir transcends its moment."

For the most part, though, diaries don't make very interesting sustained reading. There are so many confessions out there that we need something arresting to make us pay attention. Often, once the diary is removed from the urgency of the moment or the direct address to readers, it begins to lose its power.

A good literary memoir, on the other hand, transcends its moment. It ultimately doesn't rely on the writer's fame or connections but on the quality of its story and language.

With memoirs, there's no avoiding questions about truth and art. Of all forms of creative nonfiction, none is more often attacked than the memoir, usually for issues of "truth." Although accusations of writers "making things up" have only recently appeared on *Oprah*, they've been hurled for decades. George Orwell embellished his memoirs; Lillian Hellman and Mary McCarthy swapped litigious accusations over one another's "lies"; Sherwood Anderson created false backgrounds for his family members. Some people object to anything being fabricated, including "remembered" dialogue and scenes. Others defend manipulating facts as essential to reaching truth. Timothy Dow Adams, a scholar of autobiography, defends Sherwood Anderson's distortions, saying that his

> cavalier way with facts, his predilection for story over history, his manipulation in print of people's characters, and his insistence that if some of the people who appear in his books did not actually say the words ascribed to them, then they should have—all of these combine to present a truer picture of Anderson than a straightforward, factual biography could.

George Orwell's memoir/journalistic account, *Down and Out in Paris and London*, published in 1933, tells his experiences as a poverty-stricken drifter who meets an array of rather sad characters. Since its publication, it has been subject to angry defenses of and objections to its recreations, exaggerations, and outright lies. The criticism begins with Orwell's presentation of himself as poor, continues through the re-created dialogue, and points out the possible fabrication of the characters. Its defenders' reactions come down to a rather vociferous "So what? It's still a great book."

In the following excerpt Orwell quotes a homeless man at a Salvation Army shelter:

> "I tell you what, boys, I'm going to get that job tomorrow. I'm not one of your bloody down-on-the-knee brigade; I can look after myself. Look at that—notice there! 'The Lord will provide!' A bloody lot He's ever provided me with. You don't catch me trusting to the —— Lord. You leave it to me, boys. I'M GOING TO GET THAT JOB," etc. etc.
>
> I watched him, struck by the wild, agitated way in which he talked; he seemed hysterical, or perhaps a little drunk. An hour later I went into a small room, apart from the main hall, which was intended for reading. It had no books or papers in it, so few of the lodgers went there. As I opened the door I saw the young clerk in there all alone; he was on his knees, PRAYING. Before I shut the door again I had time to see his face, and it looked agonized. Quite suddenly I realized, from the expression of his face, that he was starving.

Did the man's tirade take place? Did the starving man exist? Orwell would say that what matters is that men starve, and that it is crucial that this be addressed. He would say, no doubt, that the entire debate misses the point.

A number of writers have attempted to avoid the fact/fiction/ lie/truth controversy by dodging the question. They call their works "a memoir in stories," or a "fictional autobiography." Mary McCarthy originally published her classic memoir *Memories of a Catholic Girlhood* as a series of short stories; the book edition was called a memoir. Yet even writers who choose to call memoirs fiction risk accusations of fabrication by those who suspect that the events are "true." Writers may be accused of embellishing by some, withholding by others.

The question of truth haunts even the most conscientious writers. No matter how much we wish to present the clear and simple facts of our lives, it is impossible to do so. Literary writers by nature drift between the realms of imagination and "reality." As much as we try to be accurate, we will find ourselves turning those damned facts into art.

Memoirist Patricia Hampl writes, "We find, in our details and broken and obscured images, the language of symbol. Here memory impulsively reaches out its arms and embraces imagination. That is the resort to invention. It isn't a lie, but an act of necessity, as the innate urge to locate personal truth always is."

Many essayists have questioned their choices and even wondered whether writing nonfiction is ethical. Ultimately, the bottom line: They needed, for whatever reasons, to tell that particular story. The best they could do was not to tell a deliberate lie. In "Marketing Memory," Bernard Cooper scrutinizes his own motives, and then admits to the essential problem: publication.

> The process of writing a memoir is insular, ruminative, a mining of privacies; once published, however, the book becomes an act of extroversion, an advertisement to buy, a performance of self rather than its articulation. The gap between these two experiences—the creation of a memoir and the ramifications of having written one—is wide enough, it seems to me, to bewilder even the most poised and gregarious among us.

Joan Didion expressed her frustration with the whole debate by saying, "Not only have I had trouble distinguishing between what happened and what merely might have happened, but I remain unconvinced that the distinction, for my purposes, matters. . . . How it felt to me. That is getting closer to the truth."

Finally, each writer has to make her own decisions about the act of writing and the risks involved once something is written. If George Orwell had worried about achieving "perfect truth," we'd have no *Down and Out in Paris and London*; Virginia Woolf wouldn't have written her diaries. The best memoirs are so beautifully written, so fundamentally honest in spirit and import that they ultimately transcend the endless debate of truth versus lie. They are not important because of what they confess but because of their voice, style, and ability to vividly capture a particular time and place.

The Essay

By heritage, the essay is not the tormented genre of schooling and pedantic prose. As we suggested above, owing to their origin with Montaigne's "tries," essays are surely the most protean and personable of short nonfiction. However, as Robert Scholes and Carl Klaus pointed out forty years ago, *essay* came to be used as a catch-all term for nonfiction prose of limited length—including "the essay test," which has come to mean any exam that requires more than clicking buttons or penciling ovals. Such exams, which tend to have students demonstrate that they know what authorities know, actually oppose the essay tradition. The defining feature of the essay is a sense of exploration and reflection in which the author's shaping consciousness and, quite often, experience are ever present in a form that is organic to the topic and purpose at hand. Let's unpack that.

Just as creative nonfiction divides into several genres, so do essays. Scholes and Klaus offered a still useful scheme for categorizing elements of essays. "The essay as story" describes those works that are primarily—even exclusively—narrative. George Orwell's "A Hanging," a first-person account of watching a Burmese prisoner going to the gallows in the 1930s, is an example of a piece consisting almost entirely of reported events, with fairly little commentary. Annie Dillard's essay "Total Eclipse" is primarily narrative in its account of events before, during, and after watching a solar eclipse, but Dillard interrupts that narrative with reflection and even some information that doesn't seem part of the main story: information about mining and transportation to ancient Sumeria.

"The essay as poem" refers to works that use imagistic and associative language to create a mood, evoke an attitude or feeling, or form an aesthetically engaging text. Today such essays are better known as "lyric essays," and we discuss them at greater length later in this chapter.

"The essay as drama" describes works in which conversation among two or more people plays a strong role. Plato's *Dialogues* obviously fit into this category, as do interviews or profiles that rely heavily on a scene and the back-and-forth exchanges between the writer and his or her subject. Scholes and Klaus offer the example of E. M. Forster's "The Graves at Gallipoli," in which dead soldiers are represented talking to each other.

Finally, Klaus and Scholes offer the category of "the essay as essay," works that focus on presenting ideas or a particular point of view. Such essays explore topics, intermingling facts or experiences with analysis or reflections, as Montaigne did in his essay on "Cannibals" or as Gerald Early does in " 'I Only Like It Better When the Pain Comes': More Notes toward a Cultural Definition of Prizefighting" (on page 320). These essays of ideas differ from straight arguments or articles because of their imaginative qualities and their writers' presence and voice.

There are other ways of categorizing essays. One is by various traditions, typical subject matters, or approaches. "Personal" or "familiar"

essays address readers as confidants and friends, and are often about subjects that are personal or seemingly trivial. They often overlap with memoirs.
"Place essays" (we discuss later the larger category of place writing) focus
on nature, travel, or specific locations. "Profiles" focus on people, going
beyond interviews or biographies to draw out deeper qualities of the person at the heart of the work. Consider, for example, Cynthia Ozick's essay
"What Helen Keller Saw" (page 623).

While there are some "pure" examples of each type, the point is not
to sort all essays into categories. It's more useful to think of these as tendencies, and most essays combine several elements. Still, categories are a
handy point of reference, and we offer a few more that we find useful.

Critiques, Rants, and Reviews

Certain creative nonfiction writers are cranky. Their rants, complaints, and
evaluations cross all creative nonfiction lines, and are often embedded in
pieces larger than the rant itself. Nature writing, for one, has a long tradition of the tirade. While there may be long passages
waxing poetically about mountains, there are likely
also complaints about the snowmobiles cascading
down the nearby slope. Some writers thrive on their
free-flowing rages: Hunter S. Thompson and Edward
Abbey, for two.

"Some writers thrive on their
free-flowing rages."

What makes this different from, say, Ann Coulter or most ranting
blogs is that the writers couch their rampages within a good story and
among vivid descriptive passages. They give a full picture, providing
plenty of context and backing up their own personal viewpoint with a
scenic truth. The narrator usually represents herself as a distinctive character, allowing the reader to accept the rant by either identifying with the
narrator or seeing it as part of the writer's quirky sensibility.

Here is a brief excerpt from Edward Abbey's environmentalist classic,
Desert Solitaire. This rant goes on for a chapter; in this section, he offers
the third of his many suggestions for improving the national parks:

> Put the park rangers to work. Lazy scheming loafers, they've wasted too many
> years selling tickets at toll booths and sitting behind desks filling out charts
> and tables in the vain effort to appease the mania for statistics which torments
> the Washington office. Put them to work. They're supposed to be rangers—
> make the bums range; kick them out of those overheated air-conditioned
> offices, yank them out of those overstuffed patrol cars, and drive them out on
> the trails where they should be, leading the dudes over hill and dale, safely
> into and back out of the wilderness. It won't hurt them to work off a little
> office fat; it'll do them good, help take their minds off each other's wives,
> and give them a chance to get out of reach of the boss—a blessing for all
> concerned.

The reason most readers stick with Abbey on his tear is because he's already pulled us in, and because he is entertaining. By this time, we have already walked mountains, talked with miners, and observed cacti. We know Abbey's cantankerous nature, his background, and his sense of humor. If we like him, we'll ride with him through the rants and perhaps even be convinced by them. And this is how most creative nonfiction writers mount an argument: rather than diagramming it, or laying it out point by logical point, they get us to see the world through their eyes. If Abbey can convince us of the beauty of his undisturbed desert by having us experience its transcendent joys, then we will probably accept that its destruction is not a good thing. And if the reader has not been convinced, he probably will not have read long enough to get to the rant, anyway.

Another kind of argument is more subtle in tone than Abbey's but just as definite in its position. Barbara Kingsolver's piece "Household Words," found on page 471, expresses her outrage with a tone of injured compassion. She draws us into the essay by describing an event that could happen to anybody: driving home, she witnesses a violent attack against a homeless woman and does nothing. The other witnesses to the event also do nothing. "I did and I didn't leave her behind," she says, "because I'm still thinking and now writing about this scene." Yet the essay excoriates Kingsolver and, really, all of us, the witnesses. The piece moves away from the particular incident and into a larger discussion of society's responsibilities, then goes a level further to explore the very meaning of home and of its absence. At this philosophical level she enters the realm of the essay tradition, beyond what might otherwise have been an opinion item in the newspaper.

A review, on the other hand, is usually less angry or strident than an argument; they are often cooler and more reasonable in tone. Most reviews aren't creative nonfiction. They're written to a specified length for a magazine or newspaper and follow certain conventions. Most reviewers don't have a great deal of latitude in form or even time to develop an idea. Creative reviews are often longer, more complex pieces by authors established enough to be able to break usual journalistic rules. Their works often include references that seem removed from the immediate review subject, and may have an autobiographical element. An example is a piece from the *New Yorker* by Adam Gopnik, "Times Regained," which is both an objection to the gentrification of Times Square and a review of books about that place. Gopnik's piece is clearly creative nonfiction because of its style and breadth:

> Now, of course, we have the new Times Square, as fresh as a neon daisy, with a giant Gap and a Niketown and an Applebee's and an ESPN Zone and television announcers visible through tinted windows, all family retailing and national brands. In some ways, the Square has never looked better, with the diagonal sloping lines of the Reuters Building, the curving Deco zipper, even the giant mock dinosaur in the Toys R Us. There are, of course, people who miss the old Times Square, its picturesque squalor and violence and misery and exploitation. Those who pointed at the old Times Square as an instance

of everything that capitalism can do wrong now point to the new Times Square as an instance of everything that capitalism can do worse.

Clearly, someone who calls Times Square a "neon daisy" is not writing as a pure journalist or scholar. Gopnik doesn't even talk about the books until after four long paragraphs. (Few newspapers would ever put up with such a transgression.) Gopnik then compares the books in a thoughtful but irreverent way. (One book, he says, is "full of eye-opening material, if one can keep one's eyes open long enough to find it," while the other is "an engaged civics lesson.") The essay does do the proper work of a review, which is to critique the works and give a sense of their content, but it also goes much further by presenting its own opinionated description of Times Square.

When able to work in a creative nonfiction mode, critics and debaters have plenty of room to develop a subject, give context and depth, use associative and aesthetic strategies rather than formulae. Creative reviews have particularly found a place in music publications, with writers like Lester Bangs and Touré peppering their work with slang, rants, asides, and general irreverencies. Some sportswriters also have a crazy observational quality (which is probably why Hunter S. Thompson ended up working for ESPN). But it remains rare that reviewers have this liberty, and even when they do, they have the argumentative responsibility of building a persuasive case.

Lyric and Reflective Essays

Reflection is, by definition, "the act of turning back." In a reflection, the writer is usually seeking to understand an experience, observation, or text, exploring it for meanings and connections. Reflections are contemplative and often lyrical in tone. The writer is in effect gazing into a pool of water—taking a breather from the action, whether that action takes place in the essay, or in the realm of the "real" world. Reflections mirror the writer's mood and personality and the subject at hand. When part of a long piece, the reflection is most often found in place writing and memoir, the most introspective of the forms. When a reflection exists as a piece of its own and has a looping quality and minimal narrative trajectory, it has become known as a lyric essay.

The following excerpt from E. B. White's "Once More to the Lake" is a classic example of a traditional essayistic reflection:

Summertime, oh, summertime, pattern of life indelible, the fade-proof lake, the woods unshatterable, the pasture with the sweetfern and the juniper forever and ever, summer without end; this was the background, and the life along the shore was the design, the cottagers with their innocent and tranquil design, their tiny docks with the flagpole and the American flag floating against the white clouds in the blue sky, the little paths over the roots of the trees leading from camp to camp and the paths leading back to the outhouses and the canoes and the postcards that showed things looking a little better than they looked. This was the American family at play.

This lyrical piece centers around visual imagery; we can imagine standing with White and seeing, along the shore, the docks, woods, canoes, trees. It's a hopeful scene, all Americana.

But reflections don't have to be about pretty or pleasant things, or to address the subjects that might be associated with the word *lyrical*.

In the literary essay "What's Inside You, Brother?" (page 724), Touré tells of his experiences at a boxing gym (referring to himself in third person throughout much of the piece):

Sometimes Touré will be in the heart of the circle, maybe sparring with Jack, hands up, headgear laced tight, lungs heavy, ribs stinging after Jack backs him into a corner and slices a sharp left uppercut through Touré's elbows into the soft, very top section of his stomach. Then, for Touré, time stops. He loses control of his body, feels briefly suspended in air, his thoughts seemingly hollered to him from far away. Life is never faster than in the ring, except when you're reeling from a razing punch. Then, life is never slower. Sometimes Touré will be in the heart of the circle sparring, but I don't know why: he's not very good.

In "What Helen Keller Saw" (page 623), Cynthia Ozick writes about teacher Annie Sullivan's work with Helen Keller. Rather than using matter-of-fact language, Ozick captures the *spirit* of Annie Sullivan's work with the deaf, comparing her method of tapping Helen's palm with the artistic act of writing:

Like any writer, she wrote and wrote and wrote, all day long. She wrote words, phrases, sentences, lines of poetry, descriptions of animals, trees, flowers, weather, skies, clouds, concepts: whatever lay before her or came usefully to mind. She wrote not on paper with a pen, but with her fingers, spelling rapidly into the child's alert palm. Helen, quick to imitate yet uncomprehending, was under a spell of curiosity (the pun itself reveals the manual alphabet as a magical tool). Her teacher spelled into her hand; she spelled the same letters back, mimicking unknowable configurations. But it was not until the connection was effected between finger-wriggling and its referent— the cognitive key, the insight, the crisis of discovery—that what we call mind broke free.

Nature writing is particularly known for its reflective passages, since the writer often experiences long moments of contemplative solitude. Louise Erdrich's essay "Big Grass" refers to a sense (in this case, smell) and an old notion ("all flesh is grass"—a recognition of death and renewal).

It is that smell of winter dust I love best, rising from the cracked stalk. Tenacious in its cycle, stubborn in its modest refusal to die, the grass embodies the philosopher's myth of eternal return. All flesh is grass is not a depressing conceit to me. To see ourselves within our span as creatures capable of quiet and continual renewal gets me through those times when the writing stinks, I've lost my temper, overloaded on wine chocolates, or am simply lost to myself. Snow melts. Grass springs back. Here we are on a quiet rise, finding the first uncanny shoots of green.

My daughters' hair has a scent as undefinable as grass—made up of mood and weather, of curiosity and water. They part the stiff waves of grass, gaze into the sheltered universe. Just to be, just to exist—that is the talent of grass.

This passage expresses hope in the face of loss. It also has a sense of the solid and the concrete (*stiff, hair, chocolates*) along with its metaphysical qualities. The landscape Erdrich adores in this essay is North Dakota's—a place that most people would discount as empty and plain. Her reflections upon its melancholic beauties serve not only as her personal expression but as a way of showing the reader that a subject that may at first seem ordinary or bleak is filled with mystery when given a deeper look.

The lyric essay transcends reflection to emphasize language and imagery above all else. Deborah Tall defines lyric essays as those that "give primacy to artfulness over the conveying of information. They forsake narrative line, discursive logic, and the art of persuasion in favor of idiosyncratic meditation." The term is often used interchangeably with the terms "essayistic poetry" and "prose poetry." Most lyric essays are short and exist in and of themselves as a piece, centering more upon circular form than narrative line. They are strictly a literary genre, lacking, for the most part, the crossover into mainstream magazine publication. Like poetry, the lyric essay is rarely explicit in its meanings, relying instead upon suggestion, upon allusion.

What makes a lyric essay an essay? Like all creative nonfiction, it suggests an allegiance to the truth. It admits a direct connection to the writer's life and persona. Essayistic poem or lyric essay? Ultimately, it depends upon what the writer and editor choose to call it. We think that a lyric essay falls more on the side of the essay, as we've discussed it here; it tends to be less compact, more idea-centered, than poetry; usually there is a narrative line, even if it is dominated by the language, and a circular, braided structure, even if its central unity comes from a recurring image or metaphor.

An example of such a piece is Brenda Miller's "A Field Guide to the Desert." While this piece has a braided story (a mother-daughter trip, their mother's problems, the relationship between the girls and the narrator/ mother), it is brought together by key images: the water, the rock. These physical things have multiple meanings that we understand through long tradition. Miller uses each thing to imply a number of emotional experiences, but ultimately the dichotomy is life (sustenance, love) and death (deprivation, isolation). These images and others related to them carefully recur throughout the piece. There is minimal explanation; the backstory (about the mother and the narrator) and any complex discussion of the place ("the canyon with no name") are absent from this piece. Its meanings and conclusions are implied, not stated. Yet this piece would not be mistaken for a poem; it is ultimately prosaic and does contain a number of clear narrative strands, even if they aren't emphasized.

Place Writing

Writers have long been writing about the paths they encounter, whether these are found on the other side of the world or in the backyard. It's easy to make the assumption that place writing is synonymous with nature writing. Not so. A NASCAR track, the Apollo Theater, and the riverbank are all places, worthy of the same degree of absorption.

The style used in a work of place writing nearly always reflects its subject. Nature writing tends to be more lyrical and reflective than the harder-edged, more quickly paced, short-sentenced writing of the streets. Nature writing usually reflects the musical, flowing, solitary, and sometimes threatening feel of the natural world. Long descriptive passages make sense because the writer is usually less focused on people and so able to contemplate small details of the landscape. Nature writing often centers around the senses and the consideration of the small.

In *The Outermost House* (1928), Henry Beston muses upon the sea:

> Listen to the surf, really lend it your ears, and you will hear in it a world of sounds: hollow boomings and heavy roarings, great watery tumblings and tramplings, long hissing seethes, sharp, rifle-shot reports, splashes, whispers, the grinding undertone of stones, and sometimes vocal sounds that might be the half-heard talk of people in the sea. And not only is the great sound varied in the manner of its making, it is also constantly changing its tempo, its pitch, its accent, and its rhythm, being now loud and thundering, now almost placid, now furious, now grave and solemn-slow, now a simple measure, now a rhythm monstrous with a sense of purpose and elemental will.

Nearly fifty years after Beston, Annie Dillard wrote about the struggle to "see" nature closely.

> I used to be able to see flying insects in the air. I'd look ahead and see, not the row of hemlocks across the road, but the air in front of it. My eyes would focus along that column of air, picking out flying insects. But I lost interest, I guess, for I dropped the habit. Now I can see birds. Probably some people

can look at the grass at their feet and discover all the crawling creatures. I would like to know grasses and sedges—and care. Then my least journey into the world would be a field trip, a series of happy recognitions. Thoreau, in an expansive mood, exulted, "What a rich book might be made about buds, including, perhaps, sprouts!" It would be nice to think so.

Dillard uses detail to talk of what we can no longer see—what we lose in the passage from childhood to adulthood, and what, perhaps, has been lost between Beston's time and our own. By focusing on the natural world, Dillard gives us a message: this still matters. Most nature writing shares this sense of urgency, since it is becoming more difficult to find isolated natural places. Given the likelihood of interruption, it is getting difficult to focus on anything at all.

> "By focusing on the natural world, Dillard gives us a message: this still matters."

Another kind of place writing is the travelogue. Some are literary; some are not. Their aim is to render a place in time for readers who want less a "how-to" guide for a potential visit than an opportunity to experience the place secondhand. Creative travel writing has a strong narrative voice and a writer deeply and directly involved in the events of the place. The narrator is usually going somewhere new; a sense of adventuring into the unknown is nearly always the dominant tone, often inflected by physical and/or emotional risk.

British writer Isabella Bird traveled several times to the United States in the mid-1800s; for her, this was a mostly uncomfortable, though interesting, proposition. In this section, she is visiting an area near Charlotte, North Carolina:

> One day, with a party of youthful friends, I crossed the Hillsboro Creek, to visit the Indians. We had a large heavy boat, with cumbrous oars, very ill balanced, and a most inefficient crew, two of them being boys either very idle or very ignorant, and, as they kept tumbling backwards over the thwarts, one gentleman and I were left to do all the work. On our way we came upon an Indian in a bark canoe, and spent much of our strength in an ineffectual race with him, succeeding in nothing but in getting aground. We had very great difficulty in landing, and two pretty squaws indulged in hearty laughter at our numerous failures.

People appear more often in travelogues than they do in nature writing. Travel writers tend to focus more on social interactions than on the terrain. Interviews (or simple conversations) are usually an important part of the piece, giving the writing a feeling of immediacy and reality: this is what people here are like.

An example is Rory Stewart's "The Missionary Dance" on page 686. Stewart details his walk through Afghanistan, where he risks his life not only for his book, but to get to know the people. He doesn't expect the readers to literally follow him there; he does hope they will follow him into a better understanding of the Afghan people.

The City Essay

Another kind of place writing with a long, distinctive history is the city essay. These are usually tougher, blunter, bleaker, more cynical, and often funnier than most other place writing. These writings have origins in a kind of urban journalism that features a hard-bitten, opinionated columnist exploring the idiosyncrasies of urban characters. Writers such as Ben Hecht, George Ade, and Jimmy Breslin focused on the "common guy" (usually a guy, alas), who provided the writer with witty and astute observations about life. The form continues to evolve.

A classic example of the form is Gay Talese's essay "New York Is a City of Things Unnoticed":

> The roadway at the George Washington Bridge is more than 100 feet above the little red lighthouse that became obsolete when the bridge went up in 1931; its Jersey approach is two miles from where Albert Anastasia lived behind a high wall guarded by Doberman pinschers; its Jersey tollage is twenty feet from where a truck driver without a license tried to drive four elephants across in his trailer—and would have if one elephant hadn't fallen out. The upper span is 220 feet from where a Port Authority guard once climbed up to tell an aspiring suicide, "Listen, you SOB, if you don't come down, I'm going to shoot you down"—and the man crawled quickly down.

In this essay, Talese covers everything and everyone from fortune tellers, masseuses, and stray cats to escalators, Rolls Royces, and five-star hotels, to beaten piers, lingerie stores, and cardboard production factories. While Talese doesn't tell us much about himself directly, his personality and his deep affection for New York City comes through in what he chooses to show and in the way he shows it. Pieces like Talese's seem a little old-school, almost quaint now. As the cities become gentrified, a certain character has begun to disappear. While the city essay certainly still exists—after all, most people live in a city, and the publishing industry is centered in New York—it has adopted a tone of melancholy and anger.

Another kind of city essay appears in Colson Whitehead's *The Colossus of New York* (2003):

> You swallow hard when you discover that the old coffee shop is now a chain pharmacy, that the place where you first kissed So-and-so is now a discount electronics retailer, that where you bought this very jacket is now rubble behind a blue plywood fence and a future office building. Damage has been done to your city. You say, It happened overnight. But of course it didn't. Your pizza parlor, his shoeshine stand, her hat store: when they were here, we neglected them. For all you know, the place closed down moments after the last time you walked out the door. (Ten months ago? Six years? Fifteen? You can't remember, can you?) And there have been five stores in that spot before the travel agency. Five different neighborhoods coming and going between then and now, other people's other cities. Of fifteen, twenty-five, a

hundred neighborhoods. Thousands of people pass that storefront every day, each one haunting the streets of his or her own New York, not one of them seeing the same thing.

Whitehead's musings could apply to any city. In focusing on the particular urban place—a single building, a particular sidewalk—he captures a feeling experienced by all urban dwellers.

Literary Journalism

Tom Wolfe gave himself credit for inventing new journalism—he didn't; but he did provide some useful definitions. He relabeled a genre that had existed for decades and published his thoughts in an introduction to his book *The New Journalism* (1973). Once he did this, he gave other writers and critics a handy hook to hang their words upon.

Wolfe contended that new journalists use four techniques that separate their work from traditional journalism:

- scene-by-scene construction: "Telling the story by moving from scene to scene and resorting as little as possible to sheer historical narrative."
- use of dialogue: "Realistic dialogue involves the reader more completely than any other single device. It also establishes and defines character more quickly and effectively than any other single device."
- third-person point of view: Tom Wolfe is about the only person who insists upon the third-person point of view as a criterion for new journalism—probably because this was his technique. The use of the first person—the "I"—is far more common. Wolfe says that the third-person perspective is necessary to give the reader "the feeling of being inside the character's mind and experiencing the emotional reality of the scene as he experiences it." Wolfe and others point out that their subjects had all been interviewed: the "inner thoughts" are based on facts.
- the "recording of everyday gestures, habits, manners, customs, styles of furniture": Wolfe continues with a long list of things observed and recorded. Wolfe sees these common items as symbolic of people's "status life . . . the entire pattern of behavior and possessions through which people express their position in the world or what they think it is and what they hope it to be." This has long been done by writers of realistic fiction in an attempt to make a scene appear to be real and true. Such details are usually left out of traditional journalistic accounts.

Although Wolfe's contention that "new" journalism was new to the 1960s is simply not true, his definitions have been quoted and requoted and have become the standard way of defining the form.

Michael J. Arlen and others mark the beginning of literary journalism, as it's practiced today, in certain newspaper and magazine columns of the 1930s:

> The *new* thing, it seems to me, that the writer-journalist of the 1930s and 40s brought to the craft was a sense, an interest, in what went on before (and after) the Fire Commissioner came into the room. What did he do when he got on the elevator downstairs? . . . What were his *movements*? . . . Not only that, but the focus shifted away from the Fire Commissioner or the man who owned the hotel, and perhaps in the direction of the man who pumped the water, or the night clerk at the hotel across the way. Thus: reduced deference to public figures. . . . Personal touches. Dialogue—in fact, real speech, faithfully recorded.

We believe that literary journalism's beginnings go back even farther. Stephen Crane and Mark Twain certainly practiced it, although nobody was going around calling it "new journalism" at the time. Crane and other authors often had their work labeled "stories" or "travels" by editors as a way of confessing the piece's subjectivity.

The following excerpt from Crane's piece "The Scotch Express," published in 1898, focuses on a man who might usually go unnoticed. Crane, like many literary journalists, was fiercely concerned with social justice. His way of expressing this concern was not through argument, but by showing ordinary workers and crises, particularly war. The style is lyrical, moving.

> This driver was worth contemplation. He was simply a quiet, middle-aged man, bearded, and with the little wrinkles of habitual geniality and kindliness spreading from the eyes toward the temple, who stood at his post always gazing out, through his round window, while, from time to time, his hands went from here to there over his levers. He seldom changed either attitude or expression. . . . This driver's face displayed nothing but the cool sanity of a man whose thought was buried intelligently in his business. If there was any fierce drama in it, there was no sign upon him. He was so lost in dreams of speed and signals and steam, that one speculated if the wonder of his tempestuous charge and its career over England touched him, this impassive rider of a fiery thing.

The term "the new journalism" was commonly used in Victorian America; it applied at that time to what we call the "feature article." The reporting was personal and, in the mid-Victorian age, often done by women, according to Margaret Beetham. Beetham says that this "new journalism" "personalized both parties involved, the public figure being interviewed and the journalist/interviewer." It often appeared in women's magazines and occasionally crossed over into the land of the gossip column. After falling out of usage, the term "new journalism" eventually came around to apply to a form that is similar in its personal approach but more ambitious in its stylistic techniques.

The journalistic process is always flawed; literary journalism, its practitioners believe, is simply honest about its embellishments. Barbara Herrnstein Smith writes that all journalistic reports are composed of "general and imprecise recollections; scattered and possibly inconsistent pieces of verbal information; and various visual, auditory, and kinesthetic images—some of which, at any given time, will be more or less in and out of focus and all of which will be organized, integrated, and apprehended as a specific 'set' of events only in and through the very act by which we narrate them as such."

Russell Frank points out that "the old legman/rewrite system was predicated on reconstruction." He's referring here to the old *Front Page*–style journalism—the only kind that existed prior to e-mail. "The person who wrote the story never even left the office," he says. "The person who phoned in the facts got most of them from the cops or whichever officials were managing the incident in question; the legwork mostly consisted of going to the police or the courthouse or city hall, rather than to the scene itself. Once the rewrite man had the basic facts in hand, his job was to 'make it sing.'"

Apparently, journalists have always been singing. Usually, though, they didn't admit it.

The need for good social observers to get out on the streets or into the fields hasn't changed since the days of Stephen Crane. Tom Wolfe, in his praise of those "new" 1960s journalists, describes this tried and true approach: "[Jimmy] Breslin would go up to the city editor and ask what stories and assignments were coming up, choose one, go out, leave the building, cover the story as a reporter, and write about it in his column. . . . Breslin made it a practice to arrive on the scene long before the main event in order to gather the off-camera material, the play-by-play in the make-up room, that would enable him to create character. It was part of his modus operandi: to gather 'novelistic' details, the rings, the perspiration, the jabs on the shoulder."

In the works of Crane, Breslin, and the literary journalists since and between, that need to create a convincing character, drawn in a compelling way, trumps any tendency toward an unembellished description. Readers will read the piece if they are involved and immersed. If they aren't, most won't. Common people and events are not news. They only become "news"—relevant—if someone can use the techniques of art to bring them to life.

> "Literary journalism focuses on the small incident and detail—the individual instead of the 'trend.'"

Literary journalism focuses on the small incident and detail—the individual instead of the "trend." In an interview with us, Sheryl St. Germain says that creative nonfiction allows you to

> focus on something small that gets you deeper into the event. For example, instead of the loss of the city of New Orleans, I might write about the way my mother was worried about losing my brother's ashes, which were stored

in her house as the water rose during the levee breaks of [Hurricane] Katrina, or about her wedding rings. . . . In telling your own story as truthfully as you can, and by focusing on the objects that have meaning for you, you will effectively bring the reader into the larger context that the media may have already covered, but your narrative may be the one the reader remembers because you have not just given them facts, but a story.

See page 690 for a piece by St. Germain and page 696 for our interview with her.

Creative nonfiction always allows for individual subjectivity—we're all different, all biased, all blind to some things and overly attentive to others. Yet some types of creative nonfiction are more concerned with factual accuracy than others; literary journalism, by definition, is one of these. The writer relies upon both research and observation to make the piece as accurate as possible. Most include interviews that are either recorded verbatim or reconstructed through immediate recollection and notes (part 3 of our book addresses the techniques involved in collecting information). The writer must take pains to validate what she has learned. This reportorial approach can be used throughout an entire piece or may appear in a work that is primarily personal.

Writers may lean toward literary journalism because it is the best way to explore their own lives. Oddly, the act of centering a piece around a particular journalistic subject can give writers a door into their own selves. A writer who may not want to write a revealing memoir can use this as another means of self-exploration. Steve Almond expressed this well in an interview with us:

> I didn't really make a conscious decision [to write literary journalism]. I knew I wanted to write about candy in a way that honored my autobiographical experiences, but also allowed me to understand the industry and its history. So I just proceeded logically, initially writing about my own relationship with candy, then moving on to document my journey through all these factories, which became, in an odd way, a journey into my own past.

A piece from his book *Candyfreak* is on page 157, and the full interview is on page 169.

Some writers use the new journalism form because they can best provide information on a subject by focusing on the story of a real person. An example is John McPhee's well known essay "Atchafalaya," which shows the effects of damming the Mississippi River near the Gulf of Mexico. (It was written several decades before Katrina.)

> It was at Old River that the United States was going to lose its status among the world's trading nations. It was at Old River that New Orleans would be lost, Baton Rouge would be lost. At Old River, we would lose the American Ruhr. The Army's name for its operation there was Old River Control.

> Rabalais gestured across the lock toward what seemed to be a pair of placid lakes separated by a trapezoidal earth dam a hundred feet high. It weighed five million tons, and it had stopped Old River. It had cut Old River in two. The severed ends were sitting there filling up with weeds. Where the Atchafalaya had entrapped the Mississippi, big-mouth bass were now in charge.

McPhee's essay is packed with information, yet it doesn't come across as primarily informative in purpose. The piece casts Rabalais as a kind of character; we come close to entering his point of view as he gestures toward the lakes. It maintains the tension between river and human, circa the late twentieth century, and carries a subtle note of caution regarding the impossibility of controlling nature. As McPhee delivers his warnings, he presents us with interesting people, a sense of movement, description, dialogue, and a dense style. This is clearly not a newspaper report, an argument, a fiction, or a history. It speaks, and lets its characters speak, with authority.

Another kind of literary journalism is typified by its sense of urgency. It forces our attention onto a social problem by the use of compelling storytelling and the way it makes visible and immediate the people who we choose not to see. The subject may be politically controversial. An argument is made in part by the piece's very existence. The writer's opinion on the matter is not disguised.

Luis Alberto Urrea's book *Across the Wire: Life and Hard Times on the Mexican Border* (1993; a selection is on page 739) tells the struggles of Mexicans who live in Tijuana. The book compiles articles that the author published in the *San Diego Reader,* yet he observes the events not as a professional journalist but as a church aid worker.

> The family was living in a shack on a hillside across the highway from the dump. It could be reached only after a long and confusing drive through crooked alleys and ridgetop dirt paths. Lean-tos thrown together by junkies and winos surrounded their shack. You could smell the booze and urine coming through the slats. There was a small goat tied to a stake in the dirt, and no lights brightened the neighborhood save for small fires and the occasional flashlight. The men's voices were thick; they cursed and broke glass in the dark. In the shack hid Socorro, the thirteen-year-old daughter. The men wanted her.

Urrea's involvement in the events around him and the personal decisions he is forced to make are revealingly detailed in the book. But aside from his own personal involvement as narrator, the piece is clearly creative nonfiction in terms of its dramatic style. He compels us to curiosity about Socorro and her family through traditional fiction techniques such as foreshadowing. Urrea takes the sense of conflict beyond the basic depiction of poverty into the lives of individuals, their friends, and their enemies. Each chapter has a story arc; each chapter has distinctive, and usually ingratiating, characters. The fact that we come to know these people whose lives unfold on a literal garbage heap makes the events far more shocking than if Urrea had dispassionately reported the ugly effects of poverty.

Another kind of new journalism focuses on a political crisis. These pieces certainly report "news," but the author is directly involved in the story. In 2005, *Rolling Stone* magazine published a compelling series of articles by Evan Wright about American soldiers serving in Iraq. These were later collected into the book *Generation Kill*. The articles bring us close to a small group of soldiers and use description and dialogue, fiction-style, to immerse us in their situation. Wright puts himself at risk and doesn't refrain from telling us so, which only increases the dramatic tension: Will he die? Be wounded? Quit?

> While two First Recon companies are instructed to set up positions on the banks of the Euphrates, Bravo Company waits at the foot of the bridge, about 200 meters away from the river's edge. No sooner are we settled than machine-gun fire begins to rake the area. Incoming rounds make a zinging sound, just like they do in Bugs Bunny cartoons. They hit palm trees nearby, shredding the fronds, sending puffs of smoke off the trunks. Marines from Task Force Tarawa to our right and to our left open up with machine guns. First Recon's Alpha and Charlie companies begin blasting targets in the city with their heavy guns.
>
> Enemy mortars start to explode on both sides of Colbert's vehicle, about 150 meters distant. "Stand by for shit to get stupid," Person says, sounding merely annoyed. He adds, "You know that feeling before a debate when you gotta piss and you've got that weird feeling in your stomach, then you go in and kick ass?" He smiles. "I don't have that feeling now."

Joe Sacco uses a similar approach in his graphic (illustrated) journalism. *Safe Area Gorazde: The War in Eastern Bosnia* (2000) and *Palestine* (2001) chronicle the effects of the wars in these countries. (An example of his work is on page 656.) In creative nonfiction fashion, Sacco focuses on a few individuals and on his role as observer to make what is ultimately a searing political statement. Although he is not trying to mask his political point of view, he uses almost cinematically displayed events to make his case. Of his approach, Sacco says,

> I went to Palestine with the conviction that Palestinians had been historically wronged. What was important to me, however, was to keep my eyes and ears open and report honestly—as opposed to "objectively." In other words, if Palestinians said something that I knew would sound harsh or ugly to an American ear, that wouldn't keep me from reporting it. No one is an angel, and we certainly cannot expect history's victims to fit into that category. I don't think of my book as an argument or a statement so much as presenting a reality as lived by a dispossessed and sometimes bitter people. I don't know what change I'm trying to effect except to provide a greater feeling for the humanity of a people who have been pushed into a desperate corner.

We've offered a long tour through many types of creative nonfiction. You'll be relieved to learn there is no exit exam—but perhaps dismayed that neither is there a tasting room. Our point is not to foist categories on you for some mere pedantic purpose. Rather, we think that knowing traditions and genres has generative power, opening a range of possibilities for your writing. We began chapter 1 by noting the dangers of defining something by what it's not. Now that we've elaborated more what creative nonfiction is, we hope you'll enjoy exploring this widely varied terrain.

Creative Nonfiction Referenced in This Chapter

Abbey, Edward. *Desert Solitaire*. Tucson: University of Arizona Press, 1988.

Bahrampour, Tara. *To See and See Again: Life in Iran and America*. New York: Farrar, Straus and Giroux, 1999.

Beston, Henry. *The Outermost House: A Year of Life on the Great Beach of Cape Cod*. New York: Henry Holt, 1928.

Bird, Isabella. *The Englishwoman in America*. Carlisle, MA: Applewood Books, 2007.

Crane, Stephen. "The Scotch Express." In *Crane: Prose and Poetry*. New York: Library of America, 1996.

Didion, Joan. "On Keeping a Notebook." In *Slouching Towards Bethlehem*. New York: Farrar, Straus and Giroux. 1990.

Dillard, Annie. "Seeing." In *Pilgrim at Tinker Creek*. New York: Harper Perennial, 2007.

Eggers, Dave. *A Heartbreaking Work of Staggering Genius*. New York: Vintage Books, 2001.

Doucet, Julie. *My New York Diary*. Montreal: Drawn & Quarterly, 2004.

Gopnik, Adam. "Times Regained." *The New Yorker*, March 22, 2004.

Hampl, Patricia. "The Need to Say It." In *I Could Tell You Stories: Sojourns in the Land of Memory*. New York: Norton, 2000.

Hemley, Robin. *Nola: A Memoir of Faith, Art, and Madness*. St. Paul: Graywolf Press, 1998.

McCarthy, Mary. *Memories of a Catholic Girlhood*. New York: Harcourt, 1972.

McPhee, John. *The Control of Nature*. New York: Farrar, Straus and Giroux, 1989.

Miller, Brenda. "A Field Guide to the Desert." In *Season of the Body*. Louisville: Sarabande, 2002.

Orwell, George. *Down and Out in Paris and London*. New York: Harvest Books, 1972.

Pollan, Michael. *The Botany of Desire: A Plant's-Eye View of the World*. New York: Random House, 2001.

Price, Jennifer. *Flight Maps: Adventures with Nature in Modern America*. New York: Basic Books, 1999.

Sacco, Joe. *Safe Area Gorazde: The War in Eastern Bosnia*. Seattle: Fantagraphics Books, 2002.

Talese, Gay. "New York is a City of Things Unnoticed." In *The Gay Talese Reader*. New York: Walker and Company, 2003.

White, E. B. "Once More to the Lake." In *The Essays of E. B. White*. New
    York: Harper Perennial, 2006.
Whitehead, Colson. *The Colossus of New York: A City in 13 Parts*. New York:
    Doubleday, 2003.
Wright, Evan. *Generation Kill*. New York: Putnam, 2004.
Yamashita, Karen Tei. *Circle K Cycles*. Minneapolis: Coffee House Press, 2001.

Works about Writing and Literature

Adams, Timothy Dow. *Telling Lies in Modern American Autobiography*.
    Chapel Hill: University of North Carolina Press, 1990.
Arlen, Michael J. "Notes on the New Journalism." *The Atlantic*, May 1972.
Beetham, Margaret. *A Magazine of Her Own? Domesticity and Desire in the
    Woman's Magazine, 1800–1914*. New York: Routledge, 1996.
Birkerts, Sven. As quoted by Peter M. Ives in "Roundtable Expert: The Whole
    Truth." In *Fourth Genre: Explorations in Nonfiction*, Vol. 7, No. 2, 2005.
Cooper, Bernard. "Marketing Memory." In *The Business of Memory: The Art
    of Remembering in an Age of Forgetting*, edited by Charles Baxter.
    St. Paul: Graywolf Press, 1999.
Dillard, Annie. *Teaching a Stone to Talk: Expeditions and Encounters*. New
    York: Harper & Row, 1982.
Frank, Russell. "You Had to Be There (and They Weren't): The Problem with
    Reporter Reconstructions." *Journal of Mass Media Ethics*, Vol. 14, 1999.
Gass, William H. *The World Within the Word*. New York: Basic Books, 2000.
Gelderman, Carol. *Mary McCarthy: A Life*. New York: St. Martin's, 1988.
Scholes, Robert and Carl Klaus. "Elements of the Essay." In *Elements of
    Literature*. New York: Oxford University Press, 1991.
Smith, Barbara Herrstein. Quoted in Frank, above.
Tall, Deborah. Definition of the lyric essay. *Seneca Review* Web site.
Wolfe, Tom. *The New Journalism*. New York: HarperCollins, 1973.

PART **2**

Craft

CHAPTER **3**

Form

If works of creative nonfiction were rambling series of disconnected musings, nobody would read them. At the same time, there is no structural template that must be followed: no formal introduction, three paragraphs, and conclusion. No thesis sentence. Yet there is a beginning and end, and in between a space to be filled. It's up to you to decide upon the design.

Beginnings and endings impose structure upon a work of art. The literary critic Edward Saïd wrote that a beginning comes from a "primordial need for certainty" from which we find coherence. All of us seek form in our experience; we all run on the clock and follow the seasons. An eternity, a life without end, is beyond our comprehension. Margaret Atwood has said that without the reality of mortality:

> We'd become a different species—one living in eternal bliss, in the eyes of its proponents; sort of like—well, angels, or superhuman beings anyway. It would certainly mean an end to narrative. If life is endless, why tell stories? No more beginnings and middles, because there will be no more endings. No Shakespeare for us, or Dante, or, well, any art, really. It's all infested with mortality, and reeks of earthiness. Our new angel-selves will no longer need or understand our art. They might have other art, though it would be pretty bloodless.

We hope this chapter will give you ideas for shaping information and ideas, stories and facts, into pleasing, effective, maybe even surprising forms.

Elements of Form

On the face of it, talking about form should be easy. You characterize the parts of a piece of writing and the arrangement of those parts. Of course, generating those parts and settling on a satisfying proportion and order is trickier, and therein lies the art of creative nonfiction.

It's possible to sort the elements of creative nonfiction into two rough piles: "information" and "idea." The information pile would contain things like stories, facts, reports, descriptions, and so on: relatively concrete stuff, often observable. The idea pile would contain interpretations, reflections, analyses, and so on: relatively more abstract stuff, the thoughts the writer has generated. Here's a quick example from Steve Almond's "In the Belly of the Freak" (page 157), as he's getting ready to leave Sioux City, Iowa, and thinking on his decision not to fly or rent a car.

> "It's possible to sort the elements of creative nonfiction into two rough piles, 'information' and 'idea.'"

> But I was, instead, in a gravel lot, shivering alongside a group of passengers with duffel bags and battered plastic sacks. If you ever want to know what America really looks like—and I direct this chiefly toward the residents of the coastal cities who tend to write about America most frequently—I would suggest you abandon the airports. The only people in airports are rich people. Take a bus from Sioux City to Kansas City, via Omaha and Maryville.

The amount of information here is relatively slight. He describes the scene in the gravel lot. The rest is "idea," what he thinks of that scene and its broader implications.

What we're lumping together as "information" comes from many sources. One, obviously, is lived experience, preserved in memory. These don't have to be "big deal" experiences of momentous events; what writers do with an incident or memory is generally more important than the subject matter itself.

Another source of information is direct observation. Instead of recollecting past experiences, writers can create new ones by paying close attention to the immediate world around them, recording their impressions in a journal or blog or just on a napkin. They can also walk into situations with the express purpose of recording them, whether a Cinco de Mayo celebration, a gun show, a beauty pageant, a concert by a band they hate, a pet store. You know going in that you may write about it, and this will have an impact on what you notice and experience. As observations become more involved and sustained, you can draw upon interviews that you record through notes or after the fact. We discuss interviews at greater length in chapter 9.

Finally, there's information gained through reading. You obviously don't know or remember—or haven't experienced—everything, but fortunately for all of us, others have, at least in bits and pieces. All writers do research in libraries and bookstores, in archives, and online—so much research that we've written about it in chapter 8.

Finding ideas is a more ambiguous, even mysterious process. A few questions may help you generate ideas about your amorphous subjects. Let's say you want to write about your mother. You don't know exactly what you want to write about her—there are so many stories to tell, so many things she's told you, so many things you've experienced with her. You might think about the stories that truly characterize her; which of these are the most dramatic and poignant and meaningful? Which are you willing to tell in public? What is driving you to want to show this? What do you want the reader to feel and think? What do you want to find out in the process of retelling the story? Why is this important? What does this mean? How is this like something else? What's the connection between this and that? What are the implications of what took place? How does it fit into the bigger scheme (outside of this one story)? Why should someone know about this? Most importantly, why should *you* know? How would someone in a different situation see this? What were and are the consequences? What is so vivid that you can't shake it? Are you sure the story will sustain you through the process of writing and revising this piece (because if you're bored, everyone else will be, too).

Sketch down all of the situations that come to mind, underlining the ones that in the act of jotting seem to carry the most power. Put them in one kind of order. Then put them in another. Remember that you can always change the order later. Take the situation or idea or vision that grips you the most. Start telling that story.

Beyond asking questions or sifting and sorting situations until the combinations stir ideas, read. Read things along lines similar to what you're doing and pay attention to the stories those writers choose to tell and how they tell them. What's the interplay of narrative and thought? Consider, too, all of the ideas, images, and incidents that the writer may *not* have included. (Of course, you can't really know, but use your imagination.) Why these particular choices? Try to get into the writer's head and feel the choices that were made, the situations that were chased. Notice where they stopped.

General Principles

Four main strategies organize most writings: logical, lyrical, spatial, and narrative. Creative nonfiction uses all four in various proportions and combinations, but narrative is often the most important, and that's where we'll focus most of our attention.

Logical (or propositional) works have skeletons of several statements that are usually designed to prove a main assertion. Once upon a time you were probably taught to write paragraphs with topic sentences followed by other sentences that provided evidence, illustration, or support. Such papers often had this form: "There are three reasons to do X. The first is. . . . The second is. . . . The final is. . . . Because of reasons 1, 2, and 3, it is clear we should do X." While this form is useful for some kinds of academic writing (but not nearly all), and while some creative nonfiction gets organized this way, straightforward thesis and support mostly doesn't get creative nonfiction writers very far because it's artificial and not "organic" to the subject matter or the writer's voice. When a creative piece is organized around ideas, those ideas generally get embedded in stories, descriptions, and other information so that the skeleton is carefully concealed.

Lyrical writings, on the other hand, are organized to achieve aesthetic effects. Images, scenes, or ideas are joined to each other by association, as in a lyric poem. Those associations are rarely logical; in fact, creative nonfiction writers often use a striking juxtaposition of dissimilar materials to create a collage in which seeing "this" against "that" forms compelling connections. Such lyrical elements are part of many creative nonfiction works and occasionally the whole piece works lyrically. Take a look at Sharon Solwitz's essay "Abracadabra" (page 671), which has several disconnected texts under such headings as "Dialogue between Two Halves of a Brain," "Advice," "This Is Not Making Me Happy," "Jesse's Hair: A History," and so on. Given her subject matter, a child dying of cancer, and her aim to render what that experience was like, a logically tidy organization just isn't going to do it. Here's a sequence:

JESSE'S HAIR: A HISTORY

. . . At Dave'n Busters they played laser tag, and Jess so tired he could barely move, but he trained that fatigue into focus and got his man, every man, his score twice as high as the next closest. But the next game he lost, got wiped out by his laser-armed enemies, and the day after he was in the hospital with hemoglobin 7, half what it should have been, a wonder he could speak, let alone stand and shoot.

OH, JESSE

I want other people to miss him, to be affected, hurt, overwhelmed by the loss of him. Nick cries in his room, Meesouk's grades have gone down, my friend Sheryl has upped her Zoloft. Good. Good, good, good.

ADVICE

You sound angry. You can write your anger.

I HATE

Grocery shopping, the process of selection that I used to love even in Jesse's last days when I thought flax oil or raw organic garlic or taro root ground up and mixed with ginger would start the long process of restoring his health.

I hate buying clothes.

Spatial organization is apparent when writers follow the physical arrangement of things, as in a description that says, "To my left. . . . Ahead. . . . To my right. . . . " A tried and true structure might follow the writer on a walk or a trip, and the journey provides the line onto which they can hang stories, reflections, ideas, and so on. Writers also sometimes use the spatial formation of the map, not only because it is a handy organizing tool but because it serves simultaneously as a metaphor. While a map is directional and might in one sense appear to be linear, it can also branch into many areas from a single point, or can wind and meander like a river and dump into the big sea. Yet the very fact of the map's existence provides reassurance that there is an order to things. Emily Hiestand's "Maps," on page 428, relies in part upon the use of the map to guide us through the sequences of a child's life.

Graphic memoir and journalism put a new twist on spatial form because the layout of the page directs readers as they make their way through the work. For example, contrast the ways that the drawing styles in *Palestine* by Joe Sacco (page 656) and *Cancer Made Me a Shallower Person* by Miriam Engelberg (page 368) influence how readers make their way through these works while still following the standard comics panel structure.

A spatial organization follows the traditional story arc, with a definitive beginning, middle, and end that lets readers feel that ideas and events lead to one another and everything comes to a satisfying conclusion. Sometimes the narrative is pushed forward by a sense of reportage: this happened, then this, and as a result this. More often, however, the creative nonfiction plots depend only partly on a literal report of events.

> "Most creative nonfiction relies, almost inevitably, upon *narrative*."

Most creative nonfiction relies, almost inevitably, upon *narrative*. Narrative is story. We've all been taught the basic story arc. Different theorists use different terms, but it usually comes down to something like this:

action → complication → climax → resolution/aftermath

Basically, something happens, the character (or narrator) is confronted, there's a crisis point, things crumble or blossom, then all is resolved. This is the arc found in most novels and movies, and while there are moments of genre-busting, of scrambling the momentum, this, still, is what the reader expects. We can try to break this form, but in doing so we're still working against standard expectations.

Creative nonfiction usually follows this same basic arc. The pace and build of dramatic tension, though, are often quite different from what you find in most fiction. Nonfiction is often more evenhanded and emotionally level in the development of the story; anything that seems highly emotive is often downplayed or treated with suspicion. The reader, though, reads on for the same old reasons: it's nearly always because we want to know what happens next, in the case of events, or how it resolves, in the case of ideas.

Suzanne Keen wrote that people read stories not only to know what happens (and to whom), but to find the "answers to enigmas large and small." Essays delve into mysteries, less in an effort to "solve them" but to grasp them and to show the process of grasping. This is particularly true of creative nonfiction, which focuses as much on "what does it mean" as on "what happened." Readers ask such questions and confront such enigmas themselves, and they enter into this quest with the writer. The story of an essay, then, can often be understood as the story of how finally to make sense of information, ideas, and people, how to configure them into a whole.

Making sense, though, does not mean making it dull. Often, the pieces loop about, using imaginative structures that mix all of the four elements just mentioned. The writer may begin with a story, then include information or reflection that isn't directly part of it, then return to the story later. The writer may begin with reflection or ideas and only later tell about an incident. The writer may include several incidents, each of them a short story in itself, all organized into some longer frame. The piece should come together with a sense of cohesion and shape. In a way, it takes life as an independent being.

Beginnings

Although there's no perfect trick to help you start a piece, one bit of advice is consistent across genres: get the reader's attention and don't let go. Unlike the introduction of formulaic academic essays, you shouldn't lay out the template of your entire work. You needn't announce what is to come, but simply offer that first hint. The voice in that first paragraph is the one the reader will expect throughout; if you start out slowly and drily, the reader won't stay with you. Your voice shouldn't put people to sleep.

The beginning of a literary work arises from the piece's deeper meanings, emotions, and intentions, which may not be clear to you until after everything's written. For some writers, the beginning is the last thing they write. Others rewrite their beginnings over and over again before going forward. Some get it right the first time, maybe by running it through their heads before putting pen to paper. Everyone and every piece is different.

The beginning usually reveals the tone and style of the piece and hints at the subject and setting. It introduces the narrator (at least through the voice) and often one of the other people in the story. A setting that is emphasized in the beginning signals that the place itself is a kind of vital character. It may introduce a recurring metaphor or motif. A motif or metaphor may appear in the beginning, then repeat throughout the piece, much like the refrain of a song.

Works of contemporary creative nonfiction usually don't start at the chronological beginning and then progress linearly. (Older autobiographies plow from birth through death far more often than contemporary nonfiction.) Pieces travel through time, starting *in media res*—mid-scene and mid-thought and mid-act—snatching up past and present and tangling them.

Once the piece is finished and you read your beginning again, ask yourself: would you keep reading? If you wouldn't, then the true beginning lies deeper in the text. Beginnings in first drafts are often false starts; you write them to get yourself going, and they're as disposable as all of those wads of paper in your wastebasket.

Examples of Beginnings

The first beginning we'll look at is from the essay "A Picture of Us" by Robyn Moreno.

> I'm not sure exactly whose idea it was to celebrate my mom's fifty-fifth birthday at Graceland. But somehow I found myself standing in front of Elvis's rather modest mansion with a candle in my hand, along with my family and the thousands of other lunatics who had come to pay homage to the King. After three hours of worship, I was fantasizing about peanut-butter-and-banana sandwiches when my older sister, Nevia, snapped me out of my reverie. She asked me to take her picture with a suspiciously effeminate Elvis impersonator. Like a true king, he grabbed her by the waist and started serenading her with "Love Me Tender." Her squeals of delight caught the attention of my other two sisters, Yvette and Bianca, who ran up and joined in the fun. After the impromptu performances, they cheered and clapped loudly. "Elvis" bowed his head humbly and mumbled a "Thank you, thank you very much." As they huddled into a photogenic position, I realized this particular Elvis had breasts. Hmmmm. Either no one noticed or, more likely, no one cared. As I peered through the camera at the three girls and the lesbian Elvis, I saw the truth. No matter which road I travel, all paths lead me back to my crazy family.

Moreno packs a lot of cues into this; we find out that:

- there are five main characters, the narrator and the members of her family;
- the setting is Graceland, where her mother is having a party;
- the narrator likes peanut-butter-and-banana sandwiches (as did Elvis, which says something about her, and probably also about her family);
- Mom's hung up on Elvis;
- her sisters are bold enough to join an Elvis impersonator and have the event documented with a photograph;
- the narrator has a sense of humor and likes quirky situations; and
- the narrator has affection for her "crazy" family.

It's clear that Moreno doesn't seem to be embarrassed by her relatives, and that "crazy" is probably not a bad thing. You can be fairly certain that this essay won't take the form of a tragic family exposé.

Some beginnings are fairly straightforward and gain strength from an apparently simple laying out of the facts:

> On the night of 13 February 1992 two hundred armed Untouchables surrounded the high-caste village of Barra in the northern Indian state of Bihar. By the light of burning splints, the raiders roused all the men from their beds and marched them out into the fields. Then, one after another, they slit their throats with a rusty harvesting sickle.

This introduction, to William Dalrymple's book *The Age of Kali*, is gripping in part because it is horrible. Most readers will be curious about what has happened here. It is elegantly written, not a "just the facts" news account; the phrase "by the light of burning splints" is rather lovely, an appalling contrast to what then occurs. By reciting the full date, the author makes clear that this is a significant event, one recorded in historical accounts. The place is very specific (no general town, no vague "India"), another indication that this is a report with historical basis.

Another straightforward approach comes in Frederick Douglass's 1845 autobiography:

> I was born in Tuckahoe, near Hillsborough, and about twelve miles from Easton, in Talbot county, Maryland. I have no accurate knowledge of my age, never having seen any authentic record containing it. By far the larger part of the slaves know as little of their ages as horses know of theirs, and it is the wish of most masters within my knowledge to keep their slaves thus ignorant. I do not remember to have ever met a slave who could tell of his birthday. They seldom come nearer to it than planting-time, harvest-time, cherry-time, spring-time, or fall-time. A want of information concerning my own was a source of unhappiness to me even during childhood. The white children could tell their ages. I could not tell why I ought to be deprived of the same privilege. I was not allowed to make any inquiries of my master concerning it. He deemed all such inquiries on the part of a slave improper and impertinent, and evidence of a restless spirit. The nearest estimate I can give makes me now between twenty-seven and twenty-eight years of age. I come to this, from hearing my master say, some time during 1835, I was about seventeen years old.

The first line lays out Douglass's birthplace in a way that echoes thousands of historical accounts. Yet it becomes clear that there is far more at stake here than a record of facts. He points out that slaves know "as little . . . as horses" of their own births, and that this is terribly deliberate. The list of the seasons, which for slaves were the planting and harvest cycles, is lyrical and all the harsher because of it. This introduction shows that no matter how straightforward a piece may appear, the levels can be deep, and the reader can feel fairly certain that these complex levels will build throughout the book. We also get a sense of Douglass's will, intelligence, and directness, not only in the complexity of his language and thought but in the way he expresses his frustration and challenges the slavemaster.

The next beginning is from a more introspective and traditionally structured piece, Sven Birkerts's "Reflections of a Nonpolitical Man" (found on page 217). This essay explores the author's own lack of active political involvement. He isn't arguing that everyone should be apolitical; he is explaining the legitimacy of his own lack of action and defending the value of art as action. This piece begins with a conflict:

> I have a friend who wants me to be more political. He doesn't specify, but I know what he means: He wants me to do things, take conspicuous stances, have a more engaged posture in the world. And he's right. That is, he must be right—otherwise why would I feel such a prickling of guilt whenever he brings the subject up? And these days he seems to bring it up all the time. When he does I naturally become defensive; I scramble toward the familiar silence of not being understood.

Birkerts begins with the story of a friend. He doesn't describe the friend, but you can easily imagine them facing one another, having a debate. It's clear that this essay won't be about the friend, though, because Birkerts doesn't linger on him or even give him a name; instead, the friend is a catalyst for the author's internal conflict. While there is no clear thesis statement, we get a sense that this will be a deeply personal perspective of a man grappling with questions of politics and philosophy. That this is a personal approach and not a traditional argument is clear by the emphasis on emotion and relationships. Birkerts tells us he feels defensive, and we suspect this essay will be the defense. He never says, "I will now tell you why being nonpolitical is a good thing." In fact, for all we know, he may come around to the friend's way of thinking. We read the essay, in part, to find out.

A strong literary beginning usually doesn't explicitly reveal the essay's intentions. Sometimes mysterious or beautiful can be enough. James Baldwin's rambling essay "Take Me to the Water" has a subtle start that in itself gives little indication of the subject of the piece. The intention is to evoke a sense of lovely ominousness:

> "That is a good idea," I heard my mother say. She was staring at a wad of black velvet, which she held in her hand, and she carefully placed this bit of cloth in a closet. We can guess how old I must have been from the fact that for years afterward I thought that an "idea" was a piece of black velvet.

The beginning brings to mind a simple relationship: that of the link between "idea" and "black." In this way, it captures the essence of the essay, which is a disjointed series of experiences that begin with the personal loss of family and progress through the civil rights movement. It also presents the sad image of Baldwin's mother, whom he is forced to leave at a young age. Ultimately, the beginning's power comes from this puzzling and rather melancholy velvet image.

Middles

Northrop Frye wrote that "when a historian's scheme gets to a certain point of comprehensiveness it becomes mythical in shape, and so approaches the poetic in structure." Creative nonfiction writers are not historians, not journalists, and not simple chroniclers of events. The shape of their work is "poetic"—or, put another way, told in the shape of a story or a prose lyric. The plot is shaped less by

> "The tension comes from the leap into ambiguities."

information and more by the melding of information and imagination. Works of creative nonfiction, like fiction and poetry, nearly always feature a search for answers to questions both obvious and obscure. The tension comes from the leap into ambiguities. Along the way, the writer usually meets other people who are similarly struggling, and their struggles, too, add to the tension of the plot.

In an essay, the "dramatic" moments are not usually wildly dramatic; they are subtle and broad, and they tend to repeat and loop, with the many small moments of external and internal conflicts coming together to form a turning point, a moment of meaning, and a resolution that may or may not be satisfactory to the writer.

Events cannot be controlled in nonfiction—we're supposed to be telling the truth—but the timing and telling of the events can (and should) be controlled. The writer determines which conflicts are important and the extent to which they are lengthened and shortened in time. To say that the telling is strictly true is an obvious lie. Every telling of a story involves selective inclusion and exclusion, a pace and rhythm, an expanse and truncation of time. We emphasize some events by description, repetition, by simply lingering on them; we leave out others that would be irrelevant, slow, just plain boring. Most creative nonfiction writers give themselves latitude to manipulate the chronology to allow a dramatic build. In real life, a climber may have slipped two feet down the rock face within the first hour of his walk; in the written version (or filmed one), it's quite possible that the climber shows that slip happening five hours into the walk. (Are such changes in details ethical? We won't enter into that debate here—it would take far too long—but be assured that writers commonly make such changes.) They also flip the timing with the use of flashbacks and flashforwards, which we will discuss momentarily. What we choose to embellish and expand and what we ignore give an event its particular stamp and style.

Narrative theorists have carefully explored the difference between "events as they happened" and "events as they are put into a plot." Consider the difference between:

My girlfriend left me one night. The next day I walked to the coffee shop. The barista said, "Good morning." I said, "Not for me," and I walked away, leaving the coffee steaming on the counter. [Events as they happened]

and

"Not for me," I said, turning toward the door. The barista looked puzzled, a little worried, as I left behind the coffee I'd just bought. She had merely said, "Good morning." What she didn't know is that my girlfriend had left the night before. [Events put into a plot]

Both versions draw upon the same events. The first relates them in the order they happened. The second, by rearranging the time sequence, creates a sense of mystery. Admittedly, it's a fairly short-lived mystery, the reason for the narrator's response getting revealed in the fourth sentence. But imagine these events drawn out and expanded over a couple of pages, and you'll note quite different effects from the same materials. Peter Brooks calls plot the "shaping force" of the story that puts together and molds random events. While we usually don't think of nonfiction as having a "plot"—we've been taught since grade school that this is the realm of fiction—creative nonfiction writers inevitably create a pattern into which they place the events, people, and places in their lives. It's how we all think, how we create coherence from chaos.

All creative nonfiction, like fiction, has a turning point, a climax, a realization. This may or may not be the dramatic turning point of popular fiction, in which the hero is pushed off a building or decides to take sleeping pills; it may be a quiet realization about one's own life or the revelation of some intriguing information. Mikhail Bakhtin, a philosopher and literary theorist, called these turns the threshold, "the breaking point of a life, the moment of a crisis, the decision that changes a life (or the indecisiveness that fails to change a life)." They are moments of change for the narrator or the characters (or place-as-character), or both. Without these moments, the piece is static, unsatisfying for both the writer and the reader.

Along with compression and expansion, time can be manipulated using flashbacks and flashforwards. Nearly all essays exhibit this fluidity in moving from present to past. Flashbacks allow the narrator to travel backward, using full scenes or quick references to provide context about herself and the situation at hand. The following short flashback is informative, providing history about the practice of Western firefighting. In it, Kim Barnes describes the fate of those who fought a massive blaze seventy-five years earlier. (The full essay, "The Ashes of August," is on page 188.) While we may traditionally view a flashback as a device that illuminates a fictional character by explaining a previous experience, this factual event serves a similar function by illuminating the danger to a group of firefighters. Without this understanding, the contemporary crisis would lack resonance; while it might be exciting, it would lose the sense of meaning that comes when we know that this has happened before and will happen again.

> The Mann Gulch smoke jumpers were young and had dropped onto a terrain that may have seemed at the time less threatening than the densely wooded ridge in the distance. They were at a point where the tree-studded mountains broke open to grassy plains dried to amber. Perhaps they believed themselves safe amid the loose-rock slope and low-lying vegetation, but they were tragically mistaken. They had their tools—their shovels and Pulaskis—but what they did not have was knowledge of the ways of this fire and of how, within an hour, it would cross the gulch and push them screaming up the steep hill, crest at the top, and die there with them. Bunch grass, cheat grass, some immature pines mixed in with older growth—these were all that was needed to create the blowup that engulfed the men. Two of the three who survived did so by racing the fire to the ridge and winning; the third, the crew's foreman, saved himself by escape of another kind: instead of running, he stopped, struck a match, set fire to the grass at his feet, then stepped into the flames he had created. He lay face down on the still-smoking earth, covered his head with his hands, and waited for the main fire to catch and sweep over him. And it did.

Barnes then connects this past event with the blaze that threatens her home and her husband: "A steeply pitched basalt-strewn slope covered with dry grass and scattered patches of timber—the very terrain Bob was headed into. As I watched him pull away, I prayed that he would have the foreman's presence of mind should the fire overtake him." This reminds us of the very real risk involved in her husband's job, and of the family members who have waited behind in every Western summer.

Flashforwards are often used when the essay is centered around a particular scene, with the narrator acknowledging that the piece is written in some "future" time—future in relation to the primary events. Flashforwards in creative nonfiction remind the reader that the narrator is a writer, working now; it is a reminder that the piece is true *to memory and experience* and that the scene at hand is not an exact photo rendition of the event as it happened.

Li-Young Lee's memoir *The Winged Seed* (a chapter of which appears on page 490) covers key periods of Lee's and his family's lives. Most of this chapter centers on a visit that the child Li-Young and his preacher father made to the home of an aged parishioner. Halfway through the piece, Lee travels back in time, first referring to one of his father's sermons in Hong Kong, then to the day his sister finds a leaflet of their father's ministry, then to the time that the photograph on the leaflet was taken, then to the testimony his father gives at a revival meeting. Finally, he proceeds to a point "many years later" and "five years after my father had died." This future period, set long after all of the other scenes in the piece, is a flashforward, told long after the writer has become an adult.

By the time it appears, we have already experienced the fluidity of Lee's story, and are not confused or surprised.

Endings

Endings are tricky, even frustrating. How do you know when you've said all that needs to be said? How do you know when you've said too much? As usual, the best answer is to read widely and try to understand how that good ending may have come about.

The best endings arise organically, from what we instinctively sense is the proper moment to end. In all ways, literary endings are the opposite of the "in conclusion" paragraph that you were forced to write in high school. While you may have a sense of the general direction in which you're traveling, you may not know exactly where the path will end. For many writers, knowing the ending defeats the purpose—they write to find out. Others begin knowing how the story starts and how it concludes, and very little in between.

The right ending sometimes comes on the first draft; sometimes it comes after many adjustments or wholesale cuts. It's not unusual to pass the moment of the best ending; it's also not unusual to end too abruptly, without taking the piece to the most powerful conclusion. While it would be great to offer a formula that would tell you when you'll feel that right ending, there, of course, isn't one. Keep in mind that the ending should leave the reader with a strong statement or mood; it's what the reader carries away. And don't be afraid to show your drafts to readers who will let you know what they think.

> "Real life is not predictable, and writers have to be ready to adjust their plans."

Most creative nonfiction uses endings to draw connections between the essay's ideas, rather than to conclude a series of statements. Sometimes a clear state of "conclusion" never comes because an event is still unfolding. Real life is not predictable, and writers have to be ready to adjust their plans. Because a straightforward conclusion may not be possible, creative nonfiction pieces usually end on notes of emotional or philosophical implication.

Examples of Endings

When Denis Johnson researched his essay "Run, Rudolph, Run" (see page 451) about the anti-abortion bomber Eric Rudolph, he didn't know if or when the killer would be captured. He was unable to interview Rudolph, because the man had disappeared into the Appalachian caves, and locals were largely unwilling to give him information. What Johnson does is absorb the town's atmosphere, making the piece a study not only of a murderer but of a place and a certain type of American. Johnson might have used the essay to take a stand on Rudolph's actions or his politics, but the piece isn't out to build a political statement. This is clear from both the beginning and ending, which are unified by the metaphor and reality of the cave. The conclusion, at first, might seem to have little to do with the subject of the essay, since Rudolph's name is not even mentioned:

> In 1914 Count Bégouën and his three sons discovered the Trois Frères Cave in the Pyrenees. A tunnel that can only be wriggled through ends in a massive chamber covered with Paleolithic 12,000-year-old images of the hunt, including a creature half-man, half-beast: a chamber used for initiating adolescent boys in a ritual of death and rebirth. Students of humankind have long seen the link between the cave and the womb. In 1956 the anthropologist Jean Gebser suggested in a piece called "Cave and Labyrinth": "The cave is a maternal, matriarchal aspect of the world. . . . To return to the cave, even in thought, is to regress from life into the state of being unborn."

A careful reading shows that Johnson is indeed talking about Rudolph's situation: death, rebirth—the need to return to a state of unknowing. In fact, these, more than Rudolph the killer, are the true subjects of this essay. The reference to the unborn reminds us of Rudolph's anti-abortion violence, and the reference to the maternal cave points to Rudolph's disrupted childhood and what he seeks. This is Johnson's commentary on the situation. The reader, however, must draw her own conclusions about just what Johnson means by this. This is another difference between creative nonfiction and an academic essay: in creative nonfiction, much can and should be left to the reader's understanding.

Creative essays often end on a philosophical note, relaying emotion with a focused meaning. In 1932, the German writer Walter Benjamin wrote a lyrical essay in praise of hashish. It is a deep look at an experience, culminating in a final declaration of joy:

> The trance abated when I crossed the Cannebiere and at last turned the corner to have a final ice cream at the little Cafe des Cours Belsunace. It was not far from the first cafe of the evening, in which, suddenly, the amorous joy convinced me that the hashish had begun its work. And when I recall this state I should like to believe that hashish persuades nature to permit us—for less egoistic purposes—that squandering of our own existence that we know in love. For if, when we love, our existence runs through nature's fingers like golden coins that she cannot hold and lets fall to purchase new birth thereby, she now throws us, without hoping or expecting anything, in ample handfuls to existence.

The piece builds as the writer draws us through what he observes and feels and ends on a literal high note in praise of the ability to notice the minute and to transcend mundane worries and obsessions. Benjamin leaves us with a thought to reflect upon, rather than a final action or daydream.

Sometimes a work of creative nonfiction ends on an emotionally powerful, unsettled, inconclusive scene. It may be such a turning point that we have no way of knowing for certain what will happen next. Such an ending usually implies that profound disturbance lies ahead.

Such is true of Marjane Satrapi's graphic memoir *Persepolis*, the story of a girl's childhood and young adolescence during the Iranian Revolution of 1980. The story begins with happy stability and culminates at a point of repression and disintegration. The book ends with a literal separation, as the young Marjane is forced to leave her family and homeland for life as an exile in a French boarding school. The final panel shows Marjane casting a last glance over her shoulder at her parents in the airport; her mother has fainted and is being carried in her father's arms; the caption says, "It would have been better to just go." While this is a logical conclusion, a natural place to stop, it is also jarring.

A different kind of ending punctuates Lillian Ross's classic essay about writer Ernest Hemingway, "How Do You Like It Now, Gentlemen?" A series of nearly constant scenes and dialogue build to leave the reader with a sharp and honest picture of that ordinary guy, Hemingway:

> "Shooting gives me a good feeling. A lot of it is being together and friendly instead of feeling you are in some place where everybody hates you and wishes you ill. It is faster than baseball, and you are out on one strike."
>
> The telephone rang, and Hemingway picked it up, listened, said a few words, and then turned to us and said that an outfit called Endorsements, Inc., had offered him four thousand dollars to pose as a Man of Distinction. "I told them I wouldn't drink the stuff for four thousand dollars," he said. "I told them I was a champagne man. Am trying to be a good guy, but it's a difficult trade. What you win in Boston, you lose in Chicago."

The ending has a bit of a "Huh?" quality, but so does the entire essay; this is part of its charm. The casual cadence of the dialogue goes far in humanizing the "great writer"—a writer who turned himself into a Hemingway knock-off. The ending obliquely reveals that Hemingway is trying to be true to himself, even as his fame conspires against that. He's feeling the pressure of being unable to please anyone. Nowhere in the essay does Lillian Ross directly say this; in fact, she is absent from the piece as a direct presence. Instead of using "I," Ross uses the common pronoun of the *New Yorker* magazine, the royal "we." It's clear, though, that Ross is a comfortable enough presence that Hemingway reveals himself, and she is enough of a straight shooter to describe him honestly, even brutally. And for the purposes of our discussion on endings, it shows that a snippet of well-chosen dialogue can reveal far more than two pages of well-constructed "conclusion."

Finally, even writing that we think of as technical, like popular science writing, can have a catchy ending. It needn't be dry and overstated to get its point across. Most commonly this is done through a close first-person point of view, with the writer turning the narrative to himself. Michael Pollan's book *The Botany of Desire* is a fascinating look at the ways that people and plants maintain a mutual relationship. To enforce the commonness of this relationship, Pollan chooses to discuss plants that are found in homes: apples, tulips, potatoes, and marijuana. The book is full of short histories, factual tidbits, and personal ruminations. The author's presence, while not announced on every page, is always behind the language, keeping the discussion comfortable and wry. The ending comes as a short personal scene:

> But I was still left with my bag of NewLeafs sitting there on the porch. And there they sat until Labor Day, when I got an invitation to a potluck supper at the town beach. Perfect! I signed up to make a potato salad. The day of the supper, I brought the bag of spuds into the kitchen and set a pot of water on the stove. But before the water even had a chance to boil, I was stricken by the obvious thought: Wouldn't I have to tell people at the picnic what they were eating? I had no reason to think the potatoes weren't perfectly safe, but if the idea of eating genetically modified food without knowing it gave me pause, I couldn't very well ask my neighbors to do so. (That would be rather more potluck than they were counting on.) So of course I'd have to tell them all about the NewLeafs—and then, no doubt, bring home a big bowl of un- touched potato salad. For surely there'd be other potato salads at the potluck, and who, given the choice, was ever going to opt for the one with the biotech spuds? I suddenly understood with perfect clarity why Monsanto doesn't want to label its genetically modified food.
>
> So I turned down the flame under the pot and went out to the garden to har- vest a pile of ordinary spuds for my potato salad. The NewLeafs went back out in the limbo of my porch.

And so Pollan sums up the piece with a portrayal of the human/plant dance—while he has argued throughout the book that we are plants, and vice versa, he is hesitant to take a chance on the "advancement" of genetic modification. Ample weight is put on that single word "limbo," thus summing up an entire political state of affairs.

Formal Options

At the beginning of this chapter, we noted that creative nonfiction has no consoling (or constricting) structural templates, and we stand by that. Writ- ing these pieces involves far more art than science. Still, it can be useful to think of some structural options, and it can even be useful—in the sense that an artist's sketchbook is useful—to play around with some of these patterns with a given body of material.

1. Straightforward Story
Story beginning
Story middle
Story end

2. Manipulated Story
Story middle (first part)
Story beginning
Story middle (more)
Story end

3. Story and Idea (Reflection) I
Story beginning
Idea
Story middle
Idea
Story end

4. Story and Idea (Reflection) II
Idea
Story beginning
Story middle
Idea
Story end

5. Story, Information, and Idea
Information
Story middle
Information
Story beginning
Idea
Story end

6. Multiple Stories and Idea
Story 1 beginning
Story 2 beginning
Idea
Story 2 middle
Story 2 end
Idea
Story 1 middle
Story 2 end
Idea

7. Etc., Etc., Etc.

The permutations are endless; we've kept things simple just to be suggestive, though you can certainly play this game further. The point is that writers can endlessly arrange elements of creative nonfiction to achieve effects. You can deploy the narrative events of a story in different sequences, depending on the dramatic effect you want to create. You can interrupt stories with related—or even seemingly unrelated—information or with overtly reflective passages, shifting from "telling" to "thinking." You can begin a piece in a heavily informational mode, then insert a story to change pace or create depth. You can put more than one story into a single work, perhaps telling all of A, then all of B (or C or even D), perhaps juxtaposing elements of these various stories.

In the end, a writer must enact Kenneth
Burke's definition of form: the arousing and fulfill-
ment of desires. How this happens depends on one's
experiences and sensibilities, informed by reading and
practice, developed by exploring the many options
available to see what works best.

Creative Nonfiction Referenced in This Chapter

Almond, Steve. "In the Belly of the Freak." In *Candyfreak*. Chapel Hill:
    Algonquin Books, 2004.
Atwood, Margaret. "Arguing against Ice Cream." Review of *Enough: Staying
    Human in an Engineered Age,* by Bill McKibben. *New York Review of
    Books* 50, no. 10 (2003).
Bakhtin, M. M. *The Dialogic Imagination: Four Essays*. Edited by Michael
    Holquist. Translated by Caryl Emerson and Michael Holquist. Austin:
    University of Texas Press, 1981.
Baldwin, James. "Take Me to the Water." In *James Baldwin: Collected Essays*.
    New York: Library of America, 1998.
Benjamin, Walter. *On Hashish*. Cambridge, MA: Belknap Press, 2006.
Brooks, Peter. *Reading for the Plot: Design and Intention in Narrative*.
    Cambridge, MA: Harvard University Press, 1992.
Burke, Kenneth. *Counter-Statement*. Berkeley: University of California Press,
    1968.
Dalrymple, William. *The Age of Kali*. Oakland: Lonely Planet, 2000.
Douglass, Frederick. *Narrative of the Life of Frederick Douglass*. West Berlin,
    NJ: Townsend Press, 2004.
Frye, Northrop. *Anatomy of Criticism*. Edited by Robert D. Denham. Toronto
    and Buffalo: University of Toronto Press, 2006.
Keen, Suzanne. *Narrative Form*. New York: Palgrave Macmillan, 2003.
Kermode, Frank. *The Sense of an Ending: Studies in the Theory of Fiction*.
    Oxford and New York: Oxford University Press, 2000.
Lee, Li-Young. *The Winged Seed: A Remembrance*. St. Paul, MN: Hungry
    Mind Press, 1999.
Moreno, Robyn. "A Picture of Us." In *Border-Line Personalities: A New
    Generation of Latinas Dish on Sex, Sass, and Cultural Shifting*, edited by
    Michelle Herrera Mulligan and Robyn Moreno. New York: Rayo, 2004.
Pollan, Michael. *The Botany of Desire: A Plant's-Eye View of the World*. New
    York: Random House, 2001.
Ross, Lillian. "How Do You Like It Now, Gentlemen?" In *Life Stories: Profiles
    from* the New Yorker, edited by David Remnick. New York: Random
    House, 2000.
Saïd, Edward. *Beginnings: Intention and Method*. New York: Columbia
    University Press, 1985.
Satrapi, Marjane. *Persepolis*. New York: Pantheon Books, 2003.

CHAPTER 4

Description

Description brings readers into the sensations of a particular time and place and state of being.

Contemporary writers tend to keep descriptions compact, using words precisely to get across the sensory details and set the tone. Creative nonfiction is more prone to long descriptive passages than current fiction, to the point that this has become an identifying characteristic of the essay. The immediate visual settings of TV and film have made many people impatient with long, lyrical, winding descriptions, which can add to the perception that the essay is a more "intellectual" form than fiction. It takes a certain patience to slow one's reading pace to concentrate on complex descriptive passages.

One reason that novels and essays from the pre–World War I era can seem ponderous is those elaborate descriptions. They use those adverbs and adjectives that we assiduously eliminate from our work today. In that period, works that we might now call creative nonfiction were usually labeled fiction. A classic example of this is the French writer Marcel Proust's series of novels, *Remembrance of Things Past* (1913–27). While most literary scholars assert that the books are fiction, they are written in the first person, reflect events and people in Proust's life, and dwell at length on minute details and sensory impressions. Some sections were originally composed as essays, but upon publication were labeled fiction, since the marketing umbrella of creative nonfiction didn't yet exist. Proust ultimately decided to call the book a novel because, he said, it was the form from which "it departs least." *Remembrance of Things Past* is, as Proust's translator Lydia Davis asserts, "art's transformation of life," in which Proust took his experiences and "altered, recombined, and shaped" them. The result certainly could be called a memoir, or, at the very least, a nonfiction novel. Whether the reader wishes to see Proust's work as fiction or nonfiction, his passages are wonderful examples of elaborate prose description:

> At the hour when I usually went downstairs to find out what the menu was, dinner would already have been started, and Francoise, commanding the forces of nature, which were now her assistants, as in fairy plays where giants hire themselves out as cooks, would strike the coal, entrust the steam with some potatoes to cook, and make the fire finish to perfection the culinary masterpieces first prepared in potters' vessels that ranged from great vats, casseroles, cauldrons, and fishkettles to terrines for game, molds for pastry, and little jugs for cream, and included a complete collection of pans of every shape and size. I would stop by the table, where the kitchen maid had just shelled them, to see the peas lined up and tallied like green marbles in a game; but what delighted me were the asparagus, steeped in ultramarine and pink, whose tips, delicately painted with little strokes of mauve and azure, shade off imperceptibly down to their feet—still soiled though they are from the dirt of their garden bed—with an iridescence that is not of this earth. It seemed to me that these celestial hues revealed the delicious creatures who had merrily metamorphosed themselves into vegetables and who, through the disguise of their firm edible flesh, disclosed in these early tints of dawn, in these beginnings of rainbows, in this extinction of blue evenings, the precious essence that I recognized again when, all night long following a dinner at which I had eaten them, they played in farces as crude and poetic as a fairy play by Shakespeare, at changing my chamber pot into a jar of perfume.

Proust's books capture not only a time and place now lost to us but a time and place that were also falling away for Proust. They are long, loving memories of a man who allowed himself the room to follow his visions to the end. While the descriptions are long, they don't waste their impressions; the words have purpose, all serving the image at hand. Had he dwelled upon the publishability of these books as he was writing them, they would never have been written. Getting them in print was difficult; they were rejected at several houses on the basis that they were "different from what the public is used to reading." Proust ultimately had to pay a publisher to print them. When the books became important, publishers who rejected them expressed their regret.

A description can be pages long, like Proust's, or a sentence of carefully chosen words. It can provide a fully formed and elaborate conception or present a bare glimpse. What the writer chooses to include and not include has everything to do with his individual manner of observation and interpretation. Just as a director and cinematographer decide what is relevant enough to include in a frame, so the writer chooses what part of the sensory experience to show and what part to drop away. Each word reveals something not only about what is observed but also about the author. It is our interpretation of our way of seeing, involving an immersion in and translation of the observed experience.

Description arises from the need to fully capture the situation. It comes naturally during the act of visualizing a scene or an individual. When description has to be added after an early draft, it's usually because we've failed to fully show what it is that we knew all along. As a writer grows more adept, the descriptions often become more complex, gaining multiple levels of meaning; they don't necessarily become longer. While there are notable exceptions (see Proust, again), most writers don't have the stamina to become truly immersed in long descriptions, and most readers don't have the patience to read them. Most young writers cut their descriptions too short out of the fear that they'll "be boring" (or, worse, bore themselves). As time passes and we read and watch in bursts between Internet clips, the art of the long description is dying away.

> "Description arises from the need to fully capture the situation."

E. L. Doctorow attributes the decline of exposition in writing to the rise of film, saying that this comes from "a kind of filmic exposition compact between writer and reader that everything will become clear eventually." Rather than having a long descriptive transition between scenes, writers now use what Doctorow calls "the instantaneous reposition in space and time: the cut." Most readers expect to have those people, places, things inferred, not told to them. Thus much literary prose writing now moves from action to action. Our descriptions have to pack a lot of meaning into fewer words. These words have ramifications and can't be wasted. This doesn't mean that you can't write with long descriptive passages. It does mean that the description should move the story forward and cast meaning. There are always exceptions, but you'll need Proustian language abilities (and a terrific imagination) to pull it off.

This doesn't mean, though, that your first drafts should hold back. Don't worry about being boring; although you know how someone or something looked/felt/sounded/smelled, the reader is unfamiliar with the particulars of your world. Without that slow line, you may never come to the jewel that is just right. The full description can also help us to see our observation objectively, as if we are viewing it for the first time. In the process of picturing the event or person we may realize something that we didn't know before. The act of writing about what we see changes the way we see.

We're including here examples of various kinds of passages in the hopes of showing some of the descriptive range and possibilities.

Description of a Place

While we tend to think of place descriptions as being a part of nature or travel narratives, the reality is that we are always in a place, and it's pretty much impossible to set any kind of scene without at some point

evoking a sense of physical space. Certainly place can be described mini-
mally, but since this is a chapter on description . . . well, our selections go
into a bit of detail:

> A circus is high and low, piccolos and trombones. The edgy tiger roars and
> charges, but then licks her trainer at the end, as if they had been friends all
> along. A clown meanly tricks his chum, dunks him treacherously in a barrel
> of water, and gloats for the crowd, but then the high-wire walker steals all
> his thunder as soon as the whistle blows. The ringmaster, though he seems
> the boss, is curiously not the star; the saddest puss gets the biggest laugh; and
> the innocence is raunchy (those leggy girls who strut their stuff alongside a
> whiteface Bozo so that dad has his own reasons to snicker). The clowns teach
> most memorably that if you trust anybody he will betray you.

This scene, from Edward Hoagland's "Circus Music" (found on
page 442), uses specific detail to evoke a circus—an any-circus. It brings
together all of the familiar circus tropes, but uses language that is distinctly Hoagland's own. These words would probably never find their
way into anyone else's work in quite the same combination ("whiteface
Bozo," "clown meanly tricks his chum," etc.). He slips in a few ominous
notes: the mean trick, the thunder-stealer, the betrayal. While this scene
of the circus is a common one, universally understood to most North
Americans, its portrayal is not; it plays on the familiar and the strange
simultaneously.

Another approach to place description is in Gerald Early's essay "'I
Only Like It Better When the Pain Comes': More Notes toward a Cultural
Definition of Prizefighting," found on page 320. It comes as part of a
memoir interlude.

> In the neighborhood where I grew up there was a block called Firhill Street.
> Every black American ghetto must have one of these streets, where the
> houses are so dilapidated, so absolutely ruined that the bricks bulge out in a
> manner that suggest a kind of sterile pregnancy. Even the inanimate objects
> seem swollen with grief. Many of the houses, as I remember, were boarded
> up with wood or sheets of metal, and yellow paper signs would be posted on
> the front doors which read: THIS PROPERTY IS DECLARED UNFIT FOR
> HUMAN HABITATION. Of course, people continued to live in these build-
> ings and no one thought anything at all about it.

In this description, Early is focusing on one neighborhood, his own;
yet he takes it a step further by saying that this neighborhood is like any
other "ghetto." The lines that follow are used to describe both his own
and all tough neighborhoods. The metaphoric language in this section is
striking and unusual, taking what might be a generic description into another realm. Most of us don't think of bricks bulging in "a kind of sterile
pregnancy" or find objects to be "swollen with grief"—yet we can visualize this now that he's pointed it out; it is recognizable in its uniqueness.

Description of an Ordinary Thing or Activity

Description certainly doesn't have to be about pretty or entertaining things and phenomena. It can concern mundane objects and processes placed in the piece because they need to be there and perhaps because the writer just found them fascinating. Anything is worthy of description, if the writer feels the need. The smallest detail and most insignificant event can be made beautiful or intriguing; it is all in how we see and the way that we show.

Here is a lyrical description by the writer Lia Purpura, from her essay "Recurrences/Concurrences":

> Frost on the bathroom window this morning burgeons and twines in winged fleur-de-lis. Astonishing frost on this, the same morning I discover my mother's old cigarette case: the same, precise blooms but in silver-etched motion. How the mind of frost, the form reaches out, draws its heirs close; from anywhere, cracked riverbeds and leaf-veins in sun. From a few blocks away, wrought-iron fish on the Roland park schoolyard fence. From childhood, Dead Man's Finger, *Codium fragile*, common seaweed, washed up on any Long Island beach.
>
> And this afternoon, sitting down to work, a plastic bag catches in a bare tree and stays. I can see it from up here, from my second floor window. Up here, it's Baltimore. The middle of winter. But I know this thing, puffed full of air, the four corners taut, is a swollen egg case, a skate's or a ray's: *Mermaid's Purse* we'd find at low tide, shining and black and tangled on shore.

In this, Purpura uses apparently simple and familiar imprints and things—frost, a bag—and uses them to travel to other things in other places and times (to the fence down the street, the seaweed on a childhood beach, the egg casing). While an essay may be about the real, we are certainly never held to the real immediate present, just as our minds will naturally travel backward and forward in any moment of daydream, any time of day. A description that begins with a pattern of frost branches into multiple patterns. A plastic bag becomes a treasured egg case. Any "thing" is a connection of something and someplace beyond what it seems to merely be.

In a different kind of example, Kate Simon in her memoir *Bronx Primitive* describes the needlework done by Jewish seamstresses at the turn of the twentieth century:

> We girls had small embroidery hoops, a few hanks of colored thread, and a stamped bit of cloth to work on. In for the sociability rather than the craft, a number of us settled for fast cross-stitching. When confronted with a leaf or flower, some would make a loop, catch it with a stitch at the end, and there it was, a petal. Those of us who, like myself, came from houses of dexterous, admired hands filled in leaves and petals laboriously and with satisfaction as the spaces became shape and color, the cloth stippled with French knots and its edges tastefully tassled.

While needlework involves a long and fairly tedious process, Simon uses this common activity to describe not only a design, but a community. Her actual description of the product is brief, yet pretty and clear. She doesn't belabor us with visions of florets, but instead simply reveals the appearance of a petal, created from a series of loops that become "shape and color." She also hints at her own particular home with women whose work she modeled. A description doesn't have to be elaborate to be vibrant and to carry information about the writer and her times.

Description of a Person

Nearly all essays have, at some point, a description of a person, even if that person is the narrator. Capturing someone in a description that is both accurate and inventive is not easy—we've read so many of them that it's hard to get the cliches out of our heads. The responsibility of writing about a person who may well read the piece adds another level of stress to what is already a challenge. (On the other hand, it's nearly certain that the person being written about will not accept that they are anything like the description, so it's best not to obsess about it.)

> "It's nearly certain that the person being written about will not accept that they are anything like the description."

It's helpful to read a lot, so that you can spot just what is overused in description. Going on at length about someone's eyes while using various synonyms for the word blue is not going to be very interesting. It's also a good idea to avoid adjectives and adverbs unless you are experienced enough as a writer to keep them under control. The description should be distinctive and as unique as possible to the unique person at hand.

In this passage from the book *The Invention of Solitude*, Paul Auster presents a vivid description of his father. This is a very short section from a very long description:

> When I was twelve or thirteen, and wanted desperately to go somewhere with a couple of my friends, I called him at work to get his permission, and he said to me, at a loss, not knowing how to put it, "You're just a bunch of greenhorns," and . . . for years afterward, my friends and I (one of them now dead, of a heroin overdose) would repeat those words as a piece of folklore, a nostalgic joke.
>
> The size of his hands. Their calluses.
>
> Eating the skin off the top of hot chocolate.
>
> Tea with lemon.
>
> The pairs of black, horn-rimmed glasses scattered through the house: on kitchen counters, on table tops, at the edge of the bathroom sink—always open, lying there like some strange, unclassified form of animal.
>
> Watching him play tennis.

The way his knees sometimes buckled when he walked.

His face.

His resemblance to Abraham Lincoln, and how people always remarked on it.

His fearlessness with dogs.

His face. And again, his face.

Tropical fish.

The tone is distant, matter-of-fact. While it is a tribute to a loved one, it is hardly gushing and embellished. It is through the unusual details and their juxtaposition that we get a sense of who this man was and what the narrator noticed of him. The details are everyday, but oddly evocative; the thought of a man, long dead, eating the skin from the hot chocolate reminds us of people we have known. The emotion is subtle, coming from what the narrator shows; he has no need to be demonstrative, and it would actually be out of character if he were. Auster comes back, three times, to the face, but doesn't go on about it. There is something poignant in the simplicity of this; to say more would take it over the top.

Contrast Auster's contemporary description with one written by Virginia Woolf more than sixty years ago.

Mrs. Grey sat on a hard chair in the corner looking—but at what? Apparently at nothing. She did not change the focus of her eyes when visitors came in. Her eyes had ceased to focus themselves; it may be that they had lost the power. They were aged eyes, blue, unspectacled. They could see, but without looking. She had never used her eyes on anything minute and difficult; merely upon faces, and dishes and fields. And now at the age of ninety-two they saw nothing but a zigzag of pain wriggling across the door, pain that twisted her legs as it wriggled; jerked her body to and fro like a marionette. Her body was wrapped round the pain as a damp sheet is folded over a wire. The wire was spasmodically jerked by a cruel invisible hand. She flung out a foot, a hand. Then it stopped. She sat still for a moment.

In "Old Mrs. Grey," Woolf uses simple and careful language to describe what could be a maudlin scene of pathetic decrepitude. Because it is relatively simple (especially for the time it was written), and because it inventively plays upon the electrical spasms of the woman's body, the piece is moving. Woolf also doesn't linger in a melodramatic way on the spasm; she shows it, then quickly leaves it again. Although the form of this piece is different from Auster's, the two pieces are effective because they imply, rather than spell out, the emotion driving the description.

A description of a person is often used as a striking beginning to a book or essay. It can bring us immediately into a situation by raising our curiosity about the person who will serve as the driving character. The person may be the narrator herself, viewing her life from a distance, or someone outside the self who will become the center of our attention. What follows is the beginning of Therese Svoboda's *Black Glasses like Clark Kent* (2008), a retelling of her uncle's war experiences:

> My uncle is Superman. With black Clark Kent glasses, grapefruit-sized biceps, lots of brilliantined thick dark hair, and a solid jaw, six-four and as handsome as all get-out, he's the perfect match for Kryptonite. He even keeps a photo of himself as a high school Adonis, veins bulging. Now, in 2004, after making millions in farming, restaurants, and real estate, instead of swooping down and rescuing people from burning buildings, he volunteers for Meals on Wheels, just what Superman would take on in his advanced years. I suspect this Superman schtick also has something to do with Nietzsche's "will to power." After all, Grandma had more than a whiff of German in her Czech fierceness. Make the best better reads the ornately written note I find in her purse after her funeral. My uncle was her baby, he bore a golden sheen that lit his life, made him special, a man with muscle.
>
> A few years ago he tried to convince me that his eighteen months in the army would make a terrific movie, or at least a great book. "I was there during the occupation of Japan, right after World War Two," he said. "They found out we were less barbaric than they were taught. It's quite a story."
>
> I rolled my eyes. Superman had gone too far.

When we write about people whom we admire, we can easily make the mistake of drawing them as flawless, saintly, ultimately dull. In this, Svoboda admits right up front that she sees her uncle as a superior being, as Superman—and he apparently truly is strong and steady. Yet she also describes this Superman image as being her uncle's self-perception and, apparently, her grandmother's (as he was her "baby" with a "golden sheen"). Svoboda admits that his confidence may arise from the "will to power," a Germanic drive to achieve and control, which in historical terms is not exactly a positive. And then, when the adored uncle attempts to get her to write his life story, she rolls her eyes. Superman becomes, well, another guy trying to wheedle a writer out of a few years of her life.

This beginning is risky because it sets up an expectation in the reader's mind that this is an extraordinary man with an extraordinary story; because of this, the writer has to truly have a story worth telling and the ability to tell it well. We will read on to find out, and if the writer gives us something to hold on to, we continue beyond, as we do with Svoboda's book.

When writing a descriptive passage, we can reveal things to the reader that we may not have fully realized about ourselves and the situation. When we write about the people close to us, we may not at first know the meanings of what we describe. We write to see and better understand these people and ourselves, and we write to better understand what took place. In the act of describing that person, we provide a frame and context that never before existed. The Superman does indeed become human, and the story that was a diffuse series of events takes on a new circumscribed existence. A person in a memoir has the opportunity to live on, and in that way we hold on to others just a little bit longer; a lost and forgotten event can be reimagined and re-experienced.

Description That Moves the Action

Most essays at some point use description to push forward the action, increase the tension, and help the reader identify with the scene. In this paragraph from Laurence Gonzales's "Firefighters," the narrator and a firefighter enter a burning house:

> Before I knew it, I was going up a stairway. I recognized that stairway. I had lived with one just like it when I was a little boy, narrow, with a round wooden handrail, only this one was like the bottom of a back yard charcoal barbecue grill: It was glowing. We were encased in our protective clothing, but I wondered what a little boy in his pajamas and socks would do here: Everywhere I looked, everything, the walls, the floor, the ceiling, the woodwork, was glowing embers. Coiled snakes of smoke issued forth as if the wood had rotted before our eyes and maggots filled its blackened flesh. I was hit by wave after wave of heat that knocked the breath out of me, and when I gulped to catch my breath, I inhaled something noxious. It was not air; it was some superheated admixture of poisons. In all my lessons during the nights and days with the firefighters, there was nothing that could have prepared me for this. I felt that I'd been dropped onto the surface of Mercury, and we were burning in a methane sea.

By quickly relating the stairway in the burning house to the one in his childhood home, Gonzales reminds us of fire's vulnerable victims. He cements this vision when he refers to backyard barbecues and pajamas. He also connects us to a memory (the stair rail, the grill) and an imagining (the boy). This reminds us of the narrator's own possible peril; it becomes more difficult for the reader to separate from the narrator and to see this as just another fire on TV. We identify.

The description quickly covers significant ground, much as the fire spreads. Smoke is referred to in one brief line. Gonzales wants us to notice what threatened him most: the smell of the poisonous gases. As happens in moments of crisis, everything narrows to this point. What the narrator smells is more important than what he sees. The author could have spent pages showing everything he remembered seeing and hearing, and those might well have made some interesting pages. But if he had done this, "Firefighters" would have been a different story. Instead, he keeps a fast pace and focuses on what he believes to be the most essential elements. The fire, which involves several floors of a building, is discussed in only two pages.

Description for Its Own Sake

Our final example is the sort of thing we usually expect from a descriptive passage: a lyrical evocation of nature. This excerpt is from Jamaica Kincaid's *My Garden (Book):*

> The month of May comes on suddenly and moves along swiftly, and each day pleasure after pleasure is flung before my eyes with such intensity that after the barrenness and harshness, in varying degrees, of the months before, it seems mocking, a punishment, to look out and see the bergenia, pink and white against the bleeding heart, pink and white; the stiff pink flower of the umbrella plant (Peltiphyllum peltatum, a plant introduced to me by Joe Eck and Wayne Winterrowd), followed by large leaves held up by long, elegant stems; the pink and blue, white and mauve of the pulmonarias ('Mrs. Moon,' 'Janet Fisk,' 'Sissinghurst White'); the emerging green tips of the hosta, missile-like in shape, slow in progress as the snails who so like to nibble at their tender shoots; the flowering apple trees.

In this, the description exists for its own sake. The season and the flowers—and the narrator's reaction to them—are what matters. The pace is leisurely and the phrasing lyrical, befitting a garden. She feels no particular need to rush through her description to get to the action—the description, with its sense of the season's evolution and its effect upon the narrator, *is* the story. The complication comes in the writer's reaction to the blooming flowers: she initially views the contrast between the harshness of winter and the life of spring as a punishment. After this hint of tension, she then moves into a long, lyrical descriptive sentence in which phrases are linked by semicolons. The language has a rhythmic sway, each specific word contributing to the musical effect. She is trying to create a sentence as beautiful as the garden. This sort of lyrical passage is a stylistic convention of nature writing, with the startling loveliness of place reflected in the rhythms and tones of each sentence.

> "To describe is to offer an interpretive representation of an aspect of experience."

Because no mode of representation—film, photo, sound, word—can exactly reproduce lived experience, the goal of description is hardly to re-create reality in anything approaching its fullness. To describe, then, is to offer an interpretive representation of an aspect of experience. What we choose—and, especially, what we don't choose—is what turns a record of scattered impressions into an artistic form.

Creative Nonfiction Referenced in This Chapter

Auster, Paul. *The Invention of Solitude.* New York: Penguin, 2007, 1982, 1988.

Gonzales, Lawrence. "Firefighters: On Fire." In *Hero's Apprentice.* Fayetteville: University of Arkansas Press, 1994.

Kincaid, Jamaica. *My Garden (Book)*. New York: Farrar, Straus and Giroux, 1999.

Proust, Marcel. *Swann's Way*. Translated by Lydia Davis. Edited by Christopher Prendergast. New York: Viking, 2003.

Purpura, Lia. *On Looking: Essays*. Louisville, KY: Sarabande Books, 2006.

Simon, Kate. *Bronx Primitive: Portraits in a Childhood*. New York: Harper & Row, 1983.

Svoboda, Therese. *Black Glasses like Clark Kent: A GI's Secret from Postwar Japan*. Saint Paul, MN: Graywolf Press, 2008.

Works about Writing and Literature

Davis, Lydia. "Introduction to *Swann's Way*." In *Swann's Way,* by Marcel Proust, translated by Lydia Davis, edited by Christopher Prendergast. New York: Viking, 2003.

Doctorow, E. L. "Quick Cuts: The Novel Follows Film into a World of Fewer Words." In *Writers on Writing: Collected Essays from the* New York Times, introduction by John Darnton. New York: Henry Holt & Company, 2001.

CHAPTER **5**

Dialogue

Dialogue, as we all know, is the sound and language of people talking as interpreted in a literary work. We hear so much unadulterated jabber—from cellphone monologue to television repartee, to friends' giggle-fest, to the intense conversation of partners—that it just blends together. The interpretation of this mess is what gives dialogue the particular stamp of the artist; the task involves finding, imposing, making sense of the cacophony. This is no less true in creative nonfiction than in fiction; dialogue is not simply an accurate transcription. If it were, we'd all be bored, as anyone who has read an entire court transcript can attest.

We tend to take dialogue in our fiction and creative nonfiction for granted; we usually only notice it if it's bad. "Realistic dialogue involves the reader more completely than any other single device," wrote Tom Wolfe; it puts us in the scenic moment. When characters are talking, our attention is usually diverted from the writer. We are forced to try to visualize these people, to supply the setting—the effect is as scenic as it is aural. We notice dialogue when it "sounds wrong," which generally means untrue to the character—in Wolfe's view, when it is unrealistic. It may also mean that it seems inconsistent to whatever style the writer has established. We notice when the writer has drawn attention to his own involvement through stylistic innovation or stylistic error.

Contemporary creative nonfiction uses dialogue far more often than essays of previous decades. While we can only conjecture about the reasons for this, it is most likely connected to our increasingly film-oriented culture. We are far more accustomed to watching a scene unfold on a screen than we are to reading a writer's commentary and analysis of that scene. We are less patient about reading long descriptive or analytical passages that aren't broken up with action and dialogue. So it's best to learn how to work with dialogue, even if it isn't your strength. A line or two, appropriately placed, can throw open a window onto a scene.

So what counts as "good" dialogue? How do you get it? You listen for the best line: the most revealing or quirky, from the most interesting person—the line that sums it all up. And how do you know what that is? Well . . . the more you learn to listen for it, the better you'll get at hearing it. Eudora Welty wrote that good lines come from listening "for the right word." This involves attentiveness, instinct, and editing skills.

> "When you decide what matters and what doesn't, you're shaping your written world."

You'll want to use the lines that contribute to the focus and meaning of your piece. When you decide what matters and what doesn't, you're shaping your written world. Nobody can tell you whether that shape is a circle, square, spiral, or blob. "Sometimes I needed to make a speech do three or four or five things at once," Welty said, "reveal what the character said but also what he thought he said, what he hid, what others were going to think he meant, and what they misunderstood, and so forth." In creative nonfiction, dialogue has to carry not only the weight of information but also the traditional demands of storytelling. It has to cast light upon events and people and it needs to move the piece forward.

The best way to understand how dialogue is written is to read some. (This is a bit different from having an ear for dialogue, which requires close attention to real people and writing down what they say and how they say it.) Read fiction and nonfiction that shows people talking. Take note of what the dialogue includes, and imagine all that it doesn't, and what this infers about the story and the character. Observe how the quotation marks (if any) are used, how the paragraphing is done, how the "he says" and "she says" and other information clue us in to the speakers. Particularly notice the way that the author summarizes what is not directly attributed to the dialogue and how the action and thoughts are worked in around the spoken language. In this chapter, we'll elaborate upon what to watch for.

Dialogue Tags

When you write dialogue, you not only have the challenge of getting the language to sound natural and true but you also have to clue in the reader as to who is speaking. While this sounds simple, it can be a struggle for unpracticed writers. Signaling the speaker without overshadowing the dialogue can be tricky. The way it's done is a strong demonstration of the writer's personal style. For good or ill, it's noticeable. If in doubt, keep it simple. Don't toss in adverbs as a way of avoiding the more complex challenge of showing the action.

The most common way to demonstrate who is speaking is to use "he said/she said." These are known casually as dialogue tags, and are used so often that most readers don't notice them. Other useful tags are "agreed," "told," and the like. There are variations, such as "he exclaimed," "she shouted," etc.—but use these sparingly, if at all. They tend to come off as forced—artificial—overly dramatic. If the line "No!" appears in an argument scene, and is accompanied by, say, the character throwing a vase, we don't need the added tag of "he shouted angrily." The shout and the anger are already clear. And a word like "exclaim" is rather archaic; how many times do you go around saying that your friend "exclaimed" that he was upset. You'd be more likely to say, "He was screaming and running around the room like an idiot." It's far more interesting to *show* what your friend was exclaiming and doing (running like a giraffe, crashing into the coffee table). Even worse is a tag like "exclaimed loudly" or "whispered quietly." Whispering *is* quiet. Exclaiming *is* loud. Words ending in *-ly* should be abolished from tag lines. Seriously.

You don't want the tags to stand out unless there's a good stylistic reason to do so, or unless they relay a meaning that can't be shown in any other way.

Here is an example of a standard "he said/she said" construction, from William Langewiesche's essay "Columbia's Last Flight":

> Kling said, "Flight, Macs."
> Cain said, "Go."
> "We just lost tire pressure on the left outboard and left inboard, both tires."
> Cain said, "Copy."

Langewiesche doesn't provide any tag at all to mark the third line of dialogue. We know by then that Kling and Cain are having a two-way conversation, and it's Kling's turn to talk; the author doesn't have to remind us. We also know that the speaker has changed, because traditionally every time the speaker changes, we get a new paragraph. Also note (you probably already have) that at the beginning and end of each person's speech is a double quotation mark. This, too, is the conventional way of marking the beginning and ending of one person's statement. (There are exceptions to all dialogue conventions, done by practiced writers for stylistic reasons. We'll discuss these near the end of the chapter.)

A more complex example comes from Edward Abbey's nature classic *Desert Solitaire* (1968):

> "There's a horse living up that canyon," I announced; "a wild horse. And a big one—feet like frying pans."
> Slowly Mackie turned his head and looked where I pointed. "Wrong again," he said, after a moment's consideration.

"What do you mean, wrong again? If it's not a horse it must be a unicorn. Or a centaur? Look at those tracks—unshod. And from the wear and tear on that trail it's been living out here for a long time. Who runs horses out here?" We were about twenty miles from the nearest ranch.

"Nobody," Mackie agreed.

"You agree it's a horse."

"Of course it's a horse."

"Of course it's a horse. Well thank you very much. And no shoes, living out here in the middle of nothing, it must be a wild horse."

"Sorry," Mackie said. "Wrong again."

"Then what the hell is it?"

"Old Moon-Eye is what you might call an independent horse. He don't belong to anybody. But he ain't wild. He's a gelding and he's got Roy Scobie's brand on his hide."

Abbey uses only the tags necessary to distinguish between the two men. As the dialogue gets going, he no longer needs the tags, not only because we can follow which two people are talking, but because each man speaks in a distinctive way. "I" (Abbey) challenges Mackie—and not only that, he's longwinded about it. Mackie is quiet, a "man of few words," befitting our usual vision of the cowboy.

To reflect the casual speech of the two men, the piece occasionally skips standard punctuation marks and grammar usage. In standard usage, you'd put a comma after the interjection *well*. A man who wasn't a salt-of-the-earth type like Mackie probably wouldn't say "He don't belong" or "ain't." This usage, while realistic, also helps to distinguish his speech from Abbey's, since we can assume that, being a writer, he generally avoids the "ain't."

Abbey uses only two tag words other than *said*: *agreed* and *announced*. And these are chosen deliberately, to indicate something specific. When Abbey says "announced," he is poking fun at the way he's talking (authorities make announcements); he uses *agreed* to make a deadpan joke.

The dialogue serves not only to characterize the men but to impart information: there is a large gelding, marked by a particular brand, leading an independent life on the trail. By showing this through the dialogue, Abbey doesn't have to bore us with a list of facts.

If we can figure out who is talking, or if it doesn't matter who is talking, you don't need to explicitly identify the speaker. In this excerpt from the book *Motel Nirvana*, Melanie McGrath describes her visit to the Biosphere, an artificial habitation à la bubble located near the New Age mecca of Sedona, Arizona. The tour group hopes to spot one of the eight people who are said to live in the Biosphere:

There is absolutely nothing visible of a remotely prurient nature. Whoever heard of such a thing? There are murmurs of significant disquiet. . . . The guide tries her luck at mediating through the incipient mutiny by climbing down beyond the cordon and screwing her head to the glass in anticipation of a sighting. After a minute or so she comes up for air and says:

"I seen one, planting crops."

A shrunken ghost-face appears at the window and peers out briefly, causing the fattest man in the party to raise his eyes from the Coke and comment:

"Looks damned near dead to me."

"Surprisingly," counters the tour guide, supposing she has the fattest man's attention, "each Biospherean has lost on average only fourteen per cent of their original body weight."

The ghost-face retreats back into a simulated salt marsh behind the glass.

"What d'they eat anyway?" asks a fat woman dressed in pink shorts.

"Well . . ." pipes up the tour guide. Something in her tone alerts pink shorts to the disturbing possibility that she is staring a lecture right in the face, when all she had been expecting was a sound-bite.

"I guess they eat just the same as anyone else," says pink shorts, cutting off the lecture at the knees.

"Well, you'd be surprised," perks up the tour guide. Jeez, she must be new on the job.

"Meat?"

The tour guide smiles. Poor creature. So amiable, so anxious to please.

"How'd they kill it?" asks the fat man, sweating luxuriantly.

The tour guide swallows.

"Gross," says pink shorts.

And for a single moment we tourers are of one triumphant fraternity, basking in the illusion of a common victory.

By not identifying the speakers, our British author probably feels a bit freer in insulting the size, clothing, and eating habits of American tourists, not to mention the guilelessness of eco-tour guides in Arizona. Although McGrath could have gotten the names of the speakers, there is really no need to do so, and in fact it would have defeated her purposes. By keeping everyone anonymous, we can identify with the tourists' desire to undermine the silly experience and be less inclined to feel sorry for the guide. The writer is under less obligation to take the Biosphere concept and its adherents seriously; she invites us to identify with the tourists by further trivializing the absurd situation. McGrath's offhand insulting labels for the overweight tourists might seem pointless, except that they provide a living, blustering contrast to the anorexic "ghost-like" inhabitants behind the barrier. They, not the ghosts, are the ones with whom the writer identifies. And the language is consistent with the author's voice and personality, which are dry and sarcastic.

Dialogue can even exist entirely without tags or description, as it does in this excerpt from Dave Eggers's book *A Heartbreaking Work of Staggering Genius*:

Today is Friday, and on Friday he gets out of school at noon, so I usually come home early, too, if I can. We are in his room.

"Where are they?"

"They're in there."

"Where?"

"Hiding."

"Where?"

"In that mountain thing we made."

"Inside the papier-mâché?"

"Yeah."

"When was the last time you saw them?"

"I don't know. A while. A week maybe."

"You sure they're still in there?"

"Yeah. Almost positive."

"How?"

"They still eat their food."

"But you never see them?"

"No, not really."

"What crappy pets."

"Yeah, I know."

"Should we return them?"

"Can we?"

"I think so."

"Stupid iguanas."

The spare patter is appropriate to this scene; it moves quickly and captures the rhythm of casual talk. We don't so much need to know who is saying what as we need to hear their kid-ness, and to get a sense of the symbiotic relationship between the two.

> "The most common dialogue pattern mixes speech with brief description."

The most common dialogue pattern mixes speech with brief description. The description can not only reveal the tone and emotion of the speakers but can signal who is speaking. This eliminates the need for the "he said/she said" tags. This scene comes from Sheryl St. Germain's essay "Trying to Sing":

Maw-Maw pops an artichoke ball into her mouth too, and between chews notes how fine Ricky's uniform is and how beautiful my engagement ring is.

"Where's Paw-Paw?" I ask.

Maw-Maw swallows, sips her beer, and looks at my mother. My mother, in turn, looks at her hands. "He's in the back bedroom." She means my parents' bedroom.

"Oh, is he okay?"

"Well, he's tired, and can't really get up, but I'll tell him you're here, and y'all can go back and say hello." My mother steps carefully over my sister and brother and the trucks and dolls on the kitchen floor and makes her way down the hall to her bedroom.

This interaction involves three speakers—the narrator, her mother, and her grandmother—and mentions two additional characters (the narrator's boyfriend and grandfather). This scene can be characterized as much by what is not being said as by what is said.

First, Maw-Maw's (the grandmother's) dialogue is summarized; she is never directly quoted. Instead, she is described as drinking, eating, and talking. The narrator's question is answered not by her grandmother but by her mother, who is cued by the grandmother's look. The act of the mother staring down at her hands indicates that she's avoiding something. When asked if the grandfather is okay, the mother says he is tired and can't get up, "but"—then she never says whether he is "okay" or not. The way the mother abruptly leaves the room implies that he is not well. Neither the dialogue nor the narrator directly explains to the reader what is going on.

Showing a disturbance in this way is more effective than if the writer had said, "My mother was acting really strangely. She wouldn't answer my question and it really made me wonder if something more was going on here." By showing us the scene, St. Germain brings the reader into the situation; we, like the narrator, watch and wonder. A deeper interaction is created between story and reader; we are participants, actively questioning, rather than behaving as passive receivers. And we get a look at "Maw-Maw" (who chews tobacco and drinks beer) and the mother (who steps around the toys) that we otherwise wouldn't get. Dialogue shouldn't tell us everything; it should show us just what we should know, and no more. The desire for verisimilitude is no reason to use digressive or repetitive language.

Creating Mood through Dialogue

The following scene by Luis Alberto Urrea (found in full on page 739) provides emotional resonance and creates an unnerving mood. The scene is less important for the information it provides or what it says about the characters than in the disturbance it creates in the narrator and the air of foreboding it provides:

"Is she drunk?" said Juanita. I said something, no doubt a joke, and leaned into the van. I worked the box I was looking for free by shoving one of the heavy bags of beans out of the way. When I turned around, the woman was standing right beside me, staring into my face. She snarled.

I stumbled back from her. Her hair stood straight off her scalp as though she were taking a heavy charge of electricity through her feet. She was wheezing.

One of the women said, "She's crazy, Hermano."

"Fuck you," she snapped. Her voice was deep, like a man's voice. "*Vete a la chingada.*"

She leaned toward me. "We know you," she said. "We know who you are. We know what you're doing."

I laughed nervously. "What?" I said.

"You'll pay for this."

I put down my box. "I don't understand," I said.

She began to rasp obscenities in her man's voice. "We know you. We'll get you."

She spun around and jerked away from us, very fast. She stumbled over rocks in the road, but kept moving, shouting all the time, "*¡Vas a ver!* You'll see! We'll get you. We'll stop you."

She paused in front of Pacha's house at the top of the hill, gesturing at me and yelling her strange threats. The hair at the back of my neck began to rise.

"Is she drunk?" Juanita repeated.

The woman threw her head back and screamed.

Urrea introduces this section as "a record of a small event that happened on a typical spring day." He makes no commentary about its importance and draws no conclusions about it. Yet the woman's accusations, punctuated by her scream, create its own disconcerting commentary on the dire conditions of the trash dump and, possibly, on the writer's sense of guilt. The crazy lady's accusation—*we know who you are, we know what you're doing*—is one that haunts many ethical journalists and creative nonfiction writers who question their own motives as they take note of others' lives. The feeling the scene creates lingers long after it has ended.

Dialogue can be used not just to build tension but to deflate it. It may be deliberately mundane, even dull, existing for a specific reason, such as to indicate the speaker's intelligence, or show something deadening about the situation at hand. It's a risky device, because the writer can end up being as dull as the speaker.

Joan Didion is expert at letting the characters in her pieces expose their own insipidness. In the following scene from "The White Album," Didion observes the Doors in the act of recording an album. She does this not because she is a fan, but because she is capturing a picture of Southern California in the Sixties—and, possibly, because she is a working journalist and knows she can publish a piece about a celebrity. In this bit, Jim Morrison slumps on a couch and closes his eyes while everyone else in the band continues to work:

An hour or so passed, and still no one had spoken to Morrison. Then Morrison spoke to Manzarek. He spoke almost in a whisper, as if he were wresting the words from behind some disabling aphasia.

"It's an hour to West Covina," he said. "I was thinking maybe we should spent the night out there after we play."

Manzarek put down the corkscrew. "Why?" he said.

"Instead of coming back."

Manzarek shrugged. "We were planning to come back."

"Well, I was thinking, we could rehearse out there."

Manzarek said nothing.

"We could get in a rehearsal, there's a Holiday Inn next door."

"We could do that," Manzarek said. "Or we could rehearse Sunday, in town."

"I guess so." Morrison paused. "Will the place be ready to rehearse Sunday?"

Manzarek looked at him for a while. "No," he said then.

I counted the control knobs on the electronic console. There were seventy-six.

So why didn't Didion do the expected: describe Morrison's physical beauty or voice? Why does she include only dull conversation that reveals no fun celebrity facts? Given the rest of the essay, it's likely that Didion's goals were to:

- deflate the Morrison mythology,
- show that rock musicians are unimpressive if you actually have to talk to them,
- demonstrate that celebrity means nothing,
- show that nothing happened while she was in the studio, and
- prove that she is above infatuation with the famous.

She is alienated by the culture around her, by celebrity life in this essay, and by Southern California in the book as a whole. The scene ends with the lines: "There was a sense that no one was going to leave the room, ever. It would be some weeks before the Doors finished recording this album. I did not see it through." By including this mundane bit of dialogue, we can understand why.

Thus far, we have covered dialogue that is written in a traditional fashion (with a new paragraph for each speaker, double quotation marks, etc.). Yet sometimes writers abandon conventional dialogue structures to gain a stylistic effect. Writers who do this well are usually those who have written long enough to know the standard approach and to break it consistently.

> "Sometimes writers abandon conventional dialogue structures to gain a stylistic effect."

In "Busted in New York," Darryl Pinckney runs dialogue together in paragraphs. Rather than cuing a change in speaker, the paragraphing signals a change in the action:

"Been smoking something?" No answer. "Put your hands flat on the trunk of this car." The women, my friends, were side by side at the back of the car. I was on the sidewalk and had to bend over. Other undercovers quickly appeared. "We're going to empty your pockets." A woman had taken up position behind Rona and Billie. I felt a hand go into my pocket. My total financial assets held by a faded money clip hit the trunk of the car. "Did you all just meet tonight?" a new voice demanded. "No." My own voice was thin and completely lacking in the authority of outrage. The money clip was followed by a pack of menthol cigarettes, a disposable lighter, a case containing reading glasses, a John Coltrane–Johnny Hartman CD—"You listen to some good music," a head of hair said—and a mobile phone. "Where's your beeper?" He patted me down. "You got a beeper." "No," came the thin reply.

The effect of blending the dialogue is to quicken the pace. Instead of every speaker standing as an individual, there is a sense of forced sameness. The police become faceless authority. We can't tell who is talking. Physical details come in the items that the narrator knew he was carrying in his pockets. This highlights his unfamiliarity with what is happening and the need to focus on the familiar; it also sets up the beeper comment. It emphasizes the narrator's fear and lack of control. The effect for the reader is disorientation.

Pinckney isn't the only nonfiction writer who changes up the dialogue format, but the practice is fairly rare. Perhaps because of creative nonfiction's historical link to the magazine market—or because of the need to accurately represent the speech of real people—there are not a great many examples of experimental breaks in the dialogue format. As creative nonfiction is increasingly embraced by literary magazine publishers, this may change.

Dialogue lets the writer quickly create a scene that moves beyond the immediate subjective mind-scape. After a long period of reflection or analysis, its appearance can come as a relief for both reader and writer—it can let the air into the room. Dialogue adds a new dimension (much like putting on those 3-D glasses) and, when done well, adds an element of what feels like external truth: this is what people said, how they sounded, as they spoke during a single moment in time. Dialogue can help you, the writer, to see events a bit more clearly, too, as you take that double-step outside yourself. And it can be fun to write. Let's hear it.

Creative Nonfiction Referenced in This Chapter

Abbey, Edward. *Desert Solitaire*. Tucson: University of Arizona Press, 1968.

Didion, Joan. "The White Album." In *The White Album*. New York: Simon and Schuster, 1979.

Eggers, Dave. *A Heartbreaking Work of Staggering Genius*. New York: Vintage Books, 2001.

Langewiesche, William. "Columbia's Last Flight." In *The Best American Magazine Writing 2004*, compiled by the American Society of Magazine Editors. New York: HarperCollins, 2004.

McGrath, Melanie. *Motel Nirvana: Dreaming in the New Age in the American Desert*. New York: St. Martin's Press, 1996.

Pinckney, Darryl. "Busted in New York." In *Best American Essays 2002*, edited by Stephen Jay Gould and Robert Atwan. Boston: Houghton Mifflin, 2002.

St. Germain, Sheryl. "Trying to Sing." In *Swamp Songs: The Making of an Unruly Woman*. Salt Lake City: University of Utah Press, 2003.

Urrea, Luis Alberto. *Across the Wire*. New York: Anchor Books, 1993.

Works about Writing and Literature

Welty, Eudora. *Conversations with Eudora Welty*, Edited by Peggy Whitman Prenshaw. Jackson, MS: 1984.

Wolfe, Tom. *The New Journalism*. New York: Harper & Row, 1973.

CHAPTER **6**

Style

We don't know about you, but the first thing we think of when we hear the word *style* is attitude as expressed through clothing, hair, jewelry (through cartilage or otherwise), cars, songs, and technological gadgets. It's an advertising word, practically synonymous with pop culture trends.

Only academic sorts—and writers—think of style in terms of writing. Yet the word "style" derives from a Latin word meaning an instrument for writing, a manner of writing, a mode of expression. Philosophers and scholars from the classical age onward took pains to distinguish between style variations and to study the most effective styles for writing and speaking. Even then, style implied the capacity for artifice—a kind of artificial, trend-based self-expression. This tendency has always been no less true of writing as anything else, with philosophers arguing against trying to adopt a writing style the same way we might pick out a new shirt. It's long been known that real style must come from something sincere, something inside, or it doesn't work. To have true style, we have to know ourselves. And then we have to find out how to express that.

Style signals who we are; it is a way of understanding ourselves and approaching others. Style in creative writing should be true to the writer, the meaning of the piece, and the musicality of language.

While most of the public has lost the conscious connection between style and language, writers still believe that what Walter Raleigh said was true—that all style stems from our delight in language: "The pen, scratched on wax or paper, has become the symbol of all that is expressive, all that is intimate, in human nature; not only arms and arts, but man himself has yielded to it." Let's believe for at least the space of this chapter that this remains true.

Whatever the mode, whatever we create, our style expresses who we are at that moment in time. While we can't avoid being aware of an audience (the reader, the viewer, the judge), we need to try to push that observer out of our mind's eye while we are working. Writing creatively is not the same as writing as a journalist, theorist, or technical writer, bound by an audience awareness and writing conventions. With creative work we have the latitude to express our own voice. The most destructive thing a writer can do is to write to please—to write primarily for acclaim. Writing to please others will not carry you through the difficulties and commitment involved in literary work.

> "To find your own writing style, you have to understand and love language."

To find your own writing style, you have to understand and love language. You have to read, listen to, and obsess over words, syllables, vowels, phrases, short and long sentences, the timing of periods, and endless other details. Writers have to fall in love with words that are concrete, deceptively simple in sound; we have to love putting them together in unique ways. We have to enjoy the challenge of trying to express intangibles in ways that are comprehensible. We have to compare one thing, one idea against another, compare solids and fluids—juxtapose words and images. In the process, we learn to see differently. We learn to be specific rather than vague, and in that honing we're forced to define what had previously been overlooked. And just when we think we've grasped it, styles and words change.

Words "wax, and wane, they wither and burgeon," wrote Raleigh. "From age to age, from place to place, from month to month, they are never at a stay. They take on colour, intensity, and vivacity from the inflections of the neighborhood; the same word is of several shapes and diverse imports in the same sentence; they depend on the building that they compose for the very chemistry of the stuff that composes them. . . . For words carry with them all the meanings they have worn."

To write, we have to pay attention to the word.

The more you write, the better your style will get. Choices in language that you once labored over will become subconscious and will be replaced by more new choices and challenges. If this isn't fun for you, then you're probably not meant to be a writer.

Writing creatively isn't safe and isn't easy. You're out in the middle of nowhere, without guidelines, no matter how many useful craft books you read. You don't have the secure boundaries supplied in the worlds of academia, business, and journalism. Institutions demand a proscribed style that masks the writer's voice. In these worlds, the information or theory is supposed to stand apart from the writer, who lacks personal identity. Words that create emotional reactions are to be avoided, unless they are written to manipulate (as in advertising or speechwriting).

Creative nonfiction falls on the other end of the style spectrum, using imagistic, sensory, and emotional language to express the writer's vision. This doesn't mean that you have to write using complex poetic sentences and multi-syllabic words. Trying To Write Like An Author is nearly always counterproductive; the idea is to both reveal and develop individual voice and style. The language should be truly your own, whatever that may mean.

Finding voice takes practice and a letting go of outmoded learning. You won't get to it in a day, and if you were to write all of your life, you'd still be trying to get closer to that "real voice." This search for identity and understanding is part of the reason we write. (It certainly isn't for the money.) For some, this voice will be conversational and immediate; for others, elaborate and distant. And that voice will change over time and by piece, as you change. The more you write, the more the written language becomes the natural one. It's as simple and complex as that.

Varieties of Style

Writing styles used by creative nonfiction writers are as various as the individuals who write the pieces. This is the beginning of Joan Didion's essay "The White Album":

> We tell ourselves stories in order to live. The princess is caged in the consulate. The man with the candy will lead the children into the sea. The naked woman on the ledge outside the window on the sixteenth floor is a victim of accidie, or the naked woman is an exhibitionist, and it would be "interesting" to know which. We tell ourselves that it makes some difference whether the naked woman is about to commit a mortal sin or is about to register a political protest or is about to be, the Aristophanic view, snatched back to the human condition by the fireman in priest's clothing just visible in the window behind her, the one smiling at the telephoto lens. We look for the sermon in the suicide, for the social or moral lesson in the murder of five. We interpret what we see, select the most workable of the multiple choices. We live entirely, especially if we are writers, by the imposition of a narrative line upon disparate images, by the "ideas" with which we have learned to freeze the shifting phantasmagoria which is our actual experience.

Didion's style has been called formal, aloof, certain, spare, exact, controlled. Didion has probably never been accused of sounding sloppy, friendly, or conversational. What is it about her language that gives us this impression? On the most obvious level, Didion uses language that isn't found in daily conversation. Accidie? Aristophanic? She clues us in to the seriousness of her topic by bringing up sin, a priest, a sermon, and social and moral lessons, not to mention exhibitionists, suicides, and murders.

We expect that this will not be a freewheeling adventure story. Given her overtness—she isn't trying to imply or show here, she's telling you—you might well expect a logical philosophical essay, and you'd be right. But we might not expect to find some of the things that do make an appearance, like the Doors and the Black Panthers. These political and cultural referents of the sixties exist in juxtaposition with, at odds with, the writer's elegant, cool distance. This adds intrigue and tension to the essay: what is this woman doing in this psychedelic world, and how will she survive?

Didion's beginning has no "I" in it; it does use plenty of "we"'s. It's a broad "we," implying all of us, the "we" of humanity, and, by extension, the "I" of the writer. From this beginning, we might not expect Didion as a character to appear. But she does, in fact, eventually emerge as the "I" who interacts with the musicians and drives her car, while still occasionally speaking for us all. The switching from the inclusive to the personal adds to the overall effect of discomfort.

Didion uses short sentences with rather odd, ambiguous images. The princess, she says, is not in the tower, but the consulate. The man lures children not into a car, but into the sea. They're mysterious, these images, and, Didion seems to indicate, we will not be able to make sense of them. As the paragraph goes on, similarly strange images are linked by commas, rather than separated with periods (the fireman in priest's clothing; the telephoto lens). A long, flowing line is broken by a short one. Using crisp, dissecting language ("multiple choices," "narrative line," "disparate images"), Didion tells us that our "ideas" (in quotation marks) are there to "freeze" our experience. Is she implying that ideas aren't valid? Does she imply that what she will write in this essay won't be true? The words she uses to evoke emotion and action are short and simple: We tell. We see. We interpret. We look. We live.

Our perception of a writer's style changes with the times. An approach that once seemed simple and accessible might, in time, seem wordy or even outdated. An example of a style that manages to be both earthy and (to contemporary ears) rather elevated is Mark Twain's. The following excerpt, from Twain's essay "Corn-Pone Style," was written late in the author's career:

> A political emergency brings out the corn-pone opinion in fine force in its two chief varieties—the pocketbook variety, which has its origin in self-interest, and the bigger variety, the sentimental variety—the one which can't bear to be outside the pale; can't bear to be in disfavor; can't endure the averted face and the cold shoulder; wants to stand well with his friends, wants to be smiled upon, wants to be welcome, wants to hear the precious words, "He's on the right track!" Uttered, perhaps by an ass, but still an ass of high degree, an ass whose approval is gold and diamonds to a smaller ass, and confers glory and honor and happiness, and membership in the herd. For these gauds many a man will dump his life-long principles into the street, and his conscience along with them. We have seen it happen. In some millions of instances.

Twain's satirical style and emphasis on political injustices and ineptitudes has had a considerable influence on American essayists. His combination of sharp wit, complex and nearly lyrical sentences, the random bit of conversation, and the slam-it-home paragraph ending led the way for thousands of political columnists of varying degrees of eptitude. It's hard to comprehend that at the time Twain wrote, his style seemed simple, breaking the model of clunky Victorian prose. This is a measure of the extent to which the passage of time changes our perception of style, as the new becomes the taken for granted.

It's now common for contemporary writing to be conversational in tone, as if the writer were sitting in the room consuming mass quantities of coffee or beer. C. Tyler's graphic memoir "Sub Zero" (found on page 732) reads almost like a diary entry. The narration on its first page is hand-written, not typeset or carefully printed; sentence fragments and abbreviations are used; slang pops up in the narrative. Although many people still believe that the essay is a formal and elevated form, it is often relaxed, using commonplace speech and place and people. And it has been since its inception.

Here's a selection from Thomas De Quincy's piece "The English Mail-Coach," written more than 150 years ago, in 1849:

> Did I then make love to Fanny? Why, yes; about as much love as one could make whilst the mail was changing horses—a process which, ten years later, did not occupy above eighty seconds; but *then*—viz., about Waterloo—it occupied five times eighty. Now, four hundred seconds offer a field quite ample enough for whispering into a young woman's ear a great deal of truth, and (by way of parenthesis) some trifle of falsehood. Grandpapa did right, therefore, to watch me. And yet, as happens too often to the grandpapas of earth in a contest with the admirers of granddaughters, how vainly would he have watched me had I meditated any evil whispers to Fanny! She, it is my belief, would have protected herself against any man's evil suggestions. But he, as the result showed, could not have intercepted the opportunities for such suggestions. Yet, why not? Was he not active? Was he not blooming? Blooming he was as Fanny herself.
>
> "Say, all our praises why should lord—"
>
> Stop, that's not the line.
>
> "Say, all our roses why should girls engross?"
>
> The coachman showed rosy blossoms on his face deeper even than his granddaughter's—*his* being drawn from the ale-cask, Fanny's from the fountains of the dawn.

Certainly, this piece still has that Victorian tone (indicating the author's aristocratic British background as much as the time period), but the direct questioning of the reader, the dashes, and (as the piece goes on) its downright drug induced bizarreness makes it as contemporary in tone as anything written by David Foster Wallace, Hunter Thompson, or Rick Moody.

Punctuation

The unusual use of punctuation is common in literary writing. Some writers use punctuation inventively and wonderfully, breaking the standard rules in ways that are clearly not mistakes. The rule breaking is done consistently and for a reason. Other writers try to experiment with punctuation and do it so badly that they come off as people who can't place a comma. Developing a rule-breaking style is, despite appearances, difficult and developed through reams of pages of writing and editing. It's a sophisticated expression of the writer's voice; a style that draws attention to itself had better be good enough to stand up to the notice.

Rick Moody has the kind of distinctive style that people seem to love or hate. His book *The Black Veil*, excerpted on page 603, uses such nonstandard approaches as the very, very long paragraph, the very, very long sentence, italics for emphasis (where you might not expect them), italics to indicate dialogue, etc. While the story itself is not especially unusual, its style stands out enough to bring some critics to paroxysms of spit-slinging invective. (After reading *The Black Veil*, novelist and critic Dale Peck notoriously called Moody "the worst writer of his generation.")

Yet Moody's approach isn't terribly far away from Virginia Woolf's. While Woolf wrote a good many conventional reviews and think-pieces, she occasionally wrote nonfiction that is as experimental in style as her fiction. The following long paragraph is from her essay "Street Hauntings":

> How beautiful a London street is then, with its islands of light, and its long groves of darkness, and on one side of it perhaps some tree-sprinkled, grass-grown space where night is folding herself to sleep naturally and, as one passes the iron railing, one hears those little cracklings and stirrings of leaf and twig which seem to suppose the silence of fields all round them, an owl hooting, and far away the rattle of a train in the valley. But this is London, we are reminded; high among the bare trees are hung oblong frames of reddish yellow light—windows; there are points of brilliance burning steadily like low stars—lamps; this empty ground, which holds the country in it and its peace, is only a London square, set about by offices and houses where at this hour fierce lights burn over maps, over documents, over desks where clerks sit turning with wetted forefinger the files of endless correspondences; or more suffusedly the firelight wavers and the lamplight falls upon the privacy of some drawing-room, its easy chairs, its papers, its china, its inlaid table, and the figure of a woman, accurately measuring out the precise number of spoons of tea which—She looks at the door as if she heard a ring downstairs and somebody asking, is she in?

Woolf's lyrical selection is strung with images broken up by commas, semicolons, and a single early-falling period. Unusual stylistic approaches are hardly rare in creative nonfiction, now or in the past. Often what appears new or strange is simply following in a tradition that has been lost to casual readers.

"There's something chatty and enthusiastic about the dash."

Another favorite punctuation mark of the innovative stylist has long been the dash. There's something chatty and enthusiastic about the dash, which is a useful device for breaking rhythm without coming to a full stop. It looks less formal than the semicolon; it has energy, a breathlessness. The following is from *Dreamthorp*, written by Alexander Smith in 1864. He is referring to the writer Montaigne:

> He mocks and scorns his deeper nature; and, like Shakespeare in *Hamlet*, says his deepest things in a jesting way. When he is gayest, be sure there is a serious design in his gaiety. Singularly shrewd and penetrating—sad, not only from sensibility of exquisite nerve and tissue, but from meditation, and an eye that pierced the surfaces of things—fond of pleasure, yet strangely fascinated by death—skeptical, yet clinging to what the Church taught and believed—lazily possessed by a high ideal of life, yet unable to reach it, careless perhaps often to strive after it, and with no very high opinion of his own goodness, or of the goodness of his fellows—and with all these serious elements, an element of humour mobile as flame, which assumed a variety of forms, now pure fun, now mischievous banter, now blistering scorn—humour in all its shapes, carelessly exercised on himself and his readers—with all this variety, complexity, riot, and contradiction almost of intellectual forces within, Montaigne wrote his bewildering Essays—

If done consciously, lyrically, unconventional punctuation shows that we've moved from the realm of the conventional to the literary. Stylistic expression is at its essence an act of rebellion, often a necessary one.

Rhythm and Style

> Why do rhythms and melodies, which are mere sounds, resemble dispositions, while tastes do not, nor yet colors or smells?
> —*Aristotle*

Writers and artists have long noted the similarities between the arts of writing and music. The poet Paul Valery once described music as the organization of "pure" sound different from "the world of noises." This kind of sound commands our attention, promotes feeling, and changes us. We identify it as the beginning of a creation rather than an accident, and we know it will have an end. Valery contrasts this musical sound with a sudden noise in a concert hall, like a slamming door, which makes us feel that "something within us is broken, that there is a breach in some kind of substance or law of association; a universe is shattered, a spell is abolished."

In creative nonfiction, the author brings us into the concert and just as willfully shatters the tone with grating reality. Usually, the nonfiction writer wants the reader to think; they don't want him to entirely suspend his disbelief, as most fiction writers do. Creative nonfiction shifts between music and noise.

Just as music has a beat and flow, so does writing. The dullest writing has rhythm, even if it is a monotonous series of whole notes. The best of it sends us into reverie or rips us into awareness, depending upon the writer's intention. Rhythm creates a sense of motion and emotion, reaching us in a physical way. Novelist John Gardner believed that sentence rhythms should "fit what [the writer] is saying, rushing along when the story rushes, turning somewhat ponderous to deal with a ponderous character, echoing the thunder of which the story tells, or capturing aurally the wobble of the drunk, the slow, dull pace of the tired old man." Poet Ezra Pound said that writers should strive for an "absolute rhythm" that corresponds to whatever emotion the writer wishes to express. Creative nonfiction nearly always tries to elicit feeling from the reader, even while, more often than fiction, it asks the reader to join in rational contemplation of an idea or to simply appreciate a bit of information.

To get a sense of the variety of written rhythms, and the impact that rhythm can have on a piece, let's look at James Alan McPherson's essay "Ivy Day in the Empty Room."

> About six years ago, at a time when the issues clustered around race still simmered on the back burners of national consciousness, I had a fierce argument with one of my oldest black friends. He had called me from his home in Lansing, Michigan to report about a conflict between members of his group, people devoted to the memory of Malcolm X, and a group of black ministers who were partisans on the memory of Martin Luther King, Jr. At issue between the two groups was the naming of a street in Lansing, one of the early homes of Malcolm Little, now known as Malcolm X. The black ministers wanted the same street named for Martin Luther King.

This passage adopts a conventional rhythm based on complex, grammatically constructed sentences. There is not much variation from sentence to sentence; the effect is that of measured, straightforward statements. The sentences aren't broken by dialogue, fragments, or wordplay. There are no question marks, exclamation points, dashes, or even semicolons. Nothing exists to draw particular attention to the rhythm. This measured quality helps to establish a tone of authority. The steadiness coaxes the reader into a possible agreement with its calm, reasoned presentation.

This rhythm and style continue until the end of "Ivy Day"'s first section, when McPherson suddenly shifts in another direction. The use of italics signals that we're to read this in a new way. This section is more personal, telling the story in a far more immediate and dramatic fashion:

> *Ahead of us, in the night, traffic and crowds of silent people. One crowd is moving as a group, a body, seeming to stop and accost other people in cars and on the street. This moving crowd is white. I tell Devorah, "We must keep walking past that crowd. White people are capable of anything! If they try to stop us, I'll throw this television and try to fight them while you run." This becomes our plan. The crowd seems to get larger and larger and whiter and whiter as we approach. We cross Massachusetts several times to avoid it. Then we are spotted and the crowd crosses after us.*

In this passage, the dialogue doesn't break conventionally into paragraphs. The rhythm shifts to short, rapid bursts, building tension. The sentence structure is simple, using a noun-verb construction ("We must," "We cross," "The crowd seems"). Later, McPherson returns to a measured, rational rhythm as he examines the social implications of the riot and builds toward his point.

The following excerpt from Lawrence Weschler uses one particularly long, melodic sentence that creates a lulling rhythm:

> His hands trembled, perpetually; he moved about in minced and shuffling ministeps, sometimes quite quickly (as if being propelled down a steep incline), other times slowly and yet more slowly still; sometimes, in mid-gesture, in mid-sentence, he'd freeze up altogether, for minutes on end, before somehow jump-starting himself back into the world and resuming wherever he'd happened to leave off. Seated at his dining-room table, his body would occasionally (especially as he grew more intellectually excited) give itself over to a veritable tempest of tics and tremors, the wooden chair under him creaking so violently you expected it to come shattering apart at any moment (several had), and he'd pop the lid off a plastic container of variously shaped and colored pills, shakingly spearing a precise one or two after the downing of which he'd gradually proceed to calm down, at least for a while. All of which he took in stride, utterly unself-consciously, not as much resigned as resolutely, obliviously sovereign.

Weschler's "A Parkinsonian Passion: Ed Weinberger" has a rhythm that moves forward and then breaks off jerkily (using parentheses), rattling and lulling, mimicking the physical effects of Parkinson's disease. The sounds of the words with the *t*s and the *sh*s (hard to soft), the alliteration, the soothing *o*s and the sharp long *e*s, come together to create just the right sound to show the man's orchestrated attempt to open a pill bottle. This is a lovely example of the way that the melody and rhythm of the language can directly tie in with the subject or person being drawn. It's a piece that, especially when read aloud, is strikingly musical.

In contrast, the writer Deborah Tall uses short, definite, noun-verb sentences and numerous paragraphs to create a vaguely ominous and oddly empty effect in her short essay "The Dream of Family":

> He is emaciated, mangled by age and disease, unable to rise from his thread-bare chair. His hands tremble wildly and tears stream down his cratered face as he gazes at us.
>
> His name is Charles.
>
> The word *grandpa* self-consciously crosses my lips for the first time in my life.
>
> This specter, the grandfather I supposedly take after. I confirm that his eyes are green.
>
> My mother acts as casually as if she'd seen him last week.
>
> My father stands nervously aside.
>
> I can't understand much of my grandfather's slurred speech, and I'm frightened by how longingly he clings to my hand.
>
> I am trying hard to bring my fullest concentration to this moment, to be sure I remember him, after.
>
> I am trying to look as moved by our meeting as he is.
>
> But I remember so little.

The white spaces explicate the great distance between people and emotions in Tall's piece. Much is clearly held back in this space, which becomes a dominating presence of its own. The short beats and the constant periods establish a somber sameness that emphasizes the lack of color or sound. The creation of emptiness is quite deliberate.

Repetition

Most music has a refrain. Pop songs repeat lines over and over (sometimes until you want to scream). Orchestral music has motifs that circle throughout the piece, usually with variations. Literary writing does this, too. We recognize these repetitions and we feel them, sometimes without being aware we are doing so.

All forms of literary writing have these returning words and motifs, images and metaphors, fragments of conversation, conversation, statements, and situations. These repetitions can be used to frame the piece (occurring at the beginning and the end but not in between). They can be scattered throughout. All remind the reader that the essay (or book) is unified. They're signposts that mark the path (even if the path is crooked or divergent).

Our first example is from David Foster Wallace's essay "Consider the Lobster" (found in its entirety on page 755):

> 2003 Festival headlights: concerts by Lee Ann Womack and Orleans, annual Maine Sea Goddess beauty pageant, Saturday's big parade, Sunday's William

G. Atwood Memorial Crate Race, annual Amateur Cooking Competition, carnival rides and midway attractions and food booths, and the MLF's Main Eating Tent, where something over 25,000 pounds of fresh-caught Maine lobster is consumed after preparation in the World's Largest Lobster Cooker near the grounds' north entrance. Also available are lobster rolls, lobster turn-overs, lobster saute, Down East lobster salad, lobster bisque, lobster ravioli, and deep-fried lobster dumplings. Lobster thermidor is obtainable at a sit-down restaurant called the Black Pearl on Harbor Park's northwest wharf. A large all-pine booth sponsored by the Maine Lobster Promotion Council has free pamphlets with recipes, eating tips, and Lobster Fun Facts. The winner of Friday's Amateur Cooking Competition prepares Saffron Lobster Ramekins, the recipe for which is now available for public download-ing at www.mainelobsterfestival.com. There are lobster T-shirts and lobster bobblehead dolls and inflatable lobster pool toys and clamp-on lobster hats with big scarlet claws that wobble on springs. Your assigned correspondent saw it all, accompanied by one girlfriend and both his own parents—one of which parents was actually born and raised in Maine, albeit in the extreme northern inland part, which is potato country and a world away from the touristic midcoast.

There is something funny about the repetition of the word *lobster*. This undoubtedly has something to do with the very look of lobster and possibly with the fact that it is boiled alive and that we consume the creature while wearing bibs. The point is that a word brings with it a series of associations, and its repetition brings attention not only to the sound but to the meaning of the word. The repeated word has to be a good one and it has to be worth saying over and over again. It has to suit the purpose. Wallace shows his ability to use nearly every possible synonym for *lobster*; nobody would ever accuse him of linguistic laziness. The language and story surrounding the repetition give the repetition purpose.

> "A word brings with it a series of associations, and its repetition brings attention not only to the sound but to the meaning of the word."

While repetition may be used for comic effect, it can also be used to add a sense of solemnity. Such is the case with Leslie Marmon Silko's memoir, "Uncle Tony's Goat." In this, the word *goat* is repeated, helping to give the piece the tone of an oral folk story:

The billy goat never forgot the bows and arrows, even after the bows had cracked and split and the crooked, whittled arrows were all lost. This goat was big and black and important to my uncle Tony because he'd paid a lot to get him and because he wasn't an ordinary goat. Uncle Tony had bought him from a white man, and then he'd hauled him in the back of the pickup all the way from Quemado. And my uncle was the only person who could touch this goat. If a stranger or one of us kids got too near him, the mane on the billy goat's neck would stand on end and the goat would rear up on his hind legs and dance forward trying to reach the person with his long, spiral horns. This billy goat smelled bad, and none of us cared if we couldn't pet him. But my uncle took good care of this goat. The goat would let Uncle Tony brush him with the horse brush and scratch him around the base of his horns. Uncle Tony talked to the billy goat—in the morning when he unpenned the goats and in the evening when he gave them their hay and closed the gate for the night. I never paid too much attention to what he said to the billy goat; usually it was something like "Get up, big goat! You've slept long enough," or "Move over, big goat, and let the others have something to eat." And I think Uncle Tony was proud of the way the billy goat mounted the nannies, powerful and erect with the great black testicles swinging in rhythm between his hind legs.

There are a good many opportunities for Silko to substitute other words for *goat*. Yet she chooses to use this same one. This repetition is a device that she uses throughout all of her work, to an almost trance-like effect. The word *goat* is loaded with associations; in most cultures, it is a sexual image, and often an evil one, and Silko directly ties into this sexuality in this segment. The repetition also reflects a pattern found in Native American stories—and, most likely, the way that Uncle Tony speaks.

Repetition can also occur on the level of the full essay. This recurring motif might be a single word, or it might be words with similar meanings. One word might be seen as primary, with the others falling into the subset.

Michael Martone's essay "Manufacturing Place," on page 571, uses the word *wire* and variations on wire throughout. He creates a network of wire, connected by switches which are operated by people. The physical wiring becomes cybernetic wiring becomes human wiring. The word is carefully chosen. The switchroom, the author says, is both a "real" place embedded in his own wiring, and "a cybernetic node." The wiring is not only what unifies the piece—it is the essence of the piece. Without it, there would be no essay.

Emily Hiestand says that her essay "Maps" is "put together something like a roadmap, with different segments, folds and creases." The map organizes the piece; Hiestand calls this organization "organic," reflecting biological order. She sees the map structure as a visual one because she tends to "perceive and decipher the world visually—gleaning for the ideas, clues, pleasure, and information embodied in shape and color, shadow, design, physical forms and gesture."

While the word *map* is repeated in "Maps," the mapping motif is seen through the repetition of names and landscape characteristics. She speaks of the code names (and numbers) used by the Atomic Energy Commission, contrasting these with the names given by the original Scotch-Irish settlers. The family and its names are also mapped, marking the distance to be travelled from origin to end. The highways and mountains are mapped. There is a map of her father's life that runs from his ancestors' homes to Normandy to Atom City. Hiestand particularizes all of the maps into the story of her father's love for maps, which comes up late in the essay. Finally, the piece acknowledges the impossibility of going back, turning the map ultimately into a relic. While she does not always say "map," we are never able to entirely lose sight of that map, of places marked and recorded, of reference points that remain despite the changes.

Rhythm, especially combined with the use of repetition, has been used since the classicists to build the intensity of a discussion and emphasize particular ideas. While political speeches often use this tactic to make absolutist declarations, the structure can also be used in more nuanced arguments. A contemporary example is found in "Sisterhood," an essay by the writer/columnist Katha Pollitt.

> Perhaps the way women think about love is part of that slave religion Nietzsche talks about, a leftover from the days when you needed a man to survive; but of course you couldn't put it like that, even to yourself, much less to him, or the spell wouldn't work. Maybe romance really is the velvet glove on the iron fist and Utopia would be everyone living in their room, and visiting the rooms of others. Maybe, in the future, when women's psychology catches up to their material circumstances, we'll live in sugar-cube cities made up entirely of studio apartments. I could hardly say that I found domesticity erotic, once I got over the sheer miracle of having my beloved right there, to be touched and looked at and talked with whenever I wanted. I would have been a good girlfriend for a political prisoner, writing long letters and living in a fever of anticipation—*just think, darling, only fifteen more years!*—and having the intoxication of romantic love without the loss of self it seemed to entail.
>
> What would the world be like if women stopped being women—shut the tea-and-sympathy shop, closed down the love store, gave up the slave religion? Could the world go on without romantic love, all iron fist, no velvet glove? . . . . Yet, in the end, nobody loves a victim, even—especially—the other victims. "Down among the women," as Fay Weldon wrote, back when she still was one. "What a place to be!" Now she writes books telling women to fake orgasms because nature has designed them to hardly ever have them and why make a man feel bad about something that isn't his fault? In other words, practice the slave religion; just don't believe in it yourself. But why would anyone do that if they can buy their own shoes?

Pollitt's rhythmic repetition of the "perhaps's" and the "maybe's" reflect the questioning that at first seems tentative but culminates in a statement of (almost) independence. The relatively short sentences hit again and again, like a nagging thought (or a headache) that won't go away. The questions never end, and while there is an implication of an answer, it hardly feels assured. All of this is in keeping with her subject, which is women's self-doubt and deception when faced with romantic love. The existence of the piece, which discusses the place and agency of women, alone puts it in the category of persuasion, even when the author herself is not entirely certain that a conclusion can ever be reached.

Every essay in this book uses repeated words and images. They're the connectors, working on the reader in ways that go beyond statements of intent, of points, of fact.

Point of View

Since whole books have been written studying the ramifications of point of view, we'll clearly not do justice to the subject in these few pages. Our discussion will stick to the choice of working in the first person ("I"), the third person ("he/she"), or the second person ("you").

There's a perception that all creative nonfiction uses the first person—that it's all, necessarily, about the "I." Beyond the use of the pronoun, there seems to be a sense that the writer has to be directly present, as a character, in the piece. Not so.

A good literary writer uses voice to project himself into the piece, no matter the point of view chosen. The decision to use "I" relies primarily on the needs of the story and the writer's need to distance himself from the material.

Although nonfiction writers can write in the third person, the first-person point of view remains by far the most common approach. In memoir the "I" is a necessarily central character and voice. Without the author as subject, there would be little story to tell; the actions and events rely upon the presence of the author/narrator as witness and actor. The writer's experiences and reactions are paramount (even if the writer tries to side-step the matter). Switching to the third person, the "she," doesn't remove the presence of the writer from the reader's mind.

First-person point of view moves the writer in close and invites the reader to experience himself as that "I." The writer is forced into accountability; it is an admission that what is written is the writer's actual experience. Personal essay, too, relies nearly exclusively on the use of the "I." In the essay, it's often the entryway into thoughtful, reflective, or opinionated passages. The use of fictionalizing techniques (particularly dialogue) is often played down or absent altogether. In the personal essay, the reader is invited to share the writer's couch; we don't necessarily become the writer (as we would in memoir), but a friend and listener.

Most examples of third-person creative nonfiction fall under the sub-genre of literary journalism. This choice of perspective puts the characters in the forefront of the narrative, as the subjects of the piece, and the author in the background, as the disembodied voice. It is a permutation of the distant stance traditionally adopted in journalism.

The best known work of creative nonfiction that avoids the "I" narrator is Truman Capote's *In Cold Blood*. For Capote to directly write himself into the story would have turned the book into, well, something like the movie *Capote*. The book wouldn't have been about Perry Smith, the killer, or even about the victims of the crime. It would have gone into the situations surrounding Capote's relationship with Smith and with the local residents, and with the decisions he made in the writing of the book. This is not the story Capote wanted to tell.

Memoir, too, can be told in the third person, although this approach is uncommon. Some memoirs switch from the first person ("I") to third ("she"), often representing a time change and a younger or older version of the author. The use of the third person gives the writer more latitude to see

> "Memoir isn't fiction, and the use of the third person doesn't absolve the writer of the need to tell the truth."

the situation clearly and to rely more heavily on scenes with dialogue and description. The third person provides a degree of distancing between the writer and the material, the writer and her reader, and the material and the reader. Previously, such books probably would have been published as fiction. Memoir isn't fiction, though, and the use of the third person doesn't absolve the writer of the need to tell the truth. Readers will interpret that "she" as an "I" in a way that doesn't happen in fiction.

Finally, some writers use the second-person point of view, the "you." This is rarely done throughout full essays; usually it comes in short passages within longer pieces. The use of "you" can be done conversationally, bringing in the reader; it can also have an oddly distancing effect, representing the gulf between the writer and the past or the writer and her emotions.

No matter which pronoun is chosen, the writer still serves in some way as the witness (however secondhand) to real events. Whether we write in the first, second, or third person, we need to develop the distance to see the story as a story—not *as* us but separate from us. The closer the story is to incidents in our personal lives, the harder it is to make the separation. The writer should choose the point of view that allows her to do this. Vivian Gornick describes this struggle beautifully in her book *The Situation and the Story*:

> To tell that tale, I soon discovered, I had to find the right tone of voice; the one I habitually lived with wouldn't do at all: it whined, it grated, it accused; above all, it accused. Then there was the matter of syntax; my own ordinary, everyday sentence—fragmented, interjecting, overriding—also wouldn't do; it had to be altered, modified, brought under control. And then I could see, this as soon as I began writing, that I needed to pull back—way back—from these people and these events to find the place where the story could draw a deep breath and take its own measure. In short, a useful point of view, one that would permit greater freedom of association—for that of course is what I have been describing—had to be brought along. What I didn't see, and that for a long while, was that this point of view could only emerge from a narrator who was me and at the same time not me.

Finally: choose the point of view that allows the story to tell itself—to take off, to fly. If it does this for you, it will probably do it for the reader, too.

How nice it would be to have a handy concluding statement that neatly summarizes style in literary writing and in life. Yet style is all about self-expression. It can involve everything from calculated flair to deliberate understatement to a sad capitulation to pack mentality. Voice, on the other hand, is so much a part of us that only elocution lessons can fix the stammer, and even then we can't do much about the timbre. We can't even hear our own voice clearly unless it is played back to us, and its appalling sound can often be blamed upon the electrical device that did the recording. We barely recognize ourselves.

And so: while style can to some extent involve conscious decision (pinstripe or floral?), voice is our mysterious uncontrollable self. Like a singer, we can learn to modulate and project that voice. Our voice and, to a lesser extent, our style emerge from a combination of physical, emotional, and spiritual phenomena that nobody really understands. To ask how we create a style is similar to the question of creating a personality. We can imprint habits upon ourselves, we can reform our most obnoxious tendencies, we can even throw away the polyester, but certain fundamental preferences drive our decisions. We like blue. Why? Who knows? And why did we like blue at the age of ten but now prefer yellow? Our style changes by age and place and era and who we are near and why and just how free we feel to go with what we truly love. We learn to incorporate that style, add flourishes, and simplify. What remains through our changes is our voice, and if we work hard and are lucky, we can learn to accept it, reveal it, and project the best of it.

Creative Nonfiction Referenced in This Chapter

Capote, Truman. *In Cold Blood*. New York: Random House, 1966.

Didion, Joan. "The White Album." In *The White Album*. New York: Simon and Schuster, 1979.

De Quincey, Thomas. "The English Mail-Coach." In *The English Mail-Coach and Other Essays*. London: J. M. Dent, 1961.

McPherson, James. "Ivy Day in the Empty Room." In *The Best American Essays 1994*, edited by Tracy Kidder. Boston: Houghton Mifflin, 1994.

Pollitt, Katha. "Sisterhood." In *Learning to Drive: And Other Life Stories*. New York: Random House, 2007.

Smith, Alexander. "Dreamthorp." In *Dreamthorp: A Book of Essays Written in the Country*. Boston: J. E. Tilton, 1864.

Tall, Deborah. "A Dream of Family." In *A Family of Strangers*. Louisville: Sarabande, 2006.

Twain, Mark. "Corn-pone Opinions." In *The Complete Essays of Mark Twain*, edited by Charles Neider. New York: DaCapo, 2000.

Weschler, Lawrence. "A Parkinsonian Passion: Ed Weinberger." In *Vermeer in Bosnia: Selected Writings*. New York: Vintage, 2005.

Woolf, Virginia. "Street Haunting." In *The Death of the Moth and Other Essays*. New York: Harcourt, 1942.

Works about Writing and Literature

Gardner, John. *On Becoming a Novelist.* New York: Norton, 1999.

Gornick, Vivian. *The Situation and the Story: The Art of Personal Narrative.* New York: Farrar, Straus and Giroux, 2001.

Peck, Dale. "The Moody Blues." *The New Republic.* July 4, 2002.

Pound, Ezra. "A Few Don'ts from an Imagiste." In *Literary Essays of Ezra Pound.* New York: New Directions, 1968.

Raleigh, Walter. *Style.* Whitefish, MT: Kessinger Publishing, 2004.

Valery, Paul. *The Art of Poetry.* Princeton, NJ: Princeton University Press, 1989.

CHAPTER **7**

Revision

Like most writers, we have a love/hate relationship with revision. On the happy side, there's the consolation of words on the page, which signal we've actually written something. On the sad side, those words may prove to be not very good; worse, they may seem perfectly brilliant even when we sense that they probably aren't.

Once you become a professional writer, you won't have a teacher forcing you to hand in previous versions, a workshop instructor giving you revision suggestions, a chairperson forcing you to finish by spring. You are, lucky you, your own boss. You can ask friends and family what they think you should do, but ultimately, you have to make your own choices and find reasons to go on. At some point, editors do help—and push—professional writers, but writers have to get themselves and their work into good shape before sending it on to editors.

It's at the point of revision that many writers quit. They like the creative rush and the workshop but grow impatient with the lonely phase of refinement. They don't want to spend the time, or can't stand having to reread their old work (and realize its weaknesses). They either love their words or hate them and can't gain distance from them.

Early drafts are cluttered with words that get us from there to here. They have holes that need to be filled, startling ideas, pretty lines, flashes of insight. But much of the draft probably won't end up in your final version—unless you're one of those writers who intensely plans and internally revises even before writing or you happen to have the spark that day.

At times, though, you might welcome revision because the danger of the first idea has passed. Susan Sontag found the first draft hardest because "if you have the idea of 'literature' in your head, [it] is formidable, intimidating. A plunge in an icy lake." Revising, she said, is "the warm part: when you already have something to work with, upgrade, edit." At its best, it can be a time for play; even at its worst, it's still a creative act filled with possibilities.

While some people emerge from hovels with a polished first draft, most of us come out with what former *New Yorker* writer Ved Mehta calls a "vomit draft," in which we "pour out everything [we can] think of without worrying about sense or grammar." After this, Mehta revises. "Cutting and shaping my thoughts help[s] me learn what, if anything, I [know] about the subject," he writes. He then develops "telling arguments" to support his points—this is where the research comes in. Then he "put[s] aside the essay and return[s] later to cast a cold eye on it."

> "A first draft is the messy phase of fortuitous accidents and utter slop."

A first draft is the messy phase of fortuitous accidents and utter slop, often within the same paragraph. It's risk time, no waiting, forging ahead without fear. You learn to suspend self-censorship.

The best writing in a draft often comes only after the mediocre. It may take paragraphs or pages before you get into the rhythm of the writing, before you become productive. Besides, nobody has to see your bad writing. It's yours until you decide to hand it away—after you revise it. As Sontag (again) says: "What I write about is other than me. As what I write is smarter than I am. Because I can rewrite it."

Figuring Out What It Needs

Steve Almond claims that "every single time you sit down to write, you're faced with, like, a bazillion decisions. Sometimes you make good ones, sometimes bad ones. But the only way to know the quality of your decisions is to develop what Hemingway called—in that restrained way of his—'a bullshit detector.'" The technical term is probably something closer to 'a critical faculty.'"

Writers acquire this detector by reading the work of other writers, whether in published books or workshop manuscripts. Workshops (or working as editors) can help us develop that critical eye; you can "note all the ill-advised decisions they made, and explain to them—in a constructive but explicit way—why those decisions won't work," says Almond. Seeing the common mistakes made by others can help you see the same ones in your own work.

It's important, too, to read published writers with an eye to how their work was put together. By reading, you learn the language, letting yourself absorb and listen. Without loving to read, there is no reason to write. On a workaday level, reading everything possible helps you to understand what you like and dislike beyond the surface level of taste. Try to figure out why you've had this reaction. Try to avoid doing what David Foster Wallace used to characterize to students as "lit crit." Don't analyze the work's deeper meanings and its historical and theoretical context. Instead, read as a writer, looking at every level of the text. What could the writer cut? rearrange? add? Look at the beginnings, transitions, endings. If it works, why? If it doesn't, play around with the language; what do you think would have made it better? Don't dodge all of this with the excuse that you don't know, don't have the expertise. You have perceptions; the better you learn to question and articulate these, the better you can apply them to your own work.

It's easy to become intimidated by your favorite writers, to believe that all of this "genius" sprang fully grown from their massive brains. A look at iconographic writers' edited manuscripts can be instructive. F. Scott Fitzgerald was a diligent perfectionist. The notes he wrote on drafts of his unfinished novel *The Last Tycoon* show that he not only commented on his weaknesses but considered ways to change the manuscript. The notes take the tone of a teacher to a student; his rational editorial self steps forward, giving advice to the writer self. "Rewrite from mood," he tells himself. "Has become stilted with rewriting." He advises himself as to character: "This chapter must not devolve into merely a piece of character analysis." "Where will the warmth come from in this? Why does he think she's warm?" And to plot:

> The problem is that the reader must not turn to Chapter X and be confused, but, on the other hand, the dramatic effect, even if the reader felt lost for a few minutes, might be more effective if he did not find at the beginning of the chapter that the plane fell. . . . I must find a method of handling it in that fashion. There must be an intervening paragraph to begin Chapter X which will reassure the reader that he is following the same story, but it can be evasive and confine itself to leading the reader astray. . . . ACTION IS CHARACTER.

You can use these same strategies when editing your own work. Read your work aloud to catch digressions and repetitions. Better yet, read it aloud in front of someone else; this is an act of distancing, as you hear and imagine your words being comprehended (or not) by the listener. Better yet, have someone read your work aloud to you. Barring that, read your work into a tape recorder and play it back. These acts put you in the role of the reader and listener, separating you from your personal attachment.

Revision Challenges Confronted by All Writers

The poet William Carlos Williams believed that a good writer

> writes as he does because he doesn't know any better way to do it, to represent exactly what he has to say CLEAN of the destroying, falsifying, besmirching agencies with which he is surrounded. . . . Everything, every minutest thing that is part of a work of art is good only when it is useful and any other explanation of the "work" would be less useful than the work itself.

If it isn't necessary—if it doesn't matter—if nothing is lost by cutting it, it shouldn't be there. This is the best revision advice we can give.

Of course, we will try to give you a little more.

If you know you have a writing weakness, admit it and read for it. Once you know that weaknesses have patterns, you can sidestep some of them as you write and catch the rest upon revision. There are certain problems that nearly all writers face, and we discuss some of them below.

Lacking Focus

Revision first involves understanding what your piece is about—and, once you know, making sure you've focused on that. While you might think you already know the meaning and subject of your own writing, in reality we often stray from our original intentions. The real story may be the one you never saw coming.

Long pieces follow tangents; some digressions will be fruitful, and others won't. Some of the characters and subtopics will likely have to be excised. Cris Mazza said that when she wrote the essay "Homeland" she wanted to include

> my mother's history . . . but couldn't find a focus, a core, what it was really about. . . . It somehow became about how a slightly off-kilter notion about women's roles in her childhood was carried on into mine. . . . It was the essay in my book with the least "centralization" because it started with an "I need to include X, Y, and Z" and then I had to discover some kind of core.

Jonathan Raban, who writes "on the road" travel narratives, drafts from notebooks packed with "long descriptions of landscape and character; some fuzzy intellection; scraps of conversation; diagrammatic drawings; paras from the local paper; weather notes; shopping lists" and more. He calls the notebooks a reflection of his "dim-bulb alter ego" who is

> short-sighted and long-winded . . . bogged down in the quotidian details . . . short of wit, and rarely passes up an opportunity to whine. . . . He's [his alter ego's] at his worst when trying hardest to "write": I have to skip page after page of phony lyricism, in search of one memorable fact. The chipped flint of

the waves? Give me a break. The mauve ring on the page, left by a glass of British Columbian plonk (than which no plonk in the world is plonkier) is more articulate than my man's laborious notebook.

This problem is endemic to creative nonfiction. We know that we want or need to tell a particular person's story or include a necessary scene, but we don't know what this means to the piece or (sometimes) to ourselves. "Truly, life is just one damn thing after another," wrote memoirist Dorothy Gallagher. "The writer's business is to find the shape in unruly life and to serve her story. Not, you may note, to serve her family, or to serve the truth, but to serve the story. There really is no choice."

Finding the story through the competing facts and personal loyalties can be difficult. While the information needs to be there, its meaning may elude us. The act of writing can seduce and beguile, causing us to love our worst lines. The lived experience that seems most wonderful may not provoke the most evocative or even interesting writing. We have all gazed at the waves; we have done this so many times, seen it in movies, and read about it that it is almost impossible to capture that moment in a unique, specific way.

It can take years to reconcile the meaning of a particular moment in our lives. It is no less difficult to understand our own work.

Making a piece cohesive isn't a simple or single process. Getting a conscious sense of the shape that best suits your final version is an intuitive act. Try to keep in mind that you can't take form for granted just because your nonfiction is "real" and it happened "just this way." We don't read to find affirmation of the vague amorphousness of life. Let it be clear that you have made your writing choices deliberately, and not because you were in a hurry or were in love with the sound of your own words.

Putting in Too Much Because It's True

When we write about ourselves, "Everything seems of almost equal value," David Madden says. It's difficult to know what to emphasize, what to objectify, how to keep the tone from becoming monotonous. If, on revision, you sense a dull sameness, it may be that you haven't gotten enough distance on the material or (because you are trying to be diligently honest) you aren't allowing the scene to come alive.

You may also be indulging in therapy, writing to work through confusion or trauma. This is a reasonable and occasionally necessary thing to do—it can help you get from one emotional place to another, allowing you to finish your narrative—but it probably needs to be cut from your final draft.

Whining and hand-wringing must go. Emotion and urgency don't automatically transfer effectively to the reader. In fact, a stretch of highly introspective material will usually distance the reader from you. The reader has to be actively involved, drawn in. If he remains on the outside, hearing you emote, he will probably feel like an unsatisfied voyeur.

Blaming, too, should go. "Literal truth-telling and finding fault with a culprit for his good are out of place in an essay, where everything should be for our good and rather for eternity," wrote Virginia Woolf. Cris Mazza says that

> with the personal essay, the question "what is this piece about?" is so crucial, because the answer can't be "me" or "something that happened to me," and once the author is aware of what the piece is really about, certain revisions are going to become evident. The "whole truth" is no reason to leave something in a piece, if it doesn't aid in creating coherence and unity.

We discussed in chapter 6 how Vivian Gornick had to modify her true tone of voice ("the one I habitually lived with") for her memoirs because "it had to be . . . brought under control." To achieve this she had to gain distance "from these people and these events to find the place where the story could draw a deep breath and take its own measure." Only this allowed her to find the narrator "who was me and at the same time not me."

Shifting from Job Prose

Many of us have jobs that require us to write. Technical manuals, reports, speeches, academic papers, even memos have conventions. These conventions are usually the antithesis of what you want for creative nonfiction. Structurally, most work and school writing insists on directness, plainness, and overt telegraphing ("There are three main points. First . . . "). These are anathema to your creative nonfiction work. For most of us, the style we use on the job is more stilted, conventionalized, labored than the one we use for literary work. It would be nice if we all had switches to turn off that forced voice and language at will. But we don't, which means that we have to find ways of getting out of the enforced rhythm and language that become second nature when we've been writing in job mode for eight hours a day.

If you're struggling to sound complex and formal, you'll sound like a fraud; if you're substituting your own inclinations with long words, you will make your work bland. Conversely, someone who thinks formally and eloquently shouldn't try to talk in a colloquial, down-home dialect. The language has to express image, idea, attitude—all of the complexity carried by a simple word. This is done by the complexity of your vision, not by the artificial complexity of jargon.

Going for the literary jargon of supposedly "beautiful" language doesn't work, either. Overly elaborate and ultimately meaningless sentences and phrases won't show anybody anything. Georges Simenon would cut "adjectives, adverbs, and every word which is just there to

make an effect. Every sentence which is just there
for the sentence. You know, you have a beautiful   "If it doesn't fit with the rest of
sentence—cut it." If it doesn't fit with the rest of   your language, it doesn't
your language, it doesn't belong; it will sound la-   belong."
bored and out of context and silly.

Katherine Anne Porter claimed that "you have to speak clearly and
simply and purely in a language that a six-year-old child can understand;
and yet have the meanings and the overtones of language, and the implications, that appeal to the highest intelligence—that is, the highest intelligence that one is able to reach." While we wouldn't go so far as to say
that you must be understood by six-year-olds (or all adults, for that matter), we would agree that your own intelligence is not necessarily revealed
by the use of multisyllabic adjectives.

Transition/Juxtaposition

A transition is that gooey matter linking two scenes or ideas or facts; it
gets you from one point to another. A juxtaposition deliberately leaves
out the transition lines while implying a connection between the related
pieces. Transitions and juxtapositions are often honed in the revision
phase.

This transition is from Rory Stewart's essay "The Missionary Dance,"
found on page 686:

> The lavish domes make clear that the Ghorids had a particular affection for
> this dancing sect. It was a relationship they advertised by placing the domes
> so visibly at the entrance to their lands and engraving them with long pas-
> sages from the Koran. . . . Once again I was looking at evidence of a very dif-
> ferent society and a very different Islam from what existed on the same site
> today.
>
> The police chief at Chist had a generator, a VCR, and a black-and-white tele-
> vision. Twenty of us gathered to watch filmed dancing.

In this section, Stewart uses the line about the changing society to
signal a connection between the ancient traditions of the dervishes and
the contemporary secular men turning on a video. With that connecting
line, he can show the two scenes side by side and have no need to explain
just how these scenes are different.

An example of juxtaposition comes in "Next Year in Jerusalem,"
page 594, when Brenda Miller moves from one section to another by infer-
ring the relationship between subjects. Look at the shift from the end of
the section titled "Next Year in Jerusalem!" and the one that follows,
"Why Is This Night Different from All Other Nights?" Both sections deal
with passages that are literal (travel to Europe/travel to Israel) and spiritual (choosing not to make the journey/choosing to cross the River

Jordan). The ramifications of her decisions are complex, having everything to do with identity. The juxtaposition emphasizes the gulf between
who the narrator was then (when she avoided the crossing) and who she
is now (when she seeks an understanding of her Jewish identity).

When creating a juxtaposition or transition, figure out what the sections mean. There should be a metaphoric or literal connection between
them; if you don't yet know the connection, your transitions will be clunky
or missing. Those old "in additions," "in conclusions," "for examples" will
not do. You're creating a bridge between actions and ideas in each section;
if there is no bridge, then you should acknowledge this.

Transitions and juxtapositions are difficult, since you're usually trying to create a sense of flow. You don't want to say too much, over-
explaining an already apparent connection, and you don't want to say
too little, leaving the reader confused. You're wanting to lead the reader
in a direction without sounding like you're leading her there.

No writer is above the struggle. Gustave Flaubert was plagued with
frustrating transition problems while writing the canonical favorite *Madame
Bovary*. It took him three days to nail down an eight-line transition between
scenes. "There is not a superfluous word in it, nevertheless I have to cut it
down further because it drags!" he moaned in a letter.

Luckily, it's one of those problems that friends or workshop colleagues can point out with some clarity; there's something very nuts-and-
bolts, very obvious, about the use and misuse of transitions.

Generally, you'll want to see if you need the first few lines, or even
paragraphs, of a new section. If the reader can grasp the connection without you giving an explanation, then cut the language.

If there really is nothing there to link section A to section B, even
metaphorically—if there isn't even a thin sense of tension—then maybe
you need to get rid of A or B or both and rethink the whole thing. While
a fragmentary style can be powerful, there should be something compelling in the way the sections grate against one another. The resulting
feeling may be as abrasive as a rock in your shoe, and that's great. It's
when there is nothing at all—when it's boring and repetitive—that you
have a problem.

An Overabundance of People

Early drafts can go in many directions, trailing this person here and that
person there, each interesting in his own way, and you also interesting in
your beguiling role of narrator. By the end of the piece, you have thirty
interesting people all vying for attention, all telling different stories, and
creating of the whole a general mess.

Unless you are constructing a book of linked essays, you'll probably
need to pick a few characters and let them dominate. One of them may be
you, the narrator. The other characters may still be around, but they'll
have to take on supporting roles. The people you choose to amplify will

be the ones who matter most to the story you're trying to tell. If you can take someone out and the meaning or progression of the story doesn't change, then he doesn't need to be in there. If you just can't give up that guy and the great little joke he tells, use him in something else.

A Failure of Imagination

Though you may be trying to hew to what's factually true, more or less, you shouldn't suppress your imagination. You need it no less in creative nonfiction than in fiction; without it, your writing will be akin to newspaper journalism or academic writing or business writing: informative but hardly entertaining. Imagination doesn't necessarily mean manufacturing fictional characters or changing the truth of what happened. It means fully envisioning what once existed. You shouldn't turn off your sight and insight in an attempt to be literally, blandly "factual."

Creating a style involves imagination. Re-creating dialogue takes imagination, too, since you will have to re-see and re-hear and then relay this in the fullest and most evocative way. Bringing real people to life is much like creating fictional characters—it means letting them breathe, showing them just as you see them in your mind. Putting the pieces together into a whole, giving it meaning, means making crazy leaps. It takes a particular kind of bravery to make a true story compelling. Imagining how your piece will be if you add this and take away that is an act of creativity; you are displaying faith that a random series of events has meaning.

When you write about real situations, whether personal or outside your own experience, you use imagination to select events and to re-create that time and place. Patricia Cornwell wrote that

> memory for me is like one of those Civil War greenhouses sadly built of daguerreotypes instead of glass panes. If I walk into my thoughts and quietly sit, I suddenly find myself surrounded by haunting faces and harrowing tableaux. I conjure up soldiers who have run into bayonets—bodies of young people who fight believing they will never die. I see mere boys giving their last Rebel Yell, and they are not so different from last week's teenager who decided to stand up suddenly in the back of a pickup truck, not realizing it was about to go under a bridge.

These associations are vivid and true, even though Cornwell never herself witnessed the Civil War. It is no less real for being secondhand.

Titles and Subheadings

The title is the first glimpse of an idea—the whole piece can be hung upon what it implies. Some writers begin with the title, and the story emerges from that. Others labor over the "right" title, revising it many times before finding one with which they can live. Ideally, the title should resonate with the ideas and mood of the piece.

E. L. Doctorow came upon the title of his novel *Loon Lake* when driving through the Adirondack mountains and spotting a sign. He said,

> I've always been moved by that part of the country but my strong feelings for its woods and streams suddenly intensified and seemed to cohere on those two words, which I said aloud as if they were the words of a poem. . . . They became my title, and were endlessly suggestive, yielding a period of time, the Great Depression, a setting, the remote mountain retreat of a very wealthy man, and a number of characters of different moral sizes.

There is no method for finding the perfect title. It can come to you, as it did for Doctorow—and if it does, you're lucky, and you've been paying attention. To see such things, it can be helpful to read poems, stories, and essays, noticing how a striking title works with the imagery of a piece.

Subheadings are more commonly found in magazine pieces than in longer creative works. These are often suggested by an editor as a way of breaking a longish essay or chapter into palatable bits. Subheadings still aren't commonly found in literary work, although they're sometimes used for stylistic effect. David Foster Wallace and Dave Eggers both have made ample use of headings as signal and commentary on what is to come. Brenda Miller's essay "Next Year in Jerusalem," on page 594, uses headings in the form of questions that show the importance of each topic, echo the possible questions of the reader, and guide us into each personal illustration. In literary work, the headings act as more than informational markers— they have a meaning and style that reflect the material to follow.

Chapter Breaks and White Space

For most writers, the revision stage includes inserting chapter or section breaks. While some writers have all of their chapters planned out before they begin writing, most don't—or, if they do, they don't stick to the plan as the work evolves. Every time you take out or add significant information, the form shifts. Changing emphasis from one character to another means that the chapter divisions change, too. Many writers figure this out after the project is finished and they can see it as a whole.

No handy rule will guide you toward the "proper" insertion of a chapter (or, in a short piece, a major break). It depends on your project, your inclination, and possibly the kind of reader you envision.

Breaks usually come when the subject changes, or when a character takes the stage, or when time passes or place shifts. Their distribution is usually logical, evenhanded, and fairly obvious. They often come at a point when the writer wishes to build suspense; there may be a feeling of suspended animation at the end of a chapter, emphasizing a question that remains unanswered.

Some books use breaks in a kind of "flash" approach. The chapters are short and snappy, with chapter titles that serve as commentary on what is to come. The form can be akin to poetry, and the writing may be highly metaphorical. Karen Tei Yamashita's "June: Circle K Recipes" on page 779 is built in this way. The headings are there to catch the eye and arouse the reader's attention and comment on what is to come. They are never random. Sometimes this approach is used for writing aimed at a highly literary audience or at a young Internet-raised one. The approach is also common (and probably necessary) in graphic memoir, in which the banner headlines signal a change in scene.

Within the text of a chapter or essay, we have to decide where the white space goes—what pauses are added and why. What isn't there is as important as what is.

White space serves as a musical rest or a stop, as long as a breath or a collapse. If you don't want the reader to pause—or you don't want to catch his or her attention—don't insert a break.

Flat-Out Errors

As we all know, revision involves that nitty-gritty of checking grammar, punctuation, and spelling. This is so routine that it's easy to overlook obvious mistakes. Yet there is nothing so necessary, since a manuscript with errors won't get published.

Everyone has ingrained grammar and spelling problems; never assume that you've conquered your little mind-glitches. And don't leave them to your online grammar checker; those give bad advice. Run a literary masterwork through your grammar checker and the program will cut lovely run-on sentences and stylistic turns of phrase. And while the spellchecker is a useful backup, it won't catch everything.

Buy at least one book about grammar and style. There are a number of good ones. (Doug Hesse, one of the writers of this book, has a grammar handbook that he coauthored with Lynn Troyka, and there are others.) Find one that includes plenty of examples and a complete index. Then use it.

The days when editors held the hand of a writer with grammatical problems have passed. Editors are overwhelmed with work; they don't have time for the added burden of your problems. Literary presses are in the same bind as mainstream presses in this regard.

Announcing What You're Going to Write about without Actually Writing about It

Almost everyone does this. It's part of the "figuring out" draft. You're spelling out what you want to do and perhaps why you're going to do it. You announce why someone should read the piece and why they should agree with you. You may think that readers need to know all of this. They do not.

People read because they are curious—about a subject, idea, character, style. Over-explanation creates distance; it prevents the piece from being a discovery for the reader and for you. You may need to explain your purposes to yourself, though, and this is why you may need to let yourself do some overstating in your early drafts. You may think that some of your most profound material is in this explanation and analysis. But you would almost always be wrong. If you can describe it, if you can show it in a scene—create a picture rather than a linear explanation—you should do it. And if you have any gemlike lines in this explanation/summary/announcement, they can always be moved someplace else.

Revising after a Piece Is Accepted

Creative nonfiction usually has a wider market than other literary forms, meaning that the editors of mainstream magazines or commercial presses must respond to a host of business pressures. Most need to make your work accessible to as many readers as possible, and this may mean a shortening or a watering-down of the original manuscript.

Should you choose to publish in a mainstream magazine, you'll have to be ready to make changes. Editors may ask you to condense language, switch paragraphs, change words, and simplify sentences. As more graphics and advertising appear in magazines, less space is available for writing. Most magazines include (maybe) one or two in-depth pieces in an issue; the rest are informative, catchy little things.

> "You need to have your own voice and follow your own genuine interests."

In an effort to be published, it's tempting to write short and trendy—to minimalize your own style. It's what Daniel Harris has called "underwriting, the triumph of a blandly tasteful styleless style . . . prose packaged and sold by the column inch." We're not here to say that pursuing this approach is necessarily bad; it's simply out of the realm of this book to tell you how to do it. It will usually change a literary and creative piece into, well, magazine journalism. There are other guidebooks about this. Careful reading of magazines, the focusing of the subject, and mimicry of the dominant style may get you there.

Keep in mind, though, that a spot-on imitation of a magazine's or writer's style usually won't work. You need to have your own voice and follow your own interests. Unless you are a tried and true journalist living in the publication's home city, you will probably not break through by toeing what appears to be the line. Most routine assignments from major magazines go to a cadre of trusted writers. These are basically subcontracted employees who can reliably cover a particular topic in a certain length of time in a certain way. Trying to copy, say, Dave Eggers's style doesn't mean that you will get Eggers's success. Even Dave Eggers doesn't want to copy his own style.

However you get a piece accepted, it is true that once a contract is signed, your work is the magazine's property, at least until the piece is published and often as long as it's in print. The magazine can change the piece as they choose unless your contract stipulates otherwise.

Take consolation that editors' changes often improve the original. Luckily, too, the relationship between writer and editor is nearly always a dialogue, not a list of demands. This dialogue begins from the time the piece is accepted, through galleys and page proofs, until the piece is bound and published.

Two Examples of Revised Work

When we asked writers for copies of their early drafts for use in this chapter, most declined, which we well understood. Some said they didn't keep their drafts; some cited the difficulty of finding that draft in the bottom of the box; a few said their revisions were too routine to make for interesting reading. A few even admitted that the publication of their original versions would be embarrassing. Nobody likes to admit just how bad their first drafts can be.

A terrific out-of-print book, *Creative Writing and Rewriting* (edited by John Kuehl, 1967), shows multiple drafts made by famous writers. If you can find a copy in the library or a used bookstore, it's a helpful read.

For our book, two writers bravely, even enthusiastically, agreed to submit early and final versions of their essays and to comment on them: Paul Lisicky and Leila Philip.

Paul Lisicky, about "Captain St. Lucifer"

Paul Lisicky generously provided his first and his final draft from the opening of "Captain St. Lucifer":

CAPTAIN ST. LUCIFER — ORIGINAL ROUGH DRAFT

There's a baby grand in the lounge of the dorm with yellowed ivory keys and a squeaking pedal. I'm the only one who seems to know that it's more than something to rest their beer bottles on, and tonight, just as I've played the first few bars of "Don't Rock the Boat," Mark Norton and two fratboys whom I recognize from Madame Sommerfeldt's Introduction to French class walk through the front doors, stop abruptly, lurch forward, glance at each other, then pull up folding metal chairs, sitting on them backwards. One swigs from a bottle of beer, with an expectant look. The three of them together have the lazy-eyed carnality of frat boys looking for something to make fun of, to jerk them out of boredom, but for some reason, I don't feel the expected stripe of heat down the back of the neck. Trust these guys. They have heard about my playing from their friends. Ever since I've been here, I've made sure to let people know that I play the piano and guitar, and the second I receive my degree I'll be swept up . . . certainty of one who knows exactly how his life is going to turn out.—as I've already established my credibility. I have no doubt, I will be a known quantity. As far as I know . . , that I've spent my musical background in church music. FOLK Masses, that I've been writing and published, which cause me much embarrassment.

I start singing the first verse, letting myself relax, my eyes close when I get to moments of appropriate intensity. (I've reinvented myself totally for them; they couldn't have known about the) By the time I get to the third verse, I'm craning my head back, looking at the ceiling. My song's three weeks old. I'm liking the arc of its melody, the harmonic structure, its harmonic rhythm . . . in spite of my grave worries that it sounds far too much like a Laura Nyro song. I love Laura Nyro. I love her mixture of Philly soul, Broadway show tune, jazz, folk, Curtis Mayfield, Moss Hart, The Young Rascals, Bob Dylan, Burt Bacharach, and all found themselves inside a fat girl's skin . . . She's even more alluring to me in that she remains an essential mystery . . . SONG WILL GO IN A COMPLETELY DIFFERENT DIRECTION IF SHE'S BORED WITH IT . . . RHYTHM WILL CHANGE, ETC. AS MUCH AS I ADMIRE THOSE QUALITIES AND THINK THEY'RE ALL GREAT, I WANT TO KNOW WHAT'S RIGHT, TO BE A PART OF THE COMMUNITY.

CAPTAIN ST. LUCIFER—FINAL VERSION

We're grouped around the battered piano in the dorm lounge. Though outwardly we're working out the harmonies of Ann and Nancy Wilson's "Dog and Butterfly," we each perform something else on our private interior stages: Bernardine's picks her 12-string Gibson to Pure Prairie League's "Amy"; Kevin's perfects his monotonic nasal stupor to "One More Cup of Coffee for the Road"; Grace's vibrato comes from a deeper, more womanly place (she has to stop listening to Streisand Superman). And I'm doing my own music, a romantic, violent mishmash which borrows fiercely from Laura Nyro and Joni Mitchell. In our best moments, the four of us are capable of bringing a rowdy crowd of undergrads to reverent, bewildered silence (see them rest their beer bottles on their tables, their eyes filling, blinking), though when we're off, we're really off. No wonder the two fratboys—our audience— wince every time Grace raises a splayed palm toward an imaginary spotlight, suggesting in no uncertain terms that her feelings are the most important ones in the room.

Once we've gravelled our vocal chords, Bernardine asks to hear "Long Train Comin'," the song I finished while I was home at my parents' last weekend. I slide onto the piano bench, shoulders falling forward, feigning indifference, though my brain's screwed so tight, I might as well be running a fever. I start the first verse, my eyes squeezing shut as my throat strains for the high notes. My fingertips stick. No focus. What's that outside? Dog? Church bell? I think of the big, ponderous bell swinging left, right, left, right, pushing back the air on either side as if it's massive, heavy as water. By the time the rhythm shifts, though, and the key changes to B minor, E, then back to B minor, I'm entirely inside the music, throwing my head back, stunned by the lights above until my eyeballs ache. When did I become this person? I'm still trying to get the hang of it—the authority others give up to me, this unnerving privilege and power.

LISICKY'S INTERPRETIVE PARAGRAPH ABOUT THE REVISION

When I compare the original draft of this passage to the published version, I'm struck by the clumsiness, the fragments, the lousy grammar. It's clear to me that the writing is grappling toward a voice. The construction of that voice depends upon summoning up the memory for the first time—hence the unedited quality of the account. I want the final product to be energized with effortlessness and spontaneity, as if it's come into the world unbidden.

Until I revisited this, I'd almost forgotten that I'd changed the content of the scene over time. In the first draft, the speaker is a solo performer; in the final he's playing with a group. In the first, the focus is on the audience; in the second, the other musicians. The piece is very much about the struggle between the individual artist versus the group performer, and I think the change in focus allows for more self-deprecation and comedy. I'm sure I was impatient with the elevated, self-involved quality of the speaker's perceptions; I wanted to bring him back to earth, to make him more welcoming as a character. So aside from the obvious work of sentence-making, I needed to bring the voice and the speaker's character into an artful alignment with the scene at hand.

Leila Philip—Versions of "Green Tea"

Leila Philip offered the following insights about writing and revising her book *The Road to Miyama*:

In general, I imagined the first audience for the book to be more academic and more focused on the ceramic history of the village than the final version, which was published by Random House. Because I was writing what I knew was going to be the first book published in English that engaged the history of Miyama, a history which included decades of discrimination against Koreans living in Japan, I was keenly aware of my obligations to that larger story. That said, when I finished the first version, I knew that I hadn't quite hit my ambitions for the narrative; I had just hit my deadline. The first version was submitted as my senior thesis at Princeton in 1986. The first chapter, "The Road through Miyama," won an international essay contest for which the prize was an all-expenses-paid trip back to Japan. Then the work as a whole received the Senior Thesis Prize in East Asian Studies.

Still, I always considered that version to be round one because I wanted to publish it as a book. After graduation, I worked as a journalist for a Japanese newspaper and began sending the manuscript out to publishers. Without an agent I got numerous rejection letters. Then I got some good advice and began looking for an agent instead of a publisher. The Candida Donadia Agency took me on, and within months they had placed the book with Random House. Then the revising began.

For this second version, which came out in 1989 as the book *The Road through Miyama*, I imagined my audience to be more of a general reader than a reader interested in Japanese ceramics and, most important, a reader of literary nonfiction. I wanted to try out more inventive and what for me at the time were more challenging approaches to shaping narrative. In general, I was working to deepen the sense of story and flow so that the reader would feel more transported into the world of the book.

I find Vivian Gornick's way of describing literature as having levels of "situation" and "story" to be useful in thinking about how narratives are made. In my case, the "situation" was my experience of apprenticing to a master potter, all the cross-cultural experiences that involved, the almost four hundred-year-old history of the village as a pottery-making center, and then all the information about making pottery. The "story" was what I wanted to convey about my experience, that information, the village, and the wide swath of history that entailed.

In other words, in the second version, I was consciously working to pull the "story" out so that it propelled the information, not the other way around. I had the good luck of working with a great editor, Becky Saletan, who was at Random House at the time. She helped me see new ways to draw out my thematic concerns within the material. I rewrote the second version by looking at the first. I had the text all marked up in different colors depending on the kinds of edits I was making. Some edits were on the level of work adjustments, but others, as in the chapter "Green Tea," involved completely rewriting the beginning and end and reordering much of what came in between.

All of this took time, about six months. When Random House purchased the book, I used my small advance to go part-time at the paper where I was working and concentrated on the revision. My advice is to let work sit for as long as you can. That time away from the manuscript enabled me to come back with fresh eyes; I was a little less enchanted with the words I had already labored over, and thus more able to cut them out when the need arose.

This is the original beginning of Leila Philip's chapter "Green Tea" (found in its full final version on page 643):

OPENING—FIRST DRAFT

May: month of camellia and bloom
azure sky and bamboo breeze
rustle of fern, tea harvest

12:00 Through a thick layer of spattered clay the old electric clock above Nagayoshi-san's wheel reads noon. Today's work of small plates line a long board. Each plate, waiting to be trimmed with a raised foot at the base, has been turned carefully upside down so that the base dries evenly. For trimming, the clay must be hard enough to sit on the wheel without deforming. But not so brittle as to crack under the force of the steel-bladed trim tool.

Yesterday I had bungled the job miserably, leaving a board of untrimmed plates outside too long in the afternoon heat. Instead of peeling off clean lines of clay like shaved chocolate, the trim tool bounced off the hard clay surface with a high-pitched screech. One by one the entire batch crumbled. Around the base of my wheel a mound of cracked plates grew. Clay crumbs filled my ankle cuffs; the trimming tool left a burning red streak in my forefinger. In the hot and empty workshop my mind wandered . . . there was a solution. Carrying the board with the ten remaining plates, at shoulder height like a chef with dish of fine raw shrimp, I stepped outside. The yard was empty. As they slipped under the brown water of the recycling vat, the ten plates gurgled and then disappeared in a slow, downward spiral dives. But a calm voice form the showroom interrupted my thoughts.

Would you do that to your children?. . . asked Nagayoshi-san, looking out from the window. Words caught in my throat. I didn't wait to see his smile, but went quickly back to work. My face felt scarlet, but the long board in hand was empty and light.

Today I carefully put all plates in the damp holding room and then clean up in a rush. Sweeping the clay shavings from the bench I find my three trimming tools and place them with a sponge next to a small white kitchen scale. The April days of rain have passed; in May the sky is azure. Today I am going out for lunch.

Outside the world is startlingly green. From the dark confined space of the workshop I walk into a burst of light. In the distance Sakurajima stokes a lazy plume of gray above the waves. My silver bicycle wheels spin. The road stretches dull and straight, a lazy snake of black tar basking before the mid-day sun. I pass by a group of old men and women picking tea. To escape the sun, women wear cotton bonnets and gloves, men sport wide-brimmed straw hats. All have bamboo baskets or plastic buckets slung over their shoulders. The noon siren blows—lunchtime for the fourteen potteries in Miyama—and the street wakens. Speeding by on his green scooter, the mailman passes. His white gloves shine. The black mailbags, once bursting with mail, flap empty in the wind. In the center of town chattering workers from the Jukan workshop spill out through tall, roofed wooden gates. Across the street at the Kirin store a crowd gathers. Mold pourers from the Katasuragi workshop, a group of six women in loose polyester slacks and smocks, tease each other like school children as they pick out soft drinks and hot canned coffee. Fukushima-san, the head painter at the Jukan workshop, walks out slowly. In his mid-thirties, he is tall and thin, wearing thick eyeglasses to hold back his longish black hair. Across the front of his blue t-shirt appears in bright yellow letters: "ENJOYINGLY."

OPENING—FINAL DRAFT

May; month of camellia and bloom
azure sky and bamboo breeze
rustle of fern, tea harvest

Suzuki-san, in a wide straw hat, bends down over the narrow black tar road, cracked and twisted where thick bamboo shoots push toward April light. Beside him, on her knees, is his wife in her faded blue bonnet. On either side frail bamboo poles hold the living grove back, away from the road. New shoots will grow twelve inches a day, ten, twenty feet in two weeks, pushing through gardens, roads, walkways, anything in their way.

Armed with short-handled sickles and blades, the old couple attacks the irreverent plants in a silent fury.

Whack. Rip. Whack. Splinters of bamboo shoot fly from their tools. I stand in the warm sun and watch.

"*Ohayō gozaimasu.*"

"*Ohayō gozaimasu.*"

"Need some help?" I ask casually, in Kagoshima ben. For the first time both heads rise. Okusan lifts the rim of her blue bonnet to get a better look. "Ah . . . *hora* . . . Ri-ra-san!" she exclaims, sitting back on her heels and smiling. "*Yōka, yōka.* It's okay." She wipes her brow with the back of a gloved hand before resuming her work. Her husband, who has looked up only once during our exchange, continues his furious reaping. I step forward to pass by, but Okusan looks back up, her eyes bright. "Where are you going?" she asks suddenly.

PHILIP'S COMMENTARY ON THE OPENING REVISION

I felt that the original beginning, which, as you can see, started with pot making and the lessons of the apprenticeship, was both too narrow and too detailed. My aim for the book was to show how cycles of pot making were integrated with cycles of agricultural life in the village. The giving and receiving of bamboo shoots, or *takenoko,* was an important spring ritual in Miyama, and like the tea harvest it was in many ways a symbol of the rural life that was even in 1983 fast disappearing. Thus, I decided to open the chapter with a scene of villagers cutting bamboo shoots. I also realized that I wanted that chapter to start outside, on the road, and then circle back to end with a scene of me inside the workshop, working as an apprentice. In that sense the original beginning—a scene of me trimming pots—becomes the end in the finished version.

I think it's important when revising to think of re-envisioning before you start tinkering with word changes. When I went back into the chapter I made big cuts like the ones I describe above before even beginning to cut down on detail or making line edits. If material didn't absolutely have to be in the narrative, didn't somehow propel it forward, I took a deep breath and cut it out. Some material—scenes and vignettes—I used other places, but mostly I condensed as rigorously as I could and tried to remember that every anecdote I included had to be strong enough to stand for the five or six others that I was leaving out. Thinking of what I couldn't put in the final narrative helped me see what was most important.

Here is a brief section from the middle of the essay.

PHILIP'S MIDDLE SECTION—FIRST DRAFT

Yamamura-san races by on her red scooter, high-heeled silver sandals flashing in the sun. She is on her way home for lunch from the Sataro workshop. From today on she will help at home during the two weeks of tea harvest. May is the month of the first tea harvest. Three times a year the long shed behind Yamamura-san's home transforms into a tea processing factory. For generations her family has run the only tea-drying business in Miyama. Her family moved to Miyama long ago, but she insists that they are Japanese and not Korean. Usually Yamamura-san works six days a week, eight to five, at the Sataro workshop.

Once harvesting begins, tea leaves must be immediately dried and processed. The factory will run twenty-four hours a day when cloth bags of tea leaves stand waiting at the entrance. Villagers bring their freshly-picked tea leaves and, after careful weighing, leave them at the factory. Green tea comes in many grades, ranging from expensive powdered green tea, *matcha*, for the tea ceremony down to coarse, daily use *bancha* tea. All Miyama villagers grow *bancha*, but even so the tea leaves are carefully separated into bags according to grower. Next tea is sent through a churning series of gas-heated drums for drying, through cutters, brush-like tea rollers, conveyer belts and gears. When the tea is spread out on the entering conveyer belt, it looks like a giraffe's green picnic. When it emerges at the other end it has been cut, dried, and rolled into tiny balls that resemble freeze-dried vegetables.

Tea was first cultivated in Japan with seeds brought from China at the beginning of the Heian. In Kagoshima, drinking tea has many meanings, according to context. Drinking the tea offered by clerks in kimono shops in Kagoshima city means that you have come to buy. Eating the accompanying sweet signals clerks to wrap up everything you have seen. When offered tea, it is customary to refuse three times. Green tea is listed along with coffee and coke at the McDonald's—popularly known as "Macudonarudu." The Dunkin' Donuts store, popular among high school girls for its stylish decor in hot "pinkkkkuuu," sells green tea doughnuts. Prior to the Edo, 1600–1868, tea was known only to the ruling classes. Today, teatime in country villages such as Miyama is ten o'clock and three sharp. Cups of green, caffeine-rich tea also appear at breakfast, lunch and dinner.

PHILIP'S MIDDLE SECTION—FINAL DRAFT

April gives way to May, bamboo gives way to tea. May is the month of *shincha*, the first tea. Every spring Yamanaka-san, who works six days a week, from eight to five, at the Sataro workshop, takes two weeks off from her job to help with the tea harvest. For generations her family has run the only tea-drying business in Miyama. Yamanaka-san's house is in the old style, with a mongamae entrance and a once ornate formal garden denoting old village wealth, but she insists that her family is of Japanese, not Korean, descent. Three times a year the long shed behind her home transforms into a tea-processing factory, but the first crop, the shincha, is considered the most delicious.

Tea was first cultivated in Japan with seeds brought from China in the late eighth century. Prior to the Edo period (1600–1868) it was a beverage known only to the ruling classes. Today, teatime in country villages such as Miyama is ten o'clock sharp in the morning and three in the afternoon. Cups of caffeine-rich green tea also appear at breakfast, lunch and dinner. Squat green rows of tea bushes line yards and gardens, and on the hillcrest below the shrine, narrow hedges of pruned tea stretch as straight and long as racetracks.

Once harvesting begins, the tea leaves must be immediately dried and processed. The factory will run twenty-four hours a day as long as villagers continue to bring the freshly picked leaves to the entrance. First they are weighed, then carefully separated into net bags and labeled by grower. The grades range from the expensive powdered *matcha* for the tea ceremony down to the coarse *bancha* for daily use. All Miyama villagers grow bancha, but each swears by the taste of his or her particular leaves. The tea is sent through a series of churning gas-heated drums for drying, then through cutters and brushlike tea rollers, all connected by a network of belts and gears. It enters the conveyer belt looking like a giraffe's green picnic, and emerges at the other end cut, dried and rolled into tiny balls that resemble freeze-dried vegetables.

Last month after morning services at the shrine the Shintō priest climbed into the back of a waiting blue Toyota truck, one hand still holding his conical black plastic priest's hat. The truck roared off, the priest's white robes flowing jauntily behind him, and stopped at the other end of the fields. From his perch the priest scattered rice and blessings over a waiting tea combine. He waved his wand of white paper over the new machine, read a prayer, and clapped solemnly. The farmer was elated.

PHILIP'S COMMENTARY ON HER REVISION

If you are using a first-person narrative, the rhythm of when to interrupt the scenic material with digression is key. I love books that work seamlessly back and forth, delivering scene as the building block, then expanding those scenes out through digressions into factual material. I also love writers that push the factual material for its metaphoric resonance, so I'm always keeping those things in mind when I work and aspiring toward them.

I wish I had some hard and fast rules to pass on that work to accomplish these goals. I don't. In my experience, finding this rhythm, which is really the pacing of the narrative, varies with each piece I write and it is something that as I'm working, I have to listen hard to catch. I read my drafts aloud at this stage. If I hear any little bit of drag, I begin to cut. Every bit of information has to develop the larger narrative pull and thematic concerns otherwise it has to be used somewhere else, otherwise it has to go. In general, for the beginning writer, working with smaller bites of digression are usually best. I often tell my students to think about how to sprinkle factual information throughout a given piece rather than inserting big chunks.

Finally, this is the original ending of "Green Tea," before final revisions.

ENDING OF "GREEN TEA" — FIRST DRAFT

Kirei desne . . . It's pretty . . .

Hirashima-san offers, looking over her bifocals. Her politeness makes it worse. The top of the dome now looks like it has been pecked by a ravenous crow. I begin to wonder about the price of the piece I have ruined.

No one can do it at first you know.

That's not bad for a start . . .

No one can do it at all if they don't like it.

Hirashima-san adds turning it over in her hands.

A sudden crunching of gravel startles us both. Peering in through the window are two businessmen in dark blue suits, white shirts, and neckties, with identical black glasses. They stand and gape. The windows grow suddenly larger, I feel caught in a giant fish bowl.

Hey . . . look over here!

one of them calls over his shoulder. The gravel crunches as two more men arrive. Hirashima-san smiles. I rush to put away my attempted lid and gather hastily sketched notes. More men in the same clothing appear.

Don't worry I'll fix this for you.

Hirashima-san says quickly.

Go on. You'll be late if you don't hurry . . . Come and see the tofu shop sometime . . .

They are waiting for you . . .

Don't forget to tell your teacher . . . Thank-you!

I barely hear her words in my hurry to collect lunchbox and notebook. At the entrance I bow down low and thank her. She smiles.

Outside the workshop is a sea of blue suits—a bus tour from Kumamo-to. Businessmen carry pamphlets about the Jukan workshop and bags of purchased pottery. Chin Jukan often appears on T.V. as a spokesman for Miyama and its Korean heritage. Bus tours arrive daily. Luckily the men at the window have left for the showroom. I slip out the wooden gates and dart across the sunny street. Down the road I see Yamamura-san on her green scooter headed back to work. Inside her store, Kirin Obahsan is laying out cans of cold juice for the newly-arrived bus tour. The May breeze is warm and full. I pull my bicycle out from the bushes and turn onto the road just as the fish truck, still blaring music, heads for Ijuin. Teapickers line the road, deftly plucking the new green leaves to fill their shoulder-slung baskets. 12:55: today I take the back road home.

ENDING OF "GREEN TEA"—FINAL DRAFT

At the crossroads of the Kirin store I see Yamanaka-san racing down the road on her red scooter, high-heeled silver sandals flashing in the sun. By the end of the week she will be busy at home with the tea harvest, but today she hurries back to the Sataro workshop from lunch. Inside the store, Kirin Obasan lays out fresh cans of cold juice for the tourists. Music still blaring, the fish truck turns right at the store, heading for the coastal town of Kaminokawa.

Sakanaa! Sakanaa! Sakananaa-san! blares the truck's loudspeaker. Today I turn right as well and take the back road home.

Back at the workshop I park my bicycle behind the kiln and step inside. Through a thick layer of spattered clay the old electric clock above Nagayoshi-san's wheel reads one. Next to my wheel sit three trimming tools, a sponge and a small white kitchen scale. Today's work—small plates— waits in the damp holding room to be trimmed, each turned carefully upside down so that the base dries evenly. For trimming, the clay must be hard enough to sit on the wheel without deforming, but not so brittle as to crack under the force of the steel-bladed trimming tool.

Yesterday I left a line of plates out drying too long in the sun, and by the time I brought them in they were a row of plaster-hard disks. When Nagayoshi-san saw what had occurred, he laughed. "That happens to me sometimes too," he said, and carefully dipped each one in water to wet the stiff clay before I trimmed them. But instead of peeling off clean lines of clay like shaved chocolate, the trim tool bounced off the hard surface with a high-pitched screech. Around the base of my wheel a mound of cracked plates grew. Clay crumbs filled my cuffs; the trimming tool left a burning red streak in my forefinger. In the hot, empty workshop my mind wandered. I already had enough plates to fill the order; trimming the rest felt like a waste of time. Carrying the board of ten remaining plates at shoulder height, I stepped outside. The yard was empty. The ten plates slipped under the brown water of the recycling vat, gurgled and disappeared in slow, downward spirals.

When Nagayoshi-san discovered my empty board, he frowned and said nothing. But at dinner that night Reiko delivered a brief lecture: if I was going to be a craftsman, then all my pots, no matter how small, were *sakuhin*—"works of art."

This time I have carefully covered my plates with a damp cloth before leaving for lunch. Opening the door to the holding room, I pull the remaining board of plates. From inside come the sounds of intermittent laughter, the clanking of the kettle on the stove. Pottery guests: once again time for tea at the Nagayoshi workshop.

PHILIP'S COMMENTARY ON THE ENDING REVISIONS

The different focus of the final version was deliberate. I wanted to show through the structure of the chapter, a sense of the relief I was feeling at being outside, no longer constrained both literally and metaphorically by the social rules and etiquette that surrounded the tea ceremony. I wanted the reader to feel that too. Thus, I worked to shape the narrative so that it took in a wide swath of life around the village—stepping back in a way to gain perspective—before I headed back into the Nagayoshi workshop. I thought it was important to end back in the workshop because that was where I would integrate all that I had learned by going to the tea at the Jukan workshop and receiving instruction on carving techniques from Hirashima-san.

"Green Tea" is one of the most information-packed chapters in the book, and the whole subject of the tea ceremony with its long history and complex philosophical and aesthetic ideals, and then the inevitable commercialization of tea ceremony ware could be the subject of many books in themselves. My challenge was to touch upon what was important and relevant to the story I was telling without getting bogged down in the larger topic. In the end, I had fun with this chapter, but I remember it as being one of the most challenging to shape.

Works about Writing and Literature Referenced in This Chapter

Arana, Marie, ed. *The Writing Life: Writers on How They Think and Work.* New York: Public Affairs, 2003.

Cornwell, Patricia. "The Passionate Researcher." In *The Writing Life*, edited by Marie Arana.

Doctorow, E. L. "From the Will-of-the-Wisp to Full-Blown Novel." In *The Writing Life.*

Fitzgerald, F. Scott. "Notes to *The Last Tycoon.*" In *The Last Tycoon*, edited by Edmund Wilson. New York: Charles Scribner's Sons, 1941.

Flaubert, Gustav. *Selected Letters.* Translated and edited by Francis Steegmuller. New York: Farrar, Straus and Cucahy, 1953.

Gallagher, Dorothy. "Recognizing the Book That Needs to Be Written." In *Writers [on Writing] Volume II: More Collected Essays from the* New York Times.

Gornick, Vivian. "A Narrator Leaps Past Journalism." In *Writers.*

Harries, Daniel. "The Writing Life: Envy and Editing." *Antioch Review* 62.4 (fall 2004).

Hesse, Douglas, and Lynn Q. Troyka. *Simon and Schuster Handbook for Writers.* New York: Simon and Schuster, 2006.

Kuehl, John. *Creative Writing and Rewriting: Contemporary American Novelists at Work.* New York: Appleton, 1967.

Madden, David. *Revising Fiction.* New York: Plume, 1988.

Mazza, Cris. "Homeland." In *Growing Up Californian.* San Francisco: City Lights, 2003.

Mehta, Ved. "Lightning and the Lightning Bug: The Craft of the Essay." *American Scholar* 67.2 (spring 1998).

Porter, Katherine Anne. *Writers at Work: Second Series.* Edited by George Plimpton. New York: Viking, 1963.

Raban, Jonathan. "Notes from the Road." In *The Writing Life*, edited by Marie Arana.

Simenon, Georges. Interview with Carvel Collins in *The Paris Review* (summer 1955): 70–90.

Sontag, Susan. "Directions: Write, Read, Rewrite. Repeat Steps 2 and 3 as Needed." In *Writers [on Writing] Vol. II.*

Williams, William Carlos. "The Basics of Faith in Art." *Selected Essays of William Carlos Williams.* New York: New Directions, 1954.

Woolf, Virginia. "The Modern Essay." In *The Common Reader.* New York: Harvest, 2002.

Writers [on Writing] Volume II: More Collected Essays from the New York Times. New York: Henry Holt, 2003.

PART 3

Research

CHAPTER **8**

Written Sources

Some people welcome the notion of "creative writing" with relief: "Man, all I have to do is record my experiences and feelings and never have to hit the library again!" It doesn't quite happen this way. Writers live not only in their own heads but also in the world around them. No writer's direct experience can comprise more than a tiny fraction of that world. They examine, explain, dissect, and try to comprehend by reading and researching. Even when writers don't refer directly to written sources, their researched knowledge provides the context for the story.

Some genres of creative nonfiction rely more on written sources than do others; people who read science, nature, and travel writing expect to find interesting facts explained in an engaging way. Nonfiction that deals with social and cultural conflicts often refers to historical accounts, news sources, and documents.

Even memoirs benefit from documents that contextualize and validate memories, everything from a grandmother's diary to local newspaper archives to high school yearbooks. Annie Dillard's essay "An Expedition to the Pole" intertwines two strands. One is a narrative of her attending a church service which has, to her, a troubling informality; the other tells of polar expeditions in which slipshod planning resulted in tragedy and death. (Dillard is employing an extended analogy that mindless worship is as foolhardy as ill-considered travel.) At one point she notes that the Franklin expedition of 1845 (138 dead) carried only a twelve-day supply of coal but carried with it "a 1,200 volume library, 'a hand-organ playing fifty tunes,' china place settings for officers and men, cut-glass wine goblets, and sterling silver flatware." Clearly Dillard researched the provisions for the voyage, and clearly the essay is richer for these details.

Types of Sources

To write creative nonfiction, you need the curiosity and drive to chase down information in libraries, historical societies, governmental archives, Web sites, and places you'd never expect. Not only will you look at books, but you might also scan government reports, brochures, photographs, maps, newspapers, film clips, sound recordings, journals, court transcripts, and who knows what. All creative nonfiction writers are detectives. For them, research isn't an odious, dreaded task but an adventure in finding an answer and getting a fuller picture.

> "Books remain the best sources for in-depth, contextual information."

Books remain the best sources for in-depth, contextual information. Nearly all other sources are short-form and time-specific. Internet documents are often shallow and unreliable. A magazine or newspaper is limited by space, which keeps a single article from going into much depth. For more-complete and often better-validated information, books remain the best way to go.

While the best libraries are usually attached to large research-oriented colleges and universities, people at small schools can usually request books through the interlibrary loan system. Don't discount public libraries, many of which have good selections and belong to statewide systems through which you can order and borrow a needed book. Most libraries still have open stacks where you get the call number, find the book you want, and then browse through books in the vicinity. This is a great way to find unexpected resources.

Bookstores, of course, are full of books (and coffee shops, movies, music, and games—but that's another story). If you're lucky, you'll live near one that allows you to browse (and sometimes even read) the books at your leisure. If you're lucky, you can afford to buy the book you need. At the very least, bookstores can give you a sense of the most recent work published on your subject. Used bookstores have troves of peculiar materials—old postcards, magazines, programs, posters, and all sorts of printed artifacts. Used books can also be purchased through Internet services that compile works from independent sellers. The best of these (at this writing) are alibris.com, addall.com, and Amazon Marketplace. Out-of-print works can be especially useful for understanding the subject's historical context.

Magazines and newspapers are useful not only for facts, topical quotations, and explanations but also for the names of experts. General databases like Academic Search Premier cover thousands of periodicals intended for broad public readerships; LexisNexis is useful for identifying newspaper articles, business news, and legal information. Academic and scholarly journals are indexed in more limited databases. Reference librarians are happy to point you in the right direction and help with research questions; they'll be relieved to answer questions more interesting than how to load paper in the printer or where you can find a restroom.

All of us have searched for information on the Internet, and there's no doubt that this can be a convenient resource. We're confident that you're familiar with all the caveats to ensure the quality of any materials you turn up there. Obviously, sites and documents produced by reputable organizations and publications will generally be trustworthy. Wikipedia is often reliable, but its sources should be checked if you plan on using the information. "Bob's Immigration Statistics and Opinions" probably won't. Beyond texts and images, the Web's increasing repository of sound recordings and videos can be helpful. Perhaps it's online. National Public Radio, for example, has thousands of interviews and stories online in sound archives.

Various governmental records, from court transcripts to real estate transactions, can prove useful. Governments collect lots of data—census figures, wage information, housing trends, weather conditions—and produce lots of reports. The Library of Congress makes legal information available through its "Thomas" (as in Thomas Jefferson) Web site at http://thomas.loc.gov/. Various agencies and departments (Interior, Health, Education and Welfare) compile and present studies in their areas of jurisdiction.

Historical documents and records can add vitality to a writing project. The specific wording of a letter, will, sermon, or proclamation carries flavor and nuance. More and more such materials are getting digitized and put online. Consider, for example, the ambitious Library of Congress project on "Primary Documents in American History." A number of historical and professional organizations have been digitizing materials as part of their missions and mandates. But the sheer volume of such materials makes the task daunting, and often the most intriguing documents are less popular and may not yet exist online. Special collections in libraries, local historical societies, courthouses, or city and state archives are frequently a better bet. Sometimes just browsing one of those places can generate ideas for a writing project that you didn't expect when you walked in the door.

Other kinds of documents, gathered under the charming label "ephemera," likewise add texture to creative nonfiction. Handbills, posters, brochures, concert programs, church bulletins, postcards, recipes, photographs—the list goes on and on. There is something satisfying about the tactile experience of working with physical documents found only in local archives or, even, personal collections. Even flea markets, thrift shops, and antique stores are useful.

Incorporating Sources

Traditional school research papers have formal procedures for citing material, preparing a bibliography, and so on. Creative nonfiction works differently. Consider this excerpt from Charles Bowden's "The Bone Garden of Desire":

> King Solomon's palace was probably one warm home. He lived with seven hundred wives and three hundred girlfriends and somehow everybody tore through ten oxen a day, plus chunks of gazelles and hartebeests. The Bible said the wise old king had twelve thousand horsemen charging around the countryside scaring up chow for the meals back home.

Maybe Bowden was already familiar with the King Solomon story and is reciting facts from memory, but it is more likely that he checked a Bible. Which version? What page, chapter, and verse? We don't know. Bowden does not supply us with MLA or APA citations, as you would with a term paper. We are expected to believe, as part of the truth compact, that he reliably asserts that King Solomon ate hartebeests. Since those who read Bowden's piece are assumed to do so for enjoyment and curiosity, it's considered unnecessary to give the same source details as you would for an essay written expressly for scholars. This is one way that the conventions of literary and academic writing differ.

Here is another bit of historical information from the same essay:

> In 1696, Mme. de Maintenon, Louis XIV's longtime mistress, writes, "Impatience to eat [peas], the pleasure of having eaten them, and the anticipation of eating them again are the three subjects I have heard very thoroughly dealt with. . . . Some women, having supped, and supped well, at the king's table, have peas waiting for them in their rooms before going to bed."
>
> Peas are new to the French court and all those lascivious mouths and expert tongues are anxious for this new sensation. I applaud this pea frenzy. Who would want a stoic as a cook?

Because Bowden is using a direct quotation from published material, he quotes Mme. de Maintenon within the text. But, as is typical in creative nonfiction (and journalism), there is no parenthetical citation or footnote. We don't really know where Mme. de Maintenon's quote came from. We don't know whether Bowden found this quotation in a book by Mme. de Maintenon, about Mme. de Maintenon, about her friends, or about French cuisine. Maybe the quote is previously unpublished, and he found it among Mme. de Maintenon's papers. Most readers find this ambiguity acceptable; they don't expect the source to be noted in a literary work. They trust that the author, being a respected writer, would not make up Mme. de Maintenon's quotation. Publishers, however, usually request from the writer a list of sources, which they use to fact-check the information. The reader trusts that the editor has taken pains to validate the information in the publication.

> "Information per se is rarely fun."

Why, in literary nonfiction, is the writer free not to attribute the source? People read these pieces for different reasons than they do objective journalism, scholarship, or reference works. Dropping lengthy references into the text breaks the flow of the language and indicates that the piece is academic. MLA-style parenthetical citations, for example, break concentration. They literally intrude and remind readers that this is information, and information per se is rarely fun. Most readers don't want to be distracted from the point that the writer is trying to make and the story he or she is telling.

In creative nonfiction, the information is not the focus. Bowden's piece is about food, yes, but it is more about dying and living. He wants us to pay attention to, and feel, what he feels as he faces the deaths of his friends. He discusses food because this is something that makes us want to live—not because he wants us to understand the culinary tendencies of the French court.

So why bring up Mme. de Maintenon at all? Bowden is describing, in a number of ways, a lust for life that comes in the face of death. And by using historical references and scientific facts, he can ground an emotional subject in reality. He also probably just likes the juxtaposition of contemporary, day-to-day life with seemingly disconnected facts—certainly, we live in a world in which we face hundreds of facts and pseudo-facts in the course of a day. And linking peas in France to salsa in America shows us that appreciation for life has never changed. But this is only our conjecture; really, you'd have to ask Charles Bowden—and even he may not exactly know why and how he did it.

One last example will illustrate how research functions in creative nonfiction. Near the beginning of Laurence Gonzales's essay "Marion Prison," which we've included in our anthology (page 403), is the following paragraph:

> There are many ways to make alcohol in USP-Marion, but the simplest is to take two small boxes of Kellogg's corn flakes and dump them into the toilet bowl in your cell. Let them fester for a week, and the result will get you drunk. Some inmates are more ambitious than that. From the prison log: "August 5, 1982: Approximately four gallons of brew found in cell of Ronnie Bruscino, 20168-148."

How does Gonzales know what he reports here? Most obvious is information from the prison log, which he quotes directly but without detailed citation in a "works cited" page. How did he get access to it? The log doesn't show up in a Google search online, and he likely didn't find a copy at the local library. Instead, Gonzales must have read the log itself, probably by going to the prison and gaining the warden's trust.

Indeed, firsthand observations and interviews play a strong role through-out his essay, and our next chapter talks about these kinds of research. Perhaps interview is how he learned how to make homebrew in a toilet; perhaps this came from published sources. The point is that Gonzales included with little fuss some researched information, and the paragraph is livelier than if he'd merely said, "Alcohol is a problem in prisons, and inmates make it through creative means."

When Do Writers Research?

Research in creative nonfiction happens in three modes that often inter-mix. Some writers have a well-mapped set of questions at the outset of a project; for example, they're going to write about a place and before typing a word they study its history, its climate, its geology, its famous residents. More often, the act of writing itself generates a need to learn. A memory of watching a particular television show as a child, for example, might lead to checking what night the show was broadcast, how long it was on the air, even what types of advertisers typically bought commercial time. Such "digressions" add texture and interest. Finally, reading and research precede and prompt the idea for a writing project. Coming across a fact that American participation in bowling leagues has declined in the past twenty years may inspire a profile of a local bowling team. It might lead to inter-views, observations, and immersion in bowling alley culture—with fur-ther research on the history of bowling leagues.

Our point is that research can bring not only credibility but also creative energy. It can impel writing as well as enhance it.

Creative Nonfiction Referenced in This Chapter

Bowden, Charles. "The Bone Garden of Desire." In *The Best American Essays 2001*, edited by Kathleen Norris and Robert Atwan. Boston: Houghton Mifflin, 2001.
Dillard, Annie. "An Expedition to the Pole." In *Teaching a Stone to Talk: Expeditions and Encounters*. New York: Harper & Row, 1982.

CHAPTER 9

Interviewing

An interview involves talking to someone who knows something that you need to find out. It's a conversation in which you, the interviewer, prompt the other person to talk. You listen closely, think quickly, and keep good notes—but none of this means much if you don't ask the right questions.

You'll want to get the person to reveal himself. You might have to talk to many people, if your piece takes on a broad subject; occasionally, you'll focus on a single one. Much of the interview will never be directly used, and that's okay; it may take a lot of questions before you hear the truest and most intriguing line.

An interview is a discovery process; you can't predict where it will go or how it is going to fit into the overall essay or if it will fit at all. In creative nonfiction, what is unexpected often turns out for the best. An interview can't and shouldn't be strictly controlled.

> "Interviewing is less stressful than you might think."

Interviewing is less stressful than you might think. It isn't you, personally, on the line—you have the protection and the liability of taking on a role. The interviewee will see you as a journalist (even if you aren't), and you will probably start feeling a bit like Woodward and/or Bernstein. The interaction, even with someone you know well, will take on a certain objective feel, since you are distancing yourself, weighing what they say, and putting it in the context of your project.

An interviewer should be curious and (at least on the surface) easygoing, able to question in a way that encourages people to trust her. The writer has to adapt to each person's idiosyncrasies and be flexible enough to change questions accordingly. The process takes patience; yet everything that comes of it, even if you can't use it directly, helps you to better understand the topic (or person) about which you're writing. Since this is creative nonfiction and not feature writing, all interviews contribute to the context, the backstory, the mood. Whatever a person says or does adds to the impression of the whole; it becomes part of an artifact.

The manner in which an interview is approached comes out of the writer's experience, journalistic background, the publication for which she is writing (if any), and her views about literal truth.

Choosing People to Interview

Most writers, if they have time, talk to as many people as possible. The more viewpoints you gather, even if they conflict, the better equipped you'll be to decide upon your own version of the truth. Not only that, but the people who you think will be helpful may not be; the people from whom you expect little may tell you interesting things. You can never assume that the "authority" has the knowledge or the willingness to share it. Writers have long known that the most entertaining and revealing perspectives usually come from the person on the street: from the dockworker to the nosy neighbor to the secretary to your younger sister.

The search for the great quote can involve considerable legwork. Jon Krakauer contacts "every single person I've read about or heard about who has any connection to the story. . . . Often, after conducting a whole bunch of long, exhausting interviews . . . I've thought, 'What is this next gal on my list really going to know? Why should I waste my time calling her?' But I make myself call her anyway, and that interview will turn out to be amazing."

When Tara Bahrampour began developing her piece "Persia on the Pacific" (on page 174), she knew few Iranians in Los Angeles—she had to introduce herself and her project to a community: "I initially spent a couple of weeks there talking to as many Iranians as I could from many different backgrounds—rich, poor, Muslim, Jewish, male, female, old, and young. I wanted to find a family whose child had never been to Iran but was dying to go there." She finally decided on a young man named Parshaw, whose story "seemed most interesting and emblematic of what I was looking for. They [Parshaw and his family] were also extremely open and generous with their time, and Parshaw himself had an appealing personality and a sweetness that worked well for the story."

Assuming that there are many people who might shed light on what you want to know, you have to decide with whom to spend your time. The best choice often becomes apparent because you have a strong sense of what you're looking for. When Jennifer Kahn was writing "Notes from a Parallel Universe," she sifted through a "huge pile of letters from cranks" that was kept by the University of California–Berkeley. She found that most of the letter writers were "monomaniacal to the point of tedium." The focus of her piece turned out to be Eugene Sittampalan, who "by contrast seemed essentially normal, though clearly obsessed. He was intelligent and not easy to categorize." If she had wanted to write a piece that ridiculed the letter writers, she could easily have chosen some of the "cranks"—but this wasn't what she wanted. The process is a matter of discovery that begins with a broad field and then winnows itself. The focal person is chosen through a process involving luck, timing, and a certain sense of inevitability.

Unfortunately, not all of us have the time or money to spend on interviewing a spectrum of people. Assuming you don't have an expense-paid contract or a hefty trust fund, you have to narrow your choices while keeping your ends open for whatever comes up. Generally, you'll choose people who you genuinely find interesting, who have "good lines" (or just like to talk), and who can best contribute to the focus your story will take. Some of your choices will be obvious—they're the ones who you know have the answers—others, less so. You'll keep a sense of limits in your head—you know how much time and money you have to work with, and you have to discipline yourself to know when to stop. It's important to prioritize, with the ones that *must* be contacted coming first on your list.

Composing the Questions

Rather than working from a preconceived list of questions, most writers come up with (as Calvin Trillin said) a sketch of "specific things I really need to know." This blueprint helps them to keep more or less on track and to feel comfortable and relaxed during the interview. Lists tend to be more formalized if the person interviewed is powerful and the piece is to be written for a publication with journalistic expectations. If you need solid, accurate quotes from an expert, or if the topic is one you don't understand, it's best to be prepared.

The questions you plan in advance are, obviously, the ones for which you need answers. Without a central question, the meaning remains elusive and the piece lacks focus. Lawrence Weschler thinks in terms of one big question that provides "a point of access to the complexity of what is." For his book *Boggs: A Comedy of Values*, about a financial scandal, that question was "where does all the money go when there is a bust?" Once he realized that the money was never really there—that the businessmen were operating on speculation—the story fell into place.

As in any conversation, the best lines usually come by surprise. That's one reason why it's better to respond spontaneously with follow-up questions than to hold yourself to a strictly planned list. William Langewische advises that you should "let the guy talk" and listen carefully to his response. "You never know where they're going, and it gets really interesting when you let people run on." The more people talk, the more they tend to reveal themselves. Jane Kramer says it this way: "I'm interested in people at that moment their cover slips, when the seamlessness of their self-presentation slips and you can enter that margin of psychic space between who they are inside and who they are outside. It's in that space—that negotiated space—that you find the person."

Any interviewee may at times give you incomplete, confusing, or false information. If you get a sense that someone is hedging, or if something just doesn't make sense, you need to ask more questions. If you're confused, repeat what the person said in your own words and ask if this is what she meant. This isn't rude; it's better than writing up a misconception.

If you ask difficult questions, you may get hostile answers. That's okay—it tells you something. Journalist Deborah Blum says that when she runs into a negative response, she goes "from chatty to straightforward. I try to get all my points in. . . . I save the most difficult questions for last." While it may not feel nice to receive the ritual booting, it's part of your job, and it isn't personal.

Since the interview process is fluid, writers often have to change and refine what it is they need to know. No amount of planning will keep this from happening. Lawrence Weschler begins with "a battery of questions the size of a huge block," but as the project progresses he learns which to cut and which to keep. This is not a failure of planning but a sign that the project is going well.

Face to Face or Far Away?

Once you know who you want to interview, you have to decide when and how to do it. If time allows, it's best to meet directly; that way, you can gauge physical reactions. This will help you weigh whether your subject is being honest or holding back, and you can weave sensory description throughout your dialogue.

Many writers find setting up the interview to be more intimidating than the interview itself. If the person is a stranger, you can try to get an introduction through an intermediary. If this isn't possible, call or write letters to arrange a time. The science writer Mary Knudsen says that she introduces herself in person and conducts the interview later. Gay Talese hung around the scene, leaping into interviews as they came along. (We've all seen movies wherein the intrepid journalist lurks in a bar, getting only slightly buzzed until he can talk to the military officer, public official, fellow cynical journalist, and/or love interest. Apparently such things really happen.) However it's done, it's a good idea to honestly identify your purpose: you're a writer and you may be publishing what they have to say.

You don't need six years of unfettered immersion time for the hang-around method to work. Let's say, for instance, that you want to write an essay about the kinds of people who go to NASCAR rallies. You've been to a few, but aren't a follower; you just find the whole milieu interesting. So you go to a rally and are barraged by noisy adults and kids from all dif- ferent social backgrounds. You want to get a sam- pling. How do you walk up to the woman consum- ing that cheese dog? Just do it. You're a writer, you have a role, and this role makes it easier. It isn't as if you want to steal her food. You're honest, self- effacing, unaggressive, friendly—an adventurer, out to find answers. While you may experience a moment of terror as you near the Cheez Whiz, remind yourself that people really want to talk— especially about their passions—and will probably be flattered to be asked. And if she says no, so what? Just walk away.

> "How do you walk up to that woman consuming that cheese dog? Just do it."

In the course of writing a book about a woman's execution, Beverly Lowry had to learn to talk to every type of person, from criminals to cops. She wrote of her own method:

> You marshall your wits, gather up your best imitation of nonchalance, turn the door handle, step in.
>
> You are operating on instinct and the need to know.
>
> One foot in front of the other. Let them do the talking.
>
> One question may not lead to the next. You ask it anyway. Hope for the best, swing with the results, follow up with another.
>
> This never changes.

Scrawls and Transcriptions

An interview is a transcribed conversation; you have to document what you learn. Nearly all writers do this by taking notes: words and phrases that jog their memory when they type them up later. The more official the inter- view, the more journalistic the piece; the more public the person, the greater the level of literal accountability; the more technical the subject, the more you will want to make sure that you understand the information.

Jane Kramer calls note-taking "a kind of editing process in itself. I write down only what I must, at some level, be hearing as important or notable." Most writers' notes look like nonsensical scribbles of peculiar code. (It's difficult to take word-for-word notes when you're floating down the Columbia River or standing on the fringes of a fight.) Then they type them up as soon as possible, adding the physical details of the encounter and filling in the gaps as they go.

While recorders are being used more often, most writers choose not to use them. Some publications require their use; most don't. If you are concerned about libel charges or your ability to accurately remember the interview, however, you should do what makes you comfortable.

Many writers find the recorder an incursion on their freedom. Gay Talese believed that they lead to a "once-over-lightly dialogue that—while perhaps symptomatic of a society permeated by fast-food computerized bottom-line impersonalized workmanship—too frequently reduces the once-artful craft of magazine writing to the level of talk radio on paper." Other writers disagree equally strongly, arguing that without a recorder, small revealing details will be lost.

This debate leads to the inevitable question of whether you can accurately quote someone when you're reconstructing from notes. The reality is that no one is ever quoted completely, even when their words are taped. Readers would not want to read page after page of unedited tape transcripts. Digressions are cut unless they contribute to the whole. The quotes that end up in the published version reflect the writer's (or publisher's) vision. The editing of information is a creative act in itself—there is no way to avoid this, no matter how "accurate" you want to be.

Literary Journalism and the Interview

Journalists, far more than other kinds of writers, have been trained to stick to a strict truth standard. A quote isn't recollected; it's literal, attributed to a source, and transcribed from accurate notes or a tape. It takes a rebellious spirit to approach journalism otherwise; as more lawsuits are levied, the more accountability that magazines demand. The glory days of Gay Talese/Tom Wolfe/Hunter S. Thompson's noteless, recollected "new journalism" may well be over for those who publish in national nonfiction magazines. Literary journals, on the other hand, rarely fact-check, since most of their editors see creative work as "hands off" in terms of editorial intrusion. Literary journals, though, rarely include journalism, preferring works of personal essay and memoir.

A journalistic piece based upon recent events—no matter how creative it may be in approach—relies upon the writer's observation and research. Even a writer as seemingly flaky as Hunter Thompson took notes, and then ran to his hotel room to tap his recollections into a typewriter. Magazine and newspaper editors expect at least a semblance of validity, and any good nonfiction writer expects the same from himself.

Interviewing People You Know

Family and friends will have a hard time separating your everyday self from the writer who wants to publish their statements. They may not take to the idea of you-as-writer/reporter; they may find it hard to believe. While your family may be easier to approach initially, they may be far more practiced at knowing how to avoid your questions.

Some memoirists and essayists would never formally "interview" people they know well. They engage in casual conversations with family members, neighbors, townspeople, and others to double-check their memories and get a deeper sense of the situation. They aren't necessarily looking to confirm their memories, since everyone observes things differently, but even a contradictory observation can shed new light.

You may hesitate to ask questions that might make your best friend uncomfortable. It may be hard to focus the information onto a narrow subject (if your friend is chatty), or to get any information at all (if your friend doesn't want to talk). Even if you don't get what you had hoped, the interaction can be valuable in both a personal and artistic sense. The interview may reveal things you never knew before and can send you on the track of other information, such as letters and photographs. (The use of personal memorabilia in research is discussed in chapter 8.)

For his book *Colored People*, about his childhood in West Virginia, Henry Louis Gates, Jr., talked with his father. Gates knew when he began that his father was a prolific storyteller; what he didn't know was how much he would discover. Gates said, "Be prepared for the revelation of things you don't even dream are going to come up." Once this happens (and it probably will), you have to decide how much of this to put in your account.

When talking to family members, most writers reconstruct that material impressionistically, gathering snips and sensations and scraps of phrases. Most publications would not expect memoirists' work to include verbatim quotes, and so recorded conversations aren't required. If you *are* considering recording Mom, you might consider the purpose of the piece, the reliability of your own memory, your mother's feelings on the matter, whether or not she'll sue you, and your own views on the necessity of verifiable fact.

Usually, "interviews" with family members arise unexpectedly and informally. There is no chance to take notes. Some writers just think like interviewers; they keep records of their lives. Russell Baker's book *Growing Up* began nearly by accident on a visit to his hospitalized mother:

> She was suffering from something I have since come to recognize as very common to elderly folks but that I had never seen before and certainly had never thought would happen to my mother. I was so astonished that my only reaction was to start taking notes on what she was saying. I had stopped at the hospital gift shop . . . to take some knickknack up to her, not realizing what I was going to find, and I tore the paper bag open so that I could write on the back of it. And I started making a record of our conversation. It's a reporter's reflex. . . . When I left I stuffed it in a raincoat pocket and forgot about it. . . . I found it many weeks later. . . . And that turned out to be the conversation that appears in the first chapter of *Growing Up*.

Had Baker not gone on to talk with other people from his life, his book would have had far less color and depth. Robin Hemley, for his book *Nola*, pulled dialogue not only from his mother but from the landlord, his brother, a policeman, a doctor, a cousin, a friend of his mother's, and his wife and daughter. The resulting conflicts in information contribute to a sense of mystery and discovery in this book about his mentally ill sister.

Putting It All Together

Now that you have your interviews finished and transcribed, what do you do with the information?

Find the focus. The shorter the piece, the more focused it has to be. What's the story? Who are the essential characters? What are the lines that shed light? What must you directly quote and what can you paraphrase? What doesn't need to be there?

You'll have to reconcile yourself to the fact that much of what you've accumulated will never appear in the piece. This can be frustrating, particularly after you've spent all that time on talking and note-taking, but that's the way it has to be. This cutting takes ruthless discipline.

> "Much of what you've accumulated will never appear in the piece."

You'll have to decide who, of all the people who *could* be in the piece, *will* be in the piece. You will probably focus on only one or two central characters—the rest, if any, are peripheral. Most of your interviewees' lines won't appear as direct quotes. They will be paraphrased or will be there as background knowledge.

An interview is truly a quest. You'll find out at least as much as, and possibly more than, you ever wanted to know. What you don't use becomes the context, the tone, and the meaning. And that's a lot to get for talking to people.

Creative Nonfiction Referenced in This Chapter

Baker, Russell. *Growing Up*. New York: New American Library, 1982.
Gates, Henry Louis. *Colored People: A Memoir*. New York: Vintage, 1995.
Hemley, Robin. *Nola: A Memoir of Faith, Art, and Madness*. St. Paul, MN: Graywolf Press, 1998.

Works about Writing and Literature

Baker, Russell. "Life with Mother." In *Inventing the Truth: The Art and Craft of Memoir*, edited by William Zinsser.
Blum, Deborah, Mary Knudsen, and Robin Marantz Henig, eds. *A Field Guide to Science Writers*. Oxford and New York: Oxford University Press, 2006.
Boynton, Robert S., ed. *The New New Journalism: Conversations with America's Best Nonfiction Writers on Their Craft*. New York: Vintage Books, 2005.

Gates, Henry Louis. "Lifting the Veil." In *Inventing the Truth: The Art and Craft for Memoir*, edited by William Zinsser.

Kramer, Jane. Quoted in *The New Journalism*, edited by Robert S. Boynton.

Langewische, William. Quoted in *The New Journalism*, edited by Robert S. Boynton.

Lowry, Beverly. "The Shadow Knows." In *Writing Creative Nonfiction: Instruction and Insights from Teachers of the Associated Writing Programs*, edited by Philip Gerard and Carolyn Forche. Cincinnati: Story Press, 2001.

Talese, Gay. "Not Interviewing Frank Sinatra." In *The Essayist at Work: Profiles of Creative Nonfiction Writers*, edited by Lee Gutkind. Portsmouth, NH: Heinemann, 1998.

Trillin, Calvin. Quoted in *The New Journalism,* edited by Robert S. Boynton.

Weschler, Lawrence. Quoted in *The New Journalism,* edited by Robert S. Boynton.

Zinsser, William, ed. *Inventing the Truth: The Art and Craft of Memoir.* New York: Houghton Mifflin, 1998.

CHAPTER **10**

Ideas for Writing

In Class or on Your Own

These exercises can be used in the classroom or by writers working on their own. They follow the order and progression outlined in the previous chapters.

1. Mini Memoir

Write a brief memoir about yourself—and we mean really brief, about five hundred words. To do this, come up with the things that are most truly you—quirky examples, illustrative situations. Do it with a style that shows your attitude; we don't want dry "just the facts" writing here. Approach it in any way you choose. Have no fear.

2. Describing an Individual

Think of someone you have seen within the past year.

Describe that person fully—physical details, of course, but also include little details that portray her essence. Include things around her, the way she speaks, habits, places you find her, whatever comes to mind. This can be stream of consciousness, not necessarily straightforward. You can write it in paragraphs or separate lines. Keep this to no more than two pages.

3. Observing the Countryside

Hang out in a public area such as a mall, a park, a bus station, a concert hall. Absorb what's going on around you in a broad sense, as if you were a complete outsider to this scene. Write this down in your notes.

Then pay attention again, focusing particularly on what you hear. Grab snippets of conversations as they go by. Write down some of these, reproducing them as exactly as you can.

Now pay attention to a few particular people. Take notes. Then take all of these notes and build a creative nonfiction piece from them. You can put yourself in the essay, but you don't have to. Describe the place in detail, giving us a feel of its character. The narrative thread can appear not only in what you witness but also in the story of your own reactions, thoughts, and movements. (2–4 pages)

4. Grey Areas

Think about specific works you've read and list at least three that *you* would classify as creative nonfiction. Then go to a bookstore and pick three specific texts: one that you think is clearly creative nonfiction, one that you know is clearly not, and one that falls into a grey area. Briefly describe why you have classified them in this way. Then discuss the book that might or might not be creative nonfiction, considering the following questions: Is it true? Is it factual? (These are not always the same thing.) Does it come from a personal point of view, and what does this mean? Does it have a literary style? If you do have a strong opinion about where this "grey area" piece falls, feel free to construct an argument. (3–4 pages)

5. Family: Dead or Alive

Write a scene from the point of view of a family member, alive or dead. The scene should be set at least ten years in the past and should be based on a "true" event (or as true as you know it to be). It can be a family member you know well or one you've only heard stories about. Try to imagine how that person views things, and use the kind of language you think that person would have used. Try to capture a sense of the time period through examples of what the person sees or does. (3–4 pages)

Variation 1: Consider a specific memory that involves one or more of your family members. First write about the event from your perspective. Then write about it from the point of view of another family member present at the event. Consider interviewing the family member to gain insight into what he or she was thinking. Remember to write it as he or she would speak, using the language that is familiar to him or her. Consider the facts as your family member would have seen them, the sounds the way he or she would hear them. Most of all, remember *he or she is not you.* (3–5 pages)

Variation 2: Write a scene that you've heard your family talk about, but you were not present to witness. This can be anything: how your grandparents first met, how your uncle got his Purple Heart, the time that cousin Cindy shot off her own toe. Try to write it in real time; try to avoid language like "One time my cousin . . . " or "Back then Cindy was a real contortionist." It should feel as if the event is happening or just happened, even if it actually took place years ago; use the literary skills that you've learned in this book to make the piece come alive. (4–5 pages)

6. The Autobiography of ?

Read the creative biography excerpted from *Louis Riel* by Chester Brown (page 224). Then write a scene for an autobiography of a real person who is not you (think *The Autobiography of Malcolm X*). Even if you interview someone, this scene will involve a bit of imagination: you should try to re-create something that happened to him or her by using description, dialogue, the person's thoughts, and the like. The figure can be living or dead, someone you know or someone you'll never know, famous or not famous. This should be written in the first person or in a very close third-person perspective. (Don't *tell* us about the person; get into the person's mind. Also: don't concern yourself with whether this is an exercise in fiction or nonfiction. This is just an exercise, and it's up to you whether you want to develop it into more than that.) (2–3 pages)

7. A Childhood Kitchen

Write a short piece set in a kitchen of your childhood. The piece should be highly detailed but also have a sense of movement and meaning (that is, something should happen, even if it is something that seems insignificant). Try to stay in the general point of view of your child self, perceiving as you might have then—as you remember yourself perceiving. (1–2 pages) (This exercise was adapted from one used by John Bowers at Wilkes University's creative nonfiction class.)

Variation: This exercise can be written alone or in the classroom. Take thirty minutes and write the following, without thinking too much about it before you begin: Picture yourself at the age of nine. Picture your residence at that time. Write a half- to full-page description of each room and one brief incident that happened there. Go with your first impressions. Use all your senses in your descriptions.

8. La La La

After reading chapter 6, "Style," think of particular songs that have special meaning to you and find their lyrics. (These are usually easy to find on the Internet.) Take a few lines from one of the songs, write them at the top of the page (or scatter them throughout the piece as "subheadings"), and then write a scene set in your past. (Avoid high school, but any other situation is fair game.) The piece should not be *about* the song but should use its words and music to evoke tone, mood, emotion, and rhythm. (2–3 pages)

9. Newsworthy

Take any news event you've heard about—national, international, important, trivial, whatever. Write a piece that reflects your own interaction with that event (or your own interpretation of that event). Approaches might include a partly fictionalized re-creation, a *creative* opinion piece involving personal examples, a memoir, observations (if an event had an effect on people around you, re-create the situation). Try to stay away from traditional logical arguments and rants. *Do not write about September 11.* (3–5 pages)

10. What a Couple of Writers Might Say

Write an imaginary conversation between two creative nonfiction writers whose work you've read. (If you haven't read much creative nonfiction, then pick two writers in this book and read their work.) These writers can talk about anything—it doesn't have to be writing. Of course, this is basically a fiction exercise, since you are making it all up, but that's okay— as long as you try to capture the sense of who they might be, and what perspectives they hold. Don't look up interviews with the writers to get this information. (2 pages)

11. A Trip Never Taken

Read the Brenda Miller essay "Next Year in Jerusalem" (page 594) and the section of the book that discusses lyric essays (page 20). Using a structure similar to Miller's, write about a trip you imagined but never took. Be precise and succinct; pay close attention to language and make every word count. (2–3 pages)

12. Based on a True Story?

Select two readings from this book. Write about how the two writers handle their portrayals of "true" events. In what ways does each writer use imagination and literary technique to tell the story? To what extent do you feel that the work is fictionalized? To what extent did this get in the way of your involvement with or acceptance of the piece? (2 pages)

13. Foregrounding Place

Read "The Ashes of August" by Kim Barnes (page 188) and the excerpt from *Pyongyang* by Guy Delisle (page 272). Then write a piece that puts a place in the foreground. The place should be one that has an impact on the narrator; it should dictate the action, not merely serve as a setting.

The kind of place you choose is up to you. Just make sure that you describe it fully and include your own reactions to the space, so that we understand the way this place exists and has an impact on the people in it. (3–5 pages)

14. Cultural Tastes

Using a format like Karen Tei Yamashita's in her "June: Circle K Recipes" (page 779), write about the food of a particular place and describe it in a way that reflects that particular subculture. Be specific; describe the food at an event or a gathering spot rather than pointing out, say, the cuisine of an entire country. (2 pages)

15. Witness

Read the excerpt from Dennis Covington's book *Salvation on Sand Mountain* (page 257). Write a piece in which you serve as a witness to a dramatic event. This drama could come from something as seemingly mundane as a family argument or as startling as a car accident. In this witnessing, you can serve either as a distant witness or someone who is directly involved. Either way, you should describe the scene fully. You are free to include information or a backstory as context, but try to keep such references relatively brief. Be cognizant of when time is slowed and when it races, of the way that a dramatic event is not always experienced as dramatic. Let the structure be as disjointed as the event itself may have been; capture the sense of how a witness feels and perceives in such a situation. (3–5 pages)

16. Ideas

Read chapter 1, "Defining Creative Nonfiction." For each of the types of creative nonfiction (literary, journalism, travel writing, memoir, etc.), write a brief proposal of ideas for pieces you would like to eventually write. Let yourself be imaginative—you won't be held to anything. For *each type*, give your thoughts on how you might pursue one or two pieces and why. Write about a paragraph per subgenre of creative nonfiction.

17. Beginning

Read the material on "Beginnings" on pages 42–46 of chapter 3. Then choose a good beginning from a work of creative nonfiction. (You can use the pieces in this anthology, or something from your own library.) Explain why this beginning grabs you. Talk about what you see as the qualities of a good beginning.

Next, write a beginning (three paragraphs) to a longer piece of creative nonfiction. Then state in general terms the direction you think this piece may take.

Variation: Explore the differences (if any) between a nonfiction beginning and a fictional one. How are they the same? How are they different? Why do you think the differences exist (if they do)? (1–2 pages)

18. Middle

Read the material on "Middles" on pages 46–49 of chapter 3. Then look through some works of creative nonfiction (from either your class texts or books or essays of your own). Pick a piece you think has a particularly strong middle section. Why do you think the middle of this piece works well? How might the writer have kept the piece moving? Can you imagine what was *not* included in this middle to keep the piece interesting? What details are focused upon? Would you say that the piece reaches some kind of climactic point, and what would that be?

Then write a middle section to the piece that you began in exercise 17. Make this three or four paragraphs in length. (It's likely that the piece is actually longer—go ahead and keep writing it if you like, but don't end it yet.)

19. End

Read the section on "Endings," pages 49–52 of chapter 3. Then look through some works of creative nonfiction (either those included here or books or essays of your own). Pick a piece with a strong ending. Talk about why this ending is effective. How does it build upon what came before? Does it wrap up the topic, or is it more open ended? What tone do you think the writer wanted to leave with the reader? What mood did it leave you in? How would you describe the author's style? How do the language and structure used in the ending contrast with what came before? Then write an ending to the piece you wrote in exercises 17 and 18. If your middle section is incomplete, you may want to write several paragraphs leading up to the ending, and then add your final words.

20. Responsibility

Read the chapter from Dave Eggers's book *A Heartbreaking Work of Staggering Genius* (page 342). Then write a creative nonfiction piece about being confronted with an overwhelming responsibility. Taking your cue from Eggers, use description, dialogue, and other techniques to bring this scene to life. (3–5 pages)

21. Semijournalistic Observer

Read "A Place Called Midland," by Susan Orlean (page 615), and "The Faith of Graffiti," by Norman Mailer (page 537). Now write your own piece of literary journalism. That is, observe an event and write about it from an involved but unobtrusive perspective. This event can be significant or insignificant—a reading, political rally, sales convention, gun show, department store opening—anything. The key is in the way you tell the story. You should be involved, if not as an actual character, then through the force of your style and voice. Try to capture the essence of what you observe, so that someone in thirty years might use your piece to understand a time period or type of people. What you shouldn't be is flat and disinterested. (3–5 pages)

22. Drawing an Interaction

Talk with someone who knows something you want to know. This can be anyone from a stranger to a close friend, and the topic can be intimately personal or not personal at all. Ask questions, paying attention to the person's reactions, inflections of voice, choice of language, and so on. Then write a piece that not only highlights some of the information but also reveals the nuances of this person's character. Equal consideration should be given to the information itself and your descriptions of the person giving you the information.

Variation: Do the above assignment but place the emphasis on the narrator (you) as you go through the process of talking with this person. This variation works best when you are on that person's own turf and you can work in impressions of the sights and sounds around you. (For example, when interviewing an athlete you can enter that person's gym, revealing your own insecurities about former PE classes while also giving us a picture of your interviewee.)

23. A Site or Museum

Writing based upon historical events is a popular subgenre in both creative nonfiction and fiction. Some creative nonfiction writers weave their own stories and perspective through the information, as the writer Tony Horwitz does in his book *Confederates in the Attic.* Other writers compose from the point of view of a historical person. Whatever the approach, writing about historical events requires not only knowledge of the historical facts but a projection into a time and place that has passed.

For this exercise, write about a visit to a historical site or museum. Think about a time when you made such a visit—or, if possible, visit the place and take notes. Mix your personal reflections with actual historical information. Contrast the physical reconstruction of events (the design and presentation of the site) with the events as you understand them. For instance, watching historical reenactors at a Civil War battle site, as Tony Horwitz did in *Confederates in the Attic,* is very different from being a soldier on an actual field of battle. What do you feel about the gap between what really occurred and the way we present that event for "education and entertainment"? Try to avoid using the device of putting all of the information in the mouth of the tour guide or filmstrip.

Your desire to inform should be outweighed by your willingness to tell a good story—to entertain and interest. That said, try to avoid outright errors of fact. (4–5 pages)

24. Historical Scene

Read S. L. Wisenberg's essay "Holocaust Girls/Lemon" (page 774). Write a piece in which you turn a historical conflict into a scene. You'll be walking the line between fiction and fact in this one, and that's okay. The factual basis of this scene can be pulled from any book, documentary, Web site, or other source. Your job is to bring the situation to life by adding details, description, and dialogue. Fictionalize the scenario without straying from the essential facts. (2–3 pages)

25. Dialogue

Read chapter 5, "Dialogue." Think of a situation you witnessed in which something interesting happened. The situation should involve discussion, heated or otherwise, between two or more individuals. The conflict should lead to some kind of resolution, even if it is not a tidy or clear one.

Write up this scenario using *as much dialogue as possible*. The dialogue should serve to move forward the incident and show us little things about the speakers. You can include occasional explanation to direct the reader toward what is happening, but there shouldn't be any paragraph-long explanatory descriptions. Just tell us enough to have your dialogue make sense (like adding a little visual description here and there, along with reminders of who is speaking). Write this in prose (not play) form. (3–4 pages)

26. Pop!

This can be in any form you choose; be inventive. The only criterion is that it needs to deal in some way with an aspect of pop culture. So it could be a nonfiction story with a pop-culture setting or context; it could be a creatively written review; it could be reflective/poetic; it could be a "think piece," an analysis; it could be about a particular pop-culture–obsessed group of people. It might be all of these. Use sources if you think you need them to make your point. (3–4 pages)

27. Calm Persuasion

Read "Reflections of a Nonpolitical Man," by Sven Birkerts (page 217), and "Caring for Your Introvert," by Jonathan Rauch (page 652). Then write your own persuasive piece that defends a belief in an interesting—but not bombastic or aggressive—way. The piece might have a reflective or thoughtful tone, but should be informative enough to bring the reader to understanding. Avoid the tendency to overstate or to fall into the old "thesis-body-conclusion" structure. And, taking a cue from the readings, you should be present in the piece as a persona. (2–3 pages)

28. Topical Event

Read "Run, Rudolph, Run," by Denis Johnson (page 451), "Palestine," by Joe Sacco (page 656), and "*Nigger:* Notes from a New Orleans Daughter," by Sheryl St. Germain (page 690). Then write a piece in which you are an observer or a participant in a topical event. (This could be anything from a demonstration to a town meeting to an accident to a storm.) Include your personal involvement and viewpoints to whatever extent seems right to you. A piece like this should include observations about individuals and should include dialogue. Even if you are only on the outskirts of the event, your perceptions are relevant. (4–6 pages)

29. Edgy Third Person

Write a piece in which you are referenced not as "I" but by name, initial, or *she/he.* Make this sound like fiction, but have it be your reality. Rely upon the literary devices of dialogue, description, action, and conflict to make this piece active and lively.

Stay focused on one situation. You might take this opportunity to write about an edgy, disturbing subject that you might avoid if you were working in the first person.

Once you finish, write a paragraph about the ways that changing the point of view did or didn't alter the way you felt as you told the story. (2–3 pages)

Variation: Write a brief scene using the first-person point of view. Then write that same scene from the third-person perspective. Do not simply rewrite what you just wrote—re-envision it. (Generally, the first-person point of view allows you to be more direct about providing information or telling your feelings; in third person, more will need to be shown and less explained.) (3–4 pages)

30. Waking Dream

Read Gary Panter's graphic piece "Nightmare Studio" (page 637). Then write a scene in which a dream becomes a nightmare, or a nightmare becomes a dream. Allow yourself the freedom to delve into it deeply and strangely, letting go of the notion that it has to make sense. (2–3 pages)

31. Destructive Nature

Read "The Ashes of August," by Kim Barnes (page 188) and "*Nigger:* Notes from a New Orleans Daughter," by Sheryl St. Germain (page 690). Then write your own essay that tells the story of a time that nature became a dominant, perhaps even destructive, force. This can be based upon your own experience or upon a researched event, told from the imagined point of view of someone who would have experienced it. (For instance, a piece about the Johnstown flood could use research to illustrate what a girl living in the town might have experienced. If you take this approach, attempt to use a "close" point of view, seeing things the way this child might have seen them.) Try to avoid a distant, academic tone. Remember to include details and descriptions of the phenomenon itself. (3–6 pages)

32. Anthropology

While reading "Rock Paintings" by Louise Erdrich (page 379), take careful note of how she explains each painting, analyzing it in terms of historical fact and symbolic meaning, using personal feelings and literary description. Then find an object in your house/apartment/dorm and write your own anthropomorphic study on it. Don't write from the perspective of present-day you, but rather as a future you, looking at a relic from the distant past. Be creative! Analyze it in all the ways that Erdrich uses to approach the rock paintings. And never come out and tell us directly what that object is. (4–5 pages)

33. Strange, Unusual, Uncomfortable

Read the excerpt from Dennis Covington's *Salvation on Sand Mountain* (page 257) and the essay by Laurence Gonzales, "Marion Prison" (page 403). Write about a place that you consider one of the strangest, most unusual, most exciting, or most uncomfortable places you have ever been. It doesn't have to be an exotic location, although it could be; it could be as everyday as a car or a room. In the course of your essay, describe the place so that your reader can get a sense of it. Use sensory detail. You can include other people and yourself in the essay, if you like, using dialogue, conflict, or whatever else it takes to bring the piece to life. Something should happen in the essay, even if it only happens internally to you. (3–5 pages)

34. Interviewing Universally

After reading Jennifer Kahn's "Notes from a Parallel Universe" (page 463), try interviewing your own "expert" on a topic. This can be in regards to a serious subject (your professor's studies in molecular physics), an ordinary but underdiscussed subject (a kindergarten teacher's methods for working with gifted children), a rather silly but inventive subject (your little brother's recipes and methods for making mud dinners), or an obvious one (your roommate's methods for making hard lemonade). Note the way that Kahn works her own presence and opinions rather subtly into the piece, then do the same when writing your essay. (3–4 pages)

35. Maps

Read Emily Hiestand's "Maps" (page 428). Notice the way that she uses the car trip as a means of telling us about her family, her family's history, and the places seen outside the car windows. Then describe your own excursion to visit family, reflecting upon the experiences of the trip itself (interactions between family members, what is seen beyond the window) and the ultimate destination. (2–4 pages)

Variation: Describe a road trip you shared with somebody else. It can be a friend, family member, coworker—one other person or an entire busload. Use your depiction of the journey as a way of revealing something (flattering or not) about the people on the trip. (3–4 pages)

36. Circuses, Fairs, and Other Freaky Shows

Taking a cue from Edward Hoagland's "Circus Music" (page 442), describe in vivid detail a circus, fair, sideshow, or theme park. Think about and describe the workers and customers, and try to capture the flavor of the environment. (If you have been a worker at this place, delve into your experience as an employee.) Include (briefly) a bit of the background of this event or place—where it is, what it is (Six Flags? Disney World? A small local fair?), and what makes it like and unlike others of its kind. Especially remember to include yourself—to keep these impressions ultimately your own, allowing us to share in your experience. (3–4 pages)

37. Heroes and Villains

Read "Traveling Light" from Amitava Kumar's *London-Bombay-New York* (page 484). Consider the way that Kumar deconstructs the cultural icon that Gandhi has become. Then think of a figure who has symbolic importance among a particular group or a country with which you identify. Like Kumar, use portrayals by the popular culture, the literary culture, and the views generally held by everyday people to put together a picture of this individual as held by the contemporary imagination. (4–5 pages)

Variation: Everybody has some sort of idol. This may be a friend, a family member, a celebrity, a historical figure, even a fictional character. In this exercise, choose an idol and retell a time when you realized this figure was flawed. What's important is the effect of the realization on you. Questions you may consider: How did this change your perception of the idol? Did it make you suspicious of idolizing anyone? How did others react? Did you agree with their reactions? Where do the realities of the private person and the fantasies of the public persona meet? Were you able to resolve this split between the fantasy and reality and accept that reality? (4–5 pages)

38. Memorial Day

After reading Maya Lin's essay about creating the Vietnam War Memorial, "Between Art and Architecture" (page 499), write about your own experience of visiting a memorial commemorating a tragic loss of life. Delve into not only your emotional response but also a description of, and ultimately the meaning of, the memorial itself. You will probably need to include historical background on the event, but don't make that your focus. Don't forget to include glimpses of others who are also there experiencing the site. (3–5 pages)

39. Machinery

Read Michael Martone's essay "Manufacturing Place" (page 571). Then write a piece in which what a thing is made of and what it does or how people work in it or with it becomes a reflection of your own experience. One example is a computer: a machine of wire and boards and light—which becomes a conduit for an international communications network, and for which we modify the way we physically sit and maneuver as we use the machine and respond to its various demands—which affects the way we feel and think.

Virtually any technology or tool can be used in an essay in this way. Allow yourself to try writing this piece without overthinking it, without worrying about whether you're doing it "right." (2–3 pages)

40. Competition

Read Cris Mazza's "A Girl among Trombonists" (page 577). Write a piece that explores one or more incidents of formal competition in school. While Mazza writes about band competitions, you can write about sports, spelling, art fairs, theater auditions, or anything else you can think of. Keep it focused on one type of event. While you'll be writing about yourself, try to make broader points about the ramifications of competition and judging upon you and others. Try to avoid the urge to complain or rant; be reflective in an attempt to seriously explore the subject. (3–4 pages)

41. Family Ramifications

Read Paul Lisicky's "New World," a complex depiction of the ways that the weight of family history and experience affect our lives (page 509). Write a scene that shows the way one generation continues to have an impact on those that follow, even when that generation is dead or incapacitated. This piece should include at least one fully developed scene; don't try to summarize decades of generational interactions. (2–3 pages)

42. Staying Out of the Way

Notice the way that Norman Mailer stays out of the limelight as narrator in "The Faith of Graffiti" (page 537) and the way that Denis Johnson does the same in "Run, Rudolph, Run" (page 451). Their attitudes aren't revealed through a dominating first-person presence but through style, tone, and the information they choose to include. Write a piece in which you interact with a group of people whom you don't know well or at all (examples: class, parties, public events). Describe these people and the place, implying your attitude without including yourself as an "I" or going on about your opinion. (4–5 pages)

43. Injustice

Read Demetria Martinez's short essays "Inherit the Earth" (page 567) and "The Things They Carried" (page 568). Then write a piece that explores what you see as an unjust and inhumane situation. Focus your writing on one or two specific scenes—preferably, situations that you have personally witnessed or experienced. Include yourself as narrator, even if you aren't personally receiving poor treatment. Try to avoid the temptation to lecture or even state your opinion overtly. It's important to *show* the injustice, letting this become your means of persuasion. (2 pages)

44. Things Carried

After reading Demetria Martinez's essay "The Things They Carried" (page 568), write a scene in which the circumstances of a group are revealed by what is carried into a place. Your piece should be detailed and specific, relying for meaning upon what is shown rather than what is explained. (1–2 pages)

45. The Boring Job

After reading Rick Moody's chapter from *The Black Veil* (page 603) and C. Tyler's "Sub Zero" (page 732), write your own account of a job that was tedious or difficult but can be made interesting because of the people you met, the techniques you learned (no matter how mundane and repetitive), and especially the way that you turn it all into a story. Keep in mind that an experience that was dull to you may not be to the reader because he or she has never done that task (and will be learning something), has never met those people, and doesn't have to experience it for nearly as long a time as you did. Give the reader a sense not only of the task itself, but of a few of the people around you (coworkers, customers). Try to focus on one or two scenes that exemplify the experience—and include a sense of conflict, even if it is only within you. (3–4 pages)

46. Creation and Collaboration

Does anyone really "create" alone? To delve into this question, try to find an example of a creative person (artist, musician, writer, or inventor) who did his or her best work with, was inspired by, or was spurred on by a rivalry with another person. To better understand the possibilities of this assignment, read Cynthia Ozick's essay "What Helen Keller Saw" (page 623). Don't use yourself as the example of the "creative person." (2–3 pages)

47. Transcendent Moment

Read "Missionary Dance" by Rory Stewart (page 686). Write about a time when an activity (artistic, spiritual, physical) had a moment of the sublime (beauty, transcendence, joy). Focus on the sensory details of the experience, paying attention to your use of language. Don't explain or analyze the event. Don't worry about having a linear structure. Keep the piece contained to one or two moments explored in depth. (2–3 pages)

48. Groups Watching

Read "Missionary Dance" by Rory Stewart (page 686). Then write about the way that a particular group of people collectively shares a creative experience. (One example: a music festival. Another: a movie watched with a noisy group of friends or fans.) Try to bring us into that experience by showing us both the group of observers and what they are seeing and by allowing us to share in their collective reaction. We should come to better understand this group by learning about what they are watching and how they react to it. (2–3 pages)

49. Two Graphic Memoirs

Read the excerpts from Craig Thompson's *Blankets* (page 699) and Guy Delisle's *Pyongyang* (page 272). Discuss whether you think the comic or "graphic novel" format is effective for memoir writing. Think particularly about what can be shown in a visual medium as opposed to a text and vice versa. Be sure to use examples to explain your perspective. (3–4 pages)

50. Losing My Religion

Read the excerpt from *Blankets* by Craig Thompson (page 699) and "The Dead of Winter" by Debbie Drechsler (page 295). Write a memoir about a time when you gained or lost faith. (This doesn't necessarily have to be a religious faith, although it can be.) If you have the ability to draw, compose it in your own graphic memoir format. (3–4 pages)

51. Insider/Outsider

Read the excerpt from Luis Alberto Urrea's *Across the Wire* (page 739). Write about an experience you've had among a subculture that is generally overlooked, ignored, feared, hated, or dismissed by the mainstream. This can be a culture or group of which you consider yourself a part, or it can be one that you experienced as an outsider. Don't make any direct judgments, pronouncements, or defenses (the way you might in an argument). Instead, reveal these people (and yourself) by the story that you tell about them. Try to keep the piece contained by focusing on a particular time period or incident. (3–5 pages)

52. Childhood Wants

Read the excerpt from Steve Almond's *Candyfreak* (page 157). Then write about a product that obsessed you as a child: food, candy, toys, sports equipment, a song or band, cigarettes—anything. It can be a product that you had or that you never had. Write about this obsession from a child's point of view, delving into the particular feelings, fantasies, and sensory experiences that surrounded this product for you at the time. Give us a sense of why this obsessed you. (2–3 pages)

Variation: After reading the selection from Steve Almond's *Candyfreak* (page 157), write about something that obsessed you as a child or adolescent and that *continues* to obsess you. This should obsess you to the point of actually researching it, training in it, perhaps even working or majoring in something connected with it. Write about this in a way that delves into your obsession and also gives us some information about it (as Almond does in *Candyfreak*). (3–5 pages)

53. Writing Life

Read "A Path Taken, with All the Certainty of Youth," Margaret Atwood's essay about her evolution as a writer (page 171). Then explore how you came to write or became "a writer." (If you write stories for yourself or only in a journal, it counts.) If, despite reading this anthology, you don't feel that you have a writing life or even an interest in writing, then write the memoir of your life as it involves any artistic endeavor. (3–5 pages)

54. Interviewing beyond Your Norm

Read Tara Bahrampour's "Persia on the Pacific" (page 174), Norman Mailer's "The Faith of Graffiti" (page 537), or Joe Sacco's *Palestine* (page 656). Then read chapter 9 on interviewing. Interview someone who lives in a place that you would never enter or engages in an activity that you would never do—unless you had this assignment. Try to get a picture of this place, culture, activity not only from what the person tells you but by what you observe by visiting the place, engaging in the activity (if possible), and observing your interviewee. The goal is to try to come to an understanding in some small way and to communicate that to the reader—or, if an understanding could not be reached, why.

After completing this essay, briefly write about the experience of doing the interview itself—your expectations, the process, and what you feel about the result. (5–7 pages)

55. Lucky

Read the excerpt from Gabrielle Bell's graphic memoir *Lucky* (page 206). Describe your own experience of fantasizing your way through a mind-numbing class, job, conversation, or other situation. The description of the fantasies should be vivid and inventive. Show enough of the situation for us to understand what's going on (and to frame your essay), but keep any overt complaining to a minimum. The emphasis should be on the fantasies. (3–5 pages)

56. Vocalizing Loss

Think of somebody you once knew and have lost. This might be through death, but can be for other reasons, too, as with a friend you've lost contact with, a teacher with whom you had a connection, or a cousin who has moved away. Read Sharon Solwitz's moving essay "Abracadabra" (page 671) and construct your own fragmentary, stream-of-consciousness "memorandum" to that lost person. It can be as lyrical or straightforward as you choose; use the voice that is honest to you. The piece should reflect your feelings toward that person and should indicate at least one change in those feelings. (3–6 pages)

57. Working on Your Pastime

Read Touré's personal essay "What's Inside You, Brother?" (page 724) In this piece, Touré uses boxing as a way of both understanding and coping with racism and identity. The following exercise is two-fold. On one level, describe a pastime of yours. It must be something that you do (acting, fighting, running) and you must describe yourself doing it. On another level, you should use your action as a way to delve into your motivations for the activity. For instance, if you run every day to work off stress, tie in the process of running with the reasons why you must take that run and the feeling you get while running. Finally, delve into all of this while referring to yourself by your own name (rather than I), as Touré does in his essay. (2–3 pages)

58. Interpreting a Lobster

Read David Foster Wallace's essay "Consider the Lobster" (page 755). Take a usually unnoticed living thing (animal, plant, fish, protozoa, insect, parent [just kidding]), and write about it in the most complex fashion you can come up with for a four-to-six-page space. Think carefully about your subject. Do some research about it; pull up the most intriguing, the oddest, the most overlooked facts. Attach this to your own experiences with and feelings about the subject. Try to meld all of this into something coherent, bringing it to some final statement or image or emotional meaning. (4-6 pages)

Classroom Ideas for Writing

These group and individual exercises can be used in class.

59. Defining Creative Nonfiction in Various Media

Come up with a list of books or movies or TV shows that you think might count as "creative nonfiction." Also throw in a few that might or might not be—where you're just not sure. Your selections can be as literary or lowbrow as you wish (think Nabokov and "reality TV"). Be prepared to discuss the lines between fiction and nonfiction and the ways that this distinction plays out in a variety of media.

60. Genres and Definitions

Think about the types of writing that might fall under the umbrella of "creative nonfiction." To do this, think about the way bookstores and libraries shelve materials; while there is a fiction section, bookstores rarely have a "creative nonfiction" section. So where do you go to find it? And how do you know you've found it?

Jot down some of the places where creative nonfiction is shelved and think about how you tell the difference between the "creative" things and the other stuff on the shelf.

61. Chain Essay

This is a kind of chain essay. One person begins the piece, and when your instructor calls time you'll pass it to the person on your left; that person will continue the piece where you left off, taking it in his own direction, and when your instructor calls time, it gets passed again; the next person writes more; and so on until your instructor calls the conclusion, and the final person writes the end. Then some (or maybe all) of them will be read aloud.

The essay begins with this phrase:

When it happened, at first I could not believe it.

After that, you can take it anywhere. And remember, even though it's nonfiction you can have your main character have fantasies, you can write a conversation, describe in detail, move back and forth in time, and write in the point of view of someone who isn't you. And when you take the story over, you will have to somehow shift the piece over to something that you know about, while still picking up the thread of where the previous writer left off.

62. Cyberworld

This exercise spans two class periods, and there's no length limit. This piece should reflect and comment on the effects of the cyberworld (especially the Internet) in our lives. It can be directly personal to the extent that you want it to be. It can have any shape or style you choose, but it should in some way include samples pulled off the Internet to paint a picture of the cyber experience and your reaction to it. The samples can be directly personal to you (as in MySpace, e-mail, IMs), things that are more general, or, preferably, a mix.

Assuming you have in-class Internet access, get together in pairs or groups and start searching for and saving things you might want to include. It may well be that the person you're searching with will want to see some things that aren't relevant to you. That's okay; you'll just have to take turns, and it all adds to the hodgepodge effect that always happens with the Internet.

Your piece can be an argument, a personal reflective essay, a lyric essay (running close to a prose poem), a satire, a kind of "found" essay (a conglomeration of source material you found and put together in an interesting way, which serves as art and commentary), or a combination of all of these. Whatever it is, it should be an honest reflection of your own impressions of and reactions to electronic media.

63. Cut and Glue

Using scissors, glue, tape, or other materials, compose a creative nonfiction collage that features the use of words, letters, or images cut from a newspaper or magazine. Use the clipped words as a part of the story. You can write words on the page, too, but they should fit into the overall design, not dominate it.

64. Objects, Associations

Take one object from your backpack, purse, or pocket. Write down, off the top of your head, the associations that come to mind when you look at this item. These can be recent or old memories, random words, stray images, or lists of other things of its kind. Let one thing lead to another without worrying about whether you are "on topic." Some of these may come to you in full sentences; others may be more fragmentary.

65. Bring in a Book

Bring in a book you like that you think falls into the category of creative nonfiction. (If you don't have the book on campus, then be prepared to talk about it.) Discuss some of the inventive ways that the writer told this "true" story that takes it from the realm of standard nonfiction, and try to explain why the book had an impact on you.

66. Places That Publish

Go to a bookstore or a college library and pick two magazines in which you think you might eventually like to publish your creative nonfiction. (These should be magazines that publish creative nonfiction, obviously. Journalists: unless the magazine publishes literary or "new" journalism, don't include it.) Describe the information that you find in the masthead (which lists the editors, contributing editors, and staff). Tell us if you are able to find guidelines for submissions (which are often found underneath the masthead). Describe the general length of the pieces and talk about whether you have pieces that fit the length expectations. Talk about the kinds of pieces included, the number of authors, the range of styles, the balance between the informative and the "creative." Talk about whether the magazine is heavy on graphics. Take notes. Be ready to present your information in class.

67. Creative Publication Reviews

This is a project for several class periods. You can work in pairs or alone—your choice.

   Research Web sites for literary and arts magazines. (Your instructor will probably have a list.) Pick two that you find the most interesting or wonderful or annoying. If you are already familiar with some online sites that publish literary work, you can review these, too—but you should also look over a few sites that you've never checked out before. Write a review and description of your chosen online publications. These reviews can be as creative (or weird) as you want them to be in structure and style, and you don't have to like the magazine to review it. Be sure to note submission policies (that is, how you go about submitting a manuscript to these magazines). Each description should take about one single-spaced page.

68. Groupwrite

On slips of paper, respond to the following prompts (one on each slip). They should all be real, something that you have actually experienced. Don't write your name on these.

- a time of day
- an example of weather
- a place (major: a specific city, school, town)
- a place (minor: a room, a beach, a park)
- one violent or extremely dramatic action
- one positive action
- an ending or resolution

When you're finished, collect each category facedown in a pile (like the weather pile, the ending pile, and so on). Then you'll break into groups of three. One person from each group will come and collect a slip from each of the seven piles (without reading the slips). Each group will then write a group story based on the information on the slips of paper. Everyone should write together, dictating the story to whoever is typing. The piece should be about three pages long and should include dialogue, description, and so on.

69. McSweeney's

Go to the Web page for McSweeney's magazine, mcsweeneys.net. Look it over. Then spend about twenty minutes writing your own versions of the pieces you find there.

70. Projection

The group should come up with an organization (of any type, such as a club, business, or school) that none of you would currently choose to join. Try to find something that is quite unlike your own interests and values. It should be something specific (examples: the Red Hat Society, IBM, the cast of *Cats*, the Vancouver Tap Dance Society). Find the organization's Web site and read over it for weird or useful facts. As a group, write a piece that uses the point of view of a person (real or fictional) who would be a member of that organization. This essay (which should be at least two pages long) should give a sense of the workings of the group based on their Web site (or your own knowledge). Try to avoid blatant stereotypes by using details that make this person an individual.

You can all write this together using one computer, or write different aspects of it separately and put it all together. However you do it, it should read as a whole.

PART **4**

Anthology

Steve Almond

From *Candyfreak*

Steve Almond grew up in Palo Alto, California, and received degrees from Wesleyan University and the University of North Carolina at Greensboro. He taught creative writing at Boston College and Emerson College and spent seven years as a newspaper reporter in El Paso and Miami. He is the author of two short story collections, *My Life in Heavy Metal* (2002) and *The Evil B.B. Chow* (2005); the 2004 nonfiction book *Candyfreak: A Journey through the Chocolate Underbelly of America*, from which the following excerpt is drawn; the novel *Which Brings Me to You* (2006, cowritten with Julianna Baggott); and a collection of essays, *Not That You Asked* (2008). His short stories have appeared in *Zoetrope, Tin House, Ploughshares*, and *Playboy*, among other magazines. He lives in Massachusetts with his wife, Erin, and daughter, Josephine.

   Candyfreak is a bit of memoir, a bit more of new journalism; in it, Almond rambles across the country in search of the inner workings of obscure candy producers. He still eats a piece of candy (at least one) every day.

Interview with Steve Almond, p. 169.

In the Belly of the Freak

Long before I began to visit actual candy factories, I harbored elaborate fantasies about visiting candy factories. The earliest of these involved a vague plan to track down the company that had produced (and ceased producing) the epic Caravelle. I assumed the operation was located in northern California, where I had grown up, and that it was run by a kindly old gentleman named Guipetto with whom I could discuss my allegiance to the Caravelle, the truly special nature of that bar, and that he would be so moved by my account that he would tear up and nod and say, "You're right, dear boy. Caravelle is the best bar we ever produced. I've always known that. But the board of directors told me it wasn't making enough money. Well, damn those vulgarians all to hell! We're going to reintroduce the Caravelle!" Then he would lean over his desk and press a button on his intercom and bark: "Miss Swanson! Get in here. I need to dictate a memo. Pronto!"

   This was my fantasy. In my fantasy, Mr. Guipetto said *pronto*.

   As my knowledge of the candy landscape became a bit more refined, I shifted to a somewhat less crazy plan: I would embark on a cross-country Candy Fellowship. The idea was that someone (a charitable foundation underwritten by the American Dental Association perhaps) would pay for me to take a coast-to-coast trip with stops at every candy company along the way.

This was clearly ridiculous. At the same time, it had become obvious that trying to visit factories one at a time, then returning to Boston, was even more ridiculous. So I laid plans for a final assault on the chocolate underbelly of America.

My criteria were pretty exhaustive:

1. Does the company manufacture a regional candy bar?
2. Will they let me in?

I contacted half a dozen companies, four of which showed the poor judgment to extend me an invitation. These were, in order of appearance:

- Palmer Candy of Sioux City, Iowa (Twin Bing)
- Sifers Valomilk of Merriam, Kansas (Valomilk)
- Idaho Candy Company of Boise, Idaho (Idaho Spud)
- Annabelle Candy of Hayward, California (Big Hunk, Rocky Road, Abba-Zaba)

The itinerary ran like so: On Monday, I was to take a 6 A.M. flight out of Boston to Milwaukee, then on to Omaha. From Omaha, I would have to find my way up to Sioux City, Iowa, then back down to Kansas City. On Tuesday, I would fly from Kansas City to Boise, via Denver. On Wednesday, I would fly from Boise to San Francisco, spend Thursday in Hayward, then catch the red-eye back to Boston, via Chicago's Midway Airport, in time to get myself to the class I was teaching at Boston College on Friday at noon. To save money, I had purchased plane tickets from a fast-talking Indian woman named Shirley, who had managed to book me (at a total cost of $992) on four different airlines, none of which I recognized. A couple of the connecting flights had a perilous half-hour layover, an arrangement that, as Shirley explained in her courteous-though-severe accent, could not be avoided.

Why did I take this trip? There are obvious answers: the sense of adventure, the free candy, the camaraderie. I hoped to seek out other purebred candyfreaks, men and women who still made bars the old way, in small factories, and who did so not primarily for profit but out of an authentic passion for candy bars.

This all sounds fabulous. But it was only a part of the truth. The whole truth would have to include the fact that a depression had been building inside me for some months. My journey began in early November and by this time there was a good deal of November in my heart. I mean by this that my life had taken on a gradual aspect of grayness, matched by the clouds which hovered outside my windows and dispelled a wearying rain. The ancient sorrows had resurfaced—the loneliness, the creeping sense of failure—and I felt doomed by the oncoming winter, trapped in

"So I allowed myself to hope, as I had in childhood, that the pleasures of candy would help me beat a path from my despair."

the clutter of my apartment, frantic to escape. So I allowed myself to hope, as I had in childhood, that the pleasures of candy would help me beat a path from my despair.

On the eve of my departure I discovered, in the course of packing, at midnight, that I had lost my driver's license. I spent the next four hours ransacking my apartment. If you had had the ill fortune to be walking past my house at 4 A.M., you would have encountered a curious sight: a thin, anguished-looking man hunched inside a battered Toyota Tercel, lighting matches one by one, in a hopeless final attempt to locate his license. This was me, shivering in my bathrobe and weeping a little.

The Unstoppable Freak Energy of Mr. Marty Palmer

The irony of the situation is that I lost my driver's license at the Arlex Driving School, where I had come for an all-day driver retraining course at the behest of the Registry of Motor Vehicles. The alternative was to surrender my license and go to jail. But that's another story. The point is that I arrived in Omaha, after a lovely sunrise layover in Milwaukee, with two hours of sleep under my belt and no clear idea of how I was supposed to reach Sioux City, 100 miles north. I'd been able to board my flights with a passport. But no one was going to rent me a car without a license. I spent fifteen minutes loitering around the rental car desks, asking various terrified midwesterners if they were heading to Sioux City. They were not.

Eventually, I headed to the bathroom, and I mention this only because I saw in that bathroom the most quintessentially American artifact I have ever encountered: a bright blue rubber mat resting in the bottom of the urinal emblazoned with the following legend:

EPPLY
WORLD'S CLEANEST AIRPORT
OMAHA, NE

God bless our relentless idiotic optimism.

What did I do? I found an airport travel agent who informed me that there was a shuttle to Sioux City. My driver was a man named Bill who looked a great deal like Phil Donahue—the same big square face and snowy helmet of hair—if you can imagine Phil Donahue in a state of perpetual road rage. Bill had a voice like a coffee grinder. He had served in the military since Vietnam. When I asked him in what capacity, he responded, "Let's just say I was defending the interests of our country, alright?"

Oh, alright.

We bombed north up I-29, the cruise control set to 77 miles per hour. It was a bright, cold day and the sun beat down on fields of hacked cornstalks. "Feed corn," Bill said. "That's most of the business around here. It's all subsidized. You also got some pork futures. Those are pig farms. Only they don't like to say pig farms. It sounds degrading."

As we approached Sioux City, a giant refinery rose up on the right. This was Morrell, the meat company. The slaughtering, Bill informed me, was done at night. He often made late runs to the airport and assured me that the stench was overpowering, "a urine/fecal type stench."

It occurred to me that Bill wasn't necessarily what the chamber of commerce had in mind when it came to promoting the greater west Iowa basin. Then again, I had dated a woman from Sioux City and she made a great point of noting that the acronym for the Sioux City airport is SUX. It seemed to be that kind of place—prone to self-denigration.

Palmer Candy was located in a squat, brown brick warehouse on the western fringe of downtown. Marty Palmer himself met me at the door. He looked like an anchorman, tall, athletic, excellent teeth, and he was superfriendly in that guileless midwestern fashion that always makes me feel guilty for thinking such lousy things about the world. Marty had a total can-do attitude and no apparent neuroses and I didn't like him so much as I wanted, instantly, to *be* him. He was also, at 45, about 20 years older than he looked. (I found this to be a consistent attribute among the folks I visited; working with candy appeared to keep them preternaturally young.)

"I think they're doing the Twin Bings right now," Marty said. "So why don't we head into the factory and take a look?"

It is difficult to explain a Twin Bing to those who've never eaten one, because they are so spectacularly unlike other bars. Imagine, if you will, two brown lumps, about the size of golf balls, roughly textured, and stuck to one another like Siamese twins. The lumps are composed of crushed peanuts and a chocolate compound. Inside each of the lumps is a bright pink, cherry-flavored filling.

The filling, Marty explained, was actually a combination of two in-gredients: nougat and fondant. Nougat, which contains egg whites, is fluffy. Fondant is a heavier, taffylike substance composed of sugar, corn syrup, and water. Together, they compose a cream. Marty made this quite clear as he led me into the brightly lit Cream Headquarters: I was to refer to the center of a Twin Bing as a *cream*.

He pointed to a circular steel table about two feet off the ground. "This is called a ball beater. It's where we prepare our fondant." The ball beater was not one of your more sophisticated machines. It had a set of giant plows that went round and round at about two miles per hour, so that, technically, it didn't really *beat* the fondant so much as shove it around. Eventually the fondant, which began as a viscous fluid, began to crystallize and thicken. At this point, a young guy hunched over the beater and pulled off hunks with his bare hands. Because the fondant was so sticky, he kept having to dip his hands in a pail of water. From a distance, he appeared to be heaving fish from a giant frying pan. Across the way, an industrial mixer was whipping up a batch of nougat. The two ingredients were blended in a giant kettle, along with the flavor and coloring. The result, a bright pink syrup, was then loaded into a depositor and squirted into molds. Marty and I stood watching a batch of cream centers being flipped from their molds and dropped into small white buckets, which were carried up an elevator and zipped into the next room.

Overseeing all this was a friendly older gentleman with a giant whisk in his hand. This was Paul, the Cream Center Manager. He had been working at Palmer from the time he was 18 years old. He was now 75. "I've hired five or six guys who were hoping to take over as manager, but Paul keeps going strong," Marty said.

Paul smiled shyly. "Well, everyone needs a little exercise," he said.

In the next room, a thousand cream centers had been piled into a glorious pink mountain. The centers, which looked like supersized gumdrops, were being directed onto a conveyor belt and carried under a curtain of chocolate coating. Next to this assembly line were two rows of women at workstations. Each woman had a stainless steel slab in front of her, shaped like a school desk. On these desks were two things: several dozen finished centers, now sheathed in a thin brown coat of chocolate, and a pile of chunky brown—well, what was it?

> "Marty's feelings about the Bing ran deep and sentimental."

"That's called hash," Marty said. "It's a combination of crushed peanuts and chocolate compound."

These women (the Bingettes?) each held ice cream scoopers, which they plunged into the hash with one hand while, with the other, they pressed a center into the middle of the scoop. This caused an overflow of hash, which they smoothed down with a single, elegant backhand swipe. It was this swipe that covered over the cream center and created the flat bottom of the bar. The entire process took about two seconds. The finished Bing was then plopped onto a slowly moving assembly line. Another Bing was quickly set beside the first, close enough that they would stick together after being cooled.

"As far as we know, we're the largest handmade candy bar left in America," Marty said. "I know it's ridiculous, but there's really no other way to do it. Hash is very hard to work with, because it doesn't really flow. You can't really extrude it. You can't run it through an enrober. You have to handle it by hand. But that's alright, because we're having a good time using our hands." He looked up cheerily, as if he expected his workers to sing out their accord in unison. But these women were grim and otherwise absorbed. Their white smocks and blue rubber gloves were stained brownish red with hash, like field surgeons fresh from the front.

Marty's feelings about the Bing ran deep and sentimental. It was the most direct link to his legacy. The bar was introduced by his great-grandfather William Palmer in 1923, during the height of the candy bar craze. Of the original flavors (vanilla, maple, pineapple, and cherry) only cherry proved popular enough to survive. "We use the same wrapper my great-grandfather did," Marty explained, as we watched the Bings emerge from the cooling tunnel. "The Bing is the one thing we never mess with."

This was not entirely true. A couple of years ago, Marty introduced a Peanut Bing. But the combination of the peanuts in the hash and the peanut center "was just too much peanut for people," so Marty looked for another flavor. The result was the Crispy Bing, which features crisped rice around a peanut-flavored caramel cream center.

It is worth asking, at this point, how the Twin Bing actually tastes. The answer here is somewhat complicated. I found the bar disappointing initially. The compound had a waxy feel; it lacked the inimitable kick of real chocolate, the richness of the cocoa butter. The hash wasn't sweet enough. The whole crushed-peanut thing was weird—I was used to full or half nuts myself, and had come to assume the pleasure of grinding them up with my teeth. The cream center was too sweet, and its consistency was disorienting: heavier than a nougat, but chewier than a cream. This is to say nothing of the bar's appearance. And here I think it might be best to quote a friend of mine's nine-year-old son, who took one look at the Twin Bing and said, "What are those, gorilla balls?"

What I can't quite explain is how the bar managed to beguile me. It was sort of like that girl at the party who's so strange looking you can't stop thinking about her, until you realize that, despite all indications of good sense, you sort of dig her. This is what happened with me and the Bing. I ate a second bar purely to confirm my initial distaste. But after the third bar, and the fourth, there was no such excuse. I had begun to relish (secretly) the salty zest of the peanuts, the sugary bite of the cream center, which called to mind cherry bubble gum. In the end, what charmed me about the Bing was the melding of fruit and nuts, which is so rare among mass-produced candy bars. (I had high hopes for the Crispy Bing, because the bar bore an obvious similarity to the Caravelle. But the crisped rice hash lacked the desired snap, and the chocolate compound, without the rescuing bouquet of the peanuts, tasted like, well, compound.)

Marty was done with the Bing part of the tour. We were only getting started, though. Rather than taking the lean-and-mean approach of the Goldenbergs or relying on contract work—an honest but inevitably degrading arrangement—Marty had created a general line house of the old variety.

He marched me upstairs to the brittle room. Marty, I should note, was in sensational shape. He walked with that springy, pigeon-toed gait favored by ex-jocks. I figured he'd played soccer. "We didn't have soccer here when I was growing up," he said. "But I did run cross-country and I swam and raced sailboats."

The main thing Marty wanted to emphasize about his brittle was that the peanuts should be floating in the middle, which could only be achieved by a precisely timed hand-stretching of the brittle. Baking soda caused the brittle to aerate, or, in laymen's terms, to *puff up real fast,* so fast that I was briefly afraid the kettle being prepped would overflow and my shoes would be singed off by molten brittle. Instead, a couple of gloved workers grabbed the kettle and hoisted it over their heads and raced down the length of a cooling table, pouring the liquid brittle as they went. Now a flurry of activity began: one worker flattened the brittle with boards, a second, trailing behind, cut the brittle into squares, or hides, another flipped these over.

"See! The peanuts are starting to sink!" Marty explained. "What these guys are going to do is stretch the brittle, which lifts the peanuts up. If they wait too long, it'll harden up." In the 30 seconds Marty had taken to explain the process, the workers had finished. Marty stepped to the table and broke off a piece of brittle and held it very close to my face. "See," he said. "Floating!"

Was Marty maybe going a little overboard on the floating peanut thing? Sure. But this was how he differentiated his product from the dozens of other brittles on the market. And more so, the story he told about his brittle was, in a sense, the story he was telling about himself. He was a craftsman. He regarded attention to detail as sacred. He took me to examine the copper kettles he used (the same kind as his grandfather) and the huge, scary peanut roaster, where redskins tumbled hypnotically around a bank of blue flame. He showed me the likewise huge and scary peanut fryer, which looked oddly like an ice cream cooler. Most of all, Marty wanted to emphasize the utmost importance of using these ingredients in an expeditious manner, to keep the "nutmeats from oxidizing" and becoming rancid. (I found myself repeating the word *nutmeat* for several weeks afterwards.)

As it should happen, we followed the fried peanuts downstairs, to the enrobing room on the first floor. Here, they were funneled into tiny metal baskets about the size of quarters. These baskets trudged along a conveyor belt and into a machine that drenched them in milk chocolate then lifted them off the conveyor belt, allowing the excess chocolate to drizzle off. This process—one I watched in a state of rapture for several minutes—created a spiffy little circular cluster. I have never been especially fond of peanut clusters, which always seemed a bit dry to me. Now I know why: because I had never eaten a cluster with *fried* peanuts.

On the line next door to the clusters, pretzels were being drenched in peanut butter. Another line had just finished a batch of pretzels enrobed in yogurt, with red and green Christmas drizzles. After Nestlé, Palmer was the nation's largest producer of coated pretzel products. Actually, Marty couldn't say this for sure, because there are no government statistics on coated pretzel products. But he was pretty sure.

The chocolate for all this coating came from a 60,000-pound vat in the basement. It was pumped upstairs, into an elaborate system of overhead pipes, then dumped into kettles for tempering. In the old days,

Marty said, his staff had done all this by hand: broken the chocolate, melted it down, and slopped buckets from station to station. I found myself imagining a kind of Oompa Loompa free-for-all, with creepy green-and-orange dwarfs skating across floors slick with chocolate. It was not a pleasant vision.

"What do you mean by the 'old days,'" I said. "Like, the fifties?"

Marty laughed. "Oh no, our new chocolate delivery system is six years old."

In the repackaging department, a tall, ornate machine with steel pincers fed bulk candies into two-for-a-buck sacks. Repackaging, Marty explained, was another way for his company to eke out some profit. We watched batch after batch of gummy bears drop down onto the electronic scales.

When we got back to his office, I assumed Marty would tell me some heartwarming tale of visiting the factory as a kid and vowing someday to run the show. In fact, after high school Marty went off to the University of Colorado and spent five years there, collecting two degrees, one in engineering, the other in business. He interviewed with several companies after college. "I viewed the family business as an overgrown candy shop," Marty said. "It wasn't like: 'Boy, I'd like to come out of college and run *that*.' It was just a funky little deal."

Then fate intervened. Or, well, maybe not fate. More like a management crisis. The two gentlemen running the candy company retired. They had assumed Marty *would* return home to take over. Or, more precisely, that he would return home to oversee the sale of the business: "People figured we were just going to let it go under and milk it for what we could." Marty decided to do just the opposite.

When I asked him if he'd studied the recent history of the candy industry, and specifically the gradual extinction of smaller companies, he nodded eagerly. "Yeah, I didn't care. I realized there was huge growth possible and there was going to be risk to it, but it *could* work, if we were willing to work hard. And the reason was this: the bigger the big guys get, the bigger the crumbs they leave on the table. Because frankly, if you're Mars or Hershey's, you don't even want to bother with a $10 million line." Marty paused and smiled broadly. "Well, *I* can make a fat lunch on that."

Marty knew that the Twin Bing was his flagship product. There were similar products on the market, such as the Cherry Mash down in Missouri, and the Mountain Bar, out in the Northwest. Bings dominated the ten northern midwestern states. His first impulse was to maximize sales within that zone. But the Bing, as it turned out, was already doing pretty well. It was the number four bar, for instance, in South Dakota. The real problem was that *no one lived in South Dakota*. Marty had a grand total of 5 million people within 400 miles of his plant. So he realized pretty quickly that he was not going to keep the lights on only doing Twin Bings.

Instead, he looked back at the history of the business, which his great-great-grandfather Edward Cook Palmer began, back in 1878, as a wholesale grocery. Edward's son, William, had made the move into candy at the turn of the century. Back then, Palmer was a general merchandise house. This was the strategy Marty adopted. His logic was simple: If you're a retailer, you only want to buy from one candy guy.

Marty was not blind to the realities of competing against companies a thousand times his size. But his tone conveyed the unmistakable swagger of an underdog who gloried in the odds against him. It occurred to me, as I watched him lean across his desk to emphasize his points, that he had probably been a very good athlete. "When we go knock on the door of the buyer, one of our biggest strengths is that we're *not* Mars or Hershey's. These guys say, 'Geez, you guys are the old style aren't you? Just making a go of it. That's great!' They'll look right at me and say, 'You can't really pay a $20,000 slotting fee, can you? How about $5 off the first 100 cases?' So we play let's make a deal. I truly believe, if a buyer is faced with a pretty level field and if it's close on cost they'll buy from me, because they've got an American flag tattooed on their heart."

This wasn't to say that Marty hadn't felt the squeeze of the Big Three. The example that leaped to mind was his chocolate-covered pretzel. For years, it had been a strong seller. Then Nestlé came along with Flipz. They spent millions of dollars in advertising to establish a national brand, and they took away a lot of Marty's business. The battle for seasonal sales had been vicious, as well. "The big guys can always come in and say: 'Would you like a better price on your everyday Butterfinger? Okay, but you need to buy fifteen items from us. How about if you buy this Butterfinger in a Christmas wrapper?' They can bring the power of their other brands to bear, because retailers can't live without Snickers or M&M's." Marty didn't sound bitter about any of these practices. Hell, they were simply good business. Such competitive disadvantages only made him more determined to turn Palmer into a regional powerhouse.

Over the years, Marty had received a lot of offers from people who wanted to buy the business, or a portion of it. It was their assumption that Palmer, as a small, independent candy company, was on its last legs. Marty's standard response was to agree to sell the business if the potential buyer agreed to pay him what he knew the business was going to be worth in ten years. He would then provide an estimate—rather a large estimate—and the buyer would, often in a state of pique, demur. Marty enjoyed these exchanges a great deal. They were one of the dividends of his hard work.

Another was the chance to produce—or, at least, to fantasize about producing—new products. He realized that kids these days were more interested in handfuls of things and sours. But Marty himself favored "the old soldiers," vanished candy bars of yesteryear. His most cherished dream was to reintroduce a bar called the Walnut Crush, which had been made by the Fenn Brothers, up in Sioux Falls, 100 miles north. "That was a delicious bar," Marty said, a little dreamily. "It was kind of like a 3 Musketeers, but the filling was bright white and it had a walnut flavor and a different texture, what we call 'short,' which is a baking term, meaning that it bites off cleanly, it doesn't pull. It was covered in dark chocolate. A very unusual piece."

The Fenn Brothers went out of business in the early seventies. When Marty took over, he tracked down the old formula and found a few former employees, who described how they made the Walnut Crush: laying the centers on cookie sheets and drying them for three days. That process had given the Crush its distinct snap, but it also made the bar impossible to mass produce, at least profitably. Marty's heart seemed to sink a little at the memory.

He was, after all, being asked (or asking himself) to play two conflicting roles simultaneously: Guardian of the Past and Forward-Thinking Business Owner. This duality was apparent everywhere, in his business decisions, in the factory's mish-mash of new and old equipment, even in the decor of his office, which included a sleek computer as well as a framed piece that I'd been eyeing curiously. It appeared to be an aged strip of cloth stitched with the Palmer name, along with the legend DELICIOUS CHOCOLATES SOLD HERE. "Actually, that's a branded calfskin," Marty said. This was a nod to Sioux City's legacy as a leader in the meat industry. Back at the turn of the century, Palmer delivered its candies as far as a horse-drawn wagon could travel in a day. These wagon jobbers would often nail a calfskin sign to a post out front of the dry goods stores they visited. "These guys were the Bud signs of their day." He had framed his.

> "'You'd get arrested today for doing things that used to be good marketing.' Marty shook his head."

He had a lot of other relics, too, stuff he couldn't quite bring himself to throw out, though he knew he probably should. "It is nice to have a little history around," he said, almost apologetically. "It helps you remember where you came from. My grandfather used to come in all the time to chew the fat. He told me about this promotion they used to run for a boxed chocolate product called Lucky Day, or Golden Strike, something having to do with luck. What he would do is cook up a batch of 300 pounds of soft nougat and throw a handful of gold coins into the batch and then of course they'd be made into candy. As a consumer, you knew you might get a piece of gold. You'd get arrested today for doing things that used to be good marketing." Marty shook his head.

While we'd been talking, a secretary had appeared and placed a box of chocolate pretzels and clusters on his desk. These were my parting gifts. We climbed into his SUV, which was about the size of my apartment, and cruised toward town.

Sioux City is best known, historically, as the starting point of Lewis and Clark's westward expedition. There is a large, phallic monument not far from the Morrell plant commemorating the explorers, as well as a business park environment named after them. In fact, Sioux City had been the biggest town between Chicago and Denver at the dawn of the twentieth century. But then someone had paid off someone else and the railroad had gotten routed through Omaha and Sioux City had gone into a steady decline.

The city was enjoying a renaissance, though, in part due to Gateway, which had come to town and brought 7,000 jobs. Marty cited the restoration of the Orpheum Theater, where he had gone the previous evening to see *Riverdance*. The city was also hard at work on a 10,000-square-foot events center. Marty was especially pleased by this project, because it was being built right next to the old Palmer factory, the first floor of which was still being used as a candy shop. We paid the shop a brief visit so Marty could show me the cracks in the tiled floor, the result of two errant boxcars which, back in 1931, bounded across the street and crashed into the front of the building.

Just before he dropped me off at the Greyhound bus station, I asked Marty if he ever questioned the decision he'd made to return to Sioux City. He said no, not really, that he realized the place wasn't Paris, but this is where his factory was and he felt a responsibility toward the 100 workers he employed. He had no delusions about the future. "It would be neat to have a sixth generation," he said, gazing at the fleet of gantry cranes that loomed over his downtown. "But you never know what kids will want to do." It seemed to me, in that moment, that Marty Palmer was straddling the two worlds that compose our lives, the past and the present, with tremendous grace.

Southbound with the Hammers Down

So I left Marty riding a high of borrowed optimism. Great things seemed possible. What I needed was a positive attitude, an appreciation of my own history, a sense of possibility. This lasted 23 minutes.

I was four hours early for my bus, so I wandered down Sixth Street, past the hospitals, toward the wide and muddy Missouri River. Sioux City reminded me of El Paso, weirdly, because of the various down-in-the-mouth Mexican restaurants, but also because of the low-slung dustiness of the place, the proximity of a strong-smelling industry (in El Paso it was lard), and the general sense of lassitude. It even looked like El Paso on a map: the convergence of three states around a river. North Sioux City was actually in South Dakota. South Sioux City was in Nebraska. Neither of these states, thankfully, had felt it necessary to post guards at their border. Last of all, there was the bus station itself, which I initially mistook for an abandoned dwelling. It was a fantastically grim little spot at the top of a ragged bluff, full of tired, yellow air.

I thought about the rental car I might have been driving, had I not lost my driver's license, had I not hated myself quite so much, had I grown up in a different family, one with a finer appreciation for the simplicities of love. By now, just after four, I'd be on the outskirts of Kansas City already, checking into a hotel room, settling into a bath, with one of the *Rocky* pictures blaring on cable.

But I was, instead, in a gravel lot, shivering alongside a group of passengers with duffel bags and battered plastic sacks. If you ever want to know what America really looks like—and I direct this chiefly toward the residents of the coastal cities who tend to write about America most frequently—I would suggest you abandon the airports. The only people in airports are rich people. Take a bus from Sioux City to Kansas City, via Omaha and Maryville. Here is where America lives, more often than not overweight, beset by children, fast-food fed, television-dulled, strongly perfumed, running low on options and telling their stories to whomever will listen, hatching schemes, self-dramatizing, preaching doomed sermons, dreaming of being other people in other lives.

The woman next to me, thickly shadowed about the eyes, munching on a fried fish sandwich, told me she'd been in Sioux City for the weekend, up from Council Bluffs to visit her boyfriend, who hadn't seemed to love her so well when they were living in the same town, had even mistreated her, but was now pledging undying love, had asked her to move in actually, and even proposed marriage, though without a ring.

"I'm waiting for the ring," she said.

"That sounds like a good idea," I said.

I thought about my own romantic history, such as it was. I'd been no better than this fellow in most cases—a little slicker, maybe, a little cagier. My last serious girlfriend had been the woman from Sioux City. She was the one who had turned me on to the Twin Bing, a few months before I politely bailed on her. Recently, she'd sent me an e-mail to let me know she was getting married, and this note, more than I liked to admit, had contributed to my blue mood. It occurred to me that I was envious of my neighbor. She was, at least, engaged in that most human of struggles, toward love, while I was playing it safe in solitude, keeping my hands busy, my heart on ice.

The bus hurtled on toward Omaha, where we took an hour break. The station there was bigger, full of ancient video games and vending machines, a bacterial snack bar, and crowded with people in an amped state of transit. The kids were running wild as a response to all the anxiety and their parents were overdoing the discipline—tears, recrimination, the white-hot building blocks of future arrests. On the grainy TV overhead, an anchorwoman was waxing eloquent about the next day's elections. Her demeanor suggested the basic message: *Isn't democracy neat?* Democracy is neat. The notion that the poor man's vote counts as much as the rich, that the poor might band together in order to choose benevolent leaders; this is as neat as civilization gets. But you would have never known that the election had anything to do with the people gathered in that station.

Outside, in the cold clear night, an old man, drunk to the point of disorientation, kept trying to board the bus. When the driver approached him, he would back away, hands up, and mutter into his sleeve. There was a family of six, no dad in sight, who seemed to be moving their entire estate south, suitcase after battered suitcase, even the little ones with their load to bear, midwestern refugees.

The driver for the second leg of our trip was a jovial fellow who looked like Ichabod Crane and sounded like Louis Armstrong, a combination I found disorienting. "Howdy back there," he growled into his intercom. "We're headed southbound with the hammers down. So just re-lax and leave the driving to yours truly."

All around us, darkness was coming to the plains. The children were settling down to sleep and a few adults were murmuring in their little cones of light. I tried for sleep, but the night had called my anxiety out of hiding. I could feel it rippling my stomach, whispering its ancient incantations. *You are unworthy of love. Candy will not save you.* We barreled south into Missouri and detoured at Maryville, through a freak hailstorm that clattered off the roof of the bus and frightened the children from their dreams.

Interview with Steve Almond

BECKY BRADWAY: This book is clearly one man's pursuit of an obsession. Would you advise writers to follow their obsessions (when writing, anyway)? How can that obsession be kept under control in the course of working? (That is: it seems that there could be many, many books written about candy. How were you able to eat just one?)

STEVE ALMOND: I think nearly all great literature is obsessive in nature. It's about obsessive love, or hate, or jealousy. This is because most readers turn to literature for a depth of emotion that they don't experience in other parts of their lives. So yes, I do suggest that writers follow their obsessions. As for the "keeping under control" part, that's a little trickier. The idea, I guess, is to step back from your obsession enough that you can explore what it's all about, and that does require some perspective. For *Candyfreak*, I tried to show the reader the depth of my obsession, but also explore why candy has played such a (pathetically) large role in my life.

BB: Did you conduct all of your research before writing the book, or did you continue doing research while writing?

SA: I did all the research before I sat down to write. But, you know, when you're doing research, you tend to know what the good material is — the stuff you found most arresting. And it's really a matter, in the writing, of getting that material down on the page.

BB: Most people might be afraid that an entire book about candy would be too much information. They would worry about writing such a book because of its narrow focus and may well not even begin because of this fear. How did you get past any hesitation you may have had that people might not be interested in this subject? (Or was this never a problem for you?)

SA: I try not to worry about what readers will think—let alone editors or agents. My job is to let it rip, to get down on the page all the most compelling sights and sounds and thoughts and feelings. In other words, my chief obligation is to honor the material, not to shape it so that someone else will find it palatable (or salable). You really can't write well if you're nervous or scared. It turns your prose self-conscious, which is the death knell of your prose.

BB: *Candyfreak* brought back plenty of childhood memories involving candy hoarding and consumption. Candy is a topic just laden with nostalgia. Yet you never cross the line into the sappiness, cuteness, or longing that might infect most creative pieces about candy. Did you deliberately avoid going into the realms of the sweet and sticky— and, if so, how did you manage to pull it off?

SA: My work always runs the risk of sentimentality, because I'm an emotionalist by nature. I'm interested in feelings more than ideas. The idea is to be brutally honest about those feelings, not just indulge the ones that will make you look noble or wise or (worst of all) heartwarming. People don't often comment on this, but *Candyfreak* is really a book about depression as much as it is about candy. If I was going to be honest about my relationship to candy, most of it was going to be imbued with dark feelings. As for the cutesy stuff—of course it gets onto the page. It's just a matter of getting rid of it in the editing process.

BB: This book could have been a memoir of your childhood and adolescent encounters with sweets. Why did you decide to go with more of a literary journalism approach?

SA: I didn't really make a conscious decision. I knew I wanted to write about candy in a way that honored my autobiographical experiences but also allowed me to understand the industry and its history. So I just proceeded logically, initially writing about my own relationship with candy, then moving on to document my journey through all these factories, which became, in an odd way, a journey into my own past.

Margaret Atwood

A Path Taken, with All the Certainty of Youth

A prolific poet, novelist, literary critic, feminist, and activist, Margaret Atwood didn't complete an entire year of school until the eighth grade, due to her family's constant migration between the backwoods of Ontario and Northern Quebec and Toronto. As a child, Atwood was an obsessive fan "of refined literature, Dell pocketbook mysteries, Grimm's Fairy Tales, Canadian animal stories, and comic books." In 1961, she won the E. J. Pratt medal for a privately published book of poetry, *Double Persephone*—this was also the year she graduated from Victoria University with a BA in English and two minors in French and philosophy. Atwood has since published approximately twelve novels, seventeen poetry collections, nine short story collections, twelve short stories, six children's books, five nonfiction pieces, and one comic strip—"Kanadian Kultchur Komix," published from 1975 to 1980 under the pseudonym "Bart Gerrard." Her best known novels include *The Handmaid's Tale* (1985), *Cat's Eye* (1988), and *Surfacing* (1972). She also lays claim to one invention, "The Long Pen," which she bills as "the world's first long distance signing device."

She has taught at a number of Canadian universities and at New York University. Atwood identifies herself as a "Red Tory"—among her more notable acts of activism, Atwood donated all of her Booker Prize money to environmental causes and gave up her house in France after Jacques Chirac resumed nuclear testing. An active member of Amnesty International, Atwood once promised a free subscription to its bimonthly reports to the next person who accused her of being too pessimistic; it is unknown who, if anyone, has collected. Atwood continues to live in Canada, dividing her time between Toronto and an island in Lake Erie.

The essay that we've included in this book is a short piece about coming to writing; it was originally published in the *New York Times*. In it, Atwood admits that when she looks at her childhood, she "can find nothing in it that would account for the bizarre direction I took, or nothing that couldn't be found in the lives of many people who did not become writers." She addresses the isolation of growing into an underappreciated profession, revealing the will that allows us to make the risky decision to put pen to paper. Her essay admits (a bit ruefully) to the mystery and accident involved in the process of becoming a writer.

How is it that I became a writer? It wasn't a likely thing for me to have done, nor was it something I chose, as you might choose to be a lawyer or a dentist. It simply happened, suddenly, in 1956, while I was crossing the football field on the way home from school. I wrote a poem in my head and then I wrote it down, and after that, writing was the only thing I wanted to do.

I didn't know that this poem of mine wasn't at all good, and if I had known, I probably wouldn't have cared. It wasn't the result but the experience that had hooked me: it was the electricity. My transition from not being a writer to being one was instantaneous, like the change from docile bank clerk to fanged monster in B movies. Anyone looking might have thought I'd been exposed to some chemical or cosmic ray of the kind that causes rats to become gigantic or men to become invisible.

I wasn't old enough to be at all self-conscious about what had just happened to me. If I'd read more about writers' lives, or indeed anything at all about them, I would have concealed the shameful transformation that had just taken place in me. Instead I announced it, much to the shock of the group of girls with whom I ate my paper-bag lunches in the high school cafeteria. One of them has since told me that she thought I was very brave, to just come out with something like that; she thought I had a lot of nerve. In truth I was simply ignorant.

> "If I had suspected anything about the role I would be expected to fulfill, not just as a writer, but as a female writer—how irrevocably doomed!—I would have flung my leaky blue blob-making ballpoint pen across the room."

There was also, as it turned out, the dismay of my parents to be reckoned with: their tolerance about caterpillars and beetles and other nonhuman life forms did not quite extend to artists. As was their habit, they bit their tongues and decided to wait out what they hoped would be a phase, and made oblique suggestions about the necessity of having a paying job.

One of my mother's friends was more cheerful. "That's nice, dear," she said, "because at least you'll be able to do it at home." (She assumed that, like all right-thinking girls, I would eventually have a home. She wasn't up on the current dirt about female writers, and did not know that these stern and dedicated creatures were supposed to forgo all of that, in favor of warped virginity or seedy loose-living, or suicide—suffering of one kind or another.)

If I had suspected anything about the role I would be expected to fulfill, not just as a writer, but as a female writer—how irrevocably doomed!—I would have flung my leaky blue blob-making ballpoint pen across the room, or plastered myself over with an impenetrable nom de plume, like B. Traven, author of *The Treasure of the Sierra Madre*, whose true identity has never been discovered. Or, like Thomas Pynchon, I would never have done any interviews, nor allowed my photo to appear on book jackets; but I was too young then to know about such ruses, and by now it is far too late.

In biographies there is usually some determining moment in early life that predicts the course of the future artist or scientist or politician. The child must be father to the man, and if he isn't, the biographer will do some cut-and-paste and stick on a different head, to make it all come out right. We do so wish to believe in a logical universe. But when I look back over the life I led until I began writing, I can find nothing in it that would account for the bizarre direction I took; or nothing that couldn't be found in the lives of many people who did not become writers.

When I published my first real collection of poetry at the age of twenty-six—"real" as opposed to the small pamphlet I myself had printed up on a flatbed press in a friend's cellar, as was the fashion among poets in those days—my brother wrote to me: "Congratulations on publishing your first book of poetry. I used to do that kind of thing myself when I was younger."

And perhaps that is the clue. We shared many of the same childhood pursuits, but he gave them up and turned to other forms of amusement, and I did not.

There I was, then, in 1956, still at high school, without a soul in sight who shared my view of what I should, could and ought to be doing. I did not know anyone who was a writer, except my aunt, who wrote children's stories for Sunday school magazines, which to my snobbish young mind did not count. None of the novelists whose books I had read—none that wrote for adults, that is, whether trashy books or literary ones—were alive and living in Canada.

I had not yet seriously begun to search for others of my kind, to ferret them out of their damp caves and secret groves, so my view at the age of sixteen was that of the general citizen: I could see only what was made clearly visible to me. It was as if the public role of the writer—a role taken for granted, it seemed, in other countries and at other times, or so said the potted biographies in the school textbooks—this role had either never become established in Canada, or had existed once but had become extinct.

To quote A. M. Klein's "Portrait of the Poet as Landscape"—a poem I had not yet read, but was to stumble upon shortly and to imprint on, much as a newly hatched duck may imprint on a kangaroo:

It is possible that he is dead, and not discovered.

It is possible that he can be found some place

In a narrow closet, like a corpse in a detective story,

Standing, his eyes staring, and ready to fall on his face . . .

We are sure only that from our real society

He has disappeared; he simply does not count . . .

. . . is, if he is at all, a number, an x,

a Mr. Smith in a hotel register,—

incognito, lost, lacunal.

Tara Bahrampour
Persia on the Pacific

Tara Bahrampour is half-Iranian and half-American and lived in Iran until 1979, when her family left during the revolution. She attended high school in Portland, Oregon, and Palo Alto, California, and received a BA in English from University of California–Berkeley and an MS in journalism from Columbia University. She is the author of the memoir *To See and See Again: A Life in Iran and America* (1999), which traces her family's migrations between Iran and the United States and her own journey back to Iran as an adult. She has written for the *New Yorker,* the *New York Times,* the *American Scholar,* the *New Republic, Travel and Leisure*, and other journals. She lives in Washington, D.C., where she is a staff writer at the *Washington Post*.

The *New York Times* called *To See and See Again* "a fascinating, often moving, account of her life on the boundary between two very different cultures." A *San Francisco Chronicle* reviewer wrote that "a memoir becomes rich indeed when it not only leads us through a life but also enhances our understanding of the cultural, political, and social character of the world influencing that life. To our benefit, *To See and See Again* does this with elegance."

The piece reprinted here, "Persia on the Pacific," is a work of literary journalism that appeared in the *New Yorker*. While Bahrampour only occasionally refers to herself in this piece, her use of stylistic language, her dialogue, her focus on an individual, and her way of weaving scene and information reveal an involved and honest personal voice. While her opinion is rarely overtly expressed, her point of view comes through in what she chooses to tell us of Parshaw, his family, and his community. She speaks with authority, as someone who knows about the disjunctions felt by immigrants and their children in an adopted country.

Interview with Tara Bahrampour, p. 185.

On June 21, 1998, Iran's national soccer team walked onto the field in its first World Cup tournament since the country had overthrown the Shah, installed an Islamic government, and taken fifty-two Americans hostage, nineteen years earlier. As millions watched on live television, the players handed white good-will bouquets to their American opponents. Then Iran beat the U.S. team, 2–1. From Tehran to Toronto, Iranian teen-agers danced on cars and old women in head scarves lifted their faces to the sky and praised God.

In Westlake Village, California, in a two-story stucco house on a cul-de-sac dotted with lemon trees and oversized roses, a twelve-year-old boy named Jonathan Dorriz watched the game with his father. Jonathan was born in the San Fernando Valley, and he didn't know much about soccer or about Iran, his parents' home country. But when the Iranian team scored its second goal, he jumped on his father's back and they galloped around the house, yelling until they were hoarse. Jonathan had always lived among expatriate Iranians, but that evening, on a visit to family friends, he saw them in a different light: "It was the first time I'd seen Iranians all rooting for the same thing instead of arguing about 'the Shah did this,' 'the mullahs did that.' I saw a sense of unity, and I felt like this was something important." Soon afterward, Jonathan began to go by his Iranian name, Parshaw.

"But there was something a little self-conscious about Parshaw's identification with Iran. His Farsi, which he has been improving with the help of a teach-yourself CD-ROM, was laced with charming mistakes."

Now in his senior year of high school, Parshaw is a handsome, loose-limbed boy with dark wavy hair, warm brown eyes, and a prominent nose. He wears long T-shirts and baggy jeans. He likes to cruise around the neighborhood—a circle of well-kept houses radiating out from the local elementary school—in his black Lexus GS 300, a seventeenth-birthday present from his parents. When I visited him last spring, he drove me past Westlake's jagged hills, which were dusted with a light green that set off the pink mansions along the ridges. On the main strip, Thousand Oaks Boulevard, each tree was tied with a neat yellow ribbon, and luxury-car dealerships shared street frontage with a set of international-themed gardens. Dangling one arm over the steering wheel, Parshaw sang along with Mansour, a local Iranian pop singer. He pointed out the park where a recent Iranian New Year's picnic had attracted so many people that valet parking was required. He told me about the posses of Iranian tough guys who come in from the Valley to strut in front of Westlake's Iranian girls. But there was something a little self-conscious about Parshaw's identification with Iran. His Farsi, which he has been improving with the help of a teach-yourself CD-ROM, was laced with charming mistakes. At the Iranian market on Thousand Oaks, he excitedly ordered rosewater-flavored "Mashti Malone," a locally made ice cream, and a videotape of "Noon-o-Goldoon," an Iranian movie. He smiled as he spoke, as if he were using passwords known to only a select few.

Half an hour down the 405 freeway, on Westwood Boulevard, you can tell by the way people cross the street that you're in the Iranian part of Los Angeles. Instead of waiting at the crosswalk, pedestrians dash between moving cars, careful to lock eyes with each driver before striding into a lane. This is how people cross the street in Iran, and here in Irangeles the cars slow down as if they know whom they're up against.

Two decades ago, this treeless stretch of road, just south of Wilshire Boulevard, was an unremarkable strip with a dry cleaner, a hair salon, and a restaurant called the All American Burger. My family came here regularly then. In January of 1979, my Iranian father and my American

mother moved our family from Iran to the United States and settled in
Portland, which seemed to be populated entirely by pale-skinned, third-
generation Oregonians and was as un-Iranian as a city could be. But my
grandparents lived in Los Angeles, and when we visited we would lose my
father for days at a time to two Iranian bookstores on Westwood whose
shopkeepers always had the latest news from Iran.

Today, those stores are surrounded by Farsi-scripted awnings offering photocopies, wedding videos, tailoring, ice cream, rugs, groceries, and
body waxing. The larger of the two bookstores, Ketab, now sells CDs
and videos and publishes the bilingual Iranian Yellow Pages, which has
thickened over the years to more than a thousand pages, a sixth of which
feature ads for Iranian doctors and dentists. The store also sells rustic
reminders of home: wooden backgammon sets, Esfahani printed tablecloths, and *givehs*—woven peasant shoes that most Los Angeles Iranians
would never have considered putting on their feet when they lived in Iran.
The Canary Chicken House, down the street, serves *kalepacheh*, a stew
made of sheep's head, hooves, and eyeballs, which, in Iran, is traditionally eaten for breakfast by poor laborers. Last fall, a billboard paid for by
a local exile group informed northbound traffic here that ten thousand
political prisoners had been killed by the Islamic regime.

It is not surprising that a nondescript street could be so quickly transformed into a thriving immigrant hub; what is unusual is this one's location, sandwiched between Beverly Hills and Brentwood, in one of the
world's most exclusive swaths of real estate. Here and in surrounding
neighborhoods, the Coffee Bean & Tea Leaf cafés overflow with dark-
haired men and women sipping Darjeeling and speaking the Farsi-English
hybrid Finglish. Downtown, a dilapidated alley has become a cheap
clothing bazaar where Mexican employees speak Farsi with their Iranian
bosses. In a San Fernando Valley strip mall, I came across a little market
with handwritten signs in Farsi: "Sweet Lemons Have Arrived" and
"Pomegranates Just in from Saveh" (a town in Iran that is famous for the
fruit). It was a joke; there were no sweet lemons, and the giant pomegranates arranged in a pyramid came from Mexico. "Better soil than here,"
the shopkeeper explained. "More like Iran."

Last fall, the Iranian community flocked to the Music Hall Theatre, in
Beverly Hills, to see "Low Heights," a movie about a man in Iran who,
desperate to get his extended family to a country that offers more opportunities, hijacks a plane with his relatives on board. A heated family argument ensues over possible destinations, and a young man who has never
left Iran cries out, "If anything happens to me, my last wish is that my
body be buried in Los Angeles!"

Los Angeles and Iran lie at opposite ends of the world, but for the
past twenty-five years—ever since the first Iranians fleeing the revolution
established an exile outpost in L.A.—the two places have been closely
linked. Under the Shah, when, as one Iranian writer put it, Iran suffered

from "Westoxication" (a tendency to view all things Western as a gold standard), L.A. was Tehran's sister city. Under the Islamic regime, it became a wicked stepsister. In Iran, people were arrested for possessing Western or Iranian music recorded in America, as well as for watching "Baywatch" and "Beverly Hills 90210," both of which were long-running favorites on illegal satellite TV. In L.A., especially during the hostage crisis, many Iranians began to refer to themselves as "Persian." (As one man explained, "You think of Iran, you think of crazy mullahs; you think of Persia, you think of Persian carpets, Persian cats. Which would *you* rather be associated with?")

The L.A. area is home to the largest Iranian community outside Iran. (The number of Iranians in the greater metropolitan area falls somewhere between a hundred thousand and six hundred thousand, depending on which source you choose to believe.) The city has Iranian Republican clubs, Iranian Rotary clubs, and Iranian night clubs; Iranian bank tellers, Iranian insurance agents, and even a few Iranian homeless people. For a time, Westlake Village had an Iranian mayor, and two Iranians recently ran for governor. Like Tehran, L.A. is a mountain-ringed, traffic-plagued, smog-filled bowl, where Iranian retirees putter in gardens and wait at bus stops. For exiles living elsewhere, visiting the city can feel as it might for an American who, coming across a U.S. military base in a strange land, suddenly finds himself awash in Kraft Singles and Lynyrd Skynyrd records. It can be comforting, but it can also be suffocating. Maz Jobrani, a thirty-one-year-old standup comedian who moved south from Marin County and got a job at a Westwood record store, recalled a fellow-Iranian walking in. "In Marin, you'd be, like, 'Hey, are you Iranian? What's your name? I think my dad knew your dad in Iran.' Here it was 'Hey, are you Iranian?' and the guy goes, 'Yeah, so?'"

Although many Iranians have moved out to Orange County and the San Fernando Valley, those who live in Beverly Hills—where about a fifth of the population in Iranian—have come to embody the stereotype. Their American neighbors often see them as flashy and loud; other expatriate Iranians tend to regard them as caricatures—former royal ministers and other "Shahi" types who fled the revolution with bags of jewels, leaving their Tehran mansions and Caspian Sea villas in the care of servants. Their wives shop for designer clothes on Rodeo Drive; their children grow up to be, or to marry, doctors.

Of course, most L.A. Iranians were never ministers. Like Iranians anywhere, they are rich or poor, Muslim, Jewish, Baha'i, Christian, or Zoroastrian, secular or religious, conservative or leftist, highly educated or less so. But to some extent they are all élite. In Iran, they were not maids or shepherds but people who had enough sophistication and cash to get to America. Most are Shiite Muslims, but in West Los Angeles the Jewish Iranians are the most cohesive, connected through synagogues, marriages, and jobs. Few of L.A.'s mosques are Shiite, and, in any case, the last thing that most people fleeing the Islamic revolution wanted to see was a mosque. "If you're Jewish, you have American Jews," says Mehdi Bozorgmehr, a sociologist who has studied the community. "Being Muslim, Iranian, and secular is a potent negative baggage to carry. You're secular, so where do you go?" The community was outraged last December, when men from some Muslim countries were ordered to register with the Immigration and Naturalization Service and several hundred L.A. Iranians, including many Jews, were detained on visa violations. Most were eventually released, but in a rare show of unity thousands of Iranians marched down Wilshire Boulevard in protest. The thought that they had anything to do with Osama bin Laden was, to them, an absurdity.

Since his World Cup initiation into the society of Iranian exiles, Parshaw Dorriz has cemented his membership by attending family gatherings, Iranian concerts, and meetings of the Westlake High School Persian Club, of which he and his twin sister, Parastoo, became co-presidents this year. He has taken a Persian-history class at U.C.L.A. and gone on 3 A.M. excursions with his father to a kabob restaurant in the Valley to eat *halim*, a sort of cream-of-wheat-and-shredded-turkey breakfast served in mountain teahouses in Iran. But some Iranian flavors remain elusive, like *kharbozeh*, a sweet, white-fleshed Persian melon that is now grown on farms around L.A. Parshaw hates the taste of it, but when he starts to say, "Akh, *kharbozeh*," his father cuts in. "You don't know," he says. "In Iran they taste so much better." Parshaw is used to hearing this from older Iranians, for whom food has become the touchstone for more intangible longings. "They talk about it all the time," he says. "The lamb and the meat—how it was different because the lamb had all the fat on the tail."

Someday, Parshaw wants to be a doctor, and to volunteer his services in the poor regions of Iran. For now, he'd just like to see Shemiran, the tree-shaded north Tehran neighborhood where his parents grew up. Sometimes he calls there to talk to his twenty-eight-year-old cousin, Ario, whom he has never met. "The first time I talked to him, he was, like, 'Your Farsi's so good,'" Parshaw says shyly. "He said, 'Come on over, I'll take you everywhere,' which is exactly what I want."

It is not what his parents want. They left Iran three decades ago and have never gone back. They opened their own businesses—Ali is a real-estate developer, Sholeh owns a beauty salon—and chose to bring up Parshaw and Parastoo far from revolution, war, and the strictures of Islam. They don't understand why Parshaw, an honors student and a basketball player with all the advantages of American life, would want to go to a country where he could be drafted, at a time when the U.S. government is murmuring about "regime change" there, a country that is a pariah not only to Americans but also to many of the Iranians who left it.

Unlike most exiles, Parshaw's family left Iran by design. In 1966, Ali, like many privileged young men—he was the oldest son of a wealthy

Tehran businessman—went abroad to study, travelling around Canada and the United States before earning a civil-engineering degree and settling down in the Valley. Sholeh was the daughter of an art-school administrator and a schoolteacher in Shemiran. When she finished high school, suitors were already lined up for *khastegari,* a formal courtship that is still widely observed in Iran. She chose, instead, to continue her studies in America. In 1970, at the age of seventeen, she landed in Houston. She knew only three English phrases and was so homesick that she lost thirty pounds. Over time, she adjusted, and a few years later her parents moved to America, too.

When Sholeh and Ali arrived in the United States, the few Iranians living here were considered exotic and harmless. By the time they met, in the early eighties—he was a client at the bank where she worked—Iranian refugees were pouring in, shell-shocked and rootless. Although the community eventually coalesced, Sholeh and Ali never really joined the busy circuit of dinners and parties. "If you're not a doctor, if you're not a millionaire, if you don't have a Mercedes, if you don't go on ski trips, you're nobody," Sholeh says. When it comes to business, Ali says, he keeps his distance from other Iranians. "They never work a day in their life," he explains. "They're on government benefits. They say America owes them because it took their oil." (He is not alone in his disdain. Many L.A. Iranians complain about how Iranians cheat on their taxes, cut lines, and appropriate handicapped license plates for their cars. In the same breath, many admit to having their own handicapped plates.)

> "'I'm used to my freedom,' she says. 'A woman is not a piece of furniture here. I cannot go back now and live in a society where men rule.'"

But in some ways the Dorrizes are very Iranian. Their house is filled with the Louis XIV-style furniture popular in Iran. They have antique chairs with cream-and-bronze striped upholstery, a silk Esfahani carpet, and an old-fashioned water pipe in their front window. Sholeh brought the children up on Persian food and demanded that they follow Persian etiquette. "I emphasized, 'Persians don't do this,' 'Persians don't do that,' 'When you're offered something, you talk with respect,'" she says. At the same time, she had no intention of inspiring her children to go to Iran. "I'm used to my freedom," she says. "A woman is not a piece of furniture here. I cannot go back now and live in a society where men rule."

In Parshaw's bedroom, under a poster of Tupac Shakur, is a copy of "The Complete Idiot's Guide to Understanding Islam." He says sheepishly that the book is perfect for someone like him, who has grown up knowing so little about his own religion. His religiosity isn't traditional—he sees "problems with the Shiites and problems with the Sunnis," so, like a picky diner at a buffet, he takes only what he likes from each side. He doesn't pray the requisite five times a day, and he doesn't believe in martyrdom, but whenever he runs out to school or to a friend's house he stops at the small table by the door to kiss the large family Koran.

This makes his mother uncomfortable. Five feet tall, with shaggy, wine-colored hair, Sholeh has dark, expressive eyes, and they often betray her fears for her son. "Parshaw has surprised me in so many ways," she told me as we sat together on the couch, cradling miniature glasses of hot tea. Religion has helped to make him a good kid, she says. He doesn't drink, he doesn't smoke, he doesn't run after girls; he doesn't cause her the same kind of anxiety as Parastoo, a striking girl who uses her American name, Sabrina, loves to go to parties, and chafes at not being allowed to date until she's eighteen. But Sholeh can understand Parastoo's desires. Parshaw's are more disconcerting to her. The last thing she wants, she says, is "a mullah on my hands." Last year at Ramadan, to her horror, Parshaw decided to fast for the entire month. "I said, 'I don't think that's a good idea. You play basketball and you run track.' I'm getting a little worried. He reads the Koran before he goes to bed. He wants to fast, and he doesn't touch pork. Believe me, I would like to get his DNA checked."

Ali and Sholeh often speak nostalgically about Iran, but their sentiments have nothing to do with Islam. When the family watched a movie that had been filmed recently in Tehran, Sholeh smiled and clucked her tongue fondly at shots of the snow-covered city. Ali recognized a type of door that his grandmother used to have—wooden, with separate iron knockers for men and women. Then, during a scene in which a mullah called people to prayer, Parshaw sat up. "You know that call of the muezzin?" he said. "It'll chill you to the bone. It gives me goosebumps, and I love that."

Sholeh put her head in her hands. When the film showed a group of high-school girls draped in black, she wrinkled her nose. "I don't want to see my country like this," she said.

"Like what?" Parshaw said testily.

"Those women in black chadors—it's like a herd of penguins walking."

Later, after Sholeh and Ali had gone to bed, Parshaw and I watched the characters in the film stop to light a candle at a tiny shrine built into the side of a building. Parshaw looked pained. "Did you see that?" he asked. "For me, it's such an uphill battle just to get my parents to allow me to go to mosque. They think all the radical ideas come from the mosque. But these people, they're going home, and on the way home they stop at a shrine, which I'm sure they don't even think twice about."

Parshaw has tangible objects that link him to Iran. In his bedroom, alongside his CDs of Jay-Z, Ja Rule, Marvin Gaye, and Louis Armstrong, are CDs of Iranian singers. On his bulletin board is an official photograph of the Iranian soccer team; a hand-drawn map of Iran; a picture of Googoosh, the pop diva of seventies Iran who was silenced by the Islamic regime; a flyer from his high-school Persian Club's Kabob Day. He has a photo album filled with outdated Iranian paper currency, and a twenty-rial coin with the Shah's profile, which Ali found when he knocked down the kitchen wall a couple of years ago. (It must have been built in by the former owners, who were also Iranian.) "I wouldn't spend that if you paid me," Parshaw said, placing it in my hand.

As I held the coin that I had once used to buy ice-cream cones, I felt a pang. Growing up in America after the revolution, I, too, had hoarded treasures from Iran. The items I carried onto the plane in the final week of the Shah's reign—my class notebook with its half-finished assignments, my school T-shirt, an amber-colored hand-shaped pendant that my aunt had pressed into my palm on the morning we left—were, as I saw it, the only objects that remained from my old life. The rest of my childhood was gone.

But it was hard to fathom how Parshaw, who had never been to Iran, could feel the same way. It was as if, after five years of obsession, Iran and the absence of Iran had become so tightly wound into his being that he had, in a sense, turned himself into an exile. Above his bed was a homemade poster that included both the Islamic Republic's Allah symbol and the Shah's lion and sun. To anyone who ever lived in Iran—pre- or post-revolution—this would be jarring, like seeing Castro and Batista on the same T-shirt. Also on the wall was a Shah-era Iranian flag. "That's my flag, my prize flag," Parshaw said. "It gives such a sense of strength." He sighed like a man who has seen and lost it all. "*Chi boodim . . . chi shodim*," he murmured. "What we were . . . what we became."

Iranians in the United States and Europe are often compared with Miami Cubans and exiled White Russians—not immigrants fleeing poverty or pogroms but élites wrenched from a life of privilege into a shadow existence that will never live up to the charmed world they remember. Like the Miami Cubans, L.A.'s Iranian exiles tend to be Republicans. Many blame Jimmy Carter for the revolution, saying that the Shah was soft on the revolutionaries because Carter was pressuring him to improve human rights. They were outraged last year when Carter won the Nobel Peace Prize. (This year, however, the community rejoiced when the prize went to Shirin Ebadi, an outspoken human-rights lawyer in Iran.) When President Bush named Iran a member of "the axis of evil," many cheered, and when he declared war with Iraq some hoped that he would bomb Iran, too.

In the eighties, Iran's government, like those of Cuba and the U.S.S.R., arrested, tortured, and executed suspected dissidents and blocked much foreign travel. Most expatriates were either too worried that their names were on blacklists or too ideologically opposed to the government to consider a trip home. But after Khomeini died, in 1989, return gradually became easier for all but the most vocal opponents of the regime. Passports that once cost a thousand dollars and took months to process now cost less than a hundred and arrive within weeks.

Some Iranians still refuse, on principle, to go back. Some, like a school friend of mine who came to America when I did, can't bring themselves to go for fear of disillusionment. Others simply have no interest. I met a trim, bronze-haired Beverly Hills real-estate agent in her fifties, who grew up in Iran at a time when women were expected to be only wives and mothers. Here, she socializes with prominent Iranian academics, psychologists, and journalists. "L.A., to Iranians, is like the Kaaba, like Mecca," she marvelled. "It's our second homeland." But Iranian men her age have been less ready to embrace American culture. "One of the grudges my husband is holding against me is that I brought him here," she said. "He only reads Iranian magazines, he only watches Iranian TV. He had a much better life in Iran. His passion is teaching, and he lost that here. For him, life in L.A. isn't that promising."

Her story reminded me of Andre Dubus III's novel "House of Sand and Fog," in which a former Iranian colonel puts on a suit every morning and then changes clothes on the way to his job as a trash collector on a California highway. For all the successful Iranian entrepreneurs, there are also men of a certain age who, paralyzed by the loss of their former status, came here and refused to learn English or to get driver's licenses. Often, their wives took up the slack, going to school and launching careers of their own. I have met no women older than fifty who want to go back to Iran, but I spoke with many men who longed for home. A Beverly Hills schoolteacher told me that her father, a wealthy insurance agent with an elegant condominium in Brentwood, dreams of spending his final days in a shack on the Caspian Sea. Even a man I met whose brother and friend were executed after the revolution for their leftist political beliefs still wanted to go back. "I look at life like a *ghezel-ala*," he told me. "What is this fish? Born in the river and then goes to the sea and then comes back and dies in the river."

But even today, after thousands of Iranians have returned to Iran without incident, a scrim of fear still covers those who haven't made the trip. Last year, L.A. Iranians were shaken when a well-known dance teacher with U.S. citizenship went back after a twenty-year absence to see his sick father and was arrested for corrupting the youth of Iran with his videos; he was barred from leaving Iran for ten years (though he was later allowed out). Parshaw's parents have horror stories of their own. "Sholeh's brother went back, they gave him a rosy picture," Ali says. "Then he ended up having to flee. They found a picture of him in the Shah's time with a right-hand man of the Shah. Another guy went back to bury his mother. When he wanted to leave, they made him pay ten thousand dollars. How can you trust people like that?" An Iranian travel agent told me about two friends who recently returned for the first time: "One came back, and he said, '*Khoda*, how much fun it was. People are bullshitting when they say Iran is bad. Every night we had parties, opium from here to there, vodka, girls who will do anything to come to America.' Two days later, his friend calls me and says, 'I will never go back. There is so much sadness, so much poverty. These people I was staying with had to get up at five in the morning to buy bread to give these parties.'"

Those who were adolescents at the time of the revolution feel perhaps the greatest ambivalence about where home is. Ali Behdad, a forty-two-year-old professor of English at U.C.L.A., sees himself as part of a lost generation, too young to have had an independent life in Iran but too old to feel completely at home in America. Iranians his age have trouble sustaining relationships, he says; he has been divorced three times, and recently married again. Between his marriages, his family in Iran offered to find him a beautiful wife if he would only come home. "But, especially for someone like me, who is trained in post-structuralism, feminism, Marxism, psychoanalysis, you can't go back," he says. "As they say in Iran, I'm a stick that's been dirtied on both ends—rotten on one side, forgotten on the other." Still, he adds, "there is a place I can go when I get homesick: I can go to Irangeles."

Through all the years of official silence between their two countries, Iranians in Los Angeles and Tehran have keenly watched one another from afar. In the late nineties, exiles in L.A. started beaming satellite-TV programs to Iran. This past June, when students in Iran held demonstrations against the Islamic government, the satellite stations tried to stage their own virtual-reality revolution, taking calls from Iranians who reported on the street battles, and exhorting viewers in Iran to go out and protest against the clerics. Mostly, though, the stations, which are also widely watched in L.A., broadcast ads, music videos, and talk shows featuring celebrity doctors. Young women call in to ask the TV plastic surgeon if they should get breast implants. Parents ask Dr. Holakouee, a psychologist who has a local radio show, how to handle their pot-smoking adolescents. "It's still a primitive culture," said Payam Farrahi, who hosts a radio show with his father. "There's still a concept of calling the head of the village to solve your problems."

The owners of the stations generally disclaim political affiliations, and their aesthetics are often dated—marked by layered blow-dried hair, tight pants, pointy shoes, and wide lapels that survive among older Iranians in L.A. long after they have gone out of style both in the United States and in Tehran. (Young Tehranis take their cues from MTV, not from the aging newscasters of stations like Pars TV or NITV.) The outdated styles seem to reflect a deeper inertia among the exiles—an inability to move beyond the political and social mindset of the Shah era. To Mehdi, a thick-bearded man who works at one of the bookstores in Westwood, the Iranian community's pining for the past is misguided. "They have no idea what is happening in Iran," he told me. "It's been twenty years, and nobody takes responsibility for what happened in Iran. We don't accept our dark side." Fariborz Davoodian, a forty-four-year-old Hollywood producer and actor with a shaved head and stylish black jeans, told me, "I've read somewhere that this is typical—the home country moves forward, but migrant groups don't."

Although Sholeh Dorriz assiduously heeds Dr. Holakouee's advice, she worries about the effect that the stations' nostalgia may have on her children. For a teen-age boy accustomed to the American media's dour images of Iran, the exile programs can be alluring. "They say, 'Iranians are this, they are that, they are the most educated immigrant. They have this kind of doctor, that kind of doctor.' My kids hear that there's no crime among us, that we have a good culture, a good backbone. It's constantly brainwashing the people about how good we are." Sholeh's friend Azita, a blond, well-manicured woman who lives a few blocks away from the Dorrizes, admits that she has painted a similarly romantic picture for her son, Daniel. "He says to me, 'Oh my God, you had a perfect childhood,' and I say, 'Yeah, I did,'" she says. "But now you can be arrested for listening to foreign music. I mean, I don't think my children can comprehend this. I don't think Daniel could ever comprehend that he can't wear shorts going down the street."

> "'It's constantly brainwashing the people about how good we are.'"

At Westlake High School, a clutch of low stucco structures set into a sheared-off hill, the parking lot is lined with shiny Jettas, Audis, BMWs, and one enormous black Cadillac S.U.V. with twenty-three-inch reverse-spinning rims, which, Parshaw tells me, in a hushed voice, cost five thousand dollars apiece. On the school grounds, tanned girls in tight jeans and Guess T-shirts talk on cell phones as they walk past oak trees and rosebushes. Boys in baggy shorts eat onion rings and cookies. Many are Iranian. A sign above the administration office announces that the school is a National Top 100 School. There is a rumor among the students that Heather Locklear was once enrolled here, and although the school has no record of her ever attending, the mere idea of it would thrill many boys in Iran. It does not thrill Parshaw and Daniel. Hanging out in Daniel's room after school, the boys study a National Geographic map of the world pinned above the desk, something that they say would hold little interest for most of their classmates.

"We're the political ones," Parshaw says.

"Most kids are so stupid," adds Daniel, a sturdy kid with a dark-blond brush of hair, pale skin, and red cheeks. Only his dark eyebrows hint at his mother's Iranian roots. (His father is American.) "They think Westlake is it, like the rest of the world is so far away."

"I know this sounds kind of bad, but we don't have any American friends," Parshaw says. Parshaw and Daniel are, of course, American, and so are their friends, though many have parents who come from other countries. But the boys identify with Iran, an anachronistic Iran that has more to do with their grandparents' generation than with their own. Parshaw imagines Tehran in black-and-white, as it is in his parents' old pictures. When Sholeh's father, who is ninety-four and lives in Torrance, near the Los Angeles airport, comes for dinner, Parshaw drapes his long arm around the old man's narrow shoulders and tries to memorize the Persian poetry that his grandfather carefully writes out in a shaky calligraphy. Daniel imagines Iran with nineteen-fifties-era cars, and dreams of hunting leopards with his grandfather. Those images of Iranian life are more meaningful to the boys than their encounters with the Iranian kids in the Valley who get tattoos that say "Allah" and pick fights with Iranian Jews.

Instead of a tattoo, Parshaw has a screen name, ParSHAofIRAN, which he uses to chat with other Iranian teen-agers and trade "You know you're Iranian if . . ." lists. (He is delighted to find entries that apply to him, such as "You drive a black Lexus, Mercedes, or BMW," "You rewind the movie 'Clueless' to show your friends the Persian Mafia part," "You have a hookah as a centerpiece in your living room," and "You actually like carbonated yogurt drinks.") He also has a hidden mark. "I don't show this to many people," he said softly, pulling off his heavy gold Westlake High School class ring and dropping it into my hand. On the inside, inscribed in a delicate cursive, were the words "Allah Akbar. I am Iran's youth."

When I was at the Dorriz house, Parshaw showed me a thick stack of papers lying beside the family TV: copies of his parents' expired Empire of Iran passports and blank applications for new Islamic Republic ones. The forms had been there for months, though Parshaw said that it would take only half an hour to fill them out. A few weeks ago, Sholeh said, she finally mailed them off, "simply because he drove me crazy." Parshaw is ecstatic, but Sholeh is still hoping that he'll outgrow his obsession with Iran. It is perhaps more likely that over the years Iran will grow closer to Parshaw. The real youth of Iran—the young people living there now—make up more than half of the country's population; as they come of age, they will gain leverage against the Islamic rule imposed by the older clerics. How Iran will change remains to be seen, but chances are it will become, in certain ways, more like L.A.

L.A., on the other hand, is probably as Iranian as it will ever get. In coming generations, many of the Iranians there will assimilate. Some will move back to Iran. Among those will be people like the middle-aged man in his Brentwood condo, dreaming of a beachside shack, and people, like Parshaw, whose inherited nostalgia is strong enough to pull them across the world. Once that happens, there may come a day when a child in Iran, listening to his American-born parents' tales of lemon trees and veggie burritos, will close his eyes, let out a wistful sigh, and claim Los Angeles as his own lost home.

Interview with Tara Bahrampour

BECKY BRADWAY: Why did you decide to focus this piece on Parshaw? Did you know the family prior to writing the article?

TARA BAHRAMPOUR: I did not know the family, or very many Iranians in L.A., when I started reporting the story. I initially spent a couple of

weeks there talking to as many Iranians as I could, from many different backgrounds—rich, poor, Muslim, Jewish, male, female, old and
young. I wanted to find a family whose child had never been to Iran
but was dying to go there, and who could basically represent the
Iranian diaspora in L.A. Several families I met fit the bill, but Parshaw's story seemed most interesting and emblematic of what I was
looking for. They were also extremely open and generous with their
time, and Parshaw himself had an appealing personality and a sweetness that worked well for the story.

BB: You're a working journalist who has also written a lovely memoir,
To See and See Again. What are the special challenges of working in
a personal narrative as opposed to a journalistic one? Do you prefer
writing one form over the other, or do you find there to be overlap?

TB: There is a definite line between strict journalism in the newspaper
sense, where every fact must be checked and every presentation must
be objective, and the personal narrative, in which memory and emotion and subjectivity play important roles. I don't prefer one over the
other; they are such different areas. It can sometimes be hard to
switch between them; when I started writing my memoir I had been
used to writing for a newspaper, and it took me a while to slow the
writing down and to let more creative language and thought
processes in. With newspapers (and to a lesser extent magazines),
there is limited space and the imperative is to squeeze in a lot of information with as few words as possible. With book-writing, it's the
opposite: you're going in much deeper, which can be harder, but, if
done well, it can also be more satisfying.

BB: You've done a lot of newspaper and magazine work. Do you have
any particular advice for someone trying to break in to these fields?

TB: The best advice I have is to develop an expertise, one that ideally is
both unusual and marketable. I was lucky to have come from Iran,
which ended up being a place few Americans can travel to but which
holds a lot of interest for Americans. But your expertise can be
anything—global warming, Asian music, firefighting, marine biology,
the military (several doctors, for example, regularly write fascinating
narratives for the *New Yorker* about their work). If you're in college,
I would advise you to major in a concrete subject like history, literature, political science, or biology, and really hone in on an area of
expertise. That will help make you stand out among a pool of job ap-
plicants or help you publish magazine articles on your subject (once
you've established some nice clips related to your area of expertise,
you can branch out). Of course you have to be a good writer, too,
but if you can offer an editor something on top of that, you'll be
ahead of the game.

BB: Did growing up in the Iranian American culture, with its ways of seeing
and its use of language, have an impact on your development as a
writer? By this I'm referring less to the exile experience and more to the

actual daily environment: sound, smell, speech, ways of thinking and seeing that may have affected your style and voice.

TB: I'm not sure there are enough Iranian Americans to call it a culture. Most of all, growing up Iranian American made me aware, from an early age, that wherever I was, there was always somewhere else that I wasn't. Going back and forth between Iran and America as a child, I always had that other reference point from which to see the place where I was living. So to some extent I was always an observer, never fully immersed in the culture and society that everyone around me took for granted. I think that helped steer me toward journalism, which is by its nature a field where the writer is often on the outside. Even when you're writing a personal narrative, you have to be able to step back and have some objectivity (e.g., to know which family anecdote is going to be of interest to people who don't know you, versus the ones you think are really cute but have no reason to be in the book).

As to whether there is anything specifically Iranian about my writing, that's harder to answer. I think having access to other languages can only help a writer, but I write (and read) in English, and my literary influences have largely been Western. Still, I think everything that makes up a life has some kind of influence, so probably in subtle ways my writing has been shaped by my Iranian side as well.

Kim Barnes

The Ashes of August

Kim Barnes was raised in the logging camps and small towns of northern Idaho. She is the author of two memoirs, *In the Wilderness: Coming of Age in Unknown Country* (1996), winner of the PEN/Jerard Award and finalist for the 1997 Pulitzer Prize, and *Hungry for the World* (2000). Her novel *Finding Caruso* (2003) was published by Putnam. She is coeditor with Claire Davis of *Kiss Tomorrow Hello: Notes from the Midlife Underground* (2006). Her essays, stories, and poems have appeared in a number of journals and anthologies, including the *Georgia Review, Shenandoah*, and the *Pushcart Prize Anthology*.

New York Times reviewer Christopher Lehmann-Haupt described Barnes's memoir *Hungry for the World* as "beautifully written if harrowing." *Salon.com* said that her book *In the Wilderness* "has a mythic feel" as she "transforms her family's stormy ties to the soil in a narrative filled with striking, often grotesquely comic images." In *Booklist*, Donna Seaman wrote that "Barnes is as fluent in provocative metaphors as she is in scenes of profound conflict and revelation."

She teaches writing at the University of Idaho and lives with her husband, the poet Robert Wrigley, and their family on Moscow Mountain.

"The Ashes of August" uses lyrical language and imagery to place us in an isolated Western landscape. The threat by fire is recounted almost matter-of-factly, as suits someone who has spent a lifetime facing this destructive possibility. While the piece is quite personal, it expertly intertwines historical and factual narrative into what would otherwise be a story of trepidation. The dangers are always mediated by Barnes's love for the place and the people in it.

Interview with Kim Barnes, p. 202.

Late summer light comes to Idaho's Clearwater Canyon in a wash of color so sweet it's palatable: butterscotch and toffee, caramel and honey. It is as though the high fields of wheat, the darker ravines tangled with blackberry, sumac, and poison ivy, the riverbanks bedded in basalt and shadowed by cottonwood and locust—all have drawn from the arid soil the last threaded rindles of moisture and spun them to gold. By four o'clock, the thermometer outside my kitchen window will read 105°. In another three hours, a hot whip of wind, and then those few moments when the wheat beards and brittle leaves, even the river, are gilded in alpenglow. Often my children call me to the window, and even as we watch, the soft brilliance darkens to sepia. But soon there will be the moon, illuminating the bridge that seems to levitate above the pearlescent river. Some nights my family and I spread our blankets on the deck and lie uncovered to trace the stars, to witness the Perseids of August—the shower of meteors so intense we exhaust ourselves pointing and counting, then fall asleep while the sky above us sparks and flares.

Other nights there is no moon or stars, only clouds gathering in the south and the air so close we labor to breathe. "Storm coming," my daughter announces, and we wait for the stillness to give way, for the wind we'll hear first as it pushes across the prairie and down the draws, bringing with it the grit of harvest. Bolts etch the sky, hit the ridges all around us; the thunder cracks above our heads. Perhaps the crop-saving rain will come, or the hail, leaving our garden shredded and bruised. Sometimes, there is nothing but the lightning and thunder, the gale bending the yellow pines to impossible angles, one tree so old and seemingly wise to wind that we watch it as the miners once watched their caged canaries: should the pine ever break, we may do well to seek concrete shelter.

These are the times we huddle together on the couch, mesmerized and alarmed. We know that the storm will pass and that we will find ourselves to have again survived. We know, too, that somewhere around us, the lightning-struck forests have begun to burn; by morning, the canyon will be nearly unseeable, the sunset a smoky vermilion.

The West, Wallace Stegner so famously noted, is defined by its aridity, and this stretch of north Idaho canyon land where I live is no exception. The Clearwater River is the reason for the numerous settlements along its reach as well as those of its tributaries. Logging, mining, agriculture: all are dependent on the presence and ways of water. Fire, too, defines this land, and at no time more so than in the month of August, when the early rains of spring have given way to weeks of no measurable precipitation, when the sweet blossoms of syringa and chokecherry have shriveled and fallen, when wild plums hang blistered with ferment. We must go high into the mountains where the snowpack held longest to find huckleberries, our belt-strung buckets banging our legs, our mouths and fingers stained black, and we go prepared to defend ourselves against two things: the bears who share our fondness for fruit, and fire. Our bear defense is little more than loud conversation and an occasional glance toward the perimeters of our patch. For fire, we carry in our pickup a shovel and a water-worthy bucket. If called upon to do so, we could hope to dig a fire line, or drown a few flames if lucky enough to be near a creek or spring.

"Born and raised within a fifty-mile radius of where I now live, I have memories of late summer that are infused with fire."

Born and raised within a fifty-mile radius of where I now live, I have memories of late summer that are infused with fire. As a child growing up in the logging camps of the Clearwater National Forest, I knew August meant that my father would rise at two A.M. to work the dew-damp hours before noon, when a machine-struck spark could set the wilderness ablaze. But no one could mandate the hours ruled by lightning, and with the lightning came the fires—as many as fifty or sixty from one storm—and with the fires came the pleas for volunteers to man the Pulaskis, buckets, and bulldozers. Often, the loggers were not asked so much as pressed into service, ordered from their sites and sent to the front lines still wearing their calked boots and pants cut short to avoid snags.

Like my father, my uncles had taken up the life of the lumberjack. Our communal camp was a circle of small wooden trailers, out of which each morning my cousins came, still in their pajamas, rubbing the sleep from their eyes. I remember my mother and aunts in those weeks of searing high-altitude heat, how they rose with their husbands and made their biscuits and pies so that the wood-fueled stove might cool before dawn, then loaded a pillowcase with sandwiches, fried pies, jugs of iced tea and Kool-Aid that would chill in the creek. Somewhere just over the ridge the men battled to keep the fires at bay, while my cousins and I explored the cool recesses of the stream bed, searching for mussels whose halves spread out like angel wings, prying the translucent periwinkles from their casings to be stabbed onto hooks that would catch the trout we'd have for supper. My sensory memories of those afternoons—the sun on my shoulders, the icy water at my knees, the incense of pine and camas, the image of my mother and aunts lounging with the straps of their swimsuits pulled down, the brush of skin against skin as my cousins sifted the water beside me in their quest for gold—are forever linked with my awareness of the smoke rising in columns only a few miles away and the drone of planes overhead, belly-heavy with retardant, the smell of something dangerous that caused us to lift our faces to the breeze as it shifted. When the men returned they were red-eyed and weary, smudged with pitch and ash, smelling like coals from the furnace. I watched them drink tumbler after tumbler of iced tea, wondered at the dangers they faced, and thought that I might want to be like them and come home a fighter and a hero.

As a child raised in the woods, I gained my awareness and wariness of fire by way of the stories told by my elders as they sat around the table after dinner, picking their teeth with broomstraw, pouring another cup of the stout coffee kept warm atop the cookstove. New fires brought stories of old ones, and so August was full of fire, both distant and near, burning the night horizon, burning the edges of my dreams.

There was the fire of 1910, the one most often remembered by those old enough to have witnessed its destruction, their stories retold by the generations who have sat and listened and seen with their own eyes the scars left across the land. That year, July had come and gone with only .05 inches of rain. Thunderstorms had started spot fires throughout the Clearwater National Forest; the Forest Service and its small force of men, working with little more than shovels and picks, could not hope to suppress so much flame. And then came August, "ominous, sinister, and threatening," according to Forest Service worker Clarence B. Swim's account of that summer. "Dire catastrophe seemed to permeate the very atmosphere. Through the first weeks of August, the sun rose a coppery red ball and passed overhead . . . as if announcing impending disaster. The air felt close, oppressive, and explosive."[1]

"Ten days of clear summer weather," the old-timers say, "and the forest will burn." No rains came, and the many small fires that crews had been battling for days grew stronger and joined and began a run that would last for weeks. It swept up and down and across the Clearwater drainages: the Lochsa, Warm Springs Creek, Kelly Creek, Hemlock Creek, Cayuse Creek—the Idaho sky was black with ash. One Forest Service veteran, Ralph S. Space, whose written history of the Clearwater Forest contains lively anecdotal recollections, remembers smoke so thick that, as a nine-year-old boy rising to another day of no rain, he could look directly into the sun without hurting his eyes. The chickens, he said, never left their roost.[2]

On 21 August 1910, the wind began to blow, picking up velocity as the sun crested, until the bull pine and white fir swayed and snapped, and the dust rose up from the dirt roads and fields to join the smoke in a dervish of soot and cinder. Men along the fires' perimeters were told to run, get out, it was no use. Some took to the creeks and rivers, pulling their hysterical horses along behind them. (One legend tells of a panicked horse breaking away and racing the fire some fifty miles east to Superior, Montana—and making it.) Others fled northward, subsisting on grouse whose feathers were too burnt for them to fly.

As in any war, many who fought the fires came away scarred, some bearing the marks like badges of courage while others, whose less-than-brave actions in the face of disaster had earned them the coward's stripes, hid themselves in the backrooms of saloons or simply disappeared. One man, part of a group sent to fight the blaze near Avery, Idaho, was so undone by the blistering heat and hurricane roar of the approaching fire that he deserted, pulled his pistol, and shot himself—the only casualty to beset his crew.[3]

One of the heroes was a man named Edward Pulaski. When he found himself and the forty-three men he led cut off from escape, he ordered them into the nearby War Eagle mine, believing the large tunnel their only hope for survival. As the heat rose and the fire ate its way closer, several of the men panicked and threatened to run. Pulaski drew his pistol and forced the men to lie belly down, faces to the ground, where the coolest air would gather. He hung blankets across the tunnel's entrance, dampening them with what water he could, until he fainted. By the time

[1]Stan Cohen and Don Miller, *The Big Burn: The Northwest's Forest Fire of 1910* (Missoula, MT: Pictorial Histories Publishing Company, 1978), 3.

[2]Ralph S. Space, *The Clearwater Story: A History of the Clearwater National Forest* (Forest Service USDA, 1964), 96.

[3]Stan B. Cohen and A. Richard Guth, *Northern Region: A Pictorial History of the U.S. Forest Service 1891–1945* (Missoula, MT: Pictorial Histories Publishing Company, 1991), 61; Stan Cohen and Don Miller, 18–19.

the flames had passed around them, sucking the oxygen from the cavern, replacing it with a scorching, unbreathable wind, five were dead from suffocation. Another man who had chosen to run before Pulaski could stop him was found a short distance away: the rescue party had stepped over him on the way in, thinking the blackened mass a burned log; only on their return trip did they recognize the charred body for what it was. Pulaski had stood strong in the face of events "such as sear the souls of lesser men," declared the Washington, DC, *Star*.[4] He would go on to become even more famous for his invention bearing his name, the Pulaski—a combination shovel, ax, and mattock that since has become standard equipment for fighters of wildfire.

Pulaski's story is just one of many that came from that time of unimaginable conflagration. For three days and nights the wind howled up the canyons and down the draws, taking the fire with it. The ash, caught by updraft and high current, traveled for thousands of miles before falling in places that most Idahoans had only heard of: in Saskatchewan, Denver, and New York, the air was thick with the detritus of western larch and hemlock; in San Francisco, ships dropped anchor outside the bay and waited for days, unable to sight land through the blue-gray smoke that had drifted south and descended upon the city.[5] Norman Maclean wrote that in his home town of Missoula, "the street lights had to be turned on in the middle of the afternoon, and curled ashes brushed softly against the lamps as if snow were falling heavily in the heat of August."[6] The "Big Blowup," they call it now, or the "Big Burn"—not one large fire, but 1,736 smaller ones that had come together across the Clearwater Region. By the time it was over, three million acres and many small towns across Idaho and Montana lay in ruins; at least eighty-five people, most of them firefighters, were dead.[7]

The Big Blowup of 1910 was not the last August fire to rage across the Clearwater: 1914, 1919, 1929, 1934—major fires every five to ten years. The fire of 1919 is synonymous in my mind with the North Fork of the Clearwater, where I spent much of my childhood, for it is there, in the middle of the turquoise river, that a small rise of land bears the name Survivor Island. I remember how, aware of its legendary significance, I studied the island each time we passed along the dusty road, how the heart-flutter of danger and adventure filled my chest. What written history I can find records how two packers and their packstrings, two Nez Perce, and several wild animals had found safety from the fire by swimming to the island. But the story I remember has only three characters: an

[4]Cohen and Miller, 18.
[5]Cohen and Guth, 58.
[6]Norman Maclean, "USFS 1919: The Ranger, the Cook, and a Hole in the Sky," in *A River Runs Through It and Other Stories* (Chicago: The University of Chicago Press, 1976), 140.
[7]Cohen and Miller, v.

Indian grandfather, his grandson, and a black bear, all secure upon the island as the fire raged by, the winds it generated whipping the water into
whitecaps. At some point, the story became embellished with a detail I
still can't shake—how the child, emboldened by the success of their escape, wanted to kill the bear, and how the grandfather would not let him.
Perhaps the elder understood the mythical ties he and his charge would
forever have to that bear; perhaps he believed that nothing else should die
in the face of the carnage that surrounded them.

With each year's August, I feel the familiar expectation that comes with
the heat and powder-dry dust boiling up from behind the cars and logging trucks. Expectation, anticipation, sometimes fear of what lies just
over the horizon—August is a month of waiting for storm, for fire, for
rain, for the season to change and pull us away from our gardens, our
open windows and doors, back to the contained warmth of the hearth
and the bed that comforts us.

Yet some part of me loves the suspense of August, the hot breath of
morning whispering the possibility of high drama, the calm and compla-
cency of dog-day afternoons giving way to evening thunderheads brewing
along the ridge. Something's afoot, something's about to happen, and I
shiver with the sureness of it.

Years when I have lived in town, surrounded by asphalt, concrete,
and brick, there was little to fear from the dance of electricity lighting the
sky except the loss of electricity itself. Here in the country, on the south-
facing slope of the Clearwater Canyon, what surrounds us is something
as volatile and menacing as the tinder-dry forest: miles of waist-high grass
and thistle the color and texture of straw. Just such desiccated vegetation
fueled the flames that killed the men made famous by Norman Maclean's
book *Young Men and Fire* (1992), the story of the tragic 1949 Mann
Gulch blaze.

We have no rural fire district here; those of us who have chosen to
call this small settlement home know that should a wildfire come our
way, we have only our wits to protect us—that and every available gun-
nysack, shovel, hoe, and tractor the community can provide. All through
the summer we watch from our windows as the sun leeches the green
from the hills and the color from the sky, and the land takes on a pale
translucence. Come August, we have counted the days since no rain, and
we know that somewhere a storm is building, perhaps just to the south
where the horizontal plane of the Camas Prairie intersects the vertical
thrust of the Seven Devils—the mountains whose peaks rise jagged and
white through the brown haze of harvest.

We check our flashlights, our candle supply; we fill our bathtubs with
water. There will be wind, which will switch the sumac and send the sage-
brush busting across the gravel roads; it will tear the limbs from the trees,
drop them across the power lines in some part of the county so remote
that the service crew will take hours, sometimes days, to locate and repair

them. Then comes the lightning, blasting the tops from the tallest pines, striking the poles that carry our phone and electricity. The lights will flicker, then fail; the air conditioner will moan into silence. Pumps that pull the water from the springs will lapse into stillness; our toilets and faucets will gurgle and go dry. If we're lucky, what passes over us will be nothing more than the black raft of storm clouds, and the seconds we count between lightning and thunder will never fall below five. But there have been times when the bolt and jarring crack have come simultaneously, and we have known, then, that the lightning has touched somewhere near us, and that we must watch more carefully now and smell the air and be ready to fight or to run.

The summer of 1998, on just such an evening, we sat at the dinner table with my in-laws, who had arrived from Illinois for a weeklong visit. My husband Bob and I had each kept an eye on the clouds mushrooming behind Angel Ridge; to my Midwestern relatives, the oppressive humidity seemed nothing unusual, but to us, accustomed to zero percent air moisture, the too-still air signaled a weather change. When I stepped out onto the deck, I could hear the wind coming, huffing its way up the canyon like a steam engine. Within minutes, I was hit with a blast of hot air, then felt the cool come in behind it. The first reverberating boom made the hair stand up on the back of my neck, a response so atavistic I could barely resist the instinctual urge to take shelter. Instead, I raised my face to the wind, redolent with fennel and sage, locust and mullein, the arid incense of a summer's rich dust; along the edges of the breeze, I could smell the dampness of distant rain.

"The country road, we knew, was our best hope, cutting between us and the fire, providing a fuel-free strip where the flames might falter."

Back at the table, we drank our coffee and shared stories of the past year. I got up once to fill a few pitchers with water. The lightning moved closer—only a few seconds between the flash and thunder—and then a clap so loud and close we all jumped. Not really a clap, not even a boom, but a sharp, ripping roar. Bob and I looked at one another and headed for the porch, and then we could see it: to the west, a narrow column of smoke just beginning to rise. Even as we watched, the column grew thicker, and then we felt the wind gain momentum, pushing east toward us.

The country road, we knew, was our best hope, cutting between us and the fire, providing a fuel-free strip where the flames might falter. Earlier in the summer, Bob had cut, raked, and burned a fire-line around our house, decreasing the chances that fire could reach us, but what we couldn't shield ourselves against were the airborne cinders already beginning to descend.

"It's right behind the Bringman place," Bob said. "If we don't get it stopped, they'll be in trouble."

I had a vague acquaintance with Mr. and Mrs. Bringman, a retired couple who have worked the canyon land for decades. Their house and outbuildings sit a quarter-mile above and to the west of us, in the middle of what was then a good crop of ripe wheat. We had come to know them as we have come to know most of our neighbors: by our happenstance run-ins at the PO. Mr. Bringman is also known for his homemade wine. Local history holds that his land had once belonged to a man of some note who had imported grapevines from France and planted them in the sandy bluffs above the river. "Noble vines," Mr. Bringman pronounced, and we began saving our empty store-bought bottles so that, once a month, he could swing by on his four-wheeler to collect them and drop off a sample of the wine he had put up the past summer, which we dutifully shelved, though he insisted it was quite ready to drink now.

"You get on the phone," Bob said. "I'm going up there." Already the smoke and ash had darkened the sky to a deep shade of gray.

"Wear boots," I said. "Take a wet handkerchief and gloves."

While Bob gathered his gear, I picked up the phone and dialed. Mrs. Bringman's voice came on the line, high-pitched and quavering. "Tell your husband to get here as fast as he can," she said. "Call anyone you can. It's coming our way."

I hung up, then began a series of calls, knowing that for each call I made, two more would go out, word of the lightning strike spreading faster than the fire itself, fanning out across the ridges and high prairie for miles, until every family would be alerted. I knew that every wife and mother would dial the next number down the road, that each man and his oldest sons would don their hats and boots, grab their shovels and buckets and be out the door within minutes, all guided by the pillar of smoke that marked the point of danger as surely as a lighthouse beam.

I paused in my calling long enough to kiss Bob as he hurried out the door. I could see the change in his eyes, the urgency and excitement, and I felt the regret and longing and resignation I had as a child when the men had gone into the wilderness, to the front where the stories were being made and the dramas played out.

"Remember how fast the fire can move," I said. I had a momentary image of my husband scrabbling across the canyon's steep pitch and felt my heart jerk with fear. "Do you have a lighter?"

Bob nodded, remembering, as I remembered, the story of the ranger who survived the Mann Gulch fire.

"Be careful," I cautioned.

"I will," he said, and was gone.

In *Young Men and Fire*, Norman Maclean researches and describes the 5 August 1949 blaze that caught and killed all but three of the fifteen Forest Service smoke jumpers who had parachuted into the Helena National Forest of Montana. They had been on the ground for less than two hours and were working their way down a hillside toward the fire—an error that would cost them dearly, for a fire racing uphill can easily catch even the fastest man. But what they had found was a simple class C fire, no more than sixty acres. It was a "ground" fire, one the men expected to mean hard work but little danger.[8]

Yet there is always danger when a wildfire is present, and so the crew knew that this one might "crown," as its charred path suggested it had done already before moving back down into undergrowth. The fire that has crowned is what creates the great roar of sound so many survivors describe as the noise of a fast-moving train descending upon them, so loud that communication becomes impossible. A crown fire creates its own weather system: the warmer air rises and the cooler air rushes down to replace it, creating a "fire whirl," a moving convection that can fill the air with burning pine cones and limbs, as though the forest itself has exploded. This incendiary debris gives rise to spot fires that can flare behind or in front of the fighters; crews find themselves suddenly surrounded, ringed by fire that seems to have come from nowhere, sprung up from the ground and converging.[9]

With these conditions comes the possibility of the phenomenon firefighters most fear: the "blowup." Blowups occur when fresh air is drawn into the "fire triangle" of flammable material, high temperature, and oxygen. Few have witnessed a true blowup and lived to tell of it, but those who have speak with wonder of the fire's speed. Maclean recounts the experience of fire expert Harry T. Gisborne, perhaps the first to observe, survive, and describe a blowup. The 1929 fire Gisborne detailed occurred in Glacier National Park and burned ninety thousand acres with almost incomprehensible swiftness, demolishing "over two square miles in possibly two minutes, although probably in a minute flat."[10]

The Mann Gulch smoke jumpers were young and had dropped onto a terrain that may have seemed at the time less threatening than the densely wooded ridge in the distance. They were at a point where the tree-studded mountains broke open to grassy plains dried to amber. Perhaps they believed themselves safe amid the loose-rock slope and low-lying vegetation, but they were tragically mistaken. They had their tools—their shovels and Pulaskis—but what they did not have was knowledge of the ways of this fire and of how within an hour, it would cross the gulch and push them screaming up the steep hill, crest at the top, and die there with them. Bunch grass, cheat grass, some immature pines mixed in with older growth—these were all that was needed to create the blowup that engulfed the men. Two of the three who survived did so by racing the fire to the ridge and winning; the third, the crew's foreman, saved himself by escape of another kind: instead of running, he stopped, struck a match, set fire to the grass at his feet, then stepped into the flames he had created. He lay face down on the still-smoking earth, covered his

---

[8]Norman Maclean, *Young Men and Fire: A True Story of the Mann Gulch Fire* (Chicago: The University of Chicago Press, 1992), 33.
[9]Maclean, 34–37.
[10]Maclean, 35, 37.

head with his hands, and waited for the main fire to catch and sweep over him. And it did.[11]

A steeply pitched basalt-strewn slope covered with dry grass and scattered patches of timber—the very terrain into which Bob was headed. I prayed that he would have the foreman's presence of mind should the fire overtake him. I could see the flames themselves now, flaring twenty feet into the sky. I let the screen door swing shut, went back to the phone, and began another call.

The men came in their pickups and stock trucks and cars, on their four-wheelers and tractors—a steady parade passing by our house. Having exhausted my list of numbers, I gave up my station to stand with my children and in-laws where our gravel driveway met the gravel road. We tried to determine what we could of the fire's direction. We waved our support as our neighbors flew by—driving too fast, we thought, though we understood their urgency. On the slope just above us, the Goodes and Grimms and Andersons had set their sprinklers atop their roofs, dampening the embers and sparking ash that floated and fell around us like fireflies in the darkening sky. I'd instructed my ten-year-old daughter and eight-year-old son to stand ready with the hose, knowing that should the power lines go down, our electric pump that drew water from the spring below would be useless; our only defense against the fire would be whatever water remained in the storage tank. But if we used that water for prevention, we would have none left should the fire reach us.

As twilight deepened, the fire's glow grew more distinct along the western horizon, until the last rays of sunlight were indistinguishable from the orange-red aura melding sky to land. My mother-in-law, city raised and only half understanding her son's desire to live in such a wild place, did her best to rein in her fear; my father-in-law, nearing eighty, paced in frustration: he should be out there, offering what help he could. Had it not been for the fire's location along the breaks of the canyon, our ability to keep him clear of the battle would have proven much more difficult.

We all knew the immediate danger Bob and the other men faced—the fire—but there were other concerns I kept to myself. Just down the road from our house is a jut of land named Rattlesnake Point: we kill an average of two diamondbacks per year in our yard; the annual score we spy along the roads and paths outside our property we leave be. In times of fire, every living thing flees from what threatens it—cougar, deer, elk, rabbit, pheasant, field mouse, bear, and rattlesnakes, too, slithering ahead of the heat faster than most could imagine, sometimes smoking from their close brush with death. My hope was that, should Bob encounter a snake, it would be too intent on escape to strike at the legs of a man.

---

[11]Maclean, 74–75, 102–106.

And then there was the terrain itself: fragile shelves of talus, slanted fields of scree. The land could give way beneath your feet, begin moving like a tipped mass of marbles. I have had it happen before, while hunting chukar, and found myself grabbing at the smallest outcroppings of sage and buckbrush, feeling them pull loose in my hands, the only thing below me a chute toward an outcropping of columnar basalt that would launch me into the canyon. I've always been lucky, able to catch a knob of stable rock or wedge my foot into the roots of a stunted hawthorn, but that memory of falling, of gathering momentum, of hurtling toward endless open space, has never left me. I knew that Bob was sure-footed and careful; I knew, too, that in the lapse of light, the ground's definition would fade.

The smoke thickened. We covered our faces with our hands, coughing, our eyes watering, unwilling to abandon our vigil, knowing how much more those closer to the fire were having to endure. I ordered the children back to the house, but they would not go. They wanted to be of some help, perhaps believing, as I did, that our standing guard might somehow keep the fire at bay. The glow had moved higher up the ridge; the flames leapt, receded, then leapt again. With the wind and lack of equipment, we had little hope that simple manpower could contain the fire. I estimated that a half-mile of pasture land separated us from the conflagration—that and the road—and I told myself we could hold our ground for a little while longer before loading the cars with what we most treasured: photographs, books, laptop computer, the children's most precious belongings. The possibility of losing our home and everything in it seemed very real to me, but I considered it with little emotion. What was uppermost in my mind was the safety of my loved ones: the family that gathered closer as the smoke increased, and my husband, somewhere just over the ridge, risking his life to save the nearby houses and barns, the crops and timber, perhaps even an entire small town should the fire run the ridge and drop over into the next draw. At that moment, I wasn't sure the saving was worth the risk. How could I weigh the loss of my husband against nothing more than property and economy? There was little chance that anyone other than the firefighters was in danger—by now, everyone in the county had been warned. Why not stand back, allow the fire to meet the river on one side, the linkage of creeks on the other? In the end, it would burn itself out.

But then I remembered the stories—the fire of 1910, the young men who had died so suddenly by thinking the distance between them and the fire enough—and I realized that this wasn't about the wheat field a mile down the road or the home of the family at the bottom of the draw. It was about fire. It was about crowning and whirls, convection and blowups. It was about August and a summer's long drought. It was about three million acres burned in a matter of days—the width and breadth of many whole states.

What I wished for, then, was the help of all the technology and knowledge such fires of the past had brought into being. The fire of 1910 showed everyone that crews of men scattered about the burning edges would never be enough, and then the Forest Service began its study and transformation of firefighting. But we do not live in a forest; we live on private land, too distant to warrant the protection of the city, too sparsely populated to afford the luxury of a volunteer fire department. That August of 1998, our situation was little different from the one facing the farmers and loggers and townspeople of 1910: our primitive tools had not changed, and at that moment, I began to realize that our chances of saving our home had not, either.

"Our jubilation had been replaced by a quiet fear that grew with each passing minute—fear that receded and then leapt up each time another pickup approached but did not slow and turn into our driveway."

I moved down the driveway, preparing myself to announce that it was time to pack up, to position ourselves by the river where Bob might find us. But then came the roar of something overhead—the thrum and air-beat of a helicopter. I looked up to see what I had believed would not come to us: help from the outside world.

From beneath the helicopter hung a length of cable attached to a large vinyl-and-canvas bucket. The pilot did not head for the fire but for the river, where he hovered and dropped and filled the bucket with nearly one hundred gallons of water—a half ton hoisted up and swinging from the Bell Jet Ranger. As we watched, the helicopter leaned itself toward the fire's furthest point, the bale opened, and a sheet of water rained down.

My daughter and son let loose with whoops of excitement. My in-laws and I clapped and hugged, jubilant at this unexpected turn of events. Again and again, the pilot followed his path from river to fire, until the ribbon of flame along the horizon had dimmed to a faint glow; within an hour, we could no longer point to even the smallest flare.

We stood watch as night came on, unable to see the helicopter now but tracing its direction by the deep hum that drifted to us on the smoky breeze. Although we were safe, rescued by the graces of the Clearwater-Potlatch Timber Protective Association, who had sent the helicopter because they were fighting no fires of their own, we all knew our wait was not over: somewhere in the darkness was our father, son, and husband. The line of vehicles that had sped by us earlier now came in reverse—a slower-moving column whose lights passed over us as we held up our hands in a gesture of greeting and gratitude.

"Bob will be coming soon," I said. "Let's go make him some fresh iced tea."

We walked the few yards back to the house, turned on the porch light. Our jubilation had been replaced by a quiet fear that grew with each passing minute—fear that receded and then leapt up each time another pickup approached but did not slow and turn into our driveway.

"He should be back by now," my father-in-law said, pacing from the window to the door and back again. "Maybe I should go see if I can find him."

I knew that Bob and the other men would have driven off-road and into the fields, gaining what time they could against the fire. Even if we could locate our four-wheel-drive, there was no guarantee Bob would be near it. Without light, the diminishing fire behind him and the total blackness of rural night before him, he could walk for hours before finding his way back to where he had parked.

"I think we should wait," I said. "He'll stay as long as he's needed. Someone will come and get us if there's trouble." I listened to my own words, only half believing. What if Bob had gotten turned around, fallen into a ravine, been isolated and trapped by the fire? What if he were lying somewhere in the dark, injured, unable to save himself?

I thought again of the rough terrain—familiar to me from the many walks Bob and I had taken, the many hours we had spent exploring and visually mapping the area. The fire likely would have eaten its way across Bedrock Canyon, down to the river and up to the top of the ridge, creating acres and acres of charcoal earth, charcoal sky—like a black blizzard. How could we hope to find him?

We made the tea. We gathered and washed the dinner dishes. We distracted the children with books and puzzles until none of us could be distracted any longer. We gathered outside in the cooling air, still heavy with smoke that would hang in the canyon for days.

"Come on, Bob," I whispered to myself. "Come on." I thought of my mother and aunts then, waiting as I waited, fighting the growing panic with the mundane details of daily life. How many hours had they spent watching from the window above the sink, their hands submerged in soapy water, their fingers blindly tracing the knife's edge? How many Augusts had passed in a haze of worry and despair as the lightning came down and the flames rose up and the men disappeared into that place where no one could reach them?

But then, the lights at the top of the driveway, the held breath, the release as the engine idled and died.

I let my daughter and son reach him first, escort him into the house. He was covered with soot, his white T-shirt scorched, burned through in some places; his face was red, nearly blistered beneath the ashy smudges. We hovered around him, offering tea, voicing our concern and sympathy. I stepped up close, breathed in the familiar smell of everything burned— the dead grass and live trees, the cloth on his back, the singed hair.

"I'm so glad you're okay." I wanted to cry—out of relief that he was home, out of anger at the fire, out of frustration that I had found myself caught up in the same cycle that my mother had known so well. I knew that the stories Bob would tell of the fire would become part of our family's shared history, that we would recite and embellish the narrative with each passing summer, that we would always remember the way he shook his head when he told us: "There was no way we were going to be able to stop it. But then I heard the helicopter, directly overhead. I looked up just as the bottom of the bucket opened. I've never felt anything so good in my life."

The next day, we drove downriver to view where the fire had burned—an oily pool spread across the golden hillside. After the fire subsided, Bob had found himself disoriented and had wandered in the dark for an hour before coming across several other men. Together they were able to find their way back. "I can look up there now," he said, "and have no idea where I was."

Later, when I asked my son what he remembered about the fire, he answered quickly: "I remember that I couldn't breathe." My daughter recalled the ash falling and my concern that we would lose our water supply. And she reminded me of something I had forgotten: "What I remember most," she said, "is how badly I wanted to go and help fight the fire, and how you wouldn't let me."

Perhaps she will be the one to leave the phone and go to the place where stories are being made, the one who will not be left behind. One of the most respected smoke jumping crews in the country is composed entirely of women; of the fourteen Oregon-based firefighters who died in the Colorado fire of 1994, four were female. I shudder with the thought of my son or daughter choosing to try himself, herself, against such an adversary. I wonder if I would come to dread and despise the month I love so well, for I am strangely wedded to the tyrannical heat, the thunderstorms, even the fire—the absolutism, the undeniable presence of August in my life.

Instead of wading the ashes of August, I spend many late summer days wading the river. This is Nez Perce land, and the water's flux covers and uncovers the remnants of their ancient industry: arrowheads, spear points, blades of obsidian. I come to the Clearwater armed only with a hook and line, meaning to fool the fish with a tuft of feather, a swirl of bright thread. I step in to my waist and feel the strange dissonance of temperature—my feet numbing with cold, the crown of my head hot with sun. I stand for a moment, brace myself. I am all that is still, an island anchored by nothing more than the felt soles of my boots. I load my line, cast toward the calm above the current. I imagine the fish rising, its world a kaleidoscope of shattered light.

Through the cooling nights of fall, during the long nights of winter when ice rimes the eddies, I dream of August, the water at my hips, my line lacing the sun. I wake to the odor of woodsmoke—my husband firing the stove—but for a sleepy moment it is the warm wind that I smell, the burning of yellow pine and prairie grass and wheat stubble. I smell summer sage and mullein, the licorice spice of dog fennel. I smell the cool drift of fish scent off the river. I open my eyes, expecting early light, the windows still open to the morning breeze, but what I see instead is the darkness before sunrise, the frost that glisters each pane of glass, and I am bereft.

Interview with Kim Barnes

BECKY BRADWAY: Kim, can you describe how you were able to weave historical information into your piece? In particular, was it difficult to transition from present to the personal past (your own childhood) to historical past (1910), and how did you do it?

KIM BARNES: "The Ashes of August" came out of an "assignment" I was given by Scott Olsen, who, along with Bret Lott, was editing an anthology titled *A Year in Place*. Each author was asked to pick a month and write about some aspect of that month in the context of landscape. By the time I agreed to take part in the project, only August and December were left, and I picked August. At first, I didn't know what the essay would be "about" other than the month itself. You can write beautifully about anything—or anyone—but, finally, the essay has to have some larger thematic arc: it has to be about something larger than itself, just as your story has to be about something larger than your individual experience.

In the arid West, August is always about fire. The history and mythology of forest fires has been part of my life for as long as I can remember. The scars left by the fire of 1910 were as much a part of the landscape as any mountain or stream. So, here's what I did: I thought of several personal memory scenes that take place in August and revolve around fire, some from the distant past, others more recent. Because I wanted to trace my "lineage" as a part of this story, I went to the little local library and read everything I could find on the big fires that had swept through the region. I also read about more recent wildfires in order to give my essay a larger scope and bring the concerns of the past into the present.

Then I needed the thematic idea that would hold them all together. I always tell my students: it's like fish on a stringer. The stringer is the idea on which you "hang" your scenes. If you can discern this idea, which you often cannot determine until you've actually written the scenes and allowed them to show you what they're about, you're almost home.

As I contemplated and started drafting the scenes I might include (at this point in the process, I really luxuriate in description and vivid detail, most often composing in present tense to gain immediacy), I asked myself, "Why am I telling them this?" and by "them" I mean my readers. Always, I ask, "Why is this important to know? What do the readers learn, not just about me, but about the 'big picture'?"— which is more about the human condition than it is about any one of us. Remember that any single event can be about any number of things, but our task is to impose, for a time, at least, one narrative of meaning—to look through one window of the house and describe what we see framed there.

When I'd written a few of these scenes, I saw that they were being informed by a couple of different things: the choice I have made to stay in this place and to live a rural life that is often defined by danger; and a sense of regret—not just about fire but about the stories of fire and my place in them.

There are times when a series of scenes can stand alone as an essay, times when the images, as is the case with some poems, can carry the meaning. More often, however, we must attempt to contemplate and explore the very scenes we have created. All narratives are made up of action and thought. I now had my scenes of action but was missing the authorial exposition that would help bring those scenes around and make the essay more fully realized.

What I came to see as I wove together the "old" stories with the stories of my girlhood and the more recent story of the lightning strike near our house was that my "reason" for telling these stories had to do with my role as a woman. As is so often the case, the stories of the women in my family have always been defined by domestic quietude, whereas the stories of the men have been defined by action and high drama. As I wrote the essay, I came to understand that, finally, there is little difference between my mother's life and my own when it comes to such narratives.

This, then, became the "glue" that holds the scenes together. "Glue" is often made up of "vertical movement" in the essay, and by this I mean movement that delves deeper rather than moving forward. Vertical movement is usually made up of contemplation, but it can also be seen in moments of associative memory, figures of speech, lyrical description, or direct questioning of meaning. It is this movement that can sometimes take the essay to a deeper level of emotion and narratival inquiry. Bringing the intellect to bear on the stories of our lives through contemplation, association, and context: I believe that this is the greatest challenge for the writer of personal nonfiction.

BB: Did continuing to live in the place where you grew up create any challenges for you as a writer? What are the benefits?

KB: My writing is so tied to place that I have a difficult time separating the story from its setting, just as I find it nearly impossible to separate myself from the land around me. For the most part, I've had little desire to explore settings outside the Western landscape, yet I believe absolutely in an artist's ability to imagine any landscape, foreign or familiar. Maybe this is because I'm deeply invested in the idea of myth and archetype. I believe that everything I need to know and write about exists vertically rather than horizontally—that is, I believe in the symbolic resonance of human experience in any given landscape. And even though I believe it is sometimes a good idea to "write what you know," I believe you can "know" things in ways that are not always experiential. Why are some of us innately drawn to cities, or mountains, or rivers, or Parisian cafes? Why do we sometimes feel like strangers in a strange land—the land being the very place we were born into?

Our connection to place isn't always defined by the physical and literal; sometimes, the place we know best and feel the greatest affinity for is a place we have never been.

For me, I feel the greatest affinity for the defined landscape of the West, especially mountain rivers and canyons—the type of land in which I was raised. Yet I feel that my connection to wild open spaces has less to do with having been born and raised here and much more to do with having been lucky enough to find a place that I feel intimately connected to at some deep, perhaps genetic level. It is the landscape that I find most comforting, even when it proves itself most hostile. As an adult, I have often been given the opportunity to choose the place I wish to live, and, always, I have chosen the inner-mountain West.

Because I'm primarily a memoirist and writer of personal essays, this kind of intimacy is very important to me. Writing as an outsider doesn't appeal to me, unless there is a defined transition that takes place so that "outsider" becomes "insider." I do use the idea of "outsider" to define alienation, unfamiliarity, chaos, loss of narrative. In my memoirs, I intentionally set up a kind of delineation between the wilderness and the "city"—civilization. Very Romantic. There are a number of scenes in which I describe the construction of the dam on the North Fork of the Clearwater—halfway between the wilderness and the city—as that point separating me from my childhood happiness. The scenes detail my journey toward my "new" life, which will be defined by loss of innocence, disaffection, and dislocation. I describe the pulp and paper mill at the city's edge in terms reminiscent of the Romantics' description of the Industrial Revolution: smokey, dark, mechanical, and monstrous. Hell. I am lost, an outsider, and must find my way back to some sense of who I am in this foreign place.

Here's the problem I have sometimes faced as an "insider" trying to write about place: I know it too intimately. I've taken it in, internalized it. There are times when I cannot separate myself in order to see it. I remember Mary Clearman Blew reading an early draft of *In the Wilderness*, my memoir about growing up in the logging camps and small towns of the Clearwater National Forest. One of the things she said to me was that I needed to step back and look at the landscape as an outsider might. In memory, all I could see was very close-in: the shack we lived in, the nearby trees. Nothing more. Not the mountaintops or the lay of the land. I had to look at photographs and maps. Same with the flora and fauna. I grew up calling every bush "buck brush." I never knew the name of the many birds that flitted through the forest, nor the specific names of the trees themselves. Everything was as common and unnotable as my own skin.

When I begin to write memoir, I detail the setting from a perspective that is more emotional than mental, I think. How I feel the place. Later, I go back and find the correct and appropriate terminology, and I check my facts. I don't want to have chokecherry blooming in July if it really blooms in April or May, no matter what my memory tells me, and so I've surrounded myself with reference books: Peterson's field guides, geology texts, Idaho Place Names. I had to learn the land I'd known since birth.

Writing is about art and inspiration, and it is about craft and hard work. Writing about the land also involves each of these things. Lyrical language—the putting together of beautiful words such as "chalcedony" and "Barrow's Goldeneye"—feels like inspiration. The finding of these words and the researching of their definitions and appropriateness to my story is work. No matter what you choose to include about your physical surroundings, it must inform and complete the narrative—it must serve to characterize both the people and the place as well as to further inform the thematic arc of the story.

I don't necessarily feel like I need physical or temporal distance from a place or event to write about it, but I do feel like I need enough narrative distance to see the story's archetypal rhythms and shape. When I can observe this thematic focus, I can determine what details and descriptions are important to more fully realizing the larger story. My approach is to write the story (what happened—the action) straight and simple the first time through—to just tell the story, as Bill Kittredge says. Then I try to separate myself from it, become reader rather than writer, see it as separate from my own experience, see it as an object of art. This is the point at which I start bringing in details of the land that harmonize with the story's themes. I can do this while surrounded by the very setting I'm describing, or I can do it while flying over Michigan. At this point, the details are my palette of colors. I can mix, blend, define by intentionally describing certain characteristics of the river, or the deer I'm hunting, or the incoming weather, or last summer's wildfire. I can paint the picture, make the dream visually materialize.

Gabrielle Bell

From *Lucky*

Gabrielle Bell was born in London and lived there two years before moving to Michigan and then to California. It was there that she grew up in an isolated rural community. "I spent a lot of time reading, walking in the woods and making up stories. For two summers I attended Camp Winnarainbow, a circus arts summer camp, and spent most of my time taking drama and art classes. As a teenager I attended Project Upward Bound at Humboldt University, a college program for low-income and at-risk students where I took classes in Shakespeare and composition and decided to be a writer." After high school she traveled in Europe, then moved to San Francisco, where she took art classes and began her career as a cartoonist. Her self-published mini-comics were eventually published in her first book, *When I'm Old and Other Stories* (2003).

In 2003 she moved to New York and produced her award-winning journal-comic series *Lucky*, which was released as a book in 2006 from Drawn & Quarterly. Bell currently lives in Brooklyn, contributes to anthologies, and continues to write and draw comics.

In an interview with the *Comics Reporter*, Bell said that *Lucky* began as "diary strips" that she eventually extended, making them "into something more considered, less immediate. In doing that, the visual format changed too. When I take the storytelling more seriously, I take the art more seriously with it." She added that "the uncomfortable moments in my comics are my awkward and fumbling attempts at understanding and communicating with other people, which is the best I can do for now."

The excerpt in this book is from *Lucky*. Bell's sweetness of tone and ability to tell the story through dialogue, description, and reflection make this a particularly literary-leaning graphic memoir. The illustrations whimsically comment upon what has been revealed through the language. By the end of the book, we come to know this narrator as she deals with the tension between her dreams and the mundane workplace.

Interview with Gabrielle Bell, p. 215.

When I look at it, all I see is the work I have to do on it. The trinkets are soothing to look at. They're made of nice color combinations, with curving and straight lines, and different textures to create a kind of gaudy opulence.

However, they also have in them things that embarrass me because I thought they were nice when I was thirteen: hearts, stars, crescent moons, flowers, smartly dressed women, cute animals, egyptian eyes...

It is an easy, painless, even pleasant job. But because I I have to go to it every day it is still a kind of jail to me, albeit a comfortable one. The wardens are thoughtful and trusting.

DON'T WORK TOO HARD, OKAY?

I'LL TRY TO BE CAREFUL.

The other inmates are friendly and helpful, and capable of mind reading.

SECOND DRAWER ON THE LEFT.

Fortunately, my co-worker Mei and I have a lot in common. For one thing, we both think that we are too fat.

HAVE YOU TRIED THROWING UP AFTER EVERY MEAL? I HEARD THAT HELPS.

I PREFER JUST TO NOT HAVE MEALS IN THE FIRST PLACE.

Another thing is that we both love French things.

SO YOU ARE A FRANCOPHILE TOO?

NO. IT'S JUST THAT I CAN'T STAND ANYTHING THAT ISN'T FRENCH.

In order to sustain us through mind-numbing jobs, it is necessary to tell ourselves lies, and mine is that if only I was surrounded by France, I would no longer feel perpetually ill at ease.

Of course my knowledge of the country comes only from novels, music and movies, but worst of all, Proust. As far as I know, everyone in Paris spends their time gazing at flowers and searching their memories.

Aside from having to learn the language, there are many things I have to learn before visiting France. I am sure I won't be allowed past customs without a thorough knowledge of wines and cheeses.

USE A NUMB-ER TWO PEN-ZEL END FEEL OUT ZEEZ FORM, ZEN PROCEED TO ZE CELLAR FOR ZE ORALS END ZE TASTING...

Of course, those things can be picked up or faked. The one thing that truly scares me is the French way of greeting.

VEH-REE GOOD. NOW FOR ZE FIN-ALE EXAM YOU MUST KEEZ ME GOOD-BYE.

Now, I'm a very socially awkward person, and cheek-kissing requires a grace and confidence that is dormant or lacking in me.

MWAH!

BONSOIR!

MWAH!

OH NO! I'M NEXT! WHAT IF HE SMELLS ME?

Who kisses who? Do you kiss the cheek or the air next to it? Do you say 'mwah' or are you silent? Do I start with the right side or the left? When do I know if we are friends enough to kiss?

* IT MEANS, ROUGHLY, 'FUCK OFF'

* PLEASE TEACH ME HOW TO KISS.

Interview with Gabrielle Bell

BECKY BRADWAY: This section of your book is a little episode from your life, showing a situation that everyone has experienced (who hasn't fantasized while at work?). I've had students who are afraid to write about themselves because (they say) "my life's too boring" — "I haven't done anything" — "I have nothing to say." Did you go through a stage when you were afraid of writing your book for just this reason? If so, how did you get past it enough to write and draw an entire book?

GABRIELLE BELL: I often have no confidence to write about myself. It's only when I approach it as an artist that I'm able to get over it. For *Lucky*, I would take a period of time—usually a month—and assign myself the task of turning an event from each day into a story. Then I could choose the most interesting stories for my comics. They weren't necessarily the most interesting things that happened, but the things that I hoped would interest everybody, not just myself or my friends. So for that month I would pay a lot of attention to everything around me, taking notes and writing and drawing. Once I'm in that habit, I'm too absorbed with the work to worry about whether it is a worthy subject matter. But I haven't been able to keep that sustained concentration all the time.

Another thing I do, while I'm working in this way, is to try to do things I wouldn't ordinarily do. It doesn't have to be any more exciting than my regular life, just different. Like, not being religious, I might try going to church. Something about the novelty of a situation somehow makes things automatically interesting and inspires curiosity.

BB: One of the things I love about this piece is the way all of the descriptions become designs in the background (the jewelry, the textures, etc.). I thought this was very imaginative. How did you come up with the idea to do it this way? Did you have to go through some attempts before you came to this approach?

GB: Not a lot of attempts for that particular one. That is the beauty of comics—to have both words and pictures to describe with, and it's great if you can strike a nice balance between the two, so each does its part in telling the story.

BB: The graphic writer Julie Doucet has said that she'll no longer be writing graphic novels because she has to spend too much time for too little money. Do you also feel that they are too time-consuming for too little pay? Would you write (or are you writing) another graphic novel or memoir? What was the best thing that came from writing *Lucky*?

GB: It's true that comics are enormously underpaid for, but I don't think that's the reason she decided to stop, though I am not sure of the real reason.

Perhaps they aren't compensated enough because for so long they've been considered frivolous, not a serious artform. Perhaps because they look so simple and easy to do. The amount of work that goes into conceiving and drawing a comic, let alone the time it takes to learn to do (years!), is invisible on the finished page. But I think it's getting better and will continue to get better. Yes, I am writing and drawing more comics. The best thing that came from writing *Lucky* was the confidence and skill to do more.

BB: The writing in this shows so much skill. Do you do a lot of writing, without illustration? Have you thought of writing a book that doesn't include artwork? (After all, you are obsessed with Proust.)

GB: Thank you! When I was younger I wanted to be a novelist. But I also drew all the time. When I started doing comics I never looked back. I prefer the combination of pictures and words. I wouldn't rule out the idea of writing a book without images, but right now it seems far more exciting to explore the possibilities of comics.

Sven Birkerts

Reflections of a Nonpolitical Man; or, Why I Can't in Good Conscience Write about Noam Chomsky

Sven Birkerts is the author of six books, including *An Artificial Wilderness: Essays on 20th Century Literature* (1987), *The Electric Life: Essays on Modern Poetry* (1989), *American Energies: Essays on Fiction* (1992), *The Gutenberg Elegies: The Fate of Reading in an Electronic Age* (1994), *Readings* (1999), and *My Sky Blue Trades: Growing Up Counter in a Contrary Time* (2002). He has edited *Tolstoy's Dictaphone: Writers and the Muse* (1996) as well as *Writing Well* (9th ed., 1997, with Donald Hall) and *The Evolving Canon* (1993). His publishers include Viking, Morrow, Faber and Faber, Graywolf, and Allyn and Bacon.

He has received grants from the Lila Wallace–Reader's Digest Foundation and the Guggenheim Foundation. He was winner of the Citation for Excellence in Reviewing from the National Book Critics Circle in 1985 and the Spielvogel-Diamonstein Award from PEN for the best book of essays in 1990. Birkerts has reviewed regularly for the *New York Times Book Review,* the *New Republic, Esquire,* the *Washington Post,* the *Atlantic, Mirabella, Parnassus,* the *Yale Review,* and other publications. He has taught writing at Harvard University, Emerson College, and Amherst and is currently a lecturer at Mt. Holyoke College and a member of the core faculty of the Bennington Writing Seminars. He is the editor of *Agni,* a literary journal.

The piece we've included, "Reflections of a Nonpolitical Man," is a personal essay that ruminates, in a logical manner, upon the reasons for the author's political inactivity. The essay is an apologia that ultimately celebrates a sedentary pursuit of knowledge as its own form of action.

I have a friend who wants me to be more political. He doesn't specify, but I know what he means: He wants me to do things, take conspicuous stances, have a more engaged posture in the world. And he's right. That is, he must be right—otherwise why would I feel such a prickling of guilt whenever he brings the subject up? And these days he seems to bring it up all the time. When he does I naturally become defensive; I scramble toward the familiar silence of not being understood.

This same friend, in an effort to raise my consciousness, has now asked me to write for him an essay on Noam Chomsky's and Edward Herman's latest book, *Manufacturing Consent.* In the face of such sincere concern for the fitness of my soul, I could not think of a way to refuse. I confess, too, that I hoped the book would make a change in me. It's not that I want to be nonpolitical, it's just that I am. I would give a great deal to be able to lay to rest the sickly guilt that moves through me whenever I face up to my own ineffectuality, my refusal to take any direct action against the waste, corruption and oppression that are around us like tethers.

So I read. And I read with care. Slowly, marking passages with a pencil. I paused—sometimes I made myself do so—over statistics confirming one outrage after another. I made every effort to understand, to impress on myself what this really meant in the world beyond the words. And I took pains to track the progress of Chomsky's argument: I marveled at the cool fury of the prose. I could see Chomsky's determination to avoid all rhetoric, to let the facts speak for themselves. Reading, I felt a deep respect for the dedication and will required to wage a campaign for truth in the face of near-universal deafness. I thought, too, about the points I would make and the sections I would cite to push those points home. I read, I marked, I plotted. And when I came to an end of it, I found that I stood squarely before an obstacle in myself: I could not possibly discuss this book, these ideas, in the necessary terms.

Not because I was not persuaded; not because I do not believe that Chomsky is doing a hero's work; not because the information does not need to go out to every person who thinks about anything more consequential than Friday's twilight doubleheader at Fenway Park—but because I was not an adequate vessel for Chomsky's vision. I would have to pretend to a stance or perspective that I could assent to intellectually, but that I had not earned with my heart. Indeed, the more I soaked myself in the information, and the more I thought about the implication of the analysis that Chomsky sets out—how the whole empire of our communications is tacitly and implicitly geared to furthering the vested interests of U.S. imperialism—the more I found myself coiling back upon my own blockage: my inability, unwillingness, to put myself forward in meaningful political action on behalf of anything. The two—Chomsky's thesis and my response—are very separate things, but as I read they became one. The book and its author became in my mind a single emblem of engaged activism before which I was struck dumb.

> "I faced the difficult fact: I will do nothing overt to further causes I believe in—I will do nothing *political*."

I faced the difficult fact: I will do nothing overt to further causes I believe in—I will do nothing *political*. An awful admission. Certainly there is no dearth of causes, all of them asking for our most committed support. Greenpeace, Amnesty International, pro-choice mobilization, anti-apartheid organizations, nuclear freeze campaigns. What is wrong with me that I cannot bestir myself to do anything more than sign an occasional petition, write out a small check?

I discussed my sense of handicap with my friend. He suggested that the problem was not mine alone, that it seemed to afflict a great many people, prominent among them the writers, artists and thinkers that one might expect would be closer to such consciousness and involvement. We went back and forth debating possible reasons, considering everything from cultural narcissism to spiritual detachment in the service of art, but we were not able to solve the matter. I promised him that if I could not write the essay he had assigned, I would instead set down my reasons for failure.

I would like to write about this inactivity, this political paralysis of mine, honestly. I would like to write about it without lapsing into the clever, cynical mode that comes to me so readily when I get defensive. But I am, of course, defensive. Somewhere not all that deep within I know that the blockage represents a failing. No, I correct myself: I don't *know* this, I only suspect it. And I would like to—I *think* I would like to—change myself, to think my way through to an understanding of things out of which response—action—would result naturally. For I know that nothing could be more false, and wrongheaded, than a rash effort on my part to set things right by simply deciding to *do* something. To go march at Seabrook, say.

But how to work through this tangle? First, I ought to make a clear distinction between political passivity (or paralysis) and political apathy. I am not apathetic. Certainly not about the thousand-and-one ills of the world. If I am apathetic about anything, it's political process: activity. But no, even that is not quite right. For I have great admiration for those people who feel the compulsion to act out their beliefs and who find meaningful ways to do so. I see newsreel footage of demonstrators being carted away from nuclear power plants or dumping sites and I envy them. I find myself wishing that I, too, knew my convictions in such a bodily— complete—fashion. Nothing stops me from joining the march—but I do not join. I applaud others; I cannot make myself act.

The obvious defense, the first that comes to mind, is that these activities are ultimately useless, that they will not stay the course of the world or stop the powers that be from enacting their schemes. This I can readily discard: for even if the protests availed nothing, they would still send a signal to those powers that they cannot simply railroad their designs into place; they cannot expect that everyone consents. And this is a necessary statement.

As it happens, such an argument is beside the point anyway. Protest and activism have brought about a great number of improvements in our collective situation. They hastened the withdrawal of troops from Vietnam; they brought about important legislative victories for blacks; they have put tremendous social and economic pressure on the South African government to end apartheid policies; they have forced the shutdown of flawed nuclear facilities, and so on. The charge of uselessness will not stick.

So, what stops me from signing up, from going to work on behalf of some cause that is especially important to me? In part, I know, that answer has to do with the sheer complexity of the offenses. I feel that a total situation—I mean a mesh made up of social and economic components, a labyrinth congruent with the deeper structures of society—begs a total response. And a total response is impossible for any individual. I could not give myself wholeheartedly (and what other kind of giving of oneself is there?) to the fight to preserve the snail darter while knowing that apartheid and plutonium dumping were in full swing elsewhere. That is, I could not *psychologically* do this. Logic, of course, protests—one cannot do everything; one should not therefore do nothing. I may not be able to solve all of the problems of the world (which is what I would, with my monstrous egotism, like to do), but I could put my voice and body on the line and do some good on behalf of some small part of the web. Others would be doing the same for other parts—perhaps some collective results could be achieved.

The logic is incontestable, but I remain inert. I must search further into myself. If what stops me from taking action is not apathy—and I believe I am not apathetic—then maybe the culprit is laziness. I squirm a bit as the beam of self-scrutiny probes at the crannies of the soul. Yes, to be sure, laziness is there in the character makeup. Or, to raise it to the dignity of a Deadly Sin: sloth. But pointing the finger there does not bring the matter to an end. For sloth is a disease of the will. And I have to own that I am only slothful in certain areas of my life. When I want or *will* something, I can be tirelessly active. So, my sloth in these political matters must point to some more or less unconscious refusal in myself. I am overtaken by sloth because for some reason I do not want to partake. Why not?

Selfishness? The belief that an expenditure of energy and thought will not net me commensurate return? That I will be giving out more than I get back? Maybe. It's not as though I haven't made those calculations, balancing off the time and caloric output required just to swell the ranks of a given demonstration by my humble numerical presence. Couldn't that energy be better spent elsewhere?

I may be getting closer. That is, I recognize the defensive logic as one I make use of when guilt afflicts me. I didn't go to take my stand at such and such a rally because I reckoned my time was better spent doing what I do. I hasten to clarify this. You see, I have to deem what I do—think, read, write—to be a part of the overall struggle. Not, perhaps, of the immediate political struggle, but the larger one, which works to ensure the survival of spirit, free inquiry, humanness—*value*—in a world where these qualities are under threat. There is no way to speak of this without sounding pompous or holier-than-thou. Trying to be serious about these ultimate things carries that risk.

At any rate, I am aware of making certain kinds of computations inwardly at times—that the expenditure involved in getting my body on the line, when set against what I could hope to accomplish with the same energy and focus doing what I am most devoted to, makes it more practical to continue my work. After all, I tell myself, I am not greedy of the time because I want to work on my stamp collection. No, I want to keep on with this business of thinking and writing.

Oh, but this too is somehow false. Or incomplete. The computation may happen, but it happens on a fairly superficial level. It does not really touch that level of will. The heavenly powers could grant me a series of bonus days with the stipulation that they not be used for reading or writing and I still would not hasten to the march. No, the deeper part of the business is tightly bound up with the volitional core, and it is there I must look for my answers.

"I give money reluctantly, and for the wrong reasons: to get the asker off my back."

I do not engage in political activity. I don't march or demonstrate. I give money reluctantly, and for the wrong reasons: to get the asker off my back. I rarely join letter-writing campaigns for Amnesty International or PEN; whenever I have written such letters I have had the feeling that I am lying to myself. I may say—I *did* say, earlier—that I want to get involved, but clearly I do not. My will refuses. And insofar as I believe in myself, my experience, I must trust that resistance; I have to try to understand it. More, I must consider whether the refusal is not in some way *positive*. What if I now reversed myself and actually upheld—proclaimed—my inactivity? Not in the manner of the Kantian categorical imperative, as a course for all to follow, but for myself: as the necessary, desirable, optimal position? I blanch to think of doing this. But if I am to stay with my original aim—to be entirely truthful—is this not what I have to do? For if I turn on this in myself, I turn on myself as well. I repudiate a whole pattern of inner evolution that I have followed (or that has been set for me).

Why, then, looking now from the positive side, do I insist on remaining politically passive?

I find two reasons, and they are, in a manner of speaking, joined at the hip. The first is that I do not ultimately believe that there is a division between the political sphere of life and the others, however we might name them. Rather, I see the various levels of perception, action, and consequence as interfused; they form, as does the psyche itself, a continuum. And it is therefore fundamentally—existentially and ontologically—false to mark out one such area—the political—as requiring us especially. Such a view, I realize, does nothing to end apartheid or put food into the mouths of the starving, and it will need further exploration. But let me first spell out the other, linked, reason.

My second belief, put most simply, is that human behavior not only functions along a continuum, with all its parts in relation, it also obeys what might be called hydraulic principles. That is, an excessive pressure at one point must result in diminution elsewhere. Energy given over to *works* is energy withdrawn from the work. Time consecrated to mailing petitions (and it's not just time, it's the energy of the devotion) is time taken from reflection on the larger condition of things. Again, that sounds terribly noble, but the side of me that ponders this dilemma has high-minded aspirations. I speak as one who feels a compulsion to write. I see my job (high-mindedly) as being the recognition and promotion of those values by which we live; or, to put it more conditionally, by which I believe we ought to live. Quite obviously, the goal of political engagement is to fight on behalf of the very same cause, but in immediate, tangible terms. I think that everyone who can should put a shoulder to the wheel and work to rectify abuses. I am trying to explain why I cannot.

I know this all sounds as though I put myself above the struggle, that I claim for myself some exalted, private agenda and urge on others the tasks that I cannot bring myself to do. I do not mean it this way. My point is that even in full awareness of the evils pressing on us from all sides (the evils that activism would address), I find that there is a place for some individuals—those so inclined or driven—to do the more obscure labor of perceiving and processing the larger current shifts, shifts embracing realms outside the political. For in truth, some people are bent in a certain way; they feel a call to filter the world's information in less immediate ways. It does not seem to me possible to do both—to pursue a clear picture of these inchoate weather patterns *and* engage in specified, directed activity. The continuum, the psyche's economy, will not allow it.

My place, then, is at the desk with my books and thoughts. I have to try to do what I can to explore ideas and tendencies. Some part of this activity necessarily impinges upon the terrain of the "political," and insofar as it does I hope that my words promote the humane values, that they exert some small influence on people who do act. But who can say how these indeterminate forces move through the world?

As I write this, I realize that there is a point I have been meaning to make, namely, that the commitment I claim for myself assumes the long view. That is, that I think of these values as continuities, and that I will for myself complete identification with their substance. This, no less than the "processing" I spoke of, calls for an absolute focus of energy and will. I mention this because in the course of thinking about this subject I have more than once looked back to the period of the late '60s. Not only because it was an era of conspicuous and directed political intensity, but also because I now see what happened to a great many members of my generation. Far too many of my peers have gone from vociferous front-line activism ("Free Huey!" and "If you're not part of the solution, you're part of the problem") to careers in the corporate mecca. They are now functionaries in the big machine that runs on only so long as it can exploit a class of have-nots. Well, there's politics, too. They had views and voices, and they gave them over when the prevailing winds shifted. They sold out. And they were able to do so because their convictions, though genuine, though vocally expressed, were shallowly rooted. Have they not undone twice over what they accomplished when they had righteousness in their hearts?

What consequences, then, can I claim for my brand of inactivity? A hard question to answer. I have not put food into one hungry person's mouth. But neither have I knowingly aided any of those who amass their profits by taking it away. (To be sure, I have consumed my share of societal goods and services—I am implicated.) I have not fought to close down any power plants. I have not overtly worked to end policies of apartheid or U.S. involvement in the political process of Central American countries. What have I done? Well, I have tried through teaching and writing to influence the perspectives of others; I have labored through the same channels to expose rhetoric and meretriciousness in writing, and to uphold examples of what is meaningful and sustaining—this in the belief that there *is* a continuum between words and mental processes and actions in the world. I have abstained from giving any comfort or solace to the bureaucrat. I have tried to live through the daily muddle with consistency and mental clarity. I have done everything to follow the promptings of the deeper muse. And all of this has left me very little for politics in the more immediate sense of the word. Probably I am *not* disqualified from urging on others the analysis of Chomsky and Herman, but the assignment happened to give me the pretext I needed for combing out these gnarled thoughts and protestations. They are not every person's thoughts. If they were, there would be little hope for the struggle to better the world. I hope that no one reads me as recommending the kind of stasis I am condemned to. I could not bear it if I somehow abetted the cause of our mutual enemy—the taker, exploiter, liar, polluter, rhetorician. . . .

Chester Brown

From *Louis Riel*

Chester Brown is a writer of graphic memoirs and other comics. He's been widely published since the 1980s, with a number of books coming out on the well-respected Canadian press Drawn & Quarterly. Although much of his early work is considered absurdist, he has since focused on historical graphic books, such as *Louis Riel*, from which comes our excerpt. He has also written about his own obsessions and about his mother's schizophrenia. One of his long-term projects is an interpretation of the Christian gospels.

Chester Brown's telling of the life of French Canadian mystic and activist Louis Riel was named one of the best comics of 2003 by *Time* magazine. The book has been Brown's biggest success; it sold out its first print run in two months. This complex full-length historical account runs counter to most of the usual perceptions of the "graphic novel" genre, as it isn't short, isn't fiction, and isn't out to appeal to a young or hip readership. Except for the graphic element, it is a fairly traditionally structured retelling of the life of a mystic. The idea for the book came, Brown said, after he read a biography of Riel; he was drawn to questions surrounding Riel's mystical visions and sanity.

In an interview with David Collier, Brown said, "Not too long before doing Riel, I had done this strip called *My Mom Was a Schizophrenic,* and that had mostly involved taking all this material that I had read in various books and whatnot and condensing it into a short space. . . . That was the most fun I'd had doing a comic book, so I kind of wanted to do something like that again . . . and doing a historical comic book made sense because the problem with the schizophrenia strip was that it didn't really have a story line. And, you know, story lines are good in comics, especially if they're longer strips. And history provides you with a story." Brown added that he didn't mind having a predetermined plot. "I am enjoying figuring out what I think is the most dramatic way of telling this set of historical facts. I'm not even thinking about, 'Boy, it'd be fun if I could have the ground swallow up Riel right now.'"

Our selection from *Louis Riel* comes late in the book, as our hero is expelled from the Canadian House of Commons for his political activities. He begins to have a series of mystical visions that are interpreted to be insanity, and is then imprisoned in a mental hospital. The dialogue in the book is conducted in both English and French, with the use of French indicated by brackets. In this way, Brown was able to print an entirely English version of the book while reminding the readers of the French identity of some of the characters. The passage of time is indicated by a series of sequential panels in which very little physically happens; Brown's use of panels works much as a prose writer's "white space."

Wanda Coleman

The Evil Eye

Known for both poetry and prose, Wanda Coleman has been honored with fellowships from the John P. Guggenheim Foundation and the National Endowment for the Arts. Her books include *A War of Eyes* (1988), *Heavy Daughter Blues* (1987), *African Sleeping Sickness* (1994), *Hand Dance* (1993), and *Bathwater Wine* (1998), for which she received the 1999 Lenore Marshall Poetry Prize—the first African American woman to receive the award. Her new books include *Ostinato Vamps* (poems, Pitt Poetry Series, 2003) and *The Riot Inside Me: Trials & Tremors* (Godine/Black Sparrow Books, 2005).

A native of Los Angeles, Coleman's father was an ex-boxer who worked at an advertising agency, while her mother was a seamstress and house-cleaner. Her first publications were poems published in a newspaper when she was thirteen. Coleman attended Valley Junior College in Van Nuys, California, and California State University at Los Angeles, and had two children by the time she was twenty. While a single parent, she worked at an array of jobs, including editorial coordinator of an arts newsletter (for the Studio Watts organization), medical secretary, journalist, proofreader, waitress, and Peace Corps/Vista recruiter. She wrote throughout this period.

Her first short story, "Watching the Sunset," appeared in *Negro Digest* in 1970, and her first chapbook of poems was published by Black Sparrow Press in 1977. Black Sparrow continued to issue Coleman's poetry in publications such as *Mad Dog Black Lady* (1979) and *Imagoes* (1983). She is known as a dynamic verbal performer.

To earn her living, Coleman has worked as a freelance journalist. This gave her the opportunity to publish essays of belief that have been collected in two volumes: *Native in a Strange Land* (1996) and *The Riot Inside Me* (2005). Her essays were described by reviewer Sandra K. Stanley as "hungry, restless, often angry, sometimes jubilant essays that she describes as love songs for Los Angeles, a 'lover with deaf ears.'" Of her nonfiction, a reviewer in *Publishers Weekly* wrote that "satire and journalism are alive and well in L.A., at least when Coleman is doing the biting and the reporting."

The piece included here was published in Coleman's first nonfiction collection, *Native in a Strange Land*. This personal essay relates an incident that took place while Coleman and her husband made a routine visit to an Oakland gas station.

Interview with Wanda Coleman, p. 239.

Love conquers all? Imagine factionalized living in a post-strife-torn city where those who marry across barriers of class, color and religion are discreetly tolerated in sophisticated settings but constantly denigrated in the streets. Imagine yourself—if you dare—in my skin, unable to go anywhere, day or night, without anticipating trouble.

* * *

We duck into a mid-Wilshire hang for appetizers, find the music enticing and ditch the buffet for a few rhythmic twirls. We're unaware that we've become an issue until we sense the laserlike stare of a young Black man dissecting us as we crisscross the dance floor.

I'm the object of his vibes. In the darkness he doesn't notice I'm at least 12 years his senior and sport a wedding ring. He's blinded by the sight of a mixed couple and huffs around us in a hostile orbit. We shine him on. Not to be ignored, he rudely thumps my man's shoulder. Huz grimaces and shakes his head. Youngblood stomps off to a dark corner, an altercation brewing.

Our fun spoiled, we make for the exit.

* * *

While Huz nurses his frozen yogurt at a Glendale mall rest stop, I step into a luggage boutique. I answer the ugly glare of the Semitic owner with an awkward nod, then examine the stock. I decide on a slender, wine-colored tote. At the register, I present my check and requisite IDs. "Credit card or cash," he admonishes.

Thrown, I leave, angrily swallowing epithets.

"Did you find anything?" Huz asks.

"Yeah, but my check was refused. I'm too Black for 'em."

"Ridiculous. Come on, I'll get it for you." He marches me back into the shop. "My wife was in here to buy a briefcase. Where is it?" Flustered, the owner reaches under the counter. "Sweetheart, is that the one?" I nod.

"We'll take it!" Authoritatively, he plucks a check from his wallet. Without a word, the owner bags the case. "I told you they'd take a check," Huz says when we get outside.

"Yeah," I smirk, "from *you.*"

* * *

We bogart through heavy traffic to the nearest pump at the Melrose self-serve station, unintentionally cutting off another car. My man jumps out, tugs the recalcitrant nozzle to the rear, wrestling to unlock the gas cap. There's a screech of rubber and scream of brakes. The incensed driver roars up on our bumper, threatening my beloved with below-the-knee amputations. Unintimidated, Huz shouts, "You dirty mutha—!"

The driver, an American of African descent, inches taller and out-weighing my man by 30 pounds, mushrooms out onto the blacktop. Succumbing to heat and gridlock-inspired tensions, Huz continues the tongue-lashing. The driver, insulted by being bad-mouthed in front of his family, silently goes into his trunk for a tire iron.

I scramble out of the car and buffalo up behind my man. The driver is surprised. That I'm Black matters and uncomfortably complicates his rage. A grudging truce ensues. The driver lowers the tire iron, and we finish getting our gas. But there are no apologies.

> "The driver is surprised. That I'm Black matters and uncomfortably complicates his rage."

* * *

I'm satisfied with my giant hot latte to go, but Huz wants a real breakfast elsewhere. At his favorite Los Feliz cafe, there are no more parking spaces on the lot. As we contemplate street parking, a white coupe pulls up behind us. I don't think my brimming latte will survive the gyrations so I climb out, aware that the White male driver is watching. I catch his eyes, don't recognize him and turn away.

While Huz parks the car, I wait at a nearby lamppost, taking sips of my latte. The white coupe swerves curbside in front of me, the electronic window lowered. I glance up. The driver's fly is unzipped and he's flapping his circumcision at me. I break into unrestrained laughter. He hits the accelerator and speeds off.

"What's so funny?" Huz asks. I tell him. He wants to kill the guy.

"It was an absurdly pathetic act," I say. He's amazed that I'm so philosophical.

* * *

Our favorite Thai eatery is packed, so we take a number, then briefly stroll the grungy Vermont Avenue business strip. We're in an exceptionally romantic mood, holding hands, sneaking a kiss. Suddenly, we're being stared down by a group of Latino men. As they pass, one turns and shouts at my back.

"Puta!"

* * *

At a Pacoima gathering, an old acquaintance greets me with a warm hello, then:

"Are you still with that Jewish fellow?"

I look at her thoughtfully, then smile.

"Yesssss."

Interview with Wanda Coleman

BECKY BRADWAY: You are perhaps best known as a poet. What can you do
    in the essay that you can't do in poetry (or vice versa)?

WANDA COLEMAN: I enjoy reading essays and being engaged in challenging
    thought, when that happens. Technically, I can do anything in poetry
    that I can do in the essay. However, when I write an essay, it is usu-
    ally because most nonliterary publications do not publish poems. Also,
    the finest essays are, themselves, often poetic in tone. Too, the essay
    is often more satisfactory in allowing a writer to express complex
    inner/outer turmoils and to engage the reader on a much more worldly
    level.

BB: How does your process differ when writing in the two forms?

WC: In the poem, I am often more interested in "structural effect," the
    chemistry of language, juxtapositions that evoke meaning, how lan-
    guage means, the subtle engagements between form and content,
    controlling the powers of poetry from alliteration to rhythm, how to
    approach oneself in new ways, one's point of view. Poetry is also
    where I play with language for the sheer fun and joy of it. In the
    essay, I am more interested in making an argument, engaging the
    reader with that argument, expressing myself well enough to con-
    vince, portray an actuality, and/or invite the reader into my percep-
    tions or ways of being.

BB: Do you feel that writing has the power to change readers—and, ulti-
    mately, society?

WC: Change can be terrible, not necessarily better. Had I been asked this
    question in the 1960s, the answer would have been undoubtedly and
    sincerely, "Yes, absolutely." However, part and parcel of the relent-
    less and increasingly complex war against Blacks has been the under-
    mining of America's fourth estate and the media as a whole (thus
    having an effect on everyone, from Bill Clinton to Willie Horton).
    You cannot make positive change through writing (or anything) if
    you do not have serious and weighty access! Overcoming the limita-
    tions of traditional access via invention of the information highway is
    what made Bill Gates a godzillionaire. Too, if and when successful,
    the change one brings about may not be the change anticipated. As a
    literary writer, no matter how excellent, I've found that if you don't
    have a PR firm, can't get your play produced, can't get an agent,
    can't get distribution, can't win the best prizes, can't get published in
    the magazines or periodicals that make careers, can't get celebrity
    sponsorship, then you can't attract the mass media, readership, or
    audience usually required to effect certain kinds of change. Largely,
    the nonalternative media has capitulated to the ungodly wealthy
    forces that profit by racism, that monitor and enforce the double
    standards that currently govern American lives, that reinforce the

biases and hatreds that are the foundation of racism—and just about every other -ism under which citizens are invisibly and tacitly oppressed. The trouble with a seemingly liberating Internet access is that there is too much of it—a glut of misinformation as well as information, without criteria or standards of excellence, or taste. So as of the end of the twentieth century, my answer to your question became: "One might change the world, if so disposed, if one is lucky, or if one can miraculously gain sufficient access, and attention other than the diabolical."

Frank Conroy

A Yo-Yo Going Down, a Mad Squirrel Coming Up

Frank Conroy published five books, including the classic memoir *Stop-Time*. *Stop-Time*, published in 1967, is one of the most respected full-length memoirs, based in part on its concise, lovely style and its metaphoric approach to events in his life. Of this book, author Stephen Bloom wrote, "Every shimmering word in *Stop-Time* seemed to detonate as Conroy, from a teenager's perspective, detailed the pain and legacy of an abusive, manic-depressive father and an absentee mother. The book was the best kind of fiction because it was numbingly true."

Conroy directed the influential Iowa Writers' Workshop at the University of Iowa for eighteen years, from 1987 until 2005, and directed the literature program at the National Endowment for the Arts from 1982 to 1987.

In addition to *Stop-Time*, Conroy wrote a collection of short stories, *Midair* (1986); a novel, *Body and Soul* (1993); a collection of essays and commentaries, *Dogs Bark, but the Caravan Rolls On: Observations Then and Now* (2002); and a travelogue, *Time and Tide: A Walk through Nantucket* (2004). His fiction and nonfiction appeared in many magazines, including the *New Yorker, Esquire, GQ, Harper's Magazine,* and *Partisan Review*. He was named a Knight of the Order of Arts and Letters by the French government.

Conroy was also an accomplished jazz pianist, winning a Grammy Award in 1986. This musical expertise wove itself throughout his prose not only in terms of subject matter, but in construction and style.

Conroy was not a prolific writer. When asked about this by interviewer Robert Birnbaum, Conroy said, "I have never thought of writing as a career. I really never have. Not even from the beginning. And not anywhere along."

Frank Conroy died of cancer on April 6, 2005, in Iowa City, Iowa, at the age of sixty-nine.

The piece we have included, a chapter from *Stop-Time*, opens with a slowly paced, detailed description of the art of yo-yoing, letting this seemingly simple practice represent far more. The piece is striking in the depth to which Conroy allows himself to fully remember and lyrically describe his subject. Conroy presents detailed dialogue from a time past; although it captures a certain beauty of childhood, it never slips into sentimentality.

The common yo-yo is crudely made, with a thick shank between two widely spaced wooden disks. The string is knotted or stapled to the shank. With such an instrument nothing can be done except the simple up-down movement. My yo-yo, on the other hand, was a perfectly balanced construction of hard wood, slightly weighted, flat, with only a sixteenth of an inch between the halves. The string was not attached to the shank, but looped over it in such a way as to allow the wooden part to

241

spin freely on its own axis. The gyroscopic effect thus created kept the yo-yo stable in all attitudes.

I started at the beginning of the book and quickly mastered the novice, intermediate, and advanced stages, practicing all day every day in the woods across the street from my house. Hour after hour of practice, never moving to the next trick until the one at hand was mastered.

The string was tied to my middle finger, just behind the nail. As I threw—with your palm up, make a fist; throw down your hand, fingers unfolding, as if you were casting grain—a short bit of string would tighten across the sensitive pad of flesh at the tip of my finger. That was the critical area. After a number of weeks I could interpret the condition of the string, the presence of any imperfections on the shank, but most importantly the exact amount of spin or inertial energy left in the yo-yo at any given moment—all from that bit of string on my fingertip. As the throwing motion became more and more natural I found I could make the yo-yo "sleep" for an astonishing length of time—fourteen or fifteen seconds—and still have enough spin left to bring it back to my hand. Gradually the basic moves became reflexes. Sleeping, twirling, swinging, and precise aim. Without thinking, without even looking, I could run through trick after trick involving various combinations of the elemental skills, switching from one to the other in a smooth continuous flow. On particularly good days I would hum a tune under my breath and do it all in time to the music.

Flicking the yo-yo expressed something. The sudden, potentially comic extension of one's arm to twice its length. The precise neatness of it, intrinsically soothing, as if relieving an inner tension too slight to be noticeable, the way a man might hitch up his pants simply to enact a reassuring gesture. It felt good. The comfortable weight in one's hand, the smooth, rapid descent down the string, ending with a barely audible snap as the yo-yo hung balanced, spinning, pregnant with force and the slave of one's fingertip. That it was vaguely masturbatory seems inescapable. I doubt that half the pubescent boys in America could have been captured by any other means, as, in the heat of the fad, half of them were. A single Loop-the-Loop might represent, in some mysterious way, the act of masturbation, but to break down the entire repertoire into the three stages of throw, trick, and return representing erection, climax, and detumescence seems immoderate.

The greatest pleasure in yo-yoing was an abstract pleasure—watching the dramatization of simple physical laws, and realizing they would never fail if a trick was done correctly. The geometric purity of it! The string wasn't just a string, it was a tool in the enactment of theorems. It was a line, an idea. And the top was an entirely different sort of idea, a gyroscope, capable of storing energy and of interacting with the line. I remember the first time I did a particularly lovely trick, one in which the sleeping yo-yo is swung from right to left while the string is interrupted by an extended index finger. Momentum carries the yo-yo in a circular path around the finger, but instead of completing the arc the yo-yo falls on the taut string between the performer's hands, where it continues to spin in an upright position. My pleasure at that moment was as much from the beauty of the experiment as from pride. Snapping apart my hands I sent the yo-yo into the air above my head, bouncing it off nothing, back into my palm.

"I practiced the yo-yo because it pleased me to do so, without the slightest application of will power."

I practiced the yo-yo because it pleased me to do so, without the slightest application of will power. It wasn't ambition that drove me, but the nature of yo-yoing. The yo-yo represented my first organized attempt to control the outside world. It fascinated me because I could see my progress in clearly defined stages, and because the intimacy of it, the almost spooky closeness I began to feel with the instrument in my hand, seemed to ensure that nothing irrelevant would interfere. I was, in the language of jazz, "up tight" with my yo-yo, and finally free, in one small area at least, of the paralyzing sloppiness of life in general.

The first significant problem arose in the attempt to do fifty consecutive Loop-the-Loops. After ten or fifteen the yo-yo invariably started to lean and the throws became less clean, resulting in loss of control. I almost skipped the whole thing because fifty seemed excessive. Ten made the point. But there it was, written out in the book. To qualify as an expert you had to do fifty, so fifty I would do.

It took me two days, and I wouldn't have spent a moment more. All those Loop-the-Loops were hard on the strings. Time after time the shank cut them and the yo-yo went sailing off into the air. It was irritating, not only because of the expense (strings were a nickel each, and fabricating your own was unsatisfactory), but because a random element had been introduced. About the only unforeseeable disaster in yo-yoing was to have your string break, and here was a trick designed to do exactly that. Twenty-five would have been enough. If you could do twenty-five clean Loop-the-Loops you could do fifty or a hundred. I supposed they were simply trying to sell strings and went back to the more interesting tricks.

The witty nonsense of Eating Spaghetti, the surprise of The Twirl, the complex neatness of Cannonball, Backwards round the World, or Halfway round the World—I could do them all, without false starts or sloppy endings. I could do every trick in the book. Perfectly.

The day was marked on the kitchen calendar (God Gave Us Bluebell Natural Bottled Gas). I got on my bike and rode into town. Pedaling along the highway I worked out with the yo-yo to break in a new string. The twins were appearing at the dime store.

I could hear the crowd before I turned the corner. Kids were coming on bikes and on foot from every corner of town, rushing down the streets like madmen. Three or four policemen were busy keeping the street clear directly in front of the store, and in a small open space around the doors some of the more adept kids were running through their tricks, showing off to the general audience or stopping to compare notes with their peers.

Standing at the edge with my yo-yo safe in my pocket, it didn't take me long to see I had them all covered. A boy in a sailor hat could do some of the harder tricks, but he missed too often to be a serious threat. I went inside.

As Ramos and Ricardo performed I watched their hands carefully, noticing little differences in style, and technique. Ricardo was a shade classier, I thought, although Ramos held an edge in the showy two-handed stuff. When they were through we went outside for the contest.

"Everybody in the alley!" Ramos shouted, his head bobbing an inch or two above the others. "Contest starting now in the alley!" A hundred excited children followed the twins into an alley beside the dime store and lined up against the wall.

"Attention all kids!" Ramos yelled, facing us from the middle of the street like a drill sergeant. "To qualify for contest you got to Rock the Cradle. You got to rock yo-yo in cradle four time. Four time! Okay? Three time no good. Okay. Everybody happy?" There were murmurs of disappointment and some of the kids stepped out of line. The rest of us closed ranks. Yo-yos flicked nervously as we waited. "Winner receive grand prize. Special Black Beauty Prize Yo-Yo with Diamonds," said Ramos, gesturing to his brother who smiled and held up the prize, turning it in the air so we could see the four stones set on each side. ("The crowd gasped . . ." I want to write. Of course they didn't. They didn't make a sound, but the impact of the diamond yo-yo was obvious.) We'd never seen anything like it. One imagined how the stones would gleam as it revolved, and how much prettier the tricks would be. The ultimate yo-yo! The only one in town! Who knew what feats were possible with such an instrument? All around me a fierce, nervous resolve was settling into the contestants, suddenly skittish as racehorses.

"Ricardo will show trick with Grand Prize Yo-Yo. Rock the Cradle four time!"

"One!" cried Ramos.

"Two!" the kids joined in.

"Three!" It was really beautiful. He did it so slowly you would have thought he had all the time in the world. I counted seconds under my breath to see how long he made it sleep.

"Four!" said the crowd.

"Thirteen," I said to myself as the yo-yo snapped back into his hand. Thirteen seconds. Excellent time for that particular trick.

"Attention all kids!" Ramos announced. "Contest start now at head of line."

The first boy did a sloppy job of gathering his string but managed to rock the cradle quickly four times.

"Okay." Ramos tapped him on the shoulder and moved to the next boy, who fumbled. "Out." Ricardo followed, doing an occasional Loop-the-Loop with the diamond yo-yo. "Out . . . out . . . okay," said Ramos as he worked down the line.

There was something about the man's inexorable advance that unnerved me. His decisions were fast, and there was no appeal. To my surprise I felt my palms begin to sweat. Closer and closer he came, his voice
growing louder, and then suddenly he was standing in front of me.
Amazed, I stared at him. It was as if he'd appeared out of thin air.

"What happen boy, you swarrow bubble gum?"

The laughter jolted me out of it. Blushing, I threw down my yo-yo
and executed a slow Rock the Cradle, counting the four passes and hesitating a moment at the end so as not to appear rushed.

"Okay." He tapped my shoulder. "Good."

I wiped my hands on my blue jeans and watched him move down the
line. "Out . . . out . . . out." He had a large mole on the back of his neck.

Seven boys qualified. Coming back, Ramos called out, "Next trick
Backward Round the World! Okay? Go!"

The first two boys missed, but the third was the kid in the sailor hat.
Glancing quickly to see that no one was behind him, he hunched up his
shoulder, threw, and just barely made the catch. There was some loose
string in his hand, but not enough to disqualify him.

Number four missed, as did number five, and it was my turn. I
stepped forward, threw the yo-yo almost straight up over my head, and
as it began to fall pulled very gently to add some speed. It zipped neatly
behind my legs and there was nothing more to do. My head turned to one
side, I stood absolutely still and watched the yo-yo come in over my
shoulder and slap into my hand. I added a Loop-the-Loop just to show
the tightness of the string.

"Did you see that?" I heard someone say.

Number seven missed, so it was between myself and the boy in the
sailor hat. His hair was bleached by the sun and combed up over his forehead in a pompadour, held from behind by the white hat. He was a year
or two older than me. Blinking his blue eyes nervously, he adjusted the
tension of his string.

"Next trick Cannonball! Cannonball! You go first this time," Ramos
said to me.

Kids had gathered in a circle around us, those in front quiet and attentive, those in back jumping up and down to get a view. "Move back
for room," Ricardo said, pushing them back. "More room, please."

I stepped into the center and paused, looking down at the ground. It
was a difficult trick. The yo-yo had to land exactly on the string and there
was a chance I'd miss the first time. I knew I wouldn't miss twice. "Can I
have one practice?"

Ramos and Ricardo consulted in their mother tongue, and then
Ramos held up his hands. "Attention all kids! Each boy have one practice
before trick."

The crowed was silent, watching me. I took a deep breath and threw,
following the fall of the yo-yo with my eyes, turning slightly, matador-
fashion, as it passed me. My finger caught the string, the yo-yo came up

and over, and missed. Without pausing I threw again. "Second time," I yelled, so there would be no misunderstanding. The circle had been too big. This time I made it small, sacrificing beauty for security. The yo-yo fell where it belonged and spun for a moment. (A moment I don't rush, my arms widespread, my eyes locked on the spinning toy. The Trick! There it is, brief and magic, right before your eyes! My hands are frozen in the middle of a deaf-and-dumb sentence, holding the whole airy, tenuous statement aloft for everyone to see.) With a quick snap I broke up the trick and made my catch.

Ramos nodded. "Okay. Very good. Now next boy."

Sailor-hat stepped forward, wiping his nose with the back of his hand. He threw once to clear the string.

"One practice," said Ramos.

He nodded.

"C'mon Bobby," someone said. "You can do it."

Bobby threw the yo-yo out to the side, made his move, and missed. "Damn," he whispered. (He said "dahyum.") The second time he got halfway through the trick before his yo-yo ran out of gas and fell impotently off the string. He picked it up and walked away, winding slowly.

> "'Second time,' I yelled, so there would be no misunderstanding. The circle had been too big. This time I made it small, sacrificing beauty for security. The yo-yo fell where it belonged and spun for a moment."

Ramos came over and held my hand in the air. "The winner!" he yelled. "Grand prize Black Beauty Diamond Yo-Yo will now be awarded."

Ricardo stood in front of me. "Take off old yo-yo." I loosened the knot and slipped it off. "Put out hand." I held out my hand and he looped the new string on my finger, just behind the nail, where the mark was. "You like Black Beauty," he said, smiling as he stepped back. "Diamond make pretty colors in the sun."

"Thank you," I said.

"Very good with yo-yo. Later we have contest for whole town. Winner go to Miami for State Championship. Maybe you win. Okay?"

"Okay." I nodded. "Thank you."

A few kids came up to look at Black Beauty. I threw it once or twice to get the feel. It seemed a bit heavier than my old one. Ramos and Ricardo were surrounded as the kids called out their favorite tricks.

"Do Pickpocket! Pickpocket!"

"Do the Double Cannonball!"

"Ramos! Ramos! Do the Turkish Army!"

Smiling, waving their hands to ward off the barrage of requests, the twins worked their way through the crowd toward the mouth of the alley. I watched them moving away and was immediately struck by a wave of fierce and irrational panic. "Wait," I yelled, pushing through after them. "Wait!"

I caught them on the street.

"No more today," Ricardo said, and then paused when he saw it was me. "Okay. The champ. What's wrong? Yo-yo no good?"

"No. It's fine."

"Good. You take care of it."

"I wanted to ask when the contest is. The one where you get to go to Miami."

"Later. After school begins." They began to move away. "We have to go home now."

"Just one more thing," I said, walking after them. "What is the hardest trick you know?"

Ricardo laughed. "Hardest trick killing flies in air."

"No, no. I mean a real trick."

They stopped and looked at me. "There is a very hard trick," Ricardo said. "I don't do it, but Ramos does. Because you won the contest he will show you. But only once, so watch carefully."

We stepped into the lobby of the Sunset Theater. Ramos cleared his string. "Watch," he said, and threw. The trick started out like a Cannonball, and then unexpectedly folded up, opened again, and as I watched breathlessly the entire complex web spun around in the air, propelled by Ramos' two hands making slow circles like a swimmer. The end was like the end of a Cannonball.

"That's beautiful," I said, genuinely awed. "What's it called?"

"The Universe."

"The Universe," I repeated.

"Because it goes around and around," said Ramos, "like the planets."

I pedaled out Los Olas Boulevard toward the beach, gliding along the empty sidewalk under the towering royal palms. At the drawbridge I disregarded a "No Bicycles" sign and zipped over at full speed. Even if the bridge-keeper had seen me I'd be gone before he got out the door. I took a right at Lotus Drive and coasted down to my cousin Lucky's house.

"Hey, Lucky!"

No answer. I pulled open the screen door and walked through the kitchen, dining room, and living room on my way to the front porch. From there I could see him out on the sea wall, spearfishing, a long gig held above his head as he walked along, his lean brown body bending slightly over the water.

"Hey, Lucky," I shouted, trotting out to him.

He didn't look up, but froze suddenly, staring down into the water. Just before I reached him he threw the gig. I knew perfectly well he hadn't seen a fish. There was a studied calmness, unlikely if he'd had a real target, and his throw was subtly overdramatized, like the movements of Olympic athletes. He was playing, which seemed perfectly natural to me, but he covered it up because he thought he was too old. Without actually thinking about it I understood, and never called him on his white lies. Lucky was always in rehearsal for great, unspecified trials ahead. I liked him.

"Shit," he said. "A mullet big as Shadow." (His dog.) Pulling the string hand over hand to retrieve the gig he peered into the water, feigning frustration. "Almost got him."

"Maybe he'll come back in."

We ambled along the sea wall.

"Two girls moved into one of Schmidt's cottages yesterday. Secretaries from up North on vacation."

"I got a yo-yo since I saw you," I said.

"Judy and Cissie. Judy's tits are so big she has to watch it going around corners. The other one has red hair down to her waist. I saw her take it down last night."

"What do you mean you saw her?"

"Just what I said." He gazed down into the water.

I waited a moment, but he would say no more. "How?" I felt a slight stiffening in my neck and my ears grew warm. I wasn't at all sure I wanted him to answer.

"You'll find out." He hefted the long gig in the air, tossing it lightly to change his grip. "Maybe."

"Look at the crab!" A small white crab was pulling at a pop bottle on the sandy bottom. "You going to hit him?"

He shook his head. "I hate those ugly shit-eaters. The only thing worse is a land crab."

"Or a snake."

"I don't mind snakes," he said.

"I won a yo-yo contest at the dime store today."

Once again he stopped, crouching, and motioned me back with his free hand. "Hold it, hold it."

"The mullet?"

After a moment he straightened up. "No. Just some seaweed. The hell with it."

We cut back across the neighbor's lawn, feeling the short tough grass between our toes. Lucky walked quickly. "The girls went up to the beach."

"How old are they?"

"Twenty or twenty-one."

"What do you call them girls for, then?" I said. "They're not girls."

"Well, whatever they are they went to the beach and that's where I'm going."

"Can you lend me a dime? I'll have enough for a banana split at Ray's."

"I guess so. Daddy gave me two bucks yesterday for cleaning his reels."

We dropped off the gig in Lucky's room, drank a glass of milk in the kitchen, and started for the beach. It was only a few blocks so I left my bike. I did a few tricks as we walked along.

"Hey. That's pretty good. Let me try." He threw a few times, trying for a Loop-the-Loop.

"I won a contest at the dime store," I said, pulling out Black Beauty. "They gave me this. You can't buy them."

We walked for a while, yo-yoing together, until I felt his hand on my arm. "There they are," he said under his breath, "coming right at us." He undid the yo-yo and gave it back to me. The two girls strolled toward us unhurriedly, white towels draped over their shoulders. "My God," Lucky said distantly, like a man talking in his sleep, "will you look at the boobs on her." I could feel him gathering himself. Nervous energy radiated like an electrical aureole around his body.

"Hi there!" he said in a totally false voice. "How's the water?"

"Hi," said Boobs. "Well, it's just great." They paused without committing themselves, as if just for a moment to catch their breaths.

"We're just going up for a swim ourselves," Lucky improvised. It occurred to me that he had the proper fatuous grown-up tone, but that he was saying everything too fast. The words leaped out of his mouth like machine-gun bullets.

"Who's your little friend?" asked Redhair.

"Oh, that's my cousin Frank," Lucky said quickly, like a tourist guide pointing out some dull local landmark. Staring at my toes I felt a mild anger whipping around in my heart. I might have been skinny, but I certainly wasn't little. I was five feet eight. "He's from up North too, and I sort of look after him."

Lucky was only two or three years older than me, but the process of physical maturation, only just begun in my case, had wreaked most of its changes in him. He was six feet tall, well muscled, and his voice was a smooth baritone. Had I been a little more aware of such things I would have realized that like almost all the Fouchet men he was exceptionally attractive to women.

"Well," said Boobs, moving away. "See you later. C'mon Cissie. I want to get this sand off me."

"Bye," said Lucky, with a little fluttering wave. "See you later, girls."

I tapped him on the arm. "So you look after me, do you?"

"Oh, what the hell," he said weakly.

"Hi there!" I mimicked the weird voice he'd used. "How's the water?"

"Do you realize," said Lucky, moving closer as if afraid of being overheard although we had the sidewalk to ourselves. "Do you realize that in a very few minutes little Miss Titties will be ever so gracefully slipping out of her teeny little bathing suit? Do you realize that her immense, glistening knockers will pop out like a pair of well-oiled basketballs? Do you realize that probably at this very moment she's dancing along to the shower with every last bit of razzamatazz flapping around in the open air?"

I threw my yo-yo nervously. That kind of talk had a strong effect on me. "I wouldn't mind dancing right along with her," I said, aware that I'd struck a good balance between the sort of wisecrack one was supposed to make, and my true feelings—that to be there with her, to hold her and have her like it because I was a man, to learn the mystery from her, to die inside her would be, in no uncertain terms, the best possible thing that could happen. Literally heaven on earth. Even the thought made my hands tremble. My dry throat swallowed nothing.

"You know why girls shouldn't drink beer on the beach?" he asked.

"No. Why?"

"They'll get sand in their Schlitz."

Laughing, we went into Ray's and ordered banana splits.

While Lucky took a workout, swimming parallel to the shore in a steady blind crawl down to the last hotel and back, I lolled in the warm sea, my legs dangling weightless in the sunny green water. I didn't believe in exercise, conscious exercise to build one's muscles. As a skinny kid, a kid so skinny total strangers would come up to me on the street and offer to buy me milkshakes, I had long ago learned to put up with my freak's body. The situation was embarrassing, ridiculous, sometimes unbearable, but I knew it couldn't be changed. Set very deeply in my mind was the idea that any program of self-betterment would be doomed from the start. To change from weakling to strongman, from C student to A student, from bad boy to good boy! I not only believed it couldn't be done, but even that it wasn't worth doing. Success would have made me another person, or an actor hiding the past. And I wouldn't succeed, I would fail. Failure was dangerous, threatening my only reliable source of strength, my pride. I was proud, and God knows why. I had no reason to be. I'd picked it up somewhere and it held me together. Better simply to live in my absurd body and not think about it.

One could always drift in the warm cloudy water, hearing the cries from the beach skipping out like stones over the soft roar of the breakers, watching the immense clouds, feeling the sun on wet hair. There was always the knowledge of one's shadow, an extension of oneself slanting down in a long dark bar, a black column sliding into the depths and into the darkness.

I spent the last few days before school in the woods, attempting to re-create the trick Ramos had shown me in the lobby of the Sunset Theater. I'd broken it down into three steps, the world, the solar system, and the galaxies, the sum of which was The Universe. The world and the solar system were within my abilities, but in the galaxies stage the yo-yo would run out of gas or the string would tangle. My strategy was to go back and practice the simple Cannonball for duration, snapping my throws out more and more evenly, trying for perfect balance so the string wouldn't touch the inner walls of the yo-yo. At the same time I speeded up the first two stages, attempting to feel The Universe not so much as three separate maneuvers but as one continuous rhythmic statement. Progress was slow but steady, and had I not been interrupted by the opening of school, I might have learned it in a week.

A sad fact about school was the prolonged separation from Tobey. I was a year ahead and had to attend the Central School in town while he finished his last term at the branch grammar school. We accepted it in numb silence, unable to rebel against the official powers we mistakenly believed to be so much stronger than ourselves. We couldn't even ride the same school bus. We started our days together though, meeting in the early morning for a few games of mumblety-peg or property before riding up to the bus stop a half-mile away.

A surprising number of kids gathered at the stop each morning, all of them younger than us. Some of the smallest we'd never even seen before, standing with their only slightly older brothers or sisters, clutching their lunch bags and watching us with big eyes. They were a pretty sad-looking lot, even by our standards—dirty, dressed in rags, hair stringy and uncombed, ankles black with caked dust. They came on foot, in twos and threes. We'd zip by them on the road, or if we were late (as they never were), we'd skid rakishly to a halt where they waited at the mailboxes, feeling like big shots as we hid our bikes in the woods. Luckily they all went to the branch school. At Central School they'd have been treated badly.

Later in the year those scruffy kids became a symbol of our separation, not because they forced us apart, but because they came to represent all the things in which each of us was involved without the other's knowledge. I began to notice after a couple of weeks, when the kids, at first so quiet, would smile when Tobey showed up, and even gather around his bike to push the button on his electric horn. Before long we were picking them up on the road, stacking them on the handlebars, the crossbars, and the fenders for the ride out to the highway, sometimes even carrying the smallest on our backs. They were too shy to open up with me (my Northern accent frightened them) but from overhearing bits here and there I learned that Tobey had become the champion of the whole Chula Vista contingent, and on more than one occasion had used his fists in the schoolyard protecting them. I was proud of him, but a bit sad, too, since he never mentioned what was going on, and even changed the subject when I brought it up. There was a trace of envy in my heart, probably because my own position at school was anonymous. But I was more proud of him than anything else.

My bus came first. I hoped for an accident or a flat tire, but it always appeared at the dip in the road down by the dump, yellow and inexorable, engine wheezing as it approached. My secondary fantasy, once the bus came into view, was that it would drive right past without stopping. But that never happened either.

The driver, Mrs. Moon, was short, fat, and hyperthyroid, with kinky red hair and blotched skin. She stared straight ahead every morning, her face set in an unchanging grimace of irritation. She never even looked at me, just pulled the door shut with a beefy arm and threw in the gears. As her short legs jabbed at the pedals her skirt rose under the large white dinner napkin, fresh each morning, that lay on her knees. She drove a steady thirty-five miles an hour over potholes, dead snakes, and fallen vegetation, never veering, never wavering, as if the bus represented an irresistible force separate from the petty realities of life.

I didn't like school. The kids were polite but distant. Well-dressed, healthy, athletic, always with a dollar in their pockets, they were town kids who'd known one another all their lives. I didn't fit. My Northern accent and relatively large vocabulary (from reading) must have seemed suspiciously classy, and yet I dressed like a redneck and lived in redneck territory. They didn't know what to make of me, and since there was nothing particularly attractive about me they had no great desire to find out. I'd be gone soon anyway, they assumed, back to wherever I'd come from. They were good kids, though, and had circumstances been more favorable, or had I been less shy, I'm sure I would have made friends with some of them. Although as Florida kids they were preoccupied with things physical—swimming, diving, basketball, and baseball went on all year round—they never teased me about being so thin. Instead they emanated a kind of mild concern, as if I were suffering from an illness for which I couldn't be held responsible.

The class hours merged into a day of boredom. The books were dull, mechanical texts from which the teachers rarely strayed. Voices droned at an impossibly slow pace, ideas emerged sluggishly, words and phrases repeated over and over became incomprehensible—my mind could find nothing to attach itself to. I was cast adrift, and it frightened me. One could disappear in such a state, simply cease knowing the difference between up and down, or who one was, or where one was. So I put myself to sleep and accepted the mediocre grades I'd done nothing to earn.

I liked the twenty minutes before the first bell. There was a broad-jump put in one of the athletic fields and the kids from the buses would line up for turns. I'd take a long run, kick off, and sail through the air knowing the sand would be soft at the other end. No one kept records. When you'd jumped you simply waited for the next man, marked his leap on the sand, and ran back to the end of the line. The best jump was marked by a peg or a schoolbook, but only the older kids were concerned about that. Once or twice I came within a foot of it.

Lunch hour I often went to the Y.M.C.A. and sat at a favorite table near the window where I could watch the other kids or the cars going by outside as I ate my sandwich. If I had a quarter I'd buy a deviled egg on white and an orange soda—a combination my body craved so strongly my hands would tremble uncontrollably as I unwrapped the cellophane. Most often I had a sandwich from home.

> "I am intensely hungry, and yet the hunger is held down, deep in my body, a smothered force that never reaches my mouth."

(I am intensely hungry, and yet the hunger is held down, deep in my body, a smothered force that never reaches my mouth. I've carried the paper bag all day. The top edge is rolled and crinkled, as soft as cloth under my fingers. The kids are laughing and yelling at ping-pong or the pinball machine. Why do I even open the bag? Every step closer to the sandwich drives the hunger deeper until my mouth is too dry to eat anything. The wax paper comes off. I already know the sandwich is completely unacceptable. There is no question. It's an imitation. It isn't real.

Eating it wouldn't nourish me. Look at the paper bag! Look at the wrapping! The whole thing is a fraud. I separate the bread. Bacon fat. Lunch meat. I am neither disgusted nor attracted. The sight has no meaning. It isn't food. I look up, vaguely uneasy. I should get up from the table and go away. There's no point in staying. I have no money, nor any way to get some before the hour is out. I should move, yet something holds me. I can't eat and I can't not eat. I stare into the paradox with catatonic rapture—a moment more, a moment more. Hunger is transcended as my mind achieves perfect balance, perfect stillness. The sandwich lies in its waxed paper. My hands lie on the table beside it. I can't move.)

Sometimes after school I'd hitchhike out to the beach and hang around the Olympic-size salt-water pool where all the kids were. I achieved a certain celebrity doing tricks on the yo-yo, and even though no one knew my name they accepted me as part of the scene. When it got dark I'd go over to Lucky's house.

"Frank, don't you want any more than that?" Gertrude asked. "You eat like a bird, child."

"Thank you, ma'm. I'm full."

"His stomach's shrunk," said Uncle Victor, unfolding the *Fort Lauderdale News* over his recently emptied plate. "Coffee. I'm late for the A.A. meeting."

"Leslie, would you clear the table, please?"

Lucky's sister began stacking dishes. I helped her carry them back to the kitchen. Leslie was a tall, good-looking girl, a swimming champion at sixteen. She smiled as I brought in a platter. "Thanks." I always blushed when she smiled at me, and the fact that I desperately wanted not to blush but to look straight in her eyes didn't make any difference.

Back at the table Lucky was talking to his father about Sneezy, his pet squirrel. "But Daddy, he's better since he was fixed. He gets better every day."

"A week more. Then we'll either put him to sleep at the vet's or let him go in the woods, whichever you prefer." Victor had a habit of not looking at his son while talking to him. It was odd—he'd look at everyone else, moving from face to face while addressing Lucky.

"He always minds me," Lucky said, betraying some emotion.

"It's unpleasant, but it has to be done. He bit the mailman and he bit George." (The Negro handyman.) "I could be sued." He pushed back his chair and took a cup of coffee from Gertrude's outstretched hand on his way to the living room. He walked with his head slightly bent, as if he were too tall for the house.

"Damn," Lucky said when we were alone.

"Don't let them gas him. Set him free in the woods in Chula Vista."

"The worst thing is I lose my cover."

"What do you mean?"

"My cover. My excuse if I ever get caught around Schmidt's cottages at night. I'd just say I was looking for Sneezy."

"Of course." I was struck with admiration at his thoroughness. "The girls."

"Damn." He drummed his fingers on the table impatiently. "I'll never think of anything as good."

"Are you going tonight?"

Lucky looked up, hesitating a moment before he answered. "Yes."

"I'll go with you."

"You might not see anything, you know. Sometimes the blinds are down."

"Leslie honey," Gertrude called from the kitchen. "You better hurry. I see your date coming down the drive."

I stood in the darkness doing stages one and two of The Universe. Black Beauty picked up stray fingers of light and sparkled dimly in the air like a dying fireworks wheel. My mind wasn't on the yo-yo. I waited, listening for Lucky on the other side of the hedge. He was due back from reconnaissance.

"Phsst!"

The trick fell apart in my hands.

"Phsst!" he called from the other side.

"Okay. I'm here," I whispered.

"The coast is clear. Come on through."

Bending down to get through the almost invisible break in the hedge I had a moment of panic. The idea of getting caught at something as shameful as peeping through windows was no laughing matter. I'd done bad things, but never anything to earn my parents' scorn. I'd been able to hold my head high and fight them openly. But if I got caught at this I'd be ashamed before my enemies.

Coming up on the other side, inhaling as I rose, the perfume of the flowers rushed into my brain. A lush aroma, thick with sweetness, thick as blood, and spiced with the clean acid of tropical greenery. My heart pounded like a drowning swimmer's as the perfume took me over, pouring into my lungs like ambrosial soup. Slightly dizzy, I took a step and bumped into Lucky.

"Sorry," I whispered, stepping back. His dark shape moved in front of me and I could see Sneezy riding his shoulder. "Chtt-chtt." The squirrel spat in the air.

"Follow me and stay in the shadows," Lucky said calmly, and moved quickly away along the hedge, his arm brushing slightly against the leaves. Sneezy ran over the back of his neck to the other shoulder, still spitting, his small body writhing with excitement.

As we got near the cottage Lucky stopped. "Walk naturally across the lawn. There's a place behind those bushes over there." He moved out over the grass and disappeared into the shadows. I followed an instant later, beads of nervous sweat collecting on my brow. The front of the cottage was dark, but Lucky had told me to expect that. The girls lived in back, in a large room with two windows. As I came up behind him I could see the lights winking through the bushes.

"There," he whispered, pointing to a small hollow in the undergrowth. I moved into position. Sneezy jumped from his shoulder to mine, startling me so severely I almost fell over. His sharp claws dug through my shirt into the skin. Wincing, I listened to Lucky.

"If you pull back this branch you get a clear view of both windows," he said, demonstrating. I looked out, my heart leaping like Ricardo's yo-yo. The blinds were down to within six inches of the sill. Every now and then something moved in the room. "Chtt-chtt," said Sneezy into my ear, his claws scrabbling for better balance on my small shoulder. "You keep him," Lucky said. "I'm going closer."

Alone, with the scent of flowers trickling down my throat like syrup, I watched the windows. Was that a pair of arms moving behind the blinds? Legs perhaps? An immense stone rolled over in my chest. Good God! Was that a thigh? Was that a bare shoulder? Lust exploded inside me, pure, hot lust bathing me like internal sunshine. I hardly noticed Lucky creeping through a bed of greenery to kneel at the corner of the window. "Chtt-chtt!" Sneezy ran up on top of my head and down again, his claws like needles. Lucky leaned forward, his hands touching the wall.

It was Judy! Crossing the room in a bathrobe, her bare thighs exposed with every stride! And there was Redhair in a bra and half-slip! Unable to believe my eyes, shaking from head to foot like an overbred French poodle, I leaned forward and spread the branches farther apart. Sweet Jesus! She was undoing the belt of the bathrobe! She was . . .

"Eeeyow!" I leaped into the air beating at Sneezy, who hung from my earlobe by his teeth, his hot breath roaring in my head. I screamed, crashing blindly through the bushes and out onto the lawn, swatting at him trying to find his jaws and simultaneously trying to hold him up. Lucky arrived out of the darkness at express-train speed, his face mirroring in that one brief instant before he passed all the stunned amazement that must have been in mine. For a moment we became the same person, like facing yourself in the glass with a new suit. Neither of us knew which body was his own. He reached out, plucked Sneezy from my ear, and in a single fluid movement tossed him ten feet through the air into the branches of a pepper tree.

Lights went on behind us. Doors slammed. Voices called. Lucky had disappeared ahead of me, and with fresh blood streaming down my neck I ran after him, trusting his path, hoping I could leap as high, my heart wild with fear.

One late afternoon in the woods everything fell into place. I'd been practicing for an hour, running through the easy tricks abstractedly, the way an expert mechanic might shuffle cards while waiting for his victims to take their seats, when I began to realize something special was happening. Never had I yo-yoed so effortlessly. Never had the tricks clicked with such mathematical precision. The yo-yo seemed to be playing itself as I stood waving my hands like a conductor before an invisible orchestra. The time was ripe for an assault on The Universe, not only the separate parts, but the whole trick as one unit.

Unbelievably, it came on the first try. I was flabbergasted. I'd been trying for weeks—for so long, in fact, I was reconciled to creeping up on it slowly, perhaps over a period of months—and suddenly victory was mine. Breathless, hoping it hadn't been a fluke, I threw again. As I watched the trick unfold, it came to me that a ghost or a spirit was controlling the yo-yo's movements, and that to be really good one had simply to give up one's desire to dominate the yo-yo and instead let the ghost take over. It was as if someone spoke to me through the yo-yo. See how easy, was the implication. Just practice till you get over your clumsiness, practice until you can yo-yo without thinking about it and then let me take over. I threw back my head and laughed. I danced a little dance on the sand and shouted out into the pine trees. I knew that in all of Fort Lauderdale and very probably in all of Florida there was not one other boy who could do what I had just done.

I knew I was best. As for what happened, I was no more than moderately disappointed when my supposedly unobtainable Black Beauty went on sale at the five-and-ten for sixty cents. I'd gone as far as one could go on the yo-yo. I'd learned tricks the demonstrators didn't know. So when the final contest arrived and I learned that after one or two extremely easy tricks the choice of champion would be based on the greatest number of consecutive Loop-the-Loops, when I learned that my skill counted for nothing in the eyes of the non-yo-yoing judges, when I found myself screwed once again as my string broke at seventy-three (eleven less than a muscle-bound idiot from the beach who couldn't do a simple Cannonball)—when, to wrap it up, all this reality was finally absorbed by my brain, the knowledge that I was without question the best yo-yo player around kept me from despair. There was no despair, only a mild confusion at the sloppiness of things, and a faint sickness at my own bewilderment.

I forgot it easily. That same night, hidden in the greenery under the window, I watched a naked girl let down her long red hair.

Dennis Covington

From *Salvation on Sand Mountain*

Dennis Covington is the author of five books, including *Lizard* (1993), which won the Delacorte Press Prize for a First Young Adult Novel, and *Salvation on Sand Mountain*, a finalist for the National Book Award in 1995 and winner of the *Boston Book Review*'s Rea Prize for the best nonfiction book of that year. He is coauthor, with his wife Vicki Covington, of the memoir *Cleaving* (1999). His articles and essays have appeared in the *New York Times, Vogue, Esquire, Redbook,* the *Georgia Review,* the *Oxford American,* and other magazines. He is professor of creative writing at Texas Tech University and served as a judge in nonfiction for the 2005 National Book Awards.

Covington, originally from Birmingham, Alabama, began his career as a freelance journalist. His nonfiction draws upon the journalist's ability to enter unfamiliar cultures and situations. *Sojourners* magazine called his prose "lyrical, compassionate, and full of the musicality that defines Southern speech and experience." Covington attributes the lyrical style in *Salvation on Sand Mountain* in part to the "cadences I heard in the snake-handling churches. The preaching is so musical and rhythmic and poetic. I think I patterned my own style after that . . . and after the language of the New Testament." Lee K. Abbott wrote in the *New York Times*: "It is a book of revelation—brilliant, dire and full of grace."

In this excerpt from *Salvation on Sand Mountain,* reporter Covington has his first experience as witness to a snake-handling ritual in the mountains of West Virginia. He's already introduced himself to the main characters and in this scene begins moving from distant viewer to near-participant in the emotional and physical experience of religious ecstasy. Along with the animated description of the church ritual, Covington also supplies historical context about the the place and people whose lives he has entered.

Jolo

By late summer I was feeling comfortable among the handlers. In fact, I was getting restless in my home church in Birmingham, where I'd occasionally want to put my hands up in the air. I didn't. But sometimes I'd tap my feet during the choir's anthem or mumble an amen or two. And I was pretty much obsessed with snake handling, though I had not, in fact, handled one myself. When Jim and Melissa and I found ourselves at a party together, we'd get off in the corner and talk about the handlers,

especially Aline McGlocklin, whose childlike beauty continued to arrest
and mystify us. She always seemed to be on the verge of ecstasy. Sometimes, she said, the Lord would move on her in the ladies room at work.
We'd never seen her take up a serpent, though, and we wondered if we
ever would. Other friends in Birmingham started to ask about the services. Some of them wanted to go. But soon the brush-arbor meetings
would be over. The nights would turn cool. It rains on Sand Mountain in
the fall, and there's fog. Without a church building of their own, the handlers would have to travel more often to Brother Carl's church in Georgia,
or to churches in East Tennessee, Kentucky, or West Virginia.

"You going up to Jolo?" Brother Carl asked me after one of the
brush-arbor meetings behind J.L.'s house. It was one of the last days of
summer, a dry, lingering heat, and the fields around us had turned an
exhausted shade of yellowish green.

I shook my head. I hadn't understood the question. The service had just ended, and I was watching Carl load snakes back into the bed of his truck.

"Me and Carolyn are going up there," Carl said.
He hoisted a serpent box onto the tailgate and then
slid it into the bed. Inside the box was a velvet-tailed
timber rattler that he and Charles McGlocklin had
both handled during the service that afternoon.

> "That's when I remembered Jolo was in West Virginia. There was a famous snake-handling church there."

"Charles and Aline are going, too," he said, "if she can get off
work." Carl lifted the tailgate and secured it while a trio of curious children from J.L.'s neighborhood tried to peer into the boxes.

"It's a ten-hour drive," he said to me, "but we like to take our time
going up. You and Jim and Melissa ought to come."

That's when I remembered Jolo was in West Virginia. There was a
famous snake-handling church there.

"I don't know," I said. "When is it?"

"Labor Day weekend. It's their twentieth annual homecoming. You'll
miss some good services if you don't go," Carl said. "They always have a
lot of serpents in Jolo." He stopped, smiled.

It had never come up between us before, but I knew what was on the
tip of his tongue: Maybe I'd take up a serpent in Jolo. It made me wonder
why he'd want me to. What would be in it for him if I did?

On the Friday of that Labor Day weekend, Jim, Melissa, and I left
Birmingham in a driving rainstorm, the spent fury of Hurricane Andrew.
It rained all the way to West Virginia, except for a spot in East Tennessee,
where the clouds lifted momentarily to reveal the high green walls of the
Appalachians. These mountains aren't as raw and angular as the Rockies,
or as mystical and remote as the Cascades. Instead, they seem mannered
and familiar, predictable in the way they roll westward in alternating
ridges and valleys. But in East Tennessee, the Appalachians converge in a

chaos of intersecting planes. There, the mountains still look as wild and formidable as they must have to the first Europeans who entered the New World—entered it only, in ways, to become lost in it.

In preparation for our trip to Jolo, I'd read David Hackett Fischer's remarkable book *Albion's Seed,* a treatise on patterns of immigration to America from the British Isles. I had it in mind that in going back up the spine of the Appalachians toward Jolo, I'd be retracing the route the snake handlers' ancestors had taken as they descended toward Alabama. I had not yet come to understand that these were my ancestors too.

Fischer says that most of the immigrants who settled the Appalachians arrived in waves from North Britain during the middle of the eighteenth century. Predominantly Protestant and poor, many of them had migrated first to Ireland, where they felt trapped between the contempt of their own church hierarchy and the hostility of Ireland's Catholic majority. But unlike some of the earlier immigrants to America, the Scotch-Irish, or Anglo-Irish, as they sometimes preferred to be called, were not fleeing religious persecution. Instead, their motives were primarily economic, a reaction to high rents, low wages, and scarcity of food. Their flight to America, though, suggested biblical themes.

"On Jordan's stormy banks I stand and cast a wishful eye," they would sing, *"to Canaan's fair and happy land where my possessions lie. I am bound for the promised land, I am bound for the promised land, oh who will come and go with me? I am bound for the promised land."*

That they survived the ocean crossing was itself a triumph, for the mortality rate during such ventures approached that of the slave trade. Like most new arrivals, the survivors faced discrimination because of their relative poverty and their odd appearance and behavior. The Scotch-Irish had a reputation for being noisy, quarrelsome, and proud. They were easy targets for ridicule in the streets of Philadelphia and the other eastern seaports where they first disembarked. The men, lean and angular, dressed in sackcloth shirts and baggy pants. They stood out among the neatly dressed Quakers in leather breeches and carefully cut doublets. The young Scotch-Irish women were equally inappropriate in their tight-waisted skirts, openly sensual by some accounts. The Quaker women wore handkerchiefs to cover their bodices.

The Scotch-Irish were encouraged by the more sedate Quakers to seek land on the western frontier, and after the coldness and clamor of the cities, the new immigrants, with names like Rutherford, Graham, Armstrong, and Bankhead, must have ached for familiar terrain, places like the Shenandoah Valley of Virginia, or the Sequatchie and Grasshopper Valleys of Tennessee: long, sheltered valleys between hills with rocky outcroppings, settings that might remind them of the starkly beautiful border regions they had left behind in southern Scotland and northern England. The climate here would be temperate, the water plentiful, and once the trees had been cleared, the land might roll beneath their feet as it had in the shadows of the Cheviot Hills. But to get to these interior valleys, the immigrants had to cross the mountains, a journey with dangers we are unable to fully appreciate now.

Fortunately, these were a people accustomed to privation and sudden violence. Fischer says their heritage as border dwellers had turned them into tight-knit warrior clans that feuded endlessly over matters of real or perceived violations of honor. In their homeland, leadership had been bestowed on those with the strength and cunning to enforce it. Other forms of authority were rejected, whether from the local landowner, the state, or the church, so that even minor theological disputes became occasions for war. A particularly bloody rebellion was waged by an anticlerical Presbyterian sect called Cameronians, after their leader, Richard Cameron. Unable to defeat the Cameronians in battle, the British authorities eventually made use of their temperaments by enlisting them in the army to fight against Roman Catholics in the Scottish Highlands.

Not surprisingly, says Fischer, the culture that arose in the Appalachian mountains resurrected the character of that life along the border between Scotland and England. The Scotch-Irish had brought few material possessions with them, but they did bring their feuds, their language, and their love of music, strong drink, and sexual adventure. They also brought their fear of outsiders and their hostility toward clerics and established religions. Their own brand of Anglicanism or Presbyterianism would have seemed peculiar in the population centers of the Atlantic seaboard, but it was appropriate for life on the frontier. They sometimes called themselves People of the New Light, to distance themselves from the formalities and rigidity of Calvinism. The established churches emphasized good works or election as the means of salvation. But the New Lights celebrated what they called "free grace" and often worshiped outdoors under the stars, a practice that would culminate in the phenomenon of Cane Ridge.

The rigors of mountain life came to suit the Scotch-Irish, and instead of coming out of the mountains into the fertile valleys, many of the new settlers stayed, eking out a subsistence from the thin soil of the highland slopes. They grew their own produce and slaughtered their own livestock. They built their own cabins and furniture. They wove their own clothes, made their own whiskey. They were poor but self-sufficient. And although most, by the beginning of the twentieth century, had been lured into the coal fields, the mill towns of the Piedmont, or the industrial cities of the Midwest, many never found their way out of the mountains, or found their way out too late to apprehend the culture that had grown up in the promised land around them. Shortly after the turn of the twentieth century, these descendants of fierce Scotch-Irish immigrants awoke from their sojourn in the mountains to face the bitter reality of an industrialized and secularized society. Their sense of purposeful labor was eroded in the mines and factories. Their formerly close-knit families fractured. And they confronted a largely urban culture that appeared to have lost its concept of the sacred. The hill people had awoken to discover that the new Eden they'd inherited was doomed—mechanized and despoiled beyond recognition—and that they were lost in the very heart of it.

All along the highways through Tennessee and southwest Virginia, the signs were everywhere: Crazy Joe's Fireworks, Jack Daniel's whiskey, drag racing, turkey shoots, and barbecue. The South they suggested was straight out of the movies—idiosyncratic, lazy, restless, and self-absorbed. And that was what Jim and Melissa and I talked about on the drive, the discrepancy between the South of the popular imagination and the one we lived and worked in every day. But once the road narrowed and entered the mountains, the signs disappeared, replaced by mine tipples, mantrips, and long lines of train cars filled with coal that steamed in the rain. The last motels and hospital were at Grundy, Virginia, a mining town on the lip of a winding river between mountains so steep and irrational, they must have blocked most of the sun most of the day. It is difficult to imagine how children can grow up in such a place without carrying narrowed horizons into the rest of their lives.

But Grundy was an oasis compared with the country between it and Jolo. Jim had taken the wheel on that stretch, and I was able to see the landscape for what it was. The topography was like a crumpled sheet of tin. And in that driving rain, at night, the road without guardrails seemed to be a metaphor for our condition. We were barreling down a rain-slick mountain after ten hours solid on the road, and the safe haven at the end of our journey was a place where strangers would be picking up rattlesnakes and drinking strychnine out of mason jars. We wondered if we'd lost our minds. Despite the fact that all three of us love danger, this was a little much. Plus, we were lost. When we finally came out of the mountains, we stopped at the first frame meeting house with a crowd. It sounded Holiness from the outside, all light and hubbub and an amplified nasal voice, but when I got out of the van to investigate, I discovered that it was simply a Friday night auction and Bingo game. I asked a table of players near the open door if they knew where I could find a snake-handling church.

"A *what?*" asked a woman in a United Mine Workers sweatshirt. The others at her table glanced up in alarm, and I got back in the van.

Farther on down the road, we found a man at a gas station who had heard of the church and could give us general directions. His name, Doyle, was stitched on his shirt pocket, and his forearm sported a tattoo of a sea monster. "Before you cross the bridge, take a right," he told us. "You'll see it up the road a ways. I wouldn't get near those snakes if I were you."

Doyle's directions were so vague that we missed the church on the first pass, but saw it doubling back, a small frame building perched on the edge of a ravine.

We parked and got out.

It was still drizzling. The door of the church was open. Yellow light poured out onto the parked cars. The sanctuary had paneled walls and ceiling fans. Gravel crunched under our feet as we passed a dark man in a late-model car. He cupped his hand to light a cigarette. Near the front door of the church we could see the rusted remains of a car that lay suspended just over the edge of the ravine in a net of kudzu and sweet gum.

Inside the church, the air smelled of camphor and damp wool. Nobody in the congregation looked back at us, and I didn't see anyone I recognized right off the bat. There was no sign yet of Charles and Aline. A few other photographers were present, though, so Jim and Melissa found seats near them and got their cameras ready. But just before I sat down, on a pew three away from the front, I saw Carl Porter at the front, far right. I caught Carl's eye, and when he smiled, his glasses glinted in the overhead lights. Carolyn wasn't beside him, so I looked around the sanctuary until I saw her near the back. She nodded and waved. Her red hair had been cut and styled, and she was wearing a high-necked dress trimmed in lace. Carolyn didn't handle often, but when she did, it was with frightful abandon. At the last homecoming at Carl's church in Georgia, the snakes had been piled up on the pulpit. Carolyn picked up the entire pile. A rattlesnake struck at her and missed, but it was not so much the close call as Carolyn's reckless passion that unnerved us. Red hair flying, speaking in tongues, she had lifted up the pile of snakes to eye level and shouted at them until her face turned crimson, and then she had dropped them back onto the pulpit with such force that Carl had to come over and straighten them up.

> "The more the snakes are taken out, the more the odds begin to work against the handlers."

Jim leaned over the back of the pew in front of me. "Looks like we missed the snakes," he whispered. He sounded disappointed. Like me, he'd become obsessed with the handlers. (On the way to Jolo, he'd talked about an art installation he wanted to do—a rusted-out car on blocks, with rattlesnakes coming out of its rotted front seat and Brother Carl preaching on the radio.) It's hard to know what to wish for in a serpent-handling church. You want to see the snakes taken out, but at the same time you don't. The more the snakes are taken out, the more the odds begin to work against the handlers. As an observer, you are in a moral quandary, responsible in an acute way for the wishes you make.

Four serpent boxes lay askew on a raised platform at the front, where a marionette of a man with thick glasses and the remains of a pompadour was flailing his arms in mid-sermon. "People today, they're hunting for an excuse," he said. "They want to look around and see what the other fellow's doing. They say, 'Well, I'm not doing this,' and 'I ain't gonna do that.'" He marched to one side of the platform in mock disgust. "Honey, I'll tell you what," he said. "You get the other fellow in your eye, and you'll both go to hell!" And then he hopped back across the platform on one foot while the congregation amened.

The preacher's name was Bob Elkins. A former mine superintendent, he was the official pastor of the church, which was called the Church of the Lord Jesus, but I would later find out that his wife, Sister Barbara Elkins, held true power. Sister Barbara was reportedly the last person still alive who had handled with George Went Hensley, the man legend said was the first to get the notion to take up a serpent, near Sale Creek, Tennessee, around 1910. At the time of our visit, Sister Barbara was seventy-six and so ill she couldn't attend the Friday night service. But she would be there on Saturday, as I would find out when I felt the sting of her reprimand.

As Brother Elkins brought his sermon to a close, Charles and Aline McGlocklin finally walked in. Brother Elkins pushed his glasses up onto his nose to get a good look at the couple, and then he continued preaching. Aline was wearing a satiny blue dress, and both she and Charles were spangled with droplets of rain. They sat next to Sister Carolyn.

When Brother Elkins had finished, Charles took to the platform with his guitar. I assumed that Brother Carl, the visiting evangelist for this year's homecoming, had invited Charles to sing and preach a little. Sermons at snake-handling churches are short but numerous. Nobody ever uses notes, preferring to let the Spirit move. Charles was a master of this kind of improvisation, but that night was his first visit to Jolo, and he seemed nervous. The West Virginia crowd was a hard-looking lot, stricter in dress and behavior than congregations farther South. Hand-printed signs on the wall behind the pulpit forbade such things as short hair on women, long hair or beards or mustaches on men, short sleeves on either sex, and gossip, talebearing, lying, backbiting, and bad language from the pulpit. The West Virginians had been in this thing a long time, and they'd been hurt. The year before, one of their members, Ray Johnson, had died after being bit by a rattlesnake during a service at the church. His son-in-law, Jeffrey Hagerman, a new member, had been bitten four times. Barbara Elkins's own daughter, Columbia, had died of snakebite at the church in 1961, and Barbara's son, Dewey Chafin—a handsome, disabled coal miner with broad shoulders and white hair—had been bitten 116 times.

Charles had been bitten only once, and that was when he saw a rattlesnake crossing the road in Alabama and picked it up to impress some fellows he worked with. "They were sinner men," Aline confided. Charles maintained that the bite didn't even hurt him. The dilemma was clear: Charles hadn't been hurt, and now he was fixing to preach to a bunch of strangers, at their own homecoming, who *had* been hurt, and hurt bad.

"The Bible says the Holy Ghost will lead you, teach you, and guide you," he said. "I didn't even have a map to show me this place." Despite his smile, he was greeted with silence. "I know we drove about five hundred miles to get here," he continued.

Still, nobody said anything. Charles strummed a chord on his guitar and looked out over the congregation as if waiting for the right words to come. He had, after all, seen angels and been taken out in the spirit for long messages from the Lord. "You know, there's a lot of church forms and a lot of church buildings, but there ain't but one church," he said, and that seemed to start the crowd warming to him. They knew what would follow. "There ain't but one God," Charles said. "One church."

Amen.

"One God, one Lord, one faith, one baptism, one father and God of all who is above all, and over all, and in you all!"

Amen. Yes, he had them.

"And it's time the people that's in the real church of the living God, the one that Jesus gave Peter the keys to the kingdom to in the sixteenth chapter of the book of Matthew, it's time that God's people let the world know God's the same yesterday, today, and forever!"

Amen. Thank God.

"Amen," he said back to them in relief. "That's already been worth the trip."

He had hit them with the Holiness precepts: one God, one spirit, the alpha and omega, unchanging. He did not say it then, but everyone understood what rightly followed: God had but one name, Jesus. For the church at Jolo, no matter how it differed otherwise from the churches in Alabama and Georgia, was a Jesus Name church. Instead of baptizing in the name of the Father, Son, and Holy Ghost, they baptized in the name of Jesus. To them, Jesus *was* the name of the Father, Son, and Holy Ghost. Trinitarians called them "Jesus Onlys." They called Trinitarians "three-God people."

Charles McGlocklin had staked his claim with the West Virginians as a Jesus Only like them, and riding their approval, he picked up his guitar again and started singing a song called "Like a Prodigal Son." He was accompanied on bass guitar by Dewey Chafin, on drums by Kirby Hollins, and on organ by Kirby's wife, Lydia Elkins Hollins, the grand-daughter of matriarch Barbara Elkins and daughter of Columbia, who had died of snakebite in this very sanctuary while she was in her early twenties. Charles strode back and forth across the platform as he sang. *"Well, I want to go home, and feast with the Father. The table is set, and they're waiting for me. . . ."*

The members of the congregation stood and swayed to the music, a gentle hill ballad that suddenly took, with Lydia Hollins's eccentric organ work, a dark and dissonant turn. Lydia, head cocked, seemed to be searching intently for an unexplored harmonic. Dewey Chafin, on bass, flicked his wrist spasmodically, just shy of the beat. The effect was gradual, an elevation. I felt myself moved in an unexpected way, as though the music were a mild intoxicant. Most of us had tambourines, including Brother Timmy McCoy, a red-haired man who worked in produce at the Kroger's in Richlands, Virginia. Brother Timmy was dressed in a ruffled yellow shirt, vest, and pointed shoes—the Liberace of snake handling, I thought. He threw his head back as he shook his tambourine. The light in the church seemed to have changed. It was softer, more liquid. Behind us, Aline lifted her hands into the air, reaching for the Spirit, like she had at the brush-arbor meetings. Her eyelids were closed, her fingers extended in a curiously splayed pattern that suggested desire in the process of being remedied. I felt gooseflesh on my arms as I watched her, and Melissa unobtrusively started taking photographs of her.

When Brother Charles finished his song and stepped down from the platform, it was clear he had been a success. He had invoked the Spirit and set the stage for Brother Carl, an old friend to the believers at the Church of the Lord Jesus. In typical fashion, Brother Carl seemed to be hanging back. Maybe it was modesty. Maybe he was just waiting on the Spirit. When he finally did take the platform, he was holding his Bible close. "This thing is good," he said. And by *thing*, he meant it all—the Bible, the serpent handling, the way of Holiness, the Holy Ghost. "It'll make you talk in the unknown tongue," he said. "My daddy used to say, if you want to see the devil run, shoot him in the back with the Holiness gun." And he held his Bible aloft. "This is it right here. With the word of God, you can put that devil to flight! That's what Jesus used to get the devil when he was fasting for forty days and nights. He used the Word!" *Amen. Thank God.* "He'll put the devil to *flight*. It'll make him put his tail between his legs and run like a scalded dog!" And he hopped and convulsed like it was him instead of the dog who'd been hit with the Holiness gun. "This thing is real!" *Amen. Thank God.*

"It takes the Spirit of God!" Brother Carl shouted. "They say this thing just started in George Hensley's day. Well, honey, I want you to know this thing's been around for years and years, when Moses built that graven serpent, and they looked upon it and lived! There's a hedge," he said, and he threw his arms out as though to describe its arc. "That hedge is Jesus!"

Amen. Thank God.

"And let me tell you, if we break that hedge, we'll get serpent bit!" He was pointing straight into the congregation now, crouched and red-faced. "You can leave this world, and honey, it don't take you long to do it!"

Amen. They knew how long it'd take.

Carl finished with a flourish. "We better know who our Saviour is!"

Oh, yes! they said. *We do!*

I was sweating and expectant, lifted on the general surge. I could tell something was about to break loose, but I couldn't predict its shape or form. I just knew that I was going to be part of it, and during the next song, "Everything's Gonna Be All Right," things started getting a little wild. Lydia Hollins was singing in a voice as raw and tortured as Janis Joplin's when flamboyant Brother Timmy, suddenly seized by the rhythm of the music, started dancing down the aisle toward the front, his tambourine going. I'd seen him in white patent leather shoes and a powder blue shirt with ruffles at the homecoming at Carl's church in May. Timmy had whirled in circles like a dervish, a rattlesnake in each hand. This time, though, he didn't head immediately for the serpent boxes. He just danced in front of the platform, stomping his feet and tossing his head in a step reminiscent of that old 1960s routine called The Pony.

"Everything's gonna be all right." Close on his heels came an older couple, Ray McAllister and his wife, Gracie, a woman in a simple pink jersey and flower-print skirt, her gray hair pinned in a bun. She seemed the least likely person in the world to pick up a rattlesnake, but in the midst of her dancing, she suddenly veered toward one of the serpent boxes. Unclasping its lid, she took out a two-and-a-half-foot-long cane-brake rattlesnake and held it up with both hands. Then she turned a slow circle with the snake outstretched, her face transfigured by something like pain or remorse.

It occurred to me then that seeing a handler in the ecstasy of an anointing is not like seeing religious ecstasy at all. The expression seems to have more to do with Eros than with God, in the same way that sex often seems to have more to do with death than with pleasure. The similarity is more than coincidence, I thought. In both sexual and religious ecstasy, the first thing that goes is self. The entrance into ecstasy is surrender. Handlers talk about *receiving* the Holy Ghost. But when the Holy Ghost is fully come upon someone like Gracie McAllister, the expression on her face reads exactly the opposite—as though someone, or something, were being violently taken away from her. The paradox of Christianity, one of many of which Jesus speaks, is that only in losing ourselves do we find ourselves, and perhaps that's why photos of the handlers so often seem to be portraits of loss.

By the time Gracie had passed the snake to her husband, Ray, a half dozen more of the faithful had joined them and had begun lifting snakes from the other boxes in no apparent order and with no apparent plan. They were shouting praise or praying out loud. Some were speaking in tongues. Things were beginning to spiral out of control. I came to the front then, banging my tambourine against my leg. I'd never been able to stay away from the center of storms. Brother Carl smiled at me. He was holding up a four-foot black timber rattler. He held it with reverence and a certain tenderness. I saw him stroke its chin. To my left, Dewey Chafin, the white-haired ex–coal miner, took up three rattlesnakes at the same time. He dropped one onto the floor in the confusion, and stooped to pick it back up. One of his thumbs was still bandaged from a copperhead bite he'd received a few weeks before. A few feet away from Dewey, young Jeffrey Hagerman, twenty-five, the son-in-law of the last member to die of snakebite, grasped a rattlesnake in either hand and hopped joyfully with them while his wide-eyed children, one in pajamas, watched from a nearby pew. *"Everything's gonna be all right."* Then the men passed the snakes among themselves. At one point, all six snakes wound up with Brother Charles, who was standing next to me. *"Everything's gonna be all right.*" With one of his massive hands, Charles held the snakes in a row by their tails, and smoothed them out with his other, as though he were straightening a rack of ties. I thought my eyes were playing tricks on me. The rattlesnakes seemed to have turned to rubber or gauze.

For twenty minutes, we continued to dance and sing, while the music ground on like some wacko, amphetamine dirge. Sister Lydia's voice was like cloth ripping. *"Everything's gonna be all right."* Sure it is, I thought. At one point Dewey Chafin gathered all six rattlesnakes together and held them up with one hand. Then Brother Carl took the rattlesnakes and put them on top of his head before distributing them back to the other men. The action was so wild and fast, I lost track of where the snakes were or who had them. I didn't care. Brother Timmy careened into me, his rattlesnake in my face. I caught a glimpse of Jim and his camera tumbling backward under Timmy's feet. Melissa was on her knees trying to get photos of the snakes from beneath. The Holy Ghost had descended like a hurricane, and we were all in danger of being swept away. But right at that moment when it seemed the frenzy couldn't restrain itself any longer, the lunatic music stopped, and everything seemed to go into slow motion. We'd reached the eye of the storm now. It was absolutely calm. The brothers and sisters continued to cradle the snakes as they prayed or spoke in tongues. Sister Lydia came from behind the electric organ and got herself a copperhead to stroke. The air seemed brighter than it had been before. Soothing. Clarifying. It was as though a thin, light oil had been poured down on us all.

I'd had this feeling before, under fire, in El Salvador. It was an adrenaline rush. I felt as though I were in an element other than air. The people around me were illuminated. Their faces were filled with light. And it seemed as though nothing could happen to any of us that would harm us, although in retrospect, of course, I knew that not to be the case. We felt invulnerable, forever alive. But then the music intruded again, slower, more stately this time, and without any other audible signal, the handlers started returning the snakes to their boxes. They actually stood in line, waiting their turn to guide the serpents back into the flat cages with "Jesus Saves" carved in the sides. After all of the serpents were safely inside, and the brothers had laid hands on Gracie McAllister to heal her troubled heart, I was seized by the desire to testify. It was an imperative. I seemed to have no control over my legs or my mouth. I stalked out in front of the congregation, and in what sounded to me like an unnaturally loud and guttural voice, announced that the Holy Ghost had led me to West Virginia to document these events in order that the gospel might be spread all over the country. I said it as though these were fighting words and I were daring anybody to disagree. I was astonished at myself afterward. Appalled is not too strong a word. At the moment, though, the words not only seemed right, but inevitable.

"This thing is real!" I told Brother Carl after the service. I was sweaty and ebullient.

"That's right," Carl said, pounding me on the back and looking sideways into my face, inquisitively, the way a physician studies a patient's eyes to see how the pupils are responding to light.

My most common nightmare is of having to go to the bathroom, but not being able to find one. So I wind up doing it in public, squatting on a busy street corner or in the center of the living room at a party, and I wake up utterly humiliated. Shame seems to drive my psychic engine. I don't know why this is so. All I know is that I am excessively calculating, especially when I appear not to be, in order to avoid being shamed. Early on, I learned to feign spontaneity. During my drinking days, I honed it to an art. But what happened that Friday night in Jolo wasn't calculated. I had experienced something genuine, and I was awed by what I had seen. I might as well have been watching people defy the law of gravity or breathe underwater. It was that startling, that inexplicable.

Jim and Melissa felt the same way. The mood in the van on the way back to our motel in Virginia was one of reckless exhilaration. Jim and I had seen similar displays of snake handling at the homecoming at Carl's church in Kingston, but not this close up. The handling Melissa had seen before had been nothing like this. She was duly impressed, although she confided that the snakes did not interest her as much as they did us. Maybe the snakes were a male thing, she suggested, although plenty of women do handle them. But what obsessed Melissa was Aline reaching for the Spirit. I'd forgotten about Aline during the chaos of the handling. Had she handled that night? No, Melissa said.

Whenever Jim and I had talked about the handling in the past, he would always suggest that there was a technique to it. Most of the time, the handlers held the snakes very lightly, right in the middle, about the place where you'd lift them up with a snake hook. The snakes seem balanced like

> "Something extraordinary had happened tonight. . . . A sort of group hypnosis, group hysteria."

that, and unable to strike. But tonight blew that theory. The handlers just grabbed them any old way they could and were doing whatever they wanted to them.

We posed all kinds of questions to one another: Why didn't anybody get bit? Maybe the loud music disorients the snakes? *Snakes don't have ears.* But they must be able to feel the vibrations. *What about all the times there wasn't any music, and everything was still?* I had been to scores of services by now. Something extraordinary had happened tonight. Jim and Melissa agreed, a sort of group hypnosis, group hysteria. "Of course, it could also have had something to do with"—and here I paused, not because I knew how Jim and Melissa would take this, but because I, too, was surprised by my thinking it—"the presence of the Holy Ghost."

Jim looked at me. "That's what I thought you'd say."

The rain stopped completely sometime during the night. The next morning started off cool and bright, but by afternoon the last of the summer heat had returned. The air stayed clear, though, as fine as glass, and that evening when we drove up to the church again for the Saturday night service, the light through the trees was low and red.

The crowd was larger that second night. There were many more members of the press there, among them a television crew from North Carolina who had shown up with their blinding lights and impeccably dressed Asian-American anchorwoman. Her suit was gray flannel, her hair perfectly in place. She was poised and articulate in front of the camera, but she didn't seem to have a clue about what was going on in the church itself.

Sister Barbara Elkins, the ailing matriarch, had shown up with a fruit jar of strychnine solution. She had mixed it herself. "She mixes it strong," Jeff Hagerman said to me. "If you get scared or get your mind off God, you start to feel it." Throughout most of the service, Sister Barb sat behind the pulpit with her handkerchief to her head. She was a large, flaccid woman in a black shift. She seemed to be in enormous pain. Her husband, Brother Bob, preached awhile, as did visiting pastors from neighboring states. When the snakes came out, the handling seemed a bit less spontaneous than it had the night before. Maybe it was the television crew's lights, maybe the presence of Sister Barb. I was at the front with the handlers, as I had been the previous night, when Brother Bob suddenly unscrewed the lid of the fruit jar on the pulpit and took a few swigs. He wiped his mouth on his sleeve and handed the jar down to Jeff Hagerman, who did the same. After drinking from the jar, Jeff shook his head and then started whirling with his arms outstretched, faster and faster, while he clicked his heels on the hard wooden floor. *Bless him!* someone said. *Give him victory!* said someone else. The music mounted higher. Jeff threw back his head and howled like an animal in heat. Then he careened out of his whirling dance and staggered to a nearby pew. He was smiling. He was fine, just dizzy, and the congregation erupted in amens and thank Gods.

Sister Barb stood on unsteady feet, and Brother Bob handed her the microphone. She started at one end of the platform and worked her way down. She was wincing in pain, but there was something she wanted to make clear. She'd had it with outsiders in the midst of the handlers, and she had a few words to say about the subject: "These reporters need to stay back. This up here is for the saints of God. And it's not a show. It's for people that worship God." She emphasized each word with a flick of her handkerchief. "We're not a hateful people, we're not haughty people, but these reporters, if they want to make their money, can make it back there and not up here where they endanger people's lives."

Sister Barbara walked back behind the pulpit, occasionally touching her handkerchief to her temple. Brother Timmy and his wife gave her an amen, but most of the other handlers were silent. I felt my own face flush as I realized she was talking most particularly about me.

"I've been in this little better than fifty years," she said. "I've been bit about sixteen times. It was the making of me. But I know you go down in the jaws of death. Just about all of us here that handle serpents has come to that point." She leaned into the pulpit for support. "I hope I make it. I hope we're saved." It was not rhetorical. She seemed to understand her time was short, and that she and the other handlers had better have chosen the right way. "There's more to it than handling serpents, anyhow," she said. "They come to get pictures of serpents, but you know there's more to it."

I knew that full well, but the idea seemed fresh to her. It seemed to rouse her. She brought herself up to full height and stepped back from the pulpit. "I know *my* blessing was handling serpents," she said with dignity. "Handling fire. But they was other things that went with it."

Yes there was. Amen.

"God don't play games," she said.

No, he don't.

"And if he sent me to you, I don't care what was wrong with you, you'll be healed."

Thank God.

"I just love God's people," she said. "I'm glad some of my children turned out. I noticed one of my grandsons by marriage, he had enough respect; he wanted the pictures for his own use and he stayed back."

Yes, he did.

"You know you can dishonor God."

Amen. You sure can.

She was looking straight at me, but I held her gaze. Her eyes were flat, reptilian.

For most of the rest of the service, I stayed behind an imaginary line with the other journalists. When I stepped outside later for some fresh air, I could see the mountains clearly, great black silhouettes against the sharp-edged sky. The sight of them stirred something like homesickness in me. But if it was homesickness, it was for a place I'd never been. Brother Carl had followed me out. He hugged me and said, "I knew she was talking about you. I should have come to your defense. I'm sorry."

I assured him it was all right, that I understood. Besides, my mind was somewhere else by then. The rain had moved on through the valley we were in, and the moon was visible through some high, gauzy clouds. Carl went back inside the church. As I stood in the dark outside, listening to the cicadas and the tambourines, I wondered about those border dwellers who had sailed for the promised land two hundred years before, in search of a new Eden. I thought about them finding their way through these mountains, the People of the New Light. I wondered whether they'd crossed the mountains around here somewhere, or farther south at the Cumberland Gap or Saluda Gap, or even farther still, at the great bend in the Tennessee River near Chattanooga, where the states of Alabama, Tennessee, and Georgia meet, and the last great plateau of the Appalachians, Sand Mountain, begins its dead aim straight for the furnaces of Birmingham.

When I finally went back inside the church, my mind was still lingering on the mountains and the clouds that nearly hid the moon, but when I saw what was happening at the front of the sanctuary, my heart nearly turned in my chest. Aline McGlocklin had left her seat in the middle of the congregation and was standing near the front, exactly as she had stood under the brush arbor on Sand Mountain. Her hands were raised, her face upturned. Her lower jaw was trembling, and I imagined the sound before I heard it: "Akiii, akiii, akiii. . . ." In front of Aline stood her husband Charles, with the four-foot black timber rattlesnake outstretched in his hands. He was getting ready to hand it to her.

The rattlesnake was so big Charles could hardly get a hand around it. He would later tell me that the Lord spoke to him in that moment and asked him, "Who do you love more, me or your wife?" Charles said the answer was God, and so he decided to go ahead and give her the snake. It was a moment that suggested that most ancient of stories—a garden, a serpent, a man and his wife. But now the story seemed oddly reversed, as though by giving his wife the serpent, the man could restore the communion with God that had been broken. Aline's hands, which had been stretched upward, now suddenly turned to receive. But as Charles began to hand the rattlesnake to her, it rolled. He steadied it. It rolled again, doing a full turn in his hands, as though it were on a lathe. Charles stepped back and handed the serpent to Carl Porter, who prayed over it aloud before he stepped forward and lay it into Aline's hands. Her face changed. It seemed to open out. The sound that she made did not resemble human speech. *Have your way, Lord,* someone said as Aline trembled in ecstasy with the big black rattlesnake outstretched in her hands. I was only an observer, but I felt I had been drawn into something so painfully intimate that I was morally obliged to look away even as I stared the harder. I wanted to step in and rescue Aline, but from what? Wasn't it the same thing that was happening to me?

Guy Delisle

From *Pyongyang*

Born in Quebec City in 1966, Guy Delisle, a French cartoonist and author, spent over ten years working in animation before proceeding to graphic novels and memoir. After earning a BA in animation at Sheridan College in Toronto, Delisle went on to work for the animation studios CinéGroupe in Montreal. He was later employed by studios in Canada, Germany, France, China, and North Korea. In fact, it was Delisle's newly taken job as an overseer for a French animation company that took him overseas and introduced him to a corner of Asia few foreigners ever get to see: Pyongyang, the capital of North Korea.

His experiences there are documented in *Pyongyang: A Journey in North Korea* (2005). A reviewer in the *Village Voice* observed that of all the recently published books on the politics and policy of North Korea, "[Delisle's] is the one you'll actually read." The memoir offers a visual peek into the city that other books simply cannot do; because Delisle was working as a cartoonist in their country, his movements were less restricted than those of the few traditional journalists who managed to get into the secretive nation. "Nobody (even me) knew when I was there that I would make a book about my journey," explained Delisle, whose book has already been translated into Korean. "[It was] only when I came back that I decided to do it."

He recently expressed desires to venture to South Korea or to make the most of his recent residence in Burma, but when asked whether or not he saw fit to return to North Korea, he simply stated, "I don't think I'd be welcome there anymore."

Pyongyang's traditional structure begins with Delisle's arrival in the city and ends with his departure. While it is a memoir (because it talks about a previous period of his life, when he was a cartoonist), it also functions as a work of literary journalism or place writing. The section we've included comes early in the book, as the author takes in his new workplace. While both the narrative and drawings contain wry jokes, Delisle's depiction creates an increasing sense of oppression. The straightforward account presented in the narration is belied by the drawings, which are often top-heavy and shadowed—altogether creating a tone of paranoia.

PYONGYANG: PHANTOM CITY IN A HERMIT NATION.

THE FEW DISMAL PICTURES YOU SEE IN THE WEST HAD ACTUALLY LED ME TO EXPECT WORSE.

TRAMWAYS, CARS, BUSES, TRUCKS... IT TURNS OUT THE STREETS AREN'T DESERTED AFTER ALL.

EVERYTHING IS VERY CLEAN. TOO CLEAN, IN FACT.

NO ONE LINGERS IN THE STREETS. EVERYONE HAS SOMEWHERE TO BE, SOMETHING TO DO.

NO LOITERING, NO OLD FOLKS CHATTING. TOTAL STERILITY.

IN EVERY ROOM, ON EVERY FLOOR, IN EVERY BUILDING THROUGHOUT NORTH KOREA, PORTRAITS OF PAPA KIM AND HIS SON HANG SIDE BY SIDE ON ONE WALL.

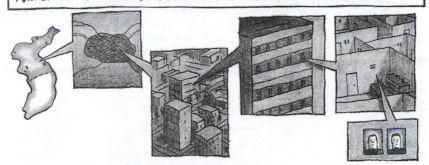

EXCEPT IN THE SHITTERS, OF COURSE.

AND SINCE "KIM IL SUNG IS KIM JONG-IL AND KIM JONG-IL IS KIM IL-SUNG", THEY'RE MADE TO LOOK ALIKE.

KIM SENIOR'S GRAY HAIR AND DEFORMING NECK TUMOR ARE GONE.

AS ARE KIM JUNIOR'S GLASSES AND EXCESS WEIGHT.

SAME SIZE, SAME AGE, SAME SUIT.

THAT WAY NOTHING EVER CHANGES — IT'S ALWAYS THE SAME HEAD AT THE HELM.

THE WORLD'S ONLY COMMUNIST DYNASTY.

HUH.

MY COFFEE BREAKS LEAD TO A FEW MORE OBSERVATIONS.

THE PORTRAITS, WHICH ARE HUNG HIGH ON THE WALLS, HAVE A WIDER EDGE ABOVE THAN BELOW.

THE ANGLE CUTS OUT ANY REFLECTIONS THAT COULD PREVENT YOU FROM CONTEMPLATING THE SUN OF THE 21st CENTURY AND HIS VENERABLE FATHER. IT ALSO INTENSIFIES THE GAZE IN THIS FACE-TO-FACE ENCOUNTER.

THERE'S A DETAIL ORWELL WOULD HAVE LIKED.

BOTH WEAR ONE OF THE OFFICIAL BADGES THAT INVARIABLY DEPICT KIM JUNIOR OR KIM SENIOR. YOU CAN'T TELL FROM THE PORTRAITS, BUT IT'S TEMPTING TO THINK THEY'RE WEARING EACH OTHER'S IMAGES, CREATING THE KIND OF SHORT CIRCUIT ANIMATORS LOVE...

SCENE (117): When the character pulls on the ribbon, keep it tight as the bow unravels.

Or else he looks like he's holding a snake and playing with it.

MISTER GUY.

Hmpf.

AFTER ASKING TWO DAYS AGO, I'M BEING TAKEN TO VISIT ONE OF THE PRIDES OF THE NATION...

THE PYONG-YANG SUBWAY.

BURIED 90 METERS UNDERGROUND, THE PYONGYANG SUBWAY CAN DOUBLE AS A BOMB SHELTER IN CASE OF NUCLEAR ATTACK. WHAT BETTER WAY TO CULTIVATE A CONSTANT SENSE OF THREAT?

THE

LONG

WAY

DOWN.

A REGULAR

MARBLE FLOORS, CHANDELIERS, SCULPTED COLUMNS. IT'S A SUBTERRANEAN PALACE TO THE GLORY OF PUBLIC TRANSIT.

EVERYWHERE, GARISH MURALS TRANSFIGURE A REALITY THAT JUST SEEMS DRAB TO ME.

IN A CITY WITHOUT ENOUGH ELECTRICITY TO POWER ITS TRAFFIC LIGHTS, THE SUBWAY TUNNELS ARE LIT UP LIKE LAS VEGAS!

STRANGE...VERRRY STRANGE...

THE TOUR ENDS AT THE NEXT STATION. OUR DRIVER PICKS US UP AT THE EXIT.

I'VE NEVER MET ANYONE WHO'S SEEN MORE THAN TWO STATIONS.

Annie Dillard

Total Eclipse

Annie Dillard's first book of nonfiction, *A Pilgrim at Tinker Creek* (1974), won the Pulitzer Prize. Since then, she has gone on to write several volumes of nonfiction: *Holy the Firm* (1977), *Teaching a Stone to Talk* (1982), *An American Childhood* (1987), and *The Writing Life* (1989, revised 1998). Her novels are *The Living* (1992), *For the Time Being* (1999), and *The Maytrees* (her most recent book, published in 2007); she also edited the anthology *Modern American Memoirs* (1996). She spends at least part of her time in a small cabin in the Virginia mountains.

Of her work, Mary Cantwell said, "What Dillard does is this: First she guides the reader through the microscope that is her eyes, enlarging frogs, bugs, spiders, water snakes—whatever flies, swims or crawls—to monstrous proportions. Then she aims that microscope, only by now it is a telescope, at the heavens. To perceive God's creatures is, in a sense, to perceive God. Except that, in the end, God defeats her (and all of us), being unknowable. Dillard speaks often of the 'created' world. To her, woods and fields, streams and oceans and creepy-crawlies are no happenstance."

Dillard grew up in Pittsburgh, the daughter of affluent, nonconformist parents. During her childhood, she developed an interest in religion and mysticism, reading widely and contemplating philosophical questions. After graduating from high school, Dillard attended Hollins College, where she studied literature and creative writing. Upon graduation, she painted and wrote. After a near-fatal bout of pneumonia in 1971, she spent four seasons living near Tinker Creek, a suburban area surrounded by forests, streams, mountains, and animals. When she wasn't in the library, she spent her time outdoors, walking, camping, and observing. After living there for about a year, Dillard began writing about her experiences near the creek; the resulting book, *A Pilgrim at Tinker Creek*, brought her the Pulitzer Prize at the age of twenty-nine.

Of her writing, Dillard recently said, "All my books started out as extravagant and ended up pure and plain. This one [a novel, *The Maytrees*] was over 1,200 pages at one point, and I just pared it back—boy did I—by the syllable. I lost some of my best metaphors, but they had to go. It's a little silly to finally learn how to write at this age. But I long ago realized I was secretly sincere."

Choosing a single Dillard essay to include was difficult, but our selection finally came down to her classic "Total Eclipse." In this lyric piece, the incident of the eclipse, its coming and going, presents Dillard a chance to enter philosophical and poetic places, bringing all together into unity.

I

It had been like dying, that sliding down the mountain pass. It had been like the death of someone, irrational, that sliding down the mountain pass and into the region of dread. It was like slipping into fever, or falling down that hole in sleep from which you wake yourself whimpering. We had crossed the mountains that day, and now we were in a strange place—a hotel in central Washington, in a town near Yakima. The eclipse we had traveled here to see would occur early the next morning.

I lay in bed. My husband, Gary, was reading beside me. I lay in bed and looked at the painting on the hotel room wall. It was a print of a detailed and lifelike painting of a smiling clown's head, made out of vegetables. It was a painting of the sort which you do not intend to look at, and which, alas, you never forget. Some tasteless fate presses it upon you; it becomes part of the complex interior junk you carry with you wherever you go. Two years have passed since the total eclipse of which I write. During those years I have forgotten, I assume, a great many things I wanted to remember—but I have not forgotten that clown painting or its lunatic setting in the old hotel.

The clown was bald. Actually, he wore a clown's tight rubber wig, painted white; this stretched over the top of his skull, which was a cabbage. His hair was bunches of baby carrots. Inset in his white clown makeup, and in his cabbage skull, were his small and laughing human eyes. The clown's glance was like the glance of Rembrandt in some of the self-portraits: lively, knowing, deep, and loving. The crinkled shadows around his eyes were string beans. His eyebrows were parsley. Each of his ears was a broad bean. His thin, joyful lips were red chili peppers; between his lips were wet rows of human teeth and a suggestion of a real tongue. The clown print was framed in gilt and glassed.

> "I watched the landscape innocently, like a fool, like a diver in the rapture of the deep who plays on the bottom while his air runs out."

To put ourselves in the path of the total eclipse, that day we had driven five hours inland from the Washington coast, where we lived. When we tried to cross the Cascades range, an avalanche had blocked the pass.

A slope's worth of snow blocked the road; traffic backed up. Had the avalanche buried any cars that morning? We could not learn. This highway was the only winter road over the mountains. We waited as highway crews bulldozed a passage through the avalanche. With two-by-fours and walls of plyboard, they erected a one-way, roofed tunnel through the avalanche. We drove through the avalanche tunnel, crossed the pass, and descended several thousand feet into central Washington and the broad Yakima valley, about which we knew only that it was orchard country. As we lost altitude, the snows disappeared; our ears popped; the trees changed, and in the trees were strange birds. I watched the landscape innocently, like a fool, like a diver in the rapture of the deep who plays on the bottom while his air runs out.

The hotel lobby was a dark, derelict room, narrow as a corridor, and seemingly without air. We waited on a couch while the manager vanished upstairs to do something unknown to our room. Beside us on an overstuffed chair, absolutely motionless, was a platinum-blond woman in her forties wearing a black silk dress and a strand of pearls. Her long legs were crossed; she supported her head on her fist. At the dim far end of the room, their backs toward us, sat six bald old men in their shirtsleeves, around a loud television. Two of them seemed asleep. They were drunks. "Number six!" cried the man on television, "Number six!"

On the broad lobby desk, lighted and bubbling, was a ten-gallon aquarium containing one large fish; the fish tilted up and down in its water. Against the long opposite wall sang a live canary in its cage. Beneath the cage, among spilled millet seeds on the carpet, were a decorated child's sand bucket and matching sand shovel.

Now the alarm was set for six. I lay awake remembering an article I had read downstairs in the lobby, in an engineering magazine. The article was about gold mining.

In South Africa, in India, and in South Dakota, the gold mines extend so deeply into the earth's crust that they are hot. The rock walls burn the miners' hands. The companies have to air-condition the mines; if the air conditioners break, the miners die. The elevators in the mine shafts run very slowly, down, and up, so the miners' ears will not pop in their skulls. When the miners return to the surface, their faces are deathly pale.

Early the next morning we checked out. It was February 26, 1979, a Monday morning. We would drive out of town, find a hilltop, watch the eclipse, and then drive back over the mountains and home to the coast. How familiar things are here; how adept we are; how smoothly and professionally we check out! I had forgotten the clown's smiling head and the hotel lobby as if they had never existed. Gary put the car in gear and off we went, as off we have gone to a hundred other adventures.

It was before dawn when we found a highway out of town and drove into the unfamiliar countryside. By the growing light we could see a band of cirrostratus clouds in the sky. Later the rising sun would clear these clouds before the eclipse began. We drove at random until we came to a range of unfenced hills. We pulled off the highway, bundled up, and climbed one of these hills.

II

The hill was five hundred feet high. Long winter-killed grass covered it, as high as our knees. We climbed and rested, sweating in the cold; we passed clumps of bundled people on the hillside who were setting up telescopes and fiddling with cameras. The top of the hill stuck up in the middle of the sky. We tightened our scarves and looked around.

East of us rose another hill like ours. Between the hills, far below, was the highway which threaded south into the valley. This was the Yakima valley; I had never seen it before. It is justly famous for its beauty, like every planted valley. It extended south into the horizon, a distant dream of a valley, a Shangri-la. All its hundreds of low, golden slopes bore orchards. Among the orchards were towns, and roads, and plowed and fallow fields. Through the valley wandered a thin, shining river; from the river extended fine, frozen irrigation ditches. Distance blurred and blued the sight, so that the whole valley looked like a thickness or sediment at the bottom of the sky. Directly behind us was more sky, and empty lowlands blued by distance, and Mount Adams. Mount Adams was an enormous, snow-covered volcanic cone rising flat, like so much scenery.

Now the sun was up. We could not see it; but the sky behind the band of clouds was yellow, and, far down the valley, some hillside orchards had lighted up. More people were parking near the highway and climbing the hills. It was the West. All of us rugged individualists were wearing knit caps and blue nylon parkas. People were climbing the nearby hills and setting up shop in clumps among the dead grasses. It looked as though we had all gathered on hilltops to pray for the world on its last day. It looked as though we had all crawled out of spaceships and were preparing to assault the valley below. It looked as though we were scattered on hilltops at dawn to sacrifice virgins, make rain, set stone stelae in a ring. There was no place out of the wind. The straw grasses banged our legs.

Up in the sky where we stood the air was lusterless yellow. To the west the sky was blue. Now the sun cleared the clouds. We cast rough shadows on the blowing grass; freezing, we waved our arms. Near the sun, the sky was bright and colorless. There was nothing to see.

It began with no ado. It was odd that such a well-advertised public event should have no starting gun, no overture, no introductory speaker. I should have known right then that I was out of my depth. Without pause or preamble, silent as orbits, a piece of the sun went away. We looked at it through welders' goggles. A piece of the sun was missing; in its place we saw empty sky.

I had seen a partial eclipse in 1970. A partial eclipse is very interesting. It bears almost no relation to a total eclipse. Seeing a partial eclipse bears the same relation to seeing a total eclipse as kissing a man does to marrying him, or as flying in an airplane does to falling out of an airplane. Although the one experience precedes the other, it in no way prepares you for it. During a partial eclipse the sky does not darken—not even when 94 percent of the sun is hidden. Nor does the sun, seen colorless through protective devices, seem terribly strange. We have all seen a sliver of light in the sky; we have all seen the crescent moon by day. However, during a partial eclipse the air does indeed get cold, precisely as if someone were standing between you and the fire. And blackbirds do fly back to their roosts. I had seen a partial eclipse before, and here was another.

What you see in an eclipse is entirely different from what you know. It is especially different for those of us whose grasp of astronomy is so frail that, given a flashlight, a grapefruit, two oranges, and fifteen years, we still could not figure out which way to set the clocks for Daylight Saving Time. Usually it is a bit of a trick to keep your knowledge from blinding you. But during an eclipse it is easy. What you see is much more convincing than any wild-eyed theory you may know.

You may read that the moon has something to do with eclipses. I have never seen the moon yet. You do not see the moon. So near the sun, it is as completely invisible as the stars are by day. What you see before your eyes is the sun going through phases. It gets narrower and narrower, as the waning moon does, and, like the ordinary moon, it travels alone in the simple sky. The sky is of course background. It does not appear to eat the sun; it is far behind the sun. The sun simply shaves away; gradually, you see less sun and more sky.

The sky's blue was deepening, but there was no darkness. The sun was a wide crescent, like a segment of tangerine. The wind freshened and blew steadily over the hill. The eastern hill across the highway grew dusky and sharp. The towns and orchards in the valley to the south were dissolving into the blue light. Only the thin river held a trickle of sun.

Now the sky to the west deepened to indigo, a color never seen. A dark sky usually loses color. This was a saturated, deep indigo, up in the air. Stuck up into that unworldly sky was the cone of Mount Adams, and the alpenglow was upon it. The alpenglow is that red light of sunset which holds out on snowy mountaintops long after the valleys and table-lands are dimmed. "Look at Mount Adams," I said, and that was the last sane moment I remember.

I turned back to the sun. It was going. The sun was going, and the world was wrong. The grasses were wrong; they were platinum. Their every detail of stem, head, and blade shone lightless and artificially distinct as an art photographer's platinum print. This color has never been seen on earth. The hues were metallic; their finish was matte. The hillside was a nineteenth-century tinted photograph from which the tints had faded. All the people you see in the photograph, distinct and detailed as their faces look, are now dead. The sky was navy blue. My hands were silver. All the distant hills' grasses were finespun metal which the wind laid down. I was watching a faded color print of a movie filmed in the Middle Ages; I was standing in it, by some mistake. I was standing in a movie of hillside grasses filmed in the Middle Ages. I missed my own century, the people I knew, and the real light of day.

I looked at Gary. He was in the film. Everything was lost. He was a platinum print, a dead artist's version of life. I saw on his skull the darkness of night mixed with the colors of day. My mind was going out; my eyes were receding the way galaxies recede to the rim of space. Gary was light-years away, gesturing inside a circle of darkness, down the wrong end of a telescope. He smiled as if he saw me; the stringy crinkles around his eyes moved. The sight of him, familiar and wrong, was something I was remembering from centuries hence, from the other side of death: yes, *that* is the way he used to look, when we were living. When it was our generation's turn to be alive. I could not hear him; the wind was too loud. Behind him the sun was going. We had all started down a chute of time. At first it was pleasant; now there was no stopping it. Gary was chuting away across space, moving and talking and catching my eye, chuting down the long corridor of separation. The skin on his face moved like thin bronze plating that would peel.

The grass at our feet was wild barley. It was the wild einkorn wheat which grew on the hilly flanks of the Zagros Mountains, above the Euphrates valley, above the valley of the river we called *River*. We harvested the grass with stone sickles, I remember. We found the grasses on the hillsides; we built our shelter beside them and cut them down. That is how he used to look then, that one, moving and living and catching my eye, with the sky so dark behind him, and the wind blowing. God save our life.

From all the hills came screams. A piece of sky beside the crescent sun was detaching. It was a loosened circle of evening sky, suddenly lighted from the back. It was an abrupt black body out of nowhere; it was a flat disk; it was almost over the sun. That is when there were screams. At once this disk of sky slid over the sun like a lid. The sky snapped over the sun like a lens cover. The hatch in the brain slammed. Abruptly it was dark night, on the land and in the sky. In the night sky was a tiny ring of light. The hole where the sun belongs is very small. A thin ring of light marked its place. There was no sound. The eyes dried, the arteries drained, the lungs hushed. There was no world. We were the world's dead people rotating and orbiting around and around, embedded in the planet's crust, while the earth rolled down. Our minds were light-years distant, forgetful of almost everything. Only an extraordinary act of will could recall to us our former, living selves and our contexts in matter and time. We had, it seems, loved the planet and loved our lives, but could no longer remember the way of them. We got the light wrong. In the sky was something that should not be there. In the black sky was a ring of light. It was a thin ring, an old, thin silver wedding band, an old, worn ring. It was an old wedding band in the sky, or a morsel of bone. There were stars. It was all over.

III

It is now that the temptation is strongest to leave these regions. We have seen enough; let's go. Why burn our hands any more than we have to?

But two years have passed; the price of gold has risen. I return to the same buried alluvial beds and pick through the strata again.

I saw, early in the morning, the sun diminish against a backdrop of sky. I saw a circular piece of that sky appear, suddenly detached, blackened, and backlighted; from nowhere it came and overlapped the sun. It did not look like the moon. It was enormous and black. If I had not read that it was the moon, I could have seen the sight a hundred times and never thought of the moon once. (If, however, I had not read that it was the moon—if, like most of the world's people throughout time, I had simply glanced up and seen this thing—then I doubtless would not have speculated much, but would have, like Emperor Louis of Bavaria in 840, simply died of fright on the spot.) It did not look like a dragon, although it looked more like a dragon than the moon. It looked like a lens cover, or the lid of a pot. It materialized out of thin air—black, and flat, and sliding, outlined in flame.

Seeing this black body was like seeing a mushroom cloud. The heart screeched. The meaning of the sight overwhelmed its fascination. It obliterated meaning itself. If you were to glance out one day and see a row of mushroom clouds rising on the horizon, you would know at once that what you were seeing, remarkable as it was, was intrinsically not worth remarking. No use running to tell anyone. Significant as it was, it did not matter a whit. For what is significance? It is significance for people. No people, no significance. This is all I have to tell you.

In the deeps are the violence and terror of which psychology has warned us. But if you ride these monsters deeper down, if you drop with them farther over the world's rim, you find what our sciences cannot locate or name, the substrate, the ocean or matrix or ether which buoys the rest, which gives goodness its power for good, and evil its power for evil, the unified field: our complex and inexplicable caring for each other, and for our life together here. This is given. It is not learned.

"The event was over. Its devastation lay round about us."

The world which lay under darkness and stillness following the closing of the lid was not the world we know. The event was over. Its devastation lay round about us. The clamoring mind and heart stilled, almost indifferent, certainly disembodied, frail, and exhausted. The hills were hushed, obliterated. Up in the sky, like a crater from some distant cataclysm, was a hollow ring.

You have seen photographs of the sun taken during a total eclipse. The corona fills the print. All of those photographs were taken through telescopes. The lenses of telescopes and cameras can no more cover the breadth and scale of the visual array than language can cover the breadth and simultaneity of internal experience. Lenses enlarge the sight, omit its context, and make of it a pretty and sensible picture, like something on a Christmas card. I assure you, if you send any shepherds a Christmas card on which is printed a three-by-three photograph of the angel of the Lord, the glory of the Lord, and a multitude of the heavenly host, they will not be sore afraid. More fearsome things can come in envelopes. More moving photographs than those of the sun's corona can appear in magazines. But I pray you will never see anything more awful in the sky.

You see the wide world swaddled in darkness; you see a vast breadth of hilly land, and an enormous, distant, blackened valley; you see towns' lights, a river's path, and blurred portions of your hat and scarf; you see your husband's face looking like an early black-and-white film; and you see a sprawl of black sky and blue sky together, with unfamiliar stars in it, some barely visible bands of cloud, and over there, a small white ring. The ring is as small as one goose in a flock of migrating geese—if you happen to notice a flock of migrating geese. It is one 360th part of the visible sky. The sun we see is less than half the diameter of a dime held at arm's length.

The Crab Nebula, in the constellation Taurus, looks, through binoculars, like a smoke ring. It is a star in the process of exploding. Light from its explosion first reached the earth in 1054; it was a supernova then, and so bright it shone in the daytime. Now it is not so bright, but it is still exploding. It expands at the rate of seventy million miles a day. It is interesting to look through binoculars at something expanding seventy million miles a day. It does not budge. Its apparent size does not increase. Photographs of the Crab Nebula taken fifteen years ago seem identical to photographs of it taken yesterday. Some lichens are similar. Botanists have measured some ordinary lichens twice, at fifty-year intervals, without detecting any growth at all. And yet their cells divide; they live.

The small ring of light was like these things—like a ridiculous lichen up in the sky, like a perfectly still explosion 4,200 light-years away: it was interesting, and lovely, and in witless motion, and it had nothing to do with anything.

It had nothing to do with anything. The sun was too small, and too cold, and too far away, to keep the world alive. The white ring was not enough. It was feeble and worthless. It was as useless as a memory; it was as off kilter and hollow and wretched as a memory.

When you try your hardest to recall someone's face, or the look of a place, you see in your mind's eye some vague and terrible sight such as this. It is dark; it is insubstantial; it is all wrong.

The white ring and the saturated darkness made the earth and the sky look as they must look in the memories of the careless dead. What I saw, what I seemed to be standing in, was all the wrecked light that the memories of the dead could shed upon the living world. We had all died in our boots on the hilltops of Yakima, and were alone in eternity. Empty space stoppered our eyes and mouths; we cared for nothing. We remembered our living days wrong. With great effort we had remembered some sort of circular light in the sky—but only the outline. Oh, and then the orchard trees withered, the ground froze, the glaciers slid down the valleys and overlapped the towns. If there had ever been people on earth, nobody knew it. The dead had forgotten those they had loved. The dead were parted one from the other and could no longer remember the faces and lands they had loved in the light. They seemed to stand on darkened hill-tops, looking down.

IV

We teach our children one thing only, as we were taught: to wake up. We teach our children to look alive there, to join by words and activities the life of human culture on the planet's crust. As adults we are almost all adept at waking up. We have so mastered the transition we have forgotten we ever learned it. Yet it is a transition we make a hundred times a day, as, like so many will-less dolphins, we plunge and surface, lapse and emerge. We live half our waking lives and all of our sleeping lives in some private, useless, and insensible waters we never mention or recall. Useless, I say. Valueless, I might add—until someone hauls their wealth up to the surface and into the wide-awake city, in a form that people can use.

I do not know how we got to the restaurant. Like Roethke, "I take my waking slow." Gradually I seemed more or less alive, and already forget-ful. It was now almost nine in the morning. It was the day of a solar eclipse in central Washington, and a fine adventure for everyone. The sky was clear; there was a fresh breeze out of the north.

The restaurant was a roadside place with tables and booths. The other eclipse-watchers were there. From our booth we could see their cars' California license plates, their University of Washington parking stickers. Inside the restaurant we were all eating eggs or waffles; people were fairly shouting and exchanging enthusiasms, like fans after a World Series game. Did you see . . . ? Did you see . . . ? Then somebody said something which knocked me for a loop.

A college student, a boy in a blue parka who carried a Hasselblad, said to us, "Did you see that little white ring? It looked like a Life Saver. It looked like a Life Saver up in the sky."

And so it did. The boy spoke well. He was a walking alarm clock. I myself had at that time no access to such a word. He could write a sen-tence, and I could not. I grabbed that Life Saver and rode it to the surface. And I had to laugh. I had been dumbstruck on the Euphrates River, I had been dead and gone and grieving, all over the sight of something which, if you could claw your way up to that level, you would grant looked very much like a Life Saver. It was good to be back among people so clever; it was good to have all the world's words at the mind's disposal, so the mind could begin its task. All those things for which we have no words are lost. The mind—the culture—has two little tools, grammar and lexi-con: a decorated sand bucket and a matching shovel. With these we blus-ter about the continents and do all the world's work. With these we try to save our very lives.

There are a few more things to tell from this level, the level of the restaurant. One is the old joke about breakfast. "It can never be satisfied, the mind, never." Wallace Stevens wrote that, and in the long run he was right. The mind wants to live forever, or to learn a very good reason why not. The mind wants the world to return its love, or its awareness; the mind wants to know all the world, and all eternity, and God. The mind's sidekick, however, will settle for two eggs over easy.

The dear, stupid body is as easily satisfied as a spaniel. And, incredibly, the simple spaniel can lure the brawling mind to its dish. It is everlastingly funny that the proud, metaphysically ambitious, clamoring mind will hush if you give it an egg.

Further: while the mind reels in deep space, while the mind grieves or fears or exults, the workaday senses, in ignorance or idiocy, like so many computer terminals printing out market prices while the world blows up, still transcribe their little data and transmit them to the warehouse in the skull. Later, under the tranquilizing influence of fried eggs, the mind can sort through this data. The restaurant was a halfway house, a decompression chamber. There I remembered a few things more.

The deepest, and most terrifying, was this: I have said that I heard screams. (I have since read that screaming, with hysteria, is a common reaction even to expected total eclipses.) People on all the hillsides, including, I think, myself, screamed when the black body of the moon detached from the sky and rolled over the sun. But something else was happening at that same instant, and it was this, I believe, which made us scream.

The second before the sun went out we saw a wall of dark shadow come speeding at us. We no sooner saw it than it was upon us, like thunder. It roared up the valley. It slammed our hill and knocked us out. It was the monstrous swift shadow cone of the moon. I have since read that this wave of shadow moves 1,800 miles an hour. Language can give no sense of this sort of speed—1,800 miles an hour. It was 195 miles wide. No end was in sight—you saw only the edge. It rolled at you across the land at 1,800 miles an hour, hauling darkness like plague behind it. Seeing it, and knowing it was coming straight for you, was like feeling a slug of anesthetic shoot up your arm. If you think very fast, you may have time to think, "Soon it will hit my brain." You can feel the deadness race up your arm; you can feel the appalling, inhuman speed of your own blood. We saw the wall of shadow coming, and screamed before it hit.

This was the universe about which we have read so much and never before felt: the universe as a clockwork of loose spheres flung at stupefying, unauthorized speeds. How could anything moving so fast not crash, not veer from its orbit amok like a car out of control on a turn?

Less than two minutes later, when the sun emerged, the trailing edge of the shadow cone sped away. It coursed down our hill and raced eastward over the plain, faster than the eye could believe; it swept over the plain and dropped over the planet's rim in a twinkling. It had clobbered us, and now it roared away. We blinked in the light. It was as though an enormous, loping god in the sky had reached down and slapped the earth's face.

Something else, something more ordinary, came back to me along about the third cup of coffee. During the moments of totality, it was so dark that drivers on the highway below turned on their cars' headlights. We could see the highway's route as a strand of lights. It was bumper-to-bumper down there. It was eight-fifteen in the morning, Monday morning, and people were driving into Yakima to work. That it was as dark as night, and eerie as hell, an hour after dawn, apparently meant that in order to *see* to drive to work, people had to use their headlights. Four or five cars pulled off the road. The rest, in a line at least five miles long, drove to town. The highway ran between hills; the people could not have seen any of the eclipsed sun at all. Yakima will have another total eclipse in 2019. Perhaps, in 2019, businesses will give their employees an hour off.

From the restaurant we drove back to the coast. The highway crossing the Cascades range was open. We drove over the mountain like old pros. We joined our places on the planet's thin crust; it held. For the time being, we were home free.

Early that morning at six, when we had checked out, the six bald men were sitting on folding chairs in the dim hotel lobby. The television was on. Most of them were awake. You might drown in your own spittle, God knows, at any time; you might wake up dead in a small hotel, a cabbage head watching TV while snows pile up in the passes, watching TV while the chili peppers smile and the moon passes over the sun and nothing changes and nothing is learned because you have lost your bucket and shovel and no longer care. What if you regain the surface and open your sack and find, instead of treasure, a beast which jumps at you? Or you may not come back at all. The winches may jam, the scaffolding buckle, the air conditioning collapse. You may glance up one day and see by your headlamp the canary keeled over in its cage. You may reach into a cranny for pearls and touch a moray eel. You yank on your rope; it is too late.

Apparently people share a sense of these hazards, for when the total eclipse ended, an odd thing happened.

When the sun appeared as a blinding bead on the ring's side, the eclipse was over. The black lens cover appeared again, backlighted, and slid away. At once the yellow light made the sky blue again; the black lid dissolved and vanished. The real world began there. I remember now: we all hurried away. We were born and bored at a stroke. We rushed down the hill. We found our car; we saw the other people streaming down the hillsides; we joined the highway traffic and drove away.

We never looked back. It was a general vamoose, and an odd one, for when we left the hill, the sun was still partially eclipsed—a sight rare enough, and one which, in itself, we would probably have driven five hours to see. But enough is enough. One turns at last even from glory itself with a sigh of relief. From the depths of mystery, and even from the heights of splendor, we bounce back and hurry for the latitudes of home.

Debbie Drechsler

The Dead of Winter

Debbie Drechsler has been combining words and pictures for most of the time she's been able to hold a pencil. The endsheets of her childhood books were filled with drawings she made to accompany the stories she told herself after the book had been read to her. These stories and pictures had nothing in common with the actual book they were drawn in. Her mother began to supply her with paper, and on a few occasions, gave her stories to be illustrated.

As an adult Debbie Drechsler has made her living as an editorial illustrator and comics creator. Her graphic novels *Daddy's Girl* (1996) and *Summer of Love* (2002) gained a following; she has been praised for her realistic, even brutal, writing style. Her work often explores the difficulties faced by young women as they are forced to face situations that include sexual abuse, abortion, and general adolescent confusion; the pieces are personal in tone. Her sensitive approach is still rare in the male-dominated action world of American graphic novels.

Andrew Arnold of *Time* called *Summer of Love* one of the best books of 2002, saying, "Though it takes place in the late 1960s, nothing much has changed about the suburban teenage life except that they apparently didn't curse as much. Kids hang out in the woods and gossip about each other. A bunch of guys have a basement band and girls come to watch. Among other things, *Summer* creates an authentic portrait of one of our great American subcultures." Drechsler has an evocative style that "shows" more than "tells," even as it delves deeply into character interactions. The same reviewer said that Drechsler's are "great comix, because, told with few words, Drechsler reveals the character's confusion and awkwardness through the details of her drawing. Her characters' body language and facial details are among the most expressive in this medium without being the least bit photo-realistic." Her style is distinctly her own.

As an illustrator, Drechsler has worked on staff for a variety of newspapers in upstate New York and the San Francisco Bay Area and freelanced for many magazines, newspapers, and book publishers. Her clients include *Business Week, U.S. News & World Report, Redbook, Sunset, Access, Parenting, Cricket, Texas Monthly,* the *Boston Globe, Organic Gardening, Natural Health, Condé Nast Traveler,* the *Los Angeles Times,* the *Oakland Tribune,* the *Washington Post, Esquire, Spy,* Avon Books, Bantam Books, Mercury Press, and the Algonquin Press.

She lives in northern California. Her web site is http://www.debdrex.com, and includes samples of her illustrations and artwork. Her books are published by Fantagraphics.

Interview with Debbie Drechsler, p. 302.

Interview with Debbie Drechsler

BECKY BRADWAY: I know that you work as a freelance artist and graphic
   designer. And that most people who write graphic novels/memoirs
   make their primary living as artists. I wondered whether you also
   have a background writing and to what extent you see yourself as a
   writer.

DEBBIE DRECHSLER: I don't have a background in writing other than the
   obligatory poetry in high school. Although I enjoyed writing the
   stories that became my comics (I haven't created a new one in several
   years), I don't really think of myself as a writer.

BB: What are the special difficulties involved in writing about highly emotional or personal subjects? (In creative writing classes, we sometimes
   talk about the need to get the distance to be able to "see" the events
   in a way that we make it interesting to the reader.) How do you get
   the distance to write this piece?

DD: The stories that I wrote were the stories that I had to write, so I don't
   really know what, if there were any, the special difficulties were. They
   were the only stories I wrote!

   I wrote them in two or three drafts. The first draft was all emotion.
   I threw myself into the heart of the story and let it tell itself to me. In
   essence, I lived it. What I had at the end of that first draft was all of
   the emotional content of the story and the bare bones of the structure.
   In subsequent drafts I began to build an actual story, giving it structure, paring it down to its essential self, and worrying about continu-
   ity and the more mundane aspects of storytelling.

BB: Why do you think the field of graphic novels/memoirs is growing in
   popularity?

DD: Oh, gosh. I think you need someone who's more of an anthropologist
   to answer this one! Or at least someone who studies comics.

BB: What are some of your favorite graphic novels/memoirs?

DD: All of Lynda Barry's work, Julie Doucet, Dori Seda, Aline Kominsky,
   Jason Lutes, Michael Dougan, Phoebe Gloeckner.

BB: When you were coming up with the design for the main character/
   narrator of "The Dead of Winter," did you go through a series of
   decisions regarding how she would look, how the surroundings
   would look (and which you would choose), etc.? Can you describe
   this, since I'm guessing it would be much the same as the way a writer
   decides upon the personality that comes through in her narrator's
   voice.

DD: Because my work has such a strong autobiographical aspect it was
   kind of a no-brainer. The narrator looked like and sounded like my
   younger self (at least as I saw and remembered her/me) and the surroundings were what I remembered from that time in my life. Much
   easier, I would say, than creating an entirely fictional character!

David James Duncan

What Fundamentalists Need for Their Salvation

David James Duncan is the author of *The River Why* (1983), *The Brothers K* (1992), *River Teeth* (1995), *My Story as Told by Water* (2001), and *God Laughs and Plays* (2006). His work has won many honors, including three Pacific Northwest Bookseller's Awards, two Pushcart Prizes, a Lannan Fellowship, the 2001 Western States Book Award, a National Book Award nomination, inclusion in three volumes of *Best American Spiritual Writing*, an honorary doctorate from the University of Portland, and (with Wendell Berry) the American Library Association's 2003 Award for the Preservation of Intellectual Freedom.

The writer Ian Frazier said that David James Duncan is "passionate, original, skillful, and funny as hell. His essays about the natural world are some of the best nonfiction around." Duncan's first book, the coming-of-age novel *The River Why*, is still in print after twenty years and has gained a dedicated following. A reviewer for *Esquire* called this book "wonderfully funny . . . imbued with a wisdom and a rather joyous ecology-minded spirit." A *Booklist* reviewer described Duncan's style as "refreshing because of its intimate tone, the simultaneously lyrical and vernacular prose, vivid description, hilarious action, spirited movement, and poignant observation."

Duncan has spoken all over the United States on rivers and wilderness, on the pathos of fly fishing, and about imaginative freedom, the nonmonastic contemplative life, and the nonreligious literature of faith. He was born east of Portland, Oregon, within view of the Columbia River near the mouth of the Columbia Gorge. He now lives outside Missoula, Montana, "in the highest headwaters of the same river, on a trout stream." He is at work on a novel called *Love on Mount Purgatory*.

The essay that we've included is from Duncan's most recent book, *God Laughs and Plays*. Bill McKibben called this book "funny, deft, ingenious, and most of all passionate. The author grew up in the fever swamps of intense evangelicalism (his branch, the Seventh-day Adventists, preach Saturday as the Sabbath) but left it all behind for a life of fly-fishing and ridge-running in the mountain West. What he didn't leave behind were Matthew, Mark, Luke and John. . . . As [a self-confessed evangelist] he is a scandal both to the institutional church and to secular snobs; a truly dangerous man." In an interview, Duncan called the worst moments of his professional life "a tie between two moments: the day I lost 12 short stories to the implosion of a computer and the day the Supreme Court appointed King George the Bush."

"What Fundamentalists Need for Their Salvation" is a classic personal essay, a reasoned argument on a timeless subject that uses personal observations to build its points. It advocates freedom of expression (which is not terribly uncommon in literary circles), but adds the complication of doing so as a fundamentalism-rejecting Christian. The piece evolves from being an anti-censorship argument to one that fights against the tenets of right-wing evangelicals, and it does so without losing a sense of structure and focus. The essay relies far more on exposition than on scenes, as Duncan doesn't step away from being overt in his intentions. Its tone fits its subject matter; at times, it sounds like a gentle sermon. Yet Duncan never presumes his reader's agreement; he simply seems to be requesting a hearing. The quiet tone only seems to enhance the power of the argument, as he draws us in through his engaging persona.

Interview with David James Duncan, p. 317.

Go forth and preach. And if you have to, use words.
— *St. Francis of Assisi*

1. Censored

A few years ago I was asked to speak to sixty or seventy high school students in a town neither geographically nor demographically far from Sweet Home, Oregon, from whence the Oregon Citizens Alliance — a fundamentalist religious group with a selective-Leviticus-quoting antihomosexual agenda — had sprung into national headlines. The high school was in a logging town and I'm a defender of our last few remaining ancient forests. I was years behind on a novel deadline, and busy with my own three kids. I accepted the invitation anyhow, when I learned that students were being forced to read a version of my first novel, *The River Why*, from which hundreds of words had been purged by a team of parents armed with indelible black felt-tip pens.

The general topic of this novel is, for lack of a better word, *redemption* — the redemption, in this case, of a young fly fisherman. The genre is ancient: the story of a spiritual quest. The novel had already been assigned, a teacher explained to me when I arrived at the school, and her class was halfway through it, when the mother of a student happened to pick the book up and discover my protagonist's use of language. By no stretch of the imagination or Bible could his language be considered obscene. Using the Hollywood rating system, I believe my novel would receive a "PG-13" — and I'm embarrassed to add that a "G" would be as likely as an "R." The passages this mother nevertheless proceeded to underline, xerox, and distribute at a P.T.A. meeting nearly caused the book to be banned outright. At the same meeting, however, a couple of brave English teachers stood up and tenaciously defended the morality of the novel's overall aims, enabling a compromise (which of course satisfied neither side) to be reached. The book was called back from the students, duly purged by the parents, and reassigned. Then, as some sort of finale (and, I think, an act of teacherly revenge upon the vigilantes), I was invited to visit.

Upon arriving at the school, the first thing I did was paw through an excised copy to see just how black my prose had been deemed to be—and more than a few pages, it turned out, looked rather as if Cajuns had cooked them. But what interested me far more than the quantity of black marks was the unexpected difficulty of the whole censorship endeavor. Hard as these parents had tried to Clorox my prose, a myopic focus on "nasty words" at the expense of attention to narrative flow had resulted in a remarkably self-defeating arbitrariness. They'd taken care, for instance, to spare their big strapping logging-town teenagers my protagonist's dislike of the Army Corps of Engineers by converting the phrase "God damn dams" to "God [beep] dams." Yet when the same protagonist, one Gus Orviston, told a story about an inch-and-a-half-long scorpion his kid brother lost inside his fly-fishing-crazed family's house, not a word was blackened out of Gus's surmise that the lonely creature had ultimately "found and fallen in love with one of my father's mayfly imitations and died of lover's nuts trying to figure out how to screw the thing."

Along similar lines, Gus was allowed, in a scene when his lady-love rejected him, to describe himself as a "blubbering Sasquatch . . . my beard full of lint, my teeth yellow, my fly open and undershorts showing there the same color as my teeth, and thick green boogers clogging both my nostrils." Yet when he attempted moments later to describe the bottom of a river as "the place where the slime and mudsuckers and fish-shit live," student innocence had to be protected by the prophylactic "fish-[beep]."

> "The students' reactions to being assigned censored literature turned out to be mild compared to their teachers'."

The pattern grew obvious: while my protagonist had been allowed to piss, puke, and fornicate, to insult door-to-door evangelists, and even to misread and reject the Bible with impunity, every time he tried to use a so-called dirty word—even the innocuous likes of "hell," "damn," or "ass"—down came the indelible markers. Some kind of "suitable-for-mixed-company" politeness was all that my censors were out to impose. It always seems to dumbfound and offend the promulgators of such cleanlinesses when the makers and defenders of literature declare even purges like theirs to be not just ineffective, but dangerous.

The students' reactions to being assigned censored literature turned out to be mild compared to their teachers'. Most considered it embarrassing to be "treated like kids" in this way, but no more embarrassing than many other facets of high school, small town, and family life. When I read to them the novel's single most censored scene—an exposé of the greed and stupidity of two drunken and foul-mouthed fishermen—with the foul words restored, the students, on a show of hands, unanimously preferred greedy drunks to sound like greedy drunks, not Sunday School teachers. They also agreed that the purge had been ineffective, since their imaginations had readily supplied every blacked-out word. But most of them were no more able than their parent-censors to perceive or articulate any real danger in the laundering of their curriculum or literature.

A parable on the danger:

When I was a kid and picked raspberries for money, some of the teenaged boys in the fields used to defy the heat, boredom, and row bosses (most of whom were staid Judeo-Suburban housewives) by regaling us with a series of ad-libbed yarns they called "The Adventures of One-Eyed Dirk." To a casual listener, One-Eyed Dirk's were some of the dullest adventures ever endured. We pickers listened with bated breath, though, knowing it was our teen raconteurs, not Dirk, who were having the real adventure. The trick to a One-Eyed Dirk story was to juxtapose strategic verbs and modifiers with names of common nouns (say, car parts, office supplies, or garden vegetables) in a way that, through the magic of metaphor, let you spout pure analogical pornography within the hearing of all, yet proclaim your innocence if confronted by an offended adult. An example might go: "Stunned by the size of the musk melons she'd offered him, One-Eyed Dirk groped through his own meager harvest, found the bent green zucchini, sighed at the worm-hole in the end, but, with a shy smile, drew it out and thrust it slowly toward her. . . ."

Silly as this kind of thing may be, it underscores the fact that there is virtually nothing a would-be censor can do to guarantee the purity of language, because it is not just words that render language impure. Even "dirty" words tend to be morally neutral until placed in a context—and it is the individual human imagination, more than individual words, that gives a context its moral or immoral twist. One-Eyed Dirk's G-rated zucchinis and wing nuts and valve jobs drive home the point that a bored kid out to tell an off-color yarn can do it with geometry symbols, nautical flags, or two rocks and a stick if he wants. The human imagination was *designed* (by its Designer, if you will) to make rapid-fire, free-form, often preposterous connections between shapes, words, colors, ideas, desires, sounds. This is its seeming "moral weakness," but also its wondrous strength. The very nature of imagination is the reason why organized censorship never quite works—and also the reason why every ferociously determined censorship effort sooner or later escalates into fascistic political agendas, burnings at the stake, dunking chairs, gulags, pogroms, and other literal forms of purge. Obviously, the only fail-safe way to eliminate impurities from human tongues, imaginations, and cultures is to eliminate human life itself.

2. The Morality of Literature

Ever since the advent of the printing press, there have been readers who slip from enthusiasm for a favorite text into the belief that the words in that text embody truth: do not just symbolize it, but *literally embody it.* Not till the past century, though, has an American alliance of self-styled "conservative Christians" declared that this slip is in fact the true Christian religion, that a single bookful of words is Absolute Truth, and that this Truth should become the sole basis of the nation's political, legal, and cultural life. The growing clout of this faction does not change the theological aberrance of its stance: fundamentalism's deification of the written words of the Bible—in light of every scripture-based Wisdom tradition in the world *including Christianity's two-thousand-year-old own*—is not just naïveté: it is idolatry.

Words in books can remind us of truth, and help awaken us to it. But in themselves, words are just paint and writers are just painters, Old Testament and gospel writers, bhakti and Sufi saints, Tibetan lamas and Catholic popes included. There are, of course, crucial differences between scripture and belles lettres, and between inspired and merely inventive prose. But the authors of both write with human hands and in human tongues.

Let us not overestimate the power of any form of literature.

Let us not underestimate it either. As readers we are asked on page one to lay our hand upon the back of an author's as he or she paints a world. If the author's strokes somehow repel or betray our trust, if our concentration is lax, or if we're biased or closed in some way, then no hand-in-hand magic can occur. But when a great word-painter is read with reciprocally great concentration and trust, a wondrous thing happens. First, the painter's hand disappears. Then so does our own. Till there is only the living world of the painting.

This disappearance—this effacement of self in the life of a story—is, I believe, the greatest truth we experience through any literature, be it discursive or dramatic, sacred or secular. It is, at any rate, the greatest *describable* truth we experience, since for the duration of our effacement we possess no "I" with which to describe anything outside the imagined world in which we've become lost. Like all great truths, this disappearance of self in an interior world requires, simultaneously, a sacrifice (of the reader's ego) and a resurrection (of the world and characters in the text). And like all great truths, it is not realized by picking and choosing certain literal meanings from the text's sentences and words: what is required is a willing immersion of imagination, intuition, and mind in the dynamic pulse and flow of living language.

In light of this truth, the most valid form of censorship is that practiced by writers upon themselves. Scrupulously revising or destroying all writing that fails to let readers vanish into the life of their language is every author's duty. What we are morally obligated to censor from our work, in other words, is our own incompetence. Nothing more, nothing less. Simple as it sounds, it keeps us more than busy. "Fundamental accuracy of statement," wrote Ezra Pound in support of this brand of censorship, "is the one sole morality of literature." If, in other words, a story requires that its author create a mountain, and further requires that this mountain be imposing, the immoral mountain is not the one with the pair of unmarried hikers copulating on a remote slope: it is the mountain that fails to be imposing. The "sole morality of literature" demands that an author contemplate his peak till frozen clouds begin to swirl round the summit, frigid stone masses haunt and daunt us, and the bones of fallen climbers and mountain goats appear not at some safe distance but in the crevasses at our very feet.

With all due apologies to literary inquisitors everywhere, the same "one sole morality" applies in regard to the imposing penis. This is not to say that all penises are, according to Pound's dictum, moral. Indeed, a gratuitously shocking penis, an extraneous-to-our-story penis, a hey-look-at-me-for-the-sake-of-nothing-but-me penis, however imposing, is literarily immoral (that is, incompetent), since by jarring the reader from the narrative flow into a mood of "What's this stupid penis doing here?" the author has undermined the greatest truth of his tale—that is, our ability to immerse ourselves in it. Once the dramatic exigencies of a story have demanded of its author an imposing penis, however, it is the apoplectic-veined archetype that has us defensively crossing imaginary legs before we know it (or opening them, as the narrative case may be) that is the literarily moral penis. And it is the church, quasi-religious political cult, or government agency that seeks to drape a cloth over it that is, literarily, immoral.

But how could the deletion of male members, filthy language, perversion, sadomasochism, sexual violence, and so on ever be criticized? Why in God's name shouldn't we censor literature, art, and human behavior itself in order to safeguard the innocence of our children and our culture? These are the "purity questions," the "morality questions"—the Jesse Helms, Jerry Falwell, Pat Robertson questions, yes, and also the Stalin, Hitler, Mao, McCarthy, Khomeini, Taliban questions. Libertarians and knee-jerk liberals need to remind themselves, however, that a lot of people besides fanatics and ideologues ask the same questions—all responsible parents of young children, for instance.

Here are two sincere answers to the purity questions, one civic, one Christian.

The civic:

To seek laws that protect each citizen's freedom of expression is not to seek a citizenry that freely expresses anything and everything. Art and literature at their worst can be depraved. But the citizens of this country *already* possess a Constitutional right to say so: we are perfectly free, regardless of our religion, to detest the work of any writer or artist we honestly detest, and to criticize that writer or artist in the most scathing language we're able to devise. I, for example, found the few chapters of Bret Easton Ellis's *American Psycho* I got through to be as sensationalistic and literarily incompetent as any novel I've ever tried to read. To "shock and awe" readers by torturing characters redundantly and without mercy is not a literary strategy to which "the one sole morality of literature" allows most writers to subscribe. But to say this much satisfies me. And it's all the fun the Constitution allows. To carry my disgust further—to try to summon the outrage, compose the propaganda, induce the paranoia, and generate the political clout that would let me and my ideological clones ban, purge, or punish one overpaid hack—is not the way people in this tenuously free country long ago agreed to do things.

The church, historically, has ruled many a state, and has generally not ruled well. This is precisely why America now does things differently.

As James Madison observed in 1785, "ecclesiastical establishments" have upheld many political tyrants, and they have created many spiritual tyrannies, but "in no instance have they been seen [to be] the guardians of the liberties of the people. . . . A just Government instituted to secure & perpetuate [liberty] needs them not." America's founding fathers decided, in short, that self-restraint, while far from perfect, is infinitely preferable to being restrained by priests and kings.

The greatest literature practices such restraint. The old Irish bards, for instance, when asked to recite certain vile stories, would often say to their audience: *'Tis an evil tale for telling. I canna' make it.* And hearing this, the crowd would request a different tale. Hyperconfessional and sensation-addicted Americans could use a dose of this bardic wisdom. But sickening stories remain an unavoidable by-product of sick cultures, and a crucial diagnostic tool for anyone seeking a cure. Writers need the freedom to invoke mayhem, sexuality, moral ambiguities, and twisted visions for as many reasons as chefs need the freedom to invoke curry, garlic, Chinese mustard, and other substances we can't tolerate in large doses, in order to produce a fine cuisine. There is no mention of jalapeño peppers in the Bible, and neither the average child or average televangelist can handle them: this is no reason to legislate them clean out of our huevos rancheros.

The Christian answer to the purity question:

In the slender classic *An Experiment in Criticism,* that indefatigably Christian lover of non-Christian literature C. S. Lewis, wrote that access to uncensored literature is crucial because we are not meant to be imprisoned in a single, isolated self. "We demand windows," he wrote. "[And] literature . . . is a series of windows, even of doors. . . . Good reading . . . can be described either as an enlargement or as a temporary annihilation of the self. But that is an old paradox; 'he that loseth his life shall save it.' We therefore delight to enter into other men's beliefs . . . even though we think them untrue. And into their passions, though we think them depraved. . . . Literary experience heals the wound, without undermining the privilege, of individuality. . . . In reading great literature I become a thousand men and yet remain myself. . . . Here—as in worship, in love, in moral action, and in knowing—I transcend myself, and am never more myself than when I do."

> "The majority of challenges to the printed word in American schools, libraries, and bookstores are made by people who call themselves 'fundamentalist' or 'evangelical' Christians."

3. Why No Argument against Fundamentalist Censorship Works

The majority of challenges to the printed word in American schools, libraries, and bookstores are made by people who call themselves "fundamentalist" or "evangelical" Christians. I've just provided two arguments against such challenges. I don't believe, however, that my arguments, or any argument resembling them in category, will persuade a single committed fundamentalist that censorship is a potentially deadly cultural strategy. The only way to persuade a fundamentalist of such a thing would be with a fundamentalist argument. And there are none. Fundamentalism and censorship have always gone hand in hand.

My focus here is literary, not theological. But for literary reasons I am compelled to point out that a theologically simplistic, politically motivated, mass-produced cult is out to simplify and "improve" our literature, art, science, sexual choices, Constitution, culture, and souls, and that I see no more effective choice, in defending ourselves against these "improvements," than to confront the theological basis of the cult itself. By confining ourselves to trying to defend those whom organized fundamentalism attacks — gays and evolutionists, for example — we feed ourselves right into the teeth of the "Christian Right's" propaganda machinery. I know poets and authors capable of making a crowd weep at the sincerity and beauty of their art. Every time I see one of them reduced to publicly explaining, via blurts of verbiage nonsensically edited by some TV news show, that they're trying to defend freedom of expression, not the freedom of perverts and pedophiles, I feel a huge strategic error being committed. Literary people, being comparatively complex, seem mystified by the adamant oversimplifications that fuel fundamentalist attacks on scientific truth and artistic and civil freedoms. Having lived among fundamentalists, I don't understand this mystification. The belligerent mind-set and self-insulating dogmas that enable politicized fundamentalism to proliferate are neither complicated nor invulnerable to criticism. To treat the earth as disposable and the Bible as "God," turn that "God" into a political action committee, equate arrogance and effrontery with "evangelism," right-wing politics with "worship," aggression with "compassion," disingenuous televised prattle with "prayer," and call the result "Christianity," is, as I read the words and acts of Jesus, not an enviable position, but a fatal one.

Rather than try to defend welfare mothers, valid science, loving gay couples, Muslim culture, fragile ecosystems, or any other scapegoat or victim of fundamentalist rhetoric, I'd like to take a closer look at the scapegoat manufacturers themselves.

4. American Fundamentalism

Most of the famed leaders of the new "Bible-based" American political alliances share a conviction that their causes and agendas are approved of, and directly inspired by, no less a being than God. This enviable conviction is less enviably arrived at by accepting on faith, hence as "higher-than-fact," that the Christian Bible pared down into American TV English is God's "word" to humankind, that this same Bible is His only word to humankind, and that the politicized apocalyptic fundamentalist's unprecedentedly selective slant on this Bible is the one true slant.

The position is remarkably self-insulating. Possessing little knowledge of or regard for the world's wealth of religious, literary, spiritual, and cultural traditions, fundamentalist leaders allow themselves no concept of love or compassion but their own. They can therefore honestly, even cheerfully, say that it is out of "Christian compassion" and a sort of "tough love" for others that they seek to impose on all others their tendentiously literalized God, Bible, and slant. But how tough can love be before it ceases to be love at all? Well-known variations on the theme include the various Inquisitions' murderously tough love for "heretics" who for centuries were defined as merely defiant of the Inquisition itself; the European Catholic and American Puritan tough love for "witches" who for centuries were defined as virtually any sexually active or humanitarian or unusually skilled single woman whose healing herbs or independence from men defied a male church hierarchy's claim to be the source of all healing; the Conquistadors' genocidally tough love for the Inca, Aztecs, and Maya whose gold they stole for the "glory" of a church meant to honor the perfect poverty of a life begun in a manger and ended on a cross; the missionaries' and U.S. cavalry's genocidally tough love for land-rich indigenous peoples whose crime was merely to exist; and, today, the Bush team's murderously tough love for an oil-rich Muslim world as likely to convert to Texas neocon values as Bush himself is likely to convert to Islam.

Each of these crusader groups has seen itself as fighting to make its own or some other culture "more Christian" even as it tramples the teachings of Christ into a blood-soaked earth. The result, among millions of nonfundamentalists, has been a growing revulsion toward anything that chooses to call itself "Christian." But I see no more crucial tool for defusing fundamentalist aggression than the four books of the gospels, and can think of no more crucial question to keep asking self-righteous crusaders than whether there is anything truly imitative of Jesus—that is, anything compassionate, self-abnegating, empathetic, forgiving, and enemy-loving—in their assaults on religious and cultural diversity, ecosystem health, non-Christian religion, or anything else they have determined to be "evil."

For two thousand years the heart of Christianity has *not* been a self-pronounced "acceptance of Jesus as my personal lord and savior": the religion's heart has been the words, example, and Person of Jesus, coupled with the believer's unceasing attempt to speak, act, and live in accord with this sublime example. (*"This life is not good if it is not an imitation of His life."*—John of the Cross) When the word "Christian" sinks beneath this definition—when a mere self-proclaimed formula is said to suffice for salvation, enabling "saved Christians" to behave in a far less Christ-like manner than millions who consider themselves non-Christian—what has the term "Christian" come to mean?

Jesus's words and sacrifice point humanity both to Himself and beyond Himself, for the Person of Jesus, traditionally, opens directly into the Unbounded. A "personal relationship" with such a being is not something one can "exclusively" own: what the Person of Jesus invites His followers into is a loving relationship with Infinite Mystery. I find it hard to see this Mystery operating in the cocksure judgments, financial scheming, and propagandizing of "evangelists" such as Kenneth Copeland, Pat Robertson, Robert Tilton, Benny Hinn, and Jerry Falwell. Indeed, Christ's Sermon on the Mount is rife with warnings against their kind of proselytizing. (*"Not everyone that saith unto me, Lord, Lord, shall enter into the kingdom of heaven." "Hypocrites . . . love to pray standing in the synagogues and in the corners of the streets, that they may be seen of men." "Whosoever shall not receive the kingdom of God as a little child shall in no wise enter." "Thou hypocrite, first cast out the beam that is of thine own eye; and then shalt thou see clearly to cast the mote out of thy brother's eye."*)

As for the political side of the neocon/fundamentalist fusion, Christ's Beatitudes bless the poor in spirit, they that mourn, the meek, the merciful, the pure in heart, and the peacemakers, among others. What merciful peacemaker can claim to see these blessings manifesting in the conservation debacles, the support of the superrich, and the war making of George W. Bush? I'm not averse to a little Bible-thumping. What appalls me is the deletion of Christ's loving example from the Jesus-character in the Bible that politicized fundamentalists choose to thump. Jesus practiced no politics, spoke of no left or right, and commited no acts of violence, however justified. His embrace of humanity included everyone, though He sternly and repeatedly warned the ungenerous rich, the self-righteously religious, and "hypocrites" of the errors of their ways. The daily stance He repeatedly encouraged was to remain childlike, grateful, loving, and endlessly forgiving. His parables were profoundly mystical, His literalism nonexistent.

Another problem with fundamentalist "tradition": a mere ninety years ago the word "fundamentalist" did not exist: the term was coined by an American Protestant splinter group which, in 1920, proclaimed that adhering to "the literal inerrancy of the Bible" was the true Christian faith. The popularity of this blunder does not change the gospel facts. Deifying the mere letter of biblical law blinds the believer to the spirit we see again and again in Jesus's loving words, deeds, and example.

This, in all sincerity, is why American fundamentalists need connections to, and the compassion of, those who are no such thing. How can those lost in literalism save one another? As Max Weber put it: "We [Christians] are building an iron cage, and we're inside of it, and we're closing the door. And the handle is on the outside."

5. Inside the Cage

Contemporary American fundamentalism is in many ways a manufactured product, and in some ways even an industrial by-product. While its grandiosity of scale is impressive, so is McDonald's, Coca-Cola's, and

ExxonMobil's. Its fully automated evangelical machinery runs twenty-four hours a day, like any factory, making "converts" globally. But to what? The conversion industry's notion of the word Christian has substituted a "Rapture Index" and Armageddon fantasy for Christ's interior kingdom of heaven and love of neighbor; it is funded by donors lured by a televangelical "guarantee" of "a hundredfold increase on all financial donations," as if Mark 10:30 were an ad for a financial pyramid scheme and Jesus never said, "Sell all thou hast and distribute unto the poor"; it has replaced once-personal relationships between parishioners and priests or preachers with radio and TV bombast, sham healings, and congregation-fleecing scams performed by televangelical "rock stars"; it has trumped worship characterized by contemplative music, reflective thought, and silent prayer with three-ring media circuses and "Victory Campaigns"; it inserts veritable lobbyists in its pulpits and political brochures in its pews, claims that both speak for Jesus, and raises millions for this "Jesus" though its version of him preaches neocon policies straight out of Washington think tanks and spends most of "his" money on war; it quotes Mark 10:15 and Matthew 5:44 and Matthew 6:6 and Luke 18:9–14 a grand total of never; it revels in its election of a violent, historically ignorant, science-flaunting, carcinogenic-policied president who goads us toward theocracy at home even as he decries theocracies overseas; it defies cooperation and reason in governance, exults in division, and hastens the degeneration of a democracy built upon cooperation and reason; it claims an exclusive monopoly on truth (*"This ideal of America is the hope of all mankind."—G. W. Bush*) yet trivializes truth globally by evincing ignorance of Christianity's historical and spiritual essence, disrespect toward the world's ethnic and religious diversity, and a stunning lack of interest in humanity's astonishingly rich cultural present and past.

To refer to peregrinating Celtic monks and fundamentalist lobbyists, Origen and Oral Roberts, the Desert Fathers and Tim LaHaye, Dante and Tammy Faye, St. Francis and the TV "Prosperity Gospel" hucksters, Lady Julian of Norwich and Jimmy Swaggart, John of the Cross and George W. Bush, all as "Christian" stretches the word so thin its meaning vanishes. The term "carbon-based life-form" is as informative. The gulf between historic Christianity and politicized, media-driven fundamentalism is *vast*. Misreading its one book, condescending to all others, using the resultant curtailment of comprehension and tolerance as a unifying principle, industrialized fundamentalism seeks to control minds, not open them; seeks the tithe-paying ideological clone, not C. S. Lewis's "windows into others"; seeks a rigidification and righteousness of self, not literature's enlargement of self, or Christ's recommended effacement of it.

"United" in this way, we shall fall.

But to merely shun those trapped inside this ideology is also futile. Those who are not fundamentalists are too often satisfied with expressing derision, intellectual superiority, or revulsion toward them and calling it good. John of the Cross proposes a more difficult but promising course of action: *"Have a great love for those who contradict and fail to love you, for in this way love is begotten in a heart that has no love. God so acts with us, for He loves us that we might love by means of the very love He bears toward us."*

6. Shame and Reverence

The hero of my censored novel, Gus by name, was a fly fisher and spiritual seeker who voiced serious reservations about the Being some believers so possessively refer to as "God." But a problem that Gus and I ran into in telling his story was that, after a climactic all-night adventure with a river and a huge chinook salmon, he had a sudden, transrational (or, in the old Christian lexicon, "mystical") experience that left him too overwhelmed to speak with accuracy, yet too grateful to remain mute. This paradox is autobiographical. As the recipient of many such detonations, I felt bound by gratitude to let my protagonist speak of such mysteries. But as a lifelong witness of the fundamentalist assault on the Christian lexicon, I felt compelled to speak in non-Christian terms. Though Gus spoke of a presence so God-like that in the end he dubbed it "the Ancient One," his account of his experience did not once invoke the word "God."

Reader reactions to this climax have been neatly divided. Those who have experienced similar detonations have sometimes been so moved by the scene that their eyes filled as they thanked me for writing it—and those who've experienced no such detonation have asked why I ruined a dang good fishin' yarn with woowoo. I admire both reactions. Both are constitutionally correct. Both are perfectly honest. What more should a writer want from his reader? What more, for that matter, can a mortal, be they skeptic or mystic, offer the Absolute?

The French novelist-philosopher René Daumal describes the paradox I faced perfectly. He wrote: "I swear to you that I have to force myself to write or to pronounce this word: God. It is a noise I make with my mouth or a movement of the fingers that hold my pen. To pronounce or to write this word makes me ashamed. What is real here is that shame. Must I never speak of the Unknowable because it would be a lie? Must I speak of the Unknowable because I know that I proceed from it and am bound to bear witness to it? This contradiction is the prime mover of my best thoughts."

Another word for this shame, in my view, is *reverence*. And fundamentalism, speaking of the Unknowable, too often lacks this essential quality. The kind of fundamentalism that now more or less governs our country does not just proudly pronounce the word "God," it defines and Americanizes "God," worships its own definition, and aims to impose that definition on all. What an abyss between this effrontery and the Christ-inspired self-giving of a St. Francis, Mother Teresa, or Martin Luther King! What a contrast, too, between this kind of Christianity and that of the Amish, who practice no evangelism, who tease those who quote the Bible too often (calling them "scripture smart"), and who consider it laughable to pronounce oneself "saved," since God alone is capable of such almighty judgments.

And what a gulf between fundamentalism and American literature. If America's writers have arrived at a theological consensus concerning what humans owe the Divine, it might be this: better to be honest to God, even if that means stating one's complete lack of belief in any such Being, than to allow one's mind and imagination to be processed by an ideology factory—be it fundamentalist, Marxist, or what have you. E. B. White said it well: "In a free country it is the duty of writers to pay no attention to duty. Only under a dictatorship is literature expected to exhibit an harmonious design or an inspirational tone."

The "inspirational art" of the Maoist opera and the "Christian Supply Store" are equally blind, in their dutiful purpose, to the truth that God works in mysterious ways. In literature as in life, for example, there are ways of disbelieving in God that are more loving, and in this sense more imitative of Jesus, than some forms of orthodox belief. There are agnostic and atheist humanitarians who believe as they do, and love their neighbors as they do, because the cruelty of humanity makes it impossible for them to conceive of a God who is anything but remiss or cruel. Rather than consider God cruel, they choose doubt or disbelief, and serve others anyway. This is a backhanded form of reverence; a beautiful kind of "shame."

It seems to upset some fundamentalists that literature's answer to "the God question" is as open-minded as the Constitution's, and that most writers remain as determined as were the founding fathers to separate church from state. There is also no doubt that the openness our literature and Constitution encourage results in a theological cacophony and mood of irritable interdependence that bear little resemblance to the self-righteousness now reigning in the average conservative church. But America remains a country that stakes its life and literature on the belief that this cacophony and interdependence are not only legal, but essential to our health.

Edward Abbey remains welcome to say: *"God is Love? Not bloody likely!"* Goethe remains welcome to reply: *"As a man is, so is his God; therefore God is often an object of mockery."* And the readers of both— provided they avoid thought-control machines—remain free to draw their own intelligent conclusions.

7. What Fundamentalists Need for Their Salvation

There is one precious Earth, and she is finite. She can absorb just so many wounds or poisons before she ceases to support life. Millions of us have recognized that in wounding the earth for centuries we have been wounding ourselves, and that the only "kingdom of God" to which Christ gives directions lies within these wounded selves. There is likewise, for most humans born on earth, just one mother tongue, and it is less widely recognized that a given tongue at a given time consists of only so many words, and that these words can absorb only so many abuses before they cease to mean.

> "America's spiritual vocabulary... has been enduring a series of abuses so constricting that the damage may last for centuries."

America's spiritual vocabulary—with its huge defining terms such as "God," "soul," "sacrifice," "mysticism," "faith," "salvation," "grace," "redemption"—has been enduring a series of abuses so constricting that the damage may last for centuries. Too many of us have tried to sidestep this damage by simply rejecting the terminology. The defamation of a religious vocabulary cannot be undone by turning away: the harm is undone when we work to reopen each word's true history, nuance, and depth. Holy words need stewardship as surely as do gardens, orchards, or ecosystems. When lovingly tended, such words surround us with spaciousness and mystery the way a sacred grove surrounds us with cathedral light, peace, and oxygenated air. When we merely abandon our holy words, and fail to replace them, we end up living in a spiritual clear-cut.

If Americans of European descent are to understand and honor the legacy of Celtic, European, Middle Eastern, and other Christian traditions and pass our literature, music, art, monasticism, and mysticism on intact, the right-wing hijacking of Christianity must be defined as the reductionist rip-off that it is. To allow televangelists or pulpit neocons to claim exclusive ownership of Jesus is to hand that incomparable lover of enemies, prostitutes, foreigners, children, and fishermen over to those who evince no such love. And to cede the word "Christian" to earth-trashing literalists who say "the End is nigh" feels rather like ceding my backyard henhouse to weasels. For my hens (and morning omelettes), such a concession would sure enough bring on "the end of the world." But neither my chickens nor I consider the end of our world something to yearn for and work toward.

The God of politicized right-wing fundamentalism, as advertised daily by a relentless array of media, is a Supramundane Caucasian Male as furious with humanity's failure to live by a few randomly selected dictums from Leviticus as He is oblivious to the "Christian Right's" failure to live the compassion of the gospels and earth stewardship of both testaments. As surely as I feel love and need for food and water, I feel love and need for God. But these feelings have nothing to do with Supramundane Males planning torments for those who don't abide by neocon "moral values." If the "Christian Right's God" is indeed God, then all my spiritual heroes from Valmiki and Laotse, Bodhidharma and Socrates, Kabir and Mira Bai, Rumi and Hafiz, Dogen and Dante, Teresa of Avila and Julian of Norwich, Eckhart and the Beguines, Sankaracharya and Aquinas, Black Elk and Chief Joseph, Tolstoy and Dostoevsky, Thoreau and Muir, Shunryu and D. T. Suzuki, Gandhi and the Dalai Lama, to Merton and Snyder, will be consigned to perdition with me—for the One we all worship is an infinitely more loving, infinitely less fathomable Being.

Based on the lives and words of the preceding heroes and on the Person and gospels of Jesus Himself, I believe humanity's situation to be rather different. I hold the evangelical truth of the matter to be that contemporary fundamentalists, including first and foremost those aimed at Empire and Armageddon, need us nonfundamentalists, mystics, ecosystem activists, unprogrammable artists, agnostic humanitarians, incorrigible writers, truth-telling musicians, incorruptible scientists, organic gardeners, slow food farmers, gay restaurateurs, wilderness visionaries, pagan preachers of sustainability, compassion-driven entrepreneurs, heartbroken Muslims, grief-stricken children, loving believers, loving disbelievers, peace-marching millions, and the One who loves us all in such a huge way that it is not going too far to say *they need us for their salvation.*

As Mark Twain pointed out over a century ago, the only truly prominent community that fundamentalists have so far established in any world, real or imaginary, is hell.

Interview with David James Duncan

BECKY BRADWAY: Is there a particular way you organized your essay to grab the reader's attention and get them to continue reading your argument?

DAVID JAMES DUNCAN: Many people sense that the blend of fundamentalist religiosity and neocon politics has harmed America, but can't articulate why. Rather than state some op-ed generality, I began with a specific, small town fundamentalist act that threatened the purposes of literature, insulted the intelligence of teenagers, undermined teachers, and ignored our constitutionally guaranteed freedoms of expression and choice. My censored novel, *The River Why*—censored partly *because* of its "dirty words" and comic and sexual situations—depicts a sincere search for a life grounded in acts of kindness and in ancient spiritual truths. By showing readers the specific words blacked out of the novel, I was able to keep the tone light even as I showed my attackers to be silly and ineffectual. At this point I figured I'd either hooked my readers or spooked them, so I had nothing to lose by diving right into a serious consideration of how religious zealotry, throughout history as well as now, has led to mental rigidity and purgings in the name of "purity" that are not only silly, but extremely deadly.

America was founded on principles intended to resist this kind of purge. Although I hated to abandon my comic tone, I grew serious in dealing with this material, because there is a lot at stake. Robin Cody recently had his novel *Ricochet River* removed from high school reading lists in Oregon by "conservative Christians" simply because its loggers swear and its teenagers are interested in sex. How can we honestly create fiction if the teenagers don't like sex and the loggers don't curse? Even the Bible is full of sex and cursings! Literature needs to be based upon our genuine nature if is to generate the identification and power and empathy to inspire and *improve* those natures. Denying teenage sexuality is akin to denying the fossil record and claiming Earth is six thousand years old—which fundamentalists also do. Robin Cody responded to being banned by concocting a new version of his novel with the sex scenes and four-letter words deleted. I admire Robin's other work but feel very strongly that this was the wrong way to go. Fundamentalists are our neighbors, not our moral police. We're told by Jesus to love our neighbors, not to kowtow to their moral edicts. I responded to being censored by reminding us that Jesus appalled the goody-goodies of his day by hanging out with prostitutes, tavern keepers and sinners, and by ignoring the "moral values" of the clergy of his day. I remind us that Americans have died by the thousand and sacrificed by the million to win and preserve our freedoms of speech, of choice, of art, and of literature. Any demagogue, ayatollah, president, or preacher who claims to know what we all ought to read is not only arrogant, he is blind to our history and to the example of Jesus. If writers want their storytelling to remain free, they've got to take a stand against all such bullying.

BB: Do you really believe an essay can change people's minds? Foolish mortal, why do you think so?

DJD: An essay, when backed by courageous action, can do more than change minds: it can forge a nation, or win a war, or reverse a centuries-old struggle. Here's an example: Ralph Waldo Emerson's essay "Nature" let the air out of the same kind of faux-Christian pompousness we see strutting round Washington, D.C., again today. "Nature" also helped a young Harvard lad named Henry David Thoreau blossom into the brave activist whose essay "Civil Disobedience" helped galvanize the abolition of slavery. "Civil Disobedience," in turn, inspired a young South African barrister named Mohandas K. Gandhi to refine a mode of passive nonviolence which, when he took it home to India, guided him through an astounding series of fasts, boycotts, marches, demonstrations, and other actions that drove the occupying British out of India via an almost bulletless, bombless war. This victory (which included many Gandhi letters and pleas that were, in fact, essays) then inspired a young Baptist preacher named Martin Luther King to deploy similar methods and ideals in the American South, and King's stupendous "sermons" and speeches all have the structure and flow of fine essays. Fired by the eloquence and courage of this man, African Americans moved en masse not only to the fronts of buses and into the polling booths but into better jobs, neighborhoods, positions of prominence, onto stages, stadiums, movie and TV screens, soon giving us the America we know today. A world with no "Nature," no "Civil Disobedience," no Indian Salt March and *datya-qraha,* no

MLK essay from the Birmingham jail, may well have led to a world with no Muhammad Ali (for what white cracker, without the break-throughs inspired by these essays, would have tolerated such a man?). These essays may be what let Lee Elder slip quietly into the Masters in Georgia, so that Tiger Woods could later wallop all comers at that long-time Bastion of Whiteness. Essays informed the Alice Walker who penned *The Color Purple,* which led to a movie that gave Oprah Winfrey a role she has ridden to fame, glory, and multicultural power. Essays inform the likes of Toni Morrison, Chris Rock, Whoopi Goldberg, all of whom have been censored by fundamentalists. But the fundamentalists of yesterday would have jailed or killed them. So we "foolish mortals" have made some progress. Still, we have more work—and more essay-writing—to do.

BB: Are there particular challenges involved in writing about spiritual matters?

DJD: Humility is extra important in spiritual writing—and is best main-tained, in my case, by invoking the fool I know best: me.

Allowing the Divine Mystery to be mysterious is crucial—and remembering that spiritual experience, soul experience, heart experi-ence, belongs to spirit, soul and heart, not to us. Being firm with regard to those we feel are stuck in arrogance, ignorance or error, without being rancorous and nasty in the way that, say, Rush Limbaugh or Ann Coulter are, is very important. In spiritual writing we set out to make *neighbors* of those with whom we disagree, not *corpses.* That's why I cite John of the Cross. *"Have a great love for those who contra-dict and fail to love you, for in this way love is begotten in a heart that had no love."* I suspect it's impossible to truly be in touch with living spirit without also being in touch with compassion and love.

I think it's important to add that we can sometimes only find our compassion through hard work. In the case of this essay, for exam-ple, my first draft was driven by sheer heat. I detest the legacy of religious zealotry: the wars, persecution of women, abuse of children, attacks on other faiths, destructions of culture, art, ecosystems, tribes. My first draft spoke of this with vehemence and little restraint. But then I found that John of the Cross quote about loving those who don't love us. It stopped me in my tracks. I pictured St. Francis bless-ing those who beat him, remembered the christlike forgiveness of the Dalai Lama, remembered Gandhi saying, "Beware of the means by which you fight the fascists, lest you become fascists yourselves." And I rewrote the entire essay, consciously turning the heat from high down to medium. I allowed myself to be critical, but didn't allow my-self to be snide or caustic. I tried to call a spade a spade, but not to name-call. A lot of evangelical Christians have responded positively to this essay. I could easily have just polarized them. It was only my second effort—the *San Juan de la Cruz*–inspired effort—that prevented me from scorching or overspicing the spiritual food.

Gerald Early

"I Only Like It Better When the Pain Comes": More Notes toward a Cultural Definition of Prizefighting

Gerald Early is the Merle Kling Professor of Modern Letters in the English department at Washington University in St. Louis. He has written *Tuxedo Junction: Essays on American Culture* (1989, the source of the following piece); *The Culture of Bruising: Essays on Prizefighting, Literature, and Modern American Culture* (1994); *One Nation under a Groove: Motown and American Culture* (1994); and *Daughters: On Family and Fatherhood* (1994) and has edited *The Sammy Davis, Jr. Reader* (2001); *Miles Davis and American Culture* (2001); *My Soul's High Song: The Collected Works of Countee Cullen* (1991); *Voice of the Harlem Renaissance* (1991); *The Muhammad Ali Reader* (1998); *Body Language: Writers on Sports* (1998); *Speech and Power: The African American Essay* (1993); and *Lure and Loathing: Essays on the Race, Identity, and the Ambivalence of Assimilation* (1993).

His accomplishments extend to other media: he has served as a consultant for a number of documentary film projects (including four of Ken Burns's films) and was twice nominated for Grammy Awards for his liner note writing. He is an elected member of the American Academy of Arts and Sciences and serves on the academy's council. He is currently working on a book about African Americans during the Korean War era as well as a novel about jazz for young people entitled *Up for It*. His latest book is called *This Is Where I Came In: Essays on Black America in the 1960s* (2003), a collection of three lectures published by the University of Nebraska Press.

" 'I Only Like It Better When the Pain Comes' " is a complex personal essay about boxing and African Americans. The piece is divided into three parts: the first, memoir; the second, a series of literary and social critiques; and the third, memoir again, this time focusing on a particular character. The beginning contains stories of a neighborhood, of a kind of ritualized fighting between those who will never be famous; the middle, about writers who perceive boxing as a formal pursuit, a classical sport, an interaction between male symbols; the end a return to the St. Louis neighborhood, to the individual who finds in boxing a kind of salvation. The second section, the critique, is primarily about the misconceptions held by certain white writers about black fighters, misconceptions that lie primarily in delusions about black masculinity. The other two sections effectively take down those misconceptions. While the essay as a whole appears to be fragmentary, it gains its meaning from the whole of these parts.

Interview with Gerald Early, p. 340.

To all the black boys of Philadelphia
who are the small princes of our wounded order

I. The Exiles

On a summer day many years ago Jeff Chandler beat my cousin Gino
Fernandez in a fight on the grounds of the Nebinger schoolyard. I think
both Jeff and Gino were nine or ten, which means that I was about fourteen or fifteen. I doubt if now it is remotely possible to recall the reason
for the fight. I lived in South Philadelphia and my cousin, who lived in
West Philadelphia, would from time to time come to visit me and spend a
few days. I remember well how we enjoyed each other as boys, finding
much to do with our days together. This was to change as Gino grew
older; toward the end of his life I rarely saw him and when I did we had
little enough to say. In recent years, I have come to feel quite bad about
this estrangement even though it was not my fault that it occurred. On
this particular day of the fight, I suppose that my cousin's being from
West Philadelphia and therefore a stranger in the neighborhood may have
had something to do with the antagonism between the boys. Jeff probably
instigated the fight because he was always, as I remember him, a very
tough small boy who took a great deal of pride in his ability to fight.

The battle was not a very long one. It started out evenly enough, but
the crowd of boys who nearly smothered the combatants was quite partisan in favor of Jeff, giving him the sort of "home-court advantage" that
revealed to me instantly that my cousin was doomed. Gino did, though,
fight quite well for several minutes. Suddenly, Jeff hit him with an uppercut to the solar plexus so perfectly executed that any prizefighter would
have been proud to have thrown it; its technique was not simply flawless,
but rich in artistic refulgence. My cousin crumpled to the ground in
agony. He was crying, a sure sign of capitulation. Jeff walked away, surrounded by his cloud of admiring and cheering witnesses. He felt no sympathy for the loser and, in truth, it was proper that he did not. After all,
each boy knew the risks of the encounter before it began, and to commit
oneself to any action is to commit oneself to the etiquette of promptly
paying certain immediate psychic costs for failure. So, after a minute or
two of taunts and jeers directed at me about my "punk cousin," I was left
alone to tend to Gino, who was now sobbing heavily, deeply ashamed. I
picked him up, extricated a balled-up, snotty handkerchief from my
pocket, and wiped his face. We walked together almost in the pose of big
brother and little brother: I held my arm around his shoulder and he
walked with his head down. I told him not to cry, that everything would
be all right, that he would surely have better days. I was quite wrong in

The title comes from an article that appeared in the March 1983 issue of *The Ring* entitled
"1982: The Year of the Notables and Quotables" (pp. 18–29). The full quotation of Frank
"the Animal" Fletcher reads as follows: "I hate to say it, but it's true that I only like it
better when pain comes."

this prediction, for if anyone was to have better days it was to be Jeff Chandler. My cousin, at the age of sixteen, was to have his head blown off by a sawed-off shotgun fired at close range by a sniper during a street-gang war. Jeff Chandler became the World Boxing Association bantam-weight champion. The fates of these boys, poor black boys of the streets, far from being unique, take on a sort of

> "The fates of these boys, poor black boys of the streets, far from being unique, take on a sort of dreary, deadening, clichéd familiarity."

dreary, deadening, clichéd familiarity. Both fought for street gangs as adolescents and either could have drawn the other's fortune or misfortune. Chandler could very easily have ended up on a slab in the morgue, and my cousin might well have become a professional fighter. This is perhaps not only how the Bigger Thomases of black America are born but also how they are made.

Although my cousin lived and died in West Philadelphia, his funeral took place in a South Philadelphia funeral home. The deep oddity of that fact is that the funeral came very close to not taking place at all in that location. The South Philadelphia street gang nearest to the funeral home was the Fifth and South Streets gang, the very gang that Jeff Chandler was then fighting for. And these boys were not going to have their turf invaded by the comrades-in-arms of a fallen West Philadelphia gang member. I remember that at the funeral there were nearly as many cops as bereaved relatives and friends, and such a guarded atmosphere that one might have thought some cruel political dictator was being buried. If there had not been so many police officers present, my cousin's funeral might very well have sparked more bloodshed.

I do not think any group of people could have felt more diminished and deranged by all this than my family did. Here, after all, was a young, wayward Jehovah's Witness boy who was murdered according to the arcane but deadly rules of the ghetto rites of passage. My family, both its South Philadelphia and its West Philadelphia branches, had never thought it even lived in a ghetto, much less that it would be brutalized by its hard reality. My mother was stunned to learn that Gino was a member of a street gang. I was an undergraduate at the University of Pennsylvania at the time, and this whole horrible incident made me feel degraded.

Jeff Chandler is a very good professional fighter, amazingly good when one considers that he has had no amateur career to speak of. He had a few amateur fights, then decided that it would be better to fight for money and glory than for trophies and glory, especially since the amount of effort would be about the same. He has beaten everyone in his weight division worth beating, and would love to fight his Latin counterpart—Lupe Pintor, the World Boxing Council bantamweight champion—in a title unification bout. But the young Mexican wants nothing to do with Chandler, so the hard Philadelphian will probably move on to the featherweight division and hope that he can make more money fighting bigger fellows. Because of the death of Tyrone Everett, the retirement of Joe

Frazier, the deterioration of Matthew Saad Muhammad and Jimmy Young, and the unfulfillment of Curtis Parker and Frank Fletcher, Chandler has become the top Philadelphia fighter. That is quite an accomplishment because that town produces many good fighters, and the training sessions, both in the gym and on the streets, are wars of the bloodiest and most demanding kind. Chandler, to put it simply, is a survivor in a place and an occupation where most are swallowed whole in mid-career.

II. The Kings in the Tower

1

Alexis Arguello, great champion of the featherweight, junior lightweight, and lightweight divisions, is known to be a friendly, easygoing fellow outside the ring. He numbers among his friends many fighters who are potential rivals. He seems particularly proud of his friendship with Sugar Ray Leonard, who despite his retirement is still a potential rival because everyone knows that retirement announcements in boxing do not mean much. The story goes that once in a social context Arguello met Roberto Duran, great champion of the lightweight and welterweight divisions, and came up to shake hands and chat with him. At this time Duran was still considered, by those who are supposed to know, pound for pound the best fighter in all of boxing, and there was more than a little talk of a possible big-money bout between him and Arguello. Duran, known for his haughty disdain for and intense dislike of opponents, looked aghast at the approaching Arguello and, while backing away from him, screamed, "Get away from me! I'm not your friend! Get away from me!"

As crazy as it seems, Duran merely took one of boxing's learned inclinations to both its neurotic and its rational limits. It would seem only to complicate matters a great deal to be friendly with the men one is required to fight. A boxer must inflict a lot of punishment in the normal course of a fight in order to expect to win, and it would seem that he might feel less compromised or uneasy in his actions if the opponent was not a friend. On the other hand, it is quite natural for people who share a particular profession also to share friendships; who can know better than a prizefighter the rewards of achievement or the frustrations of defeat in the prizefighting profession?

Duran does not wish to be friendly with boxers who may be potential opponents because it makes the psychological part of training that much harder. This is often referred to as "psyching yourself up," which means creating an artificial hatred for your opponent, so that you may more efficiently and brutally beat him up. There is more at work here than the incredibly fierce sense of Darwinian competition that characterizes the spirit of play in other professional sports. Boxing, after all, is the only sport whose object is to hurt your opponent—to place him in such pain, to inflict such severe injury upon him, that he cannot or will not continue to fight. The emotional incentive for this must be deeper than the mere quest for championship belts and big money, although, to be sure, those latter items do spur fighters on. Boxers must be driven by other needs as well when they enter the ring: they must have "something to prove," or they must "hold a grudge" against their opponent for some imaginary or petty slight, or they must feel like particularly evil bastards who can, to use John L. Sullivan's phrase, "lick any son of a bitch in the house." In short, the bouts become quests for manhood.

Former boxer Leonard Gardner's fine novel about second-rate boxers in California, *Fat City,* contains a scene in which the reader sees the pathetic desperation of this psyching up of the boxer, this dredging up of courage from the spirit to stem the tide of the deep fear of it all:

"Hoping never done nothing," [said Buford Wills.] "It *wanting* that do it. You got to want to win so bad you can taste it. If you want to win bad enough you win. They no way in hell this dude going to beat me. He too old. I going to be all over him. I going kick him so bad, everytime he take a bite of food tomorrow he going think of me. He be one sore son-of-a-bitch. He going *know* he been in a fight. I get him before he get me. I going hit him with everything. I won't just *beat* that motherfucker, I going *kill* him." Buford was small and thin. His hair, divided at one side with a razor-blade part, was cropped close. His nose turned up, his nostrils flared, his lips were soft and full and his hooded eyes were narrowed in a constant frown. The year before, only fourteen, he had lied about his age and won the Golden Gloves novice flyweight title in San Francisco. Tonight he was fighting the champion of Fort Ord. "You want to know what make a good fighter?"

"What's that?" [asked Ernie Munger.]

"It believing in yourself. That the will to win. The rest condition. You want to kick ass, you kick ass."

"I hope you're right."

"You don't want to kick ass, you get your own ass whipped."

"I want to kick ass. Don't worry about that."

"You just shit out of luck."

"I said I wanted to kick ass."

"You got to want to kick ass *bad.* They no manager or trainer or pill can do it for you."

"I want to kick ass as bad as you do."

"Then you go out and kick ass."

I have spoken in an earlier essay[1] about the general cultural significance of prizefighting, but I would like to be a bit more specific here. One of the two interrelated cultural needs that boxing serves suggests that the antagonism of the opponents is very much like that of a morality play, a morality play about the very nature of capitalistic society. Despite the fact

---

[1] "Hot Spicks Versus Cool Spades: Three Notes Toward a Cultural Definition of Prizefighting."

that boxing is an international sport, practiced everywhere on the globe, America has become and has been for some time the center of professional fighting. Most of the best fighters are Americans; most of the big money originates here, and most of the publicity as well. In short, boxing is an American pastime. Moreover, one must not lose sight of the fact that modern professional boxing in its traceable history was a product of Britain; boxing in its course to its present identity is not just Western, not simply American, but particularly Anglo-Saxon. It should come as a surprise to no one, knowing modern prizefighting's national and racial origins, that the sport extols most simply and directly the values that the Anglo-Saxon male has historically cherished most: the indomitable will of the individual, aggressive conquest, and contempt for humiliation and submission. It is, perhaps, intended to be the height of irony that Wills, the black boy, the historical victim of the Anglo-Saxon's will to power, should teach Ernie Munger, the white boy, the Western values of male conquest. Wills's little speech sounds as much like the street-corner version of the philosophy of Robinson Crusoe as it does like the advice of a senior boardroom executive to a junior upstart. It is one of the striking ironies of the novel that boxing, a sport that so ruthlessly symbolizes the success ethic of American society, produces men who are so ill equipped to be anything but failures. Thus, one of the true oddities of the symbolism of boxing is that the minority male, in becoming like the paradigmatic, mythological Anglo-Saxon male, wears a kind of white face.

Duran's little episode with Alexis Arguello might remind one of the incredible invisible burden of the champion boxer, the great "asskicker." Gardner's novel is exclusively concerned with pugs, or as Camus called them, "low-brow gods." But the intensity of emotional commitment is greater when the fights mean more; more money, more prestige for the winner, more humiliation for the loser. Duran's insecurity has its source in the very deep doubt he must have about his self-image in his chosen profession. Duran is afraid, not so much of being beaten, but of being reduced, lessened, by showing any signs that would make him less committed to his line of work. One must remember that it was Duran who once said after beating an opponent that if he had been in shape he would have sent him to the morgue, not the hospital; it was Duran who once saluted Sugar Ray Leonard's wife by pointing his middle finger and calling her *puta* ("whore"); and it was Duran who spat in Leonard's face at the end of their first bout. This need for the commitment, the overwhelming identification not with boxing but with what it means to be an asskicker, is probably the main reason that Duran is still fighting even though he should have retired a few years ago. Duran is more the mythical Anglo-Saxon male than the Anglo-Saxon himself, and if that identification proves meaningless, then Duran is forced to ask himself what his blustering quest for manhood means. This is why he is still fighting and embarrassing himself. He does not want to think about what it would mean to stop: then he would be like a soldier without a war.

2

A film that clearly presents, in a huge metaphorical gesture, the secret fear of the male is the 1950s science fiction classic *The Incredible Shrinking Man*. Slowly, as the hero's body becomes smaller and smaller, the audience finds him overwhelmed not by life generally, not by his job, his government, his culture, or by his general intercourse with other people—but by his home and his wife. The woman becomes an overprotective giant and the home a wild hive of booby traps that threaten him at every turn. One is, of course, reminded of Leslie Fiedler and his talk about those many nineteenth-century American Adams who were trying to escape the very things that Herman Melville's Tommo was returning to at the end of *Typee*: home and mother. In *The Incredible Shrinking Man* there is a parodic inversion by which the man finds himself being swallowed by his home and his wife (whose relative largeness and maternal concern make her a mother figure); he must do battle against objects of his own home: a cat and a spider. The hero thus discovers that living in his home has become the ultimate pioneering adventure as he hunts for food and water and, in the final symbol of pathetic power, uses a straight pin for a sword. Grant Williams, who portrays the hero, ultimately loses his battle and his body simply vanishes by the end of the film.

This neurotic vision, or rather this dream or parable of the neurotic trapped male, poses an essential question about the sport of boxing: What is its secret, primeval appeal to its viewers? Part of the answer, no doubt, lies in the boxer's puritanical regimen: the hard training, the abstinence from sex before a fight, the Spartan diet. The boxer's leanness and physical conditioning become a sign of his virtue, a virtue worth a great deal in a land where the fatness of sin is the sin of fatness. But more deeply, the answer rests somewhere in the fact that the male is not needed as a cultural image for his courage, stamina, and heart, all of those manly virtues about which he has woven myths; he is needed as a psychological emblem to illustrate the capacity of dumb suffering. It is the torment and disfigurement of the male body that help the male to achieve the godhead. Norman Mailer would find in a film like *The Incredible Shrinking Man* the most endearing symbolism.

The first section of Mailer's *The Fight* opens and closes with images of the male body; the opening chapter describes "the Prince of Heaven," Muhammad Ali, in a training session, the beautiful body hiding both power and grace within its limbs:

> To the degree that boxing is carnality, meat against meat, Ali was master when it was time to receive, he got the juice out of it, the aesthetic juice of the punches he blocked or clipped, plus all the libidinal juice of Bossman Jones banging away on his gut. . . .
>
> Now it was as if Ali carried the idea to some advanced place where he could assimilate punches faster than other fighters, could literally transmit the

shock through more parts of his body, or direct it to the best path, as if ideally he was working toward the ability to receive that five-punch combination (or six or seven!) yet be so ready to ship the impact out to each arm, each organ and each leg, that the punishment might be digested, and the mind remain clear. It was a study to watch Ali take punches.

The descriptions seem complementary. In the first, the body as mythic image lies between art and sex; and in the second, the body is the mechanism that must be controlled and manipulated by the mind. Both denote so precisely the precarious precision of the boxer's psychological tightrope-walk between seizing and creating the moment, and squandering it. Mailer is indeed concerned with the wider symbol of the black male's tightrope-walking. But Mailer's representation is not so much a psychology of the male body as it is an anthropology of the male body. Somehow, through the imagery at the beginning, of Ali's body as self-fulfilling sex, as art, and as machine, and the imagery at the end of the first section, of the spindly, ugly body of Ali's talkative trainer, Drew Brown, the reader is presented with the history of male culture, from prince to clown, from the improvisations of the body to the improvisations of language (when the body, as in the case of Brown, fails as adequate symbolism). The polar realities of Brown and Ali as male figures symbolize the morality of masculinity: Ali puts his body on the line and is thus a hero-warrior. Drew Brown weaves with his mouth and is like a jester, a gnome, or as Mailer calls him, the King of the Flunkies. It is Brown who creates Ali's chants and poetry and it is with Brown that Mailer "plays the dozens." So although Ali was known as "the Mouth," Mailer's fascination and that of the entire Western culture with Ali have, in truth, always been with his heroic body. Boxing becomes, for Mailer, the most primitive yet the highest moment for the male psyche. The one-on-one encounter, the rewards of its brinksmanship, the egotistic excesses of its one-upmanship are what boxing and the male body mean.

> "Yet I think writers like Mailer use Ali as an excuse to write about race, or more precisely, about blacks: what a wonderful opportunity to clear the chest and spleen of numerous phobias and neuroses!"

The major problem with Mailer's fight book is that he spends a good number of his pages, far too many really, writing about race. This comes about because this book, like most of Mailer's fight pieces, is about Muhammad Ali, and with Ali as a subject I suppose one is, perforce, confronted with the issue of race. Yet I think white writers like Mailer use Ali as an excuse to write about race, or more precisely, about blacks: what a wonderful opportunity to clear the chest and spleen of numerous phobias and neuroses! When Mailer writes about race or about blacks he invariably is going to sound like the writer who penned that inglorious essay "The White Negro"—which means that he is liable to sound foolish. He will not sound utterly foolish, just foolish enough to make any knowing reader accept his good portions with a great deal of suspicion. Consider these passages:

> But [Norman Mailer's] love affair with the Black soul, a sentimental orgy at its worst, had been given a drubbing through the seasons of Black Power. He no longer knew whether he loved Blacks or secretly disliked them, which had to be the dirtiest secret in his American life. Part of the woe of the first trip to Africa, part of that irrationally intense detestation of Mobutu . . . must be a cover for the rage he was feeling toward Blacks, any Blacks. . . .
>
> His animosity switched a continent over to Black Americans with their arrogance, jive, ethnic put-down costumes, caterwauling soul, their thump-your-testicle organ sound and black new vomitous egos like the slag of all of alienated sewage-compacted heap U.S.A.; then he knew that he had not only come to report on a fight but to look a little more into his own outsized feelings of love and—could it be?—sheer hate for the existence of Blacks on earth.

Mailer was in Zaire to report on the heavyweight championship fight between Ali and George Foreman that took place in a hastily constructed stadium in the fall of 1974. Thus, the reader is confronted with Mailer's image of the land of bogeys and boots, the land without rational order; and the image becomes a quest on Mailer's part for the legitimation of his own rational white mind and his confessed inability to understand that mind which symbolizes for him the nonwhite other. It is Mailer's being in Africa and covering a fight between two black fighters that ultimately leads to the sort of psychic flatulence that the two quotations reveal. For Mailer, the black is always the id-dominated beast, the heart of the white man's darkness; and always, in Mailer's tone, there is that juvenile penis envy that might as well be hate because it amounts to such an insulting kind of love. He writes elsewhere in the book:

> So much resentment had developed for black style, black snobbery, black rhetoric, black pimps, superfly, and all the virtuoso handling of the ho. The pride Blacks took in their skill as pimps!

It is no wonder that Mailer loves boxing, or rather loves the symbolism of boxing. His engagement with the black experience has always been limited to the male side of all matters—when Mailer says "Blacks" he means male (an observation also made by Michelle Wallace in her book *Black Macho and the Myth of the Superwoman*). And his engagement with boxing has come about largely because its symbolism can be worked out in such an exclusively male arena and in exclusively male terms. What is amazing, in this regard, is Mailer's lack of growth in the years between the publication of "The White Negro" (1957) and *The Fight* (1975). Jazz and the black subterranean urban life served the same purpose in the pages of the essay as boxing and traveling in Africa do in the book.

Consider the similarity to the book in tone and content of these quotations from the essay:

> Knowing in the cells of his existence that life was war, nothing but war, the Negro (all exceptions admitted) could rarely afford the sophisticated inhibitions of civilization, and so he kept for his survival the art of the primitive, he lived in the enormous present, he subsisted for his Saturday night kicks, relinquishing the pleasures of the mind for the more obligatory pleasures of the body. . . .

> It is therefore no accident that psychopathy is most prevalent with the Negro. Hated from outside and therefore hating himself, the Negro was forced into the position of exploring all those moral wildernesses of civilized life which the Square automatically condemns as delinquent or evil or immature or morbid or self-destructive or corrupt. . . . But the Negro, not being privileged to gratify his self-esteem with the heady satisfactions of categorical condemnation, chose to move instead in that other direction where all situations are equally valid, and in the worst of perversion, promiscuity, pimpery, drug addiction, rape, razor-slash, bottle-break, what-have-you, the Negro discovered and elaborated a morality of the bottom.

Mailer expresses a very simple and very old idea here, namely, that the black male is metaphorically the white male's unconsciousness personified. What is of deeper interest in that formulation is Mailer's homogenization of the black male personality; in effect any black male, from jazz musician to boxer to pimp to bank robber, any black male who is estranged from bourgeois culture for whatever reason (and the reasons and the choices are far from being the same) is, for Mailer, the same outcast, the same uninhibited, uncivilized self, the same untraumatized noble savage. Ironically, if the black or Latin prizefighter within the code of his own world has absorbed the masculine rites and morality of the Anglo-Saxon West, then as symbol in the larger world he is simply a new type of minstrel, a black face hidden behind an even deeper blackface: the secret shadow-self of the white man's mind. In Mailer's vision, the boxers become clockwork psychopaths; each round in a fight is nothing more than a three-minute drill in regulated aggression, orchestrated and articulated by the writers outside the ring who have come to see boxing not as a sport but as imagistic psychotherapeutic ethics. For Mailer, the good id (Ali) whips the bad id (Foreman). One wishes that Mailer had taken to heart D. H. Lawrence's warning about "cherishing illusions about the race soul, the eternal Negroid soul. . . ."

There is nothing easier than to rake Mailer over the coals for his sexism. I do not intend to do that—first of all because he has been a frequent and quite easy target for feminists in recent years. Secondly, any male who really enjoys boxing is drawn to it at least partly because it is an all-male province, no matter how silly its bravado or how pointlessly dangerous its risks.

The reason why Mailer's book would be open to attack by feminists is related to his conjuring up of Ernest Hemingway whenever he gets the opportunity. Hemingway haunts Mailer and, in this particular instance, one is apt to think that *Death in the Afternoon* looms like a large shadow over Mailer's text. And it is the image of Hemingway that makes one think that Mailer's love of the all-male world of boxing is not the simple recitation of a particular preference but an actual statement of repudiation of any sexually mixed world. To chant the name of Hemingway is merely to give the imprint of genius to any meditation on a world without women.

But in the end, Mailer did not take Hemingway's advice. He tried to write an epic about boxing. The actual fight between Muhammad Ali and George Foreman had to be one of the most boring on record. The only reason it was of any interest is that everyone in the world was convinced that Ali would lose badly. After all, Foreman had bounced Joe Frazier and Ken Norton around like rubber balls, and those two last fighters gave Ali fits in the ring. But as Angelo Dundee has said, "Styles make a fight," and for this fight with Foreman, Ali had the right style. It was exciting *that* he won, but not *how* he won. The fight took on the same pattern round after round: Ali leaning against the ropes covering up while Foreman flailed away like a windmill. Finally, Foreman was too tired to hold his arms up anymore and Ali knocked him out in the eighth round; a flyweight could have knocked Foreman out by then. Ali's strategy worked only because Foreman was such an abysmally stupid fighter. And the long-term bodily effects of the rope-a-dope strategy, which a very lazy Ali adopted as a main feature in his subsequent fights, have yet to be fully realized. Suffice it to say that in the long run Ali may be the big loser. Mailer devotes nearly forty pages in his book to describing the actual combat, a rather dangerous thing to do. A third-rate writer for *The Ring* could have described it in a thousand-word column. Mailer wants to write an epic; he wants to invest his writing with the images of larger-than-life heroes and villains and larger-than-life tragedy and drama. But as Hemingway wrote, "Nor is overwritten journalism made literature by the injection of a false epic quality. Remember this too: all bad writers are in love with the epic."

3

"I am a sports romanticist," wrote the late Nat Fleischer, great boxing historian and biographer, founder and publisher of *The Ring* magazine, "the Bible of Boxing." This statement opens what Fleischer considered to be or at least what was publicly announced as his autobiography, *50 Years at Ringside*. One supposes that Fleischer, certainly not the best of writers even by a fairly liberal standard, though a solid journalist, was indulging in a bit of grandiloquence: he might just as easily have said that he was a sports fan (or more particularly a boxing fan since Fleischer made his reputation as a writer on that single sport and nothing else) and left it at that. But "romanticist" might, after all, be the right word to capture Fleischer's obsession. For Fleischer, boxing had long ceased to be an escape from reality, an adjunct of reality, or a component of reality; the prizefight had become reality itself. Is it not one of the major characteristics of the romanticist to flood and enrich an emblem incessantly until not only does that emblem explain the world but all actions in the world, however distant, are seen as simply replicating the emblem? And is not that act seen as applying, to use Jacques Barzun's phrase, "energy, morality, and genius" to "the problem of reconstruction"? The romanticist, finally, is a reconstructionist. And surely Fleischer was quite dedicated to the task of reconstructing prizefighting.

Having described in the most minute detail in his dozens of books and in his columns and editorials in *The Ring* and other publications the thousands of fights that he witnessed or read about from the golden age of bareknuckle fighting to the era of Muhammad Ali, Fleischer seemed fairly certain that what happened in the prize ring and why it happened were the only experiences worth knowing. This devotion far exceeds that of even the most rabid fan who is usually satisfied by merely collecting and hoarding certain objects, a devotion that not only is parasitic and simply a sign of neurotic consumption but also abhors producing anything. Fleischer's obsession, not unlike that of black scholar Carter G. Woodson, was indeed most closely akin to that astringent devotion of the scholar; for what he really wanted to know was the unknowable: the essence of his love, the essence of boxing, the thing that made it what it was. And he searched for that essence as diligently as, perhaps even more so than, say, a nineteenth-century specialist would seek the essence of Victorianism or the essence of Marx or the essence of Matthew Arnold. Consequently, his production as a writer was prodigious: a five-volume set on the history of blacks in pugilism from its beginnings in England to the era of Joe Louis (which would not have been possible without the existence of Pierce Egan's *Boxiana* and other histories of British Regency boxing and the *National Police Gazette,* the best historical source of American boxing in the late nineteenth and early twentieth centuries); full-length and short biographies of Stanley Ketchel, Jack Dempsey, John L. Sullivan, James Corbett, Gene Tunney, Benny Leonard, Ben Hogan, and others; several general histories of prizefighting and the heavyweight championship; books and pamphlets on such matters as how to train a fighter, how to be a second, how to be a manager, and how to referee a fight; in addition to articles and editorials in *The Ring* for over fifty years. According to *Newsweek,* Fleischer wrote about 40 million words on boxing during his lifetime.

Of all his books, Fleischer was most proud of his multivolume set on black fighters. In the introduction to the first volume he writes:

> Now that the task has been completed, the writer believes that he has done a job for colored fighters which parallels that done by Pierce Egan for fisticuffs in general. But for Egan's splendid *Boxiana* which appeared in parts from 1812 to 1828, the story of the beginnings of the sport would have been lost.

He goes on in this vein:

> In writing the story of the negro [*sic*], the author went far beyond the method used by Egan. Pierce found his story in newspaper files. The writer had to delve through ancient pamphlets, forgotten magazines, copies of newspapers which flourished long before the United States became a nation.

And at last we arrive at the heart of the matter:

> In developing the story of the Negro [*sic*], the writer discovered that a new treatment of the subject was necessary. The model laid down by Egan could not be followed. Even more arduous research than had been gone through by Egan was necessary, because never before had anyone attempted the story of the colored fighter without prejudice to that fighter.

Within the space of a few short paragraphs, Egan is transformed from the hero historian who must be emulated to the rival historian who must be overcome or overthrown: a bold exposition of Fleischer's anxiety of influence and his vision as a reconstructionist. If Egan, now known to historians not as a historian himself but as the frivolous author of the rather minor Tom and Jerry adventures, a text Thackeray branded as not one-half so good as Cruikshank's accompanying pictures, could write the equivalent of a five-volume set on the most socially outcast men of his day, with a few exceptions (prizefighting was, indeed, a criminal offense in Regency England), then Fleischer, of course, could write a five-volume set on the most despised of the socially outcast: the black prizefighter. If Egan could describe the fights of Jack Broughton, which he never saw, then Fleischer could describe the fights of Richmond and Molineaux, the great black fighters he never saw of the late eighteenth and early nineteenth centuries. But what separates Fleischer from Egan and their monumental achievements in the fields of sportswriting and cultural history is that Egan as romantic historian was not a Puritan and Fleischer was. Egan gave the world such fanciful words as *bruiser* (boxer), *bunch of fives* (fist), *chopper* and *chops* (mouth), *clout* (blow), *conk* (head), *game* (brave), *ivories* (teeth), *up to scratch* (ready to fight), *mug* (face), *peeper* (eye), *sneezer* (nose), *upper story* (head), *lark* (adventure), *bottom* (courage), *the fancy* (followers of boxing), and a score of others. Egan loved slang, puns, and the ambience of the life of the prizefighter. Egan was a hedonist. Fleischer was an ascetic: The life of a fighter is simply the fights he has fought, a truth so fundamental that it is nearly as profound as it is simple-minded. First, for Fleischer, a fighter is good, then, at his prime, then, slowly coming apart, and finally, completely finished. The inevitable warp and woof of what to Fleischer is a commonplace tragedy is his only concern and his only pattern. Fleischer dedicated his energy and moral vision to the ultimate failed energy and partial moral vision of the prizefighter. For Fleischer, in every instance, the fighter eventually breaks the covenant with his own body, with his own athletic purity, with the sacred mission of the sport. Fleischer's writing contains no puns, no thick and hectic descriptions of the world of prizefighting, and only the most standard slang: "mitt" for glove, "claret" for blood, "orb" for eye, and so forth. In short, Egan was wildly inventive, reimagining and re-creating the fights and the fighter's world he wrote about so vividly, whereas Fleischer was ponderously consistent and prosaic; not interested in *conceiving* fights, he simply *reported* them with elephantine tenacity. During Fleischer's—and for that matter twentieth-century sportwriting's—heyday from the 1920s to the 1940s, prizefights were made a good deal more frequently than they are today. A good fighter during the twenties, except Dempsey, might fight as often as once a month; some, especially black fighters who had to overcome the constant difficulty of being demanded to throw fights to white opponents, fought almost weekly, in some cases daily. So Fleischer's mill was always, as it were, grinding, grinding away, and his writing, despite his unending opportunity to practice his craft, always had the texture of pulverized substance or in this case pulverized thought, fights so minutely described that they seemed atomized parodies of journalistic descriptions.

Of course, lost in all of Fleischer's books, in this plethora of words, this sea of comprehensive accounts of prizefighting, were the objects of Fleischer's search. In seeking the essence of prizefighting, he was searching not for more and more words about fights or more and more boring descriptions of fights or even ultimately to slay the father figure of Pierce Egan; he was seeking what every scholar truly wants: the one perfect *redaction*, that very small set of words that would say better everything contained in all of the volumes of the world.

He finally discovered one sort of redaction when he wrote "I'm a sports romanticist" to open his autobiography and then, a few pages later, added, "There is romance in boxing." He found one gesture of temperament that explained and contained all of his other gestures, that essence of eloquence that contained all his grandiloquence, the emblem in the emblem. His tautology is absolutely necessary: If he is a romanticist and he loves prizefighting, then prizefighting must have romance. And if prizefighting has romance, and he loves the sport (love is essentially a romantic pretext), then he must be a romanticist. It is substantially not only a self-justifying discourse but an ontological proposition. It is this redaction of the romantic temperament that Fleischer, a Jew, shared with the other American Jewish writers who have dreamed about and written about prizefighting, who were attracted to prizefighting because it offered a kind of solidarity beyond a Jewish sensibility or marginality, those two writers being A. J. Liebling and Norman Mailer. For these very unathletic Jews, although each of them did on more than one occasion step into the ring and train with professional fighters, to love fighting was an intellectual test of being able to explicate an inexplicable love, to justify loving an object that was surely not worthy of either the love or the justification. In a captivating way, being a Jewish intellectual in love with boxing was equivalent to replicating and mocking the aesthetic and political condition of being a Jew.

But because Fleischer is a romanticist and there is romance in boxing, because the object he loves confirms his existence as much he confirms its reality, all fighters, in the end, become simply two fighters, a winner and a loser, a bloodied specimen of humanity and one less bloody. And every fight becomes the same fight, the same tense drama, or the same relentlessly mundane factuality of socially permitted violence endlessly repeated. Only a romanticist could stand this type of repetition; indeed, only a romanticist would crave for its insistence, for the security of the one gesture being fatuously reenacted. Today we might call Fleischer not a historian or a biographer or a romanticist but rather a mythologist. For is not myth the essence of reality, the redaction, the all-consuming gesture, and is not its first and foremost requirement that it must be endlessly repeated and endlessly endured to be truly what it is? That the mythologist must be as voracious in his need to absorb the same expression as the myth is extravagant in its immutable ability to express sameness? And is not myth ultimately an attack against materialism, an attack against any reality (super, mundane, ultra) external to perception or external to the ability to idealize? And has not materialism always been the object of attack for romanticists? So what is a romanticist but someone who does not want the world or the actions of humanity to be subsumed under some impersonal reality, a materialist universe. And Fleischer's prolific endurance was his act of idealization, not to say something new about the fights he saw but to be moved, inspired that the fights so compellingly called forth the need to be witnessed in the same way. What makes Fleischer, on one level, so much more interesting as a writer than Mailer, Liebling, even Egan, was his refusal to call attention to himself as a writer, to resist utterly the attempt to make it all interesting by flights of rhetorical fancy. But there are occasions when the romanticist creates the very thing he is fighting against. Endless descriptions of fights may produce the very clockwork, depersonalized, *trivialized* reality that the romanticist wants to avoid. Fleischer did not understand this, which is why, unlike Egan, who did, he continued to report about prizefighting until the very hour of his death.

4

If Ernest Hemingway's presence overshadows Norman Mailer's fight pieces, then A. J. Liebling is haunted by the old Victorian fight journalist Pierce Egan. Liebling's book on boxing, *The Sweet Science* (the title is derived from a phrase coined by Egan), is doubtless the best nonfiction book on boxing since Egan penned pieces on the bareknuckle brawlers of England in the publication *Boxiana*. Liebling's essays, which originally appeared in *The New Yorker,* are a purist's journey through the major bouts of the fifties: Sugar Ray Robinson's fights with Joey Maxim and Randy Turpin, Marciano's two bouts with Jersey Joe Walcott, his two bouts with Ezzard Charles, and his fight with Archie Moore. Liebling also covers an early Floyd Patterson fight, Moore's battle with his arch-nemesis Harold Johnson, and a minor Sandy Saddler fight.

Liebling writes as a journalist; he is not obsessed with the epic, so his pieces are not pretentious like Mailer's. At his best, he reminds one of the best of Red Smith. Indeed, Liebling positively revels in the seedy hotel, the wrinkled topcoat, the greasy-collar persona of the boxing writer. And because he writes here in the guise of the boxing writer, he is also a purist who loves to listen to the old boys and keep a sharp eye out for the odd-balls. The book is filled with presences like Freddie Brown, old-time, raspy-voiced trainer whose last famous pupil was the foul-tempered but brilliant Roberto Duran; Al Weill, manager of Rocky Marciano and seeker of "young broken fighters"; Charlie Goldman, trainer of Marciano, who says, "One of the troubles with fighters now is they don't start before they're interested in dames"; and Runyonesque characters like Prince Monolulu, an Ethiopian prince who plays the ponies in England, preaches Zionism on Sundays, and has moderate success betting on fights.

Yet in reading this book one gets the impression that Liebling is well aware that he has approached the end of an epoch. The boxers and the bouts, the managers and the trainers, the auditoriums where the fights are held, and the audiences who witness them are all part of the past. Liebling sees televised fights as heralding the downfall of the sport:

> The immediate crisis in the United States, forestalling the one high living standards might bring on, has been caused by the popularization of a ridiculous gadget called television. This is utilized in the sale of beer and razor blades. The clients of the television companies, by putting on a free boxing show almost every night of the week, have knocked out of business the hundreds of small-city and neighborhood boxing clubs where youngsters had a chance to learn their trade and journeymen to mature their skills. Consequently the number of good new prospects diminishes with every year, and the peddlers' public is already being asked to believe that a boy with perhaps ten or fifteen fights behind him is a topnotch performer. Neither advertising nor brewers, and least of all the networks, give a hoot if they push the Sweet Science back into a period of genre painting. When it is in a coma they will find some other way to peddle their peanuts.

The purist's obsession with standards is not simply a crotchety moralism but a quest for integrity in a world where such a quality is fast vanishing. As it happened, Liebling was right; television absolutely distorted and detached the viewer's ability to see or understand prizefighting and often interfered with the boxer's ability to perform. The viewer is distanced from the struggle and the pain of the ordeal; the vibrating edge of fear and brutality is blunted, is in fact reduced and packaged. Indeed, far from being able to "experience" a fight on television, one is simply manipulated by the camera angles and the commentators. One reacts to the grossness of the occasion without sensing its subtleties. The fighters, in many cases little more than honorable schoolboys who have been advanced too many grades without benefit of instruction, are often in more danger of being seriously injured than would be the case if they were more seasoned performers. Finally, to have taken from the province of the enthusiast and put up for public sale not only the big-money and big-name fights, but the little ordinary ones as well, is to have reduced the sport to its one most prominent and marketable characteristic—the charismatic flowing of blood. As one of the characters in Budd Schulberg's novel *The Harder They Fall* puts it, boxing is "show business with blood."

In the end, it is Liebling's very self-consciousness about his quest for integrity that makes *The Sweet Science* reek of a high-brow, quaint conservatism. To Liebling, the televised boxing match might have been the beginning of a high-tech, grossly inartistic seizure of the manly art of self-defense. But it must be admitted that before television the world of boxing was one of gangsterism, fixed fights, racial baiting and discrimination, severe punch-drunkenness, down-and-out fighters without two nickels to rub together, petty whores, fleece artists, dishonest officials, and a general miasma of corruption and filth. Television was not ruining an art form; it was buying into a money-making den of iniquity. Nearly any sense of this side of boxing is absent from Liebling's essays. Boxing is not, after all, merely a series of cunningly contrived pieces about its characters written in order to make a low-class endeavor palatable to the high-brow readers of *The New Yorker*. This is where Liebling's purist bent leads him astray: the age of the 1940s and the early 1950s in pre-television boxing was not the golden age of bareknuckle fighters that Pierce Egan described during the Regency and early Victorian era. Perhaps the 1810s and 1820s were as innocently bawdy and brawling as Egan wanted his readers to believe, but the 1940s and 1950s demanded more than the picturesque. Liebling's aim, I think, is clear; *The Sweet Science* was meant to be the romance of modern prizefighting, sportswriting as *belles lettres*. Here is an overweight Jewish intellectual who imagined himself the reincarnation of a cocky, loutish nineteenth-century Irishman, emulating Egan's style of dense slang, obscure allusions, sporting-life ambience, and reemphasizing Egan's values, described by one scholar as being "acceptance of social diversity and of the divisions in society with each class pursuing its own pleasures"; "warning against tricksters, money-lenders, procuresses and con-men"; and "rejoicing in the existence of low life." But ultimately *The Sweet Science,* despite the ghost of Egan, is so much less than Egan. The book was not even meant to be historical romanticism like Egan's pieces but rather sheer requiem for the last artists of integrity. This is why the book is framed with the images of two great black fighters who are in the twilight of their careers: Joe Louis and Archie Moore, two supreme artists making their last stands. When Liebling writes that a "boxer, like a writer, must stand alone," the reader knows that the book is making an early claim to its easy moral victory. *The Sweet Science* is nothing more than an effective, long good-bye.[2]

---

[2]It is deeply ironic that the greatest fighter of all time, Muhammad Ali, should be a creature of television. The world's greatest ring artist shamelessly sold himself like any sponsor's product. Liebling died in 1963, before Ali won the heavyweight title for the first time. Wherever he is now, he must be terribly chagrined by it all.

III. Young Man Streetfighter: An American Sketch

Let me begin by warning the reader that this will not be an unhappy story.

In the neighborhood where I grew up there was a block called Fairhill Street. Every black American ghetto must have one of these streets, where the houses are so dilapidated, so absolutely ruined that the bricks bulge out in a manner that suggest a kind of sterile pregnancy. Even the inanimate objects seem swollen with grief. Many of the houses, as I remember, were boarded up with wood or sheets of metal, and yellow paper signs would be posted on the front doors which read: THIS PROPERTY IS DECLARED UNFIT FOR HUMAN HABITATION. Of course, people continued to live in these buildings and no one thought anything at all about it. If you were to ask these people why they did not move to more suitable quarters, they would tell you simply that they could afford nothing else; they had no place else to live. They were, I think, wretchedly poor, the poorest black people in the neighborhood. The young children would run around barefoot in the summer, with dirty, cut-up feet, mostly because the parents could not afford the fancy PF Flyers and Converses that I and other children wore. The girls on this block were always pregnant before the age of fifteen and the boys in jail before sixteen. In those days, people on welfare did not receive food stamps; they were given government-issued food popularly referred to as "surplus." At school, it was easy to spot the kids whose families received surplus; they always brought lunches that consisted of the whitest white bread in the world and thick, pink, rubbery pieces of Spam or potted meat. Those of us who thought we were better off than our Fairhill Street friends—if only, as in the case of most of us, by the fewest of dollars—would revel in our lunches of greasy steak sandwiches and submarines or glazed doughnuts and soda pop bought from the corner store.

On this street was an empty lot, covered with broken glass, garbage, and the occasional dead body of an animal, where one could usually find members of the Fifth and South Streets gang. And it was on this lot that I saw the greatest fistfight of my life, better than any professional fight I have seen before or since. On a certain day in my youth, Frank White, the warlord of the Seventh Street gang, and Tabu, the warlord of Fifth and South Streets gang, fought in that strange ring for the championship of the streets.

It was an extremely hot August day in my twelfth or thirteenth summer. I was loafing in the playground with the boys of the Fifth and South Streets gang. Some of them were playing basketball; most were simply lounging in the shade, listening to R&B on a transistor radio, drinking wine or soda pop, and trying to beat the heat. Tabu was sitting on a bench playing checkers. He loved playing checkers more than anyone else I knew except the old men who played on the front steps of a house on Fairhill Street. Tabu and his opponents always played by the "touch a man, move a man" rule, just as the old men did, which meant that these

games were the fastest ever witnessed on a board. Tabu liked me a great
deal and this was certainly a curious thing because I had little merit or
influence among the boys; I was simply one of the fellows who hung
around the fringes. He had a great deal of respect for my intelligence
(even in those days I was known for being a bookish boy), which I
thought surprising since virtually no one else did. It was an even exchange
since I had a great deal of respect for the way he used his dukes. It was a
nice friendship; he always called me Slim because he did not like the name
Gerald, and I always called him Tabu because I never knew any other
name to call him.

Seeing Tabu in my mind's eye, it is hard to imagine that he was the
warlord, the best fighter in the gang. He surely had the physique—he was
lean and muscular and as hard as steel. But he did not seem to have the
temperament. He loved to play basketball and checkers and talk to girls
and laugh. He never seemed angry enough with anyone about anything
to want to fight. Yet he did fight quite well and quite often and with a
bewildering sense of humor. Whenever he had an opponent—whether
in a street fight, basketball game, or checkers match—at an insurmountable disadvantage, he would shout gleefully, "It's game time and your ass
is mine!"

On this hot afternoon, word began to spread through the playground
that the Seventh Street gang was "coming down strong" looking to kick
the asses of the "punk motherfuckers of Fifth and South." The air was
suddenly electric with excitement. The boys, once assured that this was
no idle rumor, gathered their weapons and massed themselves and began
moving out of the playground to meet the enemy. I tagged along mostly
to watch. Midway up Fairhill Street we could see the crush of black
youthful humanity coming to greet us. We had about fifty members and
Seventh Street easily had sixty or seventy. I thought we were outmanned—
so much so that, discretion being the better part of valor, it was time to
consider beating a hasty retreat. No one else felt that way. When the two
gangs did meet face to face, there was no violence. The leaders from both
groups began to talk, and it was decided, surprisingly, to declare a truce,
so that both gangs could unite against the Thirteenth and Fitzgerald
Streets gang, the massively manned nemesis of both the Fifth and South
and the Seventh Streets gangs. There was some disagreement as to who
was to have leadership over this combination and it was decided to have
the warlord from each group fight to settle the matter.

The rules of the fight were simple: no kicking, no head-butting, no
hitting below the belt, no wrestling, and no rounds. Both boys were to
fight until one of them quit. Whoever quit would be the loser.

I did not know Frank White personally but I knew his reputation. He
too was lean and muscular but much taller than Tabu. And he had a face
that indicated that behind his fire-red eyes was one of the most evil dispo-
sitions in all of South Philadelphia. He had a lemon-yellow complexion
with freckles and a thick ring of scar tissue around his neck from a knife

wound. It was rumored that he had once broken a grown man's jaw in a fistfight. Another rumor was that he had killed a boy in a knife fight and had beaten the rap in court. He looked grim and merciless.

We all sojourned to the empty lot and the principals removed their shirts and shadow-boxed a bit to warm up. It was such a hot day that both boys were sweating heavily even before they faced each other. White had very quick hands and a fluid motion; he looked very, very good to me—much better than Tabu, whose facial expression did not even seem to absorb the gravity of the situation. He was smiling and jocular about all of this. I was afraid for him.

The fight started with both boys exchanging evenly; but White soon pulled out in front, using the advantage of his height and reach. He threw rapid-fire left jabs, then followed up with straight rights and left hooks. He was like a smooth-running machine and he never varied his pattern. First, Tabu's nose started to bleed, then his mouth, then little welt marks started to form around his eyes. Tabu was scoring with punches, too. But his hands were not as fast so he did not land as often. After twenty minutes, both boys were so drenched in sweat that their trousers were soaked and they were nearly exhausted. It was surely surprising that neither passed out from sunstroke. At this point, Tabu was losing badly. Suddenly, he crouched very low as if he

> "Tabu screamed out, 'It's game time and your ass is mine!'"

were going to spring or lunge a punch. That seemed a sure sign of utter desperation. He stayed in this position for a minute and allowed White to hit with a jab, then another and another. After throwing the left a half-dozen times without missing, White predictably threw a tremendous straight right; it did not miss, although White afterward probably wished that it had. It was the punch that Tabu was waiting for; he timed it so that as the punch was thrown, he jerked out of his crouch and thrust his head forward like a bull charging. The blow landed on the top of Tabu's skull and White immediately gave a howl of pain. He had either jammed his knuckles on Tabu's hard head or broken his hand. In either case, his right hand was useless. Tabu screamed out, "It's game time and your ass is mine!" Tabu swarmed all over White but the fight went on for another twenty minutes before White, after having been struck so vicious a blow on his chest that a surface blood vessel ruptured, finally sat down on the filthy ground and looked up at Tabu and shook his head. The warlord of Seventh Street had quit. It was Tabu's finest hour; he was the undisputed king of the hill insofar as we poor black boys of South Philadelphia were concerned.

As I grew older and no longer hung around with the neighborhood boys, I wondered what had happened to Tabu. About four years ago, when I visited Philadelphia, I learned the news. I was in a record store called 3rd Street Jazz looking through the stacks when suddenly I heard someone call out, "Hey, Slim. Where you been?" I knew the voice right away. I turned and saw Tabu—but what a change from the street days!

He was wearing a three-piece suit, carrying a very expensive-looking at-taché case, sporting a neatly trimmed goatee and mustache, and looked for all the world like the landed gentry of black folk. Was this the same person who had once been my hero back on Fairhill Street? He told me what he had been doing: he had a degree from Temple University and worked as an administrator for a municipal agency. He was going to law school at night and contemplated finishing that degree in two more years. He was married, with, as he put it, "four beautiful daughters," all of whom had African names that sounded like pure poetry but which I could not recall the moment after he had spoken them. I was never good at remembering poetry. He still had a good physique but he was begin-ning to develop a paunchy middle. He told me he played racquetball at a health spa he belonged to. He seemed almost sleek with success.

"I had to quit the gang in order to get serious," he said. "I had to stop fighting. You know, some of those cats are still out there. Into the dope thing. Been to prison. And still into the gang thing. Man, they never grew up. Just want to keep street fighting all their lives. You can't go around fist-fighting forever. You got to become a man and put that stuff behind you. I just decided to grow up."

We talked about jazz quite a bit. He had become a big fan of "the music." We were discussing Miles Davis's *Sketches of Spain*. Tabu shook his head in admiration: "It's the baddest album out there. Man, it's like Miles telling the other trumpet players, 'It's game time and your ass is mine.'" I smiled. Some things never really change.

As I said in the beginning, this was not intended to be an unhappy story about a ghetto boy. It is, in fact, an American success story of the most familiar sort. The lesson of the story is this: Tabu, unlike those sweet Sugar Rays (Robinson, Seales, and Leonard), is the only fighter I have ever heard of who was smart enough to quit before, as Pete Town-shend put it, he got old.

Interview with Gerald Early

BECKY BRADWAY: Every section of this piece could stand alone as a dis-tinct essay or article. Did you initially conceive of this essay as a whole, or was each section composed separately and then, later, linked thematically?

GERALD EARLY: The essay was conceived as a whole. Each part was meant to illuminate the others. The pieces were not composed separately. The entire essay was written as a whole with the vision of the separate parts. Think of them as distinct movements in a sonata.

BB: You are known both as an essayist and as a literary scholar. Does your writing process change when writing a piece of criticism as op-posed to memoir?

GE: Not really. I am trying to write as well as I can and think as clearly as I can with whatever I am writing. My job with any of my writing is to get the reader to both think and feel; that is why the autobiographical sections are included in some pieces. Autobiography enables a reader to think through his or her feelings and to identify with what is being said to him or her, to identify with what he or she is being asked to think about. I try to break down barriers between me and my reader.

BB: You hold a doctorate in literature. The number of writers who study literature seems to be dwindling. Do you feel that majoring in literature remains a relevant pursuit for writers? What is your view of the growing numbers of MFA programs?

GE: Hmmm, I don't think you can be a good writer unless you're a good reader. I earned a PhD because I wanted to become a good reader, a better reader than I was. It never occurred to me to enter an MFA program because I was convinced that as I became a better reader I would, with practice, naturally, become a better writer. There are a lot of MFA programs out there. I sure hope all those would-be writers find readers in a world where reading is dwindling fast.

Dave Eggers

From *A Heartbreaking Work of Staggering Genius*

Dave Eggers grew up close to Chicago and attended the University of Illinois. He is the author of the memoir *A Heartbreaking Work of Staggering Genius* (2000), the novel *You Shall Know Our Velocity!* (2002), the story collection *How We Are Hungry* (2004), and the novel *What Is the What* (2006). In 1998, he founded McSweeney's, an independent book-publishing house in San Francisco that puts out the *McSweeney's* quarterly literary journal; the monthly magazine the *Believer*; a daily humor Web site, www.mcsweeneys.net; and *Wholphin*, a DVD quarterly of short films. In 2002, Eggers and his friends opened 826 Valencia, a writing lab for young people located in the Mission District of San Francisco, where he teaches writing to high school students and runs a summer publishing camp; there are now branches of 826 in Brooklyn, Los Angeles, Seattle, Chicago, Ann Arbor, and Boston. With the help of his workshop students, Eggers edits a collection of fiction, essays, and journalism called *The Best American Nonrequired Reading*. He is also the coeditor of the Voice of Witness series of oral histories.

His fiction has appeared in *Zoetrope, Punk Planet*, and the *New Yorker*. He has recently written introductions to new editions of books by Edward Wallant, John Cheever, and Mark Twain. He writes regularly about art and music for magazines, including *Frieze, Blind Spot, Parkett*, and *Spin*, and his design work has been featured in many periodicals, including *Print and Eye*, and annuals, including *Area: 100 Graphic Designers* and *Reinventing the Wheel*. He has designed most of the books and quarterlies published by McSweeney's and created the templates for the *Believer* and *Wholphin*. In 2003, his designs for *McSweeney's* were featured in the National Design Triennial at the Cooper-Hewitt National Design Museum and in the California Design Biennial.

What follows is an excerpt from *A Heartbreaking Work of Staggering Genius*, his memoir that inventively tells of the responsibility Eggers takes on for his younger brother after his parents' deaths. Reviewers of the book expressed confusion: they tended to criticize the book's self-indulgence and embellishments while simultaneously applauding them as "clever" and "literary" and "youthful." They became stuck on the book's long beginning, in which Eggers explains that some parts are truer than others and that any passages that are too self-referential could be skipped. Most reviewers ended up being won over despite their resistance, as in this conclusion by the *New York Times*: "it quickly becomes a virtuosic piece of writing, a big, daring, manic-depressive stew of book that noisily announces the debut of a talented—yes, staggeringly talented new writer." Writer David Sedaris said that "the force and energy of this book could power a train."

No matter what you think of *A Heartbreaking Work*, it calls out to be noticed, and any discussion of contemporary memoir eventually has to come
around to Dave Eggers.

The selection we have included comes shortly after Eggers takes responsibility for his young brother Toph following the death of their parents. Shortly
after Eggers's graduation from college, he and his brother leave suburban
Chicago for the urban wilds of San Francisco. Here he confronts the same realities that face all young parents, with the added trial of a sudden pseudo-
parenthood that lacks authentic parental authority. He is, after all, just a
brother, and this dynamic comes across clearly in the interactions between
these two as they sort out their lives. Particularly striking is Eggers's natural
use of dialogue that seems silly but implies much about the pair. The piece
also includes Eggers's trademark use of diagrams and lists that further illuminate their daily lives.

The enemies list is growing quickly, unabated. All these people imped-
ing us, trifling with us, not knowing or caring who we are, what has
happened. The squirrelly guy who sold Toph that cheap lock for his
bike—his new bike, the one we bought last year, for his birthday, just
before we left Chicago—I wanted to punish that man—he said it was
the best lock they had, "invincible, no sweat" he said—and the bike
was stolen within the week. And that idiot in the van, who backed over
our little Civic, with both of us in it, at a stoplight, in the middle of
Berkeley, me forced to picture it happening that second, the van continuing, monster-truck-style, over the hood, onto us, Toph crushed,
slowly, me watching, helpess— And something should be done about
(or to) that gaunt and severe woman on the BART, the one with the
hair pulled back so tight she looked half-onion, who sat across from us,
kept looking over her book, at us, disapproving, as I rested my feet on
Toph's lap, like I was a molester— And the secretary at school, with
her blaming look at me when he's late for school— And that other
woman, the across-the-street neighbor, a haggy creature with the
chubby son, who stops her gardening and stares every time we leave the
house. And the owners of the Berkeley hills sublet, who kept our deposit, citing (or claiming) damage to just about everything in the house.
And most of all, those real estate people. Cruel, vicious, subhuman.
Those fuckers were unbelievable.

"Where do you work?"

"I don't have a job yet."

"Are you in school?"

"No."

"And this is your . . . son?"

"Brother."

"Oh. Well. We'll let you know."

We had no idea where to look. Toph's new school has no bus service,
so from the start I knew I'd be driving him to and fro regardless of where
we lived. Thus, in late July, when we started looking for a place for the

fall, we cast our net wide, considered, at least initially, almost every neighborhood in Berkeley, Albany, and southern Oakland. After discerning that between my income—assuming at some point that notion would become reality—and Toph's Social Security money—he's entitled to a monthly stipend, equivalent to what would have been paid our parents, we presume—we could pay about $1,000 a month, we set out.

And were soon struck with the relatively dingy reality of our new lives. There would no longer be hills, or views—that sublet was a freak occurrence. We would have no garage, no washer and dryer, no dishwasher, no disposal, no closets, no bathtub. Some of the places we saw didn't even have doors on the bedrooms. I felt terrible, felt personally responsible; I began to look without Toph, to spare him the gore. We were in decline. In Chicago we had a house, an ample kind of house, four bedrooms, a yard, a creek running behind, huge, hundred-year-old trees, a little hill, some woods. Then there was the sublet, the golden house in the hills, its glass and light, overlooking everything, mountains, oceans, all of those bridges. And now, in part due to the inevitable implosion of our household—Katie doesn't want to live with all of us, Kirsten and I need some time apart, and Beth and I, like any grown siblings with any kind of history behind them, knew one of us would be found bloody and dismembered if we continued to occupy the same four walls—we had all accepted smaller, humbler situations. Beth would live alone, Kirsten with a roommate found in the classifieds, and Toph and I would find a two-bedroom, would try to live close, but not too close, to one or both of them.

"We were in decline."

I had wanted a loft. For years I had pictured my first postcollegiate rental as a huge raw space, all high ceilings and chipped paint, exposed brick, water pipes and heating ducts, a massive open area where I could paint, could build and house enormous canvases, throw stuff around, maybe set up a basketball hoop, a smallish hockey rink. It would be close to the Bay, and a park, and the BART, grocery stores, everything. I called a few places listed in Oakland.

"What's the neighborhood like?" I asked.

"Well, it's kinda funky. But our lot has a gate."

"A gate? What about a park?"

"A park?"

"Yeah, I have an eight-year-old. Is there a park nearby?"

"Oh please. Get serious."

Even when we accepted the prospect of a one-story two-bedroom in the flatlands, people were unkind, ungiving. I had expected open arms from all, everyone grateful that we, as God's tragic envoys, had stepped down from the clouds to consider dwelling in their silly little buildings. What we were getting was something eerily close to indifference.

Early on, we had seen a listing—two bedrooms, yard, North Berkeley—and had made the call; the man sounded enthused, definitely not evil. But then, on a warm and blue day, we drove to his house. As we got out of our little red car and walked toward him, he was standing out on the porch, he looked stricken.

"This is your brother?"

"Yeah."

"Ooh," he said, with difficulty, as if the O were an egg he was forcing through his mouth. "Jeez, I expected you two to be older. How old are you guys?"

"I'm twenty-two. He's nine."

"But on the application you said he had an income. I don't see how that's possible."

I explained Social Security to him. I explained to him the inheritance of money. I was cheerful about it, emphasizing that we were well aware that it was a little unusual, but anyway, now that that's out of the way—

He tilted his head, his arms folded. We were still on the driveway. We were not being invited into the house.

"Listen guys, I don't want to waste your time. I'm really looking for a couple, an older couple preferably."

The wind sent to us the smell of those white flowers that are everywhere, the ones on the bushes. Rhododendrons?

"Can you see where I'm coming from?" he asked.

On the BART, on the way to an A's game, we sat, Toph and I, reading side by side, and across from us was a young woman, Latina, a little older than me, with her daughter, a bit younger than Toph. The woman, small and in a white shirt, was playing with the hair of the girl, who was sucking on a drinkbox. They could be sisters, with a wider age-gap than Toph and me—or could she be her mother? If she's 25 and the girl 7 . . . it could be. They seemed nice. The woman was not wearing any rings. I wondered if we could all move in together. She would understand. She would already know how it is. We could combine our households. It would be so good, we could share all the responsibilities, babysitting no problem. Toph and this girl would be friends and maybe would end up getting married— And maybe the woman and I should be together, too. But she looked like she had a boyfriend. Did she? That secure look. So at ease. Not just a boyfriend, but a good man, too. A large man maybe. A boyfriend who lifts heavy things for a living. Or could, if he wanted to. She was now turning the girl's hair around her fingers, around and around, the black threads tighter and— But we wouldn't have to be romantic. We could just have a happy household. The boyfriend, whose name could be Phil, would be a okay with it, part of the mix. But he wouldn't be living with us. That would be too much. No sleepovers, either. No underwear or bathrooms or showers. But maybe she's not with anyone. Phil went away. Phil was drafted. He was a Peruvian citizen and was drafted, and we were sad for him, but that's how it goes, sorry Phil. So. How would we decorate? That would be a problem. But I would defer. Yes, defer. To have a happy easy house with help from this woman and to have her and Toph content in their room with their stomachs on the carpet and sharing some book I would defer.

In mid-August, by now desperate, I walked into a small adobe house a few blocks from Beth's new apartment. The owner was a large, middle-aged black woman, looking not unlike the Bible-reading woman who had been with my mother at the end. The house was perfect. Or rather, it was not at all perfect, but was far less imperfect than anything else we'd seen. The woman's son had just gone to college—she was also a single mother—and she was picking up and moving to New Mexico. The house was about the right size for us, snug on a street dappled through a canopy of interlocking greenery. There was a backyard, a porch, a shed, a sunroom even, no dishwasher or laundry but it hardly mattered, with us a few weeks from school starting—when she asked about financial matters, I threw down my ace.

"I'm worried about your lack of a job," she said.

"Listen," I blurted. "We can pay. We have money. We could pay the year's rent all at once, if you want."

Her eyes widened.

So we wrote the check. At this point, all sense of thrift has fallen away. We grew up in a tightfisted house, where there was no allowance, where asking for $5 from our father elicited the heaviest of sighs, required detailed plans for repayment. Our mother was far worse—would not even shop in Lake Forest, where everything was overpriced, would instead drive ten, twenty, thirty miles to Marshall's, to T.J. Maxx, for bargains, for bulk. Once a year we'd all pile into the Pinto and would drive to a place on the west side of Chicago, Sinofsky's, where for $4, $5 each we'd buy dozens of slightly flawed rugby shirts, holes here and there, extra buttons, collars ruined by bleach, pink bleeding into white. We grew up with a weird kind of cognitive dissonance; we knew we lived in a nice town—our cousins out East often made that point to us—but then, if this was true, why was our mother always fretting aloud about not having the money to buy staples? "How will I even buy milk tomorrow?" she would yell at him from the kitchen. Our father, who was out of work a year here, a year there, never seemed impressed with her worry; he seemed to have it all worked out. Still, we were ready for and expected sudden indigence, to be forced out of the house in the middle of the night and into one of the apartments on the highway, at the edge of town. To become one of *those kids*.

It never happened, of course, and now, though we are not rich, and there is very little money actually coming in, Beth and I have tossed away the guilt associated with spending it. When it's a matter of expense versus convenience, the choice is not a choice. While my mother would have driven forty miles for a half-priced tomato, I'll pay $10 for it if it means

I don't have to get in the car. It's a matter of exhaustion, mostly. Fatigue loosens my wallet, Beth's even more, loosens the checkbook tied to Toph's account. We are done sacrificing, Beth and I have decided—at least when it's unnecessary, when it involves money, which, for the time being at least, we have. Even the larger expenditures, those that require Bill's approval, are pushed through with little resistance.

We lasted about a month without a washer/dryer. Every weekend, Toph and I would stuff our laundry into four plastic garbage bags, grab two each, his pair smaller, throw them over our shoulders and stagger, peasant-like, to the place around the corner and down the street. Because there is no way to carry two large, overstuffed garbage bags at once, after half a block Toph would have dropped one of his bags. With its cheap plastic ripped and his shorts and Bulls T-shirts spilling across the sidewalk, he'd run back to the house to get another bag to replace it. Seconds later, he'd return, with his bicycle—

"What are you doing?"

"Wait. Let me try something . . ."

—thinking he could balance the laundry bags on the seat and the frame, and of course that wouldn't work for shit, so we'd be on the sidewalk, picking it all up, four bags of laundry, the clothes stuck in his bike chain, on the neighbor's lawn, ants making homes inside—twenty minutes later and only fifty feet from our front door. There was exhaustion, there was exasperation, there were thoughts of washing clothes in the sink or shower. The next day we called Bill, hummed loudly through his mild objections, and finally bought ourselves a washer and dryer.

They're used, both found and delivered for $400, and they're loud, and they don't match—one is beige and one is white—but good lord, they're beautiful, beautiful machines.

The house is about half the size of the last place, but it's full of light, and there is room in this house, there is flow. The floors are wooden floors, and because the first room becomes the kitchen, there is room, if one is so inclined, to run from one end of the house to the other, without hitting a door or a wall. As a matter of fact, if one happens to be wearing socks, one can run, hypothetically, from the back of the house, through the kitchen, and when one gets to the hardwood of the living room, one can jump, slide, and make it all the way to the front door, sometimes still at full speed (fig. 1).

We feel temporary here, like housesitters, vacationers, and so we do very little in the way of mingling with the community.

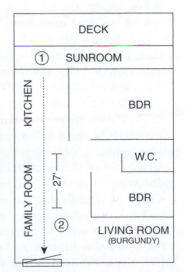

The immediate neighborhood includes an older lesbian couple, an elderly Chinese couple, a black man/white woman pair in their early forties, and Daniel and Boona next door, sandaled and beaded, unmarried—and just friends, it seems—both in some kind of social work. Elsewhere on the block are single mothers, divorcees, widows, widowers, single women living with single men, single women living with single women, and, a few blocks away, there is even Barry Gifford. Only here would we blend. Only here, by comparison, would we seem ho-hum.

We repaint the entire house. Toph and I do it all in one week, with rollers, skipping the corners, the molding, leaving the rooms loose, fuzzy, Rothkoesque. We do the family room a sort of light blue, and the living room a deep burgundy. My room is salmon, the kitchen is an off-yellow, and Toph's we leave white—until one night, the night before his 10th birthday and in the middle of a spell of nightmares, for decoration and protection I paint two huge superheroes, Wolverine and Cable, on his walls, one flying down from above, one standing over his bed. He sleeps through the entire process, the paint dripping onto his bedspread, his exposed left leg.

The place is ours now, but it's a mess.

We discuss the problem.

"You suck," I say.

"No, you suck," he says.

"No, you suck."

"Nooooo, you suck."

"Well, you suckity suck suck."

"What?"

"I said, you—"

"That's so stupid."

We are on the couch, surveying. We are arguing over who has to clean what. More important, we are debating who should have done the work in the first place, before there was this much work to do. There was a time, I am reminding Toph, when a condition of his allowance was the completion of a bare minimum of household chores.

"Allowance?" he says. "You never give me my allowance."

I rethink my strategy.

The coffee table is our home's purgatory, the halfway point for everything eaten or worn or broken. It is covered with papers and books, two plastic plates, a half-dozen dirty utensils, an opened Rice Krispie bar, and a Styrofoam container containing french fries that last night one of us decided were "too thick and squishy" and were left uneaten. There is a package of pretzels that has been opened by the one person in the house who can't open bags properly and so cuts holes in the middle with steak knives. There are at least four basketballs in the room, eight lacrosse balls, a skateboard, two backpacks, and a suitcase, still partially packed, which has not moved in four months. Next to the couch, on the floor, are three glasses that once held milk and now hold its hardened remains. The family room and its perpetual state of disrepair is the problem that we are attempting to resolve.

I have just delivered a State of the Family Room Address, sweeping in scope, visionary in strategy, inspirational to one and all, and the issue has now moved to committee. And though the committee has been looking at it from many angles, addressing matters of both the provenance of the various elements of its unkemptness and matters of precisely who would be best suited to carry out the committee's recommendations, we are stalemated, solution-wise.

"But it's mostly your stuff," he says.

He's right.

"Immaterial!" I say.

Early in the negotiations, I, the senior committee member, had proposed a plan whereby the junior committee member, Toph, being young and in need of valuable life lessons and no doubt eager to prove his mettle to his peers, would clean the living room not only this time, but also on a regular basis, perhaps twice a week, in exchange for not only $2 a week in tax-free allowance, but also the guarantee that if all expressed duties are performed satisfactorily and on time, he will not be beaten senseless in his sleep by the senior committee member. The junior committee member, insolent and obviously lacking both good sense and any notion of bipartisanship, does not like this plan. He dismisses it out of hand.

"No way" is what he said.

However, with great charity and in the spirit of compromise, the senior member immediately proposed an altered plan, a generous plan whereby Toph, being so wonderfully youthful and in need of diversion and exercise, would clean the house on a regular basis, now only once a week instead of twice, in exchange for not $2 but now $3 ($3!) a week in tax-free allowance, and along with the guarantee that if all such cleaning duties are performed satisfactorily and on time, the junior committee member will not be buried to his neck in the backyard and left helpless, able only to scream as hungry dogs tear the flesh from his head. Again, showing how bullheaded and shortsighted he can be, Toph passes on the proposal, this time without comment—only a roll of the eyes—and his refusal to consider any reasonable plan at all is what prompts the charged exchange detailed previously and which continues presently:

"You know how much you suck?" I ask Toph.

"No, how much?" he answers, feigning boredom.

"A lot," I say.

"Oh, that much?"

We are at an impasse, two parties with the same goal but, seemingly, no way to reconcile our ideas about getting there.

"You know what we need?" Toph asks.

"What?" I say.

"A robot maid."

None of it is his fault. Though he's relatively neat—brought up in Montessori, all those careful children and their butcher-block cubbyholes—

I'm converting him slowly, irrevocably, to my way, the slovenly way, and the results are getting a little gruesome. We have an ant problem. We have an ant problem because we have not yet grasped the difference between paper mess and food mess. We leave food out, we leave food on the plates in the sink, and

"We have an ant problem because we have not yet grasped the difference between paper mess and food mess."

when I finally turn myself to the task of washing the dishes, I must first wash away all the ants, those tiny black ones, off the plates and silverware and down the drain. Then we spray the ant column, which extends from the sink, across the counter, down the wall and through the floorboards, with Raid, which of course we hide when guests come—oh, this is Berkeley.

Certain things get us motivated. One day, his friend Luke, all of eleven, walked in and said: "Jesus. How can you live like this?" And for a week or so afterward we cleaned thoroughly, set schedules of maintenance, bought supplies. But we soon lost our inspiration and settled back in, allowing things to fall and stay fallen. If we throw and miss the garbage can, the item, usually remnants of a fruit item, stays where it lands, until a few weeks later when someone, Beth or Kirsten, making a big show of how appalled they are, picks it up and throws it out. They worry for us. I worry for us. I worry that any minute someone—the police, a child welfare agency, a health inspector, someone—will burst in and arrest me, or maybe just shove me around, make fun of me, call me bad names, and then take Toph away, will bring him somewhere where the house is kept clean, where laundry is done properly and frequently, where the parental figure or figures can cook and do so regularly, where there is no running around the house poking each other with sticks from the backyard.

The running around hitting each other with things is pretty much the only thing we're both interested in, and thus the rest of our operation suffers. We scrape through every day blindly, always getting stumped on something we should know—how to plunge a toilet, how to boil corn, his Social Security number, the date of our father's birthday—such that every day that he gets to school, that I get to work and back in time for dinner, each day that we cook and eat before nine and he goes to bed before eleven and doesn't have blue malnourished-looking rings around his eyes like he did for all those months last year—we never figured out why—feels like we've pulled off some fantastic trick—an escape from a burning station wagon, the hiding of the Statue of Liberty.

By mid-fall, we settle into something like a schedule. In the morning, a little after I go to bed, Toph wakes up at, say, 3 or 4 or 4:30 in the morning, so as to allow ten minutes to shower, ten minutes to dress, half an hour to make and eat breakfast and finish his homework, and at least three and a half, four hours for cartoons. At 8:45, he wakes me up. At 8:50 he wakes me up again. At 8:55 he wakes me up one more time and, while yelling at him because he's late, I drive him to school. I park our little red car next to the school, on the side I have been told, in four separate flyers and one personal note, is not to be used for the loading or unloading of children. Then I grab a piece of paper from his backpack and compose a note.

Dear Ms. Richardson,

I am sorry Chris is late this morning. I could make something up about an appointment or a sickness, but the fact is that we woke up late. Go figure.

Best,

Brother of Chris

We are always late, always half-done. All school forms need to be sent to me twice, and I have to hand them in late. Bills are paid in ninety days minimum. Toph is always squeezed onto sports teams late, and exceptions must be made—I am never sure whether our incompetence derives from our situation, or just my lack of organization—though of course I publicly blame the former. Our relationship, at least in terms of its terms and its rules, is wonderfully flexible. He has to do certain things for me because I am his parent, and I have to do certain things for him. Of course, when I am called upon to do something I don't want to do, I do not have to do it, because I am not, actually, his parent. When something doesn't get done, we both shrug, because technically, neither of us is responsible, being just these two guys, brothers maybe, but we hardly even look alike, making duty even more questionable. But when someone has to be blamed, he allows me to finger him, and when he resists, I only need to look at him that certain way, that way that says "We are partners here, little jerk, and yesterday, when I was exhausted, and sick with pinkeye, you wanted to get some of those Magic cards, absolutely had to have them for the next day, because everyone was bringing new cards in to show during lunch, and because I was afraid that you'd be unpopular and would be cast out for being a near-orphan and having funny ears and living in a rental and would grow up with an interest in guns and uniforms, or worse, I'll find you under the covers reading *Chicken Soup for the Prepubescent Soul* and lamenting your poor lot, I got dressed and went to that comics store that's open 'til eight, and we got two packs of cards and one of them had a hologram in it, and you were the envy of all, and your life continued on its recent course of ease, of convenience, of relative stardom, of charmed bliss"—and he relents.

Parked in front of the school, I try to get him to give me a hug. I reach my arm around him, pull him near and say what I find myself saying too often:

"Your hat smells like urine."

"No it doesn't," he says.

It does.

"Smell it."

"I'm not going to smell it."

"You should wash it."

"It doesn't smell."

"It does."

"Why would it smell of urine?"

"Maybe you peed on it."

"Shut up."

"Don't say that. I told you not to say that."

"Sorry."

"Maybe you shouldn't sweat so much."

"Why?"

"It must be your sweat that's making it smell like urine."

"Bye."

"What?"

"Bye. I'm already late."

"Fine. Bye."

He gets out. He has to knock on the school's door to get in, and when the door opens, the secretary tries to give me the customary dirty look but now as always I am not watching, cannot see her, no. Toph disappears inside.

On my way to whatever temping assignment I have that day or week, usually somewhere in the sweltering (Far) East Bay, I muse idly about home schooling. I have been lamenting all the time he is there, at school, being taught God knows what, away from me. I calculate that his teachers see him, on a daily basis, as much as or more than I do, and I am convinced there is something fundamentally wrong with this situation; a jealousy creeps over me, of his school, his teachers, the parents who come in and help . . .

For weeks I've been working for a geological surveying company, re-creating topographical maps, line by line, with archaic Macintosh drawing programs. It's monotonous, but also soothing and meditative, the utter lack of thinking necessary, no worry possible in the utter safety of life there, in their immaculate Oakland office, with its water coolers and soda machines and soft, quiet carpet. While temping there are breaks, and lunch, and one can bring a Walkman if one so desires, can take a fifteen-minute break, walk around, read— It's bliss. The temp doesn't have to pretend that he cares about their company, and they don't have to pretend that they owe him anything. And finally, just when the job, like almost any job would, becomes too boring to continue, when the temp has learned anything he could have learned, and has milked it for the $18/hr and whatever kitsch value it may have had, when to continue anymore would be a sort of death and would show a terrible lack of respect for his valuable time—usually after three or four days—then, neatly enough, the assignment is over. *Perfect.*

In her sunglasses and new Jeep, Beth picks Toph up from school, and he spends the afternoon at her little place, sharing her futon, the two of them studying side by side, until I get home. At that point, Beth and I do our best to fight about something vital and lasting—"You said six o' clock"/"I said six thirty"/"You said six"/"Why would I have said six?"—and once we have done so, she leaves us to our dinner.

Which we wouldn't bother with if we didn't have to. Neither Toph nor I, though raised by our mother thirteen years apart, ever developed any interest in food, and much less in cooking—both of our palates were stunted at five, six years old, at fruit rolls and plain hamburgers. And though we daydream aloud about the existence of a simple pill, one pill a day, that would solve our daily dietary requirements, I recognize the importance of cooking regularly, though I have no idea why cooking regularly is important. So we cook about four times a week, for us a heroic schedule of operation. This is the menu from which we choose, with almost all dishes modeled closely after those which our mother, while still cooking more varied and robust meals for our siblings and father, prepared specially for us, each of us at one time her youngest:

1. THE SAUCY BEEFEATER

(Sirloin strips, sliced and sautéed in Kikkoman-brand soy sauce, cooked until black, served with tortillas and eaten by hand, the tortilla being torn into small pieces, each small piece being used to envelope one, two, maybe three but no more than three beef fragments at a time. Served with potatoes, prepared in the French manner, with oranges and apples, sliced the only logical way—first in half, width-wise, then lengthwise, ten slices per—and served in a bowl, on the side.)

2. THE SAUCY CHICKEN

(Sliced chicken breasts, sautéed in Kikkoman soy sauce, cooked until tangy, almost crispy, and served with tortillas and eaten by hand in the manner described above. Accompanied with potatoes, served in the French manner—which it should be mentioned are exclusively Ore-Ida brand Crispers! frozen french fries, they being the only one of their species that actually become crispy during their oven-time. Also with sliced oranges and apples, served on the side.)

3. THE CRUNCHY CHICKEN

(Courtesy of Church's Fried Chicken, drive-through, at San Pablo and Gilman. White meat insisted on, along with biscuits, mashed potatoes, and added to, at home, with a small green salad of iceberg lettuce and one sliced cucumber. No dressing.)

4. THE CRUMBLING WALL

(Hamburger, prepared medium well, with bacon and barbecue sauce. Courtesy of that place on Solano, where, it should be mentioned, they use much too much barbecue sauce, which anyone should know has the almost immediate effect of soaking the bun, the bun becoming like oatmeal, inedible, the burger ruined, all in a matter of minutes—so quick that even when the burger is picked up and patrons attempt to save the bun ("Separate them! Quick! Get the bun away from the sauce! Now scrape! Scrape!"), it's always too late, necessitating the keeping, at home, of a stash of replacement buns, which are then toasted, heavily, to provide maximum resistance to the sauce's degenerative effects. Served with potatoes of the French kind, and fruit, as above.)

5. THE MEXICAN-ITALIAN WAR

(Tacos: Ground beef sauteed in Prego spaghetti sauce (Traditional style), served with tortillas, but without beans, salsa, tomatoes, cheese, guacamole, and whatever that white creamy substance is that is sometimes found on the dish's inferior, less pure incarnations. On the side: Pillsbury brand crescent rolls and iceberg salad. No dressing.)

6. [WE DIDN'T ACTUALLY NAME ANY OF THESE MEALS. WOULD WE SEEM COOLER, OR SOMEHOW LESS COOL, HAD WE DONE SO? I AM THINKING LESS COOL.]

(Pizza, served with pepperoni. Tombstone, Fat Slice, Pizza Hut, or Domino's, if the price cannot be resisted. With a ready-made small green salad.)

7. THE OLD MAN AND THE SEA

(Mrs. Paul's frozen fried clams, one package each ($3.49—not cheap), served with Crispers!, crescent rolls, and sliced oranges and apples. Or sometimes cantaloupe.)

8. GAVIN MACLEOD AND CHARO

(For him: Grilled cheese served with one slice of Kraft American cheese set in middle of two pieces of seeded Jewish rye, toasted in pan and cut diagonally. For other him: Quesadillas—one slice of Kraft American cheese, between one tortilla, prepared in skillet. With sliced honeydew.)

(NOTE: no spices are available, except oregano, which is shaken, sparingly, onto two items: a) pepperoni pizza; and b) sliced Jewish rye bread, which is folded around oregano, a la Tufnel. No vegetables are available, except carrots, celery, cucumbers, green beans and iceberg lettuce, which are all served raw and only raw. Unavailable is food that swims in its own excrement. Pasta is not available, especially not that regurgitated mess known as lasagna. Further, all such foods, those containing more than two or three ingredients mixed together indiscriminately, including all sandwiches except salami, are not chewed, but eschewed. All meals are served with a tall glass of 1% milk, with the gallon jug resting on the floor next to the table, for convenient refills. Alternative beverages are not available. Anything not on the menu is not available. Any complaints will be handled quickly, and with severity.)

"Hey, I need your help," I say, when I need his help cooking.
"Okay," he says, and then helps out with the cooking.
Sometimes we sing while we are cooking. We sing regular words, words about pouring the milk or getting the spaghetti sauce, though we sing them in opera-style. We can sing opera-style, too. It is incredible.

Sometimes, while cooking, we have sword fights using wooden spoons or sticks that we bring into the house for such occasions. It is an unsaid mission of mine, the source of which is sometimes clear and sometimes not, to keep things moving, to entertain the boy, to keep him on his toes. For a while we would chase each other around the house, mouths full of water, threatening to spit. Of course, neither of us would have ever thought of actually spitting a mouthful of water at the other inside the house, until one night, when I had him cornered in the kitchen, I just went ahead and did it. Things have been devolving ever since. I have stuck half a cantaloupe into his face. I have rubbed a handful of banana onto his chest, tossed a glassful of apple juice into his face. It's an effort, I'm guessing, to let him know, if it weren't already obvious, that as much as I want to carry on our parents' legacy, he and I will also be doing some *experimenting*. And constantly entertaining, like some amazing, endless telethon. There is a voice inside me, a very excited, chirpy voice, that urges me to keep things merry, madcap even, the mood buoyant. Because Beth is always pulling out old photo albums, crying, asking Toph how he feels, I feel I have to overcompensate by keeping us occupied. I am making our lives a music video, a game show on Nickelodeon—lots of quick cuts, crazy camera angles, fun, fun, *fun*! It's a campaign of distraction and revisionist history—leaflets dropped behind enemy lines, fireworks, funny dances, magic tricks. *Whassat? Lookie there! Where'd it go?*

In the kitchen, when the inspiration calls, I take out the family's seventeen-inch turkey knife, plant my legs in an A, squat a little and hold the knife over my head, samurai-style.

"Hiyyyyy!" I yell.

"Don't," he says, backing away.

"Hiyyyyy!" I yell, stepping toward him, because threatening children with seventeen-inch knives is funny. Always the best games have involved some kind of threatened injury, or near-accident, as when he was a toddler and I would run around with him on my shoulders, pretending to be dizzy, spinning, stumbling—

"Not funny," he says, backing into the family room.

I put the knife away; it clinks into the silverware drawer.

"Dad used to do that all the time," I say. "Out of the blue. He'd get this look on his face, this bug-eyed look, and act like he was going to split our heads open with the knife."

"Sounds funny," he says.

"Yeah, it was funny," I say. "It actually was funny."

Sometimes while we cook he tells me about things that happened at school.

"What happened today?" I ask.

"Today Matthew told me that he hopes that you and Beth are in a plane and that the plane crashes and that you both die just like Mom and Dad."

"They didn't die in a plane crash."

"That's what I said."

Sometimes I call the parents of Toph's classmates.

"Yeah, that's what he said," I say.

"It's hard enough, you know," I say.

"No, he's okay," I continue, pouring it on this incompetent moron who has raised a twisted boy. "I just don't know why Matthew would say that. I mean, why do suppose your son wants Beth and me to die in a plane crash?

"No, Toph's fine. Don't worry about us. We're fine. I'm worried about you— I mean, you should worry about young Matthew there," I say.

Oh, these poor people. What is to be done?

During dinner, during the basketball season, we watch the Bulls on cable. Otherwise, needing to keep constantly occupied, we play one of an endlessly rotating series of games—gin, backgammon, Trivial Pursuit, chess—with our plates next to the board. We have been trying to eat in the kitchen, but since we got the Ping-Pong net, it's been more difficult.

"Unhook the net," I say.

"Why?" he asks.

"For dinner," I say.

"No, you unhook it," he says.

So usually we eat on the coffee table. If the coffee table is beyond clearing, we eat on the family room floor. If the family room floor is covered with plates from the night before, we eat on my bed.

After dinner, we play games for our own amusement and the edification of the neighbors. In addition to the belt-cracking game mentioned earlier, there is the game that involves Toph pretending that he's a kid, while I pretend I'm a parent.

"Dad, can I drive the car?" he asks as I sit, reading the paper.

"No, son, you can't," I say, still reading the paper.

"But why?"

"Because I said so."

"But Daaaad!"

"I said no!"

"I hate you! I hate you I hate you I hate you I hate you!"

Then he runs to his room and slams the door.

A few seconds later he opens the door.

"Was that good?" he asks.

"Yeah, yeah," I say. "That was pretty good."

Today is Friday, and on Friday he gets out of school at noon, so I usually come home early, too, if I can. We are in his room.

"Where are they?"

"They're in there."

"Where?"

"Hiding."

"Where?"

"In that mountain thing we made."

"Inside the papier-maché?"

"Yeah."

"When was the last time you saw them?"

"I don't know. A while. A week maybe."

"You sure they're still in there?"

"Yeah. Almost positive."

"How?"

"They still eat their food."

"But you never see them?"

"No, not really."

"What crappy pets."

"Yeah, I know."

"Should we return them?"

"Can we?"

"I think so."

"Stupid iguanas."

We walk the two blocks, through the backyard of that one mossy gnome house, to the park with the small half court.

"Now, why do you go all the way over there when you do it?"

"All the way over where?"

"You had an open-court layup, but you went all the way over there to do it. Watch. I'll be you . . . . See?"

"See what?"

"I went all the way over—like eight feet over there."

"So?"

"That's what you were doing!"

"I was not."

"You were too."

"I was not."

"You were!"

"Let's just play."

"You gotta learn this—"

"Fine, I learned it."

"Jerk."

"Pussy."

The game invariably ends with this:

"What's the big deal?"

"__"

"You get so emotional when we play."

"__"

"C'mon. Talk. Say something."

"__"

"I have a right to tell you how to do stuff."

"—"

"Don't be such a sullen little dork."

"—"

"What's your problem? You have to walk ten feet behind me? You look like an idiot."

"—"

"Here, you carry this. I'm going to the store."

"—"

"—"

"Is the door open? I don't have a key."

"Here."

5:30 p.m.

"I'm taking a nap."

"So?"

"I need you to wake me up in an hour."

"What time?"

"Six-twenty."

"Fine."

"Really. You have to wake me up."

"Fine."

"I'll be incredibly upset if I don't get up."

"Fine."

7:40 p.m.

"Jesus!"

"What?"

"Why didn't you wake me up?"

"What time is it?"

"Seven-forty!"

"Oh!" he says, actually putting his hand over his mouth.

"We're late!"

"For what?"

"Goddamn it! For your open house, idiot!"

"Oh!" he says, again actually putting his hand over his mouth.

We have twenty minutes to make it. We are firemen and there is a fire. I run this way, he the other. Toph goes up to his room to change. In a few minutes I knock on his door.

"Don't come in!"

"We have to go."

"Hold on."

I wait by the door and the door opens. He is dressed.

"What is that? You can't wear that."

"What?"

"No way."

"What?"

"Don't mess with me. Just change, retard."

The door closes. Drawers are opened and there is stomping.

The door reopens.

"Are you kidding?"

"What?"

"That's worse than the last thing you had on."

"What's wrong with it?"

"Look at it. There're permanent grease stains all over it. And it's too big. And it's a sweatshirt. You can't wear a sweatshirt. And don't you have any other shoes?"

"No. Someone didn't get me any."

"I didn't what?"

"Nothing."

"No, tell me—what didn't I do for you?"

"Nothing."

"Screw you."

"No, screw you."

"Change!"

The door closes. A minute, then the door opens.

"That's bet— What the— Can't you tuck in the shirt? I mean, didn't anyone ever teach you how to tuck in your shirt? You look like a moron."

"Why?"

"You're nine years old and I'm going to have to come over there and help you tuck in your shirt."

"I can do it."

"I'm doing it. We've got five minutes left to get there. Jesus, we're always late. I'm always waiting for you. Don't move. And where's your belt? God, you're a mess."

7:40–7:50 p.m.

"Goddamn it. We're always late. Why the hell can't you get dressed yourself? Roll down your window. It's too hot in here. How come you refuse to open your window when it's boiling in here? And your buttons are off. Look at your buttons. Look at your collar, up around your ear. Oh my God. Now I'll have to dress you every day. At least help with your buttons. Man are they off. You missed about ten, retard."

"*Retard.*"

"*Retard.*"

"*Retard.*"

We are flying down San Pablo, in the left lane, then the right lane, passing Beetles and Volvos, their pleading bumper stickers.

"I was dressed fine."

"Dressed fine? Goddamn it, you were so not dressed fine. Open the window more. You looked like a retard. A little more. That's good. You cannot dress like that to an open house. This is what people wear. This is special occasion rules, my man. This is like, give me a break, you know? This is obvious stuff. This is just common sense. I mean, give me a goddamn break, okay? You have got to help me out every once in a while, little man. I'm exhausted, overworked, dead half the time, and I just can't be dressing someone who's nine years old and should be perfectly capable of dressing himself. I mean, Jesus Christ, Toph, give me a goddamn break every once in a while, please? Can I have a break every once in a while? A little break? A little cooperation? Jesus Christ—"

"You just passed the school."

7:52 p.m.

The open house is still full—it goes until nine, not eight, as I had thought—and we are both overdressed. We walk in. Toph immediately untucks his shirt.

The walls are covered with corrected papers about slavery, and the first-graders' unsettling self-portraits.

Heads turn. This is our first open house, and people are not sure what to make of us. I am surprised, having expected that everyone would have been briefed about our arrival. Kids look at Toph and say hi.

"We are unusual and tragic and alive."

"Hi, Chris."

And then they look at me and squint.

They are scared. They are jealous.

We are pathetic. We are stars.

We are either sad and sickly or we are glamorous and new. We walk in and the choices race through my head. Sad and sickly? Or glamorous and new? Sad/sickly or glamorous/new? Sad/sickly? Glamorous/new?

We are unusual and tragic and alive.

We walk into the throng of parents and children.

We are disadvantaged but young and virile. We walk the halls and the playground, and we are taller, we radiate. We are orphans. As orphans, we are celebrities. We are foreign exchange people, from a place where there are still orphans. Russia? Romania? Somewhere raw and exotic. We are the bright new stars born of a screaming black hole, the nascent suns burst from the darkness, from the grasping void of space that folds and swallows—a darkness that would devour anyone not as strong as we. We are oddities, sideshows, talk show subjects. We capture everyone's imagination. That's why Matthew wants Beth and me dead in a plane crash. His parents are old, bald, square, wear glasses, are wooden and gray, are cardboard boxes, folded, closeted, dead to the world— We ate at their house actually, not long ago, accepting a neighborly invitation sometime before Matthew's plane crash comment. And we were bored to tears in their stillborn house, its wooden floors and bare walls—the daughter even played the piano for us, the father so haughtily proud of her, the poor bald guy. They owned no TV, there were no toys anywhere, the place was airless, a coffin—

But we!—we are great-looking! We have a style, which is messy, rak-ish, yet intriguingly so, singular. We are new and everyone else is old. We are the chosen ones, obviously, the queens to their drones—the rest of those gathered at this open house are aging, past their prime, sad, hope-less. They are crinkly and no longer have random sex, as only I among them am still capable of. They are done with such things; even thinking about them having sex is unappealing. They cannot run without looking silly. They cannot coach the soccer team without making a mockery of themselves and the sport. Oh, they are over. They are walking corpses, es-pecially that imbecile smoking out in the courtyard. Toph and I are the fu-ture, a terrifyingly bright future, a future that has come from Chicago, two terrible boys from far away, cast away and left for dead, shipwrecked, for-gotten, but yet, but yet, here, resurfaced, bolder and more fearless, bruised and unshaven, sure, their pant legs frayed, their stomachs full of salt water, but now unstoppable, insurmountable, ready to kick the saggy asses of the gray-haired, thickly bespectacled, slump-shouldered of Berke-ley's glowering parentiscenti!

Can you see this?

We walk around the classrooms. In his homeroom, on the walls, there are papers about Africa. His paper is not on the wall.

"Where's your paper?"

"I don't know. Ms. Richardson didn't like it, I guess."

"Hmmph."

Who is this Ms. Richardson? She must be a moron. I want this "Ms. Richardson" brought out and driven before me!

The school is full of nice children but eccentric children, delicate and oddly shaped. They are what my friends and I, growing up in public schools, always envisioned private school kids were like—a little too pre-cious, their innate peculiarities amplified, not muted, for better and worse. Kids who think that they are pirates, and are encouraged to dress the part, in school. Kids who program computers and collect military magazines. Chubby boys with big heads and very long hair. Skinny girls who wear sandals and carry flowers.

After about ten minutes, we're bored. My main reason for coming has gone bust.

I was looking to score.

I expected flirting. I expected attractive single mothers and flirting. My goal, a goal I honestly thought was fairly realistic, was to meet an at-tractive single mother and have Toph befriend the mother's son so we can arrange playdates, during which the mother and I will go upstairs and screw around while the kids play outside. I expected meaningful glances and carefully worded propositions. I imagine that the world of schools and parents is oozing with intrigue and debauchery, that under its con-cerned and well-meaning facade, its two-parent families, conferences with teachers and thoughtful questions directed to the history teacher about Harriet Tubman, everyone is swinging.

But by and large they're ugly. I scan the crowd milling in the court-yard. The parents are interesting only in their prototypical Berkeley-ness. They wear baggy tie-dyed, truly tie-dyed, pants, and do not comb their hair. Most are over forty. All of the men have beards, and are short. Many of the women are old enough to have mothered me, and look it. I am disheartened by the lack of possibility. I am closer in age to most of the children. Oh but there is one mother, a small-headed woman with long, long, straight black hair, thick and wild like a horse's tail. She looks exactly like her daughter, same oval face, same sad dark eyes. I've seen her before, when I've driven Toph to school, and have guessed that she's single; the father is never present.

"I'm gonna ask her out," I say.

"Please, don't. Please," Toph says. He really thinks I might.

"Do you like the daughter at all? This could be fun—we could dou-ble date!"

"Please, please don't."

Of course I won't. I have no nerve. But he does not know that yet. We walk the halls decorated with construction paper and student work. I meet Ms. Richardson, the homeroom teacher, who is tall and black and severe—with distended, angry eyes. I meet the science teacher who looks precisely like Bill Clinton and stutters. There is a girl in Toph's class who, at nine, is taller than her parents, and heavier than me. I want Toph to be her friend and make her happy.

A woman nearby is looking at us. People look at us. They look and wonder. They wonder if I am a teacher, not knowing how to place me, thinking maybe that because I have scraggly facial hair and am wearing old shoes that I will take and molest their children. I surely look threaten-ing. The woman, this one looking at us, has long gray hair and large glasses. She is wearing a floor-length patterned skirt and sandals. She leans toward us, points her finger to me and to Toph and back, smiles. Then we find our places and read the script:

MOTHER
Hi. This is your . . . son?

BROTHER
Uh . . . no.

MOTHER
Brother?

BROTHER
Yeah.

MOTHER
(*squinting to make sure*)
Oh, you can tell right away.

BROTHER
*(though knowing that it is
not really true, that he is old
and severe-looking, and his
brother glows)*
Yeah, people say that.

MOTHER
Having fun?

BROTHER
Sure. Sure.

MOTHER
You go to school at Cal?

BROTHER
No, no, I finished school a few
years ago.

MOTHER
And you live around here?

BROTHER
Yeah, we live a few miles north.
Close to Albany.

MOTHER
So you live with your folks?

BROTHER
No, just us.

MOTHER
But . . . where are your parents?

BROTHER
*(thinking, thinking: "They're not
here." "They couldn't make it."
"I have no idea, actually; if only
you knew just little idea I have.
Oh it's a doozy, that story. Do
you know what it's like, to have
no idea, no idea at all of their
exact whereabouts, I mean, the
actual place that they are right
now, as we speak? That is a
weird feeling, oh man. You want
to talk about it? You have a few
hours?")*
Oh, they died a few years ago.

MOTHER
(*grabbing* BROTHER'S *forearm*)
Oh, I'm sorry.

BROTHER
No, no, don't worry.
(*wanting to add, as he
sometimes does, "It wan't your
fault." He loves that line,
especially when he tacks on:
"Or was it?"*)

MOTHER
So he lives with you?

BROTHER
Yeah.

MOTHER
Oh, gosh. That's interesting.

BROTHER
(*thinking of the state of the
house. It is interesting.*)
Well, we have fun. What grade is
your . . .

MOTHER
Daughter. Fourth. Amanda. If I
may, can I ask how they died?

BROTHER
(*again scanning possibilities for
the entertainment of him and his
brother. Plane crash. Train crash.
Terrorists. Wolves. He has made
up things before, and he was
amused, though younger
brother's amusement level was
unclear.*)
Cancer.

MOTHER
But . . . at the same time?

BROTHER
About five weeks apart.

MOTHER
Oh my god.

BROTHER
(*with inexplicable little chuckle*)
Yeah, it was weird.

MOTHER
How long ago was this?

BROTHER
A few winters ago.
(BROTHER *thinks about how much
he likes the "a few winters ago"
line. It's new. It sounds dramatic,
vaguely poetic. For a while it was
"last year." Then it was "a year
and a half ago." Now, much to
BROTHER's relief, it's "a few years
ago." "A few years ago" has a
comfortable distance. The blood is
dry, the scabs hardened, peeled.
Early on was different. Shortly
before leaving Chicago, BROTHERs
went to the barber to have TOPH's
hair cut, and BROTHER doesn't
remember how it came up, and
BROTHER was really hoping it
wouldn't come up, but when it did
come up, BROTHER answered, "A
few weeks ago." At that the
haircutting woman stopped, went
through the antique saloon-style
doors to the back room, and
stayed there for a while. She came
back red-eyed. BROTHER felt
terrible. He is always feeling
terrible, when the innocent, benign
questions of unsuspecting strangers
yield the bizarre answer he must
provide. Like someone asking
about the weather and being told
of nuclear winter. But it does have
its advantages. In this case,
BROTHERs got a free haircut.*)

MOTHER
(*holding BROTHER's forearm
again*)
Well. Good for you! What a
good brother you are!

BROTHER

(*Smiling. Wonders:* What does
that mean? *He is often told this.
At soccer games, at school fund-
raisers, at the beach, at the
baseball card shows, at the pet
store. Sometimes the person
telling him this knows their full
biography and sometimes she or
he does not.* BROTHER *doesn't
understand the line, both what it
means and when it became a
standard sort of expression that
many different people use.* What
a good brother you are! BROTHER
*had never heard the saying
before, but now it comes out of
all kinds of people's mouths,
always phrased the same way, the
same words, the same
inflections—a rising sort of
cadence:*

What   a   good   bro-ther you   are!

What *does* that mean? *He smiles,
and if Toph is close, he'll punch
him in the arm, or try to trip
him—*look at us horsing around!
Light as air!*—then* BROTHER *will
say the same thing he always says
after they say their words, the
thing that seems to deflate the
mounting tension, the
uncomfortable drama swelling in
the conversation, while also
throwing it back at the
questioner, because he often
wants the questioner to think
about what he or she is saying.*

What he says, with a cute little
shrug, or a sigh, is:)
Well, what are you gonna do?
(MOTHER *smiles and squeezes*
BROTHER's *forearm one more*
time, then pats it. BROTHERs *look*
to AUDIENCE, *wink, and then*
break into a fabulous Fossean
dance number, lots of kicks and
high-stepping, a few throws and
catches, a big sliding-across-the-
stage-on-their-knees thing, then
some more jumping, some
strutting, and finally, a crossing-
in-midair front flip via hidden
trampoline, with both of them
landing perfectly, just before the
orchestra, on one knee, hands
extended toward audience,
grinning while breathing heavily.
The crowd stands and thunders.
The curtain falls. They thunder
still.)
FIN

As the crowd stomps the floor for a curtain call, we sneak through the
back door and make off like superheroes.

Miriam Engelberg

From *Cancer Made Me a Shallower Person*

The following biography is from Miriam Engelberg's Web site: "I first got interested in autobiographical comics after hearing an interview with Peter Kuper on *Fresh Air*. When I originally started cartooning, in 1997, I assumed I would collaborate with someone else to create the art, like Harvey Pekar. My son was a baby at the time, and I was planning to write cartoons about parenting. After a friend suggested I do my own drawings, I decided to give it a try. Now I can't imagine doing the writing without the drawing; the two processes go together for me. When I worked a day job at CompassPoint Nonprofit Services teaching computer classes, the Executive Director, Jan Masaoka, asked me to do some cartoons about the nonprofit sector. These eventually became Planet 501c3, which has developed a following among nonprofit staff members around the world.

"When I was first diagnosed with breast cancer at age 43, I began writing comics about those experiences, just trying to document what was happening in my life for my own sanity. I would come back from doctors' appointments with little notes jotted down that said things like '3-armed gown' and 'living with statistics.' Often I'd be telling a friend something upsetting about the latest twist and turn in my cancer saga, but as the words came out of my mouth they would turn into something absurd and we'd both end up laughing.

"Have I really become a shallower person since cancer? Some of my friends beg to differ and state unequivocally that I was already shallow before cancer."

Over time those cartoons became the book *Cancer Made Me a Shallower Person*, which was published in 2006. Miriam Engelberg died of cancer in October 2006.

PERSONAL

WAITING

BIOPSY

WORK ABOVE ALL

DIAGNOSIS

I FIGURED I SHOULD JUST GIVE UP ANY PRETENSE OF RESTRAINT AND ANNOUNCE IT PUBLICLY.
HELLO, YOU'RE ON "CAR TALK."
OUR '95 SATURN GETS BAD GAS MILEAGE, AND... I HAVE BREAST CANCER!
SOB
MEANWHILE, I STILL HADN'T TOLD MY PARENTS—THE TWO MOST HEALTH-CONSCIOUS PEOPLE IN THE ENTIRE WESTERN WORLD.
WE HAVE A COMPLETELY FAT-FREE DIET, AND WE WASH ALL VEGETABLES AND FRUIT IN DISH-WASHING LIQUID.
WE WALK 3 MILES A DAY, DO TAI CHI AND TAKE MEGA VITA-MINS.
FOR YEARS THEY'D BEEN MAILING ME ARTICLES...
HOW TO TELL IF IT'S A COLD OR THE FLU
SUN DANGERS
FAT IS BAD
CHOOSING THE BEST SUN BLOCK
ZINC!
VITAMIN C PROTECTS AGAI
COLD OR FLU?
RECIPES FOR HEALTH
10 TIPS TO AVOID THE FLU
EXERC
VITAMIN E SHOWN TO
MELANOMA? BAD: OK:
CALCIUM: AVOID OSTEO-POROSIS
FAT LINKED TO CANCE
FLU SHOTS
100 EXERCISES
FLU OR COLD?
...WHILE I WORKED HARD IN THERAPY TO STOP LISTENING TO THEM.
I JUST DON'T WANT TO DEVOTE MY WHOLE LIFE TO WORRYING ABOUT HEALTH.
THAT'S GREAT! YOU'RE FINALLY LEARNING TO RELAX AND ENJOY LIFE INSTEAD OF TRYING TO CONTROL IT.
BUT NOW...
I CAUSED THIS BY EATING TOO MUCH CHEESE. MOM AND DAD WILL SAY, "I TOLD YOU SO." ALL THEIR HEALTH STUFF WAS RIGHT AFTER ALL. I NEVER SHOULD HAVE RELAXED AND ENJOYED LIFE.
VEGETABLES ARE HEALTHY, BUT THESE AREN'T ORGANIC. FISH CONTAINS TOXINS FROM POLLUTION. MEAT HAS HORMONES. DAIRY IS SUPPOSED TO BE DANGEROUS. FAT IS BAD. SUGAR IS HARMFUL. WHITE FLOUR LACKS...

Louise Erdrich

Rock Paintings

Louise Erdrich is known primarily as a novelist. Her heritage is Anishinaabe (Ojibwe, Chippewa) and German, and her Native American identity has been and continues to be at the forefront of her concerns, although she has been criticized in some quarters as being too self-referential rather than politically active. Family relationships have long been a theme of her work. Erdrich was born in Little Falls, Minnesota; her grandfather served as a tribal chairman for the Turtle Mountain Band of the Chippewa, and her parents taught at the Bureau of Indian Affairs school. She received her BA from Dartmouth College and an MA in creative writing from Johns Hopkins University.

While working various jobs, Erdrich wrote and published a book of poems, *Jacklight* (1984), and then the novel *Love Medicine* (1984), a work of interconnected stories told from the points of view of people living on a North Dakota reservation. The book was critically praised and received the 1984 National Book Critics Circle Award. *Love Medicine* was followed by *The Beet Queen* (1986), which focused largely on a North Dakota German-American community. Her more recent novels include *The Antelope Wife* (1998), *The Master Butchers Singing Club* (2003), and *The Last Report on the Miracles at Little No Horse* (2002). Her books of nonfiction include *The Blue Jay's Dance* (1995) and *Books and Islands of Ojibwe Country* (2003), from which "Rock Paintings" comes.

She owns Birchbark Books, a bookstore in Minneapolis, Minnesota, and lives in Minnesota.

Books and Islands of Ojibwe Country was written as part of a series on place published by National Geographic Books. This book is unusual for Erdrich in that it takes the form of a personal travelogue. While it is filled with geographical and historical information about the Ojibwe country of Minnesota, it comes from the personal point of view of a mother with an infant child. As with most of her writing, it has a mythic and oddly formal tone, even as Erdrich explores the subject of her and her child's identities.

The section we have included is a lyrical description of some of the rock paintings of the Anishinaabe tribe. Erdrich combines poetic impressions with historical information and descriptions of what is taking place around this ancient site. The paintings are viewed from the water, where Erdrich floats with a knowledgeable guide. Her depictions of the drawings are far from straightforward, as they move her to imaginings that seem to have their basis in a metaphoric understanding of the old symbols.

More About Age

One of the first questions people ask about the rock paintings is how old they are—complicated answer. There is no completely accurate way to date rock paintings. Some are hundreds of years old, and others thousands of years. The Anishinaabe have been in Lake of the Woods forever, according to Tobasonakwut. Since at least two thousand years before the birth of Christ, according to archaeologists. One thing certain is that the paintings were made by the ancestors of the present-day Anishinaabeg, for the ancient symbols on the rocks are as familiar and recognizable to Tobasonakwut as are, say, highway and airport and deer crossing signs to contemporary Americans. Of course, the rock paintings are not just pointer signs. They hold far more significance. They refer to a spiritual geography, and are meant to provide teaching and dream guides to generations of Anishinaabeg.

Akawe Asema

The rock paintings are alive. This is more impor-
tant than anything else that I can say about them.   "The rock paintings are alive."
As if to prove this point, we see as we approach
Painted Rock Island that a boat has paused. It is a
silver fishing boat with a medium horsepower outboard motor. A man leans over and scoops a handful of tobacco from a pouch, places it before the painting, and then maneuvers his boat out and goes on. *Akawe asema.* First offer tobacco. This makes Tobasonakwut extremely happy, as do all the offerings that we will see as we visit the other paintings. It is evidence to him that the spiritual life of his people is in the process of recovery. He swerves the boat out and chases down the man who made the offering, and then, seeing who he is, waves and cuts away. He is doubly pleased because he knows where this man sets his nets, and knows that he went ten or twelve miles out of his way to visit the rock painting. It is sunset now and will be dark before the man returns to his dock.

The Wild Rice Spirit

The long rays of the deepening sun reach through the channel. As we draw our boat up to the rock painting, the light warms the face of what was once a cliff. I am standing before the rock wall of Painted Rock Island and trying to read it like a book. I don't know the language, though. The painting spreads across a ten- or twelve-foot rectangle of smooth rock, and includes several spirit figures as well as diagrams of teachings. The deep light pulls the figures from the rock. They seem to glow from the inside, a vibrant golden red. For a long while, I am only interested in the visual experience of standing at eye level with the central figures in the rock. They are simple and extremely powerful. One is a horned human figure and the other a stylized spirit figure who Tobasonakwut calls, lovingly, the *Manoominikeshii,* or the wild rice spirit.

Once you know what it is, the wild rice spirit looks exactly like itself. A spiritualized wild rice plant. Beautifully drawn, economically imagined. I have no doubt that this figure appeared to the painter in a dream, for I have had such dreams, and I have heard such dreams described. The spirits of things have a certain look to them, a family resemblance. This particular spirit of the wild rice crop is invoked and fussed over, worried over, just as the plants are checked throughout the summer for signs of ripening.

This year, on Lake of the Woods, the rice looks dismal. Because the high waters have invaded a whole new level of recently established rice beds, the rice is leggy and will flop over before it can be harvested. Earlier in the day, we stopped to examine Tobasonakwut's family rice beds. At this time of the year, mid-July, the rice is especially beautiful. It is in the floating leaf stage and makes a pattern on the water like bright green floating hair. *Kiimaagoogan*, it is called. But upon pulling up a stalk Tobasonakwut says sadly, "There's nothing in this loonshit," meaning he cannot find the seed in the roots. All the energy of the plant has gone into growing itself high enough to survive the depth of the water. There will not be enough reserve strength left in the plant to produce a harvest. "And then," Tobasonakwut goes on, "if your parents had no children, you can't have children." In other words, the rice crop will be affected for years.

So perhaps this year it is especially important to ask for some help from the Manoominikeshii.

When the pictures were painted, the lake was a full nine feet lower, and as it is nearly four feet higher this year than usual, some paintings of course are submerged. The water level is a political as well as natural process—it is in most large lakes now. From the beginning, that the provincial government allowed the lake levels to rise infuriated the Anishinaabeg, as the water ruined thousands of acres of wild rice beds. As it is, I mentally add about one story of rock to the painting, which at present lies only a few feet out of the water.

This is a feminine-looking drawing. The language of the wild rice harvest is intensely erotic and often comically sexualized. If the stalk is floppy, it is a poor erection. Too wet, it is a penis soaking in its favorite place. Half hard, full, hairy, the metaphors go on and on. Everything is sexual, the way of the world is to be sexual, and it is good (although often ridiculous). The great teacher of the Anishinaabeg, whose intellectual prints are also on this rock, was a being called Nanabozho, or Winabojo. He was wise, he was clever, he was a sexual idiot, a glutton, full of miscalculations and bravado. He gave medicines to the Ojibwe, one of the primary being laughter.

The Horned Man

This is the figure that glows brightest from the rock. He is not a devil, and he isn't throwing away a Christian cross—the local white Christian interpretation of the painting, which has led to its close call at defacement.

(At the figure's far right, in white paint, I can still make out Jesus Christ in fairly neat lettering. But the thirty-year-old graffiti has nearly flaked off, while the original painted figures still blaze true.) As I stand before the painting, I come to believe that the horned figure is a self-portrait of the artist.

Books. Why? So we can talk to you even though we are dead. Here we are, the writer and I, regarding each other.

Horns connote intellectual and spiritual activity—important to us both and used on many of the rock paintings all across the Canadian Shield. The cross that the figure is holding over the rectangular water drum probably signifies the degree that the painter had reached in the hierarchy of knowledge that composes the formal structure of the Ojibwe religion, the Midewiwin. The cross is the sign of the fourth degree, and as well, there are four Mide squares stacked at the figure's left-hand side, again revealing the position of the painter in the Mide lodge.

I quickly grow fond of this squat, rosy, hieratic figure. His stance is both proud and somewhat comical, the bent legs strong and stocky. His arms are raised but he doesn't seem to be praying as much as dancing, ready to spring into the air, off the rock. When this rock was painted on a cliff, the water below was not a channel but a small lake that probably flooded periodically, allowing fish to exit and enter. Perhaps it was a camping or a teaching place, or possibly even a productive wild rice bed. Very likely it was a place where the Mide lodge was built, like Niiyaawaangashing. The painter may have been a Mide teacher, eager to leave instructions and to tell people about the activities that took place here.

Most of the major forms of communication with the spirit world are visible in this painting—the Mide lodge, the sweat lodge or *madoodiswan*, the shake tent. The horned figure beats a water drum. Such drums are extremely resonant, and their tone changes beautifully according to the level of the water and the player's skill at shifting the water in the drum while beating it. (Anyone curious about the sound of the water drum can buy a CD and listen to the winners of a recent Native American Grammy, the singers Verdell Primeaux and Johnny Mike, *Bless the People.*) The water drum is a healing drum. In the pictograph a bear floats over the drum, and a line between the horned figure and the bear connects them with the sky world.

The line is a sign of power and communication. It is sound, speech, song. The lines drawn between things in Ojibwe pictographs are extremely important, for they express relationships, usually between a human and a supernatural being. Wavy lines are most impressive, for they signify direct visionary information, talk from spirit to spirit. In the work of some contemporary Ojibwe artists, Joe Geshick, Blake Debassige, and of course Norval Morrisseau, the line is still used to signify spiritual interaction. Contemporary native art is not just influenced by the conventions invented by the rock painters, it is a continuation, evidence of the vitality of Ojibwe art.

The Bay of Baby Spirits

Looking on a map at the little bay we are going to travel, my friend, who is in training as a *doulah* or birth assistant, says no wonder it is known as the home of baby spirits—the bay is thin and winding and looks like a fallopian tube. The bay of little spirits is a courting bay, the water shallow and romantic. To either side, the rich young undergrowth is said to be inhabited by the spirits of babies who choose humans, as they pass, to come and live with. Traveling slowly down the shallow channel, I stroke the tender spot upon Kiizhikok's head, the fontanel, which has nearly shut. I've heard it said that until it does the baby still hears spirits talking. If they're out there, if they're talking to her, I hope they are warning her that it is dangerous to hide stones in her mouth.

Suddenly we come upon three young moose, gangly and playful. Instead of climbing onto land, one clomps into the water and then swims along beside us. Her long rabbity ears cock toward us from time to time, and she doesn't seem particularly frightened. Her Joe Camel nose held high, she rolls her eyes at us. Those odd Twiggy legs and knobby knees work smoothly, powerfully. A wonderful swimmer, she at last veers away into the reeds and cattails. I am very surprised that this happened. According to John Tanner the wary moose is the most difficult of animals to hunt. But then, these are very young moose and our baby is in the boat. I harbor the irrational notion that animals are curious about Kiizhikok and show themselves around her, that her presence is a kind of magnet to them. And it is true, not only do we see animals but they seem unafraid of her, like the otter, like the moose, and the constantly wheeling eagles and pelicans. The animals come close as if they want to get a good look at this child whose ancestors watched their ancestors, whose grandmother ate their grandmothers, whose father was stolen from among them by priests.

Mirage Islands

When the water is high like it is this year, large pieces of bog pull free of the lake bottom and drift all through the bays and channels. You fall asleep looking at a certain shoreline, memorizing the sweep of it, and by morning the shape has shifted and the bog has moved on. When these bogs attach to islands, they can change its shape instantly, but often they merely bounce against the island until they fall apart. Lodge owners get their guide boats out and push the bogs into the lake currents. Close up, rising out of deep water, they are deceptively solid looking. They are a rich biomass composed of reeds, young willow, *wiikenh*, cattails.

Cattails are a useful plant whose roots are edible, whose tails when puffed out are a perfect diapering material for the tender new bottoms of Anishinaabeg babies, used to stuff in the bags of cradleboards. Reeds were used for floor covering, woven into mats. Wiikenh, or sweetflag, is the star of the floating bog, though, a medicine with every possible use.

"Where there is wiikenh, there are Anishinaabeg," says Tobasonakwut. Wiikenh is the ultimate medicine. He investigates each floating bog, hoping to pick it easily, for when rooted it is difficult to wrench from the mud.

Looking at these bogs it is easy to see how, once, when a raiding party of Bwaanag had camped in Ojibwe country, they were driven out by use of a floating bog. The warriors entered the bog from underneath and swam it to the shore of the Bwaanag camp, like Birnam Wood come to Dunsinane. From that bog, they attacked and drove the Bwaanag out.

Massacre Island

It is not considered wise to point a finger at any island, especially this one. The Ojibwe use mouth or head to indicate direction, and are often humorously mocked for "pointing with the lips." But it is impolite to point a finger at people, and the islands as well. Pointing at the islands is like challenging them. And you don't want to challenge anything this powerful.

Massacre Island is a forbidden place. Recently, two men who tried to fast there were bothered the entire night by ghosts. As we approach the island, I feel its brooding presence. I can't tell whether this island is a formidable place because of its history, or whether it possesses a somber gravity all on its own. But the very look of the place disturbs me. Massacre Island is located where the lake deepens. Sounds travel farther, the air thins, the waves go flat. Its rocks sloping down to the water are not the pale pink flecked granite of the other islands, but a heavy gray nearly black in places and streaked with a fierce red-gold lichen.

On this island, the Ojibwe wiped out an entire party of Sioux, or Bwaanag. As Tobasonakwut tells it, the entire island was ringed by Ojibwe canoes. At a signal, the *sasawkwe*, the war whoop, a terrifying and a bloodthirsty shrill, was raised. From one canoe to the next, it traveled, a ring of horrifying sound. The canoes advanced four times. The sasawkwe was raised four times. On the last time, the Ojibwe paddlers surged all the way forward, beached their canoes, and stormed the Bwaanag. He shows where the warriors died, including one who staked himself into the earth and fought all comers who entered his circle, until he was overwhelmed.

Atisikan

The paint, *atisikan*, should be patented, says Tobasonakwut. It is an eternal paint. The Ojibwe Sharpee paint. It works on anything. When he was little he often watched the paint being prepared. It was used for other things, besides painting on rocks. For burial, for bringing people into the religion, for teachings, for decorating request sticks and Mide stakes.

The recipes for paints used by other tribes are often based on vermillion from outcroppings of cinnabar. The Inuit used blood and charcoal.

Burnt plum seeds and bull rushes were mixed into a black paint by the Klamath, and many tribes used blue carbonate of copper. Later, as we walk the Kaawiikwethawangag, the Eternal Sands, I will find some of the mysterious ingredients of the Ojibwe atisikan at my feet, then jumping from the lake.

Obabikon

On a great gray sweep of boulder, high above Obabikon channel, a rock painting gives instructions to the spirit on how to travel from this life into the next life. Such a journey takes four days and is filled with difficulties. For that reason, loved ones provide the spirit with food, spirit dishes, and encouragement in the form of prayers and songs. We climb to the painting with tobacco and leave handfuls by the first painting, a line with four straight, sweeping branches, and the second painting, which is of a *mikinaak*, or turtle.

The mikinaak has immense significance in Ojibwe life. As there are thirteen plates in its back, it is associated with the thirteen moons in the yearly cycle, and also with women. It was women, says Tobasonakwut, who were responsible for beginning Ojibwe mathematical calculations. They began because they had to be concerned with their own cycles, had to count the days so that they would know when they would be fertile. They had to keep close track of the moon, and had to relate it to their bodies in order to predict the births of their children. And they had to be accurate, so that they could adequately prepare. In a harsh Ojibwe winter, giving birth in an unprotected spot could be lethal. Women had to prepare to be near relatives and other knowledgeable women. Mathematics wasn't abstract. It was intimate. Dividing and multiplying and factoring were concerns of the body, and of survival.

Whitefish Bay

To get into Whitefish Bay from where we are will require lots of sandwiches, water, a full gas tank, and two extra five-gallon plastic gas containers that ride in front when full. We start early on a tremendously hot morning. By now, I'm much happier in a boat. I still have the usual fantasy, on starting out, involving the rock and the swim to shore towing Kiizhikok, but by now I'm used to it. I try to move on quickly and enjoy the breeze whipping with heroic freshness off the lake. Whitefish Bay connects to Lake of the Woods via a peculiar contraption called a boat trolley. This is a suspicious-looking, wood-ribbed basket that the boat is floated onto. By sheer muscle power, turning a big red metal wheel that moves the trolley basket along a set of metal tracks, the boat is painfully transferred. Once on the other side of the concrete channel, we reload ourselves and start off, into Whitefish Bay.

First, we pause at the place where Tobasonakwut was born, a quiet little bay of old-growth pine and soft duff. Just after he and his brother were born, Tobasonakwut's name was discovered by his father, who gazed out into the bay and saw a certain type of cloud cover, low and even. Tobasonakwut. His twin was named for a small bird that visited his mother shortly after the birth. She has told Tobasonakwut that as this is the type of bird who nests in the same place year after year, if he ever sees one on a visit it will be a relative of the one who named his brother.

As he is sitting beneath a tree that must have been a sapling when he was born, as he is singing to his daughter, I realize that after thousands of years of continual habitation and birth on the shores of this lake, Tobasonakwut is one of the last human beings who will ever be born out on these islands.

Wiikenh

Wiikenh tea strengthens the immune system. Mixed with a mashed waterlily root, *okundamoh*, it draws out infection and poison. Speakers chew wiikenh to keep their throats clear, and singers chew it to strengthen their voices at the drum. As we enter a long channel filled with shallow water and small flooded bays, Tobasonakwut sees vast clumps of bright green-gold reeds and mutters, over and over, "So much wiikenh!" This is not the gloating sound I've heard before in his voice when discovering so much medicine. Rather, he is distressed that it should be sprouting in such tremendous abundance and no one else has come to pick it. His tone implies that this should all have been harvested, that the endless thick fringe of plants along the shores is an almost painful sight. One thing is sure, he can't pass it up, and for about an hour we putter along, stopping from time to time for him to lean over the prow of the boat and pull up the long tough bundles of muddy roots. He slices them off with a very sharp hunting knife while I sit behind the wheel of the boat with the baby.

Wiikenh gathering is very boring to her, but she has decided to be lulled into a state of contemplation by a combination of breast milk and boat engine. Indeed, every time she gets into the boat now, she tips her head dreamily toward my nipple. I've grown used to having her there. I've filmed eagles and those young moose, dancing loons and *zhegeg*, pelicans, with one hand while she nurses away. Indeed, though I haven't mentioned it, I have been filming everything I've described all along, as well as somehow brandishing a pen and notebook, all while nursing. One grows used to it.

"Sometimes I look at men, at the way most of them move so freely in the world, without a baby attached, and it seems to me very strange."

Sometimes I look at men, at the way most of them move so freely in the world, without a baby attached, and it seems to me very strange. Sometimes it is enviable. Mostly, it is not. For at night, as she curls up or sprawls next to me and as I fall asleep, I hold onto her foot. This is as much for my comfort as to make sure that she doesn't fall off the bed.

As I'm drifting away, I feel sorry for anyone else who is not falling asleep this way, holding onto her baby's foot. The world is calm and clear. I wish for nothing. I am not nervous about the future. Her toes curl around my fingers. I could even stop writing books.

Spirit Bay

The name on the map is actually Devil's Bay, so tiresome and so insulting. Squaw Rock. Devil's This and Devil's That. Indian or Tomahawk Anything. There's no use railing. You know it as well as I do. Some day, when there is nothing more important to do, the Anishinaabeg will demand that all the names be changed. For it was obviously the rock painting at the entrance to the bay that inspired the name. It is not a devil, of course, but a spirit in communication with the unknowable. Another horned figure, only this time enormous, imposing, and much older than the one in Lake of the Woods.

This spirit figure, horns pointed, wavering, and with arms upraised, is fading to a yellow-gold stain in the rock. It is a huge figure, looming all the way up the nine- or ten-foot flat of the stone. At the base of this painting, there is a small ledge. Upon it, a white polo shirt has been carefully folded, an offering, as well as a pair of jeans. The offerings are made out of respect, for personal reasons, or to ask the spirit of the painting for help. There are three rolls of cloth, tied with ribbons. Asema. Again, here are the offerings, the signs that the rock paintings are alive and still respected by the Anishinaabeg.

Binessi

I get very excited when I see the thunderbird pictured on a cliff far above the water. It is so beautifully painted, so fluid and powerful even glimpsed from forty feet below. "Are you strong? Are you agile?" Tobasonakwut asks. "If you are you should climb up to that rock. You'll never be sorry that you did." I believe him. I grab my camera, my tobacco offering, and retie my running shoes. I already have my twenty extra pounds left over from having a baby. I am just pretending that I am strong and agile. Really, I'm soft and clumsy, but I want to see the painting. I am on fire to see it. I want to stand before that painting because I know that it is one of the most beautiful paintings I will have ever seen. Put up there out of reach or within difficult reach for that very reason. At that moment, I just want to see it because it is beautiful, not because I'll get some spiritual gift.

The climb is hard, though of course it looked easy from below. Like all women are accused of doing, I claw my way to the top. Sweaty, heart pounding, I finally know I'm there. All I have to do is inch forward and step around the edge of the cliff, but that's the thing. I have to step around one particular rock and it looks like there's nothing below it or on the other side. I could fall into the rocks. My children could be left motherless. Or I could simply get hurt, which is not simple at all. I calculate. The nearest hospital is hours away and there is that trolley contraption. So I don't go around the rock, but seek another route. I continue climbing until I'm over the top of the cliff. Still, I can't see down. I don't know how to get down to the paintings. Again, I nearly take the chance and lower myself over the cliff but I can't see how far I'd fall. Finally, looking far, far down at my baby in her tiny life jacket, I know I'm a mother and I just can't do it.

Climbing back into the boat is admitting defeat.

"Give me the camera, and tobacco," says Tobasonakwut.

"No!" I say. "Don't do it!"

"Why? If you can't make it then you'll feel bad if I do?"

"Just like a guy, so competitive! Because you *will* go around the corner of that rock and you'll fall and kill yourself."

"I will not fall. I've done this before."

"How many years ago?"

"A few."

With terse dignity, Tobasonakwut goes. He's an incredible climber and regularly shames the twenty-somethings who come to fast on the rock cliffs by climbing past them and even dragging up their gear. I know he'll make it. He'll do something ridiculous, maybe even get hurt, but he'll manage to get right next to the paintings.

He's always poking around in the islands. Once, he described a rock-slide he started coming down from a cliff like this one. Remembering this, I maneuver the boat away from a skid of rocks on the south side of the cliff, though he didn't go up that route. Anyway, he had a terrifying ski down on the boulders and at the bottom one bounced high in the air, over him, and its point landed right between the first and second toe of his right foot. He said that he'd done something mildly offensive to the rocks. He'd thrown one down to see what happened. That's how the landslide started. When the boulder bounced down on his foot, he thought it would slice his foot off. But when he looked down his foot was still there. Just a crushed place between his toes. It was as if, he said, the rocks, the grandfathers had said, "Don't fool around with us."

And now he's climbing rocks again.

It's no use. The best I can do is make sure that the baby's comfortable. I might as well be comfortable too. I take a fat little peanut butter sandwich from the cooler and munch dreamily, while nursing, and after a while the wind in the pines and the chatter of birds lull us into a peaceful torpor. I forget to watch for him, forget the all important ascent. From somewhere, at some point, I hear him call but he doesn't sound in distress so I just let my mind float out onto the lake.

Then he's back.

"Did you see me up there?"

"No!" I feel guilty, awful. Here he is about as old as I'll be when Kiizhikok graduates from high school and I didn't take the trouble to film him as he made the dangerous climb to the rock paintings. He hands over the camera. Ashamed of my distracted laziness, I put it away.

"How did you do it?" I ask quietly.

"Oh, jumped."

"What?"

"Jumped."

I'm immediately just a little pissed off. "You jumped? You could have broken your leg!"

"It was only six feet."

"More like fifteen feet."

"Well, if you hang down, it comes to . . . "

"Don't ever do that again!"

We travel for a while, heading back for the boat trolley, and I brood on his unlikely stubborn-headed insistence that he's still a young man. How long will it take before he really hurts himself? He's scarred and burnt. Just last winter a red hot stone from a sweat lodge brushed up against his calf and left a deep hole. His back and chest are pitted with sun-dance scars and one of his eyebrows was smashed sideways in a boxing match. He took so many punches to the head while a boxer that he has to take special eyedrops now to relieve the pressure on his optic nerve.

"You've got to quit doing things like this," I say softly, but I know I will have no effect, and besides, this is one of the reasons I love him. He's a little crazy, in a good way, half teenager and half *akiwenzii*.

He doesn't answer, just keeps steering the boat, munching trail mix.

When we get to the boat trolley I am further convinced that animals love the baby because it happens again. This time it is a nice fat *waboose*, a grown rabbit. The rabbit sees us from across the shallow boat channel and behaves just like a friendly little dog. It hops down onto the trolley mechanism while Tobasonakwut is laboriously turning the wheel. The little rabbit crosses the water using a rail as a bridge, and comes curiously up to me. The rabbit looks right at the baby. Just as when the otter came toward us, I'm a bit unnerved. I suddenly imagine that this rabbit will bounce charmingly close, and then bare vampire teeth. But it merely inspects us, turns, and hops away calmly.

All right, I think, animals *do* love the baby.

Now that we're over the channel and into Lake of the Woods again, I try hard to let go of my agitation about Tobasonakwut's dangerous rock climb. We start talking about the thunderbird pictured in the rock painting that I didn't get to. I did take a movie picture of it and Tobasonakwut surely snapped some up-close shots, I think, consoling myself. That thunderbird is very graceful, and there is a handprint with it. It is still the most beautiful bird I have ever seen.

Binessiwag

These spirits are particular about what they're called—they prefer *Binessiwag* to *Animikiig*. They're very powerful. Thunder is the beating of their wings. Lightning flashes from their eyes. You don't want to rile the young ones, as they are the most unpredictable. When a storm approaches, traditional Ojibwe cover all the shiny objects—mirror and cooking pans—so as not to attract the attention of the Binessiwag. A feather over the door lets them know Anishinaabeg are at home. They will avoid that house. It is important, when the Binessiwag appear, at any time of the day or night, to offer tobacco.

The only natural enemy of these immensely strong beings are the great snakes, the *Ginebigoog*, who live underwater. These snakes are said to travel from lake to lake via an underground network of watery tunnels that lies beneath northern Minnesota and Ontario. There is an ongoing feud between these two powerful supernatural beings. The young Binessiwag, those that come out in spring, are the most volatile, the most unpredictable. Anyone who has experienced a violent spring thunderstorm in the north woods can attest to this truth. As we have perfect weather, we don't need to appease the Binessiwag. Day after day the morning sun shines clear. The Earth heats up. The water gleams like metal. The sky by noon is a hot deep blue.

The Eternal Sands

Kaawiikwethawangag, they are called, the Eternal Sands. John Tanner must have approached from the south, for he said, that "this lake is called by the Indians Pub-be-kwaw-waung-gaw Sau-gi-e-gun, 'the Lake of the Sand Hills.' Why it is called 'Lake of the Woods' by the whites, I cannot tell, as there is not much wood about it." And it is true, the lake is very different in character when approached from this direction. Gorgeous and deserted sand beaches stretch around the southeast side of Big Island, the reserve that Tobasonakwut's mother, the original Nenaa'ikiizhikok, came from. The great island is now empty of people, the villages abandoned since shortly after World War II.

Even though Canada's aboriginal people could not vote and were being forced from their lands and educated by force, they fought in both World Wars. One of Tobasonakwut's uncles, a soldier, came home to Big Island much affected by the fighting. He was silent, withdrawn, and stayed away from his family. Then his little son, a small boy named Wabijiis, came down with an unusual fever.

Such was the terror of disease, at the time, that it was decided that once the boy died the village would break up and the people disperse to Seamo Bay and Niiyaawaangashing. The little boy's grave was dug with paddles—the people wanted to bury him the old way and not use metal. A prayer flag was erected near. The little boy Wabijiis was the last person buried on Big Island, and his grave and all that remains of the village is now grown over with young trees.

Nameh

All of a sudden between our boat and the fringed woods a great fish vaults up into the air. I've seen muskies. I walk around a Minneapolis lake of which signs warn MUSKELUNGE ARE IN THESE WATERS.

Once, I saw an Uptown Minneapolis type, dressed in tight black jeans and tight black T, wearing a suit jacket, fishing in a very cool way. Cool until he hooked a vast muskie. His screams echoed along the sedate bike paths and the fish he dragged forth was soon surrounded by Rollerbladers, joggers, and awestruck pink- and blue-haired teens. The fish I just saw was not a muskie. It was even bigger. Tobasonakwut sees it from the corner of his eye and slows the boat down.

> "His screams echoed along the sedate bike paths and the fish he dragged forth was soon surrounded by Rollerbladers, joggers, and awestruck pink- and blue-haired teens."

"Asema," he says, and puts the tobacco in the water. That fish was the *nameh*. The sturgeon. Tobasonakwut is happy and moved to see it because, he says, "They rarely show themselves like that."

Once again, I'm sure it is the baby. The sturgeon seemed to take flight above the water, rising in a pale thrust and falling on its back. The sturgeon is a living relic of life before the age of the dinosaurs, and to see one is to obtain a glimpse of life 200 million years ago. I've never seen one of these fish in the wild before, much less grown large. I've only seen tiny, fish hatchery, Pallid Sturgeon that a relative of mine who works for the North Dakota Department of Natural Resources was raising to stock the Missouri River. Nameh, *Acipenser fulvescens Rafinesque*, the Lake Sturgeon, is long-lived and can grow to more than eight feet. The Lake of the Woods record fish was a lake sturgeon weighing 238 pounds. Tobasonakwut says they can grow over twice that large. Males live into their forties. Female sturgeon can live over one hundred years, but they only spawn every four years, and not until they are in their twenties.

The sturgeon up here on Lake of the Woods were the buffalo of the Ojibwe. Greed and overfishing by non-Indians caused their population to crash around the turn of the nineteenth century, when, along with the Great Lakes, Lake of the Woods became one of the world's principal suppliers of caviar. The sturgeon were indiscriminately taken by the non-Indian fisheries for their roe, much as the buffalo hunters took only the buffalo tongues. They were stacked like cordwood all along the lake and often left to rot. An agonizing sight for the Ojibwe, who revere the sturgeon and who knew its secrets.

Long before fish-farming, the Ojibwe had traditional "sturgeon gardens," shallow and protected parts of the lake where they mixed eggs and sperm and protected the baby sturgeon from predators. The eggs and sperm were mixed together with an eagle feather in an act both sacred and ordinary. These days, the Ontario Ministry of Natural Resources and tribal communities raise sturgeon. A conservation program begun ninety-nine years ago, in Lake Winnebago near Shawano, Wisconsin, has provided the best example and the best hope. Wisconsin has tightly restricted sturgeon fishing since 1903, and Lake Winnebago now has the only large, self-sustaining sturgeon population in the world. A long-term program there may provide stocks that will rehabilitate sturgeon in the Great Lakes and throughout Canada.

At the base of the very first rock painting that we visited, a great sturgeon floats above a tiny triangular tent. It is a divining tent, a place where Ojibwe people have always gone to learn the wishes of the spirits and to gain comfort from their teachings. Someday perhaps Kiizhikok's children will find the sturgeon vaulting from the water around Big Island a common sight. I hope so. It was a moment out of time.

Waves

On our way to visit the island and the Eternal Sands, we experience a confluence of shifting winds and waves. Tobasonakwut shows me how the waves are creating underwaves and counterwaves. The rough swells from the southeast are bouncing against the rocky shores, which he avoids. The wooded lands and shores will absorb the force of the waves and not send them back out to create confusion. Heading toward open water, we travel behind the farthest island, also a wave cutter. We slice right into the waves when possible. But we are dealing with yesterday's wind, a strong north wind, and swells underneath the waves now proceeding from the wind that shifted, fresh, to the south. I think of what Tobasonakwut's father said, "The creator is the lake and we are the waves on the lake." The image of complexity and shifting mutability of human nature is very clear today. Eventually, we beach our boat at the first little bay. Tobasonakwut starts out, at once, to comb for treasures.

I have the same feeling when I come upon a deserted beach as I do when entering a used bookstore with promisingly messy shelves bearing handwritten signs and directions, or a rummage sale run by beaming white haired people who are handing out free coffee and look like they kept all of their forties soapbox glass dishes and their flowered tablecloths in the original plastic. As I look at the beach, strewn with driftwood and interesting rocks, I have the slightly guilty feeling that I get when I visit the gift shop before the museum. Sure enough, as baby and I beachcomb in the opposite direction from Tobasonakwut, we come across three magnificent eagle spikes, those feathers at the ends of wings, the ones used by sun dancers in their sage crowns. But the wind dies suddenly at the margin of the beach and we are edged from the fabulous pickings by biting blackflies and the big droning horseflies that drive moose insane. To avoid the flies, the baby and I take to water just like the moose do.

I plop down and let the waves crash into me at waist height while I nurse the baby. Occasionally her head is spritzed and refreshed. I am wearing a hat, lots of sunblock, dark glasses. The amber-colored water is too rough for leeches to grab onto my legs. I could sit here forever. The pelicans, zhegeg, pass over, twenty or thirty at a time, wheeling in strict formation when up high. Sometimes more casual, they sail down low and

I see the boatlike prows of their breasts and drooping gullets. Crowds of black ducks veer over, too. There is a curtain of birds along this beach. Rising and falling, the flocks constantly change and shift. Then, just before me, about seventy feet out, the great fish rears again. This time it hangs even longer in the air, catching sun on its belly, somehow joyous.

"It's all there," Tobasonakwut says upon returning, pointing behind me and then out to the open water.

"What?"

"Atisikan."

The paint that is eternal comes from the Eternal Sands. Just down the beach the waves have dragged the sand off the tough roots of a low beach plant. The roots are such a brilliant red that from a short distance it looks as though the leaves are bleeding into the water. This is a component of the sacred paint used in the rock paintings. And the fish who showed itself to me is a part of the atisikan too. Sturgeon's oil is one of the bonding agents that will not let go, one of the substances that makes the paint eternal.

Offering

I am almost asleep when I realize that I have seen all that is depicted in the first rock painting, the one that I marveled over, the one that glowed from the rock in all of its complexity. I saw the wild rice, which is the spirit of the wild rice, I saw the bear, I saw the deer, and I saw the nameh. The next morning, we go back to the painting. Tobasonakwut ties up at the base of the rock. I bring a dish of food, including asema, up to the top of the rock. I also leave my favorite ribbon shirt.

It is a leave-taking. I have to tell myself not to look back as we travel away from the rock. It is as though I've left behind something intangible — not the shirt, the tobacco, or the food. It is as though I've written a poem and burned it. Given up a piece of my own spirit. I don't understand the feeling that closes in on me. And even now, as I am writing in my study, and as I am looking at photographs I took of the paintings, I am afflicted with a confusing nostalgia. It is a place that has gripped me. I feel a growing love. Partly, it is that I know it through my baby and through her namesake, but I also had ancestors who lived here generations ago.

The Ojibwe side of my family, who ended up with the surname Gourneau, roamed from Madeline Island in Lake Superior, along what is now the Canadian border, through Lake of the Woods and down to Red Lake, and then out onto the Great Plains and eventually the Turtle Mountains. Baupayakiingikwe, Striped Earth Woman, was one of those ancestors, as was Kwasenchiwin, Acts Like A Boy. Our family was of the Ajijauk or Crane dodem, and the Makwa or Bear dodem. I can't help but imagine that these two women, whose names my mother and sister have searched out of old tribal histories, walked where I've walked, saw what I've seen, perhaps traced these rock paintings. Perhaps even painted them.

Ojibwemowin

My grandfather, Patrick Gourneau, was the last person in our family who spoke his native language, Ojibwemowin, with any fluency. When he went off into the Turtle Mountain woods to pray with his pipe, I stood apart at a short distance, listening and wondering. Growing up in an ordinary small North Dakota town, I thought Ojibwemowin was a language for prayers, like the solemn Latin sung at High Mass. I had no idea that most Ojibwe people on reserves in Canada, and many in Minnesota and Wisconsin, still spoke English as a second language, Ojibwemowin as their first. And then, while visiting Manitoulin Island, Ontario, I sat among a group of laughing elders who spoke only their own language. I went to a café where people around me spoke Ojibwemowin and stood in line at a bank surrounded by Ojibwe speakers. I was hooked, and had to know more. I wanted to get the jokes, to understand the prayers and the *adisookaanug*, the sacred stories, and most of all, Ojibwe irony. As most speakers are now bilingual, the language is spiked with puns on both English and Ojibwemowin, most playing on the oddness of *gichi-mookomaan*, that is "big knife" or American, habits and behavior.

As I was living in New Hampshire at the time, my only recourse was to use a set of Ojibwe language tapes made by Basil Johnson, the distinguished Canadian Ojibwe writer. Unknown to Basil Johnson, he became my friend. His patient Anishinaabe voice reminded me of my grandfather's and of the kindest of elders. Basil and I conversed in the isolation of my car as I dropped off and picked up children, bought groceries, navigated tangled New England roads. I carried my tapes everywhere I went. The language bit deep into my heart, but I could only go so long talking with Basil on a tape. I longed for real community. At last, when I moved to Minnesota, I met fellow Ojibwe people who were embarked on what seems at times a quixotic enterprise—learning one of the toughest languages ever invented.

Ojibwemowin is, in fact, entered in the Guinness Book of World Records as one of the most difficult languages to learn. The great hurdle to learning resides in the manifold use of verbs—a stammer-inducing complex. Ojibwemowin is a language of action, which makes sense to me. The Ojibwe have never been all that materialistic, and from the beginning they were always on the move. How many things, nouns, could anyone carry around? Ojibwemowin is also a language of human relationships. Two-thirds of the words are verbs, and for *each verb*, there can be as many as six thousand forms. This sounds impossible, until you realize that the verb forms not only have to do with the relationships among the people conducting the action, but the precise way the action is conducted and even under what physical conditions. The blizzard of verb forms makes it an adaptive and powerfully precise language. There are lots of verbs for exactly how people shift position. *Miinoshin* describes how someone turns this way and that until ready to make a determined move, *iskwishin* how a person behaves when tired of one position and looking for one more comfortable. The best speakers are the most inventive, and come up with new words all of the time. *Mookegidaazo* describes the way a baby looks when outrage is building and coming to the surface where it will result in a thunderous squawl. There is a verb for the way a raven opens and shuts its claws in the cold and a verb for what would happen if a man fell off a motorcycle with a pipe in his mouth and drove the stem of it through the back of his head. There can be a verb for anything.

Tobasonakwut delights in the language, his first language. He loves to delineate the sources and origins of words, keeps lists of new words, and creates them himself. Yet, as with many of his generation, he endured tremendous punishment for this love. He remembers singing his father's song to comfort himself as he was driven to a residential school at age eleven. The priest who was driving stopped the car, made him get out, and savagely beat him. Tobasonakwut spoke no English when he first went to school and although he now speaks like an Ivy League professor if he wants to, he stubbornly kept his Ojibwemowin. Tobasonakwut says that the beatings and humiliations only made him the fiercer in loving and preserving his language. As he says this he clutches his heart, as if the language is lodged there. From the beginning, even as a child, he determined that he would speak it as often as he could.

For Tobasonakwut, Ojibwemowin is the primary language of philosophy, and also of emotions. Shades of feeling can be mixed like paints. *Kawiin gego omaa ayasinoon*, a phrase used when describing loneliness, carries the additional meaning of missing a part of one's own being. Ojibwe is especially good at describing intellectual and dream states. One of Tobasonakwut's favorite phrases is *andopawatchigan*, which means "seek your dream," but is lots more complicated. It means that first you have to find and identify your dream, often through fasting, and then that you also must carry out exactly what your dream tells you to do in each detail. And then the philosophy comes in, for by doing this repeatedly you will gradually come into a balanced relationship with all of life.

My experience with the language is of course very different. Instead of the language being beaten out of me, I've tried for years to acquire it. But how do I go back to a language I never had? I love my first language — why complicate my life with another? I will never have the facility to really use the flexible descriptive power of this language. Still, I love it. The sound comforts me. I feel as though all along this language was waiting for me with kindness. I imagine God hears this language. Perhaps my grandfather's use of the language penetrated. What the Ojibwe call the *Gizhe Manidoo*, the ineffable and compassionate spirit residing in all that lives, is associated for me with the flow of Ojibwemowin. My Catholic training touched me intellectually and symbolically, but apparently never engaged my heart.

Ojibwemowin is one of the few surviving languages that evolved to the present here in North America. For an American writer, it seems crucial to at least have a passing familiarity with the language, which is adapted to the land as no other language can possibly be. Its philosophy is bound up in northern earth, lakes, rivers, forests, and plains. Its origins pertain to the animals and their particular habits, to the shades of meaning in the very placement of stones. Many of the names and songs associated with these places were revealed to people in dreams and songs—it is a language that most directly reflects a human involvement with the spirit of the land itself. It is the language of the paintings that seem to glow from within the rocks.

That is not to say Ojibwemowin is an elevated language of vanished spirituality. One of my favorite words is *wiindibaanens* or computer. It means "little brain machine." Ojibwe people have words for animals from other continents. *Genwaabiigigwed*, the long-necked horse, is a giraffe. *Ojaanzhingwedeyshkanaad*, rhinoceros, the one with the horn sticking out of his nose. *Nandookomeshiinh* is the lice hunter, the monkey. There are words for the serenity prayer used in twelve-step programs and translations of nursery rhymes. The varieties of people other than Ojibwe or Anishinabe are also named: *Aniibiishaabookewininiwag*, the tea people, are Asian. All Europeans are *Omakakiiininiwag*, or frog people, but the French are *Wemitigoozhiwag*, the wooden-cross people. Catholics, who included the Jesuit priests, are *Mekadewikonayewininiwag*, the black-robe men. *Agongosininiwag*, the chipmunk people, are Scandinavian. I'm still trying to find out why.

When it comes to nouns, there are blessedly fewer of them and no designations of gender, no feminine or masculine possessives or articles. Nouns are mainly designated as animate or inanimate, though what is alive and dead doesn't correspond at all to what an English speaker might imagine. For instance, the word for stone, *asin*, is animate. After all, the preexistence of the world according to Ojibwe religion consisted of a conversation between stones. People speak to and thank the stones in the sweat lodge, where the asiniig are superheated and used for healing. They are addressed as grandmothers and grandfathers. Once I began to think of stones as animate, I started to wonder whether I was picking up a stone or it was putting itself into my hand. Stones are no longer the same as they were to me in English.

Ojibwemowin was of course a language of memory, an oral language, passed on by community but not written. For most of the last two centuries, missionized students adapted the English alphabet and wrote phonetically. Ojibwe orthography has recently been standardized so that the language can be taught in schools and universities. In this book, I have tried to use mainly accepted spellings, although I've fudged a little with Ojibwe words that might be confused with English words, and done my best on words that aren't in the *Concise Dictionary of Minnesota Ojibwe*, by Nichols and Nyholm. I've mastered shamefully little of the language. I'm still working on its most basic forms. Even if I do occasionally get a sentence right, there are so many dialects of Ojibwe that, for many speakers, I'll still have gotten it wrong. And yet, as ludicrous as my Ojibwe must sound to a fluent speaker, I have never, ever, been greeted with a moment of impatience or laughter. Perhaps people wait until I've left the room, but more likely, I think, there is an urgency about attempting to speak the language.

To native speakers like Tobasonakwut, the language is a deeply loved entity. A spirit or an originating genius belongs to each word. Before attempting to speak this language, students petition these spirits with gifts of cloth, tobacco, and food. Anyone who attempts Ojibwemowin is engaged in something more than learning tongue twisters. However awkward my nouns, unstable my verbs, however stumbling my delivery, to engage in the language is to engage the spirit of the words. And as the words are everything around us, and all that we are, learning Ojibwemowin is a lifetime pursuit that might be described as living a religion.

Gigaa-waabamin

Ojibwe people don't say good-bye, that's too final. "I'll see you" is as close to good-bye as the language goes for a common parting. Some habits of Ojibwe have filtered into my English and I find that I can't say good-bye, or if I do, I have to soften it with see-you-laters and have-funs and always, to my children and Tobasonakwut, drive-carefully. *Weweni*, careful. Or, as others jokingly say, *weweni babamanadis*, which translates roughly as an admonition to be careful as you go around being ugly in your ugly life. Or *gego anooj igo ezhichigeken*. Don't do any of the weird things that I would. *Gigaa-waabamin* means "I'll see you again." That's just the way it is. He has a complicated life up north and I have a complicated life down in Minneapolis, so there is a lot of gigaa-waabamin.

Elizabeth Gilbert

From *Eat, Pray, Love*

Elizabeth Gilbert was born in Connecticut in 1969 and raised on a small family Christmas tree farm. She graduated from New York University with a degree in political science. After college, she traveled and worked random jobs, writing stories and essays. Her first story collection brought the praise of Annie Proulx, who called her "a young writer of incandescent talent." During the 1990s she was on the staff of *Spin* magazine; her pieces featured unusual people and situations, such as rodeo bunnies and Chinese dam builders. She then moved on to *GQ* where she primarily worked on profiles of the famous. Her biography of an idiosyncratic woodsman, *The Last American Man*, was a finalist in 2002 for both the National Book Award and the National Book Critic's Circle Award.

Her most recent book, *Eat, Pray, Love* (2006), is a personal account of travels following divorce. Anne Lamott proclaimed it "wise, jaunty, human, ethereal, heartbreaking." It has been optioned for a movie to star Julia Roberts.

About her nonfiction, Gilbert once told an interviewer, "Everything I learned about being a journalist I learned by being a bartender. The most exquisite lesson of all is that people will tell you anything. Want to. There's no question you can't ask if your intention is not hostile. And it's not like entrapment; it's more like a gorgeous revelation. People want to tell the story that they have."

Our excerpt is from her book *Eat, Pray, Love*. While this book tells of her personal travels, she insists that she doesn't reveal much that is actually personal. "I think I'm a fairly representative woman in many ways and what I've gone through seems to be what a lot of people go through," Gilbert told interviewer Dave Welch. "That said, I didn't put everything in the book. I was protective of certain people's privacy and very, very careful to try to say as little as possible, for instance, about my ex-husband and the circumstances of our collapsed marriage. For one thing—who wants to read that? Also, I just felt, ethically speaking, more comfortable revealing my own dysfunctions than revealing my (almost certainly biased) perspective of someone else's dysfunctions." The book has more of the tone of a chatty travelogue than of a confessional-style memoir.

Using Italy as a backdrop, our selection depicts the relationship between Gilbert and her sister Catherine. In a brief space, we gain an understanding not only of Catherine's personality, but of the relationship between the sisters, the family dynamic, and the setting. Gilbert portrays a series of brief situations that exemplify the sisters' bond, past and present, doing so in a way that keeps the narrative moving quickly and brightly.

My sister's arrival in Rome a few days later helped nudge my attention away from lingering sadness over David and bring me back up to speed. My sister does everything fast, and energy twists up around her in miniature cyclones. She's three years older than me and three inches taller than me. She's an athlete and a scholar and a mother and a writer. The whole time she was in Rome, she was training for a marathon, which means she would wake up at dawn and run eighteen miles in the time it generally takes me to read one article in the newspaper and drink two cappuccinos. She actually looks like a deer when she runs. When she was pregnant with her first child, she swam across an entire lake one night in the dark. I wouldn't join her, and I wasn't even pregnant. I was too scared. But my sister doesn't really get scared. When she was pregnant with her second child, a midwife asked if Catherine had any unspoken fears about anything that could go wrong with the baby—such as genetic defects or complications during the birth. My sister said, "My only fear is that he might grow up to become a Republican."

> "I was too scared. But my sister doesn't really get scared."

That's my sister's name—Catherine. She's my one and only sibling. When we were growing up in rural Connecticut, it was just the two of us, living in a farmhouse with our parents. No other kids nearby. She was mighty and domineering, the commander of my whole life. I lived in awe and fear of her; nobody else's opinion mattered but hers. I cheated at card games with her in order to *lose*, so she wouldn't get mad at me. We were not always friends. She was annoyed by me, and I was scared of her, I believe, until I was twenty-eight years old and got tired of it. That was the year I finally stood up to her, and her reaction was something along the lines of, "What took you so long?"

We were just beginning to hammer out the new terms of our relationship when my marriage went into a skid. It would have been so easy for Catherine to have gained victory from my defeat. I'd always been the loved and lucky one, the favorite of both family and destiny. The world had always been a more comfortable and welcoming place for me than it was for my sister, who pressed so sharply against life and who was hurt by it fairly hard sometimes in return. It would have been so easy for Catherine to have responded to my divorce and depression with a: "Ha! Look at Little Mary Sunshine now!" Instead, she held me up like a champion. She answered the phone in the middle of the night whenever I was in distress and made comforting noises. And she came along with me when I went searching for answers as to why I was so sad. For the longest time, my therapy was almost vicariously shared by her. I'd call her after every session with a debriefing of everything I'd realized in my therapist's office, and she'd put down whatever she was doing and say, "Ah . . . that explains a lot." Explains a lot about *both* of us, that is.

Now we speak to each other on the phone almost every day—or at least we did, before I moved to Rome. Before either of us gets on an airplane now, the one always calls the other and says, "I know this is morbid, but I just wanted to tell you that I love you. You know . . . just in case . . ." And the other one always says, "I know . . . just in case."

She arrives in Rome prepared, as ever. She brings five guidebooks, all of which she has read already, and she has the city pre-mapped in her head. She was completely oriented before she even left Philadelphia. And this is a classic example of the differences between us. I am the one who spent my first weeks in Rome wandering about, 90 percent lost and 100 percent happy, seeing everything around me as an unexplainable beautiful mystery. But this is how the world kind of always looks to me. To my sister's eyes, there is nothing which cannot be explained if one has access to a proper reference library. This is a woman who keeps *The Co-lumbia Encyclopedia* in her kitchen next to the cookbooks—and *reads* it, for pleasure.

There's a game I like to play with my friends sometimes called "Watch This!" Whenever anybody's wondering about some obscure fact (for instance: "Who *was* Saint Louis?") I will say, "Watch this!" then pick up the nearest phone and dial my sister's number. Sometimes I'll catch her in the car, driving her kids home from school in the Volvo, and she will muse: "Saint Louis . . . well, he was a hairshirt-wearing French king, actually, which is interesting because . . ."

So my sister comes to visit me in Rome—in my new city—and then shows it to me. This is Rome, Catherine-style. Full of facts and dates and architecture that I do not see because my mind does not work in that way. The only thing I ever want to know about any place or any person is the *story*, this is the only thing I watch for—never for aesthetic details. (Sofie came to my apartment a month after I'd moved into the place and said, "Nice pink bathroom," and this was the *first time* I'd noticed that it was, indeed, pink. Bright pink, from floor to ceiling, bright pink tile everywhere—I honestly hadn't seen it before.) But my sister's trained eye picks up the Gothic, or Romanesque, or Byzantine features of a building, the pattern of the church floor, or the dim sketch of the unfinished fresco hidden behind the altar. She strides across Rome on her long legs (we used to call her "Catherine-of-the-Three-Foot-Long-Femurs") and I has-ten after her, as I have since toddlerhood, taking two eager steps to her every one.

"See, Liz?" she says, "See how they just slapped that nineteenth-century façade over that brickwork? I bet if we turn the corner we'll find . . . yes! . . . see, they *did* use the original Roman monoliths as supporting beams, probably because they didn't have the manpower to move them . . . yes, I quite like the jumble-sale quality of this basilica. . . ."

Catherine carries the map and her Michelin Green Guide, and I carry our picnic lunch (two of those big softball-sized rolls of bread, spicy sausage, pickled sardines wrapped around meaty green olives, a mush-room pâté that tastes like a forest, balls of smoked mozzarella, peppered and grilled arugula, cherry tomatoes, pecorino cheese, mineral water and a split of cold white wine), and while I wonder when we're going to eat, she wonders aloud, "Why *don't* people talk more about the Council of Trent?"

She takes me into dozens of churches in Rome, and I can't keep them straight—St. This and St. That, and St. Somebody of the Barefoot Penitents of Righteous Misery . . . but just because I cannot remember the names or details of all these buttresses and cornices is not to say that I do not love to be inside these places with my sister, whose cobalt eyes miss nothing. I don't remember the name of the church that had those frescoes that looked so much like American WPA New Deal heroic murals, but I do remember Catherine pointing them out to me and saying, "You gotta love those Franklin Roosevelt popes up there . . ." I also remember the morning we woke early and went to mass at St. Susanna, and held each other's hands as we listened to the nuns there chanting their daybreak Gregorian hymns, both of us in tears from the echoing haunt of their prayers. My sister is not a religious person. Nobody in my family really is. (I've taken to calling myself the "white sheep" of the family.) My spiritual investigations interest my sister mostly from a point of intellectual curiosity. "I think that kind of faith is so beautiful," she whispers to me in the church, "but I can't do it, I just can't . . ."

Here's another example of the difference in our worldviews. A family in my sister's neighborhood was recently stricken with a double tragedy, when both the young mother and her three-year-old son were diagnosed with cancer. When Catherine told me about this, I could only say, shocked, "Dear God, that family needs grace." She replied firmly, "That family needs *casseroles*," and then proceeded to organize the entire neighborhood into bringing that family dinner, in shifts, every single night, for an entire year. I do not know if my sister fully recognizes that this *is* grace.

We walk out of St. Susanna, and she says, "Do you know why the popes needed city planning in the Middle Ages? Because basically you had two million Catholic pilgrims a year coming from all over the Western World to make that walk from the Vatican to St. John Lateran—sometimes on their knees—and you had to have *amenities* for those people."

My sister's faith is in learning. Her sacred text is the *Oxford English Dictionary*. As she bows her head in study, fingers speeding across the pages, she is with her God. I see my sister in prayer again later that same day—when she drops to her knees in the middle of the Roman Forum, clears away some litter off the face of the soil (as though erasing a blackboard), then takes up a small stone and draws for me in the dirt a blueprint of a classic Romanesque basilica. She points from her drawing to the ruin before her, leading me to understand (even visually challenged *me* can understand!) what that building once must have looked like eighteen centuries earlier. She sketches with her finger in the empty air the missing arches, the nave, the windows long gone. Like Harold with his

Purple Crayon, she fills in the absent cosmos with her imagination and makes whole the ruined.

In Italian there is a seldom-used tense called the *passato remoto*, the remote past. You use this tense when you are discussing things in the far, far distant past, things that happened so long ago they have no personal impact whatsoever on you anymore—for example, ancient history. But my sister, if she spoke Italian, would not use this tense to discuss ancient history. In her world, the Roman Forum is not remote, nor is it past. It is exactly as present and close to her as I am.

She leaves the next day.

"Listen," I say, "be sure to call me when your plane lands safely, OK? Not to be morbid, but . . ."

"I know, sweetie," she says. "I love you, too."

Laurence Gonzales

Marion Prison

Laurence Gonzales won the 2001 and 2002 National Magazine Awards from the American Society of Magazine Editors for pieces he wrote for *National Geographic Adventure Magazine*. Since 1970, his essays have appeared in *Harper's, Rolling Stone, Men's Journal, National Geographic Adventure, Smithsonian Air and Space, Chicago Magazine, San Francisco Magazine*, and elsewhere.

He has published a dozen books, including two essay collections, three novels, and the book-length essay *One Zero Charlie* (1993). His most recent book is *Deep Survival: Who Lives, Who Dies, and Why* (2003). He appears often as a speaker before groups as diverse as the Santa Fe Institute, Legg Mason Capital Management, and the Wilderness Medical Society. He has long lived in the Chicago area.

Kurt Vonnegut said, "The excellence of Laurence Gonzales's writing and the depth of his reporting saddened me in a way, reminding me yet again what a tiny voice facts and reason have in this era of wrap-around, mega-decibel rock-and-roll." About *Deep Survival*, Donna Seaman wrote in *Booklist*, "The study of survival offers an illuminating portal into the human psyche, and Gonzales, knowledgeable and passionate, is a compelling and trustworthy guide." A reviewer for *Kirkus Reviews* called it "a superb, entertaining addition to a nature buff's library—or for anyone not tucked safely away in a bunker."

We've included "Marion Prison," one of Gonzales's essays from his collection *The Still Point* (1989). This work of literary journalism is a complicated "you-are-there" look at life in a maximum security prison from the perspective of inmates, guards, the warden, the physician, and the author himself. The amount of detail, relayed with a relative lack of personal reflection, creates an oppressive, even creepy, tone. While the piece could have been constructed as an argument, Gonzales kept his opinion hidden, leaving only an implication of it at the end.

Next to killing someone or trying to escape, the most serious offenses that a prisoner in the U.S. Penitentiary at Marion, Illinois, can commit are drinking and being caught in possession of money.

There are many ways to make alcohol in USP-Marion, but the simplest is to take two small boxes of Kellogg's corn flakes and dump them into the toilet bowl in your cell. Let them fester for a week, and the result will get you drunk. Some inmates are more ambitious than that. From the prison log: "August 5, 1982: Approximately four gallons of brew found in cell of Ronnie Bruscino, 20168-148."

It is part of the magical transmutation of elements that occurs in the most maximum state of incarceration in America today. After an extended period of being locked up with nothing to do, cut off from the sight of other human beings, the sights and sounds of normal life, you begin to see the world transform itself. Nothing is as it seems. One thing changes into another. If you stare at a typewriter for long enough with nothing else to occupy your mind, nothing else to stimulate your senses, the platen rods begin to look like shish kabob skewers. Then one day you find yourself with one of them in your hand, and it has been sharpened, and you've wrapped a sweatband around the blunt end for a better grip, and you are plunging the point into someone's chest. Jack Henry Abbott, convicted murderer and author of *In the Belly of the Beast*, wrote, "It is like cutting hot butter, no resistance at all."

The guards come and take you away. The administration orders the typewriters removed from the library, and you are locked in your cell. You are left with nothing but the steel bunk, the three walls, the air vent, the grille. But after you've stared at the air vent for months on end, it too begins to change. Instead of the metal frame and duct, you begin to see long, gleaming isosceles triangles. You get a four-inch bit of hacksaw blade that someone at Lewisburg Penitentiary swallowed before he was transferred here and expelled from his body upon arrival, a scrap of metal that has been passed from man to man, mouth to mouth, hand to hand, by the fleeting practiced prestidigitation of inmates making contact on the way to the shower or the visiting room. You spend weeks gently sawing at the edge of the air vent with this tiny bit of serrated metal; and each day you putty the cut you've made, using a mixture of Dial and Ivory soap, blended to match the flesh-colored paint that seems to obscure everything in this prison. And when you've finally sawed the shank of metal free from the edge of the vent, you spend another week (or two or three) on your hands and knees, feverishly rubbing it against the concrete floor whenever the guards aren't looking, until it becomes pointed like that isosceles triangle you dreamed. Then you work on it some more until it is sharp enough to shave with.

You ignite a book of matches and melt your toothbrush to make a handle for the pristine knife.

Then one day you find yourself plunging it into someone's chest. And the guards take the metal beds away and replace them with concrete slabs; and they throw you in the hole with nothing but a Bible and your underwear and a bedsheet. So you soak the Bible in the toilet until it is water-logged and weighs fifteen pounds, and you wrap it in your T-shirt; and when the guard comes to get you for your weekly shower, you hit him with it and fracture his skull. All these things have happened at USP-Marion.

Another entry in the prison's log:

April 2, 1980: While being processed for a U.S. District Court appearance, inmate Bryan, Joseph 15562-175 was found to be in possession of two (2) handcuff keys made from a "Doodle Art Pen." They were found hidden in the hollowed out bottom of his tennis shoe. The keys were made to fit the S & W handcuffs carried by the U.S. Marshall's Service. Bryan was in the Control Unit (H-Unit) at the time the incident occurred.

"How does a Doodle Art Pen become a cuff key?"

How does a Doodle Art Pen become a cuff key? These are the secrets of solitary confinement at Marion that no visitor can learn. A U.S. Circuit Court Judge wrote, "On at least one occasion a [Marion] prisoner had smuggled a homemade bomb into the courtroom via a 'keister cache' lodged in his rectum. When the bomb exploded, a correctional officer lost three fingers on his right hand."

As I walked the corridors of Marion one day, I stopped to greet a prisoner in his cell. "What's happening?" I asked.

"You want to know what's happening?" he asked in outrage. "Get in that cell next door for about ten years; you'll find out what's happening."

At Marion, reality is kaleidoscopic. As I learned, a visitor does not visit USP-Marion; he is led through a warp that winds its twisting way among three dimensions the way a cavern winds through the earth. One dimension is inhabited by the prisoners; one is inhabited by the guards; and the third is inhabited by the prison officials—the warden, associate wardens, and so on down the line. Whether Marion makes you crazy or your own craziness gets you sent to Marion, once you arrive, peculiar things begin to happen; and they happen fast and all the time.

The Administration

USP-Marion is the modern-day replacement for Alcatraz. It is supposed to be so secure that the Bureau of Prisons (which provides administration for all Federal prisons) invented a new level of classification for it: It's called Level Six, the only place of its kind. Marion is the end of the line. Since there is no Federal death penalty, incarceration in USP-Marion is considered the most severe punishment that our government can mete out.

Marion sits on acres of rolling manicured lawn. To reach it, I drove about fifteen miles east of Carbondale, Illinois, and then followed the access road toward a sky-blue water tower. The tinted glass and clean lines of the cast-concrete gun towers make them look more like airport control towers than battlements. The low, louvered buildings of Marion were surrounded by a dancing silver aura that confused my eye as I approached. It was like the first brilliant reflected sunlight I've glimpsed driving toward the ocean. Then I rounded a curve, and the scene snapped into focus: thousands of yards of razor wire, each individual razor blade picking up the sunlight and reflecting it back the way rippling water does.

The light was like a glittering energy barrier around the sand-colored concrete buildings.

I couldn't tell from the road that the modern prison factories were abandoned, the new cafeteria idle, the gymnasium as silent and empty as the chapel.

In the bright, air-conditioned anteroom beside the entrance to the warden's office, a secretary sat before a large plate-glass window. Behind her was a big poster with the inscription CAUTION: HUMAN BEING— HANDLE WITH CARE. Her window overlooked the freshly mowed expanse of lawn where a helicopter had landed May 24, 1978, during an escape attempt. Barbara Oswald, a friend of one of the inmates, had hired a helicopter and then pulled a pistol and ordered the pilot to land inside USP-Marion. The pilot wrestled the gun from Oswald and shot her six times, killing her. He landed the helicopter on the grass; and when he opened the door, her body tumbled out onto the green lawn right in front of this window.

"This is the prettiest spot to be in the fall and spring," the secretary told me. "There's a lot of dogwood and redbud that come out," she said, pointing at the treeline in the distance. Between us and the treeline, a hundred yards of silver razor wire curled up and over the fence like an ocean breaker.

On February 14, 1979, two inmates actually climbed over that barrier after wrapping their arms in newspaper, which would seem to confirm what the administration says: that the typical Marion prisoner is a desperate and violent man, always on the verge of escape. To support that point of view, officials display homemade weapons—pen bombs and hacksaw blades and handcuff keys—evidence that those who are put in USP-Marion are a special breed.

John Clark, executive assistant to the warden, summed up administration policy this way: "It's a matter of who's going to run the prison, us or them."

"All of 'em are total sociopaths," said acting warden D. B. Bailes.

Marion officials stop just short of saying that there is such a thing as a born criminal, the notorious criminal type that went out of vogue among penologists and criminologists a hundred years ago.

* * *

Not many people are sent to Marion directly from court after being convicted. Most are sent there for "failure to adjust" to institutional life, which means that the prisoner has done something at Leavenworth or Lewisburg or Lompoc or some other Federal prison that made those officials feel that the prisoner needed the more secure and repressive atmosphere of Marion to make him adjust. In addition, state prisoners who fail to adjust to state institutions may be sent to Marion. Precisely what it takes to get into Marion is the subject of controversy. A U.S. magistrate in the Southern District of Illinois, in a recent decision involving transfers to Marion, cited a case called *Meachum v. Fano*, saying, "Therein, the Court held that prisoners may be transferred between or among institutions arbitrarily—for no reason at all."

It is equally difficult to say how a prisoner gets out of Marion.

When I saw it, the airy prisoner mess hall was equipped with a contemporary salad bar, red tile floors, and stainless-steel cafeteria equipment that gleamed in the noonday sun pouring through the glass-brick skylight thirty feet above. Light-orange and yellow decor made it look as if it might have been a modern hospital or university cafeteria. Some of the tables set up in a small area of the dining hall had blue-and-white checked tablecloths on them. The room was frankly inviting, and the food was more palatable than what I was served in my college dorm.

Only no one ate there. No one except a handful of men who had recently been singled out to leave Marion, having gone through a mysterious process that no one could explain—not prisoners or officials or guards—by which, the warden insisted, one can work his way out to the regular prison system.

I watched half a dozen prisoners line up for chow one day, dwarfed in that enormous echoing cafeteria. One of them, a highly educated man considered to be an escape artist, tried to explain how he achieved his status in this elite group eating lunch in the mess hall. With a wry smile, he said, "*Arbeit Macht Frei.*"

What he was saying was that Marion is the hole; people disappear into it.

There are many differences between a normal maximum-security prison (where you might be sent for murder or bank robbery) and Marion. One is cell time. A normal maximum-security prison operates this way: At 6:00 A.M. your cell door opens and you run down to the mess hall for breakfast. You then go to work in a prison factory or on an outdoor work gang. All this time you are moving around freely, within the confines of the outer wall of the prison. You go to lunch in the mess hall. You have recreation in the yard or go to the gym to punch the heavy bag or lift weights. There's a four o'clock cell count, during which time you must be in your cell. You hit the chow line again in the evening. And at some point you are locked into your cell for the night.

At Marion prisoners are locked in their cells twenty-three hours a day. One hour a day, one man at a time is removed for recreation. (The exception is the elite group mentioned above.) There is disagreement about precisely how and why this condition, known as lockdown, was put into effect at Marion; but it was, on October 28, 1983, in an atmosphere of general disruption that had been building since the summer and culminated in the killing of two guards and one prisoner. The Marion lockdown is now the longest in two centuries of U.S. prison history.

Asked who has been incarcerated at Marion to justify these conditions, the administration will list such criminal luminaries as Joe Stasi, the

French Connection; Terrance Alden, the Bionic Bank Robber (so called because he could stand flat-footed and jump right into a teller's cage); and Alton Coleman, a kidnaper who went on a six-state murder spree in 1984 and was eventually caught in Evanston, Illinois. Numerous others had cop-killing, rape, murder, armed robbery, bank robbery, and multiple escapes on their records before they got to Marion. One quarter of the men at Marion have committed murder while in prison. The average sentence is forty-one years, while some are serving multiple life sentences. Marion houses numerous members of the white supremist gang known as the Aryan Brotherhood, including the infamous Joseph Paul Franklin, who bombed a synagogue in Chattanooga, Tennessee.

One Marion inmate was serving a Federal life sentence, to be followed by a state death penalty after his release.

The administration of Marion, as well as the Bureau of Prisons, maintains that the population of USP-Marion, being radically different from all other prison populations, merits such radical conditions as total lockdown and justifies the forty thousand dollars per year per man that it costs to maintain those conditions.

Executive assistant John Clark and acting warden D. B. Bailes explained the official point of view to me as we sat on green leather couches in the gold-carpeted warden's office one sunny summer day. (Warden Jerry Williford was on leave.) Bailes was a tall, fit-looking man in a conservative gray suit, with a bald head, a big smile, and an easy manner. Clark, a former Catholic priest, was a large, bespectacled man, partly bald, with curly brown hair. He wore shirt sleeves and a tie open at the neck. He had an unflinching stare and did not laugh easily. Both prison officials had the look of hard-working, unpretentious businessmen. An architect's model of the prison was on a coffee table in the middle of the room. It had two main concourses—called East Corridor and North Corridor—from which the louvered concrete cell blocks extended like fingers.

"We don't know what causes crime," Bailes said. "We don't make any pretense at rehabilitation."

Clark said, "One of my theories about prisons is they're drama schools where people learn to act rehabilitated. They tried here for several years to operate more or less as a normal penitentiary when they didn't have a normal penitentiary population. They finally decided that just wasn't realistic."

I asked how long-term isolation affects prisoners.

"After so many years, they begin to break down," Bailes admitted. "But," he added, "the prisoners let you know when one of 'em is getting flaky," so that the affected inmate can be taken out for psychiatric treatment.

The primary emphasis was that these were desperate, dangerous men who would do anything to escape and who had no regard for human life, not even their own. Many prisoners have contraband already in their intestinal tracts when they arrive at Marion, having inserted it or swallowed it before leaving a less secure prison. Drugs, syringes, handcuff keys, and even hacksaws and carborundum rods are routinely found, Bailes said. Most prisoners are now X-rayed before being allowed into Marion. Some are dry-celled: put into a cell with no running water, so that their feces may be inspected.

"But that's not foolproof," Bailes told me. "They'll re-swallow it." To detect contraband, Bailes prefers a method he calls the "finger wave." Physicians call it a digital rectal examination. "We don't have an alternative," Bailes said.

Richard Urbanik, one of Marion's two resident psychologists, introduced himself by saying, "I'm considered the most liberal person here." He confirmed Bailes's assessment of the Marion population while admitting, "This would be a very harsh way to treat the normal prisoner." Urbanik called his 335 patients "the most vicious group of people in the United States," but disagreed with acting warden Bailes's opinion of their psychological problems. He claimed that the odds are "relatively low" that this type of inmate would suffer from a two-year lockdown. "The Marion prisoner is antisocial severe," Urbanik said. "The Marion prisoner is different. Different behaviorally. They don't feel anxiety. They don't have the capacity. That's been shown in many research studies. Psychopaths don't learn under punishment. I'm a psychologist. We look at behavior. We're not really worried about whether there's a mind."

Urbanik characterized the situation at Marion as "basically like your four-year-old being put on his bed for misbehaving." He said that immobilizing a prisoner in a six-by-nine-foot cell twenty-three hours a day does not affect him. The fact that the bureau sent him to Marion means that he is severely antisocial, and "his being antisocial buffers him against the normal effects, although," he added, "there hasn't been a lot of research into the effects of long-term incarceration."

Precisely what a Marion prisoner is and what he is not, precisely how much he can tolerate before the punishment serves to make him more violent instead of less so, are the subjects of heated debate and of at least one lawsuit that was recently settled in favor of the bureau. The official position of the Bureau of Prisons is this:

> It is the mission of the United States Penitentiary, Marion, Illinois, to provide for the safety of inmates, staff and the public through appropriately designed correctional programs and procedures for those inmates identified as the most difficult to manage. . . . Marion's success in controlling these dangerous and disruptive offenders at one location allows other facilities to continue to function as open, working institutions. . . .

In the recently-settled lawsuit (*Bruscino et al. v. Carlson, et al.*), a U.S. magistrate called the methods at Marion "prudent," while characterizing complaints by prisoners about conditions there as "vicious and unjustified attacks."

The Staff

The prison log indicated that doors were frequently found mysteriously unlocked. Everywhere I went inside Marion I saw locks being changed. It's not like changing a dead bolt; Folger Adams locks have to be burned out with a cutting torch and new ones welded back into place. The halls of Marion smell like hot flux.

The heavy Folger Adams keys come with a silver cover that snaps into place when the key is not in use, because for some of the inmates, just one glance is enough: They can memorize the steps and then cut a copy out of anything—plastic, metal, wood, glass.

In the guard office at the end of each cell block is a board with little cards on it. Each card has a prisoner's cell number and a note that might say, "Killed Staff" or "Caution!" or "Bad Fight" or some other warning. One had a skull drawn on it.

The guards go around tapping the bars with rubber mallets once a week to check for any odd sounds and look for metal filings. Someone is always cutting his way out.

Nail clippers and Bic razors are kept on little numbered hooks in a locked case at the end of the range.

There is a wire litter for carrying wounded.

The attitude of the guards toward the prisoners is implicit in the language they use. Beating a prisoner is called "counseling." The inmates don't eat; they feed. When the stress of continuous solitary confinement becomes too much for an inmate and he does something rash—anything from refusing to go back into his cell after a shower to hitting a guard with his shackled hands—they say he "went off." As an unexploded bomb will finally go off if you agitate it enough.

> "One of his best friends was a guard named Merle Eugene Clutts. He was murdered by inmate Thomas Silverstein."

The guards understand the stress. They suffer from it, too. It is possible to get the idea that the guards (who prefer to be called correction officers, in keeping with bureau policy) are hired by the pound and are nothing but big, ignorant bullies; but that, like most stereotypes, is not the entire picture.

Not only do the guards understand the nature of stress—theirs and that of the prisoners—but they also have a deep and subtle understanding of their relationship with the inmates. Most of them expressed undisguised loathing for them.

One guard, who had been at Marion for fifteen years, said, "The only thing wrong with this system is that we don't have the death penalty." He was a controlled and good-humored man most of the time, but when he spoke of inmates, his whole body tensed. He trembled as he told me, "I hate inmates." One of his best friends was a guard named Merle Eugene Clutts. He was murdered by inmate Thomas Silverstein.

It wasn't always that way at Marion, said J. B. Killman, a guard who had been at Marion for seventeen years. "You never completely relax around inmates. But it used to be inmates would speak to you. We were on a first-name basis with them." He recalled a time when the staff and inmates lived in a kind of uneasy detente. "They had things to do then. There was leather craft. They'd have movies on Friday nights with hot buttered popcorn. Basketball. Outside entertainment would come in. Sixty people worked in the kitchen and dining room. It was a nice institution back then. It started to change in the late seventies when a different type inmate began to come here."

What Killman noticed was one of the periodic shifts in penological practice that has been taking place since the 1600s. Prisons go back and forth between rehabilitation and repression. In the 1930s, Alcatraz was the repressive model of a prison. It caused a scandal (as such prisons eventually do), and during the 1960s the United States tried rehabilitation. Since that never works, the pendulum swings back. Marion is the new repressive model. When it causes enough of a scandal, another rehabilitation model will replace it.

***

The guards know that the administration holds the view that everything that happens to a prisoner is his own fault. But they also know that they can control inmate behavior to an extent. Probably without being aware of it, they are masters of practical behavior-modification techniques. A guard can make an inmate go off or he can help to defuse him before he goes off. A guard can overlook a rule infraction. (You can be thrown in the hole, for example, for having an extra pair of socks.) Or he can overlook the fact that your toilet doesn't work; he can make you live in your own waste. Of all the powers that anyone has in the world over us, no one has the broad discretionary powers of a prison guard. The guards know their own power, and like all people everywhere, some abuse it, some respect it.

They carry black Lifetime riot bludgeons, three-foot-long weighted hardwood bats with a round steel ball protruding from either end. The metal ball is there so that the bludgeon won't break ribs. The steel ball separates the ribs, tearing the intercostal muscles, and then pops out. While the pain from it can be intense for weeks and months afterward, the bludgeon tends not to leave obvious marks. But if a guard really wants to hurt an inmate, he doesn't need to touch him. Under the right circumstances, he can take his life simply by letting one inmate out while another is handcuffed and helpless.

And yet the guards and prisoners are often nothing more than reflected images of one another. Often they come from the same backgrounds, and the factor deciding who becomes a prisoner and who becomes a guard is often blind luck. One former Marion guard, speaking of his job at another prison, told me of a case in which one of the inmates turned out to be a boy he'd grown up with in a small town in southern Illinois. He caught the inmate with drugs and had to report him. "He was my best friend as we were growing up," the guard said. "We just took different roads in life. Because my friend was busted by me, he was beaten, raped, and turned into a punk for the rest of the inmates. I was told by my captain that I was a rotten son of a bitch for setting up a friend like that."

One of Marion's two prison chaplains, Gavin O'Conner, said, "Most prisons operate on the good will of the inmates."

Executive assistant Clark agreed. "At any time the inmates could take over because they've got you outnumbered."

Any guard who has been in a prison takeover or riot knows that. Several of the guards I talked to had been surrounded by prisoners at Marion, and they described it in the same terms I had heard used in descriptions of men surrounded by the enemy in war. In a typical prison situation (the way Marion was before the lockdown), the guards—one or two or three at a time—wade in among the unrestrained prisoners— dozens, sometimes hundreds—and simply hope that nothing happens. They avert fear by blocking it from their minds. Once the idea of fear enters, however, they are marked men.

One such marked man was David W. Hale, who had been a prison guard since he was eighteen years old. At the age of twenty-eight he left Marion. The administration, which was forced to ask Hale to resign when Hale admitted beating prisoners, says he was an officer with many problems. The stress got to him, they say. He began abusing his powers, mistreating prisoners, and refusing orders from his superiors. The U.S. magistrate in the *Bruscino* case (which involved a long list of complaints by prisoners about conditions and practices at Marion) said, "The Court has serious reservations regarding the entirety of the testimony of former correctional officer David Hale."

Others, including former guards who knew Hale, claim that the administration was angry with him for what they called "spreading rumors to frighten other officers." Inmates, Hale claimed, were telling him that they were going to kill guards and take over the prison. Hale was on the yard one day before the lockdown, when he was surrounded by inmates. He called 222, the emergency number—"dialed deuces," as the guards say— but no one came. A guard of twenty years experience stood and watched. It was at the discretion of the inmates that Hale lived to tell about it.

Hale and others have claimed that the Bureau of Prisons was intentionally trying to provoke an incident at Marion, which would provide an excuse for a protracted lockdown. That would, say the guards, serve the dual purpose of getting the administration a bigger budget and realizing the ultimate repressive model of a prison: total control.

When I met Hale, he was living on unemployment compensation with his wife and children in a frame house beside a pond, an hour's drive from Marion. Young and boyish, he seemed deeply disillusioned with what he had fully expected to be his career for life. "When I started working there," he said, "it was like any other penitentiary. The inmates were all out; they were working in the factories. Sure, there'd be stabbings, fights, and stuff, but that was to be expected. The staff was never involved. It was between inmates. And then [former] Warden [Harold] Miller started taking more and more stuff away from inmates. Like you're going to work longer hours, we're going to cut your pay; you're gonna have less time on outside recreation. And he just kept taking and kept taking until finally the inmates went on strike."

Hale said that the atmosphere at Marion in 1979 and 1980 was one of increasing terror and intense frustration for the guards; there were almost daily assaults on the staff, but the staff could not fight back. The administration did nothing to try to stop the disruptions and would not allow staff retaliation, even though, according to Hale, inmates were often shackled to their bunks or beaten for minor rule infractions.

Hale finally decided to take matters into his own hands. He felt that if the staff didn't respond to inmate aggression, the prison would go out of control and there would be widespread killings of guards. Hale was going to beat an inmate who had assaulted a guard to demonstrate that these attacks would no longer be tolerated. The lieutenant stopped him, and Hale requested to be taken out of the cell block at that point. The significance of his action was not lost on Hale's fellow officers: It was tantamount to desertion in the face of the enemy. It was career suicide.

Hale said, "I was so mad I was crying, because I knew what was going to happen and nobody was going to listen to me. I said, 'Why don't you tell these officers that these inmates are going to take this place over and they're going to kill every fucking one of us? And you people don't care. We're like a bunch of meat on a hook you're dangling in front of them to see what they're going to do.'"

Roger Ditterline became a guard at Marion in 1980 after six years as a state trooper. He is now retired with total disability. He was one of three officers stabbed when Robert Hoffman was killed by inmate Clayton Fountain. He said, "There weren't any controls. When you have this many murderers, rapists, people doing hard time, antisocial characters, you try to keep a lid on them fairly tight, but it didn't seem to be that way." At that time the guards did not even have riot batons. "We were moving these guys all the time up there with their handcuffs locked in front of them. Now, that goes against everything I was ever taught in law enforcement."

One day before the lockdown, when prisoners were allowed to walk freely to the mess hall for meals, Ditterline found himself surrounded by seventy or eighty inmates when he and another officer were sent in to get a bowl of beans a prisoner had taken from the cafeteria to his cell in defiance of the rules. The prisoners could have killed the two guards, but they did not. Some say it is this very balance of terror and respect between guard and prisoner that makes a normal prison system work. The guards cannot brutalize prisoners too much, because they know that one day they may face being surrounded by those same prisoners and be judged on the spot. When that even strain between guard and prisoner goes out of balance, the system breaks down; and riots or takeovers result. Ditterline, Hale, and other Marion guards believe that the administration and the Bureau of Prisons may have intentionally allowed Marion to go out of balance.

Ditterline said, "It seemed like the administration was trying to get something to happen, and we couldn't figure out why."

Ditterline and Hale said that under Warden Miller, rule changes seemed capricious and designed to frustrate prisoner and guard alike. One day the guards would be ordered to remove all sugar packets from the cells. The next day it would be salt. One day razors were issued; the next day they were prohibited. "It was crazy," Ditterline said.

During the winter months, when the wind blew through the louvered windows along the ranges, the administration would allow inmates to hang blankets on their cell bars to stop the wind. The inmates would get used to that for three or four weeks, and then a memo would come from the warden's office: Immediately confiscate all blankets hanging up.

Although the guards may have seen a conspiracy, it could just as easily have been the typical workings of a bureaucracy.

Jim Hale is another former Marion guard (no relation to David Hale). The day after the killing of officers Clutts and Hoffman at Marion, he claims that he began carrying a knife for his own protection because he felt the administration was not sufficiently concerned about staff safety. He was forced to resign when a fellow officer reported him. It is illegal for a guard to carry any weapons other than those issued by the prison, such as the riot batons (or guns in the gun towers).

When I visited Jim Hale, he was living in a motel room on the outskirts of Marion, Illinois, in a room not much larger than a prison cell. The shades were pulled tight against the white hot light reflecting off the highway outside, and the room was dense and dark with his belongings. The air was still and thick. Clothes, combat boots, dishes, and magazines were everywhere. He had an unusually large number of knives. There was a Bowie knife on top of the television and a machete propped up by the door. A Gerber boot knife was on the nightstand. The closet shelves were stacked high with junk food, and Hale and I sat on the bed while we talked. He was a large, soft man in his twenties and was wearing an undershirt. His pale arms were tattooed.

"The administration was just waiting and hoping for somebody to get killed so they could lock it down," he said.

"Why?" I asked.

"I don't know," Jim Hale said. "I can't really say much about that. Harold Miller has a reputation throughout the Bureau; you hear people talk about him: When they want a place locked down, they send Harold

Miller there. And it gets locked down. When he left Marion [shortly after the lockdown began], he went to Lewisburg. Within two weeks after he got to Lewisburg, they locked the place down because they had a work strike."

Referring to the day when two guards were killed at Marion, Hale said, "The associate warden, a guy named Ken Stewart, told the crew that was working H-Unit [the hole] that night to go ahead and run it like it was normal routine. Take these guys to Rec; put them in the showers. Now that doesn't make a lick of sense. They should have locked that unit down—it doesn't have to be the whole joint, just that unit [i.e., cell block]. Lock that unit down and shake it down. It wasn't locked down; it wasn't shook down. OK, Tommy Silverstein killed a guard that morning. That made him a big shot, the way the cons think. Well, here's Clay Fountain sitting upstairs [in the same cell block]. And he's a rabid little bastard if there ever was one. There's no way in hell he's going to let Tommy Silverstein have all the glory for killing a guard. If he got the chance that night, he was going to have to have some of that glory. Well, he got his chance. Bob Hoffman was killed because of it."

Later I asked John Clark why Fountain had to kill a guard. He said, "To keep the body count up, I guess."

"Then why weren't normal practices followed?" I asked. "Why weren't the cells searched after the first murder of the day?"

"That's the first time I've ever heard that even mentioned," Clark said.

Jerry Powless was the officer escorting Fountain when Fountain stuck his hands into another inmate's cell. Fountain spun around with one cuff off and a knife in his hand. Before he could get to Hoffman, however, he had to face Powless and Ditterline. He plunged the knife into Powless's chest and Ditterline stepped between Powless and Fountain.

When Ditterline told me about this, his voice dropped almost to a whisper and tears came to his eyes. "I remember blocking a couple of the blows, but he nailed me a couple of times and I fell backward. I was kicking at him, trying to keep him at bay as best I could." Fountain rushed past Ditterline and Powless to attack Hoffman, fatally stabbing him.

"And you know who the first person through that front grille was?" Ditterline asked. "Hoffman's boy. His son. He saw his father die."

Hoffman's son was also a guard and the first person to respond when David Hale dialed deuces. When Clay Fountain saw him come in to help his father, he hollered out, "Come on! I've never gotten a father-son combination before." And then Fountain did a little victory dance down the range, laughing, amid cheers from the other inmates.

The Inmates

When a person has passed through five grilles, he can say he's been in Marion, and he can look back out to the front door and see what effect all that steel has on sunlight. The world he knew—the bright, new, air-conditioned front vestibule, which with its magnetometer and guard looks like an airport terminal—is dimmed and shattered into an alien logarithmic crosshatching on the mirror-polished floor. But even there he is still not really in Marion. He is protected from it by his mind, which keeps alive the images of what he just left outside.

On the other hand, if he were to stay in Marion for a very long time and had to move past those grilles, it would be very difficult to remember what was out there, the white parking lot glittering with red and blue and tan automobiles—models he has never seen, which will come into and go out of style before he is released—and beyond that, the Crab Orchard National Wildlife Refuge with more than forty thousand acres of forest and lake, deer and opossum, fox and quail.

When a prisoner goes off at Marion, he is taken from the east corridor "normal" population to the north corridor "special housing"; he passes those grilles on his way into solitary confinement. You have to wonder if the designers planned it this way, but a man going to the hole can actually see outside, almost into the parking lot.

I saw a young black man being dragged there, shackled hand and foot. He was moved along by three guards. One held the handcuff chain behind his back to jerk him flat on his face at a moment's notice, while two others held their clubs at the ready to strike him down if he made a move. As the prisoner passed the divided shafts of sunlight on the gleaming yellow linoleum, he strained to look out beyond the grilles. After long enough inside Marion, the inmates simply call everything out there "the street."

"Being in the hole twenty-three hours a day for two and three years is a son of a bitch," said Garrett Trapnell, who is serving life for hijacking. "Some men are over in H-Unit today, and the only way they're ever going to see a skirt or ride in a car or eat at McDonald's is by killing somebody. So in our society, here, there's no punishment for murder. For murder you get rewarded. I've seen guys talking: 'I wanna see a girl, man! I wanna smell the world, I wanna see the grass; I wanna ride in a car. How am I gonna do that? I'm gonna kill this motherfucker.' An automatic trip—it's court time."

> "'I have never seen procedures so extreme and so seemingly designed to degrade and aggravate the prisoners.'"

Dr. Frank J. Rundle, a psychiatrist who visited Marion, described "security conditions of a degree I have seen nowhere in ten years of visiting prisons around the United States." He added, "If more humane conditions are not soon restored there will be a catastrophe."

Joseph G. Cannon, a professor in the administration of justice at the University of Missouri in St. Louis, wrote, "I have worked in and around prisons and jails for the greater part of my life (now in my sixtieth year) and I have never seen procedures so extreme and so seemingly designed to degrade and aggravate the prisoners. . . . If the present procedures at this prison are permitted to continue, violence will be the consequence."

Craig Haney, a social psychologist specializing in prisons, said, "Unless the draconian and Orwellian conditions that now prevail [at Marion] are significantly abated, I believe that major outbreaks of violence will result."

What they mean is that one prisoner who escapes could pull a lever and let out eighteen prisoners on a range. Those eighteen could overwhelm the three to five guards at the end of the range and then let out an additional fifty or so prisoners. Those fifty could overwhelm guards on another cell block, and so on, until the entire prison was in the hands of the inmates. What they are saying is that even the tightest security must slip up once in a while, and then, if you haven't already developed the good will of the prisoners, you'll have a prison takeover on your hands. Marion could be the next Santa Fe. At that prison, inmates murdered thirty-three guards in a thirty-six-hour siege in 1980. Some guards were tortured with electric drills before being killed.

* * *

I walked along the ranges, passing cell after cell. Hot moist waves of air moved through the flesh-colored bars like vapor sweat. There was the faint scent of burning paint and the resin binder of a grinding wheel. A lock was being changed somewhere on the corridor. The smoke drifted to us and mixed with the sublimated sweat that poured off guards and prisoners and rolled down the hall like a fog.

In some of the cells inmates had been allowed to fashion ducts out of laundry-bag plastic to direct air from the vent toward the bunk; these looked like giant condoms protruding from the walls. Each six-by-nine-foot cell had a vent and a bunk, a combination sink and toilet, and a cardboard locker about three feet wide and eighteen inches deep. The cells face out onto the range and a concrete wall with louvered windows. If the louvers are opened (at the guards' discretion), the prisoners can see across to the next louvered concrete cell block. The prisoners cannot see one another; they carry on conversations by shouting up and down the ranges.

Sometimes the inmates would not even look up to see who was there as I passed. At other times they would loom up out of the darkness, tattooed and apparitional and white, like rare fish surfacing from the ocean depths. A skull and death's head mask came up out of one cell, and I read beneath the blue hallucinations the words WEISS MACHT, German for "white power."

Then I saw that it was tattooed on a man's stomach, and I shifted my eyes to see his face. He might have been in his middle thirties. His head was nearly shaven; his well-developed upper body was covered with tattoos. He had so many tattoos it appeared that his clear, pale skin was turning blue from within—the last stages of some disfiguring disease. He looked up from a copy of Edward Abbey's novel *The Monkey Wrench*

Gang and stared out at me. Swastikas had been hammered into his skin here and there, single-needle work; skulls and images of the Grim Reaper squirmed on rippling white flesh. There was a deep mass of scar tissue on his left arm near the elbow, and I asked him what had caused it. He said he'd removed a tattoo. I asked why.

"I thought it might cause me some trouble in here," he said.

"What did it say?"

"Oh, nothing. Just some initials."

"What initials?" I asked.

"A. B.," he said.

I walked away. I didn't get it until I had seen two or three men adorned as he was. Then it hit me: Aryan Brotherhood.

Some inmates came right up to the bars talking, as if I had been there all along. They did not touch the bars. They behaved, in fact, as if the bars were not there, passing papers through the bars, shaking hands with a casual, graceful ease that could have come only with long practice. An eight-and-a-half-by-eleven-inch sheet of paper was deftly folded with the fingers of one hand, then passed through the bars and unfolded again as if by magic.

Henry B. Johnson, a mild-mannered, clean-shaven black man wearing black horn-rimmed glasses and a forest green knit ski cap, came up out of the darkness of his cell, chattering softly in a long enunciated drawl, and didn't stop talking until I walked away. ". . . Leavenworth, Atlanta, Terry Haute, Lewisburg, El Reno, I done twenty years flat. They say I robbed a Safeway, a stickup, armed robbery, right? I originally started my time in the state of Virginia, then transferred to Federal system. I came here, moved to El Reno, El Reno to Leavenworth, Leavenworth to Atlanta, Atlanta back up here, to Terry Haute, back to Atlanta, Atlanta to Lewisburg, Lewisburg back here, Otisville to Lewisburg, and back. Now, the flux of the situation that I like to bring to hand is this here: The reason that the prisoners are locked down in this facility has nothing to do with the prisoners per se. It's the economics of the thing, the politics. You know anything about politics? Here's what I'm saying: What took place in the Control Unit—which is the last stop in this particular facility, right?—has no bearing on the population in this particular facility, right? It was an isolated incident. Now it's my understanding that the alleged officers that they claimed was murdered in the Control Unit should have been dealt with at that end. Since then, the past twenty-one months, we've been locked in our cells twenty-three hours a day, right? And a long period of incarceration without proper medical diet breeds psychosis. You know what psychosis is? It makes one become predatory, compulsive—his behavior is other than normal. So what I'm saying is if they plan to relieviate the situation, try to get things back into control, they should open the facility up. In my particular case, right now, I'm seven years overdue for being released. I come in when I was eighteen. I'm thirty-nine now."

Paper is the currency of prison; it was paper that got them into this fix; and paper, they hope, will get them out. An administration memo can grant a privilege or take it away. Almost all the prisoners I spoke to showed me something on paper—a writ, a lawsuit, a plea, a letter, a shot (citation for rule infraction), even a poem.

Clark sneered at the legal actions brought by prisoners. "It's part of the way they structure their time," he said. It is also their only hope.

On the other hand, the librarian told me of those inmates who simply request one legal volume after another—"sequence readers," he called them—one a day, until they've run through every volume on the shelves. He has to answer every request, or they'll file a suit saying they're denied legal counsel. As a result, with an inmate population of only 335, he processed ten thousand requests for books in 1984.

A lawsuit is no trivial matter. I visited one room in the prison stacked hip high with some forty thousand pages of documents involved in *Bruscino*. The case contended that the harsh conditions of USP-Marion violate a wide range of constitutional rights. The room was dark, abandoned looking, with a paper wasp pelting its body in vain against the bright metal mesh of a single window up near the ceiling. The long tables where researchers had sat, the high yellow ceilings, the dust, all contributed to the impression that this was what remained of a vanished civilization. "The only option they have at this time to change their self-imposed plight," said the magistrate in that case, "is to manipulate the judicial system for their benefit. This Court will not be a party to such manipulation." And, he added, "Conditions at USP-Marion, singularly or totally, are constitutional."

* * *

As I walked the ranges, I saw one man sitting on the toilet, staring out. We might have been shadows on a scrim. The only privacy in prison is the privacy you create by refusing to see.

Another inmate sat bolt upright on the edge of his bunk with his face just inches from the television set, staring with rapt attention at the close-up face of a soap opera heroine. Channel ten is a closed circuit on which the prison broadcasts religious services and, now and then, the Jane Fonda workout tape first thing in the morning. It was once a favorite, but after two years of solitary confinement, the inmates have become inured even to that. Prison authorities decide who can have a television set or a radio—or any possession, for that matter. A list of approved articles is distributed. Anything not specifically approved is forbidden. In the hole, there is nothing.

A big, white, freckled kid with red hair cut marine style squinted, pacing angrily in his cell. He looked as if he were about to hit someone, only no one was in there but him. When I approached, he spun on me accusingly, his fists balled. "There's no sense in me talkin' to you," he said.

He had an eye tattooed in the center of his hairless chest. He was almost shouting. "I've been here for five years!"

Another man rushed the bars, saying, "Yeah, don't believe anything they tell you. They're just covering their own asses. I was roughed up in Lewisburg and protested. I fought back. I was charged with assault and sent here." Behind him on his shelf was a copy of *Art through the Ages*. Some prisoners are allowed to have books sent to them from outside. "Now what sound man is going to attack ten officers?" he asked.

Michael Price had WEISS BRUDER tattooed across his stomach and a little swastika needled into the tender flesh just outside his right eye. Elsewhere on his body: a skull, a Grim Reaper, and the word DAGO. I thought it remarkable that a white racist would use ink to make his skin darker.

Glen West said he'd committed robberies, escaped from prison, and taken policemen hostage since his career of crime began. "I'm not saying I don't belong in here," he told me as I passed his cell. "I don't care where they put me. But isn't it funny that the Bureau of Prisons hires nothing but perfect people? None of them make mistakes." He couldn't read when he was first put in prison. He taught himself during the rehabilitation fad.

He handed me some papers. They magically folded on his side of the bars, passed through, and unfolded again in the air before me. It was a trick as neat and unconscious as a cowboy rolling a cigarette with one hand. I read the BP-DIR-9 form, "Request for Administrative Remedy," which has two parts, one labeled Part A—INMATE REQUEST—and the larger labeled Part B—RESPONSE. In the top portion West had written:

> I have been told by both the Warden and now the counselor that even though we have a cabinet in our cell which can be used as a table to eat our meals on they won't allow us to. We are being told to either eat out of our laps or off the floor. This simply because they think the cell looks neater if the cabinet is where we can't use it. We can't eat out of our lap like a sea otter because often the trays have food or water all over the bottom of them. Besides to say eat out of your lap because we like the way the cabinet looks over there is ridiculous. Why not just give us a bowl and we can eat off the floor like a dog.

The warden wrote back, "This is in response to your request for administrative remedy receipted 5/31/85, in which you request to be allowed to use your storage locker to eat off of. Lockers presently issued to inmates are designed for storage of personal property, also a shelf for televisions. Shelves are presently being considered for placement in each cell which will serve the purpose for eating, writing, etc. Accordingly, your request is denied."

It's the sort of treatment that is so difficult to define, so gentle is the method, like the Chinese water torture, or the death of ten thousand cuts. Each cut is so clean that you never feel a thing.

I watched an inmate go off one day at Marion. (The administration calls it "acting out.") He was a black man in his mid-thirties. He'd been let out of his cell for his sixty minutes of indoor recreation, and he was walking up and down the range in his bare feet, cackling and howling, refusing to be locked up again. He didn't realize he was more locked up than most of us will ever know. Freedom to him was an hour out on the range: A yellow-painted steel screen at the far end covered a ventilation shaft; a sliding grille of prison bars blocked his way out past me and the guards. Still he wouldn't go back into his cell—I guess freedom is a relative thing—and no one was about to go in there and talk to him until the riot squad came. So he was allowed to hoot and carry on until he wore himself out. Then the SORT team came and did a forced cell move on him: held him down and carried him away. SORT stands for Strategic Operations Response Team. Inmates call it the Goon Squad. When the SORT team comes to get you, all your possessions are removed and taken to the second floor of the hospital, where they're stored in an abandoned ward.

After the guards were killed, inmates say, there were widespread recriminatory beatings of the prisoners by the guards. Mike Sizemore, a young white man, was one of the alleged victims. He told me his version of the events: "Shortly after the lockdown they moved us early one morning. I was dressed in shorts, T-shirt, and shower shoes, nothing else. And this was the middle of November and all the windows were wide open and they were writing up shots left and right." A prisoner is never given explanations, such as why he's being moved, or to where, or why he's being made to stand nearly naked in a November breeze. "I asked if they could close the windows," Sizemore said, "and the guy jabbed me through the bars with his stick and told me to shut up."

The next day the SORT team came for him.

While they were moving him, someone "hit me in the back of the neck and knocked me to the floor. And then it started. It was a long way to the hole. They beat me up all the way, throwing me into the walls. They still didn't handcuff me, but I saw no point in fighting back. I'm not a man who will let a man smack me in the face and not do anything. But they were all dressed out [in riot gear], and I couldn't have hurt them if I tried." When they got him to H-Unit, the hole, the guards punched him around some more, Sizemore said, and asked why Clutts and Hoffman had been murdered. Later a physician's assistant happened to be passing his cell and Sizemore asked to see a doctor. He was told he could not see one.

The U.S. Court ruled in the *Bruscino* case that such charges by prisoners were untrue and without foundation in fact.

* * *

By a mysterious paradox of the rule system, if you go off frequently enough, unless you kill or maim someone, the guards finally back off and leave you alone. Describing "the process of dissolution" that takes place after long incarceration, Jack Henry Abbott in his book *In the Belly of the Beast* wrote, "The pigs can sense it and they pass the word. They place you on the *pay-him-no-mind* list. You are allowed to roam the prison and do and say *anything* you care to and the guards overlook it; ignore you as if you were not even there. Only if you commit an act of violence do they pounce and drag you to the hole."

Danny Atteberry, known as Schemo to his friends, is a white inmate with long black hair hanging down past his shoulders. He paced his cell, bobbing and smiling and laughing. He had set his steel bunk on end in an attempt to make the most of the fifty-four square feet of floor space. Atteberry had hung his clothes on the steel bedframe and rolled up the mattress in a corner. Like so many inmates I saw, Atteberry was doing his paperwork when I walked up to his cell—preparing or reading or researching various legal documents. Tom Krajenta, unit manager and immediate superior of all the guards on the unit, stood behind me, facing Atteberry, as we talked. I asked Atteberry why his cell was arranged the way it was.

"I'm living in the bathroom, in the shitter," he said. He laughed: A-hilk! "I mean this is where I've got to live. There ain't nothing I can do, I'm in here twenty-three hours a day. And so I'm gonna live however I want. Now, they're putting guys in the hole if they don't set their bed up here, if they don't put their TV back." A-hilk! A-hilk!

"So how come you're not in the hole?" I asked.

"I generally stay in the hole. I've gotten like twenty shots in the last eighteen months for calling them turds and shit-eaters and maggots and for putting up a sign on my locker that says FUCK AUTHORITY. They take me away from my constitutional rights and put me in the hole."

"So how come you're not in the hole right now with your bunk up on end like that?" I asked.

Atteberry got a wild grin on his face and edged closer to the bars. "Because they're treating me real nice. They don't want to put me in the hole for some reason. I don't know." A-hilk! A-hilk!

I turned to Krajenta and asked why Atteberry wasn't in the hole.

"In this unit the regulation as far as the actual furnishing—we just don't enforce it. The other unit manager or I have the discretion to say if you don't have your bed down you're going to go to the hole, but I haven't done that in this unit because I don't have any problems in this unit."

"I'm the only one that fucks up," Atteberry added. A-hilk!

"How do you feel about being called a turd by Atteberry?" I asked Krajenta.

"I just totally disregard anything that comes out of his mouth."

I asked Atteberry what he'd done to get into prison in the first place.

"I was a youngster. I've been here seventeen years. I went down when I was twenty-two on a robbery charge. After that I escaped and caught a robbery and assault on a police on escape. And then after that I took hostages and stabbed nurses in a prison takeover in 1974 in Walla Walla, Washington."

I asked him how long he might be in prison, and he said he didn't know.

I went down into I-Unit, a cell block containing seventy-two strip cells, what used to be called Oriental cells at Alcatraz, with nothing in them but a toilet and a bunk. B-Range of I-Unit contains the boxcar cells, which have closed fronts to cut off sound and ventilation. There are the bars, as on a regular cell, and then a few feet in front of that—just far enough so that the prisoner can't reach—is a second set of bars covered with plexiglass. A door can be closed so that the inmate's screams are muffled, so that air flow is cut off, so that he can't throw food or feces out of his cell. As I walked down the range, I could hear the last man in the last cell hollering, "Hey! Lemme speak to you for a moment! Hey, newspaper boy! Open the door! Open the door!"

"The door's open," I told him.

"Oh," he said, as if he'd just noticed.

I went through the door and stood in the small space between the two sets of bars.

"My name is Abdul Salam, a.k.a. Clark." A piece of paper materialized on my side of the bars. It said he was once Jesse James Clark but had become Muhammad Mustafa Abdulla. He was an enormous black man, perhaps 230 pounds; but very little of it was fat. In the middle of his stomach he had an enormous scar blooming like a pale flower from the dark flesh of his navel. Smaller scars adorned his arms and upper body. "Now, tell all the women that they gonna send me to Springfield," he said.

"Can we take your picture?" I asked Abdulla.

He hollered up at the ceiling, "Hey Price-Bey! Hey Price-Bey!"

A voice drifted down from D-Range above us: "I heard dat."

"You gonna let 'em take a picture of you, man?"

"Yeah, I am!"

"OK," he said. Abdulla's cell was littered with clothes and bits of torn-up paper. The walls and ceiling had been smeared with something dark. He showed us his prayer rug and Koran. He insisted on putting on his shirt and shoes before having his photograph taken, saying he was a religious man; and he held his worn, green-bound Koran and posed deliberately for each shot. One of his sneakers was laced halfway up and untied. The other was completely unlaced. As he moved his enormous bulk in that cramped and littered space, he lurched and staggered; though he never quite hit the walls or the bars. Even for Abdulla the bars seemed not to be there.

"Hey, Clark," Abdulla said to the warden's assistant. "I know ya'll sending me to Springfield for a medical, for a mental, and you know I don't have no mental problems. You ought to send me back to D.C."

"I'm not sending you anywhere," Clark said.

Abdulla suggested this caption for his picture: "I want you to put in there that I am trying to get back to D.C. and that any Muslim that desire to contact me that it's cool and I'm tryin' to do right but Marion is holding me here as a contract prisoner and don't want to turn me loose."

"Tell me about your stomach scar," I said.

"Naaah!" Abdulla said modestly. "I don't want to talk about that. You know, because that involved me getting shot and then I shot somebody else, that's all. But lemme tell you: They keep my door closed twenty-four hours a day. I been on lockup in this place right here for three months."

He kept on talking as the associate warden and I walked back up the range. Jesse James Clark was taken away the following week to the hospital facility at Springfield, Missouri, for a psychiatric examination.

While I-Unit is known as the most disruptive and rowdy in the prison, D-Unit, which the guards call Dog-Unit, is just the opposite. No radios or televisions are allowed on I-Unit. They are allowed on D-Unit, yet it's surprising how quiet D-Unit is. I never heard music as loud as you might hear it on any bus or subway. There was an almost monastic feel to D-Unit.

There were only forty-five men on Dog-Unit, although it can hold seventy-two. One of them was Frank Lewis, a soft-spoken thirty-year-old black man, who looked weary and contrite. He had robbed a bank with someone in New York in 1977, and when I asked him to tell me about it, he said, "I'm not proud of it." He smiled slightly when I asked him to tell me if there was anything good about being in Marion. "It makes you think much more. Think about your life and how things are fucked up—how you fucked up. And you start saying, 'Wait a minute, I've got to do something about this.' Most of the guys here are in the hole. I've been around. I've been to plenty of institutions, and this one here is tight. It's very tight." He said he didn't mind Dog-Unit because it was quieter. "There's a great deal of maturity over here; guys can somewhat deal with it."

I asked Lewis to compare Marion with Leavenworth, which is where he was serving his sentence before being transferred to Marion.

"Ah, no comparison. At Leavenworth there's much more freedom. You can move around. There's a lot of programs, and you can pretty well occupy yourself. Here there's nothing, so if you can't read, you can't write, and you have no discipline, you're in trouble. It's dangerous in the sense that a lot of guys don't have any money, been down awhile, they've lost contact with their girlfriends; and a guy reaches a level of frustration. So it does present a large amount of danger. In fact that's why I'm over here, because the guys can handle it." Dog-Unit is designated for those the administration identifies as gang leaders.

I asked him if there was any violence when he robbed the bank.

"Well, a gun was used and the threat was there."

"How long did you get?" I asked.

"I got twenty-five years," he said, "because it was the second time."

"So what got you to Marion?" I asked.

"I got in a fight with some officers," he said. "Or a struggling match anyway. But it doesn't take anything major to come here."

It just takes something major to get out.

I visited John Greschner in the hole, which has many names: H-Unit (we were on A-Range), the Control Unit, disciplinary segregation, solitary, strip cell, Oriental cell. Whatever you call it, Greschner put it this way: "There's nothing in there but me." Even when an H-Unit inmate is let out of his cell for his hour of recreation, he is only put in a larger cell.

> "Even when an H-Unit inmate is let out of his cell for his hour of recreation, he is only put in a larger cell."

Greschner stood in the exercise cage as I spoke to him, an elongated steel-mesh box along the range of eighteen cells. In the box was an exercise bike, a chinning bar, and nothing else. If he requested a jump rope, I was told, the guards would give him one. Then again, maybe they wouldn't. Prison authorities gave me their point of view on a few of Greschner's activities since he was sent to Marion in 1976:

> November 18, 1979: At approximately 3:30 P.M. on "A" range of "H" Unit Greschner, John 2550-135 attacked and stabbed Logan, John Henry 87870-132 with a sharpened weapon fashioned from a round metal rod. Logan received approximately twelve wounds to the chest and upper part of the body. The wounds required that Logan be transported to Marion Hospital for treatment.

> April 28, 1980: Inmates John Greschner, Reg. No. 02550-135, and Clayton Fountain, Reg. No. 89129-132, escaped from their cells in the Control Unit by way of the air vent system in the rear of their cells. Using the air vent system, they gained access to the pipespace in the Control Unit and attempted to escape from that area. Squads of officers had to go into the pipespace using riot batons, plastic shields and tear gas guns to force the inmates to leave the pipespace.

When I saw Greschner, he was very pale and sweating from exercise. He had black hair and a goatee. His shirt was off, and he was holding it around the back of his neck to absorb the sweat. He pointed across the range at his cell. "I'm down here for insolence and use of morphine or heroin."

"How do you get morphine in here?" I asked.

"Well, that's what I was trying to explain to them, how do I get morphine in here? You know, they've got it locked down. I don't have any contact with anybody in the streets, I don't have any visits, I don't have anything." Balancing on the balls of his feet, he smiled and shrugged as we struggled to see each other through the steel mesh. Like the bars, it seemed designed to frustrate human contact. The bars and screens seemed always to be just at eye level and spaced so that you could never quite see anyone with both eyes at once. Like everything else at Marion, the effect was disorienting.

"But this is no good here," Greschner said. "They lay people on these shelves for years and years. As a matter of fact, they've got a new shrink here. He's been placed in this unit since the killing of the guards

and the allegations by the prisoners that people deteriorate down here—
long term isolation, sensory deprivation. There is no TV, no radio, and if
they consider you're disruptive, even if you're in the cell and you can't get
out of the cell, they will run in and jump you with a Goon Squad [SORT
team] and beat that ass and tie you to a bunk. So they brought a shrink in
here and the first time I seen him I asked him, 'You know there's a lot of
things been happening here and you've been getting a lot of testimony [in
Bruscino] by psychiatrists that these units are harmful. They aren't doing
any good. Also, a personal friend of mine named Silverstein, who ya'll got
for killin' one of these guards, was down here for years on end, and they
knew that was going to happen with that guard because he told them it
was going to happen with that guard if they didn't get that guard off his
back. And I was there when he told the unit manager that after months
and months and months and months of the harassment from that guard,
Clutts, finally he says, 'I can't take it any more. If you don't get this guy
off my fuckin' back, I'm gonna have to do it.' He told J. T. Holland that.
That was the Control Unit manager. They never did it. I went to Leavenworth. Six months later I hear they got Silverstein for killing Clutts."

As Greschner talked, he became more animated, pointing his finger at
the flesh-colored steel mesh that separated us. "Now, I have no problems
with a guard doing his job. That's what he's here for, to make sure we
ain't sawing windows out and all that. But when you start poking at a
motherfucker and start fucking with a motherfucker all the time, you
know, putting shit in his food, fucking with his rack, harassing him, shaking his shit down—you go in and you find pictures of your old lady, or
your mom, with boot prints on 'em. Then you go to his superior and say,
'Hey, look, check this out, look what he's doing in there,' and they don't
do nothing; finally, it reaches the point where you're either going to take
it or you're going to do something.

"Now, I'm trying to explain this to this shrink. I told him, 'Yeah, I
did almost nine years in solitary confinement, I went down to Leavenworth, yeah, I'm annoyed and fucked up, man, and . . . I'm doin' OK . . .
but I'm fucked up and having a hard time navigating, man. I been away
from people so long, you walk up and I don't know you, I'm kind of annoyed with you. . . .' You know what I'm saying?"

"Yeah," I said.

"And consequently, I'm down here for four months, and I get in a little old beef with this dude, man; I get in a killing. Now I'm back here.
They gimme a double life sentence. And I'm saying, 'What do you think
of that? What do you think of the detrimental effects of a unit like this?'
And he says, 'You know what, Greschner? You just gimme good reason
to keep you locked up in here forever.'"

* * *

Being in the hospital was like being on the bottom of a swimming pool, an indistinct green coolness after the oven of the cellblocks. The physician's assistant in charge of rectal searches carried a radio and a set of keys like a guard. He said, "I have yet to see a beating here."

The dentist, a civilian drawing lieutenant-colonel's pay, said, "I've got the needle, the ultimate persuader." And he laughed.

I took the armored elevator to the second floor, a ward that used to house inmates but is now deserted except for one guard and one prisoner behind a steel door for his own protection while he's testifying. Federal witness protection. He squinted out through a slit at us. A walking dead man.

At the end of the corridor were two large hospital wards now piled high with upturned hospital beds, discarded IV stands, old duffel bags, and the belongings of prisoners who were being kept in strip cells.

I asked the fat, boyish guard, "What do you two talk about up here?"

"I avoid talking to most of these convicts," he said.

"Don't you talk to him at all?"

"When I have to."

"Why?"

"You start off talking about apples and pretty soon you're talking about oranges. The next thing you know you're talking about tangerines," he said. He turned the key and sent me on my way in the steel elevator.

I went out of the hospital and down the corridor and back out through the magnetometer and into the world. The parking lot, the cars, seemed dazzling and fantastic after days inside USP-Marion. As I stood on the brink of the Crab Orchard Wildlife Refuge, I thought how cruel it seemed to deprive someone of all this. Then I remembered one prisoner I'd asked what he thought his punishment should have been for all he'd done.

"What do you think they ought to do to you?"

"By the code that I live, I would have done something. I expected it. I'm not in here unjustly. I stabbed the officer and that's what I'm in here for. Wasn't nothing unjust about that. It was just something that happened at the time. I couldn't get around it. I have my own code of ethics I live by on the streets. I don't live by society's laws, so when society catches up with me, I got to be punished. I accept that. It ain't no big deal. I accept what's coming to me according to the society."

"Would you try to escape?"

He looked up suddenly and angrily, as if to see whether or not my question was serious. "Would I try to escape? Of course."

Emily Hiestand

Maps

Emily Hiestand is an essayist, poet, and photographer. Her photographs are collected, exhibited, published, and available as archival prints from Ebb Tide Editions. Hiestand is the author of three books: *The Very Rich Hours* (1992, travel essays); *Angela the Upside-Down Girl* (1999, memoir); and *Green the Witch Hazel Wood* (1989, poems). She is a contributor to a book of American landscape terms, *Home Ground* (2006). Hiestand's writing has appeared in the *Atlantic,* the *New Yorker,* the *Nation,* the *Georgia Review, Salon,* and *Best American Poetry*, among many other publications. Her honors include the Whiting Award, the Pushcart Prize, National Poetry Award, National Magazine Award, numerous awards from the Boston Art Director's Club, and grants from the Massachusetts Cultural Council and the National Endowment for the Humanities. Hiestand works as a communications planner, writer, editor, and art director in Boston.

Our selection, "Maps," is part of Hiestand's collection of interconnected essays, *Angela the Upside-Down Girl*. Colette Kelso, reviewing for *Agni Review*, called Emily Hiestand "a wizard of imagery, conjuring . . . with smooth moves," adding that the pieces in *Angela the Upside-Down Girl* are "truly edifying . . . fully rounded, mindful observations that create a fine detailing of the places we could call home." They combine to form a map of place, family, and time. "Maps" centers on a particular dot, that of Atom City, Tennessee.

People think they're very close to the answer, but I don't think so. . . .
Whether or not nature has an ultimate, simple, unified, beautiful form is
an open question.
—*Richard Feynman*

I grew up in the 1950s in a small town in Tennessee. I lived there with my mother and father and two younger brothers in a house with a nice yard and three big trees. My brothers were Cub Scouts. We all learned to swim. My dad wore a coat and tie and walked to work. My parents gave a cocktail party at Christmastime with fancy cookies and ice clinking in the drink glasses. Amidst all the abiding normalcy of those years, our family did something, repeatedly, that defied the laws of physics, space, and time.

Twice a year, and sometimes more often, the five of us climbed into a time travel machine, a device that my parents kept parked on the street, as if it were a normal pale blue Chrysler sedan, and we set out in it on journeys that took us from The Atomic Age, in which we lived, to The

Age of Mule Agriculture. Once we arrived in the agrarian age, we listened to stories told in wondrous accents, we were hugged and kissed, we ate coconut cakes, and sat in parlors (not living rooms) lit by glowing hurricane lamps. There was no Danish furniture to be seen. After about a week, we reluctantly reboarded the time machine and returned to our own house, which was located on a street in the heart of America's Technological Future.

Each of our travels was accomplished by traversing the three hundred miles from Oak Ridge, Tennessee, to Tuscaloosa County, Alabama, the land of my mother's people. Motoring on the slow, two-lane highways of the day, our journey took nine hours each way. To the naked eye, it was standard Fifties road fare, with stops for food and gas, and many "Are we there yet?" called out from the back seat, and everyone involved acted as if it was perfectly normal to transport ourselves from the future to a world that clocked the past, most especially our own particular past, its every magnifying glass, courtship, and thimble.

These repeated family journeys began in a new and uncommon town tucked into a remote fold between the Cumberlands and the Great Smoky Mountains. Built in the early 1940s, Oak Ridge emerged in secrecy and haste, and for more than a decade after its creation, appeared only on military and specialized government maps. The new town occupied a beautiful land rippling with black oak and chestnut ridges, a territory that had once been home to the Cherokee Nation, and later to Scots-Irish settlers who came to the hills and valleys with their north-country ballads and recipes for clear whisky. The secluded terrain in Tennessee also had the precise qualities a group of federal agents were seeking when they came to assess the region in 1942: it was sparsely populated, not far from a rail line, and close by the clean, abundant waters of the Clinch River and the new Tennessee Valley Authority lakes. Vast amounts of water would be needed for the wartime project that was to be conducted in this place.

There were three hypothetical, complex, and immensely expensive schemes for the unprecedented mission that would be conducted in this quasi-wilderness in Tennessee. Each of the schemes was so tenuous, so unfounded and so speculative as to sound now like a kind of fantasy or surreal dream, rather than the considered plan of a responsible government. But in an action characteristic of the entire undertaking, the directors of the project, the Manhattan Project, decided against testing or assessing any of the schemes in advance. They decided there was simply not time to choose among them, and so the directors called for a ferociously expensive, technologically innovative plant to be built for *each* of the three unproven techniques.

Three colossal plants were built and were given the code names that my brothers and I would hear throughout our childhood—K-25; Y-12; and X-10, names that we came to say as easily as we said Lone Ranger,

Tonto, or Fudgesicle. Y-12 was the site of the ca-
lutrons, electromagnetic devices made of a vacuum
chamber and ten-thousand-ton magnets wrapped
in miles of silver coils, the silver delivered directly
from the vaults at Fort Knox. K-25 housed an
immense cascading arrangement of microscopic fil-
ters, through which individual molecules of a cor-

"During the war years, the Oak
Ridge plants used one-seventh
of the entire electrical capacity
available in the United States."

rosive gas could be filtered, one by one. During the war years, the three
Oak Ridge plants used one-seventh of the entire electrical capacity available in the United States. The scientists and workers who were there
when the K-25 plant and its exotic equipment began to operate remember
that the plant emitted a deep hum along its entire long length, a sound,
many would say, like an enormous hive of bees preparing to swarm.

In August 1945, only three years after the federal agents first chose
the hills of eastern Tennessee for their secret work, a wristwatch was
found in the debris of the city of Hiroshima. The watch still exists—an
old-fashioned watch with a round face and Arabic numerals, thin hands,
and a wind-up spring; and although the timepiece is badly burned and
blackened, the hands of the watch are still readable, stopped at 8:16 A.M.
Only after that hour, on the morning of August 6, 1945, an hour which
began to alter our idea of time itself, did most of the workers in the plants
in the eastern Tennessee hills learn what it was that they had been making, what they had been doing, and why. In the secret plants, physicists,
engineers, industrialists, and busloads of young women from the east
Tennessee countryside had successfully separated enough U-235, a rare
isotope of uranium, to provide the fissionable matter for the atomic bomb
named Little Boy.

* * *

My mother and father arrived in Oak Ridge, Tennessee two years later, in
1947, when my father took a job lawyering for the Atomic Energy Commission, the new government agency that had been formed to manage the
atom. There were other job offers for a young WWII veteran and legal
scholar who had been editor of his law review, but this one appealed
most to a couple of modest means, with a newborn baby, because the job
for AEC came with a house. It was a simple house—a "C" house in the
lingo of Oak Ridge—one of the eight pre-fab patterns for the instant
town, from tiny As to larger Ds and Es. Like all the Oak Ridge dwellings,
our C house was built using wood framing covered with panels of new
product called Cemesto Board, a novel sandwich of cement and asbestos.
In September of 1947, when my parents arrived in a green Ford, there
were physical gates at the entrances to Atom City, guarded night and day
by armed sentinels. My mother and father had clearance passes that allowed them to enter their new home, and I was waved into town with
them, two months old, asleep on the back seat.

My hometown would struggle, one of the town managers wrote in his memoirs, to keep up with the U.S. military's eagerness for the gray-black powder called "enriched uranium." After the war, the fact that nuclear weapons work was performed at Oak Ridge was not itself a secret, but the how-to for separating uranium was, and is, intensely guarded information, so the doings and even the purpose of the plants in Oak Ridge were seldom discussed socially, and never mentioned to children. The people of our town, like Americans elsewhere, then believed in the promise of the atom, and in the story that the new weapons were a deterrent to war. But even if you believed the prevailing national stories about atomic weapons, why would anyone in 1952 especially want to mention to a child turning five, and wearing a shiny pointed hat, dazed by a birthday cake and its candles, that the island of Elugelab in the Marshalls had just been vaporized by the first test of a thermonuclear bomb, a bomb 450 times more destructive than the one that had destroyed Nagasaki? And so my brothers and I, and our friends, Christine Barnes, Amanda, and the Nelson twins, and all of the kids on Gordon Road heard nothing about the ferocious weapons that were even then being made in our town. Instead, we grew up thinking of the unseen plants only as the mysterious places where the energy that was "too cheap to meter" came from.

That was the hope in those days, in the 1950s, when the atomic scientists, many of whom had petitioned with President Truman not to use their brainchild on the innocents of a city—demonstrate it in a deserted place, they had urged—longed for some redemption, some humane and useful purpose and application for their epic work. In that first decade of the nuclear age, official American nuclear language focused on the potentials of the atom to generate plentiful energy, as well as the radioisotopes that could offer new healing techniques for the body. Everyone likes to point to the latter program, an unequivocal good that made a menu of isotopes available for medicine and research—including californium-252, which has been so useful in cancer therapy. The scientists of Oak Ridge have also done invaluable work in the areas of bone-marrow transplants, energy conservation, and the messenger role of RNA. They made the boxes that carried the moon rocks back to Planet Earth. And so well did the "Atoms for Peace" part of the story obscure the other part, that I had been active in nuclear disarmament work for years before I understood that I was working to end the primary bread-and-butter activity of my hometown.

Today Oak Ridge and the Oak Ridge National Laboratory is a hub of scientific and technological innovation, generating new knowledge in genetics, biofuels, robotics, and medicine. Although the process of uranium enrichment has shifted to other sites around the country, Oak Ridge remains home to the nation's largest storehouse of weapons-grade uranium. The town's culture has changed some, of course, since the 1940s and '50s. The Department of Energy has opened many of its old files (thanks to former Secretary of Energy Hazel O'Leary), which will offer information for historians and environmentalists about operations and practices once cloaked in secrecy. For the 50th anniversary of Oak Ridge, the town chose the theme: *Born of war, living for peace, growing through science.* For the same occasion, the town catalyzed and installed the first monument in history to link a Manhattan Project city and the nation of Japan; located in Bissell Park, surrounded by a grove of young locust trees, the monument is an enormous dark, bronze temple bell, about seven feet high, and five feet in diameter, a wonderful bell with a deep-throated sound, cast by Soutetsu Iwazawa, one of Kyoto's master bell-makers. Few knew at the time, and not many remember now, that for many months in 1945, Kyoto, like Hiroshima and Nagasaki, was a target for the atom bomb; the old cultural city was spared only because of personal intimate knowledge, the kind that comes from travel; by chance, Truman's Secretary of War, Henry L. Stimson, had spent his honeymoon in Kyoto, had seen and loved the city, and managed to remove its name from the fateful list. Describing the bell he cast for Oak Ridge, Iwazawa says that in Japan during the war, many ancient bells were melted down to make weapons, and that for this symbolic bell, he wanted to reverse the process.

We will need all forms of imagination now to reverse the effects of decades of nuclear weapons manufacturing. Today, anyone who knows the way can drive a few miles out of my hometown through one of the loveliest woods on earth, turn onto a narrow paved road on the side of a ridge, and look out on what locals call simply "the barrels"—76,000 steel drums stacked several high, squatting on the land as far as the eye can see, each drum filled with a stew of radioactive waste, chemical toxins, and hot rags, wrenches, and liquids, various materials and tools that became radioactive in the course of being used.

Estimates to clean the place (to remediate, decontaminate, incinerate and dispose of the waste, and figure out what to do with the waste that cannot be incinerated, buried or disposed of) run into the hundreds of billions of dollars. Too much for government these days, and the current plan is to invite bids from private contractors. How long will it take? "I don't think any one knows," one DOE official in Oak Ridge tells me with a candid sigh. "It will just be years and years."

This town in Tennessee, so steeped in the specific hopes and horrors of the last century, is also for me the landscape of first, and most enduring, affection, the place of wonder lodged so deeply that it exists not only in my mind and my mind's eye, but in the body's own physical memory. I found that out when I returned to my first home after thirty years of northerly migrations. On the day my husband and I arrived, and I stood again at the base of the hill that leads up Georgia Avenue, the door of memory opened wide suddenly without warning, and I was trudging up that hill carrying a cabbage from the grocery store for my mother: in my body, in its muscles and limbs, arose the exact feeling of that long ago walk, fresh and complete. In my hands, there was the feel of the dense, round, pale green cabbage. Unbeknownst to me, my body had been holding, all that time, a perfect memory of the contour of the hill of Georgia Avenue, and of the thickening grove of trees and the shade that began near the left turn onto Gordon Road. I cannot say for sure how old I was that day, maybe six, young enough that I had mistakenly bought a cabbage instead of a lettuce, which is what my mother had sent me for.

"Up and at 'em, Atom City!" the radio deejay called each morning in my hometown. As a young man, my father disappeared each weekday morning into a building everyone called the Castle. It was a simple building, plain vanilla barracks architecture, but it was labyrinthine and sited atop a hill, and as well protected as any castle in history. Only adults with clearance passes could go beyond the lobby of the Oak Ridge castle, and so the lobby was the feature of the building I knew best, especially the floor. Many afternoons, while I sat on a wooden bench waiting in the lobby for my father to emerge from his office, I watched a janitor wax and buff the olive-green floor with a round machine that moved over the linoleum like a serene animal, leaving glossy patterns of circles being absorbed into other circles, endlessly. The security officer at the dark metal desk would talk to me to put me at ease, I think: "I can't let you in there, you know," he would say, kindly, nodding to the closed, locked door. "You might discover secrets," he added, winking in a way that suggested to me that A) he was totally kidding, and B) that I might really be, as I dared to hope, as intrepid as Nancy Drew.

I did often try to imagine the unseen interior rooms where my father did legal work for the AEC: arranging for the millions of troy ounces of silver (once coiled around the calutron devices) to be returned to Fort Knox; telling some project directors that no, it was definitely not legal for them to sell a herd of accidentally irradiated pigs on the Tennessee livestock market; also investigating the alarming plutonium fire at Rocky Flats, Colorado; and always being so scrupulous and Dust Bowl–boy honest that he would not bring home so much as a pencil from his office. "That's government property, kids," he explained. A patient man in the bureaucratic vineyard, called "the peacemaker" by his colleagues, the first of my civics teachers and the only one who taught me how to fish.

"Our town was then a kind of modern frontier village, insular and close, full of purpose and people pulling together, like immigrants to a new land."

Our town was then a kind of modern frontier village, insular and close, full of purpose and people pulling together, like immigrants to a new land. The day that my brother Andy, age four, wearied of coloring the disciples, wandered out of Sunday School, and started walking home along the turnpike that ran through town, he was scooped up in only a few blocks. "Aren't you Sparks Hiestand's little boy? Let's get you home." When not in school my brothers and I were rustling on feral quests along the namesake ridge of our town, and when night closed around us we were at home in its shadows and folds. The town that cradled the abyss also gave us that—a voluptuous ease and comfort in the night, in its cool, loamy, porous smells; its grays, green-blacks, and slates; its shards of light seen through ink-dark hydrangeas. On Halloween Eve, all the front doors of Atom City opened for us; voices in the doorways admired our pumpkin heads and black capes, large hands came toward us dropping popcorn balls into our brown paper grocery-store bags. And each ordinary day, Monday through Friday, someone called "He's home!" the moment one of us saw our father walking over the hill onto our street. I hold these few simple things to the center of remembrance to say that the atomic town had many things in common with other villages.

But only ours was the home of "the technological fix"—that phrase that would shimmer over years like a promissory note, the phrase coined by Dicky Weinberg's father, who was a physicist. How we liked that word "physicist," partly because it began in delight, with "fizz," and was a series of buzzy, hissy sounds, and also because to be a physicist then in Oak Ridge was to be a local god. In such a town, the school science fairs were the *fiestas* of our culture. By junior high, a good science project was a route to popularity—"Did you see DeDe's magnet experiment!"—and for several summers beginning when my best friend Ellen Jane and I were eight, we were overjoyed to be drafted into a real-life research project.

The lab at X-10 was investigating sources of cold light, and scientists there had the idea to enlist children to collect the common lightning bug, needed for some of the experiments. They paid us a penny a bug—which sum amazed and conflicted us, because we caught fireflies anyway, for fun (that quick lunge at a wink of light, and with luck your palm closes around a fluttering, ticklish set of wings), and we would have given our catch to science for free. Many nights we slept next to our jarred collections of *Lampyridae,* the creatures exuding their acrid smell, weakly lighting up the books on our nightstands, in my case, *The Mystery of the Brass-Bound Trunk, The Secret of the Old Clock, The Clue of the Velvet Mask,* stories of the daring girl sleuth who drove a blue roadster.

Childhood in Atom City also had the usual amount of making things out of gimp, playing Clue, and roller skating. For several years, like girls all over America, Ellen Jane and I had skate keys slung nearly permanently around our necks, but we must have been among the only girls on earth who went regularly to the Atoms for Peace Museum to practice being nuclear engineers: slipping our hands into sets of lead-lined gloves, manipulating the bright fuel rods of a simulated graphite reactor, and saying out loud the words "fission," and "critical mass." After practice, we went to the theatre of the silver Van de Graaff dome, a large generator on a pedestal that was a demonstration of static electricity. The man exhibiting the generator spoke seriously for a few minutes about "a force that could kill a person," then beckoned a child in the audience onto the platform, toward the quiescent silver dome. "Go on, honey. It's all right," he'd say.

So you took a breath, put the palm of your hand on the cool dome, and then your hair began to stand straight up, like the quills of a porcupine on alert, or a spiny urchin. It was funny; it was hilarious, and Ellen Jane and I began to call it "doing the dome." (An instance of early geek chic.) Other days we skated to the shoe store to slip our feet into the fluoroscope and stare at the bones of our feet. The fluoroscope, a metal device that resembled the fortune-telling machine and scale outside the grocery store, was an X-ray tube with a fluorescent screen at one end and an eyepiece at the other. Any body part placed between the tube and the screen produced a clear image, even in a lit room, and for a few years before it was quietly pulled out of shoe stores, the fluoroscope—which, of course, gave off a considerable slug of radiation—was considered the ultra-scientific way to size a shoe to a child's foot.

Growing up in Oak Ridge, we knew we were modern. We understood that the future was going to be spotless, that energy would flow like golden rain over the earth, bringing a peace and level of comfort never before known. No teacher had to urge us, on our own we pored over the periodic table, memorizing rare earths and noble gases, the atomic weights of argon, europium, molybdenum, xenon, and zinc. The atom was our turf—as native to us as steel to Pittsburgh, cheese to the village of Brie—and it was perhaps inevitable that we would make an important scientific discovery.

It happened the summer we were nine, and smitten with the card game canasta, which we had just learned from David Bailey. One afternoon, while lying on our stomachs, playing canasta in my mother's living room, we noticed that if we stared very hard at the frozen discard pile, or at the rug, at the Cumberland Mountains out the picture window, the television, even at our own arms, we could see minute semi-transparent vibrations. Everywhere. They weren't specks and they weren't particles; our discovery looked more like spaces between things, maybe it was the field in which grains of matter were sliding around, attracting and repelling one another. What was happening? Were our own eyes like electron microscopes? Were we seeing into what the exhibits at the museum called "the very structure of the universe"? We had no way to test our discovery that summer, and no one we told about it seemed to recognize its incredible significance. But I did not forget about the dancing transparency we saw that summer. In hindsight, I could say it was obviously some summer heat induced optical illusion, or I could say, why not, that Ellen Jane and I had glimpsed a primitive version of string theory—the idea that each of the fundamental particles is generated by an infinitesimal string of pure energy, each of which has a particular, generative vibration.

The canasta discovery was surprising—less because we were nine-year-olds whose background in physics was listening to jokes about the half-life of the neutrino at our parents' cocktail parties than because, at that date, the only model of the atom we had seen was the atom as tiny solar system: the pop-icon atom with a central nucleus circled by electron planets in shapely orbits. That was the folk atom pictured on our school notebooks, on the swim team's nylon suits, and on the municipal town seal. It was also the inspiration for the full-figured atom we saw one evening near dusk in a town parade: a plump man tossing hard candies into the crowd from a float. His head, encased in a round mask like a diving helmet, was the nucleus, and the electron rings were made of hula hoops looped around his body, bobbing as he danced—the whole effect less like an atom than a sable snowflake or lanky spider. But then what *did* atoms really look like? It was the same question that the nuclear physicists were then asking. Theoretically, the solar system model of the atom had collapsed, long before, long before it was being sewn onto our swimsuits, and the "basic building block" idea was giving way to the slippery house of quarks—to mesons and gluons, and to particles named color, charm, and top quark, all entities with only a tendency to exist.

At nine, ten, and eleven years old, Ellen Jane and I assumed that the true atomic structure, when found, would be a kind of Rosetta Stone for our lives, would clarify the jumbled macroscopic world, too—the world of piano recitals, the need for starchier crinolines to hold up our circle skirts, the sad, frightening madwoman who lived on Indian Lane, the wars crackling on the radio news, a place called Cyprus, my tragically straight hair, Ellen's tragically curly hair. Scientists, I later learned, were divided on this point: some dismissed such extrapolation as a naive over-interpretation of the very specific atomic realm. Other scientists went much further than we had—speculating, for example, that human free will itself might be beholden to the uncertainty principle.

Though I had embraced the atom as a boss metaphor for life, and a sciency little pal, I knew—we all knew—that it was also more swift and terrible than lightning. How did we know that? No child of Oak Ridge had yet seen the images of Hiroshima and Nagasaki, pictures that operate on us now with the force of the sacred. But our elders had. And some of them had also witnessed Trinity, and the thermonuclear tests, and one day the hands that had placed the sphere of plutonium into the case of the Fat Man bomb would place a dinner plate in front of me, and touch my shoulder kindly. Not for many years would the children of Oak Ridge read the eyewitness descriptions of the nuclear blasts and bombs, but some sense of what our elders had seen and felt had already transferred to us—in the way they spoke, tones of voice, in their eyes, in sentences interrupted, also in the evacuation drills, marches down a dirt road into nowhere, the cognitive dissonance of ducking and covering, the idea that desks that did not stop spitballs would shield us from "the flash" at the window. Don't look, the teacher said, if there is an atomic flash. And so years later when I did read the accounts, I felt the formal pain so exactly described by Emily Dickinson—"The Nerves sit ceremonious" she wrote—but I was not surprised to hear how the cold of early morning went blindingly bright and hot with a light that "bored its way right through you"; how the *Journada del Muerta* desert was filled with luminescent purples, with a parasol of spectral blue, with swirls of flame, and ball of fire that grew and rolled, that kept coming and coming, one man said, closer and closer and how the path of the shock waves was visible through the morning clouds; how a thunder kept echoing back and forth across the desert floor.

✳ ✳ ✳

Our town was also a normal American town in having the normal amount of denial about these weapons. (Even now, they come and go in the national conscience, and it proves hard to hold in mind how they are real, in real places: 2,850 of them in New Mexico, 2,000 in Georgia, 455 in Louisiana; 12,500 in all, each one geometrically crueler than Little Boy, many loaded and unloaded at the "hot cargo pad" at Albuquerque Airport and transported along Interstate 40.) But it is undeniable that our normal town, one ground-zero of the technological future, was very different from its nearest neighbor, the hamlet of Oliver Springs, where a turkey shoot was held each Saturday morning—which did not mean, our father explained, shooting *at* turkeys but at targets *for* turkeys, which were the prizes. Our town was unlike the nearby towns of Clinton and Sevierville, where the yards held cobalt-blue gazing balls, and unlike the genteel Upper South cities of Chattanooga and Memphis.

Growing out of none of these earlier realities, our town was more like a spaceship that had landed, not very softly, in an alfalfa or tobacco field. And what did the older Tennessee towns think of Atom City? Many of the families who had once lived where Oak Ridge was built, and been removed from their land by eminent domain, were understandably bitter. Other natives were merely worried and skeptical. When Cas Walker, who sponsored a TV variety show, campaigned against fluoridation, he could count on reaching his viewers by describing the plan as "a communist plot started by those foreigners in Oak Ridge." And once a mountain blacksmith who took the time to explain to my brothers and me that red-hot was not the hottest fire, who awed us by bringing the tip of a white-hot poker close to our noses, told us that we were what his people called "fotched up"—the mountain phrase for *outsiders*.

If the scientific methods and modernist tastes of our community distanced us from the older Tennessee cultures, they did not shield us from the slow effects of the land itself, the hills and high mountains that hold the most flowery forests in North America, thick with redbuds, dogwoods, sourwoods and tulip trees blooming over a prolonged spring. Thick with mosses, a capillary lace of streams, and snakes shedding papery skins, the forests of east Tennessee gave any wandering child a regard that seemed to preexist even that of her human family. But in those early, postwar years, the living rooms, patios, and lawns of Atom City itself, though immensely historic, were too new to actually *hold* any history, any layers of time or conservatory custom. In that atmosphere, I had the sense that we had all risen up out of the ground overnight, like mushrooms after hard rain. And in fact I suppose we had.

* * *

Perhaps that is one of the reasons I especially loved to get in my father's car and endure sitting with my two brothers in the back seat for nine (or seven hundred) hours as we drove to Alabama, because we were traveling then into deep memory, and history, and time. When our car arrived on the Callahan land in Tuscaloosa County, we walked with great-uncles who spoke in a familial way to paw-paw trees and animals. We walked a red field where first my great-grandmother, and then my grandmother in turn, had planted seeds, my grandmother Frances dropping kernels in a row so straight that her father claimed she was the best corn planter in the county. "Better than any of my *boys*," he had boasted. My grandmother was proud of that praise well into her nineties. In red-clay Alabama we sat in parlors, not living rooms, and listened as our grandmother and her twelve siblings remembered. Their mother was the late Nancy Augusta Speed, a redhead and writer of romantic fiction, a mother then undergoing the final stages of beatification. Their father was a newspaper editor, a man "of strong opinions strongly held," who when his lungs sickened from printer's ink, sold his beloved *Eutaw Mirror* and gamely took up farming. "Papa learned most of it from farm journals and books," said his youngest boy, Artemas, then newly elected to the Alabama state legislature.

On the Callahan porches and in the Callahan parlors, the basic building block of the universe had long ago been discovered and named. It was Talk, and its constituent elements were Mama and Papa, yellow-dog Democrats, grits and red-eye gravy, and, of course, God Almighty, who was before all building blocks and all universes, and did not approve of gambling—a point on which Albert ("God-does-not-throw-dice") Einstein and the Callahans of Tuscaloosa saw eye-to-eye.

The Callahans were not an insular people; they all set out at times into the larger world, one of them as far as Alaska, but when they gathered together they liked to remind themselves who they were and how they had come to be who they were. When a very large family enjoys its saga, when segments are told and retold, with disputes over crucial details and with laughter rippling around a circle of men and women, a listening child might get the idea that that place was the center of the world. In Alabama, I often felt like a small boat on the sea of their beautiful sounds—Scots-Irish and African cadences met in the Southern new world—and I assumed those sounds would be as constant and enduring as the sea.

The automobile route from Atom City to the center of the world ran south-southwest alongside the Tennessee River, taking Highway 27 through Spring City and Dayton (site of the Scopes Trial), then through

Soddy-Daisy, and the gap at Lookout Mountain. From the Cumberland Plateau, we descended into miles of poison-dusted cotton fields, where my younger brothers and I were watchful for the Burma Shave signs then dotted along Highway 11. Whenever a series appeared we sprang into action, chanting the verses. A few of them dealt the good things that will happen only to a smoothly shaven man, for example: "It gave / McDonald / That needed charm / Hello Hollywood / Good-bye farm." But the anonymous poets of Burma Shave were primarily concerned with two great subjects: getting the girl and staying alive on the road. Here is an example of each theme:

A beard

That's rough

And overgrown

Is better than

A chaperone.

Angels

Who guard you

When you drive

Usually retire

At 65.

We thrilled to those fractured couplets, to the lame verse itself, and also, I think, to the sheer idea of fitting rhymes to the speed and scale of the highway. We felt the American cleverness in those red-and-white signs, and we were proud to be part of such a country—a witty country, with its poetry inked along the road. *Are we there yet?* Gondolas of coal, and cabooses flew by our windows, and my mother remembers a carful of children who pleaded with their father to stop at every alligator game park, Indian wigwam motel, and fireworks stand along the road. It must have been a nearly continuous pleading, for if the 1950s highways were slow, they did not lack for that sort of wonder.

On our trips South to Tuscaloosa, lunch was always at a roadside restaurant called Ruby's Chicken-in-a-Basket, because we reached it just about noontime. No sooner were we settled in our booth at Ruby's than my father would spread his Texaco road map over the table. Was my mother impatient with him for reading the map during lunch, rather than talking with us, impatient for his tracing again the well-known route, and during a meal which even on the road she felt should have a certain tone. I do not remember, exactly, what she said. I only recall my father's determined reply: "I need to know where I am, Dear." And his hand on the map, deliberately tracing and retracing the tangle of red and blue lines.

For as long as I have known him, my father has liked maps, and I have liked to look at them with him—beginning at that roadside lunch stop—me hoping to puzzle out a connection between the clear lines marking our location on the map and, say, Ruby's, a place where the food came in red plastic baskets, which gave rise to many questions, including: Why didn't they just give us our lunch on plates? And if it was going to be a basket, why not use a real straw basket? Or, if you wanted to use plastic, why not make the plastic into something that wasn't a fake something else? And there was also the question of our father's intense concern with location and safety, his constant cautiousness, which seemed so tedious to his smooth, unlined children.

When we were young my father spoke only rarely about his war, and then always in fragments, whose bone-clean form I have come to admire. Normandy. After the landing at Utah Red Beach. At a fork in the road, and my father's infantry unit is moving into the interior. He is driving ahead, with several other men, to set up communications lines. That's his job. He's the communications officer. The other men call him "Sparks." It's a small convoy and my father is in the last jeep. He and his

> "Only much later would I begin to know how war steals some things from people, and gives them other things instead."

pals—he loves these men—had reviewed the map earlier, and agreed to go right at this fork. It's important. But the lead man makes a mistake, turns left, and the second jeep follows him. My father tells his driver to stop. He signals his pals by walkie-talkie, and waits at the fork for them to return. And then, out of sight, gunfire. "An ambush," my father's story ended.

Unlike the stories told in Alabama, our father's short, short story was not meant to make anyone laugh, nor remember fondly, and there was no satisfied ending, such as "And so they did dig that well, and Mama and Papa used that water all their long lives." In 1954 in the Chicken-in-a-Basket on Highway 11, I did not yet understand my father's wish to examine the map again and again, to review each detail. Only much later would I begin to know how war steals some things from people, and gives them other things instead. And now I might say that my father's scrutinizing of maps, his touching them, folding them up and tucking them in the sun visor, his getting them down and looking at them again was less a way to gauge a route, a route that he knew by heart, than it was a way to review the mystery of survival, to touch its creases as though touching an amulet.

* * *

After lunch, our father would fold up his map carefully and tuck it in the felt visor, where it stayed until we pulled into the filling station on the outskirts of Birmingham. *Are we there yet?* We were there, we had arrived when we saw the sign on the Moon Winx Motel, a heart-stopping piece of American road art, a big, double-sided, neon taxicab-yellow crescent moon shaped sign, with the face of the man-in-the-moon on each side, with a smiling mouth, a blue eye that winked, and that happy, blatant misspelling, that *x* in Winx. Two miles beyond the Moon Winx sign, and the tires of our car would be crunching the bed of river pebbles on the driveway to the Callahan land. In morning light the pebbles were many-colored—salmon, ochre, a calcium white—and the water-worn stones, from the one-time bed of the Tombigbee River, closed around our bare feet like cool pockets.

And yet this place that felt to me like the center of the world was also the place that my mother had left at twenty, had to leave, feeling some of the diffuse stifle that any young person may feel in an enmeshed society, and also wondering, she says, "what kind of life I could have there, because I didn't agree with the treatment of blacks and women." After graduate school in cold Chicago, my mother wrote for the immortal "Which Twin Has the Toni" advertising campaign, listened to jazz in good clubs, wore glamorous suits, which she had sewed herself, said yes to my father at Wrigley Field, made curtains for their first apartment out of Army surplus parachutes. Although my mother has often called me to say "Let's go home," meaning let's go to Alabama, and although the accent and manners of her first home are suffused in her every gesture, my mother has little tristesse for a lost place or past. She is the possessor of a mind so open and questing and generally with-it that I have been lulled occasionally into thinking her my complete contemporary, and have shocked her by some effluvia beneath the more dignified norms of her generation.

Neither my mother nor my father could afford to look back. It was their child, saturated from infancy in an atomized world, who was tempted to gaze at vanishing older worlds, and to bumble in vacated shadows. Taking the techno-futurism of my hometown as the norm, I was riveted by the familial rooms of the rural South, its kerosene globe lamps, the dark wood radio cabinets, shelves of yellowed sewing patterns, the intricate kinship system, the incidental, daily phrases that were like magic words. And also riveted, I think, by the feeling that I belonged, simply by virtue of being the daughter of the daughter of Frances Webb Callahan Watkins. But try as I might, I—who had touched the silver Van de Graaff generator—could never enter into the world of buggies and circuit preachers, and by eight or nine I had also begun to notice that there *were* no mules on their lands anymore, and no circuit preachers riding. My elders were conjuring a world that had already passed, that lived now in their magic words. Meanwhile, back in Oak Ridge, Arthur Snell and I were building a rocket ship, for which we had found most of the parts we needed.

As my mother and father leaned so bravely into the post-war decades, it was easy to feel us all going faster, like the agitated electrons in the museum movie, "preparing," the narrator said, "to jump into another orbit." There was little doubt that we would jump to the next orbit, even if we had only a tendency to exist.

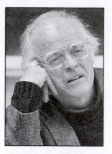

Edward Hoagland
Circus Music

John Updike called Edward Hoagland "the best essayist of my generation." Philip Roth praised the "precision" of his style. The *New York Times* said that he is "one of our most truthful writers about nature." The *Washington Post* said that Hoagland's work is "so intensely personal, so sharp-eyed and deep-sighted, so tender and tough, lyrical and elegiac, as to transmute a simple stroll into a full-blown mystical experience."

Hoagland began writing in part, he says, because his stammer inhibited his ability to talk freely. His stutter continued throughout his adult life, making it difficult for him to, for instance, make the rounds of literary parties. Writing, though, was another matter, and he developed a complex, fluid style. Though he was raised in Manhattan and went to Harvard, he had an adventurous involvement with the outdoors and a wandering spirit that led him to join the circus, fight fires, climb mountains, and above all to remain indomitable and independent.

Hoagland said in an interview that his father disapproved of his writing aspirations, fearing that his books would threaten their "painstakingly achieved social status. . . . Indeed, he specifically told me that it would destroy their social life, injure his professional career as a corporation lawyer and hurt my sister's chances of marrying well. And of course none of that happened."

Hoagland is a prolific essayist and fiction writer with a number of collections. His first book, *Cat Man*, won the 1954 Houghton Mifflin Literary Fellowship. Since then he has written nearly twenty books, including *Walking the Dead Diamond River* (a 1974 National Book Award nominee), *African Calliope* (a 1980 American Book Award nominee), *The Tugman's Passage* (a 1982 National Book Critics Circle Award nominee), *Balancing Acts* (1992), and *Compass Points*, an autobiography (2002). His essays have been collected in the *Edward Hoagland Reader* (1979) and *Hoagland on Nature* (2003). In 1982 he was elected to the American Academy of Arts and Letters. He lives (without email) in rural Vermont.

While Hoagland is perhaps best known as a nature writer, his work has covered a number of subject areas, from academic politics to marriage. The piece we've included, originally published in 2003 in *Harper's Magazine*, is about the circus.

A circus is both acrobatic and elephantine, wholesome but freakish, and that is partly why we like it so—because we are two-headed, too. A showgirl in the center ring displays her pretty legs to daddy while his children are engrossed in watching a palomino stallion dance to the band's tempo. But that, of course, is an illusion. The bandmaster, flourishing his silver cornet, is actually following the horse's mannered, jerky prance, not vice versa, which in turn is being cued by the same short-skirted lady's cracking whip. And in the old days the sideshow used to be called "The Ten-in-One" because it had "Ten Different Freaks Under One Tent for Only One Dollar! Can you beat that, folks?" as the barkers yelled. Only, I suppose, by looking inside oneself. People too fat or too small, too thin or too tall, remind us of a certain unwieldy, weird, but shrinking-violet personage whom we know all too well—as does the Knife Thrower, the Escape Artist or Contortionist, the Tattooed or Albino Lady, hefting a boa constrictor, perhaps, and the knuckle-walking Wild Man, bearded all over, or the Living Skeleton, and the kinky but outwardly clean-cut gentleman who is wed to the swords and fireballs that he swallows a dozen times a day for our entertainment. Why is it entertainment, if we're not gawking at a caricature of ourselves?

"Like actors only more so, circus performers are expected to be manic and depressive."

In the big top everybody wears a spiffy uniform, but if yours isn't a one-night stand and they stay until tomorrow, you'll see some of the circus people sleeping in the horse straw on the ground. And when the costumes come off, baby, don't imagine they'll remember you, no matter how hard you may think you clapped. Behind the greasepaint is quite a different sort of face and person. You wouldn't necessarily trust one of the clowns or animal handlers who give such intense pleasure to tens of thousands of children with the downright raising of even a couple; they might already have abandoned a family. Like actors only more so, circus performers are expected to be manic and depressive, and we accept the paradox that a real genius at making little kids laugh, like Danny Kaye or Charlie Chaplin, could verge on frightening them as a father. The funniness is vertiginous, and the hippodrome food is too sweet. Too much is going on in the rings to absorb it all, and the physical stunts sometimes edge toward the suicidal. Maybe the grisly part of the bargain is that we, the "lot lice," the Elmers, rubes, towners, hayseeds, hicks, yokels, are paying green money to watch the star troupers risk their lives. If a trapeze artist falls and hits the ground, he'll lie in front of a grandstand of utter strangers, whimpering, jactitating, and dying alone.

A circus is high and low, piccolos and trombones. The edgy tiger roars and charges, but then licks her trainer at the end, as if they had been friends all along. A clown meanly tricks his chum, dunks him treacherously in a barrel of water, and gloats for the crowd, but then the high-wire walker steals all his thunder as soon as the whistle blows. The ringmaster, though he seems the boss, is curiously not the star; the saddest puss gets the biggest laugh; and the innocence is raunchy (those leggy girls who strut their stuff alongside a whiteface Bozo so that dad has his own reasons to snicker). The clowns teach most memorably that if you trust anybody he will betray you.

We want circus people to be different from us—homeless and garish, heedless and tawdry (otherwise why pay to watch?)—yet to connect with us in deeper currents that we share. Our fear of heights and ridicule, our complicated fascination with animals (whips, but kindness), our love of grace and agility, of stylish vanity and splendid boasting, of dressing in spangles yet living in tents and trailers. As an element of rooting our children in a stable home, we nourish them with this annual spectacle of the elaborately raffish and picaresque. Therefore, we want the show people to be outlandish but never outrageous, to hide from us their perverse, larcenous, or alcoholic tendencies that may accompany the tramping life. A guy who just got out of the county jail (we hope not the Big House) for doing whatever (and we don't want to know the whatever) and then hit the road because his wife didn't want him is coiling and flinging the ropes around that keep the aerialists' rigging up; and somehow it has become the kind of responsibility he can handle. And without quite articulating it, we want our offspring to be flexible and adventurous as well as predictable, tolerant as well as ethical, capable of flights of delight as well as down-to-earth. Also, we want circus people to know us better than we know them, in a sense: to be wise beyond what their education and social status should officially warrant in gauging human nature, and cater to and inspire our children, even though we have come to watch some of them risk breaking their necks—which is base of us—and even if they can't always manage their own private behavior. People are juggling themselves, hand-to-mouth, in brassy penury, in the circus, not just tossing torches or chancing an awful clawing. Then they'll live in back-street rented rooms during the winter until they can take to the road again.

It's no coincidence that circus music is often identical to the sort of marches that soldiers used to go off to die to. The stakes are high. Bravery, resourcefulness, pinpoint concentration, and self-containment are what make it work, and one reason why so many losers and handicapped souls have found their footing in the circus may be because they see in the crowds how thin a veneer conventional society paints upon our basic greed, inertia, and callousness. So why worry that you're an oddball and have to move somewhere new every other day to keep your haywire impulses under control and sublimate them into stunts? Like rich people, you have that privilege. New audience, new town, never seen you before, never'll see you again. It's anesthetic. If you screw up one of the acts today, you'll get it right tomorrow—so, no sweat, you get it right today.

"*We have the fattest woman in the world, and the tallest man, and a girl who has no arms or legs, and midgets who are married! Have you ever seen a camel spit, or seals play catch, or elephants stand on their heads? A man with reptile's scales, who was once just like you! And the Good Lord made him. Can you finish your ice cream after you have looked at him?*"

Good question. In the pre-television era, when much of the novel technology related to transportation, not electronics, live entertainment toured between cities by train or motor vehicle. Repertory-stage and opera companies, evangelist preachers, Chautauqua lecturers, freelance physic salesmen, vaudeville magicians, humorists, and strippers, who formerly had gone by riverboat or wagon, would troop through town—as well as the more celebrated Sells-Floto, or Sparks, or Hagenbeck-Wallace, or Sam B. Dill's, or Walter L. Main, or Robbins Bros., and Christy Bros. circuses, not to mention Ringling Bros. and Barnum & Bailey, The Greatest Show on Earth. There was Downie Bros. Wild Animal Circus, The Largest Motor Circus in the World (families and brothers stuck together in business in those days), and the famous Clyde Beatty–Cole Bros. big show, and Col. Tim McCoy & His Indian Village, or his Congress of Rough Riders of the World, and Marcellus' Golden Models (with the men's pectorals as big as the women's breasts), and Tommy Atkins' Military Riding Maids.

Fortunately, we aren't entirely bereft of a visual record of these arcane marvels. A Manhattan banquet photographer named Edward Kelty, whose usual venues were hotel ballrooms and Christmas parties, went out intermittently in the summer from the early 1920s to the mid-1940s, taking panoramic tripod pictures of circus personnel, in what could only have constituted a labor of love. He was expert, anyway, from his bread-and-butter job, at joshing smiles and camaraderie out of disparate collections of people, coaxing them to drape their arms around each other and trust the box's eye. He had begun close to home, at Coney Island freak shows, when the subway was extended out there, and Times Square flea-circus "museums" and variety halls, and the Harlem Amusement Palace. Later, building upon contacts and friendships from those places, he outfitted a truck for darkroom purposes (presumably to sleep in too) and sallied farther to photograph the tented circuses that played on vacant lots in New Jersey, Connecticut, or on Long Island, and gradually beyond. He would pose an ensemble of horse wranglers, canvasmen, ticket takers, candy butchers, teeterboard tumblers, "web-sitters" (the guys who hold the ropes for the ballet girls who climb up them and twirl), and limelight daredevils, or the bosses and moneymen. He took everybody, roustabouts as conscientiously as impresarios, and although he was not artistically very ambitious—and did hawk his prints both to the public and to the troupers, at "6 for $5"—in his consuming hobby he surely aspired to document this vivid, disreputable demimonde obsessively, thoroughly: which is his gift to us.

More of these guys may have been camera-shy than publicity hounds, but Kelty's rubber-chicken award ceremonies and industrial photo shoots must have taught him how to relax jumpy people for the few minutes required. With his Broadway pinstripes and a newsman's bent fedora, as proprietor of Century Flashlight Photographers, in the West Forties, he must have become a trusted presence in the "Backyard" and "Clown Alley." He knew show business and street touts, bookies and scalpers—

but also how to flirt with a marquee star. Because his personal life seems to have been a bit of a train wreck, I think of him more as a hat-check girl's swain, yet he knew how to let the sangfroid sing from some of these faces, or simple good rolling-stone mischief, while doing justice to the ragged stringbeans ranked in another line. These zany tribes of show-boaters must have amused him, after the wintertime's chore of recording for posterity some forty-year drudge receiving a gold watch. Other faces look muddied with inchoate emotions, however, as if the man indeed had just gotten out of the penitentiary, or were mentally retarded, or could already feel the dreadful undertow of an illness like epilepsy, schizophrenia, pedophilia, kleptomania, tuberculosis, or diabetic collapse that had choked off so many fresh starts he had attempted before. You wouldn't see *him* in a hotel ballroom, even as a waiter.

The ushers, the prop men and riggers, the cookhouse crew, the elephant men and cat men, the showgirls arrayed in white bathing suits in a tightly chaperoned, winsome line, the hoboes who had put the tent up and, in the wee hours, would tear it down, and the bosses whose body language, with arms akimbo and swaggering legs, tells us something of who they were: these collective images telegraph the complexity of the circus hierarchy, with stars at the top, winos at the bottom. Except that still below the winos were the "jigs," or Negroes, whom you may notice in uneasily angular positions as they perch semi-perilously on a wagon roof behind everybody else, up in "nigger heaven" (as expressed in movie-house terms), signifying their loose-balloon moorings in this segregated world, based on the mores of winter quarters, which were usually down South. There may even be two bands in the picture, a black one and a white one, that might have sounded better playing together.

While arranging corporate personnel in the phony bonhomie of an office get-together for a company's annual report, Kelty must have longed for summer, when he would be snapping "Congresses" of mugging clowns, fugueing freaks, rodeo sharpshooters, plus the train crews known as "razorbacks" (*Raise your backs!*), who loaded and unloaded the wagons from railroad flatcars at midnight and dawn. That was the way a chug-a-lug bar fighter might wind up, in this era when "rootless" was a pejorative word, like "hedonistic" or "atheistic," and a new face in town was cause for suspicion. These ladies toted pythons, strolling around the hippodrome track, and didn't wear enough clothes; and some of the men looked as bathless as the guys from a hobo jungle who would steal your wife's apple pie that she'd left to cool on the kitchen windowsill, yet had skills you hadn't imagined. Circuses flouted convention as part of their pitch—flaunted and cashed in on the romance of outlawry, like Old World Gypsies. If there hadn't been a crime wave when the show was in town, everybody had sure expected one. And the exotic physiognomies, strangely cut clothes, and oddly focused, disciplined bodies were almost as disturbing—"Near Eastern," whatever Near Eastern meant (it somehow sounded weirder than "Middle Eastern" or "Far Eastern"), Bedouin

Arabs, Turks and Persians, or Pygmies, Zulus, people cicatrized, "platter-lipped," or nose-split. That was the point. They came from all over the known world to parade on gaudy ten-hitch wagons or caparisoned elephants down Main Street, and then, like the animals in the cages, you wanted them to leave town. Yet if you were a farmer who thought a bear that had killed a pig was scary to come to grips with, try managing half a dozen snarling lions! Or maybe you had screwed up your nerve recently to reroof the barn? Try walking the high wire, fifty feet up, with just your wife standing underneath you in case of a slip.

When it rained, the rest of us went indoors, but show folk didn't have an indoors. They were negotiating with the mud in order to hit the road. The seat men folded thousands of chairs and "bibles," or souvenir programs. The "bull hands," the elephant men, controlled the pachyderms with a club with a hook on the end as the animals pulled out the quarter poles and the center poles and any wagons that got stuck. The transience of the circus jibed better with wild nature than the closely trimmed lawns at home—and willy-nilly a circus rolled. People with survival skills pitched in to fill the gaps. The whole grew bigger than the parts, though close to nature meant close to scandal too, as they intersect in such a phrase as "Nature calls." Nature is randy as well as rainy, smelly as well as sunny. Circus Day was uncivilized like the Fourth of July, with candied apples, cotton candy, fireworks, and special dispensation for skimpy costumes, public lust, trials of strength, breakneck stunts, colossal crowds. "It was a circus," we'll still say when some ordinary scene bursts out of control. And if your blouse stuck out farther than the next girl's, that cage boy loafing over there might decide to persuade the hippopotamus to gape her mouth for you and poke his hand inside and scratch her gums the way she liked, to make you ooh and aah at how heroic he was.

I was such a cage boy myself, with Ringling Bros. and Barnum & Bailey in 1951 and 1952, and would also pet the menagerie leopards for the right admirer. I worked for two dollars per sixteen-hour day and slept two to a bunk, three bunks high, on the train, or else could rattle through the night outside on a flatcar. The faces of the drifters I was with sometimes looked as grim and bitter as a Wanted poster, and quite at their wit's end, not having had much wit to begin with, and what they might have had perhaps dispelled in prison. They'd slammed around, with their hats pulled down over their eyes, every mother-in-law's nightmare, and knew how to jump on a moving train without saying goodbye to anybody— knew the Front Range of the Rockies, and the Tex-Mex border. And not even our rumpled banquets guy with the windblown tie—a theater-district barfly and Coney Island dime-museum habitué, who scarcely saw his own sons after they were toddlers—could have coaxed a trustful look out of them.

Up on that giddy wire or the trapeze bar—or in the Iron Jaw act, spinning relentlessly by their teeth—people did things they shouldn't reasonably do, with no ostensible purpose but showing off, while the tuba oompahed, the trombone slalomed, the clarinet climbed a rope, and the cornet hit the canvas's peak line. "Flyers" and slack-wire artists and "risley" foot-jugglers and whiteface or "auguste" clowns hoarded and pruned their skills, like the humble juggler of legend, who during the night tiptoed into the empty cathedral on the Madonna's feast day after the wealthier citizens had long since delivered their heavy gifts, genuflected before her statue, and gone comfortably home. Alone and barefoot, he performed for her with whatever grace and dexterity he could muster. And for the first time in all of history, tears welled up in her stone eyes.

That's what we try to do, isn't it? Keep rolling, keep juggling and strutting our stuff, honoring our gods; then take a bow and exit smiling? But magic seldom happens unless a structure has been erected—whether a church or a tent—that is hospitable to it. Art is fragile, and a windless silence helps. Then depart just as the applause crests, leaving some emotion for the next act, because the thrust of the circus never stops, whether in mud or sunshine, whether the tickets have sold out or not. High stakes. The aerialist Lillian Leitzel, the most mesmerizing female performer ever, fell to her death in 1931, and afterward Alfredo Codona, her husband and male counterpart, at least on the trapeze, married an aerialist/ equestrienne, but injured himself while doing a triple somersault in 1933 and never flew again. Grotesquely, he became his wife's hostler on the Tom Mix Circus—until, estranged, he shot both her and himself in her divorce lawyer's office.

Karl Wallenda, the greatest wire-walker and another compulsive, fell twelve stories off a cable strung 750 feet between two hotels in 1978, at seventy-three. But for some of these plain old Okies, Arkies, Hoosiers, and Wisconsin Cheeseheads and Georgia Crackers who got the show to run on time and then maybe drove a trailer truck all night, the gamble was compelling, too. Their trajectory ran toward alcohol and the jitters of oblivion, even though they had a seaman's way with ropes. And several gaze at Kelty's camera as if reminded of a police-station booking room, whereas the performers pose in a row in profile with their biceps bulged, or ponytail pert. "Is your body as trim as mine?" they seem to ask. "I'll stand on one hand—or one finger! I'll do a back flip from one horse to another and then lie down on the ground and let the elephant put her foot on my nose, but because we're all a family she won't crush it. Instead she'll lift me onto her shoulders and we'll chase that clown until he drops his red bloomers."

The moneymen, gimlet-eyed, with peremptory chests, let their suits, cufflinks and stickpins, their oxblood shoes and railroad men's timepieces, speak for them. They owned the tents and trucks and railroad cars, of course, but also often the lions too, despite the trainer's intimacy with them. He could be fired and have to pack his kit and never see those particular cats again. Similarly, the acrobats were not terribly suited to busking for spare change on the subway. They needed complicated rigging and a spread of canvas overhead—the whole apparatus—to gather an audience sufficient to justify risking their lives, without being clinically crazy. And a run-of-the-mill hobo, who was used to sneaking across the hazardous, lightless bustle of a railroad yard to boost himself into a moving boxcar without being detected, had probably found a raison d'être with Ringling Bros., called by show people "the Big One." In my time, if he was fired with the dreaded words "No Rehire" scribbled on his pink slip to go into the company's records, it might take the little wind that he had out of his sails. The performance, the crowds and ovations, though not directly for him, had centered and justified his shaky life.

The center poles and brocaded, bejeweled elephant howdahs might be bedecked with the Stars and Stripes, and yet one knew that the entire spectacle, unlike July 4, wasn't quite *American*. The men and women holding hands in the center ring to take a bow after manipulating their bodies on the teeterboard were probably foreigners, and might not even be married to each other—and God knows where they slept. They had somehow jelled their flightiness for professional purposes, but the idea of a new town tomorrow, a new town the next day, and consorting in a business way with freaks whose very livelihood was exhibiting their disfigurements like fakirs in an Asian marketplace (freaks inherently were un-American) was not like the Home of the Brave. What demons in themselves were they trying to anesthetize by harboring values so different from ours? We, the Elmers, the hicks, the towners, the hayshakers, had just put down good money to watch somebody shoot himself out of a cannon on the assurance that it was going to be genuine and he might really die before our eyes. But he landed succinctly on his back in the L-shaped net, swung to the ground, acknowledged our claps—and didn't then thank his lucky stars and settle down to a productive existence like ours. *Eat your heart out, rube* was part of his message. *We'll be gone tomorrow. We'll see Chicago. We'll be in Florida. You stay here and milk your cows!*

To "the Strange People," misshapen on their little stages in the sideshow and peddling 10¢ likenesses of their deformities to the public, the conventional response would be, "There but for the grace of God go I." But why had He withheld His mercy when constructing *them*? Did their burden, as suggested by ancient superstitions, express a spiritual canker? Was external ugliness a punishment laid on the erring soul? My own feeling, while working next to them in Madison Square Garden and other arenas half a century ago, was that the object lesson ran deeper still. People were fascinated not just because of morbid curiosity and schadenfreude but because we saw ourselves incarnate in the Knife Thrower, the Living Skeleton (or "Pincushion," or "Picture Gallery"), the Human Pretzel, the Fat Lady, the lame and wheezing Giant, and were encouraged to stare without being rude. The foxfire flicker of ferocity and awful insecurity that so frequently subverted our genial veneer lay out there exposed—much as the bum, the coward, the fussbudget and spoilsport whom we knew all too well was embodied in some of the skits the clowns performed. (Our Knife Thrower really got to people when, as a pièce de résistance, he "horse-whipped" pretty women who volunteered from the crowd.)

A clown or Santa Claus costume, in my experience of the individuals who wear them, can conceal a multitude of sins. But so does the attire that the rest of us hide in, using blandness to mask our shamefaced failures and maladjustments. We, too, have flat feet and big asses, chalky faces and weepy tendencies when frightened of our shadows or searching through the tanbark for a nickel we have lost, a button that popped off, or a pebble that was in our shoe—we took it out but now we miss it. In the smaller tent shows the Fat Lady in the baby-doll nightie might even *show it all* in a curtained-off area, if you paid an extra four bits (and it was said you could insert them). In a circus you didn't have to— weren't supposed to—avert your eyes, and that may have been its ultimate kick. The guy might die, but without muttering the piety "Oh, I can't watch," we simply did.

> "In a circus you didn't have to— weren't supposed to—avert your eyes, and that may have been its ultimate kick."

Uzbeks rode on saddled camels. Elephants sashayed. A sway-pole acrobat almost seemed to touch the ground on each backswing, then locked his feet and slid down headfirst. A lovely woman with blond hair hanging to her coccyx adjusted her shoulder straps, kicked off her silver slippers, and gripped a knotted rope to ascend for the Cloud Swing. Over at one side, we might not notice a self-effacing clown—not bizarrely loud now to attract attention—pulling her up with considerable care, then standing underneath in case of a mishap. But if you were observant, you realized there might be some people who had a love life after all.

The black-maned lion roared with bestial fury yet soon lapsed into contented amiability, as if he might be willing to settle in our burg. And the Albino Girl and Snake Charmer and other troupers were said to have bought cough medicine, underpants, and other personal stuff in the local stores. But just when we thought they really liked us and had been converted to our home-sweet-home values, they up and did a disappearing act. Overnight, the magic cavalcade vanished to another state, another climate. We have the gimpy, haywire gene as well, the one that makes you want to hit the road each spring while you last—a hail-fellow who knows that nothing is for keeps. You do your thing, to just whatever tattoo of music and battery of lights are available to you, survive today, sleep it off, and get up on that wire again tomorrow.

Denis Johnson

Run, Rudolph, Run

Denis Johnson was born in 1949 in Munich, Germany, and raised in Tokyo, Manila, and Washington, D.C. He holds a master's degree from the University of Iowa. He has received many awards for his work, including a Lannan Fellowship in Fiction and a Whiting Writer's Award. His most famous work is the story collection *Jesus' Son* (1993); he has several other books of fiction, including *Fiskadoro* (1985), *Already Dead* (1997), and *Tree of Smoke* (2007). He has written a number of plays, and is resident playwright of Campo Santo, a San Francisco company. He also writes new journalistic essays, most of which were collected in the book *Seek: Reports from the Edges of America & Beyond* (2001). In 2006–2007, he held the Mitte Chair in creative writing at Texas State University in San Marcos, Texas.

In 2002 Johnson won the Aga Khan Prize for Fiction from the *Paris Review* for the story "Train Dreams." His book *Jesus' Son* was turned into an award-winning movie in which he took a cameo role as a man who is stabbed in the eye by his wife.

Of Johnson's nonfiction book *Seek* (2001), the source of our selection, Ted Conover wrote, "*Seek*, a collection of his forays into nonfiction, reads like an extended experiment—short and long pieces of journalism and memoir whose subjects range from wars in Africa to cards at his local bar, where the tense is usually past but occasionally present and sometimes both, and where the voice seems continually under construction. Johnson, who uses the fictional first person to impressive effect in stories like those in *Jesus' Son*, seems unable to bear the 'I' here, and so, awkwardly, refers to himself as 'the man from Idaho,' as 'Moon One,' even as one of 'a couple of American journalists.' But he is such an adept that even his failures intrigue; and when he succeeds, the results can be spectacular." Author Michael Herr said, "There isn't an American voice I love listening to more than Denis Johnson's."

Denis Johnson currently lives in North Idaho and sometimes in Arizona.

"Run, Rudolph, Run," included here, is Johnson's quest to find the truth of a bomber who attacked several abortion clinics. At the time of the essay's writing, Eric Rudolph was on the run in the hills of the Carolinas; unable to get access to the subject, Johnson tells his story through his encounters with the townspeople who once knew the killer.

Interview with Denis Johnson, p. 462.

Caves in the earth get lost and found over and over. A cave in Pennsylvania was apparently occupied by an unbroken chain of prehistoric human occupants for thousands of years, but then inexplicably it was abandoned and forgotten until white Americans stumbled onto it. The cave in western North Carolina's Nantahala National Forest where Eric Rudolph lives now with (according to the Federal Bureau of Investigation) half a year's supply of BI-LO California raisins, BI-LO Harvest Choice Cut Green Beans, BI-LO Old-Fashioned Oatmeal, Planters Peanuts, and StarKist Tuna: if anybody but Rudolph knows its location, nobody's telling, not even for one million dollars.

Eric Robert Rudolph is wanted for every bombing that somebody else wasn't already wanted for. He's charged with creating explosions that killed one person and injured a hundred others during the summer Olympics in Atlanta in '96; damaged the Northside Family Planning Services and the Otherside Lounge (described in the papers as a gay nightclub) in January and February of '97; killed an off-duty policeman and maimed a nurse at the New Women, All Women Health Care Clinic in Birmingham in January of '98. Witnesses around the Birmingham crime scene remembered seeing a Nissan pickup. Agents traced it to Rudolph. Rudolph took to the mountainous Nantahala Forest outside the town of Andrews in Cherokee County, North Carolina, where he'd lived off and on since boyhood.

The Nantahala and neighboring forests cover the corner where Georgia, North Carolina, and Tennessee come together, a region of green nappy mountains where, as of this hot Labor Day Weekend, weekend of the full moon, only a few leaves have begun to turn, and only perhaps because of thirty days of drought. Where east-west Routes 64 and 74 encounter small towns, they're lined with the appliance dealerships, Wal-Marts, and Taco Bells, the generic hair salons and the factory shoe outlets that mark out our shared national culture. But off these major arteries all of that drops away quickly into the rural South, the olive lakes and the Rebel Lanes and Johnny Reb Motels, garden patches of tobacco and sweet corn, roadside stores proclaiming BOILED PEANUTS AND PORK RINDS; and it seems every local road comes to a fork between the stairway to Heaven and the slippery slide to Hell. ETERNITY, as one bumper sticker has it,—SMOKING OR NON-SMOKING? A hand-lettered board by a house jammed close to a narrow back road says WHAT ON EARTH ARE YOU DOING FOR HEAVEN'S SAKE. Traditionally this time of year the numberless little churches hang out signs calling the faithful to renewed salvation—REVIVAL SEP 7-11—REVIVAL WITH PASTOR MIKE—REVIVAL—REVIVAL—REVIVAL . . .

Andrews is small. It looks to have no promise, with several vacant storefronts along Main Street and two digital bank signs disagreeing slightly about what time it is. The one barbershop in Andrews has only one chair—Arden the barber's done his work there on three generations of the males of Cherokee County. Where a second chair might go, a man in a hunting cap stands with his hands clasped behind his back, casually addressing the others there: a bent old man and a teenage boy on a bench, and a prosperous-looking gentleman in the chair, returned to town for his thirty-five-year high-school reunion. "They ain't going to find Rudolph up there," the standing man says. "There's seven hundred and sixty-two and one-half caves don't nobody know about them, and let me be the one to tell you, son: That country is complicated. All up and down and twisty. And full of echoes: I went hunting down in a draw there and seen a quail pop up. I pulled that trigger at six minutes to eleven. And son, it's still a-thunderin'."

The teenage boy says he makes money gathering wild ginseng in the hills, claims he's stumbled onto caves up there plenty of times. "You have to kind of get lucky," he says. Afterward he forgot where he'd seen these caves. "They seem like they move around a little bit sometimes," he says. "I know those folks are all up there hunting Rudolph, but they ain't going to find him."

Elizabeth, the young woman who keeps the desk at the Valley Town Motel in Andrews, collects such Rudolph memorabilia as the hand-drawn poster brought around a couple weeks ago by a woman Elizabeth had never seen before, a pencil sketch of Eric Rudolph with flowing hair and the mild beautiful eyes of Jesus Christ—PRAY FOR RUDOLPH the caption reads.

> "But Elizabeth says, 'Don't even *think* I'd pray for him. He's crazy. I don't care if he's handsome or not. He's a *bombist*.' "

"He was good-looking," an old friend of Rudolph told some of the countless reporters who came to Andrews and filled up the Valley Town Motel after the fugitive was spotted in July: "He could have been a movie star if he dressed up."

But Elizabeth says, "Don't even *think* I'd pray for him. He's crazy. I don't care if he's handsome or not. He's a *bombist*."

At Arden's barbershop the men say, "He's dead by now of natural causes. Anybody'd starved to death by now."

"He's dead. They killed him. He's part of some outfit like that Army of God or the militia, and they killed him to keep him quiet."

"He's got away. He's in Money Carlo or Tahiti or something. Money Carlo or the Caribbean or I don't know."

"He's still in the Nantahala. In a cave. They'll never get him."

This is the area harboring Eric Robert Rudolph, white male, thirty-one years, 5'11", 165–180 pounds, eyes blue, hair brown, part-time carpenter, accused murderer of the living and defender of the unborn, months-running Top-Ten fugitive despite the efforts of up to two hundred (but currently down to eighty) FBI agents, their choppers and vans equipped with sonar and infrared sensing technology, several dog teams from the Georgia Department of Corrections, forty uninvited civilian volunteers under the leadership of Idaho's Col. Bo Gritz (all wearing red, white, and blue) and an undetermined number of bounty hunters, both amateur and, to the extent they can be, certified (for instance by the "Fugitive Recovery and Bounty Hunters Association" of Fort Worth or the "National Association of Bail

Enforcement Agents" of Rancho Cucamonga, California). From the weekly *Andrews Journal:*

> James Robin Bach, 49, of Chattanooga, Tennessee, was arrested after a disturbance at the Andrews Post Office Friday afternoon. Officers removed a very large hunting knife strapped to his hip, found drug paraphernalia while patting him down, and found a loaded .357 Magnum hidden in his vehicle. Bach told officers he was a bounty hunter.

It wasn't Eric Rudolph himself who brought these hordes to Cherokee County, but rather George Nordmann. Mr. Nordmann, who owns the Better Way Health Food Store on Main Street in Andrews, reported in July that he had spoken with Rudolph and that the fugitive had later taken one of his trucks and what the authorities have ever since referred to as "a six-month supply of food." George Nordmann waited a couple of days before reporting this encounter. He's an earnest, very decent-seeming man in his sixties, passionate to communicate his feelings on diet and health, willing to spend an hour with a customer who buys nothing, recommending a book called *Tissue Cleansing Through Bowel Management*, showing off ten pages of color prints of people's feces and close-ups of skin sores, and citing in particular a chapter titled "Intestinal Flora and Bowel Gardening."

His kids have posted a note to the public on his storefront: PLEASE SEND OUR DAD HOME AT 5:30. He's been dogged by journalists as his former neighbor Rudolph has been dogged by the Prison Bureau's actual dogs, and the FBI is still scrutinizing his story as to how all this food got into the hands of their quarry. Woody Enderson, inspector in charge of the Southeast Bomb Task Force, said Rudolph was "given the items in an encounter with a local witness." Mr. Nordmann hasn't been charged with anything.

$$* \, * \, *$$

"This is for the FBI and the media," Daniel Rudolph, brother of Eric, said into a video camera he'd rigged in his garage near Summerville, South Carolina, last February, and then turned to a whirring radial-arm saw and cut off his left hand at the wrist. Dressed in a white shirt and tie and wearing a tourniquet on his upper arm, he wrapped his stump with a towel and drove himself to the hospital. Paramedics retrieved the hand. Doctors reattached it. The local police chief said of investigators who viewed Daniel's videotape, "They never want to see it again." Apparently feeling implicated, the FBI issued a statement: "Daniel Rudolph's decision to maim himself is regrettable and totally unexpected." Neighbors questioned by the media claimed Daniel had never struck them as anything but completely stable. Reporters hunted down a former landlady in Florida who highly recommended Daniel and his wife as tenants and said they'd once baked her elderly mother a cake. The videotape was sent to the FBI Behavioral Sciences Unit.

Soon, in October, Col. Bo Gritz, having disbanded his volunteer force, having commemorated their failure in a brief ceremony by shaking each man's hand and pinning a small decoration to his T-shirt, and having returned to Idaho to discover that Claudia, his wife of twenty-four years, has served him with divorce papers, will drive out on a back road and shoot himself in the chest, but not fatally. Claudia is fed up with the colonel's quests to rescue hostages, fugitives, people under siege. "What kind of life do I have without my bride?" the colonel will ask of an interviewer.

As a kid Eric Rudolph spent summers with a man named Thomas Branham, a close family friend, in the Nantahala area. After the death of his father, an airline pilot, mother Patricia moved from Florida with her three boys and their sister and bought a small country home near Branham's place. In 1986, when Branham was arrested on a federal firearms violation, Patricia Rudolph went his bail. Branham on this occasion refused to recognize the court's authority and described himself as a "freeman." The case was dismissed on appeal, as the agents who found Branham's machine guns were actually authorized to search his premises only, according to the warrant, for counterfeit Heinz discount coupons.

The previous year, Patricia Rudolph had taken Eric and another brother, Jamie, to a commune in Schell City, Missouri, run by the Church of Israel, which was at that time, but no longer, associated with the Christian Identity movement. Christian Identity doctrine claims that Jews descended from the union of Eve and Satan, and that Anglo-Saxons are the true Chosen People. Patricia, Eric, and Jamie stayed in the commune about six months, according to pastor Don Gayman.

In high school Eric wrote a paper arguing that the Holocaust never happened. Patricia Rudolph wouldn't disclose her children's Social Security numbers to school officials. Eric Rudolph later rented homes under aliases and registered vehicles under phony addresses. He has never applied for a credit card or opened a bank account.

While Eric may have been influenced by his early associations, his brother Jamie shrugged them off and currently lives in Greenwich Village as a techno-pop composer. He recently issued a CD entitled *Evolve Now*.

The mass media and modern mobility have homogenized the speech of the urban South, but many folks in Cherokee County still speak with an accent so thick a person not from around here is tempted to conclude they're just playing with him. Andrews, the "Little Town with a Big Heart," belongs to an area with a sense of itself, a region with a self-image, whether or not it's entirely accurate or current—a place of honest and self-reliant mountainfolk, God-fearing, Bible-believing, stubborn, exclusive, and proud. Andrews hosts the headquarters of the Southeast Bomb Task Force, a borrowed office in the local police station whose spokespeople take no questions from journalists but periodically issue upbeat statements that fail to reflect what must be a growing frustration with a populace less than cooperative in the local manhunt. At the Cherokee Restaurant in Andrews ("Home of Country Cookin") a sign out front advertises RUDOLPH BURGER, RUDOLPH BROTHER BURGER, FBI CURLY FRIES, SKY-CAM COKE WITH AN OPTION: EAT THEM HERE OR GET THEM ON THE RUN.

It's not that people are still fighting the Civil War, or even that they're mildly, vaguely antigovernment. Locals object to that kind of labeling. "Sure, I don't agree with everything the government does. But I don't agree with everything my wife does either."—"Just because people like guns and fishing doesn't mean they're antigovernment." But apparently the kind of intelligence, the tips, that a million-dollar bounty ought to be generating haven't been coming in. "We started out appealing to citizens' sense of civic duty," will be the Justice Department's statement in October, when Eric Rudolph is formally charged with the Olympics bombing; "then we offered a reward and appealed to their greed; now we appeal to their sense of conscience." But— "I don't see where he did anything so all that wrong," citizens of Andrews will tell the TV cameras. "I wouldn't turn him in for even *ten* million dollars."

An ad on the local-access cable station in Andrews: REVIVAL SEP 9-14/ WITH J.D. HOLMES/1 DOOR WEST OF NAPA AUTO PARTS/TENNESSEE ST., MURPHY, NC. Then another immediately following: YOU COULD GET UP TO $1,000,000/FOR INFORMATION LEADING TO THE ARREST/OF TOP-10 FUGITIVE/ERIC ROBERT RUDOLPH/5-11 WHITE MALE/165-180 LBS/1-800-575-9873.

In the vestibule of the Garden Restaurant in Andrews a quart-size Tupperware container painted red and blue rests on top of one of the twenty-five-cent toy machines. A six-by-eight computer-printed sign above it:

DEAR RUDOLPH,

YOU HAVE GOT TO COME HOME SOON.

AS YOU KNOW, ALL THOSE LITTLE BOYS & GIRLS WILL BE HAVING THEIR PIC-TURES TAKEN W/ME AGAIN THIS YEAR AT WAL-MART

I DON'T KNOW WHAT I AM GOING TO TELL THEM WHEN THEY ASK ME: "WHERE IS RUDOLPH?"

SO PLEASE, DROP YOUR ADDRESS IN THIS BOX SO I CAN BRING THE SLEIGH OUT AND GIVE YOU A RIDE HOME.

LOVE,

SANTA

P.S. MRS CLAUS WANTS ME TO TELL YOU THAT SHE MISSES YOU!

Beneath is a sheaf of paper for replies, each sheet headed in caps: MEMO FROM ONE OF SANTA'S FRIENDS/YOU WILL FIND RUDOLPH AT:

You bet!

I am with my Elfs in the South Pole—you can reach me at the FBI office in Andrews, SC

—offers one correspondent who didn't bother to shove his answer in the slot, but left it out on display.

The staff at the Garden Restaurant have no idea where this box came from. It wouldn't seem to have been placed there by law enforcement, who have their own tip hot lines, and another logical candidate, bounty hunter Ray Santa, claims to have no knowledge. Ray Santa has spent time in the mountains looking for Eric Rudolph on two separate visits from his home in Baltimore. He says he'll be back again soon. As he rode the fire roads through grass as high as the handlebars on his mountain bike, Santa says "I had the feeling Rudolph knew where I was."

Mr. Santa owns the Gator's Pub in Baltimore, so named because he spent time in the seventies hunting alligators in Belize. And in Costa Rica he collected poison-dart frogs, among the most toxic varieties of animal on the planet. He ended up hospitalized and semi-famous in San Jose after handling the amphibians.

"This type of adventure—I live for it." Small and well built, in his early forties, Mr. Santa nevertheless admits he was a little shaken when a man banged on his station wagon at the Bob Allison Campground in the Nantahala Forest, where Santa was sleeping alone. "It was three in the morning. It flipped me. The guy was completely drunk, that's all, it turned out. He just liked to come up there away from it all and drink, is what he said. But it definitely got the wheels motioned in me that—'what am I doing here?' But hey, if you walk out looking for poisonous snakes, and you do it the way I did—no socks, boots, or equipment, or nothin'— well, a guy, he's got to be a little crazy."

According to Mr. Santa, the night Bo Gritz's volunteers spotted someone with a lantern and flashlight off in the depths of the woods— "That was me." He refers to Colonel Gritz's force as "these clowns," and says, "At times they were right beside me and never saw me."

Ray Santa hasn't yet spotted the fugitive, but he did find two shirts spread on bushes as if to dry, deep in the thickets, as if hidden intentionally from view, one white and one blue. He believes Rudolph might have left them there. Santa didn't disturb them. He left packets of dried food out along game paths for Rudolph, but they weren't touched.

This bounty hunter travels unarmed. And what if he should find the fugitive? What then? "Well, basically I hope to see him first. That's my ace in the hole." And what about Rudolph's gun? Supposed to be an M-16 or something similar? Santa insists, "I don't think he could kill a person face-to-face."

Ray Santa claims to have seen Patricia Rudolph, sixty-nine-year-old mother of Eric, drive through the Bob Allison Campground twice in a big black Cadillac, accompanied by one man. He says that more than once the FBI sensors were turned on him from roving vans, but they never stopped him. "That Bob Allison Campground," he says, "that's the key." The FBI searchers were camped there for some weeks. Colonel Bo Gritz's volunteers also stayed there. Of Colonel Gritz and crew he says, "These clowns, they wanted to give the reward money to Eric Rudolph's mother. To me that's like—*What?* After what he did? What about the victims? What Rudolph did was absolutely wrong.

"I'm not saying abortion's right or it's wrong. Just that the government shouldn't make those rules. You look in any penal system—ninety percent are probably unwanted—I mean when they were babies—and some of them probably killed people who were pro-life!" He repeats, "This type of adventure—I live for it." And adds, "Sometimes I wonder about myself."

At the Lake's End Grille in the hills a dozen miles east of Andrews, a sign above the counter says, ERIC RUDOLPH—1998 HIDE & SEEK CHAMPION. The seekers have quartered themselves nearby at the Appletree group campground on Chunky Gal Mountain. In the September heat the FBI sentries blocking the campground's entrance spend their time chatting with each other, dressed in black T-shirts and black pants and black hiking boots—the same outfits they can be seen wearing in news footage of the disaster at the Branch Davidians's Mt. Carmel retreat in Waco, Texas—and lounging under a giant green nylon safari-style gazebo.

"They're nice fellas," says the waitress at the Lake's End. "They come down here sometimes and they've got their dogs in the back of the trucks,"—drawn perhaps by the large sign standing out front of the Lake's End: RUDOLPH IS HERE.

Meanwhile, across the road from the Piggly Wiggly supermarket in Murphy, the seat of Cherokee County, a black-lettered message on a red-bordered billboard advises IF YOU CAN READ THIS/YOU WERE NOT ABORTED./CALL YOUR MOTHER AND/ [in red italics:] *THANK HER*

One door west of Napa Auto Parts on Tennessee Street in Murphy twenty-six adults and four children have gathered for the purpose of spiritual revival with the Reverend J.D. Holmes. Men of the Barnett Construction Company are tearing up the sidewalk out front with a giant jackhammer, working on into darkness with floodlights, obscuring the sounds of the hymns and the preaching of J.D. Holmes, who has come from out of town. Mr. Holmes is a blond man in his early thirties wearing a brown suit and pale yellow shirt. Amiable and sincere, he introduces himself quietly to individual arrivals, then steps onto the small stage before an eight-foot-tall plywood cross and a brilliant metal-flake-red set of Pearl drums, as these are the premises of a local youth center, and talks for a while about his own aimless but basically harmless youth, which, nevertheless, would have led him eventually to Hell. "Do you think anybody warned me about it? Not really. What they mostly said was, 'Watch out!—or you'll get religion!' But, thank God, I didn't get religion. I got Jesus Christ.

"God cannot know of a sin that he doesn't hate," Mr. Holmes declares in the course of his sermon. He lists some sins that God hates: pride and lying and wicked imaginations expressed in pornography and bloody slasher movies; feet that run to mischief—that is, busybodies ("If you are

on God's business, you got *no time* to be in anybody else's business!")—
and above all, he says, *above all:* the shedding of innocent blood. Which
means, in our nation at this time, abortion.

"Eighty-five percent of abortions is repeat business. And more than
eighty-five percent is for convenience's sake—not to save life!" He
could easily be talking about the Northside Family Planning Services in
Atlanta about a hundred miles away. Since January of 1997, when a
bomb went off outside the clinic, the staff will disclose its whereabouts
only to women actually making appointments over the twenty-four-
hour telephone line. Despite the bombing, medical
staff at Northside Family Planning still perform
first-trimester abortions seven days a week for a
fee of $305 on weekdays, $339 Friday through
Sunday.

"This is about eternal salvation
and irremediable damnation. The
two sides to this debate have
nothing to say to each other."

"Their innocent blood cries from the ground,
like Abel's did!" On this subject J.D. Holmes gets
really *waxed*—and here is the point of describing such a gathering in
such a place: It's easy to see that tonight, at this meeting, nobody's arguing points of medical ethics or examining the right of privacy. This is
about eternal salvation and irremediable damnation. The two sides to this
debate have nothing to say to each other.

Eric Robert Rudolph will be formally charged in October for the
Northside clinic bombing. Some Bible-based Christians believe that any
business offering to stop the human organism's growth in the womb deals
in murder, and that whoever kills a man or woman working there saves
lives. This was the argument offered by Paul Hill, who gunned down a
doctor and his bodyguard at a clinic in Pensacola, Florida, in 1994. In an
article titled "Why I Shot an Abortionist," Hill wrote: "The Lord is at
work to deliver the unborn."

But did Paul Hill actually save any of the unborn? Has Eric Rudolph?
Appointments interrupted by bloodshed can be rescheduled. On the other
hand, Deborah Gaines sued Preterm Health Services Clinic in Brookline,
Massachusetts, four years after John Salvi III attacked the clinic in a brutal shoot-out that left two people dead. She was there for an abortion that
day but didn't reschedule and instead gave birth to daughter Vivian seven
months later. She claims she's entitled to compensation for the cost of
raising her daughter, says the clinic should have had better security. Two
guards on duty at the time and presumably responsible for providing that
security have sued the clinic, too, alleging emotional trauma.

Eric Rudolph may have something to say about all this should he
someday be dragged to the surface. Until now he's sent no letters to the
newspapers or to the law, posted no messages in the dead of night. He may
be long gone.

David White, of Reliable Investigations in Murphy, won't make a
definite guess as to Rudolph's whereabouts. "I learned a long time ago
not to try and predict the activity of a criminal. But if I were him I'd still

be back in those mountains." Mr. White, retired from, as he vaguely states it, "a life-long career in law enforcement," is the only private eye in, or anywhere near, Cherokee County. He's quick to disassociate himself from bounty hunters, bail agents, and the like. "We're moral, ethical, and professional."

Stephen Cochran, Nantahala area resident, knew Eric Rudolph in recent years, calls him a skilled woodsman, says Rudolph frequently camped alone in the winter with nothing but a poncho, a sleeping bag, and a rifle. "He considered himself a survivalist. He always went places in the mountains where nobody else went." Can the searchers find him? "They might be in spitting distance of him and not know it."

FBI and Georgia state investigators met with about seventy-five bear hunters recently and showed them "raisin and oatmeal canisters, vitamin bottles, and tuna fish tins" like those Rudolph has, according to hunters who attended the lecture. Bear season will open in mid-October. "He may have a nine millimeter, an M-16, or a Colt-91 automatic rifle," said Bill Lewis of the Georgia Bureau of Investigation. "This is not your typical hunting weapon. He also is likely to be antisocial." As to the FBI agents who might stop and question hunters out in the woods, Lewis made this request: "Please bear with them."

Hunters indicated they were more concerned about a lot of armed agents sneaking all around the forest. "There's going to be confusion and panic with all these hunters and all these FBI agents out in the woods," said one.

The Saturday after Labor Day, "Doc Holiday," a mesmerist from Atlanta, performs for the annual mass meeting of the area's Electric Membership Co-op at the fairgrounds outside Hiawassee, Georgia, just over the line from Cherokee County. The Doc hypnotizes a group of twenty people onstage and climaxes his act by inducing a state of "rigid body catalepsy" in a teenage girl, stretching her taut body between two stools, and standing on her belly with his arms upraised while co-op members snap photographs.

The next day the fairgrounds hosts a much smaller gathering of area musicians at a potluck lunch and dinner that lasts all afternoon and into the night. Not many more than forty people play for one another and feed themselves at long tables heaped with plates of fried okra and every other manner of vegetable, chicken — "gospel bird," because all preachers love chicken — ham, potatoes fried and mashed, iced tea, and soft drinks. Groups play such old-time standards as "Golden Slippers" and "Will the Circle Be Unbroken." There are clog dancers. Dorothy Smith, a plump grandmother with abundant black hair, sings her own composition:

> He never meant to hurt no one,
> He wouldn't harm a fly,
> The Lord knows Eric Rudolph

Didn't want that man to die,

But he could not justify

Knowin all the things they done

So to stop that baby-killin factory

He made a home-made bomb

She and her band, Scott Ferguson on bass, Don Fox and Wade Powell on guitar and dobro, have taped the song and placed it on sale at gas stations and general stores around the tri-state region. A copy costs $6.50. "They won't have it on the Murphy radio station," Dorothy says. "But it gets played around Asheville."

You gotta run, Rudolph, run, Rudolph, run

Or the FBI's gonna shoot you with his gun

A modern-day Billy the Kid

Boy you better do just like he did—

You better run, Rudolph, run, Rudolph, run . . .

"Abortion is the same thing as murder," Dorothy Smith says. "This is the same feeling of anybody around here—if you ask anybody, they'll say, 'Well, I'd take him in and feed him.' I maybe wouldn't take him in, because that's against the law. But I'd feed him." As for the deaths attributed to Rudolph's work: "He should've got up a little earlier and made sure nobody was around to get hurt when his bomb went off."

It may be a long while before we learn what's become of Eric Robert Rudolph. But we've got almost forever, because the evidence isn't going anywhere: According to speleologists, a footprint in a cave can last for 200,000 years.

The Mammoth-Flint Ridge cave system in Kentucky has 340 miles of explored and mapped passageways. Geologists think it extends much farther into the darkness under the earth. There's no telling where Eric Rudolph might have got himself to by now, and without ever having had to show himself above ground.

In 1914 Count Bégouën and his three sons discovered the Trois Frères Cave in the Pyrenees. A tunnel that can only be wriggled through ends in a massive chamber covered with Paleolithic 12,000-year-old images of the hunt, including creatures half-man, half-beast: a chamber used for initiating adolescent boys in a ritual of death and rebirth. Students of humankind have long seen the link between the cave and the womb. In 1956 the anthropologist Jean Gebser suggested in a piece called "Cave and Labyrinth": "The cave is a maternal, matriarchal aspect of the world. . . . To return to the cave, even in thought, is to regress from life into the state of being unborn."

Interview with Denis Johnson

BECKY BRADWAY: Even though "Run, Rudolph, Run" focuses on a controversial subject (Rudolph and, by extension, abortion), you manage to
keep your own opinion carefully absent. Not only do you avoid expressing views on abortion, but you manage to talk about Rudolph in
a nonjudgmental way. Did you find it difficult to keep yourself out
of this piece? Had you ever placed yourself in any previous versions of
this essay?

DENIS JOHNSON: I'd already written several first-person articles, and I
made a point of doing this one third-person just for variety's sake.
My editor at *Esquire*, when he saw what I'd done, asked for more of
me in the piece. I ended up withdrawing it, and later it was published
in *Black Book*.

BB: One thing that strikes me about this piece (and your other essays) is
how you depict locals (often working-class Westerners or Southerners)
in a manner that isn't condescending or cute. Do you find that it's
easy to fit in and talk with the locals, or does your position as a
writer (observer, chronicler) ever get in the way?

DJ: In my experience, people not in the habit of dealing with journalists
get very chatty and friendly and revealing when approached by one.
Later they're probably sorry, at which point they become people
who've dealt with journalists, who, in my experience, are generally
cagey and tight-lipped and occasionally hostile. For good reason.

BB: In my experience, writing creative nonfiction involves considerable
unpredictability. Were there times in the writing of these essays when
what actually occurred was different from what you expected would
occur? Did this ever force you to change the focus of your piece?
How might writers learn to punt in such a situation?

DJ: I intended to track down Rudolph and interview him for the story. I
failed, and the piece took another turn, but I still think it wasn't so
far-fetched an idea. I suspect the owner of the health food store in
Andrews might have been able to contact Rudolph—a sufficiently
ruthless journalist might have found a way to intimidate him into
trying.

Jennifer Kahn

Notes from a Parallel Universe

Jennifer Kahn is a contributing editor at *Wired* magazine, and also writes for *Discover* (where the following piece first appeared), *National Geographic, Outside*, and the *New York Times*. A graduate of Princeton University and the University of California–Berkeley, her work has been selected for *Best American Science Writing 2003* and *2004*, and *Best American Science and Nature Writing 2005*.

Her work has been called "genuinely thought-provoking" by *Technology Review*. While her main topic area as a journalist is science and technology, her pieces have covered subjects as wide ranging as heart transplants, cellulite obsession, the decision to be childless, and drug experimentation on the poor. Her work ranges from profiles to investigative journalism to the personal essay.

"Notes from a Parallel Universe" delves into the world of scientific "crackpots," or maverick theorists, who develop alternative ways of viewing the universe. Kahn brings us a profile of a rogue theorist who pursues his idea with "single-minded absorption," knowing that a positive reception will never come.

Interview with Jennifer Kahn, p. 469.

Eleven years ago Eugene Sittampalam was sitting in a hotel room on the Libyan coast when he stumbled, as if by fate, on the unified field theory of physics. "I was on an engineering project at the time, with hardly any social life," he says. "I would retire to my room after dinner. I would switch on the radio, relax at my table, and start doodling." The problem that occupied him has stumped physicists from Albert Einstein to Stephen Hawking: how to join together the profound yet disparate insights of general relativity and quantum theory. But Sittampalam's doodling, apparently, drew connections that the rest had missed. "One thing led to another," he says, "and before the evening was over, I had the inverse square law of gravity derived — for the first time ever — from first principles!"

Sittampalam has no advanced degrees in physics. His theory is girded by mathematics no more complicated than high school algebra. Still, his claims are modest compared with those of other "maverick theorists," or cranks, as most scientists call them. At the American Astronomical Society meeting in 1999, a freelance astronomer argued strenuously that connecting certain pulsars across the night sky made an arrow that pointed directly to a vast alien communications network. A few years before, at Dartmouth, a dishwasher swamped the Internet newsgroups with his descriptions of the universe as a giant plutonium atom. The man, who identified himself as Archimedes Plutonium, wrote songs praising this atom universe and also

463

provided stock tips. When he appeared on campus, it was in a parka covered with equations like a necromancer's robe.

Judging from the reams of odd theories sent daily
to science journals, universities, and researchers, science cranks are more prolific than ever. This is true
despite a discouraging silence on the part of the recip-
ients. The author of one atmosphere-based theory of
gravity estimates that he has mailed 5,000 copies of
his work to physicists over the past 15 years but
received just two replies. Presentation is part of the
problem. "GENTLEMEN ARE YOU INTERESTED IN SEPARATING
VALUABLE CHEMICAL COMPOUNDS FROM THE SUNSHINE RAY?"
demands one impatient correspondent. Crank papers are so consistent in
their tics that they're sometimes hung on physics department bulletin boards
and given ratings—with points awarded for bold type, multiple exclamation marks, and comparison of self to Newton, Einstein, or God. But a few,
like Sittampalam's, are more difficult to dismiss.

> "Judging from the reams of odd theories sent daily to science journals, universities, and researchers, science cranks are more prolific than ever."

Sittampalam holds a bachelor of science degree from the University of
Ceylon and has spent 20 years consulting for a number of prominent global
engineering firms. His 85-page treatise is formatted with flawless profes-
sionalism, and he has no history of psychological disorders. Yet since his
"breakthrough" in Libya, Sittampalam has all but sidetracked his career in
pursuit of his theory. He has repeatedly sent his treatise to universities, paid
to self-publish the work in paperback, and lost "a small fortune in salary"
by his own estimation. Seven years ago he even offered a $25,000 reward
to any physicist who could refute his theory and, as he puts it, "slap me out
of this obsession." So far, no one has come up with a sufficient rebuttal.

Such single-minded absorption is part of the mythology of science. It's
no wonder, then, that scientists are nearly as fascinated by cranks as cranks
are by science. "It's unnerving," says Geoff Marcy, an astronomer at the
University of California at Berkeley. "It shows how easy it is to slip from
healthy, even necessary, conviction into certainty and delusion. Plus, you
realize that you don't always know which camp you're in." There's the
rub. Science owes a good part of its success to its capacity to contend with
doubt—to engage it, respond to it, and transform itself in the encounter.
Yet there's rarely a point at which a good idea becomes clearly, incon-
testably a bad idea. Neurologist Stanley Prusiner spent 15 years arguing
that a misfolded protein called a prion caused the brain decay associated
with scrapie and mad cow disease. Researchers snickered at him. Evidence
slowly accumulated in his favor, and in 1997 he was awarded the Nobel
Prize in medicine. "It's like a ball on top of a saddle," Marcy says. "You
can't listen too closely to the establishment or you'll never be creative. But
if you don't listen enough, you fall over the edge."

I first came across Sittampalam's theory in the Berkeley physics department. There, for the past 20-odd years, the secretaries have diligently

compiled what they call the X-files: the mother lode of crankiana. Kept in a three-foot-wide cabinet, the files contain hundreds of submissions, including one man's musical CD about thermodynamics and another's explanation of relativity and quantum mechanics spelled out on six post-cards. Elsewhere on campus, researchers maintain what amount to branch libraries of the X-files. "I have an entire shelf of crank mail," MacArthur-winning physicist Rich Muller told me. "My favorite is a book written by a crank that includes all the letters she received from scientists."

Muller's office at Lawrence Berkeley Laboratory sits several hundred feet above the city, in a stolid cement building edged by eucalyptus trees. The lab's newly heightened security was in force, and I was allowed through the gate only after a lab employee turned up to vouch for my good intentions. When I arrived, Muller had everything laid out, fat folders of letters and textbooks stacked across half of a colleague's desk. "There was a poster of the universe," he mumbled, peering up at the room's highest shelf. "It was beautiful. I put it someplace special. Now I don't know where it is."

Superficially, Muller is a bit cranky himself. His hair is thin but mussed, and his office is a cave of overstuffed folders and yellowing articles tacked to a corkboard. He is the author, among other things, of the contro-versial Nemesis theory, which argues that a second sun caused the extinc-tion of the dinosaurs, and a novel that explains some biblical miracles as clever but scientifically consistent sleight of hand. Muller corresponds with cranks and has thought enough about them to sort them into a fairly elab-orate taxonomy. "The range . . . is quite broad," he says. At the top of his hierarchy are the merely misguided: retired engineers who have strayed from load-and-strain calculations into surmises about relativity. The bot-tom of the stack is hairier: the Mullerian estate of the super-crank. Some super-cranks are harmlessly delusional, others dangerously paranoid, but none are very good at listening—a trait that drives Muller bats. "You take the time to explain the mistake in their argument, and they just ignore the explanation," he says bitterly. "They don't realize how much time scien-tists spend coming up with ideas and rejecting them."

Cranks, of course, see it differently. In their view they are Davids fight-ing a Goliath. Sometimes their foes may be theorists who have gone too far ("Deception, horn-swoggling . . . Who are you fooling?" demands an op-ponent of string theory). Other times they are scientists—overeducated, institutionalized, hidebound—who don't dare go far enough.

This confusion over fundamental purpose is understandable, given that modern physics manages to seem at once simple and profoundly puz-zling. Astronomers have only recently determined that a mysterious "dark energy" is forcing the universe apart, overwhelming the equally mysteri-ous "dark matter" that seemed to be holding it together. Even gravity, faith-ful shepherd of falling rocks and fly balls, has recently gone to pieces: At small distances, it may not be constant at all. "Some of the ideas are incredi-bly counterintuitive," says Nima Arkani-Hamed, a Harvard physicist who specializes in theoretical particle physics. "And they're just getting more bizarre."

Arkani-Hamed himself believes that space contains seven extra dimensions we can't see because they're rolled up like very small window shades. His mannerisms, too, might seem suspect in someone with less impressive credentials. He talks faster than I can take notes, a kind of super-revved speech that still seems to fall frustratingly short of the speed of thought. "Certain traits of personality and character are . . . close," he admits. "The obsessive tendencies, the compulsion, the restlessness. It's not the same, but there's a resemblance." Then he adds, dryly: "A lot of scientists have traits that would be bizarre if not channeled into science. I know that's part of why cranks interest me."

After several days of reading the X-files, I felt as if I were attending school in a parallel universe. "It is imperative that we begin burning water as fuel!" one author urged. Others were more puzzling. A note written on a ripped sheet of notebook paper said only, "I contend the holes on the right side of these pants are not explainable by contemporary science." A few submissions aped the style of scholarly papers, including credentials: An outline for "Symmetrical Energy Structures in a Megadimensional Cosmology," for instance, came from the director of the Alpha Omega Research Foundation in Palm Beach, Florida. But most favored a more urgent style. Arguments crescendoed to uppercase type. Words, boxed and colored, squeezed together on the page like castaways on a homemade raft.

At times the grandiloquence was so ingenuous it was hard to hold much of a grudge. "Readers, stretch your imagination to the very limits!" the inventor of Wavetron theory implored. "Together we will batter back the barbarous hordes!" The boldface words in another paper, taken together, read nearly like verse: "The eye is low / Negative ground / Electricity compressed, dead calm, displacing space / No one knows the cause / displacing . . . / repelling . . . / Well I do." But not every crank is so poetic nor so benign. Arkani-Hamed described one author whose e-mails had become increasingly virulent. Another physicist refused to be quoted by name in this article, replying tersely: "There is no guarantee that all cranks are harmless." Still another described his feelings about cranks as "Neutral. With a touch of fear."

One case in particular has echoed down the years with the force of a small-town murder. In 1952 a man named Bayard Peakes turned up at the office of the American Physical Society at Columbia University with a gun. Peakes was frustrated at the society's rejection of his pamphlet, "So You Love Physics." Unable to find any physicists at the society's office, he shot and killed a secretary instead. (Just months before, ironically, the society had changed its policy to open its annual meetings to public speakers and accept *all* scientific abstracts—including another by Peakes that aimed to prove that the electron doesn't exist.)

The Peakes case was unique in degree but not in kind. Scientists have been heckled, cursed, and harassed at work (one crank faxed love letters to a department chair and forged the signature of another scientist at the bottom). A few have even had cranks turn up at their homes.

It was hard not to have these cases in mind when I began contacting writers from the X-files, using the information that came with some of the papers. For the most part the authors were elusive. Phones had been disconnected, e-mail addresses bounced. The few who did answer were single-minded. One retired commercial diver answered all my questions with an uninterruptible monologue on gravity (it pushes rather than pulls, he said). An elderly man in southern California called back half a dozen times, each time hinting at his latest discovery.

"With psychosis, there's a kind of pressure to push it out," John MacGregor, an expert in the "outsider art" produced by mental patients, told me. "Sometimes the manic-depressives don't even use periods. They don't want to stop writing!" The trouble starts when such zeal is spiked with paranoia. "Schizophrenics have a tremendous desire to prove that they're sane," MacGregor said. "It could be that they've adopted science in order to prove just how rational and intelligent they are." He paused. "If a paranoid schizophrenic decides that certain rays are emanating from the physics department, it could be dangerous. These are the people who might come in and shoot it up."

Compared with the people MacGregor described—even compared with some of the physicists I interviewed—Sittampalam was charming. On the phone from his home in Sri Lanka, he proved candid but not overbearing, with crisp, British-inflected English pleasantly free of run-on tendencies. He answered questions about his family (he has five brothers and has never married) and chatted easily about his current job at ElectroFlow, a Missouri-based start-up that helps companies optimize their power consumption. He maintained that his physics theories were quite accessible; indeed, he hoped to see them introduced at the high school level.

I liked Sittampalam enough to inveigle a physicist friend to read Sittampalam's paper, with the promise that he remain anonymous. I was secretly hoping the paper would have some merit, or if not, that it would contain a clear error: one that, recognized, would set Sittampalam free from his compulsion. But when my friend got back to me, the news was bad. "As I read this, I kept thinking: 'How hard can it be to prove that this paper is incontrovertibly wrong?'" he said. "But it is hard. Not because his ideas are right. They're not. But because he's created a self-consistent system of arguments."

Self-consistency is not in itself a valuable trait—the theory that aliens created Earth and continue to control its evolution is a self-consistent system—but it can make things hard to refute. "I'd love to find just one equation in here and say, 'We have observations proving that's not correct,'" the physicist said. "But there's no mathematical progression. He starts with some very basic equations from classical mechanics. He mixes, stirs, spends some time hypothesizing in a very general way about physics, and out pops another familiar equation: $E = mc^2$. But really, he's just waved his hands. He could never have gotten to that next equation if he didn't already know what it was—and he knew what it was only because other people had figured it out for him using the traditional framework of physics."

Reading Sittampalam's paper feels a bit like being in a hedge maze: Just when you think you're heading toward some grand, central idea—an explanation of the cosmological redshift, for instance—the discussion loops away for another, more distant destination. There is the matter of Earth, for example. Sittampalam claims that his theory is the only way to explain why Earth hasn't lost enough energy over the years to spiral into the sun. But a physicist who saw the paper wrote in to note that that's exactly what *will* happen—just billions of years from now. Sittampalam acknowledged that mistake but attributed it to a typo. He had mistakenly left the words "under perturbation" out of his hypothesis, he said. Revised, his theory now explained why Earth, subject to the gravitational pull of the rest of the planets, has never wandered out of its orbit.

"First, he's talking about gravitational radiation, which is a real but minute effect; now he's talking about the solar system being sensitive to small changes," the physicist said. "It's true that if you moved the Earth a little bit today, its position and velocity in a month would become quite different. But that doesn't mean the shape of the current orbit is going to fall apart. We have simulations showing just the opposite, actually: that the solar system is stable over an incredibly long timescale. But that's what I mean. Every error you find, he's just going to change the subject. It's never-ending."

> "The truth, dispiriting as it may seem, is that cranks are pretty much never right."

The truth, dispiriting as it may seem, is that cranks are pretty much never right. "We'd love it if one of these guys were right," Arkani-Hamed says. "A revolutionary idea that works—great!" But real science tends to advance by increments rather than by revolutions. The life of working scientists is long on tedium and short on glory. They write grants, sit on committees, do paperwork. There is pressure to play it safe and be competitive. Cranks, by contrast, are free agents. With no career to lose and no scientific framework to restrict them, they can publish at their own pace and dare to shoot for the moon.

All of which may explain why most cranks aren't scientists and presumably wouldn't want to be. It may also explain why some scientists, when they talk about cranks, evince something close to envy. "There's curiosity, excitement, a kind of purity of purpose," Geoff Marcy says. Unlike conspiracy theorists, science cranks inhabit a happy universe: one that's accessible to those who plumb it ("Dear universal adventurer!" one postcard about quantum gravity begins). To read their ideas is a vicarious thrill, Arkani-Hamed admits, "but eventually you go back to what you were doing. In the end, the thing that makes science so amazing is that it works."

As for Sittampalam, he suspects that the poor reception for his work is largely a political matter. "I can easily answer all the critical points he raises," he replied, when I forwarded the physicist's critique. "But will he be convinced?" In the preface to his thesis, Sittampalam quotes Sir Martin Rees, a renowned astrophysicist and Astronomer Royal at Cambridge University. "Generally, researchers don't shoot directly for a grand goal," Rees writes. "Unless they are geniuses (or cranks) they focus on problems that seem timely or tractable." When I asked Sittampalam which he is, genius or crank, he was surprisingly equivocal. "Perhaps I'm a crank, but that's left for history," he said. "I have no regrets. When your work is for the future, by necessity you are not understood in your own days."

In the meantime, he can take comfort from the case of the Indian mathematician Srinivasa Ramanujan. In 1913 Ramanujan was a clerk at Madras Port Trust—"a short uncouth figure," in the words of one contemporary; "stout, unshaven, not over clean, with one conspicuous feature: shining eyes." Although largely self-taught in mathematics, Ramanujan had the audacity to mail 120 of his theorems to the British mathematician Godfrey Hardy at Cambridge University. Hardy dismissed the pages as gibberish at first, only to find, upon careful consideration, that some of the theorems were truly revelatory. Five years later Ramanujan was elected to the Royal Society of London.

Interview with Jennifer Kahn

BECKY BRADWAY: What made you decide to write about scientific topics? Do you have a science background?

JENNIFER KAHN: My background is in astrophysics (cosmology), but I initially resisted science writing as a poor imitation of two otherwise interesting fields (science and writing). Once I allowed myself to consider it, it quickly became clear that the specialty offered a fantastic combination: all the pleasurable inventiveness of words, with the intellectual rigor of research.

BB: Is there a particular approach or level of expertise needed when writing about science (and making it accessible to a broad readership)?

JK: A science background helps. Partly that's a matter of being able to think critically about what you're told, but it's also constructive. Fears of misrepresentation—the "cancer cured!" oversimplification— are rampant among researchers, as they would be in anyone who felt misunderstood. The conversation can sprawl once that anxiety is relaxed.

BB: How did you come up with the idea for "Notes from a Parallel Universe"? How did you know where to start?

JK: When I discovered that Berkeley kept a huge file of letters from cranks, it was like getting access to the city council records of Atlantis. The fact that the mysterious civilization was a state of mind, rather than the inhabitants of a particular geography, only made it more interesting.

BB: How did you decide upon Sittampalam as the focus?

JK: Most of the crank authors I spoke with were monomaniacal to the point of tedium, and in that sense, they were less interesting. Sittampalam, by contrast, seemed essentially normal, though clearly obsessed. He was intelligent and not easy to categorize.

Barbara Kingsolver

Household Words

Barbara Kingsolver's short fiction, poetry, and articles first appeared in print in the mid-1980s. Her first novel, *The Bean Trees*, was published in March 1987. *The Bean Trees* has been adopted into core curricula of high school and college literature classes and has been translated into more than a dozen languages.

Since then, she has written twelve more books, including the novels *Animal Dreams* (1990), *The Poisonwood Bible* (1998), and *Prodigal Summer* (2001); two essay collections, *High Tide in Tucson* (1995) and *Small Wonder* (2002); and most recently, her first full-length narrative nonfiction, *Animal, Vegetable, Miracle* (2007). She has contributed to dozens of literary anthologies, newspapers, and magazines. Her books have earned major literary awards at home and abroad, and in 2000 she received the National Humanities Medal, the United States' highest honor for service through the arts.

Barbara Kingsolver grew up in rural Kentucky. She counts among her most important early influences the Bookmobile, a large family vegetable garden, the surrounding fields and woods, and parents who were tolerant of nature study (anything but snakes and mice could be kept in the house), but intolerant of TV.

She studied at DePauw University in Indiana on a piano scholarship, then transferred from the music school to the college of liberal arts because of "her desire to study practically everything," and graduated with a degree in biology. She spent the late 1970s in Greece, France, and England, then moved to Tucson, Arizona. She eventually pursued graduate studies in evolutionary biology at the University of Arizona. During her student and post-college years she supported herself in jobs that included typesetter, housecleaner, medical laboratory technician, artist's model, archeological assistant, translator, teaching assistant, and copy editor. After graduate school she worked as a scientific writer for the University of Arizona before becoming a freelance journalist.

Kingsolver is the mother of two daughters and is married to Steven Hopp, a professor of environmental sciences. In 2004, after more than twenty-five years in Tucson, Arizona, Kingsolver left the Southwest to return to her native terrain. She now lives with her family on a farm in southwestern Virginia where they raise free-range chickens, turkeys, and Icelandic sheep and have an enormous vegetable garden.

Our selection, "Household Words," is from *Small Wonder*.

I was headed home with my mind on things; I can't even say what they were. It was an afternoon not very long ago, and probably I was ticking through the routine sacrament of my day—locating every member of my family at that moment and organizing how we would all come together for dinner and what I would feed us—when my thoughts were bluntly interrupted. A woman was being attacked fifty feet away from me. My heart thumped and then seemed to stop for good and then thumped hard again as I watched what was happening. The woman was slight, probably no taller than my older daughter, but she was my age. Her attacker, a much taller man, had no weapon but was hitting her on the head and face with his fists and open hands, screaming, calling her vile names right out in the open. She ducked, in the way any animal would, to save the more fragile bones of her face. She tried to turn her back on him, but he pursued her, smacking at her relentlessly with the flat of his hand and shouting angrily that she was trash, she was nothing, she should get away from him. And she was trying, but she couldn't. I felt my body freeze as they approached. They came very close, maybe ten feet away or even less, and then they moved on past us. I say *us* because I wasn't alone here: I was in a crowd of several dozen people, all within earshot. Maybe there were closer to a hundred of us; I'm not sure. Unbelievably, most weren't even looking. And then I did my own unbelievable thing: I left. I moved forward toward my home and family and left that battered woman behind.

> "Reader, can you believe I did what I did? Does it seem certain that I am heartless?"

I did and I didn't leave her behind, because I'm still thinking and now writing about this scene, reviling my own cowardice. Reader, can you believe I did what I did? Does it seem certain that I am heartless?

Let me give some more details of the scene, not because I hope to be forgiven. I ask only that all of us try to find ourselves in this weird landscape. It was the United States of America. I was at a busy intersection, in a car. The woman had the leathery, lined face and tattered-looking hair of a person who lives her whole life outdoors beneath the sun. So did her attacker. Both of them wore the clothes that make for an instantly recognizable uniform: shirts and pants weathered by hard daily wear to a neutral color and texture. Her possessions, and his, were stuffed into two bulky backpacks that leaned against a signpost in a median dividing six lanes of city traffic. I was in the middle lane of traffic on one side. All of the other people in this crowd were also in automobiles, on either side of me, opposite me, ahead and behind, most of them with their windows rolled up, listening to the radio or talking on cell phones. From what I could tell, no one else was watching this woman get beaten up and chased across three, then six, then nine separate lanes of traffic in the intersecting streets. I considered how I could get out of my car (should I leave it idling? lock it? what?) and run toward this woman and man, shouting at him to stop, begging the other drivers to use their phones to call the police. And then, after I had turned over this scenario in my mind for eight or nine seconds, the light changed and every car but mine began to move, and I had to think instead about the honking horns, the blocked traffic, the public nuisance I was about to become, and all the people who would shake their heads at my do-gooder foolishness and inform me that

I should stay away from these rough-looking characters because this was obviously a domestic dispute.

But that could not have been true. It was not domestic. *Domestic* means "of the home," and these people had no home. That was the problem—theirs, mine, everybody's. These people were beneath or somehow outside the laws that govern civil behavior between citizens of our country. They were homeless.

In his poem "Death of a Hired Man," Robert Frost captured in just a few words the most perfect definition of home I've ever read:

Home is the place where, when you have to go there,
They have to take you in.

I wish I could ever have been so succinct. I've spent hundreds of pages, even whole novels, trying to explain what home means to me. Sometimes I think it's the only thing I ever write about. Home is place, geography, and psyche; it's a matter of survival and safety, a condition of attachment and self-definition. It's where you learn from your parents and repeat to your children all the stories of what it means to belong to the place and people of your ken. It's a place of safety—and that is one of the most real and pressing issues for those who must live without it. For homeless women and men, the probability of being sexually assaulted or physically attacked is so great that it's a matter not of *if* but of *when*. Homelessness is the loss first of community and finally of the self. It seems fatuous that I could spend so much time contemplating the subtle nuances of home (let alone buy a magazine devoted to home remodeling or decor) when there are people near me—sometimes only a few feet away from me—who don't have one, can't get one, aren't even in the picture.

Tucson, the city where I live most of the time, is often said to be a Mecca for homeless people. I don't like this use of the term "Mecca" because it suggests a beautiful holy land and a trip undertaken to fulfill the needs of the spirit. Whereas thousands of men, women, and children undertake the long journey to Tucson each winter for one reason only: to fulfill the need of the body to lie on the ground overnight without freezing to death. They come here for raw survival; their numbers swell each October and then remain through each following summer a little higher than the year before. Increasingly they have become a presence among us, ignored by most of us, specifically banned by our laws from certain places where the city council has decided their panhandling may interfere with commerce. They are banned mostly, I think, because their presence is a pure, naked shame upon us all.

Whatever else "home" might be called, it must surely be a fundamental human license. In every culture on earth, the right to live in a home is probably the first condition of citizenship and humanity. Homelessness is an aberration. It may happen anywhere from time to time, of course, but when I look hard at the world, I see very few places where there resides an entire, permanent class of people labeled "homeless." Not in the poorest places I've ever lived, not even in an African village where everyone I knew owned only one shirt (at best) and most had never touched an automobile. Because even there, as long as the social structure remains intact, people without resources are taken in by their families. Even if someone should fall completely apart and have to go to the hospital, which means a trek on foot over dozens of miles or more, the whole family goes along to make sure the sick one is taken care of. "Home," in this case, becomes portable. I know this because I lived as a child in an African village that housed the region's small, concrete-block hospital. Whenever I walked past, the hospital's lively grounds never failed to impress me. It was just a bare-dirt plaza, maybe stretching among all its corners to the size of a city block, but it was always a busy place, where dozens of families camped out around their cooking fires while waiting for some relative to have an operation, have a baby, or die. Meanwhile they passed the time by singing, mourning, washing dishes, arguing, daydreaming, or fussing at toddlers who ran around wearing nothing but strings of beads around their bellies. In the rest of my life I have never witnessed another scene so solidly founded on both poverty and security. I don't wish to glorify the impoverished half of this equation; these children had swollen bellies from kwashiorkor, and they had parasites. But they also had families they could not forget under any circumstances, or ever abandon, or be abandoned by, however they might fall on madness or illness or hard times. I don't believe that the word *homeless* as it's used in our language could be translated there.

In most cultures I have known or read about, the provision of home is considered to be the principal function and duty of human family. In rich countries other than ours, such as Japan, the members of the European community, and Canada, the state assumes this duty as well; their citizens pay higher taxes than we do, and so the well-off live with a little less. Generally speaking, the citizens of these nations have smaller homes, smaller cars, and smaller appetites for consumer goods than we do. And to balance it out they have a kind of security unknown to U.S. citizens—that is, the promise that the state will protect every citizen from disaster. A good education, good health care, and good shelter are fairly well guaranteed, even to those who have devastating illness or bad luck. The Revised European Social Charter of the Council of Europe (1996) states in Article 34: "In order to combat social exclusion and poverty, the Union recognizes and respects the right to social and housing assistance to ensure a decent existence for all those who lack sufficient resources." More recently, at the Lisbon Summit in March 2000, heads of the fifteen European Union countries agreed to develop a common strategy for providing universal access to decent and sanitary housing. These civilized nations have long agreed that homelessness simply isn't an option.

Where *does* homelessness exist? On the border between the Congo and Rwanda when those countries are engaged in protracted civil war. In Kosovo, for the same reason. In India, wherever the construction of a massive dam has inundated villages. In Kenya and other parts of Africa, where large numbers of children have lost their entire extended families to AIDS. Many were also homeless in Somalia during the drought, in the Philippines after the volcanic explosion, in Mexico City after the earthquake. In other words, homelessness as a significant problem occurs in countries stricken by war, famine, plague, and natural disaster. And here, in the USA. Why are we not carrying on with ourselves, our neighbors, and the people who represent us the conversation that begins with the question, *What on earth is wrong with us?*

This is a special country, don't we know it. There are things about the way we organize our society that make it unique on the planet. We believe in liberty, equality, and whatever it is that permits extravagant housing developments to be built around my hometown at the rate of one new opening each week ("Model homes, 6 bedrooms, 3-car garages, starting from the low $180s!"), while fully 20 percent of children on my county's record books live below the poverty level. Nationwide, though the homeless are a difficult population to census, we can be sure they number more than one million. How does the rest of the world keep a straight face when we go riding into it on our latest white horse of Operation-this-or-that-kind-of-Justice, and everyone can see perfectly well how we behave at home? Home is where all justice begins.

More than a decade ago, a government study discovered the surprising fact that some 10 percent of American families appeared to be destined for homelessness. These were working families with a household income, not qualifying for unemployment or other kinds of relief, but they had to spend more than 60 percent of that income on housing and heating; 44 percent of it on food; and 14 percent on medical care. It doesn't take higher math to show they were having to go into debt, deeper each month, to stay alive. This truth was demonstrated dramatically in more recent years by Barbara Ehrenreich, who gave two years of her life at the end of the 1990s to the challenge of surviving on the best wages she could find as an unskilled worker, and then writing about it in her remarkable book *Nickeled and Dimed: On (Not) Getting By in America*. When workers earning minimum wage can no longer meet their bills, they must decide which of the following things to give up: housing, food, medical care. That is one of the several life histories we call, collectively, the American way.

The figures above came from a book by Arthur Blaustein, who was appointed by President Carter in 1977 to chair the National Advisory Council on Economic Opportunity. The council was abolished in 1981 by the Reagan administration, which didn't like the council's findings. But Blaustein published the work anyway, in his book *The American Promise*, which outlines our nation's disastrous approach to dealing with poverty. In his introduction he mentions an interview between Bill Moyers and Robert Penn Warren, a writer I'm proud to claim as a fellow Kentuckian, who was at that time America's Poet Laureate. Mr. Moyers asked Mr. Warren, "Sir, as one of our leading writers and philosophers, can you tell me how we can resolve the terrible crises that surround us: decaying cities, terrible health care, terrible crises in education and housing, and so much poverty?"

Mr. Warren leaned forward and said, "Well, Bill, for a beginning, I think it would be good if we would stop lying to one another."

This is it. This is all. We so desperately avoid looking at the truth square on, much less saying it aloud, because it's uncomfortable for us to go about our days in relative luxury while people next door to us are dying for lack of shelter. Civic pride can lose its shine when reality is allowed a place at the table. I find it unspeakably hard to walk past someone whose life would be improved, noticeably, by the amount of spare change I could probably find on the floor of my car.

But we manage, those of us who are lucky enough, to walk on by. We live with pronounced class difference in a nation that was founded on the ideal of classlessness, and we do it by believing in a comforting mythology of genesis that is as basic to our nation as the flag and the pledge of allegiance. Here are some of our favorite fuzzy-blanket myths:

> "I take it as part of my job to examine the stories that hold us together as a society and that we rely on to maintain our identity."

1. *Anybody* who is clever and hardworking can make it in America.
2. Homeless people are that way for some good reason. They chose it, or they're criminals or alcoholics or crazy, but whatever went wrong, it's their fault. It couldn't happen to me because I'm clever, sane, and hardworking.
3. Or maybe it isn't *entirely* their fault. But the problem of poverty is so complex that it's impossible to fix.

As a professional storyteller, I take myths personally. I take it as part of my job to examine the stories that hold us together as a society and that we rely on to maintain our identity. These particular myths about poverty are probably some of the most useful tales that create our cultural persona. I also think they're individually destructive and frankly untrue, and oh, yes, they kill people. Finally, this mythology is omnipresent, embedded to some degree in virtually every heart—healthy, wealthy, and otherwise— that beats within this union. Rich people may believe it and relax; poor people may believe it and become paralyzed with self-loathing. And the rest of us just muddle on. When I drive my car through an intersection, past four more homeless men or women (out of the thirty or more I might see in a day) with four more cardboard signs poised to drive a stake of guilt through my heart, I can hear these quiet words rising up in the back of my mind:

". . . smart like me . . . hardworking like me . . . they'd have a house like me."

And here are some questions I have occasionally had to ask myself, as a counterpoint to that little song: Am I so smart that I could survive on my wits alone, without shelter, for months or years? Could I face the enormity of that loneliness and despair without emotional painkillers in the form of alcohol or drugs?

Doubtful.

Am I *hardworking* enough that I could walk ten or fifteen miles every day in the blazing sun from a shelter downtown or a camp along the riverbank to get to this intersection, and then stand here begging? Could I stand on my own two feet all day on this scorched white pavement without water or food or shade or an ounce of love, through the 105-degree heat of every June, July, and August day in Tucson, Arizona?

No.

And then I try to imagine for just a moment that I am God, or at any rate someone kindhearted and smart who is in a position to look down from above on this scenario: Four men are standing hatless on the four corners of the busy intersection at Speedway and Tucson Boulevard while a hundred passengers eye them with indifference from idling air-conditioned cars, or glance away, waiting for the light to change. Who in this scene is clever? Who is lazy? Which four people worked hardest this day to get where they are right now and to stay alive?

This problem is not complicated. First, it might be useful for us to take the advice of a wise old Kentuckian and stop lying to one another. We live in the only rich country in the world that still tolerates this much poverty in the midst of that much wealth. The European Community members and other industrialized nations have declared themselves unwilling to tolerate homelessness, and they devote the resources necessary to guarantee a "decent existence" for all. We could do the same here without all of us first having to study trigonometry or rewrite the Constitution with our bare hands. It would just take money and a shift in values. Our elected officials could allocate the money to this instead of cutting the taxes of corporations and the wealthy, and they *will*—if and when enough of their constituents demand it. In the meantime it is possible to reallocate some money with civilian hands by writing a check or volunteering. Shelters, which offer enough beds for fewer than half the people who use these services, receive about 65 percent of their funding from federal, state, and local governments but are kept in operation almost entirely by volunteer labor. This means more than kitchen work, because humans don't live by soup alone. Volunteers teach music, literacy, and job skills, plan activities for children, and register homeless people to vote. There is nothing so educational as conversing with someone who has lost the condition of home and finding no hard boundaries of virtue that divide you. As a friend who is wheelchair-bound sometimes reminds me, "Barbara, the main difference between you and me is one bad fall off a rock."

I wish I could go back to that afternoon that haunts me and do what I know I should have done: get out of my car, make a scene, stop traffic, stop a violent man if I could. Home is the place where, when you have to go there, they have to take you in. My car might have been the place she had to go, with no other earthly alternatives left to her, and so it may be that I have to take her in, take that risk, get criticized or tainted by the communicable disease of shame that is homelessness. In some sense she did come in, for she is still with me. I rehearse a different scene in my mind. If I meet her again I hope I can be ready.

It's a tenuous satisfaction that comes from rationalizing problems away or banning them from the sidewalk. Another clean definition I admire, as succinct as Frost's for the complexities of home, is Dr. Martin Luther King Jr.'s explanation of peace: True peace, he said, is not merely the absence of tension. It's the presence of justice.

Maxine Hong Kingston
A Sea Worry

Maxine Hong Kingston's nonfiction book *The Woman Warrior* has become a staple in high school and college English classes. Published in 1976, it melds her family's historical story with her own childhood accounts, infusing all with a sense of the mythological. The line between fiction and nonfiction in this book and her following nonfiction book, *China Men* (1980), is very thin. Her method of moving freely into the re-created lives of ancestors greatly influenced later approaches to memoir. Her later works include *Tripmaster Monkey* (1989), a novel, and *The Fifth Book of Peace* (2004), another genre-melding book.

Kingston has long defended her blending of fiction and nonfiction and her use of a kind of imaginative personal mythology. Some critics have complained that her Chinese and Chinese American characters are inaccurately portrayed, and that her use of Chinese myth has little relation to the "real" thing. Kingston has responded that her mythologies and characters are fundamentally American, not Chinese, and that she has modeled her approach to nonfiction on William Carlos Williams's groundbreaking book *In the American Grain* (1925).

Maxine Hong Kingston was raised in Stockton, California, and now lives in Oakland. Her first language was Say Yup, a Cantonese dialect. She received scholarships to attend the University of California–Berkeley, from which she received an English degree and a teaching certificate. She then taught school in Hawaii for a decade; some of her experience there is recounted in her book of essays *Hawai'i One Summer* (1987). "A Sea Worry," one of Kingston's earliest essays, is drawn from this collection. It is, for Kingston, a relatively simple and straightforward account, stylistically lovely and understated. Kingston was arrested in March 2003 in Washington, D.C., for crossing a police line during a protest against the war in Iraq. Yet her response to violence has primarily been an artistic one: "In a time of destruction, say something creative," she once wrote.

Interview with Maxine Hong Kingston, p. 482.

This summer our son bodysurfs. He says it's his "job" and rises each morning at 5:30 to catch the bus to Sandy Beach. I hope that by September he will have had enough of the ocean. Tall waves throw surfers against the shallow bottom. Undertows have snatched them away. Sharks prowl Sandy's. Joseph told me that once he got out of the water because he saw an enormous shark. "Did you tell the lifeguard?" I asked. "No." "Why not?" "I didn't want to spoil the surfing." The ocean pulls at the boys, who turn into surfing addicts. At sunset you can see surfers waiting for the last golden wave.

"Why do you go surfing so often?" I ask my students.

"It feels so good," they say. "Inside the tube. I can't describe it. There are no words for it."

"You can describe it," I scold, and I am angry. "Everything can be described. Find the words for it, you lazy boy. Why don't you stay home and read?" I am afraid that the boys give themselves up to the ocean's mindlessness.

When the waves are up, surfers all over Hawai'i don't do their homework. They cut school. They know how the surf is breaking at any moment because every fifteen minutes the reports come over the radio; in fact, one of my former students is the surf reporter.

Some boys leave for mainland colleges, and write their parents heartrending letters. They beg to come home for Thanksgiving. "If I can just touch the ocean," they write from Missouri and Kansas, "I'll last for the rest of the semester." Some come home for Christmas and don't go back.

> "They write about the silence, the peace, 'no hassles,' the feeling of being reborn as they shoot out the end."

Even when the assignment is about something else, the students write about surfing. They try to describe what it is to be inside the wave as it curls over them, making a tube or "chamber" or "green room" or "pipeline" or "time warp." They write about the silence, the peace, "no hassles," the feeling of being reborn as they shoot out the end. They've written about the voice of God, the "commandments" they hear. In the margins, they draw the perfect wave. Their writing is full of clichés. "The endless summer," they say. "Unreal."

Surfing is like a religion. Among the martyrs are George Helm, Kimo Mitchell, and Eddie Aikau. Helm and Mitchell were lost at sea riding their surfboards from Kaho'olawe, where they had gone to protest the Navy's bombing of that island. Eddie Aikau was a champion surfer and lifeguard. A storm had capsized the Hōkūle'a, the ship that traces the route that the Polynesian ancestors sailed from Tahiti, and Eddie Aikau had set out on his board to get help.

Since the ocean captivates our son, we decided to go with him to see Sandy's.

We got up before dawn, picked up his friend, Marty, and drove out of Honolulu. Almost all the traffic was going in the opposite direction, the freeway coned to make more lanes into the city. We came to a place where raw mountains rose on our left and the sea fell on our right, smashing against the cliffs. The strip of cliff pulverized into sand is Sandy's. "Dangerous Current Exist," said the sign.

Earll and I sat on the shore with our blankets and thermos of coffee. Joseph and Marty put on their fins and stood at the edge of the sea for a moment, touching the water with their fingers and crossing their hearts before going in. There were fifteen boys out there, all about the same age, fourteen to twenty, all with the same kind of lean, v-shaped build, most of them with black hair that made their wet heads look like sea lions. It was hard to tell whether our kid was one of those who popped up after a big wave. A few had surfboards, which are against the rules at a body-surfing beach, but the lifeguard wasn't on duty that early.

As they watched for the next wave, the boys turned toward the ocean. They gazed slightly upward; I thought of altar boys before a great god. When a good wave arrived, they turned, faced shore, and came shooting in, some taking the wave to the right and some to the left, their bodies fishlike, one arm out in front, the hand and fingers pointed before them, like a swordfish's beak. A few held credit card trays, and some slid in on trays from MacDonald's.

"That is no country for middle-aged women," I said. We had on bathing suits underneath our clothes in case we felt moved to participate. There were no older men either.

Even from the shore, we could see inside the tubes. Sometimes, when they came at an angle, we saw into them a long way. When the wave dug into the sand, it formed a brown tube or a gold one. The magic ones, though, were made out of just water, green and turquoise rooms, translucent walls and ceilings. I saw one that was powder-blue, perfect, thin; the sun filled it with sky blue and white light. The best thing, the kids say, is when you are in the middle of the tube, and there is water all around you but you're dry.

The waves came in sets; the boys passed up the smaller ones. Inside a big one, you could see their bodies hanging upright, knees bent, duckfeet fins paddling, bodies dangling there in the wave.

Once in a while, we heard a boy yell, "Aa-whoo!" "Poon-tah!" "Aaroo!" And then we noticed how rare human voice was here; the surfers did not talk, but silently, silently rode the waves.

Since Joseph and Marty were considerate of us, they stopped after two hours, and we took them out for breakfast. We kept asking them how it felt, so that they would not lose language.

"Like a stairwell in an apartment building," said Joseph, which I liked immensely. He hasn't been in very many apartment buildings, so had to reach a bit to get the simile. "I saw somebody I knew coming toward me in the tube, and I shouted, 'Jeff. Hey, Jeff,' and my voice echoed like a stairwell in an apartment building. Jeff and I came straight at each other—mirror tube."

"Are there ever girls out there?" Earll asked.

"There's a few women who come at about eleven," said Marty.

"How old are they?"

"About twenty."

"Why do you cross your heart with water?"

"So the ocean doesn't kill us."

I described the powder-blue tube I had seen. "That part of Sandy's is called Chambers," they said.

I have gotten some surfing magazines, the ones kids steal from the school library, to see if the professionals try to describe the tube. Bradford Baker writes:

> . . . Round and pregnant in Emptiness
> I slide,
>   Laughing,
>   into the sun,
>   into the night.

Frank Miller calls the surfer

> . . . mother's fumbling
> curly-haired
> tubey-laired
> son.

"Ooh, offshores—" writes Reno Abbellira, "where wind and wave most often form that terminal rendezvous of love—when the wave can reveal her deepest longings, her crest caressed, cannily covered to form those peeling concavities we know, perhaps a bit irreverently, as tubes. Here we strive to spend every second—enclosed, encased, sometimes fatefully entombed, and hopefully, gleefully, ejected—Whoosh!"

"An iridescent ride through the entrails of God," says Gary L. Crandall.

I am relieved that the surfers keep asking one another for descriptions. I also find some comfort in the stream of commuter traffic, cars filled with men over twenty, passing Sandy Beach on their way to work.

Interview with Maxine Hong Kingston

BECKY BRADWAY: "A Sea Worry" is one of your earliest published pieces. Looking back on your older work, do you feel that you (and/or your writing) have changed a great deal?

MAXINE HONG KINGSTON: I feel that my writing changes with every piece. I am constantly experimenting, traveling to and exploring new places, and inventing new forms.

BB: Your book *The Woman Warrior* is widely praised, sometimes criticized, widely taught. Has the vast attention received by this book altered your writing and your life in certain ways?

MHK: The purpose of writing is to communicate with others. I have an enormous community of readers, who affirm the power of the word. I change with every poem and story I write—growing in understanding—and the readers change, too.

BB: You are sometimes categorized as an Asian American writer, rather than simply a writer. Are you comfortable with the use of this label?

MHK: I am glad to be an Asian American writer, as long as this is not my only label. My writing is also in anthologies and courses in British and American literature, history, California history, anthropology, psychology, feminist literature, Chinese world literature, etc., etc.

BB: Your work often moves between the genre boundaries of fiction, nonfiction, and mythology. Some critics have long complained that nonfiction pushes the boundaries of some perceived factual truth; we've certainly seen this argument flaring up in the press recently. Could you please discuss that tension between the need to hew to the facts, and the need for the artist to create?

MHK: To write true lives, we need to reveal the characters' dreams and imagination and visions. I see borders as very wide, where the most wonderful stories and poems happen.

Amitava Kumar

From *Traveling Light*

Amitava Kumar is a writer and journalist. He was born in Ara, India, and raised in the nearby town of Patna, "famous for its corruption, crushing poverty and delicious mangoes." He is the author of *Husband of a Fanatic* (2004), *Bombay-London-New York* (2002), and *Passport Photos* (2000). He has also written a book of poems, *No Tears for the N.R.I.* (1996). His novel *Home Products* was published in 2007. Kumar teaches in the English department at Vassar College.

A critic in the *New Statesman* chose the nonfiction *Bombay-London-New York* as one of the best books of 2003, saying, "Amitava Kumar evokes an India of rural simplicity, ancient traditions and bewitching rituals. Through a string of stories, he shows how the Indian diaspora internalized this view and brought Bollywood, bhangra and biryani to Britain and the U.S. to create an imaginary home away from home." The *Times Literary Supplement* called it "a willful, engaging book on Indian fiction in English, where it is always clear that there is a relationship between literary journeys and those embarked on in real life, between the flow of words and the movement of people and things, and between the reader's act of finding the literary centre and the writer's task of illuminating the periphery."

The selection we have included is part of a longer chapter from *Bombay-London-New York*. In this piece Kumar provides a brief glimpse of the changing cultural perceptions of an icon, Mahatma Gandhi.

Interview with Amitava Kumar, p. 487.

Once, when I came out of the subway in New York City, I saw a sign that said "Gandhi was a great and charitable man." Beneath, in smaller type, were the words, "However, he could have used some work on his triceps." The sign was an advertisement for the Equinox Fitness Club. If you joined early, the sign said, you could save 150 dollars.

I confess I like the use to which Gandhi is put by the Equinox Fitness Club. No doubt the Mahatma would have found the price of the packet a bit steep. But I think he would have liked the thriftiness of the early-membership plan. Gandhi came from a family of traders. The name his family gave him—Mohandas Karamchand Gandhi—was translated by the writer G. V. Desani as "Action-Slave-Fascination-Moon Grocer." What a tantalizing mix of qualities! The qualities of a man of the world! This kind of man would even have understood advertising. I am sure the Mahatma would have had a witty quip for the use to which Microsoft has put his bald visage. In America, Gandhi's image appears on huge hoardings with the words "Think Different." There is a tiny logo in the corner showing a rainbow-striped apple. Salman Rushdie has commented on this phenomenon: "Once a half-century ago, this bony man shaped a nation's struggle for freedom. But that, as they say, is history. Now Gandhi is modeling for Apple."

> "Do I really want to see Gandhi selling deodorants to a guy in Dadar?"

In India, Gandhi had been a face smiling at me from the walls of the decrepit offices in the small towns of Bihar. The use of his image for a New York City gym has returned me to a different use of Gandhi, one that takes the Mahatma out of the museum. This use has not been unknown in India, it has just been ignored by official pieties. This is the irreverent Gandhi of the Indian marketplace. Long live Gandhi Safety-Match. Long live Bapu Mark Jute Bag. Long live Mahatma Brand Mustard Oil.

Do I really want to see Gandhi selling deodorants to a guy in Dadar? "Cleanliness is next to godliness. Free your body of foreign odors!" Perhaps not. But the point that I am moving toward is that a more robust, and perhaps muscular, Gandhi is visible in the pages of Indian writing in English these days. The sanitized Mahatma of early Indian fiction has given way to a maverick Gandhi. Let's take as an early example the memoirs of a writer like Nayantara Sahgal, who was also Prime Minister Nehru's niece. Sahgal described her return from New York to New Delhi in *Prison and Chocolate Cake*. India had only recently won freedom; it had not recovered from the trauma of the bloody Partition. Then, Gandhi was assassinated. In Sahgal's book, we saw Gandhi through a young woman's eyes that are full of adulation: "My own reaction was mingled with reverence. Could it be true that a man could talk of love and truth and goodness, and apply these religious terms to politics and not be laughed at? Could it be true that such sentiments could actually guide a nation's policy? Yet in India all these things were true."

A few decades into the realities of independent India, and the scene appears irredeemably altered. In Upamanyu Chatterjee's *English, August,* what we are left with is the post-apocalyptic image of the Gandhi Hall that looks like "something out of a TV news clip on Beirut." Outside this building with its broken windowpanes and bombed-out appearance is the "statue of a short fat bespectacled man with a rod coming out of his arse." This is the postcolonial Gandhi. And I like him because—I don't know how to say this without irony—nothing seems foreign to his body. Which is to say, my worry about his being used to sell deodorants is really an irrelevant question. Gandhi can take in anything and still keep smiling. A *satyagrahi* always stays on top of the world. This is also nonviolence taken to its real and proper extreme. In a country sodomized by its leaders, here is a leader who has chosen to stand among the people with a rod up his arse.

In the early 1980s, I was in college in Delhi. Each morning, I rode on a bus that took me past the memorials to national leaders, including Gandhi's. During those years in college, I came across *Kanthapura* on my required reading list in an English course. Raja Rao's *Kanthapura,* a novel about the Gandhian revolution, was first published in 1938, almost a decade before independence. The novel was about the inhabitants of a village, innocent of any history, suddenly swept by the powerful tide of Gandhi worship. Rao, along with R. K. Narayan and Mulk Raj Anand, formed the triumvirate of Indian writers in its early stages.

While our teacher discussed the book with us, in the world outside our classroom, another myth of Gandhi was being born. The British film director Richard Attenborough was shooting his movie on Gandhi in Delhi. The newspapers printed updates of the film shoot. There were complaints about Gandhi being played by an actor who wasn't an Indian; then came the giddy news that Ben Kingsley was at least half-Indian. One of my fellow students, a stocky man who studied history and rode a motorcycle, had a small role in the film. One day someone came to class with the news that there were buses waiting outside the college gates. We could all go and join the scene of Gandhi's funeral that was being shot that day. Attenborough needed a huge crowd of well-behaved extras. Hollywood was going to bring our freedom struggle alive for us. In *Kanthapura,* Rao's highly mannered syntax had conveyed to me the removed grandeur of idealism. I was discovering the past in a stylized way. Then, in the world outside the classroom, Hollywood brought peace and popcorn together, and gave Gandhi the honor he deserved. An Oscar.

It would be impossible for someone like me, born some decades after independence, to imagine Sahgal's or Rao's awestruck relationship with the Mahatma. Our freedom as a later generation of Indians has also meant a freedom from Gandhi worship. Newer Indian writers have undoubtedly played a small part in this whole process of demystification. Consider Vikram Chandra's portrait of Gandhi where he appears less a holy man on a pedestal and more a tactical mix of East and West, of high and low, of the sacred and also the secular:

> Be fearless, like that suave cosmopolitan M. K. Gandhi, that most international of *khiladis,* who told us repeatedly that while his political gurus were Gokhale and Ranade and Tilak, his spiritual gurus were Tolstoy and Thoreau and Ruskin, and that he got his nonviolence not from the Gita but from the Sermon on the Mount. Remember that Gandhi's audience was not just Indian but also everyone else; that all his actions, the spectacle of his revolution and the revolution of his self, were performed simultaneously before a local audience and a global one. He spoke to us, to those he loved, but in speaking to us he was also speaking to all the world, and in speaking to the world he wanted nothing less than to change all of it.

Chandra's Gandhi is a happy borrower. He is not unlike the Bombay criminals whom the writer describes as "those CCTV-using, Glock-firing,

Bholenath-worshipping gangsters." Chandra finds them appealing because they "do whatever it takes to get the job done." From Gandhi to the Glock-firing gangsters . . . in less than 60 seconds! This is not only taking Gandhi off the pedestal—it is more like pushing him into the ring, with red boxing gloves and a rakish grin.

The historian Partha Chatterjee has written: "The 'message of the Mahatma' meant different things to different people." According to Chatterjee, what Gandhi's words "meant to peasants or tribals was completely different from the way it was interpreted by the literati." Following Chatterjee, it is quite interesting to me how what newspaper editors call "ordinary Indians" also in their own unremarkable ways have made Gandhi their own. I think that the Gandhi of the Indian marketplace that I was earlier championing is an example of that easy accommodation.

The people, in fact, might be ahead of writers and editorialists. As the research of Shahid Amin reveals, peasants in Gorakhpur, in the eastern India of 1921, were producing a "many-sided response to Gandhi." In the spring of 1921, *The Pioneer* carried an editorial about a report in a Gorakhpur newspaper that had cited reports of miracles popularly attributed to the Mahatma. "Smoke was seen coming from wells and, when water was drunk, it had the fragrance of *keora* (pandanus odaratissimus) an aloe-like plant which is used in the manufacture of perfume; a copy of the Holy Quran was found in a room that had not been opened for a year; an *Ahir* who refused alms to a *Sadhu* begging in Mahatma Gandhi's name, had his *gur* and two buffaloes destroyed by fire, and a skeptical Brahmin, who defied Mr Gandhi's authority, went mad and was only cured three days afterwards by the invocation of the saintly name!"

In this list of magic and change, I see a lesson about our buried, peripheral modernities. The lesson becomes clear to me long after I come out of the subway and see Gandhi's name on a sign advertising a gym. But the lesson, slow in coming, is clear enough. It is about people mixing the rational with the ritual, science with séance, and politics with the poetry of magical transformation. Long before Richard Attenborough, the myth-maker, long before the admen from Madison Avenue, long before our politicians had invented the Gandhi Jayanti Samaroh, long before Indian writers had found magical realism . . . were the peasants of Gorakhpur giving life to Gandhi. Long live the peasants of Gorakhpur.

Interview with Amitava Kumar

BECKY BRADWAY: This section from your book uses images of Gandhi that might seem to be opposed to one another (posters, the movie *Gandhi*, and peasants' verbal stories)—until you show us all the ways that they are ultimately the same. Did you find this way of constructing your piece (juxtaposing images, moving back and forth through time) to be particularly difficult? Did you plan the pattern of this piece before

you wrote this essay, or did you move sections around after you wrote
the initial draft?

AMITAVA KUMAR: I was writing about travel. And movement. This idea
is present even in the book's title *Bombay-London-New York*. The
names of those places, just as they appear on my ticket. So, in a book
that was about movement, it seemed fitting to write in a way that
reflected the to-and-fro of global travel. Except that what I'm really
describing in this excerpt is the movement of an icon, an idol, and a
commodity. I was interested in talking about popular cultural constructions of Gandhi, in India where he was born, but also in the rest
of the world. Hence, the opening lines about Gandhi in an ad for the
Equinox Fitness Club.

BB: What are the particular challenges involved in writing about a home
place that is very different from the one in which you're now living?

AK: The peculiar challenge facing any writer who is documenting literature and culture in our moment of globalization is to establish the
differences between two places—and, at the same time, reveal the infinite visible or invisible connections between them. You are always
drawing maps that provide a measure of the uneven but single world.

BB: In some ways it seems to me that American and Indian cultures are
beginning to merge. (Indian music and film are entering the popular
culture—Indians take our phone orders and answer our questions—
Indians usually live on formerly all Anglo blocks, even in the suburbs
and small towns—and, in India, American movies and advertising
have long been a part of daily life in the cities.) Anyway: what's your
feeling about these blendings of cultures?

AK: The mixing of cultures is inevitable. And also interesting. What catches
my eye is less the seamless translation of one practice from one culture
to the other: rather, it is the "mistranslation" where true inventiveness
is to be found. A friend of mine told me recently that a washing machine
(something we associate as having come from the West) was being used
in a market in an Indian town to make lassi, the spin cycle being put
to use to mix the ice and the yogurt quickly and effectively for the
large number of customers.

BB: The essays in *Bombay-London-New York* are linked by references to
books and the process of writing. The little section in our anthology
smoothly integrates references to a number of literary sources. Did
you find it difficult to integrate the sources with the friendly, witty
voice that you use in this piece? Can you advise others on ways of
doing this?

AK: I always tell my students that we need to grasp as an elementary process
of writing the juxtapositions that inform our daily life and must be
made a part of our writing. Gandhi's image in an ad for Microsoft,
hanging like a banner down the side of a building in Manhattan, juxta-
poses divided realities. It is a dramatic example of what is forever
happening around us. It is also a part of what is always in our heads,

as readers and writers, and it is something that we can't only let the ad-writers exploit. In fact, we should try to describe our realities more incisively by turning the ads against the intentions of their creators. Say you are watching the reports of a riot in L.A. You flip the channels on your TV. In a piece of writing that you do about the experience, you can begin, "The flames in L.A. are melting the cheese on a burger in a Perkins commercial."

Li-Young Lee

From *The Winged Seed*

Li-Young Lee is a highly regarded poet whose books include *The City in Which I Love You* (1991) and *Behind My Eyes* (2008). While recognized largely as a poet, his memoir *The Winged Seed*, published in 1999, was warmly received by critics and readers. He is the recipient of many poetry awards, including a creative artist grant from the National Endowment for the Arts. He was also featured on the PBS series *The Power of the Word* with Bill Moyers. His work is widely anthologized.

Li-Young Lee was born in Djakarta, Indonesia, in 1957, the son of exiled Chinese parents. His maternal grandfather was the first president of the Republic of China; his father came from a family of gangsters and entrepreneurs. His father briefly served as personal physician to Mao Tse-tsung, but after a year the family was exiled to Indonesia. Indonesia's then-dictator moved against Chinese immigrants; Lee's father was arrested and the entire family joined him in exile. En route to an island prison, the family escaped to Hong Kong; not long after, they moved to Pennsylvania. Li-Young Lee began writing poetry while at the University of Pittsburgh. Lee has taught creative writing at the Iowa Writer's Workshop, Northwestern University, the University of Oregon, and the University of Texas, Austin. He lives in Chicago.

Of *The Winged Seed*, a critic from *Publishers Weekly* said, "Through the illogic and distortion of his dreams, Li-Young leads readers into the emotional landscape of his childhood. . . . in this evocative tale, politics plays a lesser role than family history and love in a world that was sad, frightening and hard for a child to understand. For the reader, however, Li-Young's portraits of the times are vividly illuminating."

The section we have included from *The Winged Seed* tells the story of Li-Young's visit with his father to the home of an elderly parishioner. The piece travels in time and uses inventive language and rhythms to get across a boy's compassion and fear.

I remember now, in his sermon on the shoes, my father exhorted the listener to build a shoe fit for a word to don and strike its way over earth. Make a shoe for a traveler word, he'd said while he was alive, a shoe for walking over the dead, lying end to end. Corpses and a great, terrible day must not keep each from walking beside words or rectitude of heart. And we must forgive a word's lameness, for it was meant to be at sea, and the price of rest inside the shoe moving over the earth was hobbling.

On communion Sundays, I went with him after morning service on his rounds through the river valley. We performed the ritual eating with those of his congregation who were "shut-ins," those who never left their

490

houses, mainly old, infirm, crazy, or dying. In town, they lived in cramped rented rooms that smelled of boiled vegetables, moldy carpeting, and musty couch cushions. Outside of town, they were the ones inhabiting broken-shingled low houses set a few feet from the road, sometimes in a field alone or next to a rotten shed or the hulks of abandoned cars. Many of them were the same people I delivered food to once a week as a volunteer for Meals-on-Wheels, riding with two men sixty years old, an ex–coal miner and a security guard at the steel mill, in a station wagon carrying hot dinners to shut-ins.

> "We headed out after lunch, around one o'clock, and with luck we'd be able to make six visits."

While my father drove, I kept my hand on the square, black leather case between us. With a handle on the top, it bore one shiny clasp in the front which, undone, freed the lid and let the bifold front open outward, revealing inside the blue velvet interior and four small wooden tiers, each holding five brightly polished communion glasses no bigger than shot glasses.

We headed out after lunch, around one o' clock, and with luck we'd be able to make six visits. My father would have liked to do more in one day, but we couldn't plan on it, since the visits sometimes dragged, the shut-ins eager to keep in their chairs any infrequent guest. With that, and the time on the road in between, we usually got home no sooner than ten o'clock. For me it was a trial, and my favorite time was in the car on the road. We passed hills and pastures, snowy for miles, and watched the white day go gray. Trees stood like old gates on white knolls, and if the weather were warm a few days in a row, black creeks appeared in gullies and blue ravines. We saw deer at the edge of trees, and drove over furry, wind-riffled carcasses of raccoons and groundhogs. Sometimes the sky turned to snow and we slowed on blind descents.

The road out of town, a two-lane black macadam, wound past a whole hillside of graves. One spring, a heavy rain washed half the hill down onto the road along with a few of the buried inhabitants. Each time we drove by the cemetery, I looked up at the one monument which only I knew my father was thinking of when one Sunday he preached, saying: *The knight on the grave of a rich man weighs less upon sons than a father who requires walking on waves, buoyancy in time!* We drove along the graveyard's iron fence until we turned the bend and saw the huge back of the sign which we knew read *Welcome to Vandergrift.* Already I was sleepy and bored, but happy to be sitting next to my silent father. Some silences between us were tense, perennial tests. But my father's silences on Sunday afternoons, after the morning of preaching and public prayer, were relaxed and easy on both of us.

On Sundays, if we weren't making rounds, we were at home observing silence. At least twice a week, our family kept a whole afternoon of quiet, neither speaking nor whispering, my father, my mother, my sister, three brothers, and I keeping everything to ourselves in the one house of three floors of square rooms and identical doors. It was clarifying, the quiet, and our stillness felt like a deep liberty. It was one more detail of my life with my father which made me feel strange in a world which found my family strange, with our accented speech and permanent bewilderment at meatloaf.

In the car, the heater hummed and I read the list of names my father had written out earlier. We'd make the rural visits first, and start working our way back toward Vandergrift around six o'clock. By then, the sun would have already fallen and our ride grown darker by hours. We'd be heading into town from the other end, opposite the way we left, and my father, as was his habit, would choose roads unlit except by car headlights, in order to drive past an old brewery and the fenced grounds of the shut-down foundries, the steel mills half manned, and through empty downtowns of places called Truxall, Moween, Tintown, New Kensington, and Apollo, my father and I tired by then and him humming as we passed streets named for trees, Maple, Elm, and Oak, or Grant, Sherman, and Polk, the names of the dead.

But our last rural stop was Ethel Black's place. A few yards down the road from a truckers' bar, her house sat behind dense trees and next to a ditch exposing a clay pipe. The ruts were deep and icy in the driveway that wound right up to the back door. By now I was hungry, impatient, my feet freezing, and my trouser legs damp. My father smiled at me and said, "One more visit, in town, after this, then we'll have done a little good." A glum fourteen, I was not cheered.

The dilapidated house had a sagging back porch and buckled aluminum siding. A silver Christmas tree from two years ago leaned against the porch railing, the brown nest in its arms abandoned. Seeds were scattered for birds among stacks of newspapers, miscellaneous junk, a vacuum cleaner, some paint cans and loose bureau drawers. Mouse and rabbit droppings were all over boxes and a black pot sprouted some frozen yellow grass. We huffed through the wreckage, my father ahead, and me balancing in both hands the blood and fresh corpse of The Resurrected Man, as my father was fond of calling the one whose body we'd been swallowing all afternoon.

Beside a rickety utility shelf of dead potted daisies, the kitchen windowpane was broken and mended with duct tape and cardboard. My father rapped at the back door and walked in calling, "Mrs. Black?" Getting no answer, he raised his voice again, "Mrs. Black?" We walked through the cramped dingy kitchen lit by the illuminated clock over the stove. The place smelled of rotting garbage and my father pointed to bags of it in the corner, reminding me to take them out with us when we left. A mound of shit sat reeking on a newspaper in the rusty sink with a trickling faucet. The kitchen was a loosely heaped firetrap of blown-out pilots and fuses and hundreds of days of newspapers stacked on the stove and tabletop. The counters were cluttered with varying sizes of colored glass paperweights Ethel Black collected before she fell down and broke her hip ten years ago. Everywhere were ashtrays heaped with ashes and butts smoked by a fat, thirty-year-old, mentally handicapped "case" from the special education program who, trained as a geriatric aide, came as a visiting nurse twice a week to Ethel's house, and sat in the kitchen and listened to her transistor radio. It was a case of the helpless helping the worse off, the variously abandoned in their like abandonment.

The living-room curtains were drawn and an antique floor lamp glowed dimly in a corner with a crocheted shawl thrown over the dirty shade. And there on the sagging ruin of a green-and-yellow couch lay the frighteningly little bag of bones which was Ethel Black. Toothless, gape-mouthed, and bug-eyed, her head was thrown back and she stared at the ceiling as if at God, and you couldn't tell she wasn't a corpse until you heard her wheeze or she smacked her lips to wet them. Mrs. Ethel Black was in this condition for as long as I knew her. Sometimes she spit up sour-smelling water, on bad days she mumbled, "Help me. Help me. Help me," until you were ready to cry or scream, unless you learned to not listen. There was no other way but the latter if I would follow my father through house after house of similar suffering, room after room of a dying congregation.

Half hag, half child, half awake or asleep, she was wrapped up to the chin in six or seven tattered, gaudy-colored afghans. I sometimes wondered if she was conscious enough to even wish she were better off, wish she might be as lucky as Bernie Flick up the road. "At least Bernie can sit up," Constance the nurse has said, and it's true I've seen him sitting and talking to himself on his bed, which his children, all grown and with litters of kids, moved into the kitchen so Bernie could be in arm's reach of the refrigerator. Bernie slept by an oven, and had bad dandruff.

Mrs. Black's hair was a yellowish gray, as if she might have been blonde once, and she kept it in a long thick dry braid tied at the end with strands of different-colored yarn. It was strange to see such a decrepit body with so much hair. She squirmed a little under layers of musty quilt. I later found out her hands were tied to her body to prevent her from scratching herself, a nervous condition the otherwise rigid eighty-six-year-old lady had which left her skin open, raw, and infected. Looking at her, I heard my father's voice say, "Our god is surely an ironic god," though I knew it was all in my head, what I wished he would sometimes say, so I wouldn't be the only one thinking it.

When I was a boy I made, as children are apt to do, lists of everything, from names of islands to kinds of stars, Java to roses, which I mistook for stars, "the ones that don't shine in the night garden," from an old Chinese lyric my mother favored. I made lists of cars, chapters-by-heart, and lists of things my father never said to me, which included "Put 'er there, Son," and "Faith is all peril, every hour."

Nevertheless, I knew he thought it, what he'd never admit to me. And I see now his faith in his God was learning to winter-out those Pennsylvania winters and those hard communions. But if those communions were difficult, were they empty? was my continual question. Was my father wasting his time? Was he wasting his life? How was I supposed to feel about it? Even now, I feel either communion happened in that room, or my memories are crushed chalk to my tongue.

When my father preached between 1963 and 1964, on the island of Hong Kong, he drew crowds in such numbers that rows of folding chairs had to be set up in the very lobbies of the theaters where his revival meetings took place, while loudspeakers were set up outside, where throngs of sweating believers stood for hours in the sun, listening to him speak and pray.

Once, while my sister and I were buying sugarcane from our favorite street vendor, the afternoon suddenly filled with red and blue leaflets dropped from an airplane. My sister snatched one out of the air and the two of us looked at a picture of our father, under which was printed, in Chinese and English, the words *Your Friend*, and then the time and place of the next meeting of the Ling Liang Assembly and Ambassadors for Christ. I recognized the photograph as the same one my mother had taken of our father a little over a year ago on the boat from Indonesia to Hong Kong. His profile, taken by the camera from a lower angle, was backed by the sky and mast, perfect for the image of a helmsman or captain of souls. Only his family knew that when the photo was taken, we were on the way to a detention center. My father and his family were being shipped from one prison in Jakarta to another on some remote island, where, so we were told, we would be given a house and yard which we would not be permitted to leave. But on the way there, a former student of his from Gamaliel University pulled up alongside the ship with a smaller boat, so my parents assembled us in the night, and one stood above the other and handed to the one below, by hoisting over a railing, one by one, each of their five children. The two boats, big and small, rocked unevenly, the gap between them closing and widening, yet less dangerous than a guard asleep somewhere, or else awake but turned away to earn my father's bribe. By the next morning we were in the home of a congregation member of the Ling Liang Assembly. It was during one of the evening revival meetings, when members from the congregation gave personal testimonies of the working hand of God, that my father, convinced we had escaped harm due to some miracle and for some higher purpose, recounted the horrors of the last three years fleeing Sukarno and our rescue. Within a year of that testimony, he was performing mass baptisms in the ocean at night. Hundreds gathered once a month on the beach to watch my father take off his silk suit jacket, his narrow leather shoes and silk socks, roll up his sleeves and wade out into the dark water, from where we could hear him beckoning, *Come! Come to me, come farther, don't be afraid.* And one by one he embraced them and plunged them backward into the surf.

Many years later in the United States, and nearly five years after my father had died, I was eating with my family in a Chinese restaurant in the South Side of Chicago when we discovered through a friendly conversation with the proprietor that he and his wife had been great fans of my father, and had left the Ambassadors for Christ after my father left Hong Kong. The man recollected our father's first testimony and remembered sermons he found particularly memorable. He recounted to us our own story as though it were someone else's: the narrow escape, the faked names, the path to freedom and God. I was filled with a mixture of sadness and disgust, even shame. He sat with us and drank cup after cup of green tea, he and my mother weeping.

Why did I feel disgust? The facts were plain enough, and my father told them plainly, and the man remembered them accurately, to all of our astonishment. And it didn't bother me much that my father or this man attributed so much to a divine hand. I too believe that we are, all of us, for the most part, carried by something beyond us. And though I'd argue emphatically about this or that aspect of God with my father, that wasn't what bothered me when I heard that man in the restaurant talk, good man that he was, kind that he was, a fellow immigrant, as lost in America as we were. Part of me felt such confusion and anger I was almost ready to disavow everything. Why? What makes a person want to disavow his own life? What did I feel so uneasy about? What was it I felt I needed to tell that man? What little detail did I need to give him, to explain he'd got it all wrong? What irked me? Why don't my shoes fit?

When I was six and learning to speak English, I talked with an accent anyone could hear, and I noticed early on that all accents were not heard alike by the dominant population of American English speakers. Instead, each foreigner's spoken English, determined by a mother tongue, each person's noise, fell on a coloring ear, which bent the listener's eye and, consequently, the speaker's countenance; it was a kind of narrowing, and unconscious on the part of the listener, who listens in judgment, judging the speaker even before the meaning or its soundness were attended to. While some sounds were tolerated, some even granting the speaker a certain status in the instances of, say, French or British, other inflections condemned one to immediate alien, as though our gods were toys, our names disheveled silverware, and the gamelan just gonging backward. And I could clearly hear each time I opened my mouth the discord there, the wrong sounds, the strange, unmanageable sharps and flats of my vowels and my chewed-up consonants. What an uncomely noise. More than once I was told I sounded ugly. My mouth was a shame to me, an indecent trench. A recurring dream of mine as a boy who'd just arrived on the continent with my parents was my mouth full of rotten teeth, hundreds of teeth in my mouth and all of them cavity-ridden, brown, chips of burnt bone embedded in my gums. I still remember the feeling of being asked a question in English and, after a brief moment of panic, starting to move my lips, contort my tongue to make the sounds, and opening my mouth nervously to answer, too shy to move my hands to help and make the point, only hoping I made sense to my American listeners, teacher or schoolmate, who were sometimes patient, but whose ears were more often so baffled by my confounded din, they winced in annoyance and asked, *What did you say?* or, turning to someone else in complete exasperation, *What did he say?*

I'm thinking of that now because my sons have just made a new friend, a Chinese boy, seven years old, who lives two houses up the street with his parents, uncles, aunts, cousins, and a grandmother, much the same way we live. I speak to him in Mandarin, but he tells me he doesn't speak Chinese, which I take to mean he doesn't speak the same dialect as me. He says this in English and as he speaks, as he struggles to make the very sounds, lowering his head and mumbling like a whipped boy, fingering his lower lip, I am suddenly returned to my own early attempts at making American sounds, and I remember my own deliberate slurring and mumbling in order to hide my mouth, to make my accent less discernible. I want to move my mouth with his, and I don't know if I want to tell him, *Don't worry, the accent wears off, no one will know you're an alien then,* or tell him how I sometimes miss my own sound. I remember how I used to hold a hand very casually over my mouth when I talked, hoping to hide the alien thing. And I grew to hate its ugliness more than anyone. It hurt my ear and I avoided as much as possible any contact with native English speakers. In their company, I said as little as possible, and over the years made no friends who didn't come from the apartments across the alley from us in East Liberty, Pennsylvania. Large families lived there, people like us, foreigners, and most of the men, like my father, were students at the Pittsburgh Theological Seminary, behind whose parking lot we lived in a big, old, falling-down, drafty, and, to my mind, beautiful house. From India, Hong Kong, Rhodesia, Chile, Taiwan, and Mexico, our neighbors' versions of English were as strangely inflected and accented as our own. The result was that while in Chinese, with my family, I rattled like any good loose child about anything at all, and spoke my broken English without embarrassment with the children on Hoevler Street, in public school or any other place where fluent English was current, I was dumb. Perceived as feeble-minded, I was, like my siblings, spoken to very loudly, as though the problem were deafness. But I was happy, content to talk to no one outside of the world defined by one alley and an empty lot of dirt where my sister and brothers, Fei, Go, and Be, and I played with the others called Raja, Baba, Yijan, and Gee, in every season, from 1964 until our father graduated three years later.

In Mrs. Black's house we kept our coats on. The room was cold. Ice formed on the glass of the paper-stuffed windows, and a stiff draft came from the chilly hallway. My father picked up from the floor a rough-knitted cap which must have slipped off the old lady. He gently slipped it back over her head.

"Hello, Mrs. Black," he said very loudly, for she was hard of hearing.

"Huh?" the woman answered.

"We could have come to rob her, which happened to many old people like her."

"Good afternoon, Mrs. Black," my father said, leaning close to her ear. "We're here to give you your communion." Then he told me to get two chairs from the kitchen and we set them up next to her couch.

She smelled terrible, had obviously soiled herself, and was half crazed, mumbling about fire under her bed or someone stealing her money. She was completely unaware of what my father and I were doing there. We could have come to rob her, which happened to many old people like her. She seemed vaguely to remember me, so I leaned over to her and called out, "Mrs. Black? Remember me? I was here yesterday."

A look came over her of complete wonder. "You remember me, boy?" she rasped. She spoke her words loud and every word with equal emphasis, so that her phrases sounded robotlike to me, or like chanting, rather than regular speech. The words didn't sound spoken to anyone.

I said, "I'm Reverend Lee's son. Remember? I was here yesterday. We talked. I came with Harry Porter. Remember? Harry says hello, says he'll be out this week to read to you."

"Is it time to go?" she asked, and then, "Who? You read to me? Is it time to go? Shoes. Where are my shoes?"

"Not this minute, Mrs. Black. We'll have communion together first."

"You read to me?" she asked, turning to my father.

"Yes, Mrs. Black, we'll read."

"Pray for me, Parson," she said.

"I pray for you each day, Mrs. Black. You are in my prayers."

"Pray for me, Parson," she repeated in exactly the same tone.

I had just been there yesterday to deliver her evening meal. Untouched, the tray sat where I left it yesterday on the television. Constance was supposed to come and feed her shortly after I left. Either she had not come, or Mrs. Black had refused to eat. My father told me to examine the tray to see if it looked as if the plastic wrap had even been opened. It had not. He made a note and I knew he would have to telephone the visiting nurse service which Mrs. Black's children, who lived far away, were paying for. He would also have to find a member of the congregation who could give up time to visit Mrs. Black to make sure she was getting her basic needs met until a reliable nurse could be found.

I opened the leather box, poured the grape, and my father broke a saltine cracker in a silver plate, said blessings, and laid a piece of the broken cracker in Mrs. Black's mouth, and very carefully held the glass thimble of dark juice to her lips and slowly poured. Then he blessed our portions, which he and I consumed in silence, and blessed our small cups, which we drained. In the car, my father drove and I read the list of names of the people we had seen and the ones we had yet to see. We would not be able to visit all of them today. After one more visit in town, the rest would have to wait until tomorrow for their communion. All of them were the "other" members of my father's congregation, the ones no one ever saw, who couldn't attend services or any of the social functions held at church. Though their names were on the registry, though they were counted, they mostly lived uncounted, discarded lives. Their existence always seemed tangential to other lives. Mrs. Black, for instance, had six children and countless grandchildren, but none of them could get along or even live in the same county without one stabbing another or beating his kin with a lead pipe. So the old woman was left in the charge of a distant cousin, who handed her over to a friend's daughter, who in exchange for room and board nursed her, only to later abandon the old lady.

Maya Lin

Between Art and Architecture

Maya Lin is an architect. She is Chinese American, raised in Ohio; she studied architecture at Yale. As a twenty-one-year-old student, she won a blind design competition for the national Vietnam Veterans Memorial in Washington, D.C.; it is her best-known work. This monument is a striking achievement that reflects the artistic philosophy expressed in her question: "What if you were to think of a place not as a still, fixed point in time, but rather as a moving, fluid site?" The essay we have included recounts controversies that ensued during and after the monument's construction.

Lin's other designs include the Civil Rights Museum in Montgomery, Alabama, and Wave Field at the University of Michigan. She is currently working on the Confluence Project, a series of outdoor installations at historical points along the Columbia River and Snake River. She served on the committee that selected the design for the reconstructed World Trade Center. She wrote: "In all my work I have tried to create works that present you with information allowing you the chance to come to your own conclusions; they ask you to think."

In *Metropolis* magazine, Christopher Hawthorne said of Lin's *Boundaries* (2000): "The book, which explores the increasingly hybrid nature of Lin's career, is itself something of a hybrid. It is not a scholarly text, not a memoir, not a flashy vanity project, but it has elements of all three genres. Until now Lin has been reluctant to talk about the controversy that surrounded the construction of the Vietnam Memorial. . . . Even discussing the purely aesthetic aspects of the design has seemed an ordeal. Now, nearly twenty years later, some of that infamous resistance has melted away." The essay that follows is drawn from this book.

Maya Lin lives and works in New York and Colorado.

I think the most important aspect of the design of the *Vietnam Veterans Memorial* was that I had originally designed it for a class I was taking at Yale and not for the competition. In that sense, I had designed it for me — or, more exactly, for what I believed it should be. I never tried to second-guess a jury. And it wasn't until after I had completed the design that I decided to enter it in the competition.

The design emerged from an architectural seminar I was taking during my senior year. The initial idea of a memorial had come from a notice posted at the school announcing a competition for a Vietnam veterans memorial. The class, which was on funereal architecture, had spent the semester studying how people, through the built form, express their attitudes on death. As a class, we thought the memorial was an appropriate design idea for our program, so we adopted it as our final design project.

At that point, not much was known about the actual competition, so for the first half of the assignment we were left without concrete directions as to what "they" were looking for or even who "they" were. Instead, we had to determine for ourselves what a Vietnam memorial should be. Since a previous project had been to design a memorial for World War III, I had already begun to ask the simple questions: What exactly is a memorial? What should it do?

My design for a World War III memorial was a tomblike underground structure that I deliberately made to be a very futile and frustrating experience. I remember the professor of the class, Andrus Burr, coming up to me afterward, saying quite angrily, "If I had a brother who died in that war, I would never want to visit this memorial." I was somewhat puzzled that he didn't quite understand that World War III would be of such devastation that none of us would be around to visit any memorial, and that my design was instead a prewar commentary. In asking myself what a memorial to a third world war would be, I came up with a political statement that was meant as a deterrent.

I had studied earlier monuments and memorials while designing that memorial and I continued this research for the design of the Vietnam memorial. As I did more research on monuments, I realized most carried larger, more general messages about a leader's victory or accomplishments rather than the lives lost. In fact, at the national level, individual lives were very seldom dealt with, until you arrived at the memorials for World War I. Many of these memorials included the names of those killed. Partly it was a practical need to list those whose bodies could not be identified—since dog tags as identification had not yet been adopted and, due to the nature of the warfare, many killed were not identifiable— but I think as well the listing of names reflected a response by these designers to the horrors of World War I, to the immense loss of life.

The images of these monuments were extremely moving. They captured emotionally what I felt memorials should be: honest about the reality of war, about the loss of life in war, and about remembering those who served and especially those who died.

I made a conscious decision not to do any specific research on the Vietnam War and the political turmoil surrounding it. I felt that the politics had eclipsed the veterans, their service and their lives. I wanted to create a memorial that everyone would be able to respond to, regardless of whether one thought our country should or should not have participated in the war. The power of a name was very much with me at the time, partly because of the Memorial Rotunda at Yale. In Woolsey Hall, the walls are inscribed with the names of all the Yale alumni who have been killed in wars. I had never been able to resist touching the names cut into these marble walls, and no matter how busy or crowded the place is, a sense of quiet, a reverence, always surrounds those names. Throughout my freshman and sophomore years, the stonecutters were carving in by hand the names of those killed in the Vietnam War, and I think it left a lasting impression on me . . . the sense of the power of a name.

One memorial I came across also made a strong impression on me. It was a monument to the missing soldiers of the World War I battle of the Somme by Sir Edwin Lutyens in Thiepval, France. The monument includes more than 100,000 names of people who were listed as missing because, without ID tags, it was impossible to identify the dead. (The cemetery contains the bodies of 70,000 dead.) To walk past those names and realize those lost lives—the effect of that is the strength of the design. This memorial acknowl-edged those lives without focusing on the war or on creating a political statement of victory or loss. This apolitical approach became the essential aim of my design; I did not want to civilize war by glorifying it or by for-getting the sacrifices involved. The price of human life in war should al-ways be clearly remembered.

> "I did not want to civilize war by glorifying it or by forgetting the sacrifices involved."

But on a personal level, I wanted to focus on the nature of accepting and coming to terms with a loved one's death. Simple as it may seem, I re-member feeling that accepting a person's death is the first step in being able to overcome that loss.

I felt that as a culture we were extremely youth-oriented and not will-ing or able to accept death or dying as a part of life. The rites of mourn-ing, which in more primitive and older cultures were very much a part of life, have been suppressed in our modern times. In the design of the memorial, a fundamental goal was to be honest about death, since we must accept that loss in order to begin to overcome it. The pain of the loss will always be there, it will always hurt, but we must acknowledge the death in order to move on.

What then would bring back the memory of a person? A specific object or image would be limiting. A realistic sculpture would be only one interpretation of that time. I wanted something that all people could relate to on a personal level. At this time I had as yet no form, no specific artistic image.

The use of names was a way to bring back everything someone could remember about a person. The strength in a name is something that has always made me wonder at the "abstraction" of the design; the ability of a name to bring back every single memory you have of that person is far more realistic and specific and much more comprehensive than a still photograph, which captures a specific moment in time or a single event or a generalized image that may or may not be moving for all who have con-nections to that time.

Then someone in the class received the design program, which stated the basic philosophy of the memorial's design and also its requirements:

all the names of those missing and killed (57,000) must be a part of the memorial; the design must be apolitical, harmonious with the site, and conciliatory.

These were all the thoughts that were in my mind before I went to see the site.

Without having seen it, I couldn't design the memorial, so a few of us traveled to Washington, D.C., and it was at the site that the idea for the design took shape. The site was a beautiful park surrounded by trees, with traffic and noise coming from one side—Constitution Avenue.

I had a simple impulse to cut into the earth.

I imagined taking a knife and cutting into the earth, opening it up, an initial violence and pain that in time would heal. The grass would grow back, but the initial cut would remain a pure flat surface in the earth with a polished, mirrored surface, much like the surface on a geode when you cut it and polish the edge. The need for the names to be on the memorial would become the memorial; there was no need to embellish the design further. The people and their names would allow everyone to respond and remember.

It would be an interface, between our world and the quieter, darker, more peaceful world beyond. I chose black granite in order to make the surface reflective and peaceful. I never looked at the memorial as a wall, an object, but as an edge to the earth, an opened side. The mirrored effect would double the size of the park, creating two worlds, one we are a part of and one we cannot enter. The two walls were positioned so that one pointed to the Lincoln Memorial and the other pointed to the Washington Monument. By linking these two strong symbols for the country, I wanted to create a unity between the nation's past and present.

The idea of destroying the park to create something that by its very nature should commemorate life seemed hypocritical, nor was it in my nature. I wanted my design to work with the land, to make something with the site, not to fight it or dominate it. I see my works and their relationship to the landscape as being an additive rather than a combative process.

On our return to Yale, I quickly sketched my idea up, and it almost seemed too simple, too little. I toyed with adding some large flat slabs that would appear to lead into the memorial, but they didn't belong. The image was so simple that anything added to it began to detract from it.

I always wanted the names to be chronological, to make it so that those who served and returned from the war could find their place in the memorial. I initially had the names beginning on the left side and ending on the right. In a preliminary critique, a professor asked what importance that left for the apex, and I, too, thought it was a weak point, so I changed the design for the final critique. Now the chronological sequence began and ended at the apex so that the time line would circle back to itself and close the sequence. A progression in time is memorialized. The design is not just a list of the dead. To find one name, chances are you will see the others close by, and you will see yourself reflected through them.

The memorial was designed before I decided to enter the competition. I didn't even consider that it might win. When I submitted the project, I had the greatest difficulty trying to describe it in just one page. It took longer, in fact, to write the statement that I felt was needed to accompany the required drawings than to design the memorial. The description was critical to understanding the design since the memorial worked more on an emotional level than a formal level.

Coincidentally, at the time, I was taking a course with Professor Vincent Scully, in which he just happened to focus on the same memorial I had been so moved by—the Lutyens memorial to the missing. Professor Scully described one's experience of that piece as a passage or journey through a yawning archway. As he described it, it resembled a gaping scream, which after you passed through, you were left looking out on a simple graveyard with the crosses and tombstones of the French and the English. It was a journey to an awareness of immeasurable loss, with the names of the missing carved on every surface of this immense archway.

I started writing furiously in Scully's class. I think he has always been puzzled by my connection to the Lutyens memorial. Formally the two memorials could not be more different. But for me, the experiences of these two memorials describe a similar passage to an awareness about loss.

The competition required drawings, along with the option to include a written description. As the deadline for submission approached, I created a series of simple drawings. The only thing left was to complete the essay, which I instinctively knew was the only way to get anyone to understand the design, the form of which was deceptively simple. I kept reworking and reediting the final description. I actually never quite finished it. I ended up at the last minute writing freehand directly onto the presentation boards (you can see a few misprints on the actual page), and then I sent the project in, never expecting to hear about it again.

The drawings were in soft pastels, very mysterious, very painterly, and not at all typical of architectural drawings. One of the comments made by a juror was "*He* must really know what he is doing to dare to do something so naive" (italics mine). But ultimately, I think it was the written description that convinced the jurors to select my design.

On my last day of classes my roommate, Liz Perry, came to retrieve me from one of my classes, telling me a call from Washington had come in and that it was from the *Vietnam Veterans Memorial* Fund; they needed to talk to me and would call back with a few questions about the design. When they called back, they merely said they needed to ask me a few questions and wanted to fly up to New Haven to talk to me. I was convinced that I was number 100 and they were only going to question me about drainage and other technical issues. It never occurred to me that I might have won the competition. It was still, in my mind, an exercise— as competitions customarily are for architecture students.

And even after three officers of the fund were seated in my college dorm room, explaining to me that it was the largest competition of its kind, with more than fourteen hundred entries, and Colonel Schaet, who was talking, without missing a beat calmly added that I had won (I think my roommate's face showed more emotion than mine did at the time), it still hadn't registered. I don't think it did for almost a year. Having studied the nature of competitions, especially in Washington (for instance, the FDR Memorial, still unbuilt in 1981, nearly forty years after it was first proposed, or the artwork Robert Venturi and Richard Serra collaborated on for L'Enfant Plaza, which was completely modified as it went through the required Washington design process of approvals), my attitude about unusual projects getting built in Washington was not optimistic. Partly it's my nature—I never get my hopes up—and partly I assumed the simplicity of the design, and its atypical form and color, would afford it a difficult time through the various governmental-approval agencies.

After the design had been chosen, it was subject to approval by vari- ous governmental agencies at both the conceptual and design development phases. I moved to Washington and stayed there throughout these phases. I expected the design to be debated within the design-approval agencies; I never expected the politics that constantly surrounded its development and fabrication.

I was driven down to D.C. the day of my college graduation, and I immediately became part of an internal struggle for control of the design. I think my age made it seem apparent to some that I was too young to un- derstand what I had done or to see it through to completion. To bring the design into reality would require that I associate with an architect of record, a qualified firm that would work with me to realize the design. I had a very difficult time convincing the fund in charge of the memorial, the VVMF, of the importance of selecting a qualified firm that had expe- rience both in architecture and landscape-integrated solutions, and that would be sympathetic to the design.

I had gone to Cesar Pelli, then dean of Yale's School of Architecture, for the names of some firms that could handle the job. A firm by the name of Cooper-Lecky was the one he recommended, and I presented its name to the fund, unaware that the competition's adviser was the fund's choice as architect of record. I was told by the fund that this person was the architect of record, and that was that.

After a few weeks of tense and hostile negotiations (in which at one point I was warned that I would regret these actions, and that I would "come crawling back on my hands and knees"), I was finally able to convince the fund to go through a legitimate process of selecting a firm to become the architect of record. The then architecture critic for the *Washington Post*, Wolf Von Eckardt, was instrumental in pressing the fund to listen to me. But the struggle left a considerable amount of ill will and mistrust between the veterans and myself.

Through the remaining phases of the project I worked with the Cooper-Lecky architectural firm. We worked on the practical details of the design, from the addition of a safety curb to a sidewalk to the problems in inscribing the names. Many of the issues we dealt with were connected to the text and my decision to list the names chronologically. People felt it would be an inconvenience to have to search out a name in a book and then find its panel location and thought that an alphabetical listing would be more convenient—until a tally of how many Smiths had died made it clear that an alphabetical listing wouldn't be feasible. The MIA groups wanted their list of the missing separated out and listed alphabetically. I knew this would break the strength of the time line, interrupting the real-time experience of the piece, so I fought hard to maintain the chronological listing. I ended up convincing the groups that the time in which an individual was noted as missing was the emotionally compelling time for family members. A system of noting these names with a symbol[1] that could be modified to signify if the veteran was later found alive or officially declared dead would appease the concerns of the MIA groups without breaking the time line. I knew the time line was key to the experience of the memorial: a returning veteran would be able to find his or her time of service when finding a friend's name.

The text of the memorial and the fact that I had left out everything except the names led to a fight as to what else needed to be said about the war. The apex is the memorial's strongest point; I argued against the addition of text at that point for fear that a politically charged statement, one that would force a specific reading, would destroy the apolitical nature of the design. Throughout this time I was very careful not to discuss my beliefs in terms of politics; I played it extremely naive about politics, instead turning the issue into a strictly aesthetic one. Text could be added, but whatever was said needed to fit in three lines—to match the height of the dates "1959" and "1975" that it would be adjacent to. The veterans approved this graphic parameter, and the statements became a simple prologue and epilogue.

The memorial is analogous to a book in many ways. Note that on the right-hand panels the pages are set ragged right and on the left they are set ragged left, creating a spine at the apex as in a book. Another issue was scale; the text type is the smallest that we had come across, less than half an inch, which is unheard of in monument type sizing. What it does is create a very intimate reading in a very public space, the difference in intimacy between reading a billboard and reading a book.

---

[1]Each name is preceded (on the west wall) or followed (on the east wall) by one of two symbols: a diamond or a cross. The diamond denotes that the serviceman's or service-woman's death was confirmed. The cross symbolizes those who were missing in action or prisoners at the end of the war. When a serviceperson's remains were returned, the diamond symbol is superimposed over the cross. If a serviceman or woman returns alive, a circle will be inscribed around the cross.

The only other issue was the polished black granite and how it should be detailed, over which I remember having a few arguments with the architects of record. The architects could not understand my choice of a reflective, highly polished black granite. One of them felt I was making a mistake and the polished surface would be "too *feminine.*" Also puzzling to them was my choice of detailing the monument as a thin veneer with barely any thickness at its top edge. They wanted to make the monument's walls read as a massive, thick stone wall, which was not my intention at all. I always saw the wall as pure surface, an interface between light and dark, where I cut the earth and polished its open edge. The wall dematerializes as a form and allows the names to become the object, a pure and reflective surface that would allow visitors the chance to see themselves with the names. I do not think I thought of the color black as a color, more as the idea of a dark mirror into a shadowed mirrored image of the space, a space we cannot enter and from which the names separate us, an interface between the world of the living and the world of the dead.

One aspect that made the project unusual was its politicized building process. For instance, the granite could not come from Canada or Sweden. Though those countries had beautiful black granites, draft evaders went to both countries, so the veterans felt that we could not consider their granites as options. (The stone finally selected came from India.) The actual building process went smoothly for the most part, and the memorial was built very close to my original intentions.

"I was so righteous in my response that my race was completely irrelevant."

As far as all of the controversy, I really never wanted to go into it too much. The memorial's starkness, its being below grade, being black, and how much my age, gender, and race played a part in the controversy, we'll never quite know. I think it is actually a miracle that the piece ever got built. From the very beginning I often wondered, If it had not been anonymous entry 1026 but rather an entry by Maya Lin, would I have been selected?

I remember at the very first press conference a reporter asking me if I did not find it ironic that the memorial was for the Vietnam War and that I was of Asian descent. I was so righteous in my response that my race was completely irrelevant. It took me almost nine months to ask the VVMF, in charge of building the memorial, if my race was at all an issue. It had never occurred to me that it would be, and I think they had taken all the measures they could to shield me from such comments about a "gook" designing the memorial.

I remember reading the article that appeared in the *Washington Post* referring to "An Asian Memorial for an Asian War" and I knew we were in trouble. The controversy exploded in Washington after that article. Ironically, one side attacked the design for being "too Asian," while others saw its simplicity and understatement not as an intention to create a more Eastern, meditative space, but as a minimalist statement which they interpreted as being non-referential and disconnected from human experience.

This left the opinion in many that the piece emanated from a series of intellectualized aesthetic decisions, which automatically pitted artist against veterans. The fact that I was from an Ivy League college, had hair down to my knees, further fueled this distrust of the design and suspicions of a hippie college liberal or aesthetic elitist forcing her art and commentary upon them.

Perhaps it was an empathetic response to the idea about war that had led me to cut open the earth—an initial violence that heals in time but leaves a memory, like a scar. But this imagery, which some detractors would later describe as "a black gash of shame and sorrow" in which the color black was called the "universal color of shame and dishonor," would prove incredibly difficult to defend. The misreading of the design as a negative political statement that in some way was meant to reflect upon the service of the veterans was in part fueled by a cultural prejudice against the color black as well as by the misreading or misinformation that led some veterans to imagine the design as a ditch or a hole. It took a prominent four-star general, Brigadier General George Price, who happened to be black, testifying before one of the countless subcommittee hearings and defending the color black, before the design could move forward.

But the distrust, the fact that no veterans had been on the jury, the unconventionality of the design and the designer, and a very radical requirement made by the Vietnam veterans to include all the names of those killed made it inevitable that the project would become controversial. I think ultimately that much of the negative response goes back to the very natural response to cover up or not acknowledge that which is painful or unpleasant. The very fact that the veterans themselves had required the listing and therefore the acknowledgment of the more than 57,000 casualties, which is a landmark in our country in terms of seeing a war via the individual lives lost, was very hard for many to face. I remember Ross Perot when he was trying to persuade the veterans that it was an inappropriate design, asking me if I truly didn't feel that the veterans would prefer a parade instead, something happy or uplifting, and I can remember thinking that a parade would not in the long term help them overcome the enormous trauma of the politics of that war.

I do not think I fully realized until the dedication and homecoming parade that the veterans needed both. In effect the veterans gave themselves their own homecoming. In November 1982, I was in tears watching these men welcoming themselves home after almost ten years of not being acknowledged by their country for their service, their sacrifice.

But until the memorial was built I don't think they realized that the design was experiential and cathartic, and, most importantly, designed not for me, but for them. They didn't see that the chronology of the names allowed a returning veteran the ability to find his or her own time frame on the wall and created a psychological space for them that directly focused on human response and feeling. I remember one of the veterans asking me before the wall was built what I thought people's reaction would be to it. I realized then that these veterans were willing to defend a design they really didn't quite understand. I was too afraid to tell him what I was thinking, that I knew a returning veteran would cry.

An architect once told me to look always at what was originally envisioned and try to keep it. I left Washington before ground breaking. I had to. The fund and I knew that we had to accept a compromise. The closer you watch something grow, the less able you are to notice changes in it. When I saw the site again, the granite panels were being put up and the place was frighteningly close to what I thought it should be. It terrified me. It was a strange feeling, to have had an idea that was solely yours be no longer a part of your mind but totally public, no longer yours.

There was always the expectation that since the war had been controversial, the memorial must be also. It wasn't so much an artistic dispute as a political one. The choice to make an apolitical memorial was in itself political to those who felt only a positive statement about the war would make up for the earlier antiwar days, a past swing to the left now to be balanced. It was extremely naive of me to think that I could produce a neutral statement that would not become politically controversial simply because it chose not to take sides.

Anyway, the push, as one congressman put it, to "politicize" the design didn't really affect the memorial in this way. The addition of the statue of infantrymen and then the addition of the female statue to make them equal are to me sad indicators that some politicians believe that you can please all of the people all of the time by compromise and conglomerate works. These statues leave only the false reading that the wall is for the dead and they are for the living, when the design I made was for the returning veterans and equally names all who served regardless of race, creed, or sex. I am only glad that the three infantrymen are not where they had been originally intended, right in the center of the memorial, heads sticking up higher than the walls, converting the walls to a backdrop and violating that private contemplative space. Ironically, the compromise memorializes the conflict in the building of the piece.

People cannot resolve that war, nor can they separate the issues, the politics, from it. As for me, the first time I visited the memorial after it was completed I found myself searching out the name of a friend's father and touching it. It was strange to realize that I was another visitor and I was reacting to it as I had designed it.

Paul Lisicky

New World

Paul Lisicky's books include *Lawnboy* (1999), a novel, and *Famous Builder* (2002), a memoir, from which we take the following selection. A graduate of the Iowa Writers' Workshop, Lisicky has been awarded fellowships from the National Endowment for the Arts, the James Michener/Copernicus Society, the Henfield Foundation, the New Jersey State Council on the Arts, and the Fine Arts Work Center in Provincetown, where he was twice a Winter Fellow. He has taught at Cornell University, New York University, Sarah Lawrence College, Antioch University, and the University of Houston, and is a member of the writing committee of the Fine Arts Work Center in Provincetown.

Lisicky's memoir *Famous Builder* was widely reviewed: "What sets this memoir apart is the lyricism, humor, and refreshing candor with which [Lisicky] describes his life" (*Library Journal*); "The warmth of the reflections and the steady pulse of humor suggest that Lisicky wasn't an unhappy boy or an unobservant one. . . . *Famous Builder* shows the . . . urge to grapple and illuminate" (*Kirkus Reviews*); "Not your average gay memoir" (the *Washington Blade*); "The appearance of a writer like Paul Lisicky—a writer who deeply respects the complexities of love and desire, who can find tragedy and transcendence almost everywhere he looks—is a rare event" (author Michael Cunningham).

In an interview, Lisicky said, "I love to make people laugh; I love to be with people who make me laugh. I hope that the humor helps to bridge the gap between the speaker and the reader, to create intimacy. Imagine a late night where you're sitting across the kitchen table from your best friend. You've had a few glasses of wine, and you've found yourself laughing over your most humiliating stories. That's how I'd like the book to make you feel."

Paul Lisicky divides his time between New York City and Fire Island Pines, New York. A new novel, *Lumina Harbor*, is forthcoming. See his Web site at www.paullisicky.com.

Interview with Paul Lisicky, p. 533.

My father won't sit still. He walks to the sliding glass door, stares out at the lagoon. He paces the bare tile floors of our summerhouse with a solemn, abstracted expression. His footsteps shake the rafters, shake us to the root. He stands in the kitchen, pulls out a sheet of paper, and writes a To Do list in his firm cursive:

—New tailpipe for station wagon
—New roof shingles

—Sprinkler system
—Spotlights
—Wire burglar alarm
—Pump out crawl space
—Jack up porch slab
—Jalousie windows for porch
—Pour concrete sidewalk
—Pour concrete driveway
—Pour concrete patio
—Creosote bulkhead
—Build outdoor shower enclosure
—Curbs?

The raft, however, rises to the top of the list. The orange foam beneath it has lost its buoyancy after two years in saltwater. "We should have bought the good stuff," he says, shaking his head. "They saw us coming." It doesn't seem to faze him that it's ninety-two degrees, the Friday before Fourth-of-July weekend. We trudge outside behind him. Two houses down the Sendrow girls lie facedown on their towels, the backs of their legs basted with Bain de Soleil. Next door Mr. Forte and his friend Fisher, just back from the Inlet, clean flounder, wrap soft filets in aluminum foil. Perspiration creeps through my hair. I touch my scalp just to make sure it's not . . . beetles? My father kneels below us on the raft, fastening the rope to a pitted ring in the corner. Bobby and I stand on top of the bulkhead. Soon enough he jumps up beside us and the three of us pull and strain with all our might. The veins in my neck thicken. I'm not even sure my exertions affect anything: I'm thirteen years old, my arms thick as drinking straws. Although Bobby is stronger, he's not doing much better. Still, just as the rope skins the flesh of my palms, just as I'm ready to let go, to say aloud that we're a doomed, foolish family giving ourselves over to chores we can't possibly complete—why can't we ever *hire* somebody?—we manage to get the wooden behemoth up onto the grass, turning it over on its back. The three of us suck in our breaths. Its underside is encrusted with the physical symbols of shame: greasy mussels, prehistoric white barnacles, and rich green seaweed. The foam has faded to a bleached pink. Exposed to sunlight, it smells like an emptied can of fish chowder.

"Holy Mackerel," says Mr. Forte, who walks over to get a look.

I lie on the grass, breathing, breathing, listening to my beating heart. My eyes follow the tiny plane towing an advertising banner overhead: FOR SUNBURN PAIN TRY SOLARCAINE. Its engine putters, then fades. My father and Bobby sit off to the side, their brows sweaty, their faces the russet of our brick patio. (What does *my* face look like? Surely, they've been responsible for most of the hefting.) Only after my heart has stilled, only after I've made a reasonable demonstration of my willingness to help, do I rise to my feet and brush off the loose grass blades sticking to the backs of my legs.

"I have to pee," I declare.

Inside, I walk past my mother, close the bathroom door, and sit on the cool tile floor. How good it feels to be by myself, to be silent, to be still again. A tingling comes back into the tips of my fingers. I'm no longer part of the larger body of my father and my family, but I'm my own body again. There is a splinter buried in the heel of my hand, which I squeeze till I wince. Things are happening inside my head. One minute I work on a new song, which I'm planning to send to the producers of *The Partridge Family*, the next I think about the street names in Cambridge Park, a development under construction near our house in Cherry Hill. Everyone who knows me knows that I want to be a builder, a famous builder, like Bill Levitt, when I'm older. I want those who drive through my communities to be socked in the head with the sheer beauty of all they see.

"His tone says it all: I'm not serious or helpful, I have a deep, self-absorbed streak."

I huddle in the coolish bathroom and murmur, moving my lips as if I'm reciting the rosary: *Pageant Lane, Pennypacker Drive, Poppy Turn, Pershing Lane.*

Footsteps heavy on the living-room floor. I rumble the toilet-paper roll, throw the unused sheets in the trash, then flush.

"Where's Paul?" my father asks gravely.

His tone says it all: I'm not serious or helpful, I have a deep, self-absorbed streak. There's a heat in my stomach, a small contraction. My mother stirs a boiling pot on the other side of the wall and makes macaroni salad for lunch.

"He's in the bathroom."

I slip out into the back hall, where I grab a broom and pretend to sweep the floor around the water heater. (His usual expression every time he catches us at rest: "What are you doing, sitting around with your teeth in your mouth?" Or worse: "CLEAN UP THIS PLACE!")

Beach sand flies up against the laundry tub, pinging.

"I need your help," says my father. He's taken off his shirt. He looks down at his nicked, bleeding hands.

"But I thought we were done."

"Done?" he says, with a soft incredulousness. *"Done?"*

I follow him out to the dock, attempting to mask my disappointment, but my face has fallen for sure. Certainly I want to help. Certainly I want to be a good boy, a generous, benevolent, dutiful son, but I want to be *myself*, too. I don't understand why we don't get to fix up our house and make things of beauty like our neighbors: the Foxes' wooden Japanese bridge, the Moores' garden of herbs and wildflowers. Even worse, why is it that we never finish anything? Although we'll work on the raft every Saturday for the rest of the summer (replacing the top boards with fresh lumber, shining the rusty bolts), it will sit on the lawn for two years until the boards silver, until the grass dies in a gray-brown rectangle beneath it.

* * *

Just as soon as our car has climbed the mountain, we go down, down into the heart of Allentown, home to all my cousins, home to more Lisickys per capita than any other place outside Slovakia. From our vantage point it twinkles with thousands of lights through a scrim of flurries, a landscape with the quality of a Brothers Grimm fairy tale. I already hear the local accent (which my father has mysteriously lost), the vowels infused with a catch in the throat, a lilt, the slightest hint of a yodel, sentences invariably rising on the last word. There's a ridged cylindrical gas tank, at least fifteen stories tall, topped with something like a flattened beret. Aunt Mary and Uncle John live behind it. To the left of that is the only skyscraper in northeastern Pennsylvania, the Pennsylvania Power and Light tower, known locally as the PP&L, a squat version of the Empire State Building, its crowned top bathed in crimson light. The redness of those lights reminds me of an interior human organ exposed to the elements, and sure enough, I feel a contained heat inside my chest in response. To the west, out of the range of our vision, there's Dorney Park, home of the oldest running wooden roller coaster in America, where I'll come down with the first symptoms of chicken pox three years in the future. But the row houses really snare my attention. We pass blocks and blocks and blocks of them (joyless, joyless), none of which seem to be individuated. Although the temperature is in the thirties, it feels like the coldest place in the world. All of it seems impossibly old, musty, dense with the smells of upholstery and cooking: holubky; apple butter; tuna, onions, and vinegar. The place says one thing alone to me: *You will always be you here.*

   Get out.

   We stop at a red light, watching a window across the street. At the Harugari, the Hungarian club, people with beer bottles in one hand wipe off their florid faces with handkerchiefs. Hands are clapped, and a middle-aged couple in the center of the floor whirls to—I can only imagine it—a manic accordion. They dance so fast that I swear their shoes are in the air more than they're actually touching the floor. "Now that's dancing," says my father. "Not like the crap you kids like." And he takes his hands off the wheel, chugs his forearms like a go-go dancer with a brain injury.

   My stomach groans with the same sensation that keeps me from eating my bowl of cereal on certain school days. If he really loves this place as much as he says he does, if he really feels the sting of its absence, then why have we been raised as if we haven't a history, in a township named for its shopping mall filled with ficus, coconut palm, and cages of leering tropical monkeys showing us the pink of their gums?

✳ ✳ ✳

My father is a storm. His presence charges the air with abstract particles: guilt, duty, fear of failure, fear of death. If he were a painting, he'd be a

Jackson Pollack, all splash and squiggle, no open spaces, no room to breathe. If he were a piece of music, he'd be a Shostakovich symphony, brash, shot through with bursts of tympany and horn. I could keep going on like this. I could keep trying to count the instances in which he simply sat down to rest his weary bones, in which he didn't read the stock-market page while shining his shoes then run down the hall to sweep off the porch, then go back to his shoes again.

The house of his childhood. 333 North Second Street, a narrow brick row house with two second-floor windows and a wide front porch, no lawn, no plants, no intimation of adornment. A sign hangs on the wooden porch rail (MODERN SHOE REPAIR), the name of my late grandfather's business, which is later taken over by my uncle Steve, then his son, Stevie. On the block all the houses are similarly sparse, with no defining characteristics other than cleanliness. The front steps sparkle in the weak sunlight that's offered. So clean, my aunt Mary says, that "you could eat right off them."

I close my eyes and hear loud, lilting voices. They shift back and forth between Slovak and English, even the occasional Hungarian and Yiddish, all rivaling for attention. Seven children live in these rooms: Anna, Mary, Steve, Joe, Catherine, Francie, and Tony, my father, the middle child. Their quarters are so cramped that several share the same bed. A modern bathroom with pink fixtures glows in the darkness. Aunt Catherine and Uncle Joe (who later move out to a newer row house close to the fair-grounds) do everything possible to make it cheery (doilies on the backs of the sofas, new curtains), but it feels as if the walls are about to compress all the life out of you.

I have to see it from the street again. I imagine my grandparents gazing out the two upper windows, my elusive grandparents about whom I know next to nothing. Alexander, my grandfather, stands in the left window, a man of medium height, utilitarian wire-frame glasses over his broad face, above thin Eastern European lips, a glass of red wine in his hand, the same wine he makes from the grapes of the back-yard arbor. (He stores huge vats of it in the cellar.) Is his smile tinged with sadness because he doesn't know how he ended up in this gritty industrial city, so far from the vineyards of his birthplace? He takes another sip of wine (why did this batch turn out so sour?), putting off work for another few minutes. It's so hot in his workshop that he sweats profusely, and in order to keep at this pace, he eats salt by the fistful to replace what he's lost. He hears his wife, Mary, who's straight-ening up the contents of the drawers, folding clothes in the next room. He doesn't even remember their quarrel anymore, but he's aimed his trademark screw-you gesture at her—he sticks out his tongue, placing his thumbs in his ears and fluttering his fingers—in full sight of the chil-dren. Tonight they'll sleep in separate beds, separate rooms, though the truth is that they haven't spent a full night together for longer than he can remember. (At some point, it will be a joke among his children that they managed to produce so many offspring. "Immaculate conceptions," says my father.) Alexander dies at least six years before I'm born and is rarely brought up at family gatherings.

My grandmother stands at the other window. She wears a light blue dress patterned with nasturtiums; she's doughy and pale in the arms. A babushka is tied beneath her chin. With her thick gray brows—she wears no lipstick or makeup or jewelry—she looks like an earthier, heavier Georgia O'Keeffe. Like Alexander, there is a tinge of sadness in her expression, but her sadness seems to run deeper, with complex chords in it. Is it that she's been fighting with her husband, who's been drinking, spending too much time playing poker with his friends? Is it that he's been indifferent to the children, and abdicated his responsibility to Steve, the oldest male child, who's begun to administer the spankings? Or is it that she, too, feels homesick and doesn't want to learn this new grammar with its irregular verbs, its blends of consonants almost impossible to pronounce? (Years later, my parents will think she's cursing until they realize that the asshole she keeps referring to is, in fact, our next-door neighbor, *Ethel* Friedman, whom she's taken a shine to.) The weather feels foreign and sticky on her skin. The air doesn't smell as it should. Where, where is the Danube? What are they doing so far from the Danube?

In the fall of 1998, at a Chinese restaurant in Fort Lauderdale, I ask my father a few questions about the grandmother who's been nothing but an outline to me. To my surprise, I learn that she actually left my grandfather for a time. Back in Baltimore, their first home in this country, she wasn't happy with the crowd Alexander was in (reportedly, there was even a shooting at their wedding reception), so she packed up Anna and Mary to stay with her sister, Tetka, in Allentown.

He stood guarding the door. "And what about me?"

"You can come live with us only when you're good and ready," she told him.

The lo mein on the buffet table across the room practically glows beneath the copper hood. For the briefest moment, I feel a presence—a warmth, pulse—then gone.

* * *

"Who do you think you are?"

My father weeps over his trig homework.

"I said, who do you think you are?" Steve walks past the humble desk on the second floor, then sits on the bed, hunching forward. He crosses his arms. "You think you're better than we are?"

"No," says my father.

"You think you're smart or something?"

My father hangs his head.

"Tony?"

"It's just—"

"You should be out helping the family."

"But *Steve*."

"You're a car mechanic, okay? You're just a Slovak. You're no better than the rest of us."

My father cries again. His eyes blur on all the red slashes and X's on the page. He can't give up now. Not after so much work, not after all those homesick, harrowing times in the War (Texas, Belgium, Germany) when he lived off pennies a week and sent his earnings back home. Wasn't that in payment for this? It had to be for something. He wipes his eyes on his fist. No, no. The work will tax him; it will come close to killing his spirit, but one day they'll see how kind of heart he is, what he's capable of giving.

No more scraps. Finally, he'll be given the prime cuts at the table, just like his older brothers.

"It's two in the morning," whispers Steve. "It's time for sleep, kiddo."

My father blows his nose. He shakes his head. He sharpens his pencil and goes back to work as his brother looks on in fury and awe.

In two years he'll earn his degree in electrical engineering and graduate, to the shock of family and friends, not far from the top of his class.

* * *

Unlike Slovak women, Anne Homan is tall with long, slender legs and thick dark hair. The daughter of a veterinarian and a schoolteacher, she's half-English, half-German, both sides of her family having lived in this country since the 1830s. Not only does she draw and paint—her pastels and watercolors grace the walls of her mother's living room—but she loves opera, Verdi and Puccini, and sings in the occasional recital. Her mother plays the piano; her older brother, Alfred, is a professional Broadway actor, now appearing in Cole Porter's *Kiss Me Kate*. My father can't help but be charmed and impressed by all these indications of culture. Although he's only known her for a few weeks (they've met on Long Beach Island at an outing of the Collingswood Catholic Club), he's eager to bring her home to his mother.

"She loves me," he says, not two minutes after he's introduced her to the family.

My mother smiles beside him, blinking, bewildered. She thinks, what a funny thing to say.

"She's not so big," says bald, red-faced Uncle John with his trademark joviality.

What has he told them about her? my mother wonders. An earlier boyfriend once called her "shapely, well-endowed," but "big?" "Excuse me for a minute," she says, and disappears down the hall to the bathroom.

"What do you think of her, Mom?" my father says.

His mother nods once, twice. She thinks, where are the broad apple cheeks, the thighs? Such a tiny nose.

"She loves me," he says again, more softly this time.

He clenches his brow. He's in awe of the fact that anyone so lovely could love him. After all, isn't he just a "dumb Slovak," as he himself would put it, from 333 North Second Street?

"Nice girl," says my grandmother.

"You like her, Mom?"

"Fancy," she says, nodding.

My father's smile is shaded with sadness. He thinks, I wish Pop were still alive.

They face each other, waiting for my mother to come back from the bathroom, unnerved by the sudden uneasiness between them—where did this dizziness inside his head come from? My dad's face glows; it's heated from within. But how he wishes everyone had more enthusiasm! Can they already tell that the children they'll bear won't ever learn Slovak, nor appreciate the sweet, granular texture of kolache in their mouths?

✳ ✳ ✳

Allentown:	**Cherry Hill:**
Cellar	*Basement*
Supper	*Dinner*
Buggy	*Shopping Cart*
Hopper	*Toilet*
To tootsel	*To snack*
They want rain	*It's supposed to rain*
on Friday.	*on Friday.*

✳ ✳ ✳

They sit side by side on the chocolate brown sofa of their one-bedroom apartment in Haddon Hills. He gazes up at the white metal kitchen cabinets, half of which are filled with tools and engineering books. He knows she'd like that space for dishes and groceries, and he knows the place is a little cramped. He places his hands on my mother's warm belly, feels a nudge, a slight kicking, then remembers the project due at work this Thursday. He smiles, though the bottom half of his face feels tight. He must do a good job, he thinks. He must present it with more authority and panache than any of his coworkers or they'll see who he really is—a fraud. He's a car mechanic, for God's sake. What does he know about engineering, anyway? He'll lose his job; he can*not* lose his job, not now, not with all these bills, especially with a baby on the way.

He gets up off the sofa and stares at the calendar on the refrigerator. "Maybe we should go to Allentown next week?"

My mother blinks. "It's such a long ride."

"*Hon—*"

"Weren't we just there?"

Yes, they were, but the visit felt careful and strained, though he couldn't bear to admit it to himself till now. Why did it seem he had nothing in common with his family anymore? When he tried to tell Steve about the jealousies he's encountered from coworkers (they cannot bear his energy and speed), Steve stared at the football game, fumbled for his cigarette lighter or the beer bottle on the end table. They must make up for it this next time. They must have a warmer, more satisfying stay.

Don't they know how much he loves them? If they only knew how much he loves them.

Maybe it will help if he gives Mom some money.

My mother pages through the new *House & Garden*. "Let's take a look at houses."

My father nods, rubbing his lower lip with his index finger.

They walk out to the parrot red Buick in the parking lot. (How did he end up in South Jersey? he thinks. Where are the mountains in the distance, all those beautiful languages—Slovak, Hungarian, Yiddish, Polish—on the streets?) In Delaware Township, on the east side of Haddonfield, they drive through the stone gates of Woodcrest Country Club Estates, "The Entrance to Elegance," as it's described in the newspaper ads. They tour the ranchers and split-levels—each decorated in a specific style—French Provincial, Danish Modern, Early American—each named for expensive cars: Fleetwood, Eldorado, Continental, Imperial. (Other developments in the area share a proclivity toward the flash and the glare. Haddontowne's models, for example, are named for Miami Beach hotels.) After talking to the salesman, they check out the houses from the curb. Actually, they're not even sure they like the place. What about those metal windows? And why do the houses look so severe from the side, like, well, bread boxes? But it *is* the up-and-coming neighborhood, says my mother. We don't have to stay here forever. She's right, thinks my father. And wouldn't the family be proud? So much to see and do nearby: the Latin Casino nightclub; the Garden State Park racetrack; the Cherry Hill Mall; the Cherry Hill Inn, and all those other restaurants: Cinelli's, Sans Souci, Irv Morrow's Hideaway, and the Hawaiian Cottage, which is built in the shape of a squat gold pineapple with a jaunty green topknot. Already celebrities are moving onto the township's curving, freshly paved streets. Walking into Shop 'n' Bag you might run into Al Martino, Connie Stevens, WFIL TV-show personality Sally Starr, and some of the major figures in organized crime.

I swim and somersault inside my mother. In but two days they'll put a down payment on a Continental, which will be ready just in time for my birth.

* * *

My grandmother is hazy, enormous as a planet. I walk into Aunt Catherine's living room to find her sitting on the red sofa before the TV, a look of emptiness on her face. She watches *Championship Wrestling*, the single program that seems to harness her attention. I'm four years old. A good boy, I kiss her on the cheek. Freshly bathed, she smells of lotion and yeast. "Hello, Grammy," I say. "Nass boy," she answers, eyes fixed to the screen. "Nass boy." It's the only thing she's ever said to me. I know she doesn't know much in the way of English, but I wish she'd try. I wish she'd call me by my name, see me as a separate being from my brothers and cousins. (Are we just puppies to her? A litter of yapping, wide-eyed puppies?) And why doesn't anyone tell us anything about her? What is her favorite food? What was it like taking a ship across the Atlantic? And does she miss the streetcars and markets, the soot and the gray skies of Bratislava?

My father stands next to her. "Mom," he says. "This is my son."

"Son?"

"His name is Paul."

I don't understand why he talks to her as if I'm a stranger. We've had this exact exchange at least twenty times in my brief life.

She looks out at me, then up at my father with a dim, apprehensive expression in her eyes. Her lips move. She mumbles something to him in Slovak.

"No, no," he says with a rueful laugh. "I'm TO-ny. Not Francie."

Aunt Catherine walks into the room, wiping her hands on a dish towel patterned with hex signs. She already looks like a younger version of her mother; in twenty years she'll have the same "Indian nose," as she calls it. She senses something about the tightness of Grammy's mouth and blinks. She lifts her up by the elbow (heavy, how heavy she's become), guiding her toward the orange potty chair tucked in the corner of the living room. Grammy's walk seems to embody a suffering larger than herself, the suffering of every ancestor who'd gone to bed hungry—the parched lips, the growling stomach—before being snuffed out. Is she getting sicker? Or dying? One thing is for sure: she must not end up at the "poor house," as she calls the nursing home. She dreads it much more than death itself, so next week she will be shunted off to Francie and Goldie's, then a few weeks later to Mary and John's. There is no denying that everyone's nerves are raw. As soon as she's comfortable in one house, learning the trajectory of its hallways, the patterns of its sofas and armchairs, she's off somewhere else, where she must start all over again, a permanent exile in the houses of her children.

Once she's back from the potty, my father sits close to his mother on the couch and whispers in her ear. He seems to express far more affection for her than do my aunts and uncles. Is his affection part display? Is he trying to prove his devotion to the rest of the family? Although her eyes are still fixed to the wrestlers' zany trunks (blues, violets, crimsons), her thoughts are elsewhere now, in happier worlds. She's either back in Slovakia, dusting the rooms of the rich people for whom she once worked, or she's already in the next world, nimble and alive, in a flowered dress and blue babushka, sweeping someone's front steps.

✳ ✳ ✳

Boxwoods, white birches, and cedar diadaras are planted in the backyard. Ethan Allen furniture is ordered from Haddon Wayside. It's Easter, and outside, there's a smell of hyacinth and lilac on the air. It's the day of our relatives' first visit to our new house, a custom-built brick rancher on an acre lot on Circle Lane in the Boundbrook section of Cherry Hill. (How quickly we've outgrown the place in Woodcrest. And those windows: my parents spent a fortune covering them with plastic in the winter.)

> "I'm old enough to know how important this house is to them. It's a symbol, a bold announcement."

I'm old enough to know how important this house is to them. It's a symbol, a bold announcement. *I am to be taken seriously; I am worthy of something more than a mere development house; I have done something in the world.* And I've had all the proof I need by witnessing an exchange between my mother and an old friend of hers in the Haddonfield Acme. When she finds out that our house is in Cherry Hill, "in the new Kresson Road area," her face opens; her bottom lip prickles and swells. "Fabulous," whispers her friend.

Aunt Mary gets out of the car first. She looks out at the expansive front lawn, the squat Colonial lampposts at the head of the driveway. She touches the back of her head, swallows. Then Goldie, Francie, Elsie, and John get out, followed by Catherine and Joe, who pull up in their red Rambler.

Once we're all in the foyer, I point to the baseboard next to the front door. "You should take off your shoes."

"No, no," my father laughs uneasily. "These kids . . ."

"But *you* make us take off our shoes."

My father smiles at his siblings through gritted teeth. *"Paul."*

The tour commences. Everyone seems quietly respectful as they follow my father from room to room—the hearth room, the sunroom, the laundry room. Their shoes wisp the gold wall-to-wall carpet. Everything is perfect; every vase, book, and picture frame in proper position. Little do they know that we don't always live this way. It must be the first time in months that my father's papers and magazines don't cover the kitchen table.

"I like the Queen Anne furniture," notes Aunt Catherine. "Nice chair."

"Pretty windows," says Mary. "Are they hard to keep clean?"

"Look at the size of this cellar!" says Uncle John, who cups his hands around his mouth. "You could sell tickets and open a movie theater down here, Tony."

Everybody laughs. I follow the grown-ups around like a spaniel with shining eyes. Afterward, I stand outside on the back patio and breathe in the brisk, lilacy air. I love seeing what we have through my aunts' and uncles' eyes; I love these physical demonstrations of our luck and our worth. The tiny leaves of the poplars glitter in the clean April light.

Once everyone has seen the house, we all crowd in our station wagon to go on a tour of our township. We walk beneath the wet, tropical trees inside the Cherry Hill Mall; we drive across the Barclay Farm development's mock covered bridge; we drive past Muhammad Ali's stucco rancher with its iron gates. We walk through scores and scores of sample houses with the latest features: wet bars, central vacuums, built-in log boxes, conversation pits. And there's something called a bidet, which brings out the suggestive and shy in everyone. "What's that for?" says Aunt Mary. "You know," says Aunt Catherine. Aunt Mary stares at the low-slung, porcelain boat. I'm not sure I know myself. I imagine it has something to do with blood, with pregnancies. Or something darker. Then: *"Oh,"* says Aunt Mary.

The Beau Rivage, The Fontainebleau, The Ambassador, The Mark 70. So much newness! So much vitality, beauty, excitement for life! No more cramped tenements and fire escapes, no more dank lightless wells. History? Who needs it. Out with the old. We're making ourselves anew. "Oooh," we say, and look up at the huge Latin Casino sign against the twilit sky. On the glittering marquee with the gold flashing bulbs: DIRECT FROM THE LAS VEGAS STRIP: STEVE AND EYDIE.

We head out to a restaurant on Route 38 with flaring torches in its gardens and shields on its fieldstone walls. It's in a round sunken pit and is known for its steaks and huge salads: an entire head of iceberg lettuce served in a teak bowl.

"Filet mignon," my father says to the waiter in his official voice. "For everyone."

"Now, Tony," says Catherine.

"I insist," he says, holding up his hand. "This is on me."

Halfway through the meal a coiffed woman in a mink stole walks down the steps. Her husband, a slight, dark fellow with nebbishy glasses, touches the small of her back. She practices an expression of sophisticated indifference as they're led to their table, but she wants us to look at her, to *see* her, more than anything else in the world. It's what she lives for, this moment, this display. I turn to Aunt Mary. The woman has certainly captured *her* attention. "Rich people," she says, her voice tinged with modesty and pain. It seems to hurt to look at them. Is she already thinking of the towering gas tank across Foundry Street, how it throws her humble house into shade?

* * *

If only Aunt Mary knew what really happens inside the houses of Cherry Hill.

I'm eating dinner at my friend Lisa's house when all the lights go off. Immediately, we know it's not a blackout; we can see the chandelier blazing through the window of the house next door. There's a cone of light on the grass. With an astonishing poise, Mrs. Marx breezes into the dark kitchen, where she opens a drawer for a box full of matches. She returns to light the candlesticks on the table while her husband sits across from us, his head in his hands. Mrs. Marx smiles, but the match trembles between her fingertips until she burns herself. "Ah!" she cries, as it falls to the silver tray beneath. The next day Lisa tells me that they haven't paid the electric bill. The card shop Mr. Marx has operated in Clementon for the past ten years cannot compete with all the chain stores that have opened at the nearby Echelon Mall.

And, of course, there's the ongoing ritual, much less dire, in our own house.

My father stands at the kitchen table with a somber expression and hunts through the bags of groceries my mother and I have just brought home from Penn Fruit. "How much did you pay for this?" he says, holding up a bag of chocolate stars. "And what about this? Why do we need more ice cream? We already have some." She runs water in the sink. She doesn't answer. Hasn't she done enough to scrimp and save? Hasn't she filled the shelves of our pantry with store brands—Bala Club, Gaylord, Top Frost, Two Guys—instead of the pricier name labels? The afternoon sun shines on the yellow kitchen walls, heats up the skin of my forehead, blinding my left eye. Boundaries break down. I cannot tell myself apart from my mother, and surely, my father's anger extends to me as well; haven't I asked my mother for the candy? He looks down at the bag of chocolate in his hands, then shakes his head. Surely, we're frivolous, extravagant. We don't understand the meaning of good, hard work. For all we know, this single bag of candy could be the one purchase that ruins us, that brings the whole tower of match sticks tumbling down to the ground in a heap.

He tears open the edge of the plastic and hands me a star, waiting for me to accept it.

Then, with troubled relish, he eats one himself.

＊ ＊ ＊

When my youngest brother Michael tells our mother she's the "most beautiful woman in the world" (something which she remembers fondly to this day), I silently agree with him. She's recently bought her first pair of bell-bottoms, and I'm quietly hopeful: Is this only the beginning? Will she start dressing like the mothers of some of our friends, like Mrs. Kasten, who walked down the Communion aisle last week in a low-cut black mohair top, demonstrating her cleavage à la Elizabeth Taylor, setting off a minor stir among the husbands in the church? My mother wears her new bell-bottoms everywhere, at choir practice, at the supermarket, and when I tell Aunt Catherine about it on the phone (she and Uncle Joe are coming to our shore house for the last week in August), she says, "Come *on*."

"We're serious," I say. "We have a very modern mother."

"Get *out*."

But two weeks later I receive a postcard from Aunt Catherine: *I'm looking forward to visiting your 38-year old, hip swinging, bell bottoms mommy.*

I love my Aunt Catherine; unlike some of my other aunts, she's like a second mother to me. But I wonder if she's making fun. I know that my father's side of the family thinks we're weird. None of us are terribly interested in football or team sports, and I know that it's part of family legend that we were given dolls to play with as children along with the tool kits and the G.I. Joes.

My mother, two brothers, and I are crouching—or hiding, to be more precise—inside the pink bedroom of Dolores Dasher's summerhouse, which just happens to be directly behind the weedy lot across from our own summerhouse. Earlier in the day we received a phone call from Uncle Steve's son, my cousin Stevie, who's been staying with his wife and his son in Wildwood; he wants to know whether they can drop by at around two this afternoon. My mother knows what this means. They want to extend their vacation for another night or two. They'll just sit there, we know it, and wait for her to suggest it, and they know she'll suggest it because my father would be upset with her if she didn't. How many relatives have been dropping by lately? My mom feels like she's always on call; more often than not, she finds herself in the role of cook, while the aunts and uncles sit around the umbrella table, where they feed the gulls and watch the boats sailing by on the lagoon.

This time the thought of it is too much for my mother to bear. It gives her a twinge in the neck—and my brothers and I feel it in the backs of our own necks, in sympathy. At the very last minute her friend Dolores Dasher offers to hide us in the hopes they'll think there's been some miscommunication.

We look up at Dolores Dasher from the floor. Like our mother, she, too, has taken to wearing striped bell-bottoms, even though she's a good twenty pounds heavier. She wrings her hands with a vexed look in her eyes and shakes her honey blond curls off her face. Plans are hatching inside her head.

"Do you want me to go over there?" Dolores paces. "I'll go over there. I'll tell them something came up. Your car broke down. You had to take it to the mechanic. It was an emergency. How's that?"

We give her the go-ahead. We sit there in silence. I get down on all fours, butt high in the air, press the corner of my cheek into the carpet, and laugh quietly. Although we're all on edge, we're having a strange kind of fun. How many mothers would do such a thing? How I love her sense of adventure.

"Get your face off the floor, dear," she whispers. "Germs."

My brother Bobby peers over the window ledge. The top of his moppy head must certainly be visible from Point Drive.

"They'll see you," I declare.

After a few minutes, however, I feel bold enough to take a look myself. Dolores Dasher stands at the fence, gesturing, while Stevie and Janice lean against their car, lifting their faces to the sun. Little Stephen tears through the gardens and smashes the portulacas and petunias like a Rotweiler on speed.

"Little Stephen's destroying the flowers!" I cry.

"Oh, this is ridiculous," says my mother suddenly.

"Don't," I say.

"I mean they're not going to go away. This isn't nice. What's the matter with us? Come on, you kids. Up, *up.*"

And just as we stand up, Dolores walks back into her house, flipping through a sheaf of envelopes in her hand. "Well, that was a flop."

"What do you mean?" I say.

"Well, I told them about the car, but"—she rolls her eyes—"they were on to me. The car was parked right in front of them."

"Oh *no!*" we all say.

"They wouldn't take the hint. I'm sorry, Anne. Those two," she says, shaking her head. "So damn blasé."

And so we go back to greet them, cheerily, as Little Stephen starts jumping up and down on the webbed lounge until he breaks through the fabric and shrieks.

*** * ***

Aunt Mary's living room is already cast in darkness, even though it's not yet three-thirty in the afternoon. Arctic clouds rush and tumble across the sky outside the north-facing window, passing over the gas tank. A gust of wind rattles the panes. The TV imbues the room with a thin, bluish light. I sit in the armchair across from Grammy, who's lying on the couch with closed eyes, moistening her lips after a shot of insulin. I hold onto the armrests and tell myself not to be frightened.

Murmured voices in the hall. I sit on the edge of my seat and strain to hear above the cries and jeers of the football game.

"It's getting to be too much, Tony," whispers Aunt Mary.

I know they're talking about Grammy. Her care is becoming more and more of an issue; it's a full-time job, especially since she fell last week. The brothers and sisters argue about who has her when. I feel something in the air when we're all together, a pulse of frustration, regret.

"We might have to take her to a home."

"No!" he cries. Don't they know how she feels about the poor house?

"What do you mean?"

"She's my *mother*," he says. "We can't just throw her away."

A pause, a pull, a catch in the throat. "She's my mother, too," murmurs Aunt Mary. "Don't you think we love her?"

Aunt Mary has stepped into the doorway, where a bar of light from the kitchen illuminates the top half of her face. It's full of suffering, a drawn-ness in the cheeks, the same suffering I've seen in Grammy's face for years. "Then you take her, Tony," she says finally.

A wave rises then falls inside my stomach. Leaves rasp against the frosty grass outside.

My brothers and I are buttoned up in our coats, our hoods tied beneath our chins. I hold the paper bag of ham sandwiches and M&M cookies she's made for the long drive home. When my father leans over to hug her, he presses a check into the pocket of her dress.

"No, no," says Aunt Mary with exasperation.

"Now listen," says my father firmly.

"It's too much, too much," she says, fingers fluttering against the front of her dress. After a minute she tosses the check at my father. "Too much."

"Now Mary," he says.

We stand in the foyer, heads lowered. I fumble inside my bag for a Hershey's Kiss and pinch a flag of foil between my fingers. The check is tossed back and forth until it's creased. Finally, Aunt Mary plunges it into her pocket. Her face is sweaty. She's breathing hard, but she's already relieved that this part of the ritual is over.

At some point in the next couple of hours, my father must bring up the possibility of taking care of Grammy to my mother (does it happen when I'm curled up in the backseat of the car, sleeping, lying beneath my coat?). She stares at the windshield; the words are dumb in her throat. Of course they took in her own mother during the last months of her life, but this feels harder, more challenging. Hasn't she given up enough of herself these last few years, poured every last ounce of her attention into us? There's hardly anything left of her. She looks at the dried maple leaves blowing along the sidewalk, and for an instant she's a maple leaf herself, scraping against the pavement, lit by the headlights of the passing cars.

Our house is electric the next several days. Every time I touch something—a doorknob, a light switch—I get a shock. I jump every time I hear something. Doors and cabinets are slammed emphatically. Even my mashed potatoes don't have much taste; I leave them on my plate until they're cold. My dad finishes them off, spoons them into his mouth, blank-eyed, with abandon.

I stand in the backyard one day when the house finally explodes. Voices thunder. "Not true." "Responsibility!" "Your mother? *My* mother." I curl up against the trunk of the crabapple, the wet ground seeping through the seat of my pants. I cannot stand fighting. *Anything* would be better than fighting. (Where do I begin or end? I *know* they're talking about Grammy, but I can't help feeling that I'm at the center of things. I bear it all like a buoy in a squall.) I keep looking over at the windows, worrying a long blade of grass in my hands.

Then peace. The house settles into an unlikely peace for the next several days. My parents are kinder, calmer; what has transpired between them? They start talking about where Grammy should sleep, how to keep her comfortable on the long car ride back to Cherry Hill. There's talk of moving her into one of our bedrooms, Bobby and I doubling up. I picture her lying on my single bed in the dark, the back of her dress pulled up to expose the crack of her naked rear end as she waits for another shot of insulin. I picture her in this land of shopping malls and racetracks and nightclubs, frightened, far from what's familiar. My stomach hurts; my meals go unfinished for days. I must stop behaving like this. Selfish, selfish, I will myself to be a better boy. Then, just as my father decides to phone the aunts and uncles, to tell them, yes, we'll take her for a while, he learns that Grammy has taken a mysterious turn for the better. No need to move her now. One day she actually carries on an extended conversation about the summer when she was sixteen, when she rolled cigars in a factory outside Bratislava. On another day she actually gets up off the couch. She walks across the room herself, stands at Aunt Catherine's picture window, and watches with amazement all the cars and buses threading down the street.

✳ ✳ ✳

The weeds are tangled around the base of the shorehouse fence. They're amazingly thick, like dried reeds. I pull them through the wire links and cut them off with the shears. A rusty smell rises from my fingers. Steve, Myra, Francie, and Goldie are due to arrive at any minute, and sure enough the mint green Valiant moves up the street at an excessively slow pace, jerking to a stop every few feet—someone's pointing inside— before starting up again. I draw my elbows closer to my rib cage and pretend to be absorbed in my task. My head's overheated like the blades of a lawn mower. A greenhead lands on the damp flesh of my neck, and I reach back to slap it, but—*pinch*—it's too late.

My parents have prepared for the visit all week. My father has made sure he's around; he's even gone so far as to do the grocery shopping himself, a task which seems about as comfortable to him as painting his nails in public. (Why does he look so dour pushing the cart through Starn's Shop Rite? Is it the outlandish numbers on all the price tags?) For Steve, he's bought Dietz & Watson, Entenmann's, Vlasic—all the brands his brother expects whenever he comes to visit. One by one he loads the items onto the conveyor belt, trying his best to seem cheerful. "Don't take this so seriously," I'm tempted to say. Fortunately, I know when to keep my mouth shut. It doesn't take much to trigger an explosion these days.

Not in the house for five minutes, Steve sprawls in one of the blue-gold armchairs, yawns, and asks to be brought a beer. The dynamics in the house have shifted. My father doesn't sound as sure of himself; my mother lifts the lid off a pot, trying to make more macaroni salad—the first batch hasn't met with Steve's satisfaction. "Are you okay, Steve?" "Would you like another beer, Steve?" "How about a nice ham sandwich, Steve?" Steve sips from his beer, asks for another before he's finished, watching our every last move—how we walk, talk. Every gesture seems to be recorded and assigned a barely passing grade. Occasionally, his eyes actually widen as if he's appalled by something. A nerve pinches the base of my neck. How are we to live through this? He's grinding us down like a pestle.

Finally, I decide, no, enough; I'm not giving in.

I pull out the poster board of New World (a name I've shamelessly stolen from the Rossmoor Corporation), the prototypical city I've been designing since the beginning of the summer. I've situated my project in southwest Florida on an immense tract of flooded sawgrass outside of Naples, where we've recently been on a family trip. I'm so proud of New World, of my skills as a city planner, that I've lost any traces of self-consciousness. Am I showing off a bit? Steve leans forward in his chair, squints slightly. I start drawing the tiny cul-de-sacs in pencil. I reach for my art markers, ink in the parks, waterways, shopping-center sites with their respective color codes. Then once I've finished, I start the naming process: *Daily Lane, Danube Lane, Dasher Drive, Davenport Drive* . . .

"What are you doing on the floor?" says Steve.

I drag the map closer to his chair, then hand it to him. In a voice more deferential than I'd intended (how does he have this effect on people?), I describe my city. His breath is scented warmly with beer; the rims of his nails are stained yellow with nicotine. Nevertheless, there's the lure of authority in his eyes, in the steely white hair combed back off his forehead. For the first time in my life I can see that he must have been handsome and full of life once. And that it couldn't possibly be easy to be in charge all the time.

"This isn't going to work," he says finally. He points to a section of the map, a little cluster of homes I've called Jupiter Shores.

"What do you mean?"

"These canals," he says, shaking his head. "Water flows *down*hill."

I don't have it in me to remind him that my city is just west of the Everglades, where there is no downhill, where the water level is only a few inches beneath the surface even during droughts. I'm merely shocked that he'd find fault with my project, that he wouldn't find a single thing to praise in it.

My mother, hearing the nature of this exchange, walks into the living room, wiping her hands on a dish towel patterned with bronze coffeepots. "Paul's been designing cities for years. The *Philadelphia Bulletin*'s even done a story on him."

"Paul should listen," says Myra, who walks into the room from the porch. "Steve *knows.*"

How can people be so sure of themselves? He goes on to talk about the nature of physics and water, about sewers, seepage, drainage. For all I know, he's made it up. He hands back my map to me, an aloof, satisfied look in his eyes. His face slackens, bluing the skin of his cheeks. I think again: how can people be so sure of themselves?

Is it even possible to reconstruct what happens next?

I can only piece it together from the bits and pieces I've heard through the wall. ("Why didn't you defend us?" cries my mom later, before taking off in the car.) Drinking, drinking through the night, Steve lays into my mother and father, in a sustained explosion of sorts. Smoke banks against the windows, stalling in the room like soot from a power plant. For some reason he's made sure Goldie and Francie sit by his side; they pull in the edges of their lips between their teeth. Their eyes dart from Steve to my parents—whom should they side with? As Myra sits on Steve's right side, blank and imperial.

The brands you buy are junk. He holds up his whiskey and jars it; the liquid sloshes over the rim. *You expect me to drink this garbage?*

You didn't even give them the right toys. I had to give them tools to let them know they were boys.

Paul. That Paul was never so smart.

How much did you pay for this place? Who needs two houses? I'll give you seven thousand for it.

All the while my parents sit there shaking inside, stunned. His tirade goes on through the night. After all, they can't get up to leave. They live here, don't they?

* * *

On one of those thick, humid summer nights when we're in Cherry Hill instead of the shore, my father tosses his camel-colored briefcase on the kitchen table, buries his head in his hands, and sobs. He sobs so hard that my brothers and I are shy about it, impatient, even resentful—fathers aren't supposed to cry. I stand at the back of his white starched shirt (it's too tight in the shoulders), wondering how I should comfort him. Sweat stains dampen his underarms. My mother walks into the kitchen, blinks, says, "Hon?"

"Ettengoff," he says to her.

We know that name like the backs of our hands. We've heard the stories about the layoff list for weeks—my father's coworkers arriving at the job one day only to pack up their things. Heads are hung in shame, fists shaken in silence, desk legs kicked. Their bosses—Ettengoff, Sorkin, Sass, Degnan, Sellars—aren't even people anymore. Their names curdle in our mouths like unrefrigerated milk.

He throws his RCA ID badge on the table.

His snapshot glimmers in its plastic sheath: the brush cut, the glasses, the stern, commanding expression above the bow tie.

We decide that we must get to the shore house as fast as we can. We drive through the scorched woods of the Pine Barrens, past the failing and abandoned businesses—Betty and Rags Diner, Finerty's Quonset Hut, Johnny Boy Farms. The worst is anticipated. There's talk of renting out the shore house, renting out the Cherry Hill house. There's talk of selling, scaling down, moving into smaller quarters. Will I go to a different school? And what about our furniture, our piano—will they go, too? A numbness takes over my right side. The pines on either side of the highway are charred. I think of the grittiest South Jersey towns—Deepwater, Penns Grove, Thoroughfare, National Park—oily neighborhoods of aluminum Cape Cods, like houses on a train set, in the swamps along the Delaware, within sight of refineries. Cat crackers flare. I see the five of us sleeping together on yellowed linoleum as my father steps over me in the middle of the night, reaching for a glass of Alka-Seltzer.

We drive to the Ocean City boardwalk the following afternoon. Spin art, Skee-Ball, popcorn in boxes of tinted blue glass—we walk by it all, downcast, as cries of pleasure drift upward from the beach. The sand's quilted with yellow blankets. Baby oil sizzles on someone's hot, freckled shoulders. Frisbees sail. It seems almost unthinkable that anyone could be having fun at this moment. Everything glimmers with the possibility of its loss: certainly, this will be the last summer I'll stroll down this boardwalk. And the sea, the breeze, the open blue sky: I can't bear the thought of them taken away from me. At Wonderland, the red cylinders of the sky divers swoop and soar, scrambling the stomachs of the kids caged inside.

My father trails behind us, face ashen and tight.

That night we eat creamed chipped beef on toast as if to prepare ourselves for the lean times to come.

It doesn't take long for our grave news to travel back to the family in Allentown. (How must they react? With surprise? Or is it laced with something else? *This is what happens when you want too much, when you travel so far from home, from your soul.*) Aunt Catherine and Uncle Joe arrive in the boxy red Rambler. Their cheerful, calm demeanors shock us. "Help take these to the kitchen," says Aunt Catherine, as she nods to the groceries in the car. The bags are filled with all the name brands— Oreos, Fritos, Viva, Hi-C—we'd never think of buying for ourselves.

They take us to the Dairy Queen, they take us to miniature golf. They take us to the beaches along the Delaware Bay, where we collect clear, sea-polished pieces of quartz. I stare at the moss-covered hull of a sunken concrete ship (an old tourist attraction) and want to know everything about it, how it landed there, how they ever got the monstrosity to float. Anything to forget what's going on at home. We go to the movies. We lower crab traps into a dim, brackish creek. Aunt Catherine and Uncle Joe do everything possible to distract and buoy us, but in spite of their kindness and goodwill, I have the sense that they don't quite know what we've lost, what's really been at stake here. "It's all going to be fine," says Aunt Catherine.

"But Catherine—" says my mother.

"Really now," she answers with the slightest impatience.

(Does she already sense that my dad will be rehired within the week, with a raise and a bonus, no less?)

But you don't get it, I want to say. *My father cannot, cannot ever live in a row house again. It would kill him.*

Instead, I rip into a bag of Lay's Potato Chips, gorging on their salty and greasy taste as if they're the last meal I'll eat.

✳ ✳ ✳

Steve and Myra's living room is newly papered with silver. A green ceramic pine, no taller than two pencils put together, blinks on top of the TV console. I'm down on the silver-blue rug, leaning back on my elbows. Ten A.M.: another game show. The whole lot of us are in this room—aunts, cousins, uncles, parents, siblings—tense, fidgeting, waiting for the phone to ring. Outside a passing truck rumbles the front porch of the house.

When it finally happens, Mary and Catherine almost push each other on the way to the kitchen. Their clothes are crumpled, their curls lank, flattened to their scalps. They've been up all night, as have most of Grammy's children—some surrounding her hospital bed, some walking up and down the waxed halls with cups of cheap coffee. It shocks them that it's happened so fast, for on Christmas Eve she'd seemed so well; she'd closed her eyes in pleasure as the hot soup was spooned into her mouth, and then the next day. . . .

The voices are low and hushed from the kitchen.

I tense my limbs tight, tighter.

Outside, a branch cracks beneath the weight of the ice.

My father walks back to the room, finally, looks at my brothers and me for a moment as if he's never known us, as if any passing resemblance between us is uncanny, a surprise. He sits on the sofa and folds his hands in his lap. "My mother died."

The plainness of his voice, the unutterable simplicity of it. (Words fall apart: the sky darkens; a clapper strikes a bell.) From across the room my mother catches my face and smiles at me with a fond sadness. Then the weeping starts, a chorus of it from Grammy's children. It sounds foreign in their throats, almost animal, haunting and deep, as if as adults they've forgotten how to cry.

My cousins turn away. Embarrassed, impatient, they punch one another on their arms.

The hours of the next days move slowly, sluggishly. Intermittent snows, freezing drizzle. Uncle Joe takes the kids to a James Bond movie—*Diamonds Are Forever*—to keep us out of the way.

We dress. (Why am I having this trouble? My pants swim above my ankles. The buttons slip through my fingers.) The inside of the funeral home glows with a rosy, burnished light. Tufted French Provincial sofas border the walls. Nothing about it has anything to do with the life that Grammy led: her troubles and compromises, her stubbornness and will. "No," she'd say, shaking her head. "Not here. Too fancy." I'm led to her casket where she lies inside a border of banked flowers marked with a single sign: FOR MOM, WITH LOVE. YOUR CHILDREN. Her face shines pinkly, emptied beneath the lights. For a moment she seems so alive that I'm certain she's going to sit up and say, "Nass boy." Then my father touches her cheek. His eyes fill; his lower lip quivers.

I mumble a prayer, in silence: *Hail Mary, full of grace* . . .

Aunt Catherine walks in through the door, stomping her feet, brushing the snow off the shoulders of her long cinnamon-colored coat. She speaks in her usual cheerful, tough voice, preoccupied with who's bringing what to lunch after tomorrow's Mass, when she spots the unlikely casket across the room. Her knees weaken, buckle. Her face contorts. "That's not her!" she cries, as Joe and Francie hold her up by the elbows.

* * *

A block in Willowdale, the development next to where we live in Cherry Hill, starts to crumble. The houses are too spacious and expensive for anyone to use the word "slum," but driving down Heartwood Drive with our mother at the wheel, we spot the unweeded flower beds, the crusty gold rags in the dirt behind the bushes. Paint is flaking off the trim boards. Storm windows are ajar. But it's not the only block in Cherry Hill that looks like this: there's Strathmore Drive in Point of Woods, Collins Drive in Holiday Estates, Latches Lane in Candlewyck, Chaucer Place in Downs Farm. And while these streets were apple orchards less than ten years ago, the houses on them seem to be tired already. *The mask is falling. Our owners can't afford us. We've had enough of trying to pretend who we aren't.*

> "And while these streets were apple orchards less than ten years ago, the houses on them seem to be tired already."

Maybe the families who live inside these houses are changing and their children don't feel the pressures that their parents once did. ("Yes, it's good to be Jewish, Italian, Polish, Greek! Watch us now. We're just as good as the rest of you!") Although there are different kinds of pressures—odder, more complicated pressures. Someone I once saw in the lunch line of my school cafeteria stabs his mother over and over in the family living room, a story that seizes the attention of the Philadelphia/South Jersey news media for weeks. Someone else flings a vial of sulfuric acid on a special-education student's back as she wanders across the front lawn of Cherry Hill High School East. Richard Dubrow, a boy in Bobby's homeroom, stands in his closet one October morning, steps off a milk crate, and hangs himself with one of his father's blue neckties. In house after house, the kids simply fall silent, holing up in their bedrooms with their doors closed, or hanging out in the parking lot of the 7-Eleven. Anything to stave off the oppressive, persistent boredom. Until they get out. *But it's all been for you,* think their parents. *You've tread on the names of your ancestors.*

Weren't you the reason we were born?

One day after school, I'm lying on my stomach, trying to work out a proof for geometry class (in which I got a D on my last test, to the horror of my mathematician father), when the sirens outside wail and fall, wail and fall. Why is it so dark inside my room? I walk through the front door, and then one by one, people run out onto their wide green lawns with their heads raised. A sooty bank of smoke covers the entire sky, blocks out the late afternoon sun. "What's burning?" I call out to a neighbor.

"The racetrack," says Mr. Coticone. "It's going up."

* * *

A parade of funerals. Every few months there's another sudden, unexpected death in Allentown. Someone goes to work and feels pins and needles in the chest, a numbness in the jaw. A crack, flash of fire, and . . . Anna. Steve. Catherine's husband, Joe. We go to so many funerals in such a short span of time that we're getting to be in practice now. We're careful of what we say to one another. We clench our shoulders every time the phone rings.

We mill outside the St. Catherine of Sienna Cathedral as Joe's silver casket is carried down the front steps by eight of my older cousins. A flock of doves scatters about us with harsh, beating wings.

Aunt Mary turns to my father. "You're next, Tony," she says.

* * *

Our car idles on the eastbound shoulder of Route 70. My brother Michael aims his camera at the lighted billboard against the winter blue sky: TOTIE FIELDS. *LAST NIGHT TONIGHT: THANK YOU FOR TEN YEARS OF PATRONAGE.*

* * *

The meat at the Bonanza Restaurant is tough, chewy, a little hard to swallow. I'd like to eat at the new restaurant on the old Hawaiian Cottage site (another arson), but this place has become so familiar, so much a part of our family ritual on Sundays that it would seem wrong to go anywhere else. And besides, it's inexpensive, so we won't have to feel anxious later about my father's cracks about the extra side salad one of us asked for and didn't finish. All five of us sit at those long, dreary wooden tables, beneath the red wagon wheels suspended overhead, when another family of five sits down beside us. I close my eyes. Don't I just know what my father's going to do? Isn't he going to talk too loudly? Isn't he going to ask the waitress for her first name, flirt with her within sight of my mother, before he asks for a refill? Isn't he going to make some observation about the length and style of my hair? All the ingredients are here: the audience of strangers to his left and his faltering son before him.

"What's the matter, Paul?" he says casually.

I shake my head back and forth.

"Paul?"

I lift my head. "Nothing."

"Can we have some of that A.1?" says the other father, leaning in over my plate.

I pass the bottle to the man. We've been talking about my lousy scores in the math segment of the PSAT, what we can do to raise them before I take the SAT in the fall. I wonder if I should just come out and say that I'm not interested in college, that I'm not obsessed with money like he is, that I don't want to build cities in South Florida anymore. All developers do is pollute and destroy. All developers do is rip people off. I'm going to be a musician and a composer. I'm going to live a life that isn't measured and determined by how much money I have in my bank account. And if I'm poor, so what. At least I won't be worried and miserable all the time.

Still, I keep all these thoughts to myself.

He's going on and on about the possibility of hiring a tutor or sending me to some remedial class that meets at 8:00 A.M. at the high school every Saturday morning.

Just as we're ready to leave, he produces the sheer plastic doggy bag patterned with blue and red asterisks he's picked up from the dispenser next to the cash register. "Come up, kids," he says. "Fill 'er up. Make Taffy happy."

Obediently we fill the bag with gristle, bone, fat—all of which will be emptied into our little collie's bowl, even though she almost choked to death on last week's scraps.

His face is calm, expectant. He glances at the family to his left, at the cast-off pieces of steak on their plates. I know that look; his eyes shine as if he's been possessed of some idea.

NO! I think.

"Would you mind if we took your scraps?" he says to the father of the family.

A wave of dread rises from my feet to my face.

He says it again. *Would you mind if we took your scraps?*

NO!

"You can't do that," I murmur.

My father glances up at me.

"You can't. You can't, Daddy. It's just not done."

"Oh, it's perfectly fine," says the other mother in a hard voice. "I'm glad someone else has the sense to ask for it. Here," she says, and scrapes the food off her plate into the outstretched bag with the edge of her steak knife.

Where *am* I? I exhale, exasperated, shaking my head back and forth.

"These kids," says my father with a smile. "Always worried about what other people think."

"You mustn't worry, son," says the other father. "We're certainly not offended."

"Don't be a snob," says the other mother. "Think about your puppy."

I look toward the door. In twenty-five years, I'll recognize him in my duty to work hard, to extend myself past my limitations, and beyond, in spite of resistance, fear—the possibilities of transformation he's offered to me! A rush of love: I thank him. But right now I can't see beyond this moment. In 1976, the whole story comes down to this moment.

My father doesn't stop. One by one he goes to the unbussed tables of the Bonanza, filling up Taffy's bag with whatever he can find—biscuits, fried chicken wings, lukewarm baked potato skins.

"Time to go," I call.

"We're going out to the car," says Michael.

My father walks to another table and starts a conversation with another family, all of whom find his request infinitely charming. My head pounds behind my eyes; my cheeks burn. Soon enough he finds more to add to the bag.

Is our embarrassment the very thing that's egging him on?

What on earth is he trying to teach us?

"Stop," Michael calls.

We cower by the front door of the restaurant.

"You're the chairman of the Cherry Hill Planning Board," says Bobby.

"You have two master's degrees from an Ivy League university," says my mother.

"We're so much better than this," I say.

But he keeps at it, determined, cheerful, until the bag is full, ready to burst from all it contains.

Interview with Paul Lisicky

BECKY BRADWAY: In what ways is writing a memoir like (or not like) writing fiction?

PAUL LISICKY: Once you recognize that you're writing a version of your life, rather than Your Life, you're one step closer to the fiction writer. Place borders around your material, in terms of time, subject matter, or theme, and you've taken another step. Any memoir is inevitably shaped by what's going on in the here-and-now of its development. I'm sure "New World" would be a much different piece if I wrote it today. I'd probably have more to say about my father designing radar for the military, given that war has been on my mind. I'm sure environmental concerns would find a place. Maybe there'd be more about the costs of mass-materialism. But the themes of shame, self-reinvention, and self-sabotage were pressing on me back in 1998, so they determined the contours of the final piece. I say all this to demonstrate that "fact" in autobiography is a wobbly proposition. If it's possible to write the story of my relationship with my father in ten different ways from ten different points in time, and all we have are versions, then aren't we practically standing inside the fiction writer's house?

If I can think of a crucial distinction between the two forms, I'd say that memoir is fueled by inquiry, a determination to make meaning of an image or situation. It's less interested in simply telling a story than in why the story is being told. Fiction to my mind is a little more stealthy than that; it makes use of indirection and wants to feel more like consciousness. Of course, I should add that "New World" asks its readers to infer inquiry from the scenes on the page. In that way it's not that much different from a short story in terms of its methods, so I've just blown my distinction making.

BB: Did you have any qualms about writing about family members? If so, how did you get past that? How did your family react to the piece? Does it matter?

PL: Writing about real people brings up complex problems. For one thing, those people probably tell the story in which they appear differently than the writer does. For another, any person is more dimensional than your ability to represent them, no matter how skilled and sensitive your writing. Your depiction of that person is shaped by a point of view. So it's never the whole story of that person. It can't be. And that's what makes it tough.

I, of course, had to write "New World" pretending my father would never read it, which was a crock because my father ends up reading everything of mine at a certain point. I tried to write from a position of benevolent detachment. I tried to be faithful to the emotional accuracy of memory without skewing it too much in the direction of the positive or the negative. Luckily, my father likes the piece, even though he ribs me and shakes his head in mock-exasperation about my including the doggy bag scene, which appears to both embarrass him and make him proud all at once. Well, that's my father.

I wouldn't want my writing to hurt anyone, but we have so little control over how others read us. I've written certain portraits of people, naively assuming that they'd be seen as flattering when they weren't read that way at all. Maybe the best we can do for those we care about is to make them engaging, as fully rounded as any character in a good novel. No reader is interested in anyone who's idealized or vilified. But "engaging" is not the same thing as "sympathetic" or "attractive." Emma Bovary is engaging, for instance, but I wouldn't call her likable.

BB: Even though you're writing about a tense father-son relationship (some-
    times), you never slip into self-pity. In fact, you are just as unrelenting
    about your own flaws and troubles as you are about your father's. Did
    your piece just come out this way, or did you write some personal or
    rambling sections that didn't make it into the final version?

PL: I wrote the piece from a point in time when I was able to admit to
    how much alike we were. Two guys born during different decades,
    both a little awkward, both with lots of energy, both hopelessly
    attached to their mommies. And they both want to reinvent their
    lives as much as they want to preserve their pasts, which is probably
    an impossible contradiction. So the whole issue of self-pity didn't so
    much rear itself, primarily because I was working with two charac-
    ters on an equal footing. I felt an urging toward contact from the
    very first sentence—there was something both scary and new about
    that. I'm sure the power-relationship would have been different if I'd
    written this material in my twenties. It just occurs to me that self-
    pity is a likely consequence of giving up your own power—on the
    page at least—to someone else.

    All that said, the piece's development was scattershot and disorga-
    nized. It was written between August 1998 and December of that
    year. Not a long time in retrospect, but at the time it felt endless,
    both involving and taxing. I always tend to overdo it in early drafts;
    I have to explore every possible road or else I'm not satisfied. I think I
    might have had a hundred pages of material after the first draft and
    I tossed out at least two-thirds of the scenes and connective tissue I'd
    written until I only had the pivotal moments left. That's the way I
    usually write.

BB: How would you suggest that someone who is writing about troubling
    situations keep from crossing the line into self-indulgence?

PL: I think the only way to avoid self-indulgence in memoir is to pay atten-
    tion to craft, not only to description, musicality, and tone, but to over-
    all structure. Artistry is the thing that differentiates our work from the
    journal entry or the diary. Not that there isn't a place for those forms,
    but I don't think there's any reason that memoir can't be as artful as
    the richest fiction or poetry.

BB: Some people writing memoirs shy away from composing dialogue or
    constructing scenes because they are afraid of "making things up."
    Obviously, we can never be sure if things happened just the way we
    remember them. What is your feeling about that?

PL: I usually default to Vivian Gornick's response whenever this question
    gets raised. "You need dialogue," she supposedly told a student once.
    And the student said, "But I don't remember any conversations." To
    which she said, "Make them up and see if they're true." In other
    words, see if they're emotionally accurate. I think it's important to
    say that memoir isn't about facts, as much as about how the writer
    feels about the facts. Marilynn Robinson has a helpful quote about

this matter from *Housekeeping:* "Fact explains nothing. On the contrary, it is fact that needs explanation." My sense is that our anxieties about the manipulation of truth in the culture are being foisted on the memoir these days. We feel helpless in the face of this situation, so we turn that energy toward a form we think we can control. I'm not at all siding with bestselling memoirists who pass off fictionalized episodes as their life experience. But once the memoirist privileges agreed-upon truths—the stuff of the journalist—to individual inquiry then his genre loses its reason for being. Frank Conroy's *Stop-Time* would not be what it is without those lengthy approximated conversations between characters.

BB: Do you think you'll write more creative nonfiction? What are you writing now?

PL: I just finished a short memoir that thinks about the structural decisions of *Famous Builder*—the book from which "New World" was excerpted—from the standpoint of five years after its publication. I also have a new novel coming out. Among other things, it's about ghosts and grief and gentrification. It's organized around a chorus of voices, two of which speak from the afterlife. My guess is that it's a fairly loony project, though I'm probably not the best authority on that matter. I think the next book, whether it turns out to be memoir or a novel, will be much closer to autobiography.

Norman Mailer

The Faith of Graffiti

Norman Mailer was one of the best known contemporary writers, respected for both his fiction and nonfiction. His blunt, occasionally combative personality gained him notoriety among the press and other writers; his strong views were sometimes oversimplified, and at times they overshadowed his best work. His most recent fiction is *The Castle in the Forest* (2007), which uses a demon narrator to examine Hitler's psychological development. Mailer's most important nonfiction is the Pulitzer Prize–winning *The Executioner's Song* (1979), a long narrative about the life and death of killer Gary Gilmore and his girlfriend. Another important nonfiction book is *The Armies of the Night: History as a Novel, the Novel as History* (1968), an account of his experiences as a Vietnam War protester that was awarded the National Book Award and a Pulitzer.

Mailer was raised in Brooklyn, attended Harvard, and published his first story at eighteen. He was drafted into the army in World War II and served in the South Pacific. In 1948, his war novel *The Naked and the Dead* appeared; it was named by Modern Library as one of a hundred "best novels in the English language."

Mailer continued to write novels, publishing *Barbary Shore* (1951) and *Deer Park* (1955). In 1959 his first nonfiction book, *Advertisements for Myself*, was published; this book combined the personal with reportage and opinion. A few of the essays in this book were controversial, both in their time and since; reaction was particularly strong toward his piece "The White Negro." Mailer was never one to shy away from public comment, however, and he continued to publish essays, which were collected in a number of books.

Mailer long enjoyed walking the line between fiction and nonfiction. *The Executioner's Song* is notable for being what Mailer called a "nonfiction novel"; written in the third person, it relies upon re-created scenes to tell the story of killer Gary Gilmore. While we have come to take these techniques for granted now, at the time of the book's publication, its fictional re-creations were quite innovative. Joan Didion called this book "absolutely astonishing," attributing this in part to Mailer's style: "It is a largely unremarked fact about Mailer that he is a great and obsessed stylist, a writer to whom the shape of the sentence is the story." In the ensuing discussion about whether the book was truly nonfiction, James Atlas of the *New York Times* said, "*The Executioner's Song* is a great book not because Norman Mailer tape-recorded his subjects, but because he imposed on the facts his unique sensibility, assembled the chorus of voices that recounts Gary Gilmore's story in his own obsessive, incantatory way."

Although Mailer focused most often on his fiction, in 1995 he published *Oswald's Tale*, which explores the Kennedy assassination.

We have included one of Mailer's midcareer essays, "The Faith of Graffiti," published in 1974. It's one of Mailer's few essays in which he plays almost-reporter and takes a back seat to his subject, a crew of young graffiti artists.

Interview with Norman Mailer, p. 557.

1.

Journalism is chores. Journalism is bondage unless you can see yourself as a private eye inquiring into the mysteries of a new phenomenon. Then you may even become an Aesthetic Investigator ready to take up your role in the twentieth-century mystery play. Aesthetic Investigator! Make the name A-I for this is about graffiti.

A-I is talking to CAY 161. That is the famous Cay from 161st Street, there at the beginning with TAKI 183 and JUNIOR 161, as famous in the world of wall and subway graffiti. Cay has the power of his own belief. If the modern mind has moved from Giotto, who could find the beginnings of perspective in the flight of angels across the bowl of a golden sky, if we have mounted the high road of the Renaissance into Raphael's celebration of the True, the Good, and the Beautiful in each succulent three-dimensionality of the gluteus maximus, why so, too, have we moved from the celebration to the name, traveled from men and women who wrested a degree of independence from Church and God down now to the twentieth-century certainty that life is an image.

A couple of stories:

The first is a Jewish joke. Perhaps it is *the* Jewish joke. Two grand-mothers meet. One is pushing a baby carriage. "Oh," says the other, "what a beautiful grandchild you have." "That's nothing," says the first, reaching for her pocketbook. "Wait'll I show you her picture!"

The second seems apocryphal. Willem de Kooning gives a pastel to Robert Rauschenberg, who takes it home and promptly erases it. Next he signs his name to the erasure. Then he sells it. Can it be that Rauschenberg is saying, "The artist has as much right to print money as the financier?" Yes, Rauschenberg is giving us small art right here and much instruction. Authority imprinted upon emptiness is money. And the ego is capital convertible to currency by the use of the name. For six and a half centuries we have been moving from the discovery of humanity into the circulation of the name, advancing out of some primitive obeisance to dread so complete that painting once lay inert on the field of two dimensions (as if the medieval eye was not ready to wander). Then art dared to rise into that Renaissance liberation from anxiety. The painterly capacity entered the space-perspective of volume and depth. Now, with graffiti, we are back in the prison of two dimensions once more. Or is it the one dimension of the name—the art-form screaming through space on a unilinear subway line?

Something of all this is in the mind of our Aesthetic Investigator as he sits in a bedroom on West 161st Street in Washington Heights and talks to CAY 161 and JUNIOR 161 and LI'L FLAME and LURK. They talk about the name. He has agreed to do a centerpiece for a book of photographs on graffiti by Jon Naar, has agreed to do it on the instant (in a Los Angeles hotel room) that he has seen it. The splendid pictures and his undiscovered thoughts on the subject leap together. There is something to find in these pictures, thinks A-I, some process he can all but name. The intellectual hedonism of an elusive theme is laid out before him. So, yes, he accepts. And discovers weeks later that his book has already been given a title. It is *Watching My Name Go By*. He explains to the pained but sympathetic ears of his collaborators that an author needs his own title.

> "One should not be able to conceive of one's bad reviews before writing a word."

Besides, there is a practical reason. Certain literary men cannot afford titles like *Watching My Name Go By*. Norman Mailer may be first in such a category. One should not be able to conceive of one's bad reviews before writing a word.

But then he also does not like *Watching My Name Go By* for its own forthright meaning. These young graffiti writers do not use their own name. They adopt one. It is like a logo. Moxie or Socono, Tang, Whirlpool, Duz. The kids bear a not quite definable relation to their product. It is not MY NAME but THE NAME. Watching The Name Go By. He still does not like it. Yet every graffiti writer refers to the word. Even in newspaper accounts, it is the term heard most often. "I have put my name," says Super Kool to David Shirey of the *Times*, "all over the place. There ain't nowhere I go I can't see it. I sometimes go on Sunday to Seventh Avenue 86th Street and just spend the whole day"—yes, he literally says it— "watching my name go by." But then they all use it. JAPAN I, being interviewed by Jon Naar and A-I in a subway, grins as a station cop passes and scrutinizes him. He is clean. There is no spray can on him today. Otherwise he would run, not grin. Japan says, with full evaluation of his work, "You have to put in the hours to add up the names. You have to get your name around." Since he is small and could hardly oppose too many who might choose to borrow his own immortal JAPAN I, he merely snorts in answer to the question of what he would do if someone else took up his name and used it. "I would still get the class," he remarks.

Whether it is one's own interviews or others, the word that prevails is always the name. MIKE 171 informs *New York* magazine, "There are kids all over town with bags of paint waiting to *hit* their names." A bona fide clue. An object is hit with your name, yes, and in the ghetto, a hit equals a kill. "You must kill a thing," said D. H. Lawrence once, "to know it satisfactorily." (But then who else could have said it?) You hit your name and maybe something in the whole scheme of the system gives a death rattle. For now your name is over their name, over the subway manufacturer, the Transit Authority, the city administration. Your presence is on their presence, your alias hangs over their scene. There is a pleasurable sense of depth to the elusiveness of the meaning.

So he sits with Cay and Junior and the others in the bedroom of Junior's parents and asks them about the name. It is a sweet meeting. He has been traveling for all of a wet and icy snowbound Sunday afternoon through the monumental drabs of South Bronx and Washington Heights, so much like the old gray apartment house ranks of Eastern Parkway in Brooklyn near where he grew up, a trip back across three generations. The Puerto Ricans in this apartment may not be so different from the poor ambitious families of relatives his mother would speak of visiting on the Lower East Side when she came as a child up from the Jersey shore to visit. So little has changed. Still the-smell-of-cooking-in-the-walls, a single word, and the black-pocked green stucco of the halls, those dark pits in the plaster speaking of the very acne of apartment house poverty. In the apartment, entering by the kitchen, down through the small living room and past the dark bedrooms in a file off the hall, all the shades drawn, a glimpse has been had of the television working like a votive light in some poor slum church chapel (one damp fire in the rainforest) while the father in shorts sleeps on the sofa, and the women congregate—the kitchen is near. The windows are stained glass, sheets of red and yellow plastic pasted to the glass—the view must be on an air shaft. No light in this gray and late winter day. It is all the darkness of that gloom which sits in the very center of slum existence, that amalgam of worry and dread, heavy as buckets of oil, the true wages of the working class, with all that attendant fever for the attractions of crime, the grinding entrapments of having lost to the law—lawyers' fees, bondsmen, probation officers, all of it.

Yet now there is also a sense of protection in the air. The mood is not without its reverence: CAY 161 has the face of a martyr. He looks as if he has been flung face first against a wall, as if indeed a mighty hand has picked him up and hurled him through the side of a stone house. He is big, seventeen, and almost six feet tall, once good-looking and may yet be good-looking again, but now it is as if he has been drawn by a comic strip artist, for his features express the stars, comets, exclamation points, and straight-out dislocation of eyes and nose and mouth that accompanies any hero in a comic strip when he runs into a collision. SOCK! ZAM! POW! CAY 161, driving a stolen van, fleeing the cops in an old-fashioned New York street chase, has gone off the road on a turn, "and right on 161st Street where he was born and raised, he hit a hydrant, turned over a few times, and wound up inside a furniture store. . . . When the police looked inside the car,"—description by José Torres in the N.Y. *Post*— "Cay lay motionless in the driver's seat, and another youth, a passenger, sprawled unconscious outside, hurled from the car by the impact." The friend had a broken leg, and Cay had part of his brain taken out in a seven-hour operation. The doctor gave warning. He might survive. As a vegetable. For two months he did not make a move. Now, six months later, Cay is able to talk, he can move. His lips are controlled on one side of his face but slack on the other—he speaks as if he has had a stroke. He moves in the same fashion. Certain gestures are agile, others come up half-paralyzed and top-heavy, as if he will fall on his face at the first false step. So his friends are his witness. They surround him, offer the whole reverence of their whole alertness to every move he makes. There is all the elegance of good manners in the way they try to conceal that he is different from the others.

But Cay is happy now. He is in Junior's house, JUNIOR 161, his best friend. They used to go out writing together for years, both tall, a twin legend—when one stands on the other's shoulders, the name goes up higher on the wall than for anyone else. True bond of friendship: They will each write the other's name, a sacramental interchange. Junior has a lean body, that indolent ghetto languor which speaks of presence. "I move slow, man," says the body, "and that is why you watch me. Because when I move fast, you got to watch out." He is well dressed, ghetto style—a white turtleneck sweater, white pants, a white felt hat, white sneakers, nothing more. Later he will step out like this into the winter streets. You got to meet the eye of the beholder with class. Freezing is for plants.

A-I interviews them. Yes, they started three years ago and would hit four or five names a day. Junior liked to work at least an hour a day. So go the questions: Cay liked to use red marker; Junior, blue. Hundreds of masterpieces to their credit. Yes, Junior's greatest masterpiece is in the tunnel where the track descends from 125th Street to 116th Street. There, high on the wall, is JUNIOR 161 in letters six feet high. "You want to get your name in a place where people don't know how you could do it, how you could get up to there. You got to make them think." It is the peril of the position that calls. Junior frowns on the later artists who have come after Cay and himself. The talk these days is of SLY and STAY HIGH, PHASE 2, BAMA, SNAKE, and STITCH. The article by Richard Goldstein in *New York* (March 26, 1973) has offered a nomenclature for the styles, Broadway, Brooklyn, and Bronx, disquisitions on bubble and platform letters. Perhaps his source is BAMA, who has said to another reporter in his full articulate speaking style, "Bronx style is bubble letters, and Brooklyn style is script with lots of flourishes and arrows. It's a style all by itself. Broadway style, these long slim letters, was brought here from Philadelphia by a guy named Topcat. Queens style is very difficult, very hard to read."

Junior is contemptuous of this. The new forms have wiped out respect for the old utilitarian lettering. If Cay likes the work of STAY HIGH, Junior is impressed by none. "That's just fanciness," he says of the new. "How're you going to get your name around doing all that fancy stuff?"

Cay speaks into this with his deep, strangled, and wholly existential voice—he cannot be certain any sound he utters will come out as he thinks. "Everybody tries to catch up to us," he says.

"You have to put in the hours?"

A profound nod.

Of course, he is not doing it any longer. Nor is Junior. Even before the accident, both had lost interest. On the one hand, the police were getting tough, the beatings when you were caught were worse, the legal penalties higher, the supplies of paint getting to be monitored, and on the other hand something had happened to the process itself. Too many names had grown—a jungle of ego creepers.

A-I queries them about the prominence of the name. He hesitates how to pose the question—he fears confidence will be lost if he asks straight-out. "What is the meaning of the name?" but, indeed, he does not have to—Cay speaks up on what it means to watch the name go by. "The name," says Cay, in a full voice, Delphic in its unexpected resonance—as if the idol of a temple had just chosen to break into sound—"the name," says Cay, "is the *faith* of graffiti."

It is quite a remark. He wonders if Cay knows what he has said. "The name," repeats Cay, "is the *faith*." He is in no doubt of the depth of what he has said. His eyes fix on A-I, his look is severe. Abruptly, he declares that the proper title is "The Faith of Graffiti." So it is.

A Sunday afternoon has come to its end. A-I walks downstairs with Junior, Cay, Lurk, and Li'l Flame, and is shown modest examples of their writing on the apartment house walls. Cay has also used another name. At times he has called himself THE PRAYER 161. They say goodbye in the hall. Cay shows A-I the latest 161st Street sequence of thumb-up finger-curled handshakes. The pistol-pointed forefinger and upraised thumb of one man touch the thumb and forefinger of the other in a quick little cat's cradle. Cay's fingers are surprisingly deft. Then he and Junior spar a bit, half-comic for he lurches, but with the incisive tenderness of the ghetto, as if his moves also say, "Size don't come in packages. A cripple keeps the menace." It is agreeable to watch. As he attempts to spar, Cay is actually moving better than he has all day.

The name is the faith of graffiti. Was it true that the only writing which did not gut one's health lay in those questions whose answers were not known from the start? A-I still had no more than a clue to graffiti. Were the answers to be found in the long war of the will against the power of taboo? Who could know when one of the gods would turn in sleep as images were drawn? Was that a thought in the head of the first savage to put the silhouette of an animal on the wall of a cave? If so, the earliest painting had been not two dimensions but one—one, like graffiti—the hand pushing forward into the terror of future punishment. Only later would come an easier faith that the Lord might be on the side of the artist.

2.

No, size doesn't come in packages, and the graffiti writers had been all heights and all shapes, even all the ages from twelve to twenty-four. They had written masterpieces in letters six feet high on the side of walls and subway cars, and had scribbled furtive little toys, which is to say small names without style, sometimes just initials. There was panic in the act for you wrote with an eye over your shoulder for oncoming authority. The Transit

"There was panic in the act for you wrote with an eye over your shoulder for oncoming authority."

Authority cops would beat you if they caught you, or drag you to court, or both. The judge, donning the robes of Solomon, would condemn the early prisoners to clean the cars and subway stations of the names. HITLER 2 (reputed to be so innocent of his predecessor that he only knew Hitler 1 had a very big rep!) was caught, and passed on the word of his humiliation. Cleaning the cars, he had been obliged to erase the work of others. All proportions kept, it may in simple pain of heart have been not altogether unequal to condemning Cézanne to wipe out the works of Van Gogh.

So there was real fear of being caught. Pain and humiliation were implacable dues, and not all graffiti artists showed equal grace under such pressure. Some wrote like cowards, timidly, furtively, jerkily. "Man," was the condemnation of the peers, "you got a messed-up handwriting." Others laid one cool flowering of paint upon another, and this was only after having passed through all the existential stations of the criminal act, even to first *inventing* the paint, which was of course the word for stealing the stuff from the stores. But then, an invention is the creation of something that did not exist before—like a working spray can in your hand. (Indeed, if Plato's Ideal exists, and the universe is first a set of forms, then what is any invention but a theft from the given universal Ideal?)

There was always art in a criminal act—no crime could ever be as automatic as a production process—but graffiti writers were opposite to criminals, since they were living through the stages of the crime in order to commit an artistic act—what a doubling of intensity when the artist not only steals the cans but tries for the colors he wants, not only the marker and the color, but steals them in double amounts so you don't run out in the middle of a masterpiece. What a knowledge of cops' habits is called for when any Black or Puerto Rican adolescent with a big paper bag is bound to be examined by a Transit cop if he goes into the wrong station. So after his paint has been invented a writer has to decide by which subway entrance it is to be transported, and once his trip is completed back to the station that is the capital of his turf, he still has to find the nook where he can warehouse his goods for a few hours. To attempt to take the paint out of the station is to get caught. To try to bring it back to the station is worse. Six or seven kids entering a subway in Harlem, Washington Heights, or the South Bronx are going to be searched by Transit cops for cans. So they stash it, mill around the station for a time painting nothing, they are, after all, often in the subways—to the degree they are not chased, it is a natural clubhouse, virtually a country club for the sociability of it all—and when the cops are out of sight, and a train is coming in, they whip out their stash of paint from its hiding place, conceal it on their bodies, and in all the wrappings of oversize ragamuffin fatigues, get on the cars to ride to the end of the line where in some deserted midnight yard they will find their natural canvas which is of course that metal wall of a subway car ready to reverberate into all the egos on all the metal of New York.

But it is hardly so quick or automatic as that. If they are to leave the station at the end of the line, there is foreign turf to traverse which guarantees no safe passage, and always the problem of finding your way into the yards.

In the A-train yard at 207th Street, the unofficial entrance was around a fence that projected out over a cliff and dropped into the water of the Harlem River. You went out one side of that fence on a narrow ledge, out over the water, and back the other side of the fence into the yards "where the wagons," writes Richard Goldstein, "are sitting like silent whales."

We may pick our behemoth—whales and dinosaurs, elephants folded in sleep. At night, the walls of cars sit there possessed of soul—you are not just writing your name but trafficking with the iron spirit of the vehicle now resting. What a presence. What a consecutive set of iron sleeping beasts down all the corrals of the yard, and the graffiti writers stealthy as the near-to-silent sound of their movements working up and down the line of cars, some darting in to squiggle a little toy of a name on twenty cars—their nerve has no larger surge—others embarking on their first or their hundred-and-first masterpiece, daring the full enterprise of an hour of living with this tension after all the other hours of waiting (once they had come into the yard) for the telepathic disturbance of their entrance to settle, waiting for the guards patrolling the lines of track to grow somnolent and descend into the early morning pall of the watchman. Sometimes the graffiti writers would set out from their own turf at dark, yet not begin to paint until two in the morning, hiding for hours in the surest corners of the yard or in and under the trains. What a quintessential marriage of cool and style to write your name in giant separate living letters, large as animals, lithe as snakes, mysterious as Arabic and Chinese curls of alphabet, and to do it in the heart of a winter night when the hands are frozen and only the heart is hot with fear. No wonder the best of the graffiti writers, those mountains of heavy masterpiece production, STAY HIGH, PHASE 2, STAR III, get the respect, call it the glory, that they are known, famous and luminous as a rock star. It is their year. Nothing automatic about writing a masterpiece on a subway car. "I was scared," said Japan, "all the time I did it." And sitting in the station at 158th and St. Nicholas Avenue, watching the trains go by, talking between each wave of subway sound, he is tiny in size, his dark eyes as alert as any small and hungry animal who eats in a garden at night and does not know where the householder with his varmint gun may be waiting.

Now, as Japan speaks, his eyes never failing to miss the collection of names, hieroglyphs, symbols, stars, crowns, ribbons, masterpieces, and toys on every passing car, there is a sadness in his mood. The city has mounted a massive campaign. There was a period in the middle when it looked as if graffiti would take over the world, when a movement that began as the expression of tropical peoples living in a monotonous iron-gray and dull brown brick environment, surrounded by asphalt, concrete, and clangor, had erupted to save the sensuous flesh of their inheritance from a macadamization of the psyche, save the blank city wall of their unfed brain by painting the wall over with the giant trees and petty plants of a tropical rainforest. Like such a jungle, every plant, large and small, spoke to one another, lived in the profusion *and* harmony of a forest. No one wrote over another name, no one was obscene—for that would have smashed the harmony. A communion took place over the city in this plant growth of names until every institutional wall, fixed or moving, every modern new school that looked like a new factory, every old slum ware-house, every standing billboard, every huckstering poster, and the halls of every high-rise low-rent housing project that looked like a prison (and all did) were covered by a foliage of graffiti that grew seven or eight feet tall, even twelve feet high in those choice places worth the effort for one to stand on another, ah, if it had gone on, this entire city of blank architectural high-rise horrors would have been covered with paint. Graffiti writers might have become mountaineers with pitons for the ascent of high-rise high-cost swinger-single apartments in the East Sixties and Seventies. The look of New York, and then the world, might have been transformed, and the interlapping of names and colors, those wavelets of ego forever reverberating upon one another, could have risen like a flood to cover the monstrosities of abstract empty twentieth-century walls where no design ever predominated over the most profitable (and ergo most monotonous) construction ratio implicit in a twenty-million-dollar bill.

The kids painted with less than this in view, no doubt. Sufficient in the graffiti-proliferating years of the early Seventies to paint the front door of every subway car they could find. The ecstasy of the roller coaster would dive down their chest if they were ever waiting in a station when a twelve-car train came stampeding in and their name, HONDO, WILDCAT, SABU, or LOLLIPOP, was on the *front*! Yes, the graffiti had not only the feel and all the super-powered whoosh and impact of all the bubble letters in all the mad comic strips, but the *zoom*, the *aghr*, and the *ahhr* of screeching rails, the fast motion of subways roaring into stations, the comic strips come to life. So it was probably not a movement designed to cover the world so much as the excrescence of an excrescence. Slum popu-lations chilled on one side by the bleakness of modern design, and brain-cooked on the other by comic strips and TV ads with zooming letters, even brain-cooked by politicians whose ego is a virtue—I am here to help my nation—brained by the big beautiful numbers on the yard markers on football fields, by the whip of the capital letters in the names of the prod-ucts, and gut-picked by the sound of rock and soul screaming up into the voodoo of the firmament with the shriek of the performer's insides coiling like neon letters in the blue satanic light, yes, all the excrescence of the highways and the fluorescent wonderlands of every Las Vegas sign frying through the Iowa and New Jersey night, all the stomach-tightening nitty-gritty of trying to learn how to spell was in the writing, every assault on the psyche as the trains came slamming in. Maybe it was no more than a movement that looked to take some of the excrescence left within and paint it out upon the world, no more than a species of collective therapy of grace exhibited under pressure in which they never dreamed of painting over the blank and empty modern world, but the authority of the city reacted as if the city itself might be in greater peril from graffiti than from drugs, and a war had gone on, more and more implacable on the side of the authority with every legal and psychological weedkiller on full employ until the graffiti of New York was defoliated, cicatrized, Vietnamized. Now, as A-I sat in the station with Jon Naar and Japan and they watched the trains go by, aesthetic blight was on the cars. Few masterpieces remained. The windows were gray and smeared. The cars looked dull red or tarnished aluminum—their recent coat of paint remover having also stripped all polish from the manufacturer's surface. New subway cars looked like old cars. Only the ghost-outline of former masterpieces still remained. The kids were broken. The movement seemed over. Even the paint could no longer be invented. Now the cans set out for display were empty, the misdemeanors were being upped to felony, the fines were severe, the mood was vindictive. Two hideous accidents had occurred. One boy had been killed beneath a subway car, and another had been close to fatally burned by an inflammable spray can catching a spark, yes, a horror was on the movement and transit patrols moved through the yards and plugged the entrances. The white monoliths of the high-rise were safe. And the subways were dingier than they had ever been. The impulse of the jungle to cover the walled tombs of technology had been broken. Was there a clue to graffiti in the opposite passion to look upon monotony and call it health? As A-I walked the streets with Jon Naar, they passed a sign: DON'T POLLUTE—KEEP THE CITY CLEAN. "That sign," the photographer murmured, "is a form of pollution itself."

3.

Since the metaphor of plant life had climbed all over his discussion of graffiti he went with profit to the Museum of Modern Art for it confirmed the botanical notion with which he began: that if subway graffiti had not come into existence, some artist might have found it necessary to invent, for it was in the chain of such evolution. Art had been rolling down the fall-line from Cézanne to Frank Stella, from Gauguin to Mathieu. On such a map, subway graffiti was an alluvial delta, the mud-caked mouth of a hundred painterly streams. If the obvious objection was that you might interview a thousand Black and Puerto Rican kids who rushed to write their name without having ever seen a modern painting, the answer, not quite as obvious, was that plants spoke to plants.

Famous plant-man Backster, attaching the electrodes of his polygraph to a philodendron one night, wonders in the wake of this passing impulse how to test the plant for some emotional reaction. Abruptly, a current courses through the philodendron at the horror of this thought. (When Backster cuts or burns the leaf, however, the polygraph registers little:

now, the plant is numb. Its sensitivity seems to be its life, its suffering an abstention from life.) By the new logic of the experiment, plants must be a natural species of wireless. (What, indeed, did Picasso teach us if not that every form offers up its own scream when it is torn?) Radio is then no more than a prosthetic leg of communication, whereas plants speak to plants, and are aware of the death of animals on the other side of the hill. Some artists might even swear they have known this from the beginning, for they would see themselves as stimulants who inject perception into the blind vision of the century.

Still, when it comes to a matter of who might influence the writers of graffiti, one is not obliged to speak only of neon signs, comic strips, and TV products, one has the other right to think the kids are enriched by all art that offers the eye a resemblance to graffiti. Which might enable us then to talk of Jackson Pollock and the abstract graffiti of his confluences and meanderings, of Stuart Davis' dramatization of print as a presence that grows in swollen proportion to its size, even include Hans Hofmann's *Memoria in Aeternum*, where those red and yellow rectangles float like statements of a name over indistinct washes beneath, or Matisse's blue and green *Dance*. (Matisse's limbs wind onto one another like the ivy-creeper calligraphies of New York graffiti.) So might one refer to work that speaks of ghetto emotion in any place, of Siqueiros' *Echo of a Scream*, or Van Gogh's *Starry Night*. If the family histories of the most messed-up families have all the garbage-can chaos of de Kooning's *Woman*, no wonder the subway writers prided themselves on style and eclat—"you got a messed-up handwriting" being the final term of critical kill.

But on reflection, was A-I trying to slip in some old piety on the distribution of art down from the museums through media to the masses?— these subway children may never have seen *Memoria in Aeternum* at the head of the stairs at MOMA, but it filtered through to them by way of advertising artists. Fell crap! Rather say art begot art, and the migrations were no one's business. For if plants were telepathic, then humans lived in a psychic sea where all the forms of art also passed through the marketplace of the dreamer in his sleep, and every part of society spoke to every other part, if only with a curse.

So he had the happy thought during his visit to MOMA to decide that some paintings might be, by whatever measure, *on the air*—leave it to the engineers of some future techno-coven to try to determine the precise migrations of Miró's *Plate 8 from Series One, 1953, "The Family"* into the head of an espontaneo with a spray can looking over his shoulder for the black mother in a uniform who will beat his own black blue.

4.

Like a good reporter he goes to see the Mayor. It is ten days to Christmas and the last two weeks of the Lindsay administration. On that Saturday morning, A-I has his appointment to visit, nearly a week from the previous

Sunday, when he talked to Junior and Cay. Again the weather is iron-gray and cold. At Gracie Mansion, the wind is driving in from the East River, and the front porch looks across its modest private lawn to the Triboro Bridge in the north. (To the west, apartment houses rise like the sheer face of Yosemite.) It is not a large lawn in front of the Mayor's residence nor even a large house. Old white Gracie Mansion might be no exceptional residence on any wealthy road in Portland, Oregon, or Portland, Maine—there is even a basketball hoop on a backboard not far from the front door, a political touch dating from recent years, when the Knicks became the most consistently successful team in New York—yet with all its limited grandeur, Gracie Mansion is still one fine Federalist of a house (built in 1799) and if the spirit of an age could have been captured by a ratio, then where better to measure this magic mean if not in the proportions of the Mansion's living room and dining room? They speak in their harmony of some perfect period of Arcadian balance between the early frontier being settled to the West and the new sense of democratic government forging itself in the state capitals of the East. How better to characterize the decorum, substance, grace, and calm center of such architecture if not to think that the spirit and style of the *prose* of the American Constitution is also in it (even to the hint of boredom in prose and buildings both), yet why not precisely these high ceilings, paucity of curves, and all the implicit checks and balances of the right angle? Lindsay, it may be said, is at home in such surroundings. They seem built to his frame. Only a tall lean man could look well-proportioned in so *enlightened* a set of rooms. Nothing like a Gothic arch is present to suggest any mad irreconcilable opposites of God and man, no Corinthian columns to resonate with praetorian tyrannies (and orgies at the top), nor any small and slanted ceilings to speak of craft and husbandry, just government here in Federal style without the intervention of Satan or Jehovah (and next to nothing of Christ), just a fundament of Wasp genius, a building style to state that man could live without faith if things were calm enough. Perhaps the economy of balance is the true god of the Wasp.

His appointment is at eleven, but it is an unusual morning for the Lindsay family, since they have been up until five the night before at a farewell party given the Mayor to honor the eight years of his administration. Lindsay has worked as hard as any man in New York for eight years, and can afford the luxury of being hungover before a reporter this Saturday morning. What a nice relaxation. Lindsay chuckles at the memory of each unexpected rejoinder of party dialogue and laughs at the expression on Tom Morgan's face, press secretary to the Mayor, a tall man with a dark brush mustache who recapitulates in the sardonic gloom of his hungover eyes the incandescence of all those good drinks at that good party. Watching them all, studying Lindsay's face with its patrician features so endowed with every purchase on the meaning of handsome that he could be not only a movie star but there at the front, right ahead of Burt Lancaster and Steve McQueen, on a par with Robert Redford, and hardly a millimeter of profile behind Paul Newman, it occurs indeed that no movie star could be more convincing than Lindsay if it came to playing some very important American politician in the quiet American years from 1800 to 1825. Even his eroded teeth—Lindsay's one failing feature—speak with authenticity of the bad teeth of those English who became the American ruling classes in that Federalist era one hundred and seventy years ago. So sitting in such a dining room, and a little later adjourned to a living room with Lindsay and Morgan to bring up the subject of his interview, he is thinking that Gracie Mansion never had a Mayor nearly so perfectly suited to itself. If there were some divine renting agency in the halls of karma, then come soon or late the post of Mayor of New York would have had to be found for John Vliet Lindsay or the house would feel unfulfilled.

For Lindsay, however, the question may have been whether an ambitious man had ever come to power at a time less promising for himself. He had labored in his two terms, innovated and negotiated, explored, tinkered, tampered, and shifted the base of every municipal machine of government upon which he could work his cadres. He had built a constituency in the ghetto. Mailer-Breslin running for the mayoralty in '69 also ran into one argument over and over in Bedford-Stuyvesant, Harlem, and the South Bronx. It was, "What do we want with you? Lindsay's our man." Lindsay had walked the streets in summer riots, and held some kind of line for decontrol, which is to say, local control, in the ghetto schools. That had taken political courage. Yet make him no saint! He had also worked with the most powerful real estate interests in the city. No question that in his eight years, the ugliest architecture in the history of New York had also gone up. The new flat tops of the skyline now left New York as undistinguished in much of its appearance as Cleveland or Dallas. It is possible Lindsay had bought ghetto relief at the price of aesthetic stultification. Call it desecration. The view of New York's offices and high-rise apartments proved sacrilegious to the mood of any living eye—WASP balance had done it again.

Still, with all this effort, New Yorkers hated him. For every intolerable reason, first of which was his defense of the ghettos. "If I wanted a nigger for Mayor, I'd have voted for a nigger," said every archetype of a cab driver to any tourist who would listen. And yet this Federalist movie star, this hard-working mayor for ghetto rights, had been the first and most implacable enemy of subway graffiti. So there was a feather falling through the mood when he told Lindsay and Morgan why he had come.

But A-I had his speech. If he thought the Mayor had done an honorable job, and was prepared to say so, he still could not comprehend how a man who worked so hard to enter the spirit of ghetto conditions had been nonetheless so implacable in his reaction to graffiti. "Insecure cowards," Lindsay had called the kids. "A dirty shame." Others in his administration offered civic blasts: "graffiti pigs"; "thoughtless and irresponsible behavior." It was surprising. While the management of a city required you to keep it

clean—where would a mayor hide if he could not get the garbage out?—
there was a difference between political necessity and the fury of this
reaction. How could he call the kids cowards? Why the venom? It seemed
personal.

Lindsay grinned. He had heard enough preambles from reporters to
know when an interview was manageable. "Well, yes," he said, "I did get
hot under the collar, and I suppose if we had to go through it again, I
would hope to lose my temper a little less, but you have no idea what a
blow that graffiti was to us." He shook his head at the memory. "You
see, we had gone to such work, such ends, to get those new subway cars
in. It meant so much to people here in the city to get a ride for instance in
one of the new air-conditioned cars. On a hot summer day their mood
would pick up when they had the luck to catch one. And, you know, that
was work. It's hard to get anything done here. You stretch budgets, and
try to reason people into activities they don't necessarily want to take up
on their own. We were proud of those subway cars. It took a lot of talking to a lot of committees to get that accomplished."

Morgan nodded. "And then," Lindsay said, "the kids started to deface
them."

A-I put his demurrer. "Deface," after all, was the core of the argument. Some people might think subway graffiti was art. He suggested in
passing Claes Oldenburg's classic remark ". . . You're standing there in
the station, everything is gray and gloomy and all of a sudden one of
those graffiti trains slides in and brightens the place like a big bouquet
from Latin America."

Lindsay smiled as if recalling the screams, moans, epithets, and
agonized squawks of every bright college intellectual on his staff when
Oldenburg's quote first came riding in. Grand division in the Establishment!
Aesthetic schism! "Yes, we remember that quote," Lindsay's grin seemed
to say. He had the most curious quality of personality. One did not know
if he was secretly more or less decent than his personality. While the personality itself was decent enough, it was also patently not the man, nor,
unhappily for him, characteristic at all of New York. He seemed now like
a Westerner, full of probity, rawhide, and something buried in the personality, a man you might not get to know at all even after a night of
drinking together. He wasn't in the least like Richard Nixon except to
share one quality. Lindsay was out of focus. He had always been out of
focus. Part of his political trouble.

Well, Lindsay suggested, they had never really wondered whether it
was anything but defacement. "People would come into new cars and suddenly they'd see them all marked up, covered inside and out, and it
depressed people terribly. You know, we have to be a kind of nerve center
to the city. Reports came in from everywhere. This graffiti was profoundly
depressing—it truly hurt people's moods. The life would go out of everybody when they saw the cars defaced, they felt it was defacement, no question of that. And we kept hearing one request over and over, 'Can't you do

something about it?' Then, too, we had our own pride in these matters. You know, you get to feel after you've put through a new municipal building that it's yours in some way. As Mayor I'd get as angry when a city building got marked up as if I owned it personally. Oh, it's easier to talk about it now, but I must say it was hard at times not to blow up."

"Actually," Morgan observed, "the Mayor would go around calming some of us down. 'Remember,' he would tell us, 'they're only kids.'"

Yes, in the framework of that time in the Summer of '71 and the Winter and Spring of '72 when Lindsay was looking to get the Democratic nomination for President, what an upset to his fortunes, what a vermin of catastrophe that these writings had sprouted like weeds all over the misery of Fun City, a new monkey of unmanageables to sit on Lindsay's overloaded political back. He must have sensed the presidency draining away from him as the months went by, the graffiti grew, and the millions of tourists who passed through the city brought the word out to the rest of the nation: "Filth is sprouting on the walls."

Of course, where was the tourist who could distinguish between men's-room and subway graffiti? Who was going to dare to look long enough to see that it was a name and not an obscene thought in the writing. Today, just before he had come to Gracie Mansion, he had stopped in the lavatory of a York Avenue bar for a minute, and there on the john wall was drawn a pure old-fashioned piece of smut graffiti. A balloon of dialogue issued out of a girl's mouth. No art in the lettering, no style. "Did you know," said her balloon, "that your clit is in your ass?" Some lost shred of fecal communion now nailed to the wall. Was there a public comfort station in America that did not have a dozen such insights— "Suck me," "Fuck you"? That was what people expected to see on the subways. They assumed the full mad explosive shithouse of America was now erupting in their faces. So they did not look but rode in the cars with their heads down, and brought the news out to the rest of America that Lindsay could not keep the city clean. No wonder he called it a dirty shame. And labeled the aplomb of the graffiti writers cowardice. That was his attempt to soothe the terror in the heart of every subway citizen who looked at the graffiti and put his head down so his eye would not meet any eye that might be connected to the hand which held a knife, yes, that was one side of the fear, and the other was fear of the insane graffiti writer in one's own self. For what filth would burst out of every civilized office worker in New York if ever *they* started to write on moving public walls, my God, the feces to spread and the blood to spray, yes, the good voting citizen of New York would know that the violent ward at Bellevue was opening its door to him on the day he would take a spray can to a subway. So, New York citizenry saw all the children as mad—and therefore saw madness, instability, and horror in the New York Transit. No wonder Lindsay had gone to war against graffiti. The city would tolerate junk, graft, insanities of traffic, mugging, every petty crime of the street, and every major pollution, but it could not accept a towering rainforest of graffiti on all the forty-story walls. Yes, build a wall and balance a disease. For the blank wall of the new architecture was a deadening agent above to balance the growing violence beneath. (Could it be said that the monotony of modern architecture increased all over the world in direct relation to the volcanic disturbances of each society it would contain?)

In the face of such questions the interview was effectively over. They chatted for a while, and got up to say goodbye. On the way out, A-I noticed there was a Rauschenberg on the wall.

Lindsay, in his courtesy, walked with him to the gate. Wearing a blue windbreaker, he looked in the gray outdoor light like a veteran big league ballplayer, tall, weathered, knowledgeable. They took leave not uncordially, and he complimented the Mayor on eight good years, even meant it.

"I wish I had the talent to write," Lindsay said in parting. Was that a politician's gift? A-I pulled back the reply that he wished he could have been Mayor.

Outside the fence, a policeman was standing with a drawn gun. It was a simple measure of the times: Be forever ready at the Gracie gate.

"No, graffiti as a political phenomenon had small hope for life."

And indeed a ten-year-old boy on roller skates cried aloud, "That's him, that's him, that's the Mayor," and promptly took out a cap pistol and fired a number of bangbangs at the back of John Lindsay going back into his house.

For a while, A-I walked, and had a little fantasy of how impossible it would have proved if the miracle worked and he had been elected in the campaign of 1969. What would he have done about graffiti? Would he have tried to explain its virtues to the people of New York—and laughed in all the pain of absolute political failure? The answer was simple— nobody like himself would ever be elected Mayor until the people agreed bad architecture was as poisonous as bad food. No, graffiti as a political phenomenon had small hope for life. His faith in the value of the question would have to explore in another place. Did the final difficulty lie in the meaning of graffiti as art? There the inquiry might become as incomprehensible as the motives of the most advanced artists. On then to the rim of the enigma, to the Sea of Vortices, where the meanings whirl with no meaning.

5.

Years ago, so much as twenty years ago, A-I had conceived of a story he was finally not to write, for he lost his comprehension of it. A rich young artist in New York in the early Fifties, bursting to go beyond Abstract Expressionism, began to rent billboards on which he sketched huge, ill-defined (never say they were sloppy) works in paint that had been chosen to run easily and flake quickly. The rains distorted the lines, made gullies of the forms, automobile exhausts laid down a patina, and comets of flying birds crusted the disappearing surface with their impasto. By the time fifty

such billboards had been finished—a prodigious year for the painter—
the vogue was on. His show was an event. They transported the billboards by trailer-truck and broke the front wall of the gallery to get the
art objects inside. It was the biggest one-man exhibition in New York
that year. At its conclusion, two art critics were arguing whether such
species of work still belonged to art.

"You're mad," cried one, "it is not art, it is never art."

"No," said the other, "I think it's valid."

So would the story end. Its title, Validity. But before he had written
a word he made the mistake of telling it to a young Abstract Expressionist
whose work he liked. "Of course it's valid," said the painter, eyes shining
with the project. "I'd do it myself if I could afford the billboards."

The story was never written. He had assumed he was proposing a
satire, but it was evident he had no insight into how painters were ready
to think. Some process had entered art and he could not discern it out.

Let us go back to the pastel by de Kooning that Rauschenberg erased.
The details, when further inquiry is made, are less impromptu. Rauschenberg
first informed de Kooning of what he would do, and de Kooning agreed.
The work, when sold, bore the inscription "A drawing from Willem de
Kooning erased by Robert Rauschenberg." Both artists are now proposing
something more than that the artist has the same right as the financier to
print money; they may even be saying that the meat and marrow of art,
the painterly core, the life of the pigment, and the world of technique with
which hands lay on that pigment are convertible to something other. The
ambiguity of meaning in the twentieth century, the hollow in the heart of
faith, has become such an obsessional hole that art may have to be converted into intellectual transactions. It is as if we are looking for stuff, any
stuff with which to stuff the hole, and will convert every value into packing for this purpose. For there is no doubt that in erasing the pastel and
selling it, art has been diminished, but our knowledge of society is certainly enriched. An aesthetic artifact has been converted into a sociological
artifact. It is not the painting that intrigues us now but the lividities of art
fashion which made the transaction possible in the first place. Something
rabid is loose in the century. Maybe we are not converting art into some
comprehension of social process but rather are using art to choke the hole,
as if society has become so hopeless, which is to say so twisted in knots of
faithless ideological spaghetti, that the glee is in strangling the victims.

But take the example further. Let us imagine a show at the Guggenheim.
It will be like many we have seen. Let us make it a plausible modern one-
man show. Nothing will be exhibited but computer read-out sheets from
a statistical operation. Hundreds of such sheets tacked to the wall. Somewhat irregularly. Attempts at neatness will be contradicted by a confusion
in the style of placing them on the wall of the Guggenheim as it spirals up
the ramp. Checkerboards alternate with ascending bands, then cul-de-sacs,
paper stapled up every way.

We try to digest the aesthetic experience. Of what do the computer
read-out sheets consist? What is the subject of their inquiry? we ask. And

what is the motive of the artist? Is he telling us something about the order and disorder of the mind in relation to a technological world? Has he presented us with an ongoing composition of exceptional cunning? Is it possible he even has set the problem for the computer himself? Maybe the endless numbers on these computer sheets reflect some analogue to the tension of major themes in his brain. Do we then have here an arithmetical display whose relation to art is as complex as *Finnegans Wake* to literature?

Bullshit, responds the painter. The computer sheets were selected at random. Because the artist did not even wish to bear an unconscious responsibility for the selection, he chose an acquaintance with whom he shared no great psychic identity to pick up the computer sheets for him. Neither he nor the acquaintance ever inquired into the subject of the statistical problem, and he never took a look at what was brought back. Rather, he spoke to the janitor at the Guggenheim by telephone and told him to tack up the pages any way at all. The checkerboards and bands and cul-de-sacs of stapled paper were merely a reflection of the personnel—the janitor worked with two assistants. One was neat, the other drunk. And the painter never came to see the show. The show was the fact that people came, studied the walls, lived for an uncertain hour in the Guggenheim, and went out again, their minds exercised by a question that not only had no answer but may not even have been a question. The artist had done his best to have no intent. Not unless his intent was to demonstrate that most of the experience of viewing a painting is the context of the museum itself. We are next to one of John Cage's compositions in silence. Art has been saying with more and more intensity that the nature of the painting has become less interesting than the relation of painting to society—we can even erase Rauschenberg's erasure. Get the artist out of it altogether, and it is still art. The world is turning inside out.

What step is left to take? Only one. A show that offers no object at all. The last reference to painting or sculpture is the wall on which something can be hung, or the floor on which a piece can sit. That must now disappear. The art-piece enters the artist: The work can only be experienced within his psyche.

From *The New York Times*, September 2, 1973, by Peter Plagens:

a marksman-friend shot Chris Burden in the upper left arm with a .22 long-jacket before an audience of 12 intimates. He (Burden) figured on a graze wound with a Band-Aid slapped on afterward, but it "felt like a truck hit my arm at 80 miles per hour"; he went to the hospital, nauseous, and filed the requisite police report ("accident").

Plagens goes on to describe other "pieces." Burden chooses situations for their possibility of danger, pain, humiliation, or boredom. There is:

"Movie on the Way Down," in which Burden, hanging by his heels, nude, six feet off a gym floor with a movie camera in his hands, is summarily chopped loose.

The movie is presumably taken on the way down (is it filmed in slow motion?) and he ends with a cut lip. There are other pieces where he rockets flaming matches "at his nude supine wife" or sets ablaze two 16-foot wooden crosses on Laguna Canyon Road at 2 A.M.—"the intended audience for that piece," says Burden, "was the one guy driving down the road who saw it first." Ah, Los Angeles! For "Endurance/real time," he 1) stays in a locker for five days; 2) does 1,600 tours of a gallery on his bicycle; and 3) remains in bed for three weeks and a day. He also pretends to be a dead man lying under a tarpaulin on the street and is arrested by the police for creating a traffic hazard. He gets a hung jury at his trial and the case is dismissed but "one of the nine votes for conviction, a stewardess, told Burden if she ever saw him under a tarp again, she'd run over him herself." He even does a study in the shift of identity. For "I Became a Secret Hippie," Burden cuts his hair short and dresses in FBI clothes. "If you want to be a heavy artist nowadays," Plagens, reporting on Burden, concludes, "you have to do something unpleasant to your body, because everything *else* has been done. . . . [Burden] may be a product of art-world art history—backed into some untenable masochistic corner because all the other novelty territory has been claimed."

At the least, Burden is fulfilling the dictum of Jean Malaquais that once there are enough artists in the world, the work of art will become the artist himself. Burden is refining his personality. Through existential tests. Burden is not exploring his technique but his vibrations. The situations he chooses are, as Plagens describes, "edgy." They have nothing remotely resembling a boundary until they are done. In "Movie on the Way Down," Burden can hardly know if he will cut his lip or break his neck, feel a live instant on the descent or some dull anxiety. When he shoots lighted matches at his nude wife the areas defined are empty before the action begins. Given every variable from Women's Liberation to the sado-masochistic tales of Wilhelm Stekel, Burden can know in advance only that a psycho-dramatic enterprise will be commenced. But where it may end, and what everybody might feel—will the matches burn her skin?— will the marriage be fortified or scorched?—no, there is no confidence which question is going to offer an answer. Perhaps he is not refining his personality so much as attempting to clear a space in his psyche free of dread. But isn't that the fundamental operation of the primitive at the dawn of civilization, the establishment of the ego? For what is the human ego but a clearing in the forest of the psyche free of dread? Money, held in one's hand, is free of time. Cash has no past; its future is assignable. It is powerful and empty. So, too, is the ego. It bears the same relation to the psyche as cash bears to the security or comfort of the body. The ego is virtually separate from the psyche even as money is still separate from every organic communicating logic of nature.

We are back to the cave man and his cave painting. His hand draws the outline of the animal in defiance of those gods who watch him. Burden is smashing his nose on the floor or displaying his wife in defiance of the last gods of conventional art. They are that audience remnant of a once-leviathan bourgeois culture. They still trickle out to see Happenings for the desire of the middle class is to preserve its last religion—the world of the artist, palette, museum, and gallery wall. Middle-class passion is to appreciate the work of art.

But art may be the little ball rolling off the table. Perhaps art now signifies some unheard reverberation from the subterranean obsession of us all: Is civilization coming to an end? Is society burning? Is the day of the cave man returning? Has our search for ego which was once so routine—a useful (somewhat heartless) ego to be fashioned for a useful (if heartless) society—now gone past the measure of our experience so that we no longer try to construct a control center at the core of the mind, but plunge instead into absurdities which offer us that curious calm we find in the art of the absurd, even as the cave man, defying his gods, discovered he was not always dead on the next day?

But we are at the possible end of civilization, and tribal impulses start up across the world. The descending line of the isolated artist goes down from Michelangelo all the way to Shoot. But Chris Burden is finally more comfortable to us than the writers of graffiti. For Burden is the last insult from the hippie children of the middle class to the bourgeois art-patron who is their spiritual parent, but graffiti speaks of a new civilization where barbarism is stirring at the roots.

If, at the beginning of Western painting, man was small and God was large; if, in the Renaissance, man was mysteriously large in his relation to God; now, in our times man has disappeared into God. He is mass-man without identity, and he is God. He is all the schizophrenia of the powerless and all-powerful in one psyche.

As we lose our senses in the static of the oncoming universal machine, so does our need to exercise the ego take on elephantiastical proportions. Graffiti is the expression of a ghetto that is near to the plague, for civilization is now closed off from the ghetto. Too huge are the obstacles to any natural development of a civilized man. In the ghetto it is almost impossible to find some quiet identity. No, in the environment of the slum, the courage to display yourself is your only capital, and in the streets crime is the only productive process that converts such capital to the modern powers of the world, ego and money. Art is not peace but war, and form is the record of that war.

Yet there is a mystery still. From which combat came these curious letters of graffiti, with their Chinese and Arabic calligraphies? Out of what connection to the past did these lights and touches of flame become so much like the Hebrew alphabet, where the form of the letter itself was worshipped as a manifest of the Lord? No, it is not enough to think of the childlike desire to see one's name ride by in letters large enough to scream your ego across the city, no, it is almost as if we must go back into some more primeval sense of existence. If our name is enormous to us, it is also not real—as if we have come from other places than the name, and lived in other lives.

Perhaps that is the unheard echo of graffiti, the vibration of that profound discomfort it arouses. Can the unheard music of its proclamation and/or its mess, the rapt intent seething of its foliage, be the herald of some oncoming apocalypse less and less far away? For graffiti lingers on our subway door as a memento of all the lives ever lived, sounding now like the bugles of gathering armies across the unseen ridge.

Interview with Norman Mailer (Conducted by J. Michael Lennon)

About six weeks after Norman Mailer's seventy-fifth birthday on January 31, 1998, I interviewed him in Provincetown, Massachusetts. A few months earlier, he had completed editing a retrospective collection of his work that he titled *The Time of Our Time*. I had been assisting him in this process by providing copies of publications now difficult to find. Containing over one hundred excerpts from his books and periodical pieces, the anthology was published on May 6, exactly fifty years after the publication of *The Naked and the Dead*. On an overcast winter afternoon in Mailer's three-story, ivy-covered, brick waterfront home, I sat with him to discuss his current sense of his tumultuous literary career.
—*J. Michael Lennon*

J. MICHAEL LENNON: Would you say something about your preparations for this book, and the effects of a new reading of all your books? What was it like to read the writing of earlier, younger selves?

NORMAN MAILER: It was an interesting summer. I had a lot of surprises because certain books were better than I remembered; others were not as good. The bonus was *An American Dream*. It may be, sentence for sentence, the best written of all my novels, and that was curious to discover. On the other hand, pieces I'd loved for years, like "Superman Comes to the Supermarket," struck me as sometimes overwritten, very good in places, turgid in others. The biggest disappointment was "Ten Thousand Words a Minute," my account of the first Patterson-Liston fight in Chicago. It had some fine nuggets but the piece as a whole showed little organization. Of course, I was looking to pick portions of essays, and excerpts of the novels, that would conform to my overall notion. We can probably get into that a little later.

JML: Is this the first time that you have systematically read everything that you have written?

NM: Well, I didn't go back to every last word I've written. Don't forget, you were reading a great deal of it first and were sending me pieces I'd forgotten. While the book is long, 1,300 pages long, I could put another one together of equal length for there was also stuff that just broke my own loving writer's heart to leave out.

JML: *The Time of Our Time* has four pieces that are subtitled "The Cold War," scattered through the first half of the book.

NM: Yes. "Cold War I," "Cold War II," and so forth.

JML: It occurred to me that many other pieces in the book could carry that subtitle just as well, pieces from *Oswald's Tale, The Armies of the Night, The Presidential Papers, The Deer Park,* many additional pieces from *Harlot's Ghost.* Indeed, one might say that your career, in a sense, has encompassed the entire Cold War. . . . Is that fair?

NM: "Reflections on the Cold War" could have been a title for the book. The Cold War is something that we took for granted most of our lives. But the crucial years of the Cold War for me were the early fifties, because the atmosphere that lay over America then was much more *directed* and overbearing and overpowering and disagreeable. It was not that we were in any way a fascistic state, except in one serious fashion, which is that people were beginning to be ready to not think freely. The Cold War impinged on our thoughts. A few liberties were taken away from people on the extreme left, and certainly from Communism. There were any number of very unpleasant aspects of it. There was the House on Un-American Activities Committee, there was Joe McCarthy, but the prevailing mood was support of the Cold War. Under everything, however, was the great guilt of America as a Christian nation. We felt we hadn't really won the Second World War; the Russians had won it. We made an enormous contribution, but if you're going to start giving percentages of credit to who won that Second World War against Hitler, you'd have to offer the Russians at least sixty percent of the whole. Think of how many American lives would have been lost if we had had to fight Hitler on our own. The war might have gone on for seven or eight years, and Europe might eventually have been flattened by atom bombs. There's just no telling what would have happened without the Russians. So there was the guilt of turning on a former ally. Now of course, we knew what that ally was. All during the war, everybody in America knew that Russia was a Communist nation, and we were not very close to communism. But there's always been a terror at the heart of capitalism which is: What if we are doing the wrong thing? What if people are not supposed to make a lot of money? What if people are supposed to make their peace with God and live simply? This tension has always been at the core of American life. America is an immensely religious nation, and it's also an immensely acquisitive nation. We are probably more divided spiritually than other countries which often have huge or deep traditions to fall back on, and so can possess a sense of the past that we don't have. Life in America is viscerally uprooted. It's worth repeating that most of the people who are here are the descendants of men and women who came from other places, and so felt uprooted. Given this condition, there was a subterranean guilt in American life. Now that we were turning on our former ally, we couldn't afford to believe there was anything remotely good about them or it would have exercised our guilt. So our former ally changed overnight into the evil empire. And this was long before Ronald Reagan came up with the phrase. Every force in American life that was conservative and rich and powerfully installed went gung-ho for the Cold War. People were afraid to think. That was the cryptofascism of the period. Everyone was scared. So, for me, the Cold War is the fifties. Hence the subtitles: Cold War I, Cold War II, et cetera. The sixties were something else altogether.

JML: You say in your preface that "our knowledge of the personality of the observer enables us to judge better the insight and accuracy of his or her writing." Yet you chose in this book to minimize your presence.

NM: I felt that I had put such emphasis on myself as the observer through these last fifty years that the reader didn't really need any more of me. Rather I wanted to show that I had also done a good deal of objective writing. The prevailing notion about me is, "He may be a good writer, but he's such an egomaniac." There are a lot of people who never read me for that reason. That's not entirely without justice. When people have a large driving ego, as I certainly did have for many, many years, it takes them over, it's a fever. They begin to see everything in terms of their own status. If they're rejected, they fight back. Muhammad Ali is the foremost example of that. He began as the leading American egomaniac, and people couldn't bear him because there is, indeed, something heartless and cold about someone who's all ego. The remarkable thing with Ali is that through the years, and through his deeds, and those deeds were heroic, the public has come to love him. The same public that hated him for being against the war in Vietnam then, now adores him. I ran into him about a year ago in a small airport in Michigan, and we chatted for a bit, and people came up to him, middle class white people, who happened to be in the airport. They approached him as if he were a saint. All of them. I've never seen anything like it. What characterizes Ali is that he's always been very generous, even in his most hateful periods. He gave you full measure of his hatred; he never held anything back. And so, when people give him their love, and everyone loves him today, he takes it in and he gives it back. His eyes are luminescent. He stands there, large, immobile, his hands shaking a little from his Parkinson's, and he signs autographs, and he looks at each person. They go away as if they've been beatified. In the phenomenological sense, he has changed from an egomaniac to a saint. Now I'm no saint, but I will say that once you've been through this huge fever of the galloping ego, and you've lived with it, and you've worked with it, and worked through it, what you develop afterward, and it's one of the virtues of living through your vices as well as your virtues, and not repressing your vices, after you live through it, you tend to have a larger objectivity and also a greater versatility than when you started. What ego gave me was the desire to write about a great many things. So when it came to putting together this book, the last thing I looked for was to bring the reader too deeply into my life. There was one moment when I had to intrude into the book, when I wrote a page or two about my marriage with Adele which ended after I made a felonious assault upon her with a penknife. I felt that had to be put in. To ignore it was to create a species of false book. But, generally speaking, I wanted to stay out of the book because the work I've done, I felt, is much, much more important than the public life I've had. As public lives go, it has been picayune. If I stand for anything, I'm going to be there for my work, not my presence on the public scene.

JML: Did that place any limitation on you when you were making the selections for the book?

NM: I didn't go at it that way. It seemed to me that over the course of my life I had written a species of social and cultural history about America and I chose pieces that contributed to such a history. That's the fundamental scheme here. I decided I would not print the excerpts in chronological order in which they were written, but to the contrary would put them in by way of the year they take place. Excerpts from *Harlot's Ghost* offer the best example. The novel was published in 1991 but deals with the period from 1948 to 1963; in the main, it deals with the fifties. So, there's a great deal from *Harlot's Ghost* in the first half of the collection. It was not a rigid scheme or I would have had to leave out books like *Ancient Evenings*. Therefore, toward the end of the formal plan, in the eighties, you have a piece set in the year 1200 B.C. Of course, I also felt that *Ancient Evenings* had a good bit to say about the eighties, a period when Americans became immensely wealthy, and the need to amass wealth became the center of the nation. There's no culture that personifies that lust more than ancient Egypt, where, indeed, only rich people ever went to the Elysian Fields after death. If you were a poor Egyptian, you were left to rot and disappear into the desert sands. Whereas the only way you could get to these Elysian Fields was to have an appropriate funeral, which was very expensive. It seemed to me that parts of *Ancient Evenings* belonged, therefore, in the book; they still have something to say about present-day America.

JML: After you finish the excerpts from *The Executioner's Song*, you turn the page, and you are in 1200 B.C. at the embalming of Menehetet II. It's a wonderful shock.

NM: Well, originally I was going to include the autopsy of Gary Gilmore, but there wasn't room to have both the autopsy and the embalming. The embalming scene in *Ancient Evenings* is one of the best things I've ever written, so I thought, let me put that in right there. It is a shock, but there it is.

JML: The book opens in 1929 with a piece on Hemingway and Fitzgerald; it opens in the same general period that *The Sun Also Rises* was set in Paris. That book always meant so much to you.

NM: I wouldn't say that. Hemingway meant a great deal to me, but I wouldn't say *The Sun Also Rises* is a large part of that. I read it in college, and like all college kids I was impressed by it. But there are other books that meant more to me then. The work of Thomas Wolfe and James T. Farrell certainly affected me. So did *The Grapes of Wrath*.

JML: And Dos Passos?

NM: *USA* meant more than all of them. Hemingway's style intrigued me, but I got as much from his short stories as from *The Sun Also Rises*. I didn't understand *The Sun Also Rises*. Even when I read it today I am not sure I understand it altogether. These people are kind of bizarre. I suppose I mean that they really are somewhat asinine. Several of them, at least, unless you are in a mood of total sympathy for them, which is not easy to find.

JML: But haven't you admired the first person narration of Jake Barnes?

NM: Well, the first person is an amazing tool. You can get to places with the first person you can't arrive at any other way. Of course, you can also injure your writing hand, so to speak. It's a double-edged instrument. Hemingway had a marvelous sense of the limitations of the first person. It virtually created his style. If you are doing a book in the first person, there are certain things you should not talk about because they're embarrassing when you have "I" going before it. So there's a tendency, most marked in Hemingway, to keep everything at arm's length.

JML: Then there was no particular symbolism implied by your opening with the piece on Hemingway?

NM: I did it like a literary mechanic. Most of the things I do in writing are not on impulse, but on instinct. It isn't even a large instinct. It doesn't say "Start here!" Rather it whispers, "Start with this." The way a mechanic putters around before going to work on a problem. It seemed to me that it was an agreeable piece. People have this big volume in front of them. I thought, "Let's start with something absolutely comfortable and agreeable," something that will make no demands on the reader, but will offer a nice insight into Hemingway, and a good one into Fitzgerald. It tells us about something we've almost forgotten, which is: what kind of boxer was Hemingway? That was really the only reason I chose it. I just thought it was a nice little piece and there were going to be a lot of big pieces later. So let's start with something small.

JML: When JFK was running for president, you compared him, in your famous piece "Superman Comes to the Supermarket," to a movie star. Not just how he looked, and he looked like a movie star as I remember the description, but also how he affected us, how he affected our unconscious. I'm struck by how many pieces there are in this collection that link politics to the movies, social issues to celebrities and movie stars. How conscious were you of this linkage between the movies and politics?

NM: I took it for granted. One reason I've always been interested in movie
stars is because of the sudden success of *The Naked and the Dead*.
I really have the inner biography, in an odd way, of some young
actor who has a hit, and is catapulted from being someone who
haunts the spiritual bread lines to someone who's worth millions—
I'm not talking now about money but of the shift in one's ego. I had
that experience. After all, I was utterly unknown. By my own lights
I'd not been much of a soldier, and that ate at me. In a squad of
twelve men I would have been number seven, eight, or nine, if you're
going to rank them by ability. I was always at the bottom half of
the squad. That hurt me; I wasn't a good soldier and I wanted to be
one. There's a remark made by somebody who went to Andover in
the early twenties. He said, "It was the worst experience of my life,
and the most valuable." That was Andover then. It's much nicer
today. I felt that way about the Army. The worst experience of my
life, and the most valuable. And I'll say it to this day. I think I'm a
better writer today for having had those two years in the Army. It
isn't that I hate the Army today, but what a savage inner experience it
was for a young spoiled ego to go into the Army then. In fact, I often
tease my sons by telling them, "You could use a year or two in the
services." So I was without any large idea of myself and my abilities
as a man, and abruptly I was catapulted upward. Suddenly I possessed a power that came to me from my work. Yet it didn't feel as if
it had come from what I had done. Indeed, I was very much like a
young movie actor who doesn't know where he is, and who he is. I
hadn't heard in those days of identity crises, but I was in one. Movie
stars have always fascinated me since. I felt I knew something about
their lives that other authors don't. Most writers go through a long,
arduous preparation before they arrive. William Kennedy, for example, worked in the boondocks for twenty years before it was recognized what a talented writer he is. By the time he arrived at his
success, he could enjoy it. He had earned it. He knew the man he
was when his success arrived. There were no shocks and surprises.
For me it was exactly the opposite. It took me twenty years to come
to terms with who I was and to recognize that my experience was
the only experience that I was ever going to have. There are other
people like me that have had a similar experience, who were also
shot out of a cannon. . . .

JML: So your experience was something you could draw on when looking
at American politics?

NM: The moment politicians run for high office, they begin to feel unreal. They are going to affect the lives of millions and what's their
sanction? What right do they have, really? So politicians have also
fascinated me, because objectively speaking, they're phony; they have
to be. If you or I were running for president, we'd be phony, we'd
be pretending to strength and knowledge we hadn't quite acquired.

There are very few presidents that have seemed right for the role. Franklin Delano Roosevelt was one of them. Eisenhower, in a way, was right; he'd been commander-in-chief of all those armies, and he had some sense that he was in the proper place. Lyndon Johnson, who had all those years in the Senate, never felt quite right as a president. Jack Kennedy was a hero in the war and he had a great deal of preparation; he had a father who was a brilliant guy; but I don't think he felt altogether in place. Jimmy Carter came out of nowhere and never felt right.

JML: Reagan?

NM: Reagan had passed the point where he could still have three consecutive thoughts. Blissfully for him it was sort of dreamy and kind of nice, an easy role. He was never sure where the director was located; it seemed to change from day to day. But he was willing to follow orders. Then Bush, in the shadow of Reagan, never felt OK. Now, we come to William Jefferson Clinton. With him we are not only dealing with movie stars, we're dealing with the number one soap opera in America. For years I've been saying that the American presidency had become America's leading soap opera. But this has increased by an order of magnitude in the Clinton administration. Television wouldn't be half as vivid, half as alive without Clinton and his troubles, without Hillary and her wonderful soap opera relation to the wandering eye of Bill Clinton. It's the best television since *Dallas*.

JML: There's a fair amount of writing about sex in *The Time of Our Time*. Excerpts from *The Deer Park, Ancient Evenings, Harlot's Ghost*, the pieces on Henry Miller and D. H. Lawrence, not to mention "The Time of Her Time," which is the Ur-title of this book. Are time and sex still very much linked in your consciousness?

NM: Well you're referring to a line at the end of *The Deer Park*, "Think of sex as time, and time as the connection of new circuits," how does it go, "the connection of new circuits was a part of the poor odd dialogues which give hope to us noble humans for more than one night." What I meant is that time is embodied in humans. Real time has nothing to do with chronology or clocks. It has to do with the passage of our beings through existence. We connect with one another and create children, or if we don't create children, we create profound friendships that carry on some conception of existence, some vision of existence that in its passage creates time. That's why time is impossible for physicists to comprehend. We don't know what time is. We don't know what space is. We don't know what light is. We don't know what any of the fundamentals are. We do know a little about electricity and magnetism and their relations to one another. If you take a wire and you pass it through the jaws of a magnet, an electrical current will start. If you wrap a wire around an iron bar and pass the current through the wire, magnetism will start at its poles. That's fascinating, but it's all we really know. No one can explain these fundamental mysteries. People walk on blindly. "Do you have a web site?" they ask.

JML: You've spoken over the years of a "navigator" in your unconscious, driving your being along by private charts, and updating those charts as it moved along. Is the historical journey charted in this book the one that the "navigator" chose, or were many of your writing projects just happenstance?

NM: Both. When I use the notion of this "navigator" at the center of each of us, what I mean is that as we come to understand our life and others, we keep on improving these unconscious charts by which we guide our actions. But what has to be recognized is that most people, particularly in their early years, are sailing across unknown seas. The navigator develops as one grows older, but the navigator always has to be prepared for extraordinary surprises. So I wouldn't say this book was put together by my navigator. That would be too grandiose. No, I put it together as a craftsman. The choices that had to be made were interesting to me, but they weren't soul-shaking.

JML: Does the book have a plot?

NM: The book is one man's vision of American life from 1948 to 1998. On May 6, 1998, it will be fifty years since *The Naked and the Dead* appeared, and I wanted to have a book out that would reflect the fact I have been writing for these fifty years. I'm proud of that. It's a little bit like being a marathoner who still runs marathons at the age of seventy-five. In that sense, it's my prize. Through the various vicissitudes that all writers have, and mine were as large as many or most, I did manage to keep writing. This book is a reflection of that. . . .

JML: Over the years there's been a lot of comment on the relative merits of your fiction and your nonfiction. It seems to me after reading this book more than once that it demonstrates the seamlessness of your fiction and your nonfiction. Would you agree?

NM: Back in 1967 when I wrote *The Armies of the Night,* I divided the book into fiction and nonfiction. I was saying, in effect, that they're equal. When you write history, you're writing a species of fiction. What one's doing, ultimately, is giving one's vision of life. And how one arrives at one's vision of life is somewhat different in a history than in fiction, but they are much more alike than people recognize. So that's why I called the two subdivisions in *The Armies of the Night,* "History as a Novel," and "The Novel as History." I've always felt they're very much related. Let me give you an example. There's something like thirty pages in *The Time of Our Time* on Marilyn Monroe and Arthur Miller taken from my biography of Monroe. It's as factual as my sources could permit, but to me it reads like fiction. That is, it's a narrative of a movie star and a talented playwright, who are not having a very happy marriage, and if it appeared in the pages of a novel and you changed the names, it would still read.

JML: The same could be said of *The Executioner's Song.*

NM: *The Executioner's Song* absolutely defies category, because I use the real names of the people. I gave it a terrible subtitle. I called it *A True Life Novel*. I regret that very much. I think it's slightly better than Truman Capote's equally awful subtitle, *A Nonfiction Novel*. I could have made it a novel by changing all the names. Call Gary Gilmore, Harry Kilmore, and so forth, and, it would have been a "key" novel. People would have said, "Oh, so-and-so is so-and-so in that book." But by keeping the same names I pushed the envelope forward on what a novel is and what it isn't. I would say that what makes a novel is not whether the facts occurred or not. You can never get the real facts. You approximate them; you approach them. What is important is the way you present these facts. I would argue then that since I wrote it in the form of a novel, it is a novel. The form, the medium, determines the message. And the message you receive from a novel is different from the message—usually less interesting—that comes to you from nonfiction. Therefore, I like my nonfiction to read like a novel. By which I don't mean that I fudge the facts. On the contrary, since I'm already out on a limb, I'm careful about the facts. When I'm writing nonfiction I have to be more careful than the average journalist. But for me fiction and history are very much alike. . . .

JML: I've come to the end of my questions, but I've got to ask you about three words that have become famous when we talk about Norman Mailer's writing these days: "To Be Continued."

NM: . . . Writers often have a deep sense of when they're ready to do a book, and when they're not. After fifty years if I don't know, I'm not that much of a writer. So I've been waiting for an indication in myself. There has to be something new in the second volume [of *Harlot's Ghost*], something larger in one way or another than the first volume, deeper, more profound. Otherwise why get into it? That first volume is already there. . . . Finally, a new set of ideas has been germinating in me, ideas that make the thought of the second volume exciting for the first time. So I'm going to make an all-out attempt to do it over the next few years. I'm appalled at what it's going to cost physically. By the time you finish a novel you are in much less good shape than when you started because the inner tension is immense. When you're making things up it's scary; the decisions you have to make are frightening. If you choose the wrong turn, you can lose months of work. So there's always dread when you do an imaginative narrative. If your characters come alive, that's fine; they carry you a part of the way. But, finally, you have to make what might be termed career decisions for your characters. Does your protagonist want to go into the foreign service, or does he want to work in New York? These are large decisions but they are also opportunities. Certain writers have the book completely in their mind before they begin and then they write it. I'm not one of them. I find my book as I go along.

JML: And your plot?

NM: My plot comes last. What I look for are the characters. I want a con-
    ception of my characters that's deep enough so that they will get me
    to places where I have to live by my wits. That means they have to
    keep on developing for me. When my characters come alive, the plot,
    I always feel, will take care of itself. I cannot write a book where I
    figure out the plot first. When you do that, you spend the rest of your
    time filling holes in rotten teeth. Because that's what characters are
    when they only have to satisfy your plot. So I've been waiting and
    waiting, with the full knowledge that I may wait too long and it will
    never get written. Seven years have gone by and now I'm seventy-five.
    If it takes me three, four, or five years to write the second volume,
    I may be at the end of my writing wherewithal by the time I do it. So
    it's scary. We'll see. Either I'll write it or I won't be able to write it.
    But I do feel—not exactly readiness, but what you always look for
    when you start a novel: anticipation.

Demetria Martínez

Inherit the Earth
The Things They Carried

Demetria Martínez is an author, activist, lecturer, and columnist. A collection of her essays, *Confessions of a Berlitz-Tape Chicana,* was published in 2005 by University of Oklahoma Press. Her books include the widely translated novel *Mother Tongue* (1996), winner of a Western States Book Award for Fiction, and two books of poetry, *Breathing Between the Lines* (1997) and *The Devil's Workshop* (2002). She writes a column for the *National Catholic Reporter,* an independent newsweekly. *Confessions of a Berlitz-Tape Chicana* was the winner of the 2006 International Latino Book Award in the category of Best Biography. She is on the writing faculty of the William Joiner Center for the Study of War and Social Consequences at the University of Massachusetts–Boston.

Martínez's novel *Mother Tongue* is based in part upon her 1988 trial for conspiracy against the U.S. government in connection with transporting Salvadoran refugees into the country. At the time, she was a religion reporter covering the faith-based Sanctuary Movement; she was found not guilty on First Amendment grounds.

Born and residing in Albuquerque, Martínez earned her BA from Princeton University's Woodrow Wilson School of Public and International Affairs. She is active with Enlace Comunitario, an immigrants' rights group that serves Spanish-speaking victims of domestic violence.

We have included two brief essays from her book *Confessions of a Berlitz-Tape Chicana.* The pieces serve as eulogies for those who have died and those who have survived the American border crossing.

Inherit the Earth

The Arizona sun is melting like a pat of butter on the mountain that flanks Tucson's west side. As the day dies away, people are gathering at an outdoor shrine known as El Tiradito, in the heart of downtown's Barrio Historico. For fifty weeks, every Thursday night, we have gathered here for a vigil to remember those who perish as they make their brutal pilgrimage across the U.S.–Mexico border.

The shrine is little more than a ruin of a wall, its pockmarked adobes licked by candlelight. Legends have multiplied around the origins of El Tiradito, which means "the castaway." Stories speak of a love triangle in 1870 gone bad, ending in murder, the body abandoned in the hard dirt.

According to the historical marker, "This is the only shrine in the U.S. dedicated to the soul of a sinner buried in unconsecrated ground."

Unconsecrated ground. Reflecting on those words, I can't help but see our border, la frontera: a militarized zone, a killing field. I think of the fourteen men who died recently in triple-digit heat—abandoned by their smuggler, abandoned by a gluttonous nation that craves cheap labor but detests the laborer.

Too, I think of the hope that guides such men, women, and children north. Only hope, biblical in proportion, would compel Yolanda Gonzales, on Memorial Day of last year, to pour the last drops of water from her plastic jug into her daughter's bottle. The mother died in the Arizona desert. The baby, named Elizama, survived.

> "To speak of an immigrant's plight only in terms of desperation fails to honor his or her full humanity."

To speak of an immigrant's plight only in terms of desperation fails to honor his or her full humanity. Of course there is desperation; everywhere it uproots and drives masses across borders in swelling numbers.

Still, whereas desperation drives people, hope guides them. With a patience that rivals that of Job's, the migrant gathers information, plans, packs, says good-bye to her family, then strikes out. It is not Disneyland she hopes for, but dignity.

Perhaps it is such hope that consecrates the blistering desert terrain where so many have fallen. Even in death, the fourteen Mexican migrants live on as a sign: The forces of militarization and xenophobia will not stop a single determined soul from putting one foot in front of the other, plastic water jug in hand.

At our vigil we hold up a white wooden cross. It is marked with the word "Presente." Yes, the dead live among us, as martyrs, as prophets. Their lives—their hunger and their hope—add up to a cry that will be heard around the globe. A cry for change. A demand that we heal our tortured border, that we reconsecrate the earth.

The Things They Carried

Is it an art installation or an altar? At First Christian Church in Tucson, a museum-quality display case holds, among a number of objects, the following: empty plastic water jugs, a backpack, a baby bottle, soap, Colgate toothpaste, a hairbrush, a sardine can, a sock, and used AeroMéxico tickets.

When Mexican migrants fan out across the treacherous Arizona desert border region, these are some of the things they carry. On foot a person might cover eight to ten miles a day—or fewer miles if carrying a baby. Many try to beat those odds. The exhibit includes a stroller. A Caribou bicycle is also on display, its tire tubes all shot to hell, punctured by cactus needles from the trek through an impossible terrain.

"We find about one hundred bicycles a week," said Reverend Robin Hoover, pastor at First Christian and founder of Humane Borders, which has maintained water stations for migrants, mostly on public lands, in the most desolate areas of Arizona for more than a year. The U.S. Border Patrol has pledged not to target the water stations, and it recently credited the availability of the large barrels of water with saving thirty-three lives in just one day. Many fear the stations will inevitably become a target for agents rounding up Mexicans.

The installation, put together by Maeve Hickey of Dublin, is called Lost and Found: Remnants of a Desert Passage. She selected items from the hundreds that Humane Borders volunteers have collected on their frequent trips to haul water to the stations.

Standing before the glass case, Hoover explained that the Caribou bike was found about twenty-three miles north of the border in Organ Pipe Cactus National Monument.

The stroller was found twenty-one miles north of the U.S.–Mexico border at the Jim Corbett water station in Organ Pipe. Named after the deceased Sanctuary Movement founder, Jim Corbett station has dispensed the most water of all fourteen stations Humane Borders maintains.

"We've even found baby's cowboy boots with silver tips," said Hoover, adding that he doesn't know what fate the owner of the stroller or the babies met.

As to the many personal hygiene items volunteers find at water stations: "Migrants think they've made it, and now they're going to freshen up," Hoover said.

In fact a lot of migrants have no idea where they are in relation to where they want to end up.

Hoover said most have their sights on Florida, the Bay Area, Los Angeles, Chicago, New York, New Jersey, and anywhere in Texas. Depending on where they started along Arizona's almost three-hundred-mile border with Mexico, they press northward: through Organ Pipe Cactus National Monument, Buenos Aires National Wildlife Refuge, Cabeza Prieta National Wildlife Refuge, the Tohono O'odham Indian Reservation, and other, mostly public, lands.

Some groups have arranged ahead of time for rides that they'll meet up with in small towns, or at appointed spots along the highway. Smugglers called "coyotes" guide other groups for a price, often proffering false promise of a nearby city where a ride awaits to take them to their destinations. And still others imagine that Phoenix is just around the bend. They push on.

Volunteers come across many socks. When feet swell, and burrs and needles collect in socks, those are left behind. The most common metal item found, Hoover said, is a poor person's version of a Swiss Army knife, with nail clippers, can opener, and knife. It is used to cut needles out of clothes or the body. People also use the instrument to modify their clothing: to cut off sleeves and shorten pants in triple-digit heat. Another item found: injectable xylocaine to deaden the pain.

The border patrol has, in the past decade, successfully sealed off traditional urban points of entry, such as Júarez–El Paso; hence the large numbers attempting the desert, which in Arizona is mostly under federal, state, tribal, county, or corporate management. The U.S. Fish and Wildlife officials have permitted Humane Borders to erect poles with flags at seven animal watering troughs. The flags bear the symbol of the drinking gourd from the abolitionist movement, with water pouring from the dipper.

Humane Borders provides water to address the immediate emergency, but its ultimate goal is, with other groups, to force changes in U.S. immigration policy—to "take death out of the migration equation," as Hoover puts it.

The length of the entire U.S.–Mexico border is almost two thousand miles; human rights groups estimate that at least one person a day dies trying to cross it.

Remarking on the display, Hoover said he was not sure why someone would carry used AeroMéxico plane tickets, although such documents are often found. Carrying them, an immigrant runs the risk of a border patrol agent using a plane ticket as evidence of country of origin, a basis for deportation. On the other hand, there is an advantage. A name on one's person can help identify remains should one die along the way.

There's much more beyond the large display case of things found in the desert, the things that migrants carry.

At Humane Borders's church office, volunteers have collected a baby's receiving shirt, business cards, a cologne bottle, wedding pictures, crucifixes, a doll, and *Five Minutes of Prayers in the Home*, a Spanish-language booklet dated March 2002.

The desert holds letters lost or left behind. "I love you," reads a handwritten letter in Spanish. "I need you. . . . I hope that very soon we can be together forever."

Michael Martone

Manufacturing Place

Michael Martone's books include *Michael Martone* (2005), a memoir made up of contributor's notes. Some of his other books are *The Flatness and Other Landscapes,* which won the Associated Writing Programs award for nonfiction (2000), *Seeing Eye* (1995), *Fort Wayne Is Seventh on Hitler's List* (1990), *Safety Patrol* (1988), *Alive and Dead in Indiana* (1984), and *The Blue Guide to Indiana* (2001). *Racing in Place*, a book of essays, is his most recent work (2008). He has also edited a number of anthologies.

Bookreporter called *Michael Martone* by Michael Martone "one of 2005's best, most interesting and hilarious collections of short stories, not only because of its bizarre, deconstructionist format, but—for true lovers of literary fiction—its unique narrative." Of *The Flatness and Other Landscapes*, a *Publishers Weekly* reviewer wrote, "What keeps the reader's interest alive is Martone's keen eye for the uncanny details of ordinary life in an agricultural community. His depiction of how the system of vacuum pipes acts in an automatic milking machine (the pipe 'runs around the barn, circles over the stalls like a halo'), his description of the process in which pigs' needle teeth and tail are snipped (so they don't bite each others' tails off when they're crowded into a pen), his account of 'walking the beans' (weeding the rows of crop beans by walking up and down with a special hoe topped with a wick dipped in an extremely potent herbicide)—all these draw the reader into a world that seems simultaneously familiar and utterly alien."

Michael Martone was born and grew up in Fort Wayne, Indiana, where he attended the public schools. Much of his writing is set in the state. He studied at Butler University in Indianapolis and graduated from Indiana University with a degree in English. He is also a graduate of the Writing Seminars of the Johns Hopkins University. He lives in Tuscaloosa, Alabama, and teaches at the University of Alabama and the Program for Writers at Warren Wilson College.

In "Manufacturing Place," taken from *The Flatness and Other Landscapes,* Martone looks at the wiring of Fort Wayne.

Interview with Michael Martone, p. 575.

My sense of place has been generated from a particular rust belt environment of manufacturing. I was aware, growing up in Fort Wayne, Indiana, that things were made there and that those made things contributed to the identity of the place. Trucks and all their parts, pistons and axles, electric motors of all kinds, rocker valves and gasoline pumps. Pumps, pumps of all kinds. Though my parents both worked in what we call now the service sector, I still have the peculiar disposition of taking the abstract and recasting it as a solid thing.

In Fort Wayne, as in many midwestern industrial cities, the factories were built on the east side of town. The prevailing winds are from the west, thus the location of a city's smokestack industry is downwind. Fort Wayne's east-end metropolis of factories and foundries informs a metaphor I find I use over and over: factories in the east manufacturing the lovely day and sending it streaming off the assembly lines out over my city. A union-made morning, a sunset built of scrap.

I heard constantly, as I grew up there, that Fort Wayne was seventh on Hitler's bombing list. It is a folk legend of course and reflects what I recognize as a midwestern combination of pride and inferiority. Fort Wayne, it says, was important enough to be

> "In Fort Wayne, wire is everywhere."

destroyed. As with many such legends, there is an element of truth in it. During World War II, Fort Wayne was strategic because almost all the magnetic copper wire was manufactured there. Today a significant percentage of wire is still made there, and the skilled craft of cutting the dies through which wire is drawn is still practiced there. I played on a Little League team sponsored by Indiana Wire and Die. Essex, Rea Magnet Wire, Phelps Dodge all sponsored such teams and were where my friends' parents worked. We all used cable spools for tables on our porches and patios. In Junior Achievement we made string-art sailboats using thread-gauge surplus wire. When the prevailing wind failed to prevail, you could taste the tang of metal in the air, it coated your tongue and plated the backs of your teeth.

In Fort Wayne, wire is everywhere.

* * *

Last Sunday, as I have for the last twenty years since I left, I called home. My mother and father are fine, thank you very much. Even though, on either end of the line now, there is the synaptic leap of our voices through space—we use cordless phones—I still like to think, as we speak over the distance, of the actual wire. I think of the wire, the thread of insulated copper, that leads the signal singularly from my home now, in Syracuse, New York, to Home with a capital H, as simple as the analog transmission of voice via some vibrating string and two resonant tin cans.

I know. I know. I know about the microwave carriers, the towers studded with the arrays of lozenge antennae. And I know about digital switching, the scrambling of our words into binary pulses and their speedy translation back to an amplified, high-fidelity proximity of our original chit-chat. And I know about fiber-optic cable, data hitchhiking on a beam of bendable light. But I can still imagine that there still exists this physical umbilical to a physical place, an actual connection several hundred actual miles in length that conducts our conversation by means of the rhythmic jostling of charged metallic molecules, my weekly verbal wave, a boosted electric wave whipping through the medium of copper wire.

My father worked for forty years as a switchman for, first, the Home Telephone Company and, then, General Telephone Company once GTE acquired Home. Growing up, I would be taken along by my father while he troubleshot in the various switchrooms around the city. Those switchrooms were everywhere, but were hard to see. Many of them were housed in houses in residential neighborhoods to blend in with the houses that surrounded them. Often they were cinder-block shacks on back alleys or were mistaken for schools and office buildings. The main switches took up floors above the business offices of a central building downtown. These switchrooms were the mechanical replacements for the human operators who sat at boards and actually spliced, by hand, a call, lifting your one cable out of a tangled trunk line and then socketing home the connection on the panel before them.

The earlier automatic switchrooms my father took me to were noisy, a constant staccato of whirs and clicks as the switches prompted by the ratchet of a rotary dial somewhere counted out the number in rapid *tsks*, spinning, then suddenly taking hold with a crack, a kiss of bare wire leads, then the next number in a switch somewhere else in the room. The call hissed its way through the building. Hundreds of simultaneous calls being dialed mixed with the sudden release of the magnetic attraction, a *cajunk* of a hang up somewhere, when the circuit let go.

My father was in a switchroom when Kennedy was shot, knew something had happened because the switches went wild, the routine stutter and pop cranking up to an unrelieved storm of hailing. It was deafening, he said. He used an instrument called a Butt-In to butt in to a series of conversations, using alligator clips to tap the lines, and pieced together the unfolding story of the assassination.

Though noisy, the switchroom looked like the stacks of a library. The thousands of switches were dust covered with gray- or brown-painted thin metal shields shaped like the bindings of books. The switches were arranged in rows that ran the length of the room and in rank on floor to ceiling bookcase frames. Sliding off the shields—they had the heft of bound periodical volumes—was like taking a book from the shelf. There were even the same library ladders running on overhead tracks down the aisles with signs swinging from the eye-level step: Look Up Before Moving.

Often, too, a conversation would be playing on the scratchy speakers. I remember two people talking about the weather, shooting the breeze, making plans for the kids to come home. The switchmen were checking a line, had run the bad order through the PA system. The droning human voices mingled with the voice of the murmuring and twitching room, the sighs and the *tsks* of the switches reacting to or commenting upon the particular conversation's own inflections and tones.

During my own weekly ritual conversations home, the "I-am-fine-how-are-you" often seeming like an elementary lesson from a language lab tape, our dialogue's Q&A allows me time to imagine my voice, its rote response, as a plosive knot racing through the tunnel of cable, up and down over hills, buried and strung, the diffuse light as it crosses the estuary near Sandusky, the hairpin curve at Angola. Is it any wonder that I linger a bit in the switchroom as my electric signature finds its way through the nest of wire there?

For me, the switchroom with its transparent skeletal construction, its bare and functional schema, has always seemed to be a factory furiously manufacturing this idea of place, which exists in spite of the entropy of distance, against the tendencies of our drifting apart. The vented sound of the switchroom's workings, not unlike the trill of a sewing machine, stitched together these tenuous connections. When we speak of place we often speak of our sense of it, its constant though peripheral presence. That is, there is no such thing as a place, only our own inscription of it we carry around in our own nervous systems.

The switchroom, an actual place for me, is a cybernetic node at the same time. The switchroom, by facilitating these connections between people both local and long-distance, participates in the abstraction of place. The switches, tiny engines, churn out permutating transcriptions, address after address, of where *where* is. At the same time, the switch-room remains for me, by accident of my birth and my father's job, a "real" place, in my own wiring, though its function is to be transparent, a permeable membrane between here and there.

I see my father at his workbench, a broken switch disassembled before him, its voice now silent, its magic gone. I can hear the conversations too, the ones playing on the speakers, casual talk he's tapped into. This is where we are when we are in cyberspace, at this particular nexus, and the apparatus there, at least at one "there," was tended and maintained by my father.

The switchroom allows meeting at an imaginary spot that seems real, places like "Fort Wayne," say, or "Indiana," creating these places out of words, strings of words, spoken or, now, typed. And in the complete and convincing virtual construction of those shared places, we forget about these little offices, the actual precincts of our connections, these little libraries of wire.

***

Wire. Connection to a place, for me, has never been difficult to grasp. That place, Fort Wayne, where wire is made and where my father spent his life parsing out pathways, that place is wired into my brain by means of its own self-produced tendrils, its gossamer of filaments and sparkling coils, a cybernetic neural net. For me to write about this place is to write about Place (with a capital *P*) itself.

Wherever I go, wherever I am, I see wire, wire that is going someplace, wire that has come from somewhere. I have seen wire strung in ancient

Attic olive trees, on the floors of oceans. And as I write, I am wire—conductive, magnetic—because even though I am here, writing, I am also always, while writing, somewhere else.

Interview with Michael Martone

BECKY BRADWAY: I know that you've long been interested in the line (or lack of a line) between fiction and nonfiction. Does this line exist? Where is it? Please describe. Are there limitations that define each form? Who dictates them? Et cetera. (I'm sure you have plenty of ways you can go with this without any prompting from me.)

MICHAEL MARTONE: I am a prose writer. I think it is interesting that this question is often asked of prose writers. But it is seldom asked of poets or seldom asked by poets about their poems. Are poems fiction or nonfiction?

A fact is a thing done. A fiction is a thing made. Funny then that the fact that we think is so real and that we associate with truth, reality, honesty, etc., really is quite unreal, over, gone once it happens. What we have, what we live with is the residue of fact—letters, newspapers, physical evidence, eyewitness accounts from memory, histories—and all of these can and are faked. A fiction is a made thing. It is fabricated and strangely because it is made, it has a reality that a fact, a thing done, does not have. For me what we call fiction and nonfiction are both made things. One job of the writer, I think, is to constantly test and tease that slight shade of difference in prose genre. It is always the job of the reader of prose to access the difference. We live in a world we like to think is empirical, that is known through our senses, through our experience. But our senses are so easily fooled, our memory of facts so faulty. We live in this strange paradox sure of the facts but also conscious of their ephemeral nature and our hobbled means of sensing them.

I actually think that the more interesting break is between story and not story, not between fiction and nonfiction.

Finally, I like to think I am a maker of prose. There are plenty of other folks who love to put things into such categories. I let them. I like to make things, wind them up and let them make their way in the world.

BB: Your pieces often seem to embrace place (Indiana in particular) while sending up the very idea that there is a real, definable place. Place has long been an underpinning (if not *the* underpinning) of the American essay. Given the cyberworld in which we live, is place still a relevant subject?

MM: Are you kidding? Even more now. The cyberworld has to be mapped too. We have just stumbled into it. These two questions are related somehow, aren't they? We worry "the real" and we worry "the made-up." Cyberspace is another dimension, is all. We call it virtual, but Hannibal, Missouri, in *Huck Finn* is virtual too. And if one goes to "the real" Hannibal today one will find "real" humans dressed as characters from a nineteenth-century novel whitewashing a real fence and telling each other lies for real. Which part of that scenario is realer or realest? At Indiana University a group of us students created a "student" out of IBM punch cards. It was easy to do. This was in the mid-seventies. The "student" today gets the alumni newsletter in his PO box in Oolitic, Indiana. It is a "real" place inhabited by "real" people.

I wrote a fiction called "The Digitally Enhanced Image of Cary Grant Appears in a Cornfield in Indiana." In it Cary Grant in the movie *North by Northwest* appears in my real fictional cornfield in Indiana doing the scene from the movie where a biplane attempts to kill him in a cornfield in Indiana. The movie was shot in Bakersfield, California. My fiction was written in Alabama. Mount Rushmore is an important place in that movie. But there were no location shots. The place is there and it is not there as place is always there and not there.

BB: You seem to be very conscious of your language, down to the importance of the individual word. Can you discuss how you make decisions regarding language?

MM: There is always something else going on in language besides content. I am interested in the sublime and subliminal. The added oomph to language. I love a line that Richard Seltzer uses in an essay. "I scraped the fat, black, scabs." Now that is a graphic image but it also uses assonance of a particular type. The aaahhh sound makes you physically contort your vocal muscles to make the sounds of illness. The sound for the sight. I love unlocking the codes of language, especially the codes that can actually effect us physically. Victorian pornography seems useless to us now. But once the very same words in that order got hearts racing, tissues hardening, breath catching. What are our codes? What language can you actually feel, can make you feel, and can make you feel feeling?

Cris Mazza

A Girl Among Trombonists

Cris Mazza's first novel, *How to Leave a Country* (1992), won the PEN/Nelson Algren Award for book-length fiction. Some of her other notable titles include *Your Name Here: ____* (1995), *Dog People* (1997), and *Is It Sexual Harassment Yet?* (1991). Her 2001 novel *Girl Beside Him* inhabits rural Wyoming. Her 2004 novel *Homeland* involves a woman and her elderly father grappling with a thirty-year-old family tragedy while they also find themselves homeless, living in the canyons of suburban Southern California alongside migrant agricultural workers. *Indigenous/Growing Up Californian* (2003), Mazza's collection of personal essays, deals with place as it anchors memory and the reconstruction of experience. *Waterbaby* (2007), a novel, looks at how local legends still live and grow in a seacoast town in Maine.

Mazza is coeditor of *Chick-Lit: Postfeminist Fiction* (1995) and *Chick-Lit 2* (1996), anthologies of women's fiction. Mazza's fiction has been reviewed widely. A critic from *Publishers Weekly* said, "Mazza continues to work with passion, insight, and a certain cold beauty." Essayist Philip Lopate wrote, "You can trust Mazza to level with you and entertain you with her stylish prose; this is an engaging collection."

A native of Southern California, Cris Mazza grew up in San Diego County. Her BA and MA were completed at San Diego State University; she then crossed the country to finish an MFA at Brooklyn College before returning to San Diego, where she lived several years training and showing her dogs, completing her first four books, and teaching. Mazza is now a professor in and director of the Program for Writers at the University of Illinois at Chicago.

The essay we've included is from *Indigenous*.

Interview with Cris Mazza, p. 590.

In my adolescent mind, I could've starred in a popular type of advertisement where a hard-hatted construction worker or jet pilot displays resplendent macho prowess. Welding a girder twenty stories up, supported only by a leather harness and mountain-climber line, boots braced against the steel frame, silhouetted in a spray of red sparks. Or in formations of fighter jets, turning in precision movements and landing against a flawless peaceful twilight; then four leather-jacketed, still-helmeted pilots in slow-motion walking from the parked jets, showing in every step the fluid comfort of their trained bodies, and the fluid ease of their camaraderie. Then in each image, the welder or one of the pilots, still in romantic slow-motion, removes the helmet—the eyes are shut in dumb animal comfort as the head shakes off

"I was a pioneer: first girl trombonist in my high school."

the feeling of shackled confinement, and the beautiful tresses of silky long hair reveal that the macho figure is a stunning, gorgeous woman.

In *my* ad, this astonishing and magnificent creature would wear a red-and-black wool military-style uniform, white gloves, white military dress shoes, carry a trombone, and, following a breathtaking performance of precision and endurance, would make her startling emergence—shaking free her long hair—from underneath a busby hat. (Gorgeous? Well, I had the long hair.)

It was often the allure of contests, of winning something, that pushed me to overcome timidity. Before marching band, the only forms of competition available to me were the junior high science fair—my projects involved spiders and bees—and swimming races at Girl Scout camp. Both involved facing down things that scared me. Joining the all-male world of trombonists also put me face-to-face with a thing that scared me. A thing harder to name than black widow spiders or jumping from the high dive. Was it *boys? Sex?* My own gender's "place" in the world of the seventies? Or my gender's new "place" in the decades to come, and the complications it would bring that hadn't even, at the time, been named yet: sexual harassment and date rape?

So, before the questions had even been asked, I was a pioneer: first girl trombonist in my high school. And in Southern California, where trends and trailblazing are often experiments before moving east, it does seem a little late for this barrier to first be crossed in the 1970s. *Crossing* the barrier took nothing—I picked up a trombone and said *I want to play this.* But life as a trombonist took a subtle kind of nerve, a courage I didn't have: to join the boys without acquiescing in various ways, without *needing* them so anxiously.

> "Marching band was and still is a competitive sport in California."

The fall of the year has had many designations for my family: dove hunting season, the start of the academic year, fire season, the time for Southern California's Santa Ana winds, and—in the late sixties and seventies, when my sisters and I began one by one to enter high school—September announced the start of marching season.

What teenager *doesn't* want to get up on Saturday at four in the morning, get on a bus at six to get to a parade route at eight, spend four or five hours on a hot September day in a decidedly unsexy wool uniform and hat, soaking undergarments with sweat and causing the gnarly-est case of hat-hair ever seen. Easy sacrifices in the honorable pursuit of excellence, improvement, accomplishment . . . the pursuit of *winning*.

Marching band was and still is a competitive sport in California. When the 1970s Title IX ensured equal funding for boys' and girls' athletics, it didn't include marching band—it didn't need to as marching band had always been a co-ed activity where boys and girls received equal funding, when the band was funded at all. Around the same time as Title IX, homeowners screamed that their property taxes were too high, and

Proposition 13 was passed as the taxpayers' reassertion of their rights. School districts reeled. I don't recall a single football program limping away with severe wounds, but many music programs were decimated to the point that it took a decade or more to bring them back. Many students couldn't play in the band when it meant as many hours in candy and T-shirt sales as in rehearsal, when instruments couldn't be repaired, when each band member's individual uniform allowance soared, when music classes were no longer offered *during* the school day so all participation (including that of the band director) was extracurricular. We thought of Proposition 13 as the voters' revenge on the band that thundered in rehearsal through their quiet tract neighborhoods every fall day from 11 to 12:30 and again after school from 3 to 5.

In competitive marching, the first requirement is precision. Bands were judged on a military standard, so precision dance-steps didn't, at the time, count. Precision was sought first of all in the obvious: straightness of ranks (individuals marching in shoulder-to-shoulder rows), straightness of files (the front-to-back lines), and even the visibility of accurate diagonals as the band passed down the street. This meant that each individual in the block band had to remain the same exact distance from all four individuals around him or her, side to side and front to back.

Precision was also desired in the less obvious: Each step had to be the proper length so that six steps fit equally in five yards. Instruments had to be carried in exact horizontal or vertical positions—each like instrument carried in a uniform way—and had to remain as stone-still as humanly possible, whether being played or not. Obviously the musician's fingers, hands, or arms could move if that was how sound came out of the horn—pushing of valves or moving of the trombone's slide—but the rest of the instrument had to stay motionless, no jazzy body language with the horn. Instruments needed to be raised into play position and lowered into carry position with identical simultaneous movements by each individual. While playing the march, all the instruments, except those played vertically like clarinet, saxophone, and baritone, had to be carried parallel to the ground, no dipping trombone slides, no trumpet bells tipping skyward, no sagging flutes. Feet had to hit pavement at precisely the same time, nothing even slightly out-of-phase in the way people clapping to music in a large auditorium can't seem to stay with the beat. And the tempo of that beat had to remain precise: 120 beats per minute. Accuracy existed in the position of each individual's torso, shoulders, arms, and rhythm of the arm-swing, in focus of the eyes and slight upward tilt of the head. Obviously there was no head-turning side to side.

And then there was the precision required by military-type inspection. Not something that could be accomplished in daily rehearsal, this entailed a clean, pristine, and spotless objective for everything from white gloves and shoes to brass instruments and surfaces of drums, to no facial hair nor hair showing on the neck or back of the head, no jewelry, no makeup. Pant cuffs had to be exactly long enough to touch the top of the shoe and cause a slight break of the pant crease, jacket cuffs exactly long enough to touch the top thumb knuckle when the arm hangs at the side.

We were trained military-style to obey the drum major's whistled commands. One whistled order meant form-up, another was for attention, another for at-ease. There were whistles for turns and countermarches, and a specific whistle calling for the "roll-off," the percussion introduction cadence that included our cue for the precise maneuver of instruments snapping into playing position just before playing the music. From afar, and to some of our nonband classmates, we may have seemed more like Nazis than kids in the seventies. But we were actually a paradox, little flower-children rehearsing marching in straight lines wearing bell-bottoms, fringed leather vests, long and loose hair on boy and girl alike, peace signs on our notebooks, distrust of "the establishment" on our lips (but no boy from this band would have to go involuntarily to Vietnam).

In fact, a microfilm of my adolescence-to-young-adulthood would show that the August before I began the eighth grade, Sharon Tate and six other people were murdered. The spring before I started high school, protests against the war in Vietnam escalated on college campuses until students were killed by National Guard troops at Kent State. From the summer before my freshman year through the following spring, Charles Manson was on trial. The summer after my sophomore year, Republican burglars broke into the Democratic Party headquarters in the Watergate Hotel. Sometime in my freshman year, the draft ended before any of the boys my age had registered or received lottery numbers. In August before my junior year, the last American ground troops were withdrawn from Vietnam; by January all military operations against North Vietnam were halted. When I was a freshman in college, Nixon resigned, Saigon fell, and an influx of Vietnamese refugees poured into this country, a large percentage coming into Southern California. My first year of graduate school, Iranian students took sixty Americans hostage. The only mob scene I recall on my campus (which doesn't mean there weren't others) was between American and Iranian students. Women were not admitted to the U.S. military academies until I was in college, but the ERA would not finish its slow death until 1982.

Meanwhile, back in the seventies, we marched and drilled and pursued military precision . . . and the victories it would bring at weekend competitions.

Most competitions were in the Los Angeles area, so this meant bands in San Diego County and counties north of Los Angeles put in the extra hours of travel. We met at our dark, cold school at around 4 or 5 A.M., boarded buses and tried not to waste too much energy on silly adolescent diversions during the two-hour trip. As we likely didn't really have the maturity to make this determination ourselves, often we were required to travel at least the last thirty minutes to the parade site in silence. For competitions in our own area we traveled the entire distance from our school to the site in complete silence, then proceeded to change into our uniforms and form up in our pre-parade location also in absolute wordless quiet.

Upon arrival at the parade site, we debarked with our cumbersome busby hat boxes, our shoes and other equipment stowed in airline carry-on bags, and immediately went to the uniform trailer where "band parents" were handing out the freshly cleaned uniforms. We each always had the same uniform assigned to us—tried on at the beginning of the season and tailored if necessary, or else a new uniform assigned. The boys must've presented quite a challenge as their cuffs continually crept up their growing legs and arms and their jackets tightened across the shoulders.

We came from our assigned locker room fully transformed into identical cogs in the band. To complete the elimination of individuality, we each had stuffed our identical, drippy long hair up into the busby hat. The use of an eight-inch segment of nylon stocking allowed us to look as though we'd shaved our heads for each important competition: we drew the segment down over our heads and pulled our long hair through so the nylon loop was around our necks like a disembodied turtleneck. Then we slowly pulled the nylon up over our faces, allowing it to gather hair as it went, continuing to stretch it until our faces were free again and the nylon tube was being worn on the top of the head like a stocking hat, and it was filled with all of our hair. The busby hat fit neatly on top, successfully androgynizing, or android-izing boy and girl alike. As we came out of the locker room, a band parent handed us a pair of baggies to slip over our white shoes. Another parent handed out the plumes—like small, straight red feather-dusters—which attached to a slot on the sides of the black busby hats.

So, trouser cuffs turned up to protect the black wool from white shoe polish, baggies covering our shoes, our gloves on our left shoulder under the epaulet, we usually had to get back on the buses at this point and be taken to the pre-parade area where a crew of band parents began to unload the instrument cases and line them up beside the buses. As soon as each gleaming instrument was taken from its case by its owner, now with gloves on, the case was loaded back on the bus because the buses would be moving to meet us at the other end of the parade route.

The whistle sounded to form up. To make it easy for 126 people to quickly form a block band the drum major blew the whistle long and steady while lifting his or her baton vertically above his or her head. The trombone rank then quickly formed, nine across, arm's length apart, the center guide directly facing the drum major. We raised our trombones over our heads, holding them by the bottom-most loop of the slide, arms fully extended, so the long instrument was extended upright over our heads. The remaining thirteen ranks could then quickly fall into position, each individual locating his or her file behind the trombonist who was at the head.

During warm-up, while the director led the band through long tones, scales, and soft tonguing exercises to limber our lip, tongue, and diaphragm muscles, a small swarm of band parents made their way through the ranks, armed with shoe polish, lint removers, hairspray, masking tape, and needle and thread. Those with the shoe polish crouched at the feet of each band member, removed the plastic baggies and touched up the white shoes as necessary. The hair sprayers went head-to-head to plaster any loose wisps up into the hat (also liberally using the long weapon on the opposite end of hairdresser's combs). The others removed specks of lint from uniforms, taped or sewed cuffs that looked too long, tightened buttons, turned trouser cuffs back down, straightened and hooked the high collars under each chin, wiped the last fingerprints off the plastic brim of the busby hat, straightened the angle of the plume as well as the hat's chin strap, and threaded the strap's end through the catch-loop. The angle of the tall busby hats all had to be the same, so several parents would go through the ranks setting hats, jamming them down so the visor came right down over our eyes.

One at a time, on a parade official's cue, like big tractor-trailers the bands pulled out of their warm-up positions and joined the parade. At first more like a traffic jam than a parade, it would be stop-and-go, each stop another opportunity for the director to continue warming us up, rehearsing troublesome sections in the music, or tuning: he would take a tuning fork with him down the center of the band, adjusting the pitch of each instrument to the fork. And every time we stopped, the parents swarmed in again, checking, fixing, polishing, adjusting, jamming hats forward and down.

Each competition *was* a real parade through the streets of a city, including spectators lining the sidewalks. Usually it was exclusively bands—no floats or (god forbid) horses. The competition part of the parade consisted of three zones: first a warm-up zone where the band halted on a line, then stepped off with its full competition fanfare and roll-off and began playing the march exactly as it would later in competition. About halfway through the warm-up area, the band would hit the silent zone—marked with a portable sign—and had to at that point immediately cut all music and drumbeat and march silently with only the tap of one drumstick on the rim of one drum to set the beat. The purpose of this was to allow whatever band was already being judged in competition, further up the street, optimum conditions for its performance.

The beginning of the competition zone was a solid line painted across the street, also marked with a portable sign. Here, with the front rank of trombonists' toes on the line, the silent band was halted and put into military "at ease," with feet apart, the left hand flat against the small of the back, and instruments in a uniform down position, with just as much precision and unwavering focus of eyes. The band waited, motionless, in this situation until another parade official gave the cue to begin the competition performance. During this last-minute delay, the band parents had their final chance to filter through the ranks, checking for smudges on shoes or untied shoe laces, water spots on the instruments, hair loosened from under hats, or lint on uniforms. Once again problematic hats were jammed down over our brows.

Judging was in four areas: music, marching precision, military inspection, and showmanship. The music and showmanship judges sat at a rostrum midway through the competition zone, the other judges stayed on the street with the band. The podium also held the drum major judges, the twirler judges, and even a judge for identification-unit competition—the girls (never boys) who carried the school's name in front of the band.

On the drum major's signal the performance began: a fanfare followed by percussion roll-off (which usually included cues for the band to come to attention) with a flashy method of popping the instruments into carry position. Then the band stepped off and snapped instruments into play position during an opening flourish by the accessory units—drum major, twirler, and "banderettes" carrying the school's name. This opening was the majority of what the showmanship judge was concerned with. He also noted the overall picture of the band and accessory units, the "entertainment value."

Our step-off was redesigned each year, usually with a trumpet fanfare during which the block band would snap to attention—raising instruments and shouting out the school's name. One particularly effective step-off had two trumpet players set up ahead of the band, ahead of the drum major, standing in place after playing the fanfare until the advancing band engulfed them and they fell into step in their positions. Meanwhile, after the percussion cadence had given cues for popping instruments up to our mouths, the band continued advancing, marching for four steps in sudden absolute silence—not even a drum tap—before the first vibrant note of music came in unison from our horns. An astonishing and potent overture, risking, of course, a nervous or overeager musician miscounting and shattering the four beats of silence with some sort of chicken squawk.

So, after all the fanfare, the band began playing its competition march. The music judge scored the band without watching, often seated with his back to the parade so as to not be swayed by the appearance of the band's performance. Musicality was judged in terms of tempo, intonation, accuracy of instruments playing together, accuracy of technique (playing all the right notes), as well as musical interpretation (not much leeway in a military band playing a march), which included use of dynamics, tone, and phrasing.

To judge marching precision, the marching judge began by falling in step beside the right guide of the front rank. For two years, that was my position. As long as the front rank—the trombonists—stayed in a straight line, that judge would stay beside the right guide. If the front rank stayed straight the whole way through the competition zone, the judge would not even look at the other ranks and the score would be perfect. As soon as the front rank bent or an individual stuck out as slightly in front or slightly behind, the judge dropped back to the second rank and stayed there until that rank was no longer straight. He continued this process until he'd finished all the ranks, then, from the back of the band, checked each file one at a time. Only after finishing with the files would the judge check diagonals. Keeping straight files and diagonals was directly dependent on the front rank—the trombonists—because, instead of following someone, we had to be sure we stayed on an invisible line stretching out directly ahead of us, maintaining the same distance between each individual in the front rank. Without precision in the front rank, files might snake, and there would be no diagonals. So the front rank bore extra responsibility in the marching score. Not only were we crucial for straight files and diagonals, the longer we kept the judge beside the right guide (me), the less time he would have to judge other ranks, files, or diagonals. He could only judge while the band was in the competition zone. I usually had an impression of what kind of marching score we might have, depending on how long I felt that judge lingering beside me through the competition zone.

The awards ceremony was usually held in a high school football stadium. For the granddaddy event at the end of the season, the Long Beach All Western Band Review, the awards ceremony took place in the evening and was held in the sports arena. Each band sat together, some in uniform, some already changed to street clothes but wearing identical jackets or windbreakers. The stadium would rock with spirit contests: one block of kids screaming in unison "*We've got spirit, yes we do, we've got spirit, how about YOU!*" then point as one to another section, a rival band. That band would then be forced to answer with the same chant, trying to make it louder. By the time I was a junior and senior, an arrogant attitude of superiority had taken over our band—we won a lot—and we felt such displays of adolescent giddiness were below us. A rival school would lay down the spirit gauntlet, and we'd stare back mutely, flexing our dignity.

> "Placements were okay, but sweepstakes was the only trophy we truly coveted."

One by one, placements for the classes would be announced. For each class (based on school size) there were placements for drum major, for twirler, for identification units, for the corps (behind the band), and the most important award, for the band itself. After each announcement, the drum major, who would've under most circumstances been a gawky teenager, would majestically march to the podium, do an elaborate salute—involving twirling of the baton or mace—then step forward to receive the trophy.

The two final awards of the ceremony would be sweepstakes trophies, one for a grouping of the three or four smallest classes, the other for a grouping of the three or four largest. Placements were okay, but sweepstakes was the only trophy we truly coveted. We often responded with more of a groan of disappointment than a wild vocal exclamation when our school's name was read for a placement in our class, because a placement meant there would be no sweepstakes trophy. *Not* having our name read for placement could only mean we were either swept out of the placements altogether, or we'd won the big one.

Despite the smugness, the attitude of superiority we'd both earned and allowed to mutate, the next weekend the same swirl of hot adrenalin would overwhelm me, as I stood on the competition line at attention in dress uniform with my glossy trombone, as my band's front-rank right-guide. The director, who marched beside the right-guide up until the competition zone, would tap my shoulder and disappear from my peripheral vision, and we were on our own to carry out what we'd trained so ardently to do.

When instrumental music entered my life in fourth grade, I didn't play the trombone. In an effort to create harmony with a violin and clarinet currently being practiced in the bedroom I shared with my sisters, I was guided toward the cello. But long before I entered high school, from my first sight of a marching band coming toward me down a street, my second-grade aspiration to play the "slide trombone" came back to me: I wanted to march in my band's front rank. No girl ever had before me. The second time I marched in the Rose Parade, my senior year, I was right guide of the front rank. Every inch of the seven-mile route was either lined with high overflowing bleachers—like marching down the middle of a narrow football stadium—or, when there were no bleachers, the streets on both sides were packed ten-deep with standing spectators. My trombone slide sometimes barely skimmed past the front row of spectators. I saw them pull their feet back toward the curb and grab their children. They could've reached out and touched me as I floated past on the balls of my feet in spotless white shoes.

Peer groups were my parents' focus when directing us into extracurricular activities: chiefly Scouts and music, with only a smattering of sports. While scouting and sports may have been gender quarantining activities, music was not. I don't think, however, my parents realized the whole learning situation that music would provide for us, beyond the noise that came out of our instruments. Marching band, it turns out, was as character-building as my parents would've wanted . . . and less.

Most of us, in adolescence, caused ourselves extra pain due to the kind of social attention we valued and thought would make us important. "You're Nobody 'Till Somebody Loves You"—like us, girls in the fifties and early sixties viewed "love" as the greatest ego-boosting attention they could earn. But in one generation, just what that thing called "love" *was* had shifted to lust. By the mid-seventies, after the Summer of Love, and the images of Woodstock, communes, and flower children, many girls' notions of what would prove their value had been modified. Protecting or preserving one's virtue was no longer part of the game. *Protecting one's virtue.* It *still* sounds like a narrow-minded morality adage from an unenlightened century, especially since "virtue" meant *only* virginity. *Virginity* wasn't what we should've been protecting; it was our dignity that some of us left open for assault, and we were both perpetrator and victim.

In California in the 1970s, although the ERA was floundering, public school dress regulations were dismantled and Title IX mandated equal funding for girls' and boys' athletics. Everywhere there were more doors opening for girls. We were free to do things and try things, but at the same time the sexual attention by which we measured our significance would likely be out of our grasp if we went ahead and did those new things. Even though the social battlefield of the era had (in addition to "free love") stressed "do your own thing," the revision of the traditional adolescent measurement of self-value—from being loved to being sexually desired—seems linked to the steady tearing down of the "no girls allowed" signs. But let me not be misunderstood: The equalization of opportunity was *unspeakably* valuable, requiring no defense. That it caused some confusion in how my breasts fit into the picture when I entered the all-male world of trombone players was an unfortunate side effect. Yes, some of us wanted to do the things boys did, things that girls hadn't been allowed to do, but we still wanted the boys to think of us as special. This created a catch-22. I *was* special to them, but was it in the way I hoped for?

The band didn't need Title IX to ensure equal funding for girls and boys, but Title IX was part of the atmosphere, along with the abrupt abolishing of all dress codes and grooming regulations the year I entered high school. No longer were girls required to only wear skirts or dresses. When a girl did wear a skirt, no longer would the length of her hem be mandated. No longer were boys required to have their hair cut short enough to be off the collar. No longer were there rules banning facial hair. Naturally, we took the freedom as far we could. Levis and corduroys were the daily uniform; with denim workshirts, army fatigues, sweatshirts, flannel shirts, or T-shirts. Shoes were desert boots or wallabies, tennis shoes, sandals made in Mexico from used tires, mountain boots, or Vietnam jungle boots. Dress code freedom that became androgyny was, in part, I think, either a symbol or result of the budding changes in attitude about gender, which even included an experiment in co-ed home economics. Still, it was only the beginning: No longer were girls directed toward typing courses and boys toward science, though I do remember a discussion in my tenth grade social science class where the topic given to us was "Should women work?" In this confused, even unprepared social atmosphere—just on the brink of what became a turbulent gender-equalization struggle—I began playing the trombone.

When I became a trombonist in tenth grade, there was no display of rejection, no dirty tricks to try to chase me away, no ugly harassment for the purpose of warning me that I had entered a domain where I didn't belong. In years since, I've heard accounts of the brutal treatment experienced by women entering certain male fields, intended to make these women give up, quit, and leave the field to its "rightful owners." Yet I was welcomed without guile into the inner sanctum of trombonehood. But not received in the way just any new male recruit was admitted. The difference was subtle. It was almost as though I'd broken up doldrums that had settled there.

Beyond the subtleties of adjusting to a girl in the trombone rank—an adjustment even we were not cognizant was occurring—gender separation in the marching band sometimes seemed to be: band members were "men," auxiliary units were "girls." September is the hottest month in Southern California, and October can offer up some equally warm days. One Saturday we were warming up for a parade with ashes from a nearby back-country wildfire raining on us like a snow squall. The temperature was close to 100 degrees. "Band parents" buzzed around the all-girl unit of "banderettes," fearing they would faint, squirting water into their mouths from special bottles with crooked-necked spouts, holding umbrellas over them, even patting their necks with damp towels. Their uniforms were little skirts and Spanish-style frilled blouses. Meanwhile *we* were out in the same sun in wool uniforms in the hottest part of the day. I think some girls in the French horn or saxophone section pretended to wilt from heat exhaustion, just to draw attention back to themselves *as* girls. I had no respect for that gesture—if the boys could survive the heavy instruments and wool uniforms, we girls certainly had the same kind of stamina. And my position as a trombonist was one step farther into the "band-equals-men, auxiliary-unit-equals-girls" rearrangement of genders, because trombonists were *always* "men." But I was one of the boys who also had girl parts.

Yet when they accepted me as a trombone player, suddenly they could *not* think of me in the same way they viewed the girls who played clarinet and flute, the saxophonists and cymbal players, the girls who carried the glockenspiel, the baton twirler and "banderettes." What does "one of the boys" really mean? And who was more confused, me or them? They knew I had girl parts, could be teased, could be shown-off to as they did with other girls. But with me in the ranks, they could still spit and swear and grab each other's crotches and make innuendoes about the "banderbutts" who marched twenty feet in front of the band, in plain view of the first rank of trombone players. They showed me how to blow out the saliva that accumulates inside a trombone slide with as much disgusting noise as possible, the "trombone handshake" (a savage goose, best administered from the rear by surprise), and the entire imaginary clubhouse of trombone brotherhood. It had been the only full section in the band, the only full rank that had remained all male up to this point, so their behavior, whether in the band formation or seated indoors in concert set-up, had always been more like a locker room than co-ed classroom. "*Trombones!*" the director would bellow and we would dive behind our music stands laughing after doing the "trombone sneeze" on the back of a saxophonist's head: you vocalize the sound of a sneeze while spraying the unsuspecting head and neck with the spray bottle a trombonist uses to keep the slide lubricated. The victim believes he has caught a juicy sneeze on his neck and hair.

And it must never be presumed the phallic symbolism of that slide escapes the trombonist. The trombone handshake could also be performed using the trombone's slide. The slide, in its different positions, is what makes different pitches come out of the horn. The slide is also used, although infrequently, for glissando—the sound made when the slide is used to slurp from note to note without breaking. This was the motion needed for the trombone handshake, which was offered to the oblivious recipient from the rear. It worked best during warm-up or outdoor music rehearsals when military rigor was dropped and the block band curled around so everyone could see the director. The trombone section could move in behind another group of instrumentalists; a slide was extended as far as possible, the end noiselessly inserted between the knees of someone standing in front (the victim's legs must be slightly spread). Then quickly, silently, the slide was pulled in while the angle of the whole instrument was raised, so as the slide slipped back into place it also zipped along the victim's crotch. Done within ranks—them to me, me to them, them to each other—just as often as to unwitting trumpet or tuba players who forgot to keep their guard up while in the vicinity of the trombone rank. But I never saw them do this to another girl.

In my junior year—after all the boys who had welcomed me to their world had graduated—I was chosen to be trombone section leader. Who was bothering to be politically correct or exercise affirmative action in the seventies? But again, as leader of an all-male section, my instructions were never ignored or ridiculed, no conspiracy of intimidation or mockery ever disrupted a sectional rehearsal. The power had a different kind of consequence. Apparently no alluring creature came from underneath that busby band hat, shaking out her mane of hair.

All of my beloved trombone buddies—each of whom I carried a special flame for—eventually had girlfriends. Girlfriends who played flute or clarinet, French horn or piccolo, or twirled a baton. Girls they could sit beside on long bus trips to out-of-town competitions, girls they could nestle beside in the dark at Disneyland or invite as dates to the annual band banquet. But they also still had me, a trombone-crony, and the girl they, more or less consciously, realized they knew best.

One day after outdoor band rehearsal—as we streamed back into the band room through a narrow corridor that extended from the parking lot where we practiced, behind the auditorium and directly into the indoor rehearsal room—Danny drew me aside. He ushered me through a side door into the dark areas behind the stage, draped with black curtains, each of us still with a trombone in one hand. Before our eyes had adjusted, he hooked an elbow around my neck, his hand hanging down over my chest, and he cupped one breast, squeezing rhythmically.

"I can't do this to Debbie," he said, seriously, calmly, "so I'll practice on you."

He practiced on me almost daily.

These boys had not yet touched their girlfriends' breasts. I was a pal, so they turned to me to rehearse male-female touching. They were relaxed, comfortable, and familiar with me, could be *themselves* with me. And I was flattered. I was touched, in more ways than one. It made me *special* that they could be themselves with me and do things with me that they were too inhibited to do with their girlfriends. I was *important*, more important than their girlfriends. But I wasn't going to be getting any other attention from them, no movies, no dances, no basketball games, no days at the beach, no . . . what *did* teenagers do for dates in the seventies? I don't know because I never went. *Because* they were free to be themselves with me, I couldn't be a girlfriend.

Naturally it couldn't go on forever with me playing surrogate girlfriend in sexual situations. When I was one year out of high school and Danny and a few others were still seniors, the girlfriends requested they stop fraternizing with me. This was long after breast-squeezing practice sessions had ceased, and, I imagine, after they'd finally put their rehearsals to use and had begun to touch their girlfriends' breasts without a go-between. The threat of losing this privilege was likely enough for them to comply with their girlfriends' wishes. Their acceptance of me turned to a form of rejection.

It was an era when the feminist movement was making us realize we could do things that had been restricted. But it was still before we knew that crossing barriers meant more than just doing the restricted thing itself. The first girl trombone player required being more than a *girl* to know how to handle it. I wasn't a lily-white victim, and the boys weren't lascivious perpetrators. Girls like me made ourselves available for the side effects of misuse and disappointment because having a boy grab a breast *seemed* like a kind of attention that made us important. Since we had been accepted as equals doing a male-only activity, why wasn't that "important" enough?

In retrospect it seems an evolutional time, both in terms of women's progress and in my generation's development into adulthood. These were just *boys*. I eventually learned that there would be men who *would* accept a woman as an equal in his world and still want her for a life partner. Not all adult males would do this, not even a majority; but *men* would. And I sometimes wonder if my trombone-boys finally turned into men.

It was a small, ironic twist of justice that ten years after I first entered the all-male world of trombonists in my high school, when I married, I married a trombonist in the San Diego Symphony. Then a few years after that, the symphony hired *its* first female trombonist—and she sat in the principal chair. I doubt she ever was a girl among trombonists. She was only a trombonist.

Interview with Cris Mazza

BECKY BRADWAY: You're primarily known as a fiction writer. What brought about this turn toward the essay?

CRIS MAZZA: An editor for a San Diego weekly that runs investigative and place-oriented new journalism wanted me to write something for the publication, but I told her none of my "real life" experiences were interesting enough; that's why I write fiction, to live vicariously something better and more dramatic. So she asked me a few seemingly benign generic questions, including how did my parents meet and what did our family do for vacations and leisure time. My parents met when they both taught and lived at a boarding school for wealthy children of celebrities in Palos Verdes, near Los Angeles. My family hunted, fished, and scavenged, most leisure activities involved the gathering of food, including the dressing, preservation, cooking, and eating. My answers immediately made me realize that what I'd always thought was mundane was not only potentially interesting, but a vein that tapped into noteworthy parts of the culture of Southern California and the baby boomer era. That is, I knew that just being interesting was not enough; it couldn't be written with the attitude that "this must be interesting to you because it happened to me." It had to have a wider-angle background; my focused examination of my own experiences had to tap into something "larger." My parents met because of and in the era of and at the epicenter of 1950s Hollywood celebrity worship, an era that has grown and mutated and taken root in mainstream media. My family practiced hunting and gathering in a terrain that two centuries before had been inhabited and unspoiled by peaceful native hunter-gatherers, but by the time we lived there, the place was experiencing the stress of sprawl and development.

Once I got started, it was easier to see the larger issues in my other experiences. My high school passion of marching band might seem trivial but was ensnarled with feminist and political issues involving gender—and my struggling marriage to a musician in a symphony.

BB: In what ways did you find writing creative nonfiction to be different from writing fiction? (Or what can you do in an essay that you can't do in fiction, and vice versa?)

CM: I felt a curious sense of freedom writing nonfiction. Curious because one would expect fiction to have that kind of unfettered independence, simply because nonfiction is seemingly bound by "what really happened" as opposed to what might possibly happen. But I felt free to stray from a story arc, from dramatized scene, from causal relationship of scenes, from story form, from fiction's brand of narrative momentum. While plowing through a first draft, I wasn't engaged in making an artistic piece of writing, but in intense memory mining—something that I feel can't or shouldn't usually be the primary focus for a writer of fiction. I could spend pages at a time examining minute details. I could stop when I reached an interesting question and do some research, then clarify what I'd found. I could allow the person I was while writing to overlay the "character" I was in the past (although this is something I also appreciate in first-person fiction). I could make asides and explanations (although a few of my best ones were cut by my editor before the book went to press). In fiction I can make something else out of an emotion or memory (or emotion based on a memory), take something inexpressible and express it in the only way I can. In nonfiction I could examine my experiences against the backdrop of what I know now about culture or politics or the ethos of my generation.

BB: Your essay combines social commentary, history of the sixties, and snippets of memoir. Do you have any advice for people who are trying to meld a number of different approaches in the same piece?

CM: Let go of "storytelling" when necessary, when the urge strikes you. Part of the freedom I felt in nonfiction was freedom to not need to turn the details and nuances of my experience into a coherent story (as in "plot"). However, my very entrenched tendency to dramatize assisted me, as I discovered that when I reached a point where an essay needed to rise, to peak, to have a sort of crisis, I naturally shifted into dramatized event. Moving in and out of "telling a story" gave me the space to thread a little history or commentary into the narrative, to make my insertions a natural part of the narrative, and to keep an essay from sounding like I was just telling a personal story to a group of friends. But when it came to a moment of power, it was always through scene and dramatization that I found the most juice.

BB: Creative nonfiction (particularly the memoir) often takes a hit in the academy, with the accusation being that the form is not artistic or innovative enough, or that it is too confessional. Any opinions about that?

CM: Sometimes the criticisms, in my opinion, are valid, when a memoir seems to hold the underlying attitude, "This should be important to you because it happened to me." I think the media and book industry have done a disservice to the creative nonfiction genre by fostering an atmosphere that says "If your mother was a drug addict or your father abused you, you're important." So confession for confession's sake, for the sake of seeking attention or feeling that kind of importance, based only on the severity of your victimhood, I believe has given memoir this mantle to overcome, whether it be in "the academy" or in the public at large.

BB: My daughter recently graduated from high school. After reading your essay, I was struck by the sense that little has changed in terms of the gender situation in bands. (I could list other areas that are still guy-dominant, like science and math, various clubs, etc.—or, going the other way, girl-dominant: theater and chorus.) As your essay discusses, it begins with the actual male/female ratio and continues into sexual perceptions (girls who play the saxophone are "pals" (if not lesbians), guys in theater are gay, etc.). Why do you think that is? Will we ever get past this?

CM: Here's where we see how a memoirist becomes an instant expert on the larger issues represented in her memoir. This is the kind of response a memoir or personal essay should evoke, because presenting the material was more than a "look at me" appeal, and I take this question to be a huge compliment to my essay! However, this memoirist doesn't have any more answers, only questions and opinions. Do girls choose the "female" musical instruments because they subliminally know it will not detract from their attractiveness to males? Do girls avoid areas, like engineering or chess, that they subliminally (or consciously) perceive will detract from their attractiveness to males? Is that why physics departments and tuba sections lack women while theaters and high school flute sections do not? I do know that young women (in their twenties to early thirties) will admit to believing in every tenet of feminism—from equal pay to no job discrimination—but will claim to not be feminists because they think the label will make them unattractive to males their own ages. I believe these things are part of a weird mixture of innate sexual/procreation urges plus what culture does to us (nature + nurture). But I have no science to back this up, only opinions based on my own perceptions and experiences. This is also my approach to creative nonfiction. It's not the only approach—some writers use a lot more research, including interviews and field work. But it's all a step away from "this is important because it happened to me."

Brenda Miller

Next Year in Jerusalem

Brenda Miller is an associate professor of English at Western Washington University. Her book *Season of the Body: Essays* (2002) was a finalist for the PEN American Center Book Award. She has received four Pushcart Prizes for her work in creative nonfiction, and her essays have appeared in such periodicals as the *Georgia Review, Prairie Schooner, Fourth Genre*, the *Sun*, and *Yoga Journal*. She is the coauthor of the textbook *Tell It Slant: Writing and Shaping Creative Nonfiction* (2003). She serves as editor-in-chief of the *Bellingham Review*, a respected literary magazine in Washington state.

Of *Seasons of the Body*, a *Publishers Weekly* reviewer wrote, "In this collection of affecting and thought-provoking essays, Miller . . . addresses how so many people try to move determinedly forward in their lives, but often find themselves 'doubling back' and 'playing out the same plots again and again.' Likewise, the forward motion of each of these essays tends to loop back and revisit themes of love, loss, loneliness and healing." *Library Journal*'s reviewer commented on the essays' "sensuality and unflinching honesty." Our selection, "Next Year in Jerusalem," is from this collection.

Why Is This Night Different from All Other Nights?

At Passover every year, I dipped the greens in salt water to remind me of my ancestors' tears, and I chewed on parsley to remind me life is bitter, and I raised my glass of grape juice and hollered "Next year in Jerusalem!," clinking my glass hard against my cousin Murray's. At Passover, no matter how much I've grown, I remain a clumsy girl in chiffon dress and opaque tights, sitting at the children's table, my stomach growling as my little brother asks a question. His voice is halting but already proud of the story for which he's responsible. I look at him with envy while I suck grape juice off my fingers.

Why Tonight Do We Eat Only Matzoh?

My cousin Murray, a small man but imposing in his navy blue suit and graying beard, refers us to our texts, the *Haggadah,* which tells us the answers to these questions, but I've stopped listening. We dip our pinkies in red wine and fingerprint the ten plagues onto the rim of our plates. What are they? Locusts swarming the fields, hail made of fire, days of total darkness, rivers turning to blood. Ho hum. I eye the roast egg, the *haroses*, the matzoh on the Seder plate. It's always dark in my cousin's house; what light there is seems reflected off the gold-foil inlay on the Passover dishes.

My cousins smell of Brut and horseradish. I eye the roasted shank of a lamb, its blood the mark of the Chosen Ones. I watch Elijah's cup. I wait for the touch of the prophet's lips.

Why Tonight Do We Eat Bitter Herbs?

> "The Seder goes on and on; the voices around me rinsed of meaning or sense."

The Seder goes on and on; the voices around me rinsed of meaning or sense. I chew on matzoh and *haroses*, imagining slaves' hands slapping mortar between the bricks, the heavy poles biting into their shoulders as they draw cartloads full of the stuff to the pyramids. Someone is talking about the Red Sea, and I think of Yul Brynner chasing the Hebrews in his chariot, leather straps around his biceps, his bare chest glistening. I think of Charlton Heston at the edge of a cliff, the frightened Hebrews clustered around his robes. The walls of the sea part, and the Chosen Ones gallop through, wild-eyed in fear and wonderment.

Why Tonight Do We Dip Them Twice in Salt Water?

As I grew older, my grape juice changed to Manishewitz wine, and I murmured the prayers dutifully with the rest of my family. When I was twelve, my parents gave me a choice: I could spend another year in Hebrew school and get bat-mitzvahed, or quit Hebrew school right away. Our school was a stuffy classroom annexed to the synagogue, with tiny desks and battered chalkboards. Every Saturday, I sat in that room and chanted the Hebrew alphabet, recited Hebrew phrases such as "Mother is making the bread," and heard the tired stories of Abraham and Isaac, Noah and his nameless wife, Moses and the golden calf.

Of course, I chose to quit the place, my freedom those mornings as miraculous to me as that of the slaves in the Sinai. But my brothers, being boys, underwent the coming-of-age ritual, and they received bags of *gelt*, gift certificates, trips to New York. They held the Torah cradled in their arms, paraded it through the aisles of the synagogue while we kissed our fingers to touch the velvet mantle.

After my brothers were officially men, the Passover Seder grew shorter and shorter—the four questions reduced to one, the matzoh on the table lying almost untouched as we snuck into the kitchen for bread and butter.

From Hebrew school I had a detailed picture of the old Jerusalem in mind: the stone walls, the arched gateways, biblical light streaming into rooms where wondrous and miraculous things happened. I imagined black-suited scholars hurrying toward the *yeshiva,* though I'd only seen such men from a distance, during my family's occasional visits back to the sooty neighborhoods of Brooklyn and Queens.

I left home and forgot about Passover most years, until the care package arrived from my mother: an orange box of egg matzoh, a sleeve of dry *mandelbrot,* a can of macaroons so sweet they made my teeth ache. I'd forgotten, I thought, those words spoken so many times during my childhood.

Next Year in Jerusalem!

The clink of the wine glasses. The open door for Elijah. The *afikomen* in its white cloth hidden somewhere behind the *Encyclopedia Britannica.* We watched *Yentl* and *Fiddler on the Roof,* the tinny klezmer music a soundtrack to our lives as Jews in America.

No one in my family had ever been to Israel. No one really wanted to go. We had reached our own Promised Land: the warm, enclosed cul-de-sacs of the San Fernando Valley, where we lived in our tract house with a Doughboy swimming pool in a spacious backyard. We lived among minor television stars (the "Jack" from the children's show *Jack in the Box;* the girl who teased Tony the Tiger on the Frosted Flakes commercial). We ate cheeseburgers from McDonald's, and brought home heavy, greasy boxes of chocolate-chip Danish from the kosher bakery.

I traveled to Europe when I was eighteen, tramping through England, France, Germany, and Italy for three months; when I returned home, my grandfather asked me about my travels. His eyes gleamed as I told him stories about drinking espresso on the Left Bank of the River Seine, and eating peaches big as grapefruit on the coast of Italy. Finally he said, "And Israel? Tell me about Israel." He sat back and folded his hands expectantly across his chest.

I told him I hadn't gone. His smile vanished. He sat forward and dismissed me by focusing his watery gaze on the far wall of the living room; there, a *Shalom!* mosaic faced the main entry, and a *mezuzah* nestled in the doorframe.

"How could she be so close," my grandfather murmured, "and not visit the land of our people?"

To get to Israel, I could have flown from Naples to Athens, perhaps ferried to Crete and then on to Tel Aviv, a distance of about 2,000 miles: hardly what a reasonable person would define as "close." But I bit back my automatic protests; even then, I knew the physical distance between Italy and Israel was not the issue. The point was that a good Jewish girl would have bypassed Europe altogether, avoided the topography of the Holocaust, and found her way to the Promised Land unimpeded.

Why Is This Night Different from All Other Nights?

On July 2, 1994, I crossed the River Jordan into the West Bank. I crossed in a Jordanian bus full of Palestinians with American passports. My boyfriend Keith and I had our names written in Arabic on a permission slip from the Jordanian Department of the Interior. The river itself was a muddy trickle I could barely see; wild reeds grew thick in the mud of its banks. Though I was a nonreligious Jew, I had still expected to feel *something* as I crossed into the Promised Land. I expected some twinge of recognition or arrival. Even more so because all through Syria and Jordan

I'd been traveling on false papers: on my visa application I'd presented myself as a married Christian woman, a teacher of English. Keith had bought me a fake wedding band made of brass.

At the time, I did not recall the book of Exodus, recounted every year at Passover, my brother asking the four questions, the ten plagues, the angel of death, the parting of the Red Sea just a hundred miles to the south. I was afraid, as my ancestors must have been, but I was afraid of bombs and gunfire, not of Yul Brynner in his gaudy chariot. I was worried about the length of my dress, and the Syrian and Jordanian visas in my passport. Arafat had just visited Jericho for the first time in twenty-seven years, and the right-wing Jews in Jerusalem responded by breaking all the windows of the Arab-owned shops outside Damascus Gate.

My rayon dress clung to my damp thighs as an Israeli soldier boarded the bus. His hair was slicked back with mousse, and his khaki shirt hung open to the navel. He smelled, surprisingly, of Irish Spring. On his chest, a golden star of David swayed between his dog tags. "Passports!" he shouted, his voice cracking like an adolescent's.

I held mine out to him. He flipped through it, stopping on the page with the thick Syrian stamps. He looked at me, holding my passport just out of reach.

"How was Syria?" he asked.

Did he know I was Jewish? Did he expect a denunciation of the Arab countries, a declaration of fealty to Israel? Or was he flirting with me, just making small talk? The Palestinian woman in the window seat steadfastly looked the other way.

"Syria was great," I finally said, directing my words to his pendant.

He said nothing, but his lips curled up in what could be taken as a smile. He tossed my passport back into my lap and continued down the aisle of the bus. His rifle swung out as he turned, butting against my shoulder, leaving the tiniest of bruises.

In 1967, I had paraded through the schoolyard with my Jewish friends during the Six-Day War; we cheered Israel, our fists raised playfully in the air. Syria was the enemy—of Israel, of the United States, of the Jews. I confused the Syrians with the Nazis, all of them in uniform, with dogs, rounding up Jews as a preface to execution. When I heard the word "Syria"—with its sibilant "s," its insinuating lilt—I saw only three things: sand, barbed wire, and blood.

I was wrong, of course. Keith and I, in our wanderings through the Arab countries, had encountered nothing but hospitality and eager friendship. In Aleppo, Syria, the streets were lined with stalls selling green soap stacked like bricks, mounds of cardamom in open bins, amber jars of rose water and orange blossom oil. We drifted by vendors selling *schwarma*, with lamb roasting on giant spits. Men lounged in the doorways of their shops, sipping tea, or they tilted backward on straight-back chairs, rocking to the rhythm of the crowd. They waved and called to us, "Where from?"

We answered, hesitantly at first, "America," and the men cried, *Welcome!* They leapt to offer a chair, a spare tire, a piece of cardboard.

Please sit! When we passed a baklava shop the owner frantically waved us in. We communicated with grins and a smattering of French. He gave us sweet pastry and fried eggplant and Cokes. His three young daughters popped inside, swirling around each other in pretty flowered dresses, their black hair bobbed short. They stopped when they saw us, eyes wary, but after conferring with their father they came to us and kissed our cheeks. Their lips were weightless as butterfly wings, and their eyes regarded me solemnly as I took each of their hands in mine.

It was a Friday, the holy day for the Muslims, and Keith and I went back into the streets, drawn by the staticky call of the muezzin. The women were dressed in their formal Friday attire—blinding white scarves edged with lace, jet-black robes, and black gloves. Heat waves rose off the broken gray asphalt, a surface that turned to smooth marble as we approached the Grand Mosque.

When we stepped into the courtyard, an old man angrily waved us into an antechamber. He plopped a heavy black robe over my shoulders, slapped up the hood on my head, demanded money from Keith, and shoved us out again. The black hood cut off my peripheral vision, so I teetered across the vast courtyard in a cocoon, my vision reduced to the patterns of white and gray tiles, squares within squares, leading to the central mosque.

Inside, thick Persian carpets cooled our feet, laid out in a tidy mosaic, greens flowing into reds into browns and maroon. Men and women crowded up against a grated window; they wiped the grate with their palms, then brushed themselves from head to toe, kissed their fingers, rocking back and forth in prayer. We inched inside the crowd and spied something the shape of a head, draped with a blue cloth. Prayers thrummed all around us.

"Welcome." A heavyset man with graying hair and a white mustache loomed over us, smiling. He shook our hands. "From where are you?" he asked. And then, waving one hand toward the pulpit, he smiled. "It is the head of Zachariah, the father of John the Baptist," he says. "A great prophet. Come, sit down."

Mehmet introduced us to his wife, a young woman with a face round as flatbread, hugging a curly-haired toddler to her hip. She smiled at us, but said nothing as we followed them outside, to a raised colonnade surrounding the courtyard. A commotion erupted by the eastern gate, and a wooden casket emerged high above a crowd, bobbing on its way toward the inner sanctum. Men in Western dress led the mob, running back and forth across the perimeter until the casket disappeared inside.

The minaret's loudspeaker emitted the soft buzz that prefaces an imminent call to prayer. From across the courtyard, the bent figure of the gatekeeper rushed toward us.

"Can we stay?" Keith asked Mehmet.

"Yes, of course. You are my guests."

The old man, furious, pushed in close to Mehmet, who spoke back to him in a low, growling murmur. Both of them shot glances in my direction, and Mehmet returned to us, shaking his head.

"You may stay, but your wife," he said, pointing to me, "must go sit with the women."

Of course I would go; I didn't mean to offend. I meandered along the edge of the courtyard, the wool cloak scratching my arms and the back of my neck, the desert light glaring off the gray tiles. Carefully smiling, I lifted my head. But only suspicious female faces regarded me from behind the pillars. As long as I had been with Keith, I realized, I was cloaked in Western privilege, but as I walked toward the women's section, looking for Mehmet's wife, I felt this privilege shearing off, bit by bit. With Keith I was a tourist, an object of curiosity. But alone, with neither a husband or a child to validate me, I became an unknown woman, possibly a prostitute, an unclean object, profane.

"I came to understand: *I am forbidden.*"

I saw Mehmet's wife hurrying toward me; she took me by the hand and led me to a colonnade at the rear of the courtyard, in the shade. She bustled me to her mat, amid hundreds of mats laid out side by side in a patchwork down the platform. The women sat cross-legged on the ground, leaning toward each other and talking, their white, green, or black scarves knotted tightly across their throats. When I sat with them, one of the women scooted away, mumbling "*Haram!*"

I would hear this word over and over in the next hour: *Haram*, with an admonitory weight on the second syllable. I later learned this word means "forbidden," but at the time I knew only that the women began to cluster around me, tugging the elbow-length sleeves of the cloak down to cover my wrists, pushing at stray hairs that wisped from my scarf, pulling the flap of the robe over my bare ankle. I came to understand: *I am forbidden.* Their hands touched me all over, patting me into place; under these hands I felt like a very small child, or a doll made of damp, still pliant, clay.

Even in my discomfort, I knew I felt only a bit of what these women endured all their lives: numerous hands pressing them into a posture of shame, submission, invisibility. If my family had been Orthodox Jews, I would have been molded the same way, shunted away from the men, bundled into a scarf, taught to keep my gaze fixed on the ground. The shame of being a woman, the dangerous sorcery of the body concealed: I would have learned these things had I been a devout follower of my own religion.

Finally the prayers began and the women turned their attention to the muezzin. At varying intervals they stood to pray, bowing from the waist, hands on knees, then kneeling on the mat, head to the ground, arms outstretched, then up again, over and over. I looked down the row and saw hundreds of women praying, their robes layered at the hips, wafting a vague scent of olive soap and laundered cotton.

Mehmet's wife, with a wave of her hand and a lift of her eyebrows, asked me to pray with her. But I shrugged and shook my head. Would it be more sacrilegious to mimic the movements of prayer, or to sit in a posture of respectful silence? "I don't know how to pray," I said in English, surprised to hear a catch in my voice. *Afwan*, I said. *Excuse me.* Sweat ran down my neck, across my abdomen. Some of the women finished early, rushing through the movements, and again they inched closer, touching me, pushing my hair back under the hood. *Haram*, they muttered, *Haram*.

On another cue, unheard, the women stood again. I saw men wandering in and out of the courtyard, some fanning themselves as they reclined near the door of the shrine. I stood up and saw, far across the courtyard, Keith laughing with Mehmet. What could they be discussing? Politics? Family? Food? I yearned to be with them, to be exempt from the rules of women, away from these women's hands. But Mehmet's wife pulled me back from the ledge. She again motioned, this time a little more forcefully, for me to pray.

So I did. I bent, placed my hands on my knees, and tried to feel something, anything resembling a prayer. I followed Mehmet's wife, moving my hands, my head, my lips. I hardly remembered praying in my own synagogue, mumbling along beside my mother and father, tired and hot and hungry, smelling the stale odors of mothballs and Emeraude, prune Danish and Folgers coffee. I remembered sitting at my Hebrew school desk while the teacher called the roll, and my own name—*Basha Leah*— ringing in my ears. *Basha Leah* drank from a sacred well. *Basha Leah* danced for the children. *Basha Leah* was cool and elegant, with wise eyes and a compassionate heart.

So, as *Basha Leah*, I prayed with Mehmet's wife—I straightened up, rocked a little on my heels, then sank to my knees and pressed my forehead to the ground. Here I could see nothing; the hood of my cloak shrouded me, blotted out the light. I faced Mecca, my arms outstretched, my head bowed in an attitude of respect and devotion. Millions of Muslims faced Mecca that same moment, sending the force of their worship in this direction, their prayers rolling over the slope of my Jewish back.

I don't know how long I stayed like this—face down, my back a shell, my eyes shut tight. But soon I heard the rustle and swish of robes, children querying their mothers for food. I sat up, my face flushed with heat. The women seemed to have forgotten me as they gathered up their mats and yelled for the children who chased each other among the pillars. A young man circulated through the women's section, selling sesame-studded bread from a stick. Mehmet's wife sat placidly next to me, her hands intertwined in her lap.

I wanted to tell Mehmet's wife I was Jewish. I also wanted to explain that I'd never been bat-mitzvahed; I was a Jewish girl, I would say, but I didn't feel like a Jewish woman. I wanted to tell her I could not bear children of my own, and so my future as a woman remained uncertain: how would I fit myself into a family history, into the traditions of my own religion? I thought she might raise her eyebrows, but she wouldn't grow angry; I thought she might smile and say something kind to me in a language we could both understand.

But I remained silent, and in silence we waited until Mehmet came to fetch us away.

Next Year in Jerusalem!

Keith and I pass through the gate into the old city of Jerusalem, inching our way through the crowded bazaar. There are dried apricots and peaches, huge bins of garbanzo beans, stacks of green soap, chunks of lamb smoking on spits. Boys career down the steep alleyways with laden carts, braking by crushing their heels against a dangling rubber tire. We step over a threshold to the Jewish quarter.

The air clears; the crowd thins; spotless windows frame gold-chunk bracelets, silver amulets, hand-painted silk. The walls are a golden-hued sandstone; tract lighting glows from the ceiling. A gaggle of teenaged girls swarms by us, followed by an escort, a man with a revolver bulging in his pocket. I see a woman browsing in a jewelry store; she's wearing a flowered-print dress, sandals, and an automatic rifle casually slung over her shoulder. A cluster of machine guns leans against a shop window; a tourist poses with an M-16 in front of a synagogue.

As if following a trail by memory, or instinct, we're drawn to a terrace overlooking the Wailing Wall. When I was a child in Hebrew school, they showed us black-and-white newspaper photos of Hasidic men davening against this wall, women crying, bar mitzvah boys hugging the Torah. My teachers spoke of the worshippers leaning so close to the stone they kissed it. The photos must have been snapped from exactly this angle: the Dome of the Rock rising in the background, and in the foreground the ruined gray wall, with its rough-cut stones and moss growing from between the cracks. And, flush to the wall, the swaying line of worshippers. As a child I thought this was the place a Jew came when he was sad and needed to cry.

When my family held their wine glasses aloft and pledged *Next Year in Jerusalem!*, they had exactly this place in mind. The men saw themselves in tallis and yarmulkes, joining Jews from around the world in a steady chant. The women imagined rejoining their mothers and grandmothers in song. Jerusalem and the Wailing Wall were identical.

Keith and I pass through a police checkpoint and hurry down the steps into the courtyard. As if by instinct, I glance up at the rim of the wall for snipers. Two police vans glide into the enclosure; a cadre of soldiers clatters down the steps, and we blend into the crowd of tourists swarming toward the wall. On one side are the men, the dark mass of Hasidic Jews on the far left, rocking rhythmically; on the other side the women mill in muted dresses and scarves. A few people sit away from the wall in dull gray folding chairs, but most are packed shoulder to shoulder along the stones.

What am I to do, now that I'm here in the land of my grandfather's imagination? Keith leans down and whispers in my ear. "We'll meet up in a bit." He wanders to the men's side, and I see a gatekeeper drop a cardboard yarmulke onto his head.

A woman approaches me as I enter the women's section. "Are you Jewish?" she says. Her face is neutral, composed. "Yes," I say, "I'm Jewish." But the woman squints at me and continues her interrogation, unconvinced.

"Is your mother Jewish?" she asks, her gaze roaming across my forehead, my nose, my mouth. "Yes, my mother is Jewish," I meekly reply. She smiles approvingly and hands me a blank slip of paper.

Then I see them—the prayers rolled up and stuck into cracks, falling in drifts at the foot of the wall. To my left, I hear the sing-song voices of the men, murmuring, and above that the occasional throaty calls of the black-hatted Hasids davening back and forth, their foreheads tapping the wall. The Hebrew sounds familiar as English, though I have no idea what it means. I watch the women on my side: their palms flat on the wall, their heads bent, their lips moving in mumbled devotion.

I've read the Wailing Wall is an ear to God, and that's why so many come to touch it, to press their lips against the mossy rocks. I watch the women reading sotto voce from their prayer books, or sometimes with no voice at all, just moving their lips and rocking back and forth on their heels. Eventually I get close enough to touch a tentative finger to the stone. This one brick is wider than my arms spread side-to-side; the surface buckles and curves. This was a stone laid down by King Herod's men, before the birth of Christ. It feels cool and comforting, and I would keep my hand there longer, but I back off quickly to allow a small woman in a gray scarf to take her desperate place at the wall.

From the men's section I hear one of the Hasids, his prayer warbling high above the muted voices, and one of the women next to me, her hands covering her eyes, cries out in response. I back away, as I see the other women have done, keeping the wall in sight. I've said no prayer, not even to myself; I've written no plea to the *Shekinah* who resides within the stones.

But even as I shuffle in humiliation away from the wall, I know on my last day in Jerusalem I'll feel compelled to revisit the courtyard alone. I'll take my place, leaning forward to touch my forehead against the wall. I might hold both palms flat against the rock. I'll smell moss and dust and the stone that still molders beneath the earth. I'll smell the breath of millions of women before me, and I'll smell the skin of the woman next to me, her lips moving, her eyes tightly closed. Prayer has an odor of devotion and righteousness, but here it's also the smell of milk and mothballs, scarves folded in a drawer, and seltzer for the grandchildren in big glass bottles next to the fridge. It's the sound of children fidgeting at the table as they listen to the stories over and over, chewing on matzoh and *haroses*. It's the sound of my mother dishing up the brisket, the roast chicken. I'll smell my grandmother, the powder behind her ears, and I'll hear my grandfather mumbling his prayer on the other side, a voice perilously close to song.

I don't know if I'll write anything down, commit my voice to a parchment scroll and leave it forever in one of the empty cracks. But I'll know how to pray. I'll turn my head slightly and press my ear to listen against the stone.

Rick Moody

From *The Black Veil*

New Yorker Rick Moody attended Brown and Columbia universities. Among his books of fiction and essay are *Garden State* (1992), *The Ice Storm* (1994), *The Ring of Brightest Angels around Heaven* (1995), *Purple America* (1997), *Demonology* (2001), *The Diviners* (2005), and *Right Livelihoods* (2007). He has received awards from the American Academy of Arts and Letters and the Guggenheim Foundation. His short fiction and journalism have been anthologized in *Best American Stories 2001, Best American Essays 2004, Year's Best Science Fiction #9*, and, multiply, in the Pushcart Prize anthology.

The piece in our book is excerpted from *The Black Veil: A Memoir with Digressions* (2002). This book won the NAMI/Ken Book Award and the PEN Albrand Prize for excellence in the memoir. While the book deals with depression and addiction, it transcends the usual recovery narrative through its style and digressive structure. A reviewer in *Library Journal* wrote, "His lyrical phrases and wry sense of humor masterfully tie together unconventional observations and disparate threads about family history, headline news, and etymology. Though he communicates much about his life, Moody . . . shrouds his existence with a filmy veil. The characters in his life (including his father) are painted with quirky details but remain in the shadows, never fully drawn. . . . Yet by using myth and truth, Moody sheds light on what lies beyond the black veil we all wear."

When giving interviews about this book, Moody said, "Literature is on a dialectic that has fiction and nonfiction on either end. Together, they form one narrative. . . . *The Black Veil* will not be shelved with my [fiction], which is incredibly irritating to me. I want people to read it in the context of everything else I've done." Much of the critical response to Moody's memoir did just this, comparing the memoir with his novels. Most reviewers preferred his novels, feeling that *The Black Veil*, while successfully experimenting with form, was "chilly" or downright "cold." Others felt that *The Black Veil* used its form to obfuscate confession. Still others thought that it was too confessional. Some thought it appeared to be too fictionalized, too clever in its references to non-personal subjects; others wanted more of that. Most critics just didn't seem to know what to do with the book. The ensuing debate reflected the problems that many seemed to have with memoir as a genre.

Rick Moody has taught at the State University of New York at Purchase, the Bennington College Writing Seminars, the Fine Arts Work Center in Provincetown, the New York Writers Institute, and the New School for Social Research. He lives in Brooklyn, New York.

Our selection comes early in the book *The Black Veil*, when the author takes a position as salesman to the world of art.

Interview with Rick Moody, p. 613.

Every young man at some time or other wonders whether he can be a salesman. Almost every man, when he is young, daydreams about making the big sale. Like I say, from salesmen have I sprung, of automobiles, of financial planning, etc. From salesmen have I sprung, from that great religion, that American system of learning. Out of school in the early part of the Reagan presidency, I was fixed on abandoning the East Coast, abandoning lineage, abandoning the prying gaze of my sets of parents, and so I conceived of a plan to go to New Zealand, or Down Under, maybe, Auckland, or Sydney, somewhere where they spoke English but that was otherwise remote. I was afraid of being stripped of my tongue, of having nothing but awkwardness with which to negotiate foreign lands. I made a few trips to the library to hunt up facts on Anglophone countries. I asked friends at barside (digging into our pockets for quarters to insert into Asteroids) if they knew anyone who had ever lived in New Zealand or Australia, and did they know anything about these regions? Did sheep really outnumber people? Average annual rainfall? Principal industries? The Maoris, the Aborigines, walkabouts, didgeridoos, great white sharks? Ultimately, I got as far as San Francisco. They spoke an English much like mine. I had never been west of Philadelphia, except for a week in senior year of high school when I was in Denver. San Francisco was farther than Denver; it was set upon hills, draped in fog, there were gay people in profusion, there were earthquakes. I was to have two roommates on this adventure, both from school *back east*. One was a director of theatricals, called Mark, the other a budding novelist, Jeff. Mark had journeyed west first and secured us an apartment. And I was to meet Jeff in his hometown of Detroit and make the drive to the coast with him in his used Volkswagen Rabbit, sorrel hued, a car that his father had helped him purchase. We would have as company on our adventure Jeff's dog, Bloom, a mixed-breed animal clearly *at wit's end* (the West Coast fleas, to which Bloom was unaccustomed, later drove her over the brink, and she could occasionally be seen foaming at the mouth and running in circles). In Detroit, upon the advent of our departure, we were faced with the difficult problem of how to get Bloom to sit in the back of the Volkswagen, under the hatchback, in a nook carved out among Jeff's modest store of possessions. She kept attempting to free herself from this confinement. Jeff's father, an affable and warm man, clearly Midwestern, *a salesman*, enlarged by a garrulity that put you totally at ease and somewhat balding for the purposes of this anecdote, stood beside me as we attempted to jam another duffel bag full of Jeff's outfits into the available space, next to the spot where there was, in Tupperware, a three-day supply of peanut-butter-and-Welch's-grape-jelly sandwiches. Next to Bloom's nook. I was trying to close the hatchback to keep the dog from escaping. The dog was escaping. Jeff's dad was squashing in a gym bag. We were trying not to crush the sandwiches. All these things at once. The outcome was this: I closed the hatchback on Jeff's father's head. And it wasn't a love tap, either. I forcefully smashed the hatchback of the Volkswagen down on the front part of Jeff's father's forehead, where all rational and abstract thinking was stored, where there was a reservoir of *sales strategies*, and there was a dull and vegetative thud, as when, for example, *you take a swing at a honeydew with an aluminum bat*. I was amazed that Jeff's dad wasn't prone on the driveway when I was through with him, but he was still standing by my side as the hatchback swung wide again and the dog took off up the road. He cried, *You're in a hurry, aren't you?* Fixing on me a stare that was suspicious and irate. There was something horribly lonely in all this. I didn't know where I was going, to what American city, I had only the name of the place, some town where I knew exactly two people and a dog, a state I had never even seen, a mythical state, a state of soft-rock renown, and I was going west for no good reason but that it was time to do something new, time to pursue uncertain prospects, great expectations. And my first performance of greatness *in the wilderness of this world*, as Bunyan puts it, in a period of rapid, unexplainable growth, was to inflict head trauma on the man who had taken me in for the weekend. Moving rapidly to add insult to the performance, I then reached out to touch the spot where a hematoma rose on Jeff's dad's brow, as if a laying-on of hands would help. This is what I would have done, anyhow, if it had been Jeff himself I had lobotomized instead of his dad, and I suppose I was trying to offer an apology, I was mumbling something *soothing and kind*, but Jeff's father recoiled from me, backing away toward his abode, through the front door, rubbing the front part of his skull. Some things *are* unforgettable, certain smells of infancy, lyrics to bubblegum Top 40 singles. I can't remember our address in San Francisco exactly, I can't remember most of the people I've met recently, but I will probably always remember Jeff's father's expression at that moment. *You're in a hurry, aren't you?*

"I was going west for no good reason but that it was time to do something new."

　　Later, in the first two hours of our drive from Detroit to San Francisco, the Volkswagen succumbed to total electrical failure. It shut itself off, and we rolled silently to the shoulder. Waited for a tow. This took time. After paying the tow truck with some of our unimpressive cash reserves, we had the battery jumped at a filling station. Bloom sniffed around the rear of the building where the men's room was located. The mechanic could not explain the origin of our problem, but he had jumper cables. Mystery unsolved, we pushed on, with our carload of bare necessities, through Chicago, into Indiana, across Indiana, all the way to Iowa City that first day. When night fell, the headlights on the car began to flicker. I was tired. I thought I was imagining it. But I began to understand fully this *intermittency* two days later in the seventy miles between the exit for Salt Lake City and the next for West Wendover, Nevada. The Salt Flats. *No exits, no standing.* Seventy miles. After dusk, I was drinking from an open container and listening to King Crimson on headphones, and Jeff drove, and I noticed this ebbing and flowing of illumination from the front end of the car, like the saraband of dusk through autumn boughs, and at first my heart sank—there was something really wrong, we would be stranded, further misfortune ahead, and Jeff was tired of my company. I didn't say anything, and he didn't either, and I drank, and we drove through the tabula rasa of Utah. In this monotony, I faced up to the truth: the Rabbit might stall out at any time. At the side of the highway, Bloom would scare up poisonous snakes. Jeff and I would retreat into our discrete anxieties. On the other hand, everything was negotiable; it didn't matter much. *The world was our oyster.* The car could be retired here or it could survive to the Bay Area (where it would have its alternator replaced), but if we had to stay in Elko, or Reno, or Sacramento for a few days, if we had to sleep in the car, call home for money, buy a new car, kill each other out of despair and poverty, what difference did it make?

This is youth wandering carelessly into an era of responsibility. The *intermittencies* of the moment were general: a car that doesn't reliably work, two writers out of work with bad work prospects, arguing periodically, a dog about to develop epilepsy, unaffordable rent in an expensive city, drunkenness, all swelling like cactus blossoms in that moment in the desert, with the headphones blaring, with open containers. The music of King Crimson, I recognize, is the kind of *noodling, pretentious music* that no one should admit listening to, even on headphones in the desert, but the particular song that I would like to claim for the moment has appropriate resonances, namely "Neil and Jack and Me," a song about the Beat writers and their relentless crisscrossing of the nation's highway infrastructure, and maybe Jeff, the budding novelist, and I had some atavistic love for the myth of writers crisscrossing the nation's highway infrastructure, drinking, thinking somber thoughts, passing through the Tetons in a day, snowfall in the mountains one night, and the next in the desert, wasting quarters in a slot machine, eating peanut-butter-and-jelly sandwiches on the prairie with a skittish mutt. Parents everywhere, *fathers everywhere*, wish better for their children after the graduation of this progeny, a reliable source of income, a credit card for emergencies, but we had none of these things, or at least I did not, and there were times on the trip west when I was afraid to stop for what I might see, a land of struggles, a land of cruelties and disconsolations. From Nevada across the Sierras we didn't talk much, and soon we were on the Bay Bridge, and trying to make it up the steep hills of San Francisco, when the car stalled at every red light and we attempted to roll it, and this was the moment of the announcement of madness, lurking around the edges of this story from now on.

Memory brings me therefore to the Lower Haight of San Francisco, California, not the part of Haight at Ashbury, where the Grateful Dead had lived, where the Summer of Love had its magnetic north, down the hill from there. In a gentrifying neighborhood. Two liquor stores right on our block, fine with me. There were always a couple of drunks weaving around on their way past. Our landlady was a psychiatrist. She let us repaint according to whim. The couple in the apartment below was a threesome, two gay men and a lesbian in *a committed loving relationship*. They were raising a child together. A daughter. They had the most violent fights I'd ever heard. Two of them would throw the third against a wall, the floor would rumble as if with the continental tremors of the Bay Area, glassware would tumble out of the cupboard. *You never loved me! You said you loved me, but you're out all hours of the night with other men! How can I live like this? You don't care about our child! You selfish person!* Two or three such altercations a month, during which you would hear bodies hurled against walls, doors slammed. Some years later, all three of them, the committed lovers, appeared on a television talk show, on one of the issue-oriented eighties talk shows. They boasted of their success with the child. They were articulate and calm. Their daughter would be a teenager now (as I write this), according to my math, just coming into the productive phase of her teen rebellion.

Our apartment was a three-bedroom, with a small living room and kitchen, and I lived in the main expanse of the apartment, next to the kitchen. Jeff and Mark were in adjacent rooms off the hall, at the top of the stairwell. Bloom, the epileptic hound, was locked in my end, where she was often looking for something to rip to shreds. She had a knack for getting into my inner sanctum—furnished only with a bed and a small shelf on which I kept my typewriter. Bloom would climb up onto my futon to scratch her suppurating wounds while I was elsewhere, and for this reason my pallet, a futon on a discarded door mounted on milk crates, was both infested with fleas and streaked with the blood of our house pet.

I spent most of my commencement gift on rent and security deposit for the apartment, so I needed a job. My father did business in San Francisco and had old associates there, and he enabled me to get a number of *promising informational interviews* with successful practitioners of West Coast finance. They were kindly, but when they agreed to meet me they had no idea of how unmarketable my skills really were. I had no idea either. All of these people tried hard to help me (the periodicals director at a very large bank told me frankly that *I should do something that would challenge me*, and then he asked for my *birth sign*), but I was ill equipped for the burgeoning global economy, although I was good at arguing about the epistemological problems raised by French literary theory. I couldn't pretend, and therefore I couldn't get *a single decent interview* out of all these busy people in their office towers with astounding bay views. When I turned up in my outgrown Brooks Brothers pinstripe suit I would forget to bring a pen, so that I had to ask to borrow one to fill out the employment questionnaire. Or I couldn't get my hair to lie down flat. Or I got the name of the interviewer wrong, or even the name of the bank. It seemed I was the sort of wet-behind-the-ears job applicant who, though amusing, does not want the job and is therefore *a drain on your time, your good mood, your productivity.* After each prospect soured, I would feel that I had made my effort that day and that I could now repair to our apartment to read the paper or go for a walk in the park or drink champagne out of plastic stemware by the Pacific Ocean. After a month or so of this, when I was down to fifty dollars in the bank and getting ready to plead for help from home, I found an advertisement in the want ads of the _Chronicle_ offering great rewards for self-starters who were interested in art. _A chance to work in an important city arts institution, unlimited museum admission guaranteed._ I was intrigued! Didn't I know a fair amount about art, because of my survey classes in art history, because of my courses in Marxist aesthetics and Continental philosophy, because of my close personal association with many promising studio artists from the Rhode Island School of Design! My enthusiasm implied that keen _salesmanship_ was reflected in the wording of that advertisement in the _Chronicle_. As one practitioner has put it, _The salesman who bursts into the prospect's office and loudly asserts that he wants to sell some life insurance rarely walks out with an order. You have to apply suction, not pressure._ Dan, my eventual boss, sure knew how to use suction on a young art lover like myself, because soon I was working at the de Young Museum, a faux-Renaissance building in the Golden Gate Park, during the run of a traveling exhibition of art from the collection of the Vatican. The job in question involved _selling recorded tours_ of the exhibition. It paid $3.25 an hour.

I was going to become a salesman! A salesman from a long line of salesmen. A persuader, a rhetorician. _Selling is believing, believing in what you have to sell_, as Edward Goeppner of San Francisco's Podesta Baldocchi Florists has said. My tenure at the de Young was at the dawn of the age of the portable cassette recorder. Technology had not yet entirely licked the bulky design of early portability. It was our job to overcome these design shortcomings. There we stood, in the front hall of the de Young, ready to sell. Behind us, behind this staff of capable and eager recorded-tour salesmen and -women, were several large varnished hardwood shelves in which the cassette players were housed, on their sides, for easy access. And at the end of each of the two rows of shelves, near the twin cash registers, were a pair of metal trees where there dangled several dozen green earphones, their cords tentacular beneath them. Like postindustrial willows. There were eight of us on a shift, four to a side of the great entrance hall of the de Young. And, using language honed by other successful recorded-tour salesmen in other cities, using a minimum of words, a mere incantation of language, we would approach _the premium exhibition customers_ as they were herded in our general direction by the crowd-control personnel at the front of the museum. As they shuffled into earshot, our voices would ring out. _Hi! Can I interest you in a recorded tour today?_ There was a moment while the violence of our ambitions sunk in. These patrons had erroneously believed themselves already separated from their cash. At which point they would a) _start irritably_ from their private aspirations for a fathomless aesthetic experience among the artworks of the Vatican collection, causing them to rush past without a word, or b) _agree or disagree immediately_, yea or nay, perceiving at once that our efforts involved getting them to part with more of their hard-earned capital, or c) _pause_, in which case we descended on them with merciless and scripted prose to persuade them that no apperception of Leonardo's unparalleled _Saint Jerome_ would be complete without the remarks of the de Young Museum's director, whose voice almost exactly resembled that of a certain whimsical television news personality, and though none of us had ever actually *heard* the entirety of the remarks of this museum director—we couldn't be bothered, really—it was our considered opinion that this recorded tour would enhance the viewing experience, the aesthetic experience, *the total art experience* here at the de Young, and in fact this recorded tour constituted an important addition to the criticism of the late twentieth century. If the wavering art patron had gotten as far as our recitation of facts, he or she usually caved. We were young. We were earnest. If necessary, we would say anything. (It's the first impression that makes the sale, as Al Burns, vice president in charge of sales at Sterling Drug, once put it, *The first twenty seconds, when you come in actual contact with the prospect on any day at any time, are, to my mind, the most exacting, exciting, and important of all.*)

> "We were young. We were earnest. If necessary, we would say anything."

One reasonable concern of many of the de Young patrons to whom we pitched our product had to do with the earphones themselves, which hung on the ear, a single ear, suspended by a plastic frame, rather than being inserted into or worn over both ears as they are now. Customers wanted to be sure that the earphones were *disinfected* after each use. Well, we were happy to report to these compulsive hand-washers that it was the responsibility of one company runner (it was the task at the de Young that I most looked forward to, because it involved no contact with the public) to collect these earpieces at the end of the exhibit, along with the cassette players. At this juncture, he or she would scientifically *disinfect* the earphones with a squirt of industrial-strength antibacterial soap before returning both players and earpieces to the staging area up front. We could therefore, in the midst of our sales meetings with the museum-going public, assure these patrons that the earpieces were fully disinfected, after which we would *reach for their ears* and hang the little plastic flap over the top of the ear, having subdued them, having clinched the sale. *You're going to have trouble*, Dan the manager had assured us, *because people are territorial about their ears, but if you are polite and patient, they will allow you to show them how to use the earpiece.* I began to take a certain pleasure in this attention to ears. The way people would hop out of reach when you tried to probe for that cartilage. Only the very secure or the heavily sedated would easily consent.

The first important skill we had to learn, as members of the Acoustiguide sales staff, was to stand still without respite for eight hours a day. This was harder than we thought. The second skill was to negotiate long, concentrated stretches of soul-slaughtering indifference to our surroundings, to the events of daily life, and, indeed, to our futures. And the third skill was to endure the erosion of what few creature pleasures remained to us during the interminable days at the museum. Because, after a few weeks, Dan said *it didn't look good* that we were talking among ourselves during the early portion of the day, before the swarms. It violated one of the principles of good salesmanship, namely *sincerity*. When there was

downtime, Dan suggested, we should be straightening the cassette players
in the racks behind us and making sure the cassettes were fully rewound.
And *it didn't look good* if we had our feet propped up behind us on the
varnished shelving. And *it didn't look good* if we wore jeans. But before he
was done with his new lecture, with whatever superficial correction he was
after today, the hordes had descended on us anew, *a thousand potential
customers in an hour* sometimes, more as we got nearer to the Christmas
holidays, and then the museum was crawling with people, all of them irritable at the density of fellow art lovers, and the line would extend out into
the hall, and they would be upon us, and we would recite the instructions—
*Up is forward, down is reverse, and should you wish to stop the tape, just
bring the lever to this middle position, and remember, the lecture is numbered to go along with the paintings, so you'll want to move in a clockwise
direction as you pass through the galleries*—and then we would hasten to
the next sale. In the midst of this grinding tedium, a customer would complain that I was *mumbling*, or that I had not completed the instructions, or
that she couldn't understand how to operate the machine, or she would
complain that I had attempted to *touch her ear*, while alongside another
was sighing, and just behind him or her two or three more of them sighing,
irritated that they couldn't secure their recorded tour and move on. *Business is more profitable when it is friendly*, or so it is said, but I remember
Christmastime, when there was the whole line of them stretched out in
front of me, hundreds of them, the thickest, densest crowd I had yet seen,
each individual with his or her uncleaned ear, each with his ear flap and
anvil and stirrup and auditory nerve, ear hair, ear wax, and into each of
these ears I would have to whisper the same sales pitch, so close that I
could have nibbled their earlobes, and at Christmas it seemed as if there
was no dignity in the job and no relief, and the crowd pressed forward in
its collective pique, and one guy ripped the tape recorder out of my hand
because he was tired of waiting, and the crowds made me think of those
factory farms where chickens, in low lighting, peck out the eyes of the
weaker chicken beside them, and then the other chickens trample this
weak bird and eat the remains, so that the next day the farmer rakes up
feathers and nothing more, and the subsequent customer was no better
than the last guy, so to her, the customer in front of me, I said, *We're having a really bad day here; do you think you might give us a little respect on
the way past?* pleading, really, because my education had cost a great deal
of money, and this was the only job that I could find in the Bay Area, to
which the woman replied, *I'm having a bad day too, and I don't need
your rudeness*, prying the tape player out of my hands, circumnavigating
the line at the register, demanding to see the manager, probably because
she'd been in crowds all morning, after which I *walked off the line*, leaving my colleagues to fend for themselves, the only time I did so during the
months I had the job, and went into the dim, plain room behind the racks
of cassette recorders where we were allowed to eat our lunches, and where
Dan and his partner counted the lucre, and I punched the wall, in front of
my boss, and said, *I can't take this shit*, a bit of drama, some gratuitous

obscenity, but evidently I *could* take that shit, because soon I was back on the line, as I was every day during the three months in which I made $26 a day, or $520 a month, for a yearly pretax wage of $6,240. *It goes without saying that a salesman should always studiously avoid offending his prospect in any way, for a sale is always easier to make when the prospect likes you.*

Who were we, the indomitable sales force of Acoustiguide, Inc.? There was a woman named Mary who worked in the perpetually under-funded world of leftist politics, perhaps for the *Committee in Solidarity with the People of El Salvador*, and who was moonlighting at the museum until the organization could afford to pay her again. And there was a blond guy who always wore leather pants, every single day I was there, and brightly colored sweaters, and who had an unctuous style that combined honeyed vowels and menace. He turned out to be a drug dealer. There was an older woman, Estelle, whose husband was retired and who just wanted the extra income. She lived over on the good side of town, in North Beach, and she was kind and maternal, but in her company I couldn't think of a single thing to say. There was a young painter, a woman, with hennaed hair whose boyfriend was Japanese. She was strapped for cash and had animosity toward *rich people*. There was an older gay man—his lover drove a Jaguar, and one evening they gave me a ride home in their capacious backseat—who had been in the military, *deeply closeted* in the upper echelons of the American military. He seemed brilliant and ambitious, and not like the kind of guy who needed to work selling recorded tours for $3.25 an hour, and when I asked him about it, about how he got to this spot, he spoke of trysts in the park near the Pentagon, about the yearning and concealment, about the intimate relationship between *signifiers of force* and homosexuality, and, with a great seriousness, he concluded these remarks by observing that *everyone needs to be loved.* There was a Valley Girl named Lulu who hated *bad smells* and who often spoke of this antipathy; there was a guy who looked like John Lennon and who had all of John Lennon's albums. He gave me a ride on his motorcycle.

I read *The Confidence Man* over lunch. It would be gratifying to claim that after I had punched out at five o'clock, I was able to *throw the switch* on this sales job, that I could touch people's ears for eight hours and then go home to read Melville and compose short stories or whatever I was attempting to compose. But the facts were these: at night I did little but drink and watch the news. As a result, I don't remember much of *The Confidence Man*, or Foucault's *History of Sexuality*, or Heinrich Boll's *Group Portrait With Lady*, or *Juliette* by the Marquis de Sade, all of which I tried to read in San Francisco. But I did learn the hard way some of Herbert Metz's essential rules of salesmanship:

1. When you are lining up a dealer, go out with him and give him a prac-tical demonstration of the market for your product by selling it to him.
2. There comes a time in many sales calls when you have to completely change your sales tactics in the same way that a fullback often reverses

his field. It is foolish and very often disastrous to lower your head and keep bucking the line in the same old place.

3. In making a sale, no matter what you are selling, keep your eyes open all the time and be alert for the "break."

4. And finally, "know your stuff," and "know it well." Believe in it enthusiastically, whole-heartedly, and sincerely. Above all, realize how important selling is to you and to the country's economy, and glory in the work you are doing to the point that you get a greater kick and thrill out of it than anything else that you could do.

One incident at the museum made a lasting impression: the day that I saw my first blind art lover. He had the cane, the dark glasses, he had the outward signs of the disability, that system of styles that enabled us to tell him apart from the able-bodied. But he was here at the show like anyone else, and he had a friend holding his arm. He was bearded, in his forties. He was eager to rent our product. He and his friend passed into our domain, made their purchase, and later, while they were looking at Poussin or Matisse, I snuck in to watch. There was a crowd-control bottleneck around the blind guy and his friend, people were having trouble negotiating this hazard, but otherwise the blind man could have been any spectator. I flagged down one of the nearby security guards. *Lou*, I said, *there's a blind guy in the galleries.* Lou was trim, good-looking, middle-aged, and he had been at the museum for years. He'd made friends with all the docents, all the society ladies, and they were always to be seen regaling him, cornering him for gossip and art appreciation. With his most serious demeanor, Lou told me that there had always been *blind persons* who attended the museum, as it was *a place of reverence.* When they brought a friend with them, the role of that friend was to explain, describe, *embellish* the riches of the centuries. It was like a sales job.

I left the museum as soon as I could. I didn't last the duration of the Vatican collection exhibition, three months, at which point I would have been let go anyway. We were subcontractors, after all, and like all subcontractors expendable. January was torrential, and the combination of rain and drudgery blunted me further, and I felt lonely, as I almost always did in California, and so I took a job offered by my roommate Mark, building sets for an avant-garde theater company. In Sausalito. That job lasted only about six weeks.

I never had the affection my grandfather had for selling, I never felt what salesmen of his generation describe, I never thought about whether sales were good for the economy, good for character building, good for the community, I never had *the inner knowledge that marks every true member of the fraternity of salesmen: the knowledge that a successful sale can give you one of the greatest "oomphs" of your life.* My grandfather liked people, liked to be out on the floor, liked the associations of his car dealership, liked to ask questions about a young couple coming in to buy their first vehicle. When he bought his dealership, after the war, selling automobiles was a matter of taking names, because there had been no new cars for so long. After the war, people came to buy cars and you put them on the list and you treated them fairly, and they bought cars from you later. You were a reliable dealer; you were a thoughtful, decent salesman. Of course, in some dealerships it was possible to purchase your way to the front of the waiting list for new vehicles, but my grandfather was *disgusted* by his fellows in the fraternity of car dealers who would accept payoffs to bump people to the front of that line. He loved the product.

Here's P. Val Kolb, former president of Sterwin Chemicals, Inc., on automobile sales: *You can, and very often do, sell a passenger car on brand name, appearance, color, or comfortable upholstery. In such cases, women are the chief buyers. The appeal is emotional. But when you sell a truck, you talk performance. You marshal facts on dependability and operating costs. You assemble figures gathered from actual tests. That's factual selling.*

So the craft is about language, by which I mean that though my father and grandfather might have more completely welcomed me into the patrimonial lineage of Moodys had I become a bona fide salesman, maybe being a writer and being a salesman are not so different: *Selling is one of the subtle arts, which throws mind against mind, tongue against tongue, firmness against firmness. The salesman has much to accomplish with spoken words; and great things, as well as small, turn on these spoken words.* It's this language that I imagine my father overheard when he was working summers in the auto body end of Moody Motor Sales, Inc., banging out dents, watching my grandfather spinning a web of suasion. Maybe he passed the lessons on to me. *Suppose, for instance, you want a shotgun. You go into a store and there is a gun for $75 and another for $35.*

Interview with Rick Moody

BECKY BRADWAY: Nearly everyone expresses the opinion that memoir must be easier to write than fiction. (I'm sure you've heard this from scholars, students, writers, Oprah addicts, and pretty much anyone who thinks that real life is easy to handle.) I wondered if this was true for you in any way—or, if more difficult, how so.

RICK MOODY: Actually, I found writing autobiographically—without the safety net of invention—incredibly difficult. *The Black Veil*, in fact, was by far the most difficult book I have written. It turns out I just don't like to talk about myself that much. The very personal passages were exactly like pulling teeth. I kept distracting myself by writing short stories (my collection entitled *Demonology* was sort of written in the middle of *The Black Veil*), so as to avoid finishing. Or at least so as to avoid talking about myself. Since then the pole has swung dramatically in the other direction: I'm writing fiction with very little autobiographical incident in it at all. My recent work has been all about imagination. In fact, I am hoping not to write another memoir until I am in my seventies.

BB: Your writing exhibits a lot of style—most obviously in the italicized phrases and lists and long sentences. I wondered to what extent this was a conscious decision, and why you wrote it that way. And I wondered to what extent it is driven subconsciously, and is just reflecting the way you think and talk. How were you able to let yourself go beyond the traditional strictures of what can or can't be done in nonfiction?

RM: I approached *The Black Veil* like a nonfiction novel, which to my way of thinking meant that it was structured as impulsively and artfully as I would have done had it been a novel. I had begun pushing the envelope on structure in *Purple America*, the novel I published before I began *The Black Veil*. I figured with the memoir that I would try to push the envelope some more. The memoir needed to have its ass kicked a little bit, just like the novel did, or so it seemed at the time. I have no allegiance to the muted and reverential simplicity that seems to be at the heart of so much contemporary memoir writing. My sentences, with their long tangles of dependent clauses and their excessive italicizing, followed upon this kind of thinking. They were as complicated as the inside of my skull. In that sense these sentences are very much true. Probably the models for working this way are European. I'm thinking of W. G. Sebald and Ryszard Kapuscinski. Their liberated ideas about genre (likewise their very elegant prose) were much behind how I thought about my nonfiction.

BB: Can memoir ever be literally true and does it even need to aspire to such? Is it necessary to fact check a memoir, or get permission, or even tell people that you are writing about them? Or does an artist have the right to let memory serve?

RM: Implicit in the question is a philosophical conundrum that I imagine I can't repel in this abbreviated space. However: if you call your book a memoir, you must believe that something approaching the truth is possible. And yet maybe it's possible to believe in the truth and be skeptical about whether the memoir can somehow capture it. This is why my subtitle on *The Black Veil: A Memoir with Digressions* disappeared from the paperback edition. I suppose I am not sure about the memoir as a form. However, I did, to the best of my ability, tell "the truth" in *The Black Veil*, and where possible I did, yes, check facts with people. It turns out that an anecdote about my grandfather falling ill that's included in the book is sourced only to me (my brother doesn't remember the incident), and this bothers me somewhat. I did not, however, massage the facts. Ever. There was one poetical exaggeration that I had in the book for a while, but it made me so uncomfortable I cut it. If I were going to make stuff up, I might as well have written another novel. But I didn't do that. The constraint of truthtelling, to whatever degree you imagine it possible, is a good exercise for people like me who are used to a lot of fibbing.

Susan Orlean

A Place Called Midland

Susan Orlean was born on Halloween in 1955 and grew up a resident of Cleveland ("back when the Indians were still a lousy team, and before they became a really good team and then again became a somewhat lousy team, although I have hope again"). She then moved on to enjoy "a happy and relatively squandered college career" at the University of Michigan in Ann Arbor; upon graduation, she migrated to Portland, Oregon, where she landed a job at a "now-defunct" magazine, followed shortly by a job at an alternative music journal, writing music reviews and feature articles. In the words of Orlean: "While I was in Portland, Mt. St. Helens erupted; I started writing for *Rolling Stone* and the *Village Voice*; I learned to cross-country ski; I failed to learn how to cook."

She has been a staff writer for the *New Yorker* since 1982, and has contributed articles to *Vogue*, *Rolling Stone*, *Esquire*, and *Outside*, gaining a certain degree of infamy for her pursuit of the "softer subjects"—cutting out windows that allow her readers a view of lives that, while unusual, are by journalistic measure "ordinary." Her books include *Red Sox and Blue Fish* (1987), *Saturday Night* (1990), *The Bullfighter Checks Her Make-Up* (2001), and *The Orchid Thief*—a profile of Florida orchid breeder and collector John Laroche (1998), which spawned the film *Adaptation*, starring Meryl Streep as a fictional Susan Orlean.

"I read fiction. It's what I enjoy the most. I think that I used to think that I would write fiction," confessed Orlean in an interview with Robert Birnbaum. "At the moment, I'm not. . . . I don't find it limiting or frustrating to do what I'm doing. And I like the mental puzzle involved with dealing with a real situation rather than one that you can just arbitrarily choose to change. And frankly I like the social mission of writing nonfiction. I think it is different, writing nonfiction pieces and they are perceived very differently because people know this is real and someone took the time to find out about that kind of person. I don't struggle with the issue. I'm very content. I love what I do."

Our selection, "A Place Called Midland," is a close look at George W. Bush's home town, which Orlean visited during the 2000 presidential campaign. It was originally published in Orlean's collection of essays, *My Kind of Place* (2004).

In Midland, Texas, it's not the heat, it's the lack of humidity. Almost total lack of it, or so it seems, especially when you first arrive and step out of the chilled Midland International Airport and into the dry-roasted air. Midland has the kind of air that hits you like a brick. After a few minutes, your throat burns. After a few days, your skin feels powdery, your eyelids stick, your hair feels dusty and rough. The longer you spend there, the more you become a little bit like the land—you dry out and cake and crack. Not until I spent time in Midland did I fully appreciate the fact that the earth has an actual crust, like bread that has been slowly baked. I became convinced that if I stayed for a while, I would develop one, too.

Midland is a city of ninety-nine thousand, in the middle of the region known as the Permian Basin, a platform of sediment and salt capped with a wedge of rock that covers roughly a hundred and twenty-five thousand square miles of West Texas. Most people, if they know about Midland at all, know that it is where Baby Jessica McClure was rescued from a well thirteen years ago and where George W. Bush grew up and later started his business career. ("I don't know what percentage of me is Midland," he once said in an interview, "but I would say people, if they want to understand me, need to understand Midland and the attitude of Midland.") Both associations suggest a city that is innocent, idyllic, congenial—the kind of place where people fish fallen babies out of wells and young men make fortunes in old-fashioned ways. But Midland struck me as weirder than that—its simplicity deceiving, its character harder to uncover and know.

Being inconspicuous is Midland's most conspicuous feature. It used to be called Midway, because it was halfway between Fort Worth and El Paso. When it was determined that there was already a Midway in Texas, it was renamed Midland, as if nothing else about it could inspire a name. A current city slogan is "Midland: In the Middle of Somewhere." Previous slogans have included "Midland: Most Ambitious City Between the Oceans" and "Midland: Oil, Livestock, and Financial Center of the Permian Basin." Recently, the more buoyant seventies slogan "The Sky's the Limit" has been revived, since Bush has said that it embodies the Midland he knew.

> "The only measure of time that matters in Midland is oil time."

Originally, Midland was a depot on the Texas & Pacific Railway. It outlived and outgrew the other flyspeck towns in the basin—now vanished cotton and cattle outposts like Boone and Slaughter and Toad Loop and Fighting Hollow and Bounce—by wooing oil companies to locate there after the first West Texas gusher, the Santa Rita, was tapped in 1923. In the late twenties, a hopeful businessman built an ornate office tower to enhance Midland's prestige and named it the Petroleum Building. And in the thirties, houses were literally picked up and moved from the neighboring town of McCamey to Midland in order to attract employees of Humble Oil. By the mid-fifties, Midland was where the oil company engineers, geologists, leaseholders, and attorneys lived; its sister city, Odessa, was home to the tool pushers and roughnecks.

The only measure of time that really matters in Midland is oil time. Recent history is divided into two periods. There was the mid-seventies through the early eighties, when OPEC was controlling the market and crude went up to an unimaginably high thirty-five dollars a barrel and was expected to go as high as a hundred: a Rolls-Royce dealership opened in town; Midland Airpark had a waiting list for private hangars;

and powerboats were beached in nearly every driveway. And then there was 1986, and the years after that, when OPEC flooded the market, the price per barrel dropped to nine dollars, and the FDIC became the biggest employer in the county.

A popular local joke is to say that the city is in the middle of the finest fishing and hunting in the Southwest. The first person to try the joke on me was an engineer named Richard Witte. Like everyone else I met, he warned me that I'd never see the real Midland on my own, and he offered to show me around. We took his pickup and rode out of the city on razor-straight roads to the oil fields—an ocean of gray dirt, unmarked, parched, spectacularly monotonous, not a ripple in it except for the occasional sunken spot of a former buffalo wallow, until you get to the edge of the Permian Basin caprock and fall off into the rest of the world. We skirted ranches on which little sprouted except for shrubby mesquite and rows of skeletal pump jacks bobbing for oil, and zigzagged across square miles so wide and empty that, even when we raced along, we seemed to be standing still. It looked like nothing, except that there were millions of dollars underneath us, sacks of money banked in stone.

Witte then took me to see the Clay-Desta Center, an office building with a fountain of silvery water and a life-size sculpture of a mother and baby giraffe in its atrium. It was a beastly day, and the gurgling sound of the water was so pleasant that we lingered for a bit; Witte said that people often came to the Clay-Desta Center just to be near the fountain. The idea of going to an office building to be near water seemed so peculiar that I asked whether there was a more natural source around. "Sure there is," Witte said. "In fact, we're in the middle of the finest fishing and hunting in the whole Southwest." Once Witte was satisfied by the look of shock on my face, he grinned. "Drive five hours in any direction and you'll find great fishing and hunting and boating," he said. "We're right in the middle of it. It's just that none of it's here." The second time I heard the joke—from a real estate broker, as I recall—I pretended to fall for it out of politeness; the third time someone—a lawyer—tried it on me, I delivered the punch line myself.

The first day I was in Midland, I stopped in an antiques store to see what passed for an antique in West Texas, which had pretty much been unpopulated until the 1920s. I dug through old copies of *Sunset* magazine and empty Avon perfume bottles while the only other customer, a heavy, red-faced woman, talked to the store clerk. "The president made a lot of people mad," the customer was saying, and I turned to listen.

"A lot of presidents do," the clerk replied.

"Well, he shouldn't have been in a convertible," the customer went on. "That was a big mistake. But, okay, let's forget about the convertible, even. My feeling is that JFK was a goner no matter what."

I had come to Midland expecting that everyone would be talking about the presidential campaign, but it was the dead of summer and little was stirring; there were no local discussions of whether Midland might become the next Hope, Arkansas, or whether there would be house tours of Bush's former residences. It wasn't for lack of partisanship: Another local joke is to say that you can name more than ten Democrats in town. It was just that the Bush candidacy seemed predestined and expected, a natural ascendancy. While I was in Midland, the big news stories were that one of the longest horizontal wells ever drilled in the area had been completed, reaching from its starting point, near Interstate 20, to a spot twelve thousand feet below the Midland Kmart; that the Midland RockHounds had beat the Tulsa Drillers, 4–3, putting them back at the .500 mark for the season; and that oil prices were creeping up to thirty dollars a barrel.

Midland is such a small city and the Bushes are so woven into it that most people seem to have had some contact with them—lived down the street from them, or belonged to the same country club, or known Laura Bush when she was a girl. The Bush family first moved to Midland in 1950, when a lot of East Coast entrepreneurs were coming to Texas and looking for oil. It was a great moment to be punching holes in the Permian Basin: Within nine years, George H. W. Bush had made his fortune and moved the family to Houston. In the mid-seventies, when George W. Bush came back to Midland and founded Arbusto Oil, it was still a good time to be in the business. But only half of Arbusto's wells hit oil or gas; eventually, the company faltered and merged with another dying company, which was then bought out by Harken Energy, and Bush moved to Washington, D.C. Virtually every oilman I met remembered George W. from his Arbusto days. The comment I heard from most of them was, "George W. was the nicest young man you ever will meet. Just the nicest. But, you know, he never did earn a dime."

I was hot the whole time I was in Midland and dying to see anything green. When I could bear the heat, I walked around the deserted downtown, or through the neighborhood called Old Town Midland, or to the Permian Basin Petroleum Museum, Library, and Hall of Fame, over by the interstate. Everything seemed bleached and lifeless. Then, one afternoon, I drove out to the Racquet Club—which used to have George W. Bush as a member—to attend a party hosted by a local mortgage company. The clubhouse was cool and whitewashed, the lawns were silken and lush, and when the kids did cannon balls into the swimming pool, the water roared like applause. All the other guests at the party were in real estate, and they gathered in the shade of a live oak tree, snacking on hors d'oeuvres and chatting about the annual performance of Summer Mummers, the local vaudeville troupe, and the upcoming season of high school football, which is by far the biggest sport around.

It is a pretty nice time to be a real estate broker in Midland. It is not as nice as it was in, say, 1980, when you could show people only two or three houses and know they would snap one up at any price. "This was not the real world back then," Kay Sutton, who owns Century 21 in Midland, explained to me. "My daughter would shop and have lunch at the country

club, and she didn't know that there was any other way people lived." Back
then, so many new houses were going up that contractors were brought in
from all over the country and had to camp out in RVs and tents.

These days are middling; still, the agents were feeling easy and the
mortgage company was flush enough to have ordered shrimp. "It's the
high price of oil," Kay Sutton said. "It makes people optimistic." When
people are extremely optimistic, they want to live in a fancy development
like Saddle Club North or Green Tree Country Club Estates, with maybe
an attached three- or four-car garage and a view of the golf course. The
best houses have swimming pools and lawns that are as soft as lamb's
wool—real luxury in a place where a gallon of drinking water can cost
more than a gallon of gas. "Of course, everyone dreams of mature trees,"
Kay Sutton said. "But it's just a dream. You can't have both a new house
and mature trees."

Right next to my hotel was a café called the Ground Floor, the unofficial
clubhouse of a different Midland. The Ground Floor was opened in 1996
by a real estate investor from Seattle named John Nute; he put in free Internet
access, sponsored live music and poetry readings, and made the restrooms
available to anyone who walked in the door. The Ground Floor is across
the street from Centennial Plaza, one of those sterile brick-and-concrete
urban parks, and once the café opened, the two places quickly filled with
kids. "A lot of us misfits sort of found each other by hanging out at Centennial Plaza and the Ground Floor," a seventeen-year-old named Barbara
Lawhon explained to me one afternoon. "We'd sit around writing poetry
and playing music. It was a really big deal."

By 1997, Nute says, Friday night crowds at Centennial Plaza had grown
to two hundred teenagers. Some of them were skateboarders and in-line
skaters, who began doing a move on the park benches called grinding, which
tears the benches to shreds. By the next summer, a city ordinance forbidding
skateboarding and in-line skating in Centennial Plaza was being strongly
enforced, and Nute's business dropped off by more than two-thirds.

The year before the ordinance was enforced was one of the only
times Barbara liked living in Midland. "Growing up here sort of sucked
for me," she explained. "We were basically poor. Midland is all about
money. All the rich kids get into upper-level classes, even though they
can't spell. In the first day of honors English in eighth grade, our teacher
made us stand up and say our names and why we wanted to be in an honors class, and then say what our parents did for a living. And your parents' occupation is listed on the roster for band and for some of the other
clubs, too. It's gross." In Midland, the nickname for spoiled preppies is
"white hats," because of the fashion for wearing white painter hats with
college logos. I told her I'd gone to the Midland Park Mall earlier in the
week and had overheard a young guy in a white hat talking to two girls
who were working at the Athlete's Foot. "Midland has a lot, a lot, of
money," the young guy was saying as the girls nodded enthusiastically.

"There are more Mercedeses here than anywhere in the country. In other places, when kids get cars it's something like, you know, a Toyota."

"There are all these rich kids here," Barbara said. "They're doing coke, drinking, partying. They're totally into football and cheerleading and into trashing cars—just trashing them, for no reason. Everything here is about being trendy. There's even a trendy church, Kelview Heights Baptist Church, which is trendy because the pastor is on TV." Barbara said that her mother was a housecleaner. For a while, she had worked at a private club in the Clay-Desta Center, and she told Barbara that many of the younger rich men who were members behaved in a disgusting way. I was lucky to have met Barbara at all, because it turned out that she was planning to move to Austin in a couple of days, and she thought she would be a lot happier there. "It'd be great to live in Midland if you were rich," she said.

After a few minutes, Barbara and I were joined by Midge Erskine, one of the few environmental activists in town. Midge is an elegant, silver-haired woman who grew up in the East but came to Midland thirty years ago with her husband, a geologist. In the late seventies, she became unpopular with local oil companies when she protested their practices of dumping contaminated water and keeping their oil tanks uncovered—both of which killed thousands of birds and other wildlife. Recently, Midge began video-taping city council meetings and set up a website, Truthmidlandtx.com, raising questions about local power. In general, the café seemed to be the place where people's dark suspicions about their hometown surfaced: Why was the Midland Airpark, which has no control tower, still operating? Who was so eager to come in and out of Midland sight unseen? Were police reporting the real crime statistics? How did So-and-so get his money, make his deals, and avoid getting busted? But if the Ground Floor is the meeting place for Midland's local hippies, poets, folksingers, and Democrats, there may not be enough of them to keep it afloat; these days, the establishment is barely breaking even. Nute blames the city, for having scared away teenagers, and the economy, for having failed to bring a spark back to the city's downtown. To keep the café going, he was forced to liquidate his investments, and now he has lost hundreds of thousands of dollars.

I went to Midland expecting to find an ordinary small city, but nothing about it was ordinary: not its weather or its topography or its history or its economy. People in Midland take in huge amounts of money, they lose huge amounts of money—then they move on to the next day. It's a manic-depressive city, spending lavishly and then suffering desperately. One afternoon, I was out with Richard Witte, looking at the fanciest neighborhoods in town. "Here's a fella who lost millions," he said, passing one sprawling Italianate ranch. "And see that house over there?" He pointed to a white-brick confection with skylights and Palladian windows. "They lost all their money, had to sell every single piece of furniture, the TV, everything. You drive past these houses and you see a big, expensive home, but you don't know how the people might be living inside."

There's a saying in Midland that whenever you strike oil you go out and get a boat, a plane, and a mistress, and when you lose your money you get rid of them one by one, starting with the mistress. No one mentioned anything to me about mistresses, but several people I met in Midland had been forced to sell their boats and planes. No one seemed ashamed about having lost money: It was like catching a cold—common and widespread and out of your control. According to Texas law, it used to be slanderous to say someone was bankrupt, but then, in the late eighties, it became part of the vernacular, so the law was changed. One day, I was talking to a local lawyer, Warren Heagy, who himself had owned and then had to sell a couple of planes. On the way out of his office, he introduced me to a colleague, who said, "I don't understand all these Internet people whining about losing money. My husband and I lost seven million dollars and you don't see us in the newspaper complaining!"

Now oil prices are cresting again, but the buzz that always follows—"like being near a beehive on a spring day," Richard Witte says—is missing. There are still thirteen pages of oil listings in the Yellow Pages—Oil Marketers, Oil Well Casing Pullings, Oil Well Log Libraries, Oil Refiners, Oil & Gas Lawyers—and there is still a special oil-and-gas section in the newspaper every week, and every day I saw pickup trucks downtown with pieces of pump riggings bouncing around in the back. But the bust in 1986 was something no one had ever seen before, and Midland has not been the same since. When oil prices dropped from twenty-seven dollars to nine dollars a barrel, as much as seventy-five percent of the rigs were shut down, and roughly ten thousand people left Midland and never returned. Mobil, Texaco, Chevron, Conoco, and other companies scaled back their Midland operations and consolidated elsewhere, taking hundreds of administrative and executive jobs out of town.

More important, there is little exploration left to do in the Permian Basin. Most of the entrepreneurial gamble is gone: All you can do these days is work on how to draw every last drop of oil out of the ground. Some scientists speculate that in the next half century or so the Permian Basin will actually run out of oil and gas. The phrase "economic diversification"—probably unheard of in town twenty years ago—was on the front page of the *Midland Reporter-Telegram* nearly every day I was in Texas. Midland may not become one of those forgotten towns that popped up on the cap rock, never took hold, and then simply vanished, as if a high dry wind had blown it away, but these days the city is trying to market itself as a retirement haven and a convention site, just in case.

It's not hard to imagine that in Midland you are seeing the end of something. The pump jacks dipping up and down in the distance look prehistoric, and the hot wind bangs on the empty windows of the now defunct Midlander Athletic Club and the long-gone Rockin' Rodeo. You even sense it in the Petroleum Club, an exclusive organization that caters to local oil executives. It must have been a great place to make an entrance in the days when oil was big and Big Oil was invincible: The club has an enormous open staircase, and when you walk up to the dining room, you feel as if you are rising to the top of the world. The day I visited, though, the club was a little vacant; the empty stairway seemed to stretch forever, and half the dining room had been sectioned off and filled with artificial palm trees. It was my last day in Midland: I was having lunch with John Paul Pitts, the oil-and-gas editor at the *Reporter-Telegram*, and he seemed to know everyone in the room. This one had been worth millions, and that one worth billions, and that one was the founder or the president of this or that oil concern. But the dining room was subdued, and many of the fellow diners who walked by were ancient, skinny men wearing string ties.

The Petroleum Club has always been for the money people in the oil business, and the money people have almost always been white. Early on, even the oil-field workers were white, but after 1986, many of them left Midland or left the industry, and in the last fifteen years or so, a majority of the people digging and servicing and repairing the rigs have been Hispanic. The population of Midland has changed as well: Now only sixty-five percent of the residents are white, and nearly all the rest are Hispanic. There are very few Hispanics at the upper reaches of the oil industry—and few Hispanic geologists or engineers—and none were in evidence in the quiet dining room at the Petroleum Club. Pitts said that he expects the next generation of Hispanics in the business to end up in the offices downtown, rather than out on the oil patch; and some Midlanders believe that in twenty years the city may be mostly Hispanic. The question is how much longer there will be oil for them to tap.

George W. Bush has said that he would like to be buried in Midland. This will not necessarily be easy to do. When you first see it, the soil here looks loose and crumbly, and you'd think digging a hole in it would be as easy as sticking a knife in a cake. But nothing in Midland, not even burial, is as simple as it first seems. The tender soil conceals a calcium deposit called caliche that is as thick and hard as bone, and it takes a tempered-steel drill bit to break through.

Cynthia Ozick

What Helen Keller Saw

Cynthia Ozick is a highly acclaimed essayist and fiction writer; a *New York Times* reviewer called her "the most accomplished and graceful literary stylist of our time." Since 1966 she has consistently published novels, criticism, essay collections, and stories. Her most recent essay collection, *Quarrel & Quandary*, won the 2001 National Book Critics Circle Award for criticism. Her classic novella *The Shawl* (1989) was adapted as a play and directed by Sidney Lumet. Among her nonfiction books are *Metaphor & Memory* (1989), *Portrait of the Artist as a Bad Character* (1996), *Art & Ardor* (1983), and *Fame & Folly* (1996). Her fiction includes *The Pagan Rabbi and Other Stories* (1971), *The Cannibal Galaxy* (1983), and *The Messiah of Stockholm* (1987). Her novel *The Puttermesser Papers* (1997) was named one of the top ten books of the year by the *New York Times Book Review, Publishers Weekly*, and the *Los Angeles Times Book Review*. Her most recent novel is *Heir to the Glimmering World* (2004); her most recent nonfiction collection is *The Din in the Head* (2006). Her most recent story collection is *Dictation: A Quartet* (2008). Her many awards include a Guggenheim fellowship and the Mildred and Harold Strauss Living Award from the American Academy and Institute of Arts and Letters.

Cynthia Ozick has lived in the New York City area most of her life. She holds a BA from New York University and a master's degree from Ohio State University. She regularly writes for the *New Yorker,* the *New York Times Magazine*, and the *New York Times Book Review*.

Her erudite, witty essays often cover the work of writers and artists; her subjects have included Henry James, Franz Kafka, and Anton Chekhov; the place and writers of Holocaust literature; and her own personal writing adventures. Her collections also include short memoirs that address her experiences as a Jewish child and woman.

The essay we have chosen, "What Helen Keller Saw," is from *The Din in the Head*. It examines the collaboration between Helen Keller and her sighted teachers, ultimately asserting Helen's independence while acknowledging that all writers (paraphrasing Henry James) "work in the dark."

Suspicion stalks fame; incredulity stalks great fame. At least three times—at ages eleven, twenty-three, and fifty-two—Helen Keller was assaulted by accusation, doubt, and overt disbelief. Though her luster had surpassed the stellar figures of generations, she was disparaged nearly as hotly as she was exalted. She was the butt of skeptics and the cynosure of idolators. Mark Twain compared her to Joan of Arc, and pronounced her "fellow to Caesar, Alexander, Napoleon, Homer, Shakespeare and the rest of the immortals." Her renown, he said, would endure a thousand years.

It has, so far, lasted more than a hundred, while steadily dimming. Fifty years ago, even twenty, nearly every ten-year-old knew who Helen Keller was. *The Story of My Life*, her youthful autobiography, was on the reading lists of most schools, and its author was popularly understood to be, if not the equal of Mark Twain's lavish exaggerations, a heroine of uncommon grace and courage, a sort of worldly saint. To admire her was an act of piety, and she herself, by virtue of the strenuous conquest of her limitations, was a living temple dedicated to the spirit of resurrection. Much of that worshipfulness has receded. Her name, if not entirely in eclipse, hardly elicits the awed recognition it once held. No one nowadays, without intending satire, would place her alongside Caesar and Napoleon; and in an era of earnest disabilities legislation, with wheelchair ramps on every street corner, who would think to charge a stone-blind, stone-deaf woman with faking her experience?

Yet as a child she was accused of plagiarism, and in maturity of "verbalism," illicitly substituting par-roted words for firsthand perception. All this came about because she was at once liberated by language and in bondage to it, in a way few other human beings, even the blind and the deaf, can fathom. The merely blind have the window of their ears, the merely deaf listen through their eyes. For Helen Keller there was no partially ameliorating "merely." What she suffered was a totality of exclusion. Her early life was meted out in hints and inferences—she could still touch, taste, smell, and feel vibra-tions; but these were the very capacities that turned her into a wild creature, a kind of flailing animal in human form.

> "Her wants were concrete, physical, impatient, helpless, and nearly always belligerent."

The illness that annihilated Helen Keller's sight and hearing, and left her mute, has never been diagnosed. In 1882, when she was four months short of two years, medical knowledge could assert only "acute congestion of the stomach and brain," though later speculation proposes meningitis or scarlet fever. Whatever the cause, the consequence was ferocity—tantrums, kicking, rages—but also an invented system of sixty simple signs, intima-tions of intelligence. The child could mimic what she could neither see nor hear: putting on a hat before a mirror, her father reading a newspaper with his glasses on. She could fold laundry and pick out her own things. Such quiet times were few. Frenzied, tempestuous, she was an uncontrollable barbarian. Having discovered the use of a key, she shut up her mother in a closet. She overturned her baby sister's cradle. Her wants were concrete, physical, impatient, helpless, and nearly always belligerent.

She was born in Tuscumbia, Alabama, fifteen years after the Civil War, when Confederate consciousness and mores were still inflamed. Her father, who had fought at Vicksburg, called himself a "gentleman farmer," and edited a small Democratic weekly until, thanks to political influence, he was appointed a United States marshal. He was a zealous hunter who loved his guns and his dogs. Money was usually short; there were escalating mari-tal angers. His second wife, Helen's mother, was younger by twenty years, a spirited woman of intellect condemned to farmhouse toil. She had a strong literary side (Edward Everett Hale, the New Englander who wrote "The Man Without a Country," was a relative) and read seriously and searchingly. In Charles Dickens's *American Notes* she learned about Laura Bridgman, a deaf-blind country girl who was being educated at the Perkins Institution for the Blind, in Boston. Her savior was its director, Samuel Gridley Howe, humanitarian activist and husband of Julia Ward Howe, author of "The Battle Hymn of the Republic": New England idealism at its collective zenith.

Laura Bridgman was thirteen years old when Dickens met her, and was even more circumscribed than Helen Keller—she could neither smell nor taste. She was confined, he said, "in a marble cell, impervious to any ray of light, or particle of sound." But Laura Bridgman's cell could be only partly unlocked. She never mastered language beyond a handful of words unidiomatically strung together. Scientists and psychologists studied her almost zoologically, and her meticulously intricate lacework was widely admired and sold. She lived out her entire life in her room at the Perkins Institution; an 1885 photograph shows her expertly threading a needle with her tongue. She too had been a normal child, until scarlet fever ravaged her senses at the age of two.

News of Laura Bridgman ignited hope—she had been socialized into a semblance of personhood, while Helen remained a small savage—and hope led, eventually, to Alexander Graham Bell. By then the invention of the telephone was well behind him, and he was tenaciously committed to teaching the deaf to speak intelligibly. His wife was deaf; his mother had been deaf. When the six-year-old Helen was brought to him, he took her on his lap and instantly calmed her by letting her feel the vibrations of his pocket watch as it struck the hour. Her responsiveness did not register in her face; he described it as "chillingly empty." But he judged her educable, and advised her father to apply to Michael Anagnos, Howe's successor as director of the Perkins Institution, for a teacher to be sent to Tuscumbia.

Anagnos chose Anne Mansfield Sullivan, a former student at Perkins. "Mansfield" was her own embellishment; it had the sound of gentility. If the fabricated name was intended to confer an elevated status, it was because Annie Sullivan, born into penury, had no status at all. At five she contracted trachoma, a disease of the eye. Three years on, her mother died of tuberculosis and was buried in potter's field—after which her father, a drunkard prone to beating his children, deserted the family. The half-blind Annie and her small brother Jimmie, who had a tubercular hip, were tossed into the poorhouse at Tewksbury, Massachusetts, among syphilitic prostitutes and madmen. Jimmie did not survive the appalling inhumanity of the place, and decades later, recalling its "strangeness, grotesqueness and even terribleness," Annie Sullivan wrote, "I doubt if life or for that matter eternity is long enough to erase the terrors and ugly blots scored upon my mind during those dismal years from 8 to 14." She never spoke of them, not even to her intimates.

She was rescued from Tewksbury by a committee investigating its spreading notoriety, and was mercifully transferred to Perkins. There she learned Braille and the manual alphabet and came to know Laura Bridgman. At the Massachusetts Eye and Ear Infirmary she underwent two operations, which enabled her to read almost normally, though the condition of her eyes continued fragile and inconsistent over her lifetime. After six years she graduated from Perkins as class valedictorian; Anagnos recognized in her clear traces of "uncommon powers." His affectionate concern was nearly a flirtation (he had once teasingly caressed her arm), while she, orphaned and alone, had made certain to catch his notice and his love. When her days at Perkins were ended, what was to become of her? How was she to earn a living? Someone suggested that she might wash dishes or peddle needlework. "Sewing and crocheting are inventions of the devil," she sneered. "I'd rather break stones on the king's highway than hem a handkerchief."

She went to Tuscumbia instead. She was twenty years old and had no experience suitable for what she would encounter in the despairs and chaotic defeats of the Keller household. She had attempted to prepare herself by studying Laura Bridgman's training as it was recorded in the Perkins archives. Apart from this, she had no resources other than the manual alphabet that enlivened her fingers, and the steely history of her own character. The tyrannical child she had come to educate threw cutlery, pinched, grabbed food off dinner plates, sent chairs tumbling, shrieked, struggled. She was strong, beautiful but for one protruding eye, unsmiling, painfully untamed: virtually her first act on meeting the new teacher was to knock out one of her front teeth. The afflictions of the marble cell had become inflictions. Annie demanded that Helen be separated from her family; her father could not bear to see his ruined little daughter disciplined. The teacher and her recalcitrant pupil retreated to a cottage on the grounds of the main house, where Annie was to be sole authority.

What happened then and afterward she chronicled in letter after letter, to Anagnos and, more confidingly, to Mrs. Sophia Hopkins, the Perkins housemother who had given her shelter during school vacations. Mark Twain saw in Annie Sullivan a *writer:* "How she stands out in her letters!" he exclaimed. "Her brilliancy, penetration, originality, wisdom, character and the fine literary competencies of her pen—they are all there." Her observations, both of herself and of the developing child, are kin, in their humanity, particularity, and psychological acumen, to philosophical essays. Jubilantly, and with preternatural awareness, she set down the progress, almost hour by hour, of Helen Keller's disentombment, an exuberant deliverance far more remarkable than Laura Bridgman's frail and inarticulate release. Howe had taught the names of things by attaching to them labels written in raised type—but labels on spoons are not the same as self-generated thoughts. Annie Sullivan's method, insofar as she recognized it formally as a method, was pure freedom. Like any writer, she wrote and wrote and wrote, all day long. She wrote words, phrases, sentences, lines of poetry, descriptions of animals, trees, flowers, weather, skies, clouds, concepts: whatever lay before her or came usefully to mind. She wrote not on paper with a pen, but with her fingers, spelling rapidly into the child's alert palm. Helen, quick to imitate yet uncomprehending, was under a spell of curiosity (the pun itself reveals the manual alphabet as magical tool). Her teacher spelled into her hand; she spelled the same letters back, mimicking unknowable configurations. But it was not until the connection was effected between finger-wriggling and its referent—the cognitive key, the insight, the crisis of discovery—that what we call mind broke free.

This was, of course, the fabled incident at the well pump, dramatized in film and (by now) collective memory, when Helen suddenly understood that the tactile pattern pecking at her hand was inescapably related to the gush of cold water spilling over it. "Somehow," the adult Helen Keller recollected, "the mystery of language was revealed to me." In the course of a single month, from Annie's arrival to her triumph in forcibly bridling the household despot, Helen had grown docile, eagerly willing, affectionate, and tirelessly intent on learning from moment to moment. Her intellect was fiercely engaged, and when language began to flood it, she rode on a salvational ark of words.

To Mrs. Hopkins Annie wrote ecstatically:

> Something within me tells me that I shall succeed beyond my wildest dreams. I know that [Helen] has remarkable powers, and I believe that I shall be able to develop and mould them. I cannot tell how I know these things. I had no idea a short time ago how to go to work; I was feeling about in the dark; but somehow I know now, and I know that I know. I cannot explain it; but when difficulties arise, I am not perplexed or doubtful. I know how to meet them; I seem to divine Helen's peculiar needs. . . .

> Already people are taking a deep interest in Helen. No one can see her without being impressed. She is no ordinary child, and people's interest in her education will be no ordinary interest. Therefore let us be exceedingly careful in what we say and write about her. . . . My beautiful Helen shall not be transformed into a prodigy if I can help it.

At this time Helen was not yet seven years old, and Annie was being paid twenty-five dollars a month.

The fanatical public scrutiny Helen Keller aroused far exceeded Annie's predictions. It was Michael Anagnos who first proclaimed her to be a miracle child—a young goddess. "History presents no case like hers," he exulted. "As soon as a slight crevice was opened in the outer wall of their twofold imprisonment, her mental faculties emerged full-armed from their living tomb as Pallas Athene from the head of Zeus." And again: "She is the queen of precocious and brilliant children, Emersonian in temper, most exquisitely organized, with intellectual sight of unsurpassed sharpness and infinite reach, a true daughter of Mnemosyne. It is no exaggeration to say that she is a personification of goodness and happiness." Annie, the teacher of a flesh-and-blood earthly child, protested: "His extravagant way of saying [these things] rubs me the wrong way. The simple facts would be so much more convincing!" But Anagnos's glorifications caught fire: one year after Annie had begun spelling into her hand, Helen Keller was celebrated in newspapers all over the world. When her dog was inadvertently shot, an avalanche of contributions poured in to replace it; unprompted, she directed that the money be set aside for the care of an impoverished deaf-blind boy at Perkins. At eight she was taken to visit President Cleveland at the White House, and in Boston was introduced to many of the luminaries of the period: Oliver Wendell Holmes, John Greenleaf Whittier, Edward Everett Hale, and Phillips Brooks (who addressed her puzzlement over the nature of God). At nine, saluting him as "Dear Poet," she wrote to Whittier:

> I thought you would be glad to hear that your beautiful poems make me very happy. Yesterday I read "In School Days" and "My Playmate," and I enjoyed them greatly. . . . It is very pleasant to live here in our beautiful world. I cannot see the lovely things with my eyes, but my mind can see them all, and so I am joyful all the day long.
>
> When I walk out in my garden I cannot see the beautiful flowers, but I know that they are all around me; for is not the air sweet with their fragrance? I know too that the tiny lily-bells are whispering pretty secrets to their companions else they would not look so happy. I love you very dearly, because you have taught me so many lovely things about flowers, birds, and people.

Her dependence on Annie for the assimilation of her immediate surroundings was nearly total—hands-on, as we would say, and literally so—but through the raised letters of Braille she could be altogether untethered: books coursed through her. In childhood she was captivated by *Little Lord Fauntleroy*, Frances Hodgson Burnett's story of a sunnily virtuous boy who melts a crusty old man's heart; it became a secret template of her own character as she hoped she might always manifest it—not sentimentally, but in full awareness of dread. She was not deaf to Caliban's wounded cry: "You taught me language, and my profit on't/Is, I know how to curse." Helen Keller's profit was that she knew how to rejoice. In young adulthood, casting about for a faith bare of exclusiveness or harsh images, and given over to purifying idealism, she seized on Swedenborgian spiritualism. Annie had kept away from teaching any religion at all: she was a down-to-earth agnostic whom Tewksbury had cured of easy belief. When Helen's responsiveness to bitter social deprivation later took on a worldly strength, leading her to socialism, and even to unpopular Bolshevik sympathies, Annie would have no part of it, and worried that Helen had gone too far. Marx was not in Annie's canon. Homer, Virgil, Shakespeare, and Milton were: she had Helen reading *Paradise Lost* at twelve.

But Helen's formal schooling was widening beyond Annie's tutelage. With her teacher at her side, Helen spent a year at Perkins, and then entered the Wright-Humason School in New York, a fashionable academy for deaf girls; she was its single deaf-blind pupil. She also pleaded to be taught to speak like other people, and worked at it determinedly—but apart from Annie and a few others who were accustomed to her efforts, she could not be readily understood. Speech, even if imperfect, was not her only ambition: she intended to go to college. To prepare, she enrolled in the Cambridge School for Young Ladies, where she studied mathematics, German, French, Latin, and Greek and Roman history. In 1900 she was admitted to Radcliffe (then an "annex" to Harvard), still with Annie in attendance. Despite her necessary presence in every class, diligently spelling the lecture into Helen's hand, and hourly wearing out her troubled eyes as she transcribed text after text into the manual alphabet, no one thought of granting Annie a degree along with Helen. It was not uncommon for Annie Sullivan to play second fiddle to Helen Keller; the radiant miracle outshone the driven miracle worker. Not so for Mark Twain: he saw them as two halves of the same marvel. "It took the pair of you to make a complete and perfect whole," he said. Not everyone agreed. Annie was sometimes charged with being Helen's jailer, or harrier, or ventriloquist. During examinations at Radcliffe, she was not permitted to be in the building. For the rest, Helen relied on her own extraordinary memory and on Annie's lightning fingers. Luckily, a second helper, adept at the manual alphabet, soon turned up: he was John Macy, a twenty-five-year-old English instructor at Harvard, a writer and editor, a fervent socialist, and, eventually, Annie Sullivan's husband, eleven years her junior.

The money for all this schooling, and for the sustenance of the two young women (both enjoyed fine clothes and vigorous horseback riding), came in spurts from a handful of very rich men—among them John Spaulding, the Sugar King, and Henry Rogers, of Standard Oil. Helen charmed these wealthy eminences as she charmed everyone, while Annie more systematically cultivated their philanthropy. She herself was penniless, and the Kellers of Tuscumbia were financially useless. Shockingly, Helen's father had once threatened to put his little daughter on exhibit, in order to earn her keep. (Twenty years afterward, Helen took up his idea and went on the vaudeville circuit—she happily, Annie reluctantly—and even to Hollywood, where she starred in a silent movie, with the mythical Ulysses as her ectoplasmic boyfriend.)

At Radcliffe Helen became a writer. She also became a third party to Annie's difficult romance: whoever wanted Annie inevitably got Helen too. Drawn by twin literary passions like his own, Macy was more than willing, at least at first. Charles Townsend Copeland—Harvard's illustrious "Copey," a professor of rhetoric—had encouraged Helen (as she put it to him in a grateful letter) "to make my own observations and describe the experiences peculiarly my own. Henceforth I am resolved to be myself, to live my own life and write my own thoughts." Out of this came *The Story of My Life*, the autobiography of a twenty-one-year-old, published while she was still an undergraduate. It began as a series of sketches for the *Ladies' Home Journal*; the fee was three thousand dollars. John Macy described the laborious process:

> When she began work at her story, more than a year ago, she set up on the Braille machine about a hundred pages of what she called "material," consisting of detached episodes and notes put down as they came to her without definite order or coherent plan. Then came the task where one who has eyes to see must help her. Miss Sullivan and I read the disconnected passages, put them into chronological order, and counted the words to make sure the articles should be the right length. All this work we did with Miss Keller beside us, referring everything, especially matters of phrasing, to her for revision. . . .
>
> Her memory of what she had written was astonishing. She remembered whole passages, some of which she had not seen for many weeks, and could tell, before Miss Sullivan had spelled into her hand a half-dozen words of the paragraph under discussion, where they belonged and what sentences were necessary to make the connection clear.

This method of collaboration, essentially mechanical, continued throughout Helen Keller's professional writing life; yet within these constraints the design, the sensibility, the cadences were her own. She was a self-conscious stylist. Macy remarked that she had the courage of her metaphors—he meant that she sometimes let them carry her away—and Helen herself worried that her prose could now and then seem "periwigged." To the contemporary ear, many of her phrases are too much immersed in Victorian lace and striving uplift—but the contemporary ear has no entitlement, simply by being contemporary, to set itself up as judge: every period is marked by a prevailing voice. Helen Keller's earnestness is a kind of piety; she peers through the lens of a sublimely aspiring poetry. It is as if Tennyson and the Transcendentalists had together got hold of her typewriter. At the same time, she is turbulently embroiled in the whole human enterprise—except, tellingly, for irony. She has no "edge," and why should she? Irony is a radar that seeks out the dark side; she had darkness enough. Her unfailing intuition was to go after the light. She flew toward it, as she herself said, in the hope of "clear and animated language." She knew what part of her mind was instinct and what part was information, and she was cautious about the difference; she was even suspicious, as she had good reason to be. "It is certain," she wrote, "that I cannot always distinguish my own thoughts from those I read, because what I read become the very substance and texture of my mind. . . . It seems to me that the great difficulty of writing is to make the language of the educated mind express our confused ideas, half feelings, half thoughts, where we are little more than bundles of instinctive tendencies." She, who had once been incarcerated in the id, did not require knowledge of Freud to instruct her in its inchoate presence.

The Story of My Life was first published in 1903, with Macy's ample introduction. He was able to write about Helen nearly as authoritatively as

Annie, but also—in private—more skeptically: after his marriage to Annie, the three of them set up housekeeping in rural Wrentham, Massachusetts. Possibly not since the Brontës had so feverishly literary a crew lived under a single roof. Of this ultimately inharmonious trio, one, internationally famous for decades, was catapulted now into still greater renown by the recent appearance of her celebrated memoir. Macy, meanwhile, was discovering that he had married not a woman, a moody one at that, but the indispensable infrastructure of a public institution. As Helen's secondary amanuensis, he continued to be of use until the marriage collapsed. It foundered on his profligacy with money, on Annie's irritability—she fought him on his uncompromising socialism, which she disdained—and finally on his accelerating alcoholism.

Because Macy was known to have assisted Helen in the preparation of *The Story of My Life*, the insinuations of control that often assailed Annie now also landed on him. Helen's ideas, it was said, were really Macy's; he had transformed her into a "Marxist propagandist." It was true that she sympathized with his political bent, but his views had not shaped hers. As she had come independently to Swedenborgian idealism, so had she come to societal utopianism. The charge of expropriation, of both thought and idiom, was old, and dogged her at intervals during much of her early and middle life: she was a fraud, a puppet, a plagiarist. She was false coin. She was "a living lie."

She was eleven when these words were first hurled at her, spewed out by a wrathful Anagnos. Not long before, he had spoken of Helen in celestial terms. Now he denounced her as a malignant thief. What brought on this defection was a little story she had written, called "The Frost King," which she sent him as a birthday present. In the voice of a highly literary children's narrative, it recounts how the "frost fairies" cause the season's turning.

> When the children saw the trees all aglow with brilliant colors they clapped their hands and shouted for joy, and immediately began to pick great bunches to take home. "The leaves are as lovely as flowers!" cried they, in their delight.

Anagnos—doubtless clapping his hands and shouting for joy—immediately began to publicize Helen's newest accomplishment. "The Frost King" appeared both in the Perkins alumni magazine and in another journal for the blind, which, following Anagnos, unhesitatingly named it "without parallel in the history of literature." But more than a parallel was at stake; the story was found to be nearly identical to "The Frost Fairies," by Margaret Canby, a writer of children's books. Anagnos was infuriated, and fled headlong from adulation and hyperbole to humiliation and enmity. Feeling personally betrayed and institutionally discredited, he arranged an inquisition for the terrified Helen, standing her alone in a room before a jury of eight Perkins officials and himself, all mercilessly cross-questioning her. Her mature recollection of Anagnos's "court of investigation" registers as pitiably as the ordeal itself:

> Mr. Anagnos, who loved me tenderly, thinking that he had been deceived, turned a deaf ear to pleadings of love and innocence. He believed, or at least suspected, that Miss Sullivan and I had deliberately stolen the bright thoughts of another and imposed them on him to win his admiration. . . . As I lay in my bed that night, I wept as I hope few children have wept. I felt so cold, I imagined that I should die before morning, and the thought comforted me. I think if this sorrow had come to me when I was older, it would have broken my spirit beyond repairing.

She was defended by Alexander Graham Bell, and by Mark Twain, who parodied the whole procedure with a thumping hurrah for plagiarism, and disgust for the egotism of "these solemn donkeys breaking a little child's heart with their ignorant damned rubbish! A gang of dull and hoary pirates piously setting themselves the task of disciplining and purifying a kitten that they think they've caught pilfering a chop!" Margaret Canby's tale had been spelled to Helen perhaps three years before, and lay dormant in her prodigiously retentive memory; she was entirely oblivious of reproducing phrases not her own. The scandal Anagnos had precipitated left a lasting bruise. But it was also the beginning of a psychological, even a metaphysical, clarification that Helen refined and ratified as she grew older, when similar, if more subtle, suspicions cropped up in the press, compelling her to interrogate the workings of her mind. *The Story of My Life* was attacked in the *Nation* not for plagiarism in the usual sense, but for the purloining of "things beyond her powers of perception with the assurance of one who has verified every word. . . . One resents the pages of second-hand description of natural objects." The reviewer blamed her for the sin of vicariousness: "all her knowledge," he insisted, "is hearsay knowledge."

It was almost a reprise of the Perkins tribunal: she was again being confronted with the charge of inauthenticity. Anagnos's rebuke—"Helen Keller is a living lie"—regularly resurfaced, sometimes less harshly, sometimes as acerbically, in the form of a neurologist's or a psychologist's assessment, or in the reservations of reviewers. A French professor of literature, who was himself blind, determined that she was "a dupe of words, and her aesthetic enjoyment of most of the arts is a matter of auto-suggestion rather than perception." A *New Yorker* interviewer complained, "She talks bookishly. . . . To express her ideas, she falls back on the phrases she has learned from books, and uses words that sound stilted, poetical metaphors." A professor of neurology at Columbia University, after a series of tests, pooh-poohed the claim that her remaining senses might be in any way extraordinary— the acuity of her touch and smell, he concluded, was no different from that of other mortals. "That's a stab at my vanity," she joked.

But the cruelest appraisal of all came, in 1933, from Thomas Cutsforth, a blind psychologist. By this time Helen was fifty-three, and had published four additional autobiographical volumes. Cutsforth disparaged everything she had become. The wordless child she once was, he maintained, was closer to reality than what her teacher had made of her through the imposition of "word-mindedness." He objected to her use of images such as "a mist of green," "blue pools of dog violets," "soft clouds tumbling." All that, he protested, was "implied chicanery" and "a birthright sold for a mess of verbiage." He criticized

> the aims of the educational system in which she has been confined during her whole life. Literary expression has been the goal of her formal education. Fine writing, regardless of its meaningful content, has been the end toward which both she and her teacher have striven. . . . Her own experiential life was rapidly made secondary, and it was regarded as such by the victim. . . . Her teacher's ideals became her ideals, her teacher's likes became her likes, and whatever emotional activity her teacher experienced she experienced.

For Cutsforth—and not only for him—Helen Keller was the victim of language rather than its victorious master. She was no better than a copy; whatever was primary, and thereby genuine, had been stamped out. As for Annie, while here she was pilloried as the callous instrument of her pupil's victimization, elsewhere she was pitied as a woman cheated of her own life by having sacrificed it to serve another. Either Helen was Annie's slave, or Annie was Helen's.

Once again Helen had her faithful defenders. The philosopher Ernst Cassirer reflected that "a human being in the construction of his human world is not dependent upon the quality of his sense material." Even more trenchantly, a *New York Times* editor quoted Cicero: "When Democritus lost his sight he could not, to be sure, distinguish black from white; but all the same he could distinguish good from bad, just from unjust, honorable from disgraceful, expedient from inexpedient, great from small, and it was permitted him to live happily without seeing changes of color; it was not permissible to do so without true ideas."

But Helen did not depend on philosophers, ancient or modern, to make her case. She spoke for herself: she was nobody's puppet, her mind was her own, and she knew what she saw. Once, having been taken to the uppermost viewing platform of what was then the tallest building in the world, she defined her condition:

> I will concede that my guides saw a thousand things that escaped me from the top of the Empire State Building, but I am not envious. For imagination creates distances that reach to the end of the world. . . . There was the Hudson—more like the flash of a swordblade than a noble river. The little island of Manhattan, set like a jewel in its nest of rainbow waters, stared up into my face, and the solar system circled about my head!

Her rebuttal to word-mindedness, to vicariousness, to implied chicanery and the living lie, was inscribed deliberately and defiantly in her daring images of swordblade and rainbow waters. That they were derived was no reason for her to be deprived—why should she alone be starved of enchantment? The deaf-blind person, she wrote, "seizes every word of sight and hearing, because his sensations compel it. Light and color, of which he has no tactual evidence, he studies fearlessly, believing that all humanly knowable truth is open to him." She was not ashamed of talking bookishly: it meant a ready access to the storehouse of history and literature. She disposed of her critics with a dazzling apothegm: "The bulk of the world's knowledge is an imaginary construction," and went on to contend that history itself "is but a mode of imagining, of making us see civilizations that no longer appear upon the earth." Those who ridiculed her rapturous

> "She saw, then, what she wished, or was blessed, to see, and rightly named it imagination."

rendering of color she dismissed as "spirit-vandals" who would force her "to bite the dust of material things." Her idea of the subjective onlooker was broader than that of physics, and while "red" may denote an explicit and measurable wavelength in the visible spectrum, in the mind it is flittingly fickle (and not only for the blind), varying from the bluster of rage to the reticence of a blush: physics cannot cage metaphor.

She saw, then, what she wished, or was blessed, to see, and rightly named it imagination. In this she belongs to a wider class than that narrow order of the tragically deaf-blind. Her class, her tribe, hears what no healthy ear can catch, and sees what no eye chart can quantify. Her common language was not with the man who crushed a child for memorizing what the fairies do, or with the carpers who scolded her for the crime of a literary vocabulary. She was a member of the race of poets, the Romantic kind; she was close cousin to those novelists who write not only what they do not know, but what they cannot possibly know.

And though she was early taken in hand by a writerly intelligence leading her purposefully to literature, it was hardly in the power of the manual alphabet to pry out a writer who was not already there. Laura Bridgman stuck to her lace making, and with all her senses intact might have remained a needlewoman. John Macy believed finally that between Helen and Annie there was only one genius—his wife. Helen's intellect, he asserted, was "stout and energetic, of solid endurance," able to achieve through patience and toil, but void of real brilliance. In the absence of Annie's inventiveness and direction, he implied, Helen's efforts would show up as the lesser gifts they were. This did not happen. Annie died, at seventy, in 1936, four years after Macy; they had long been estranged. By then her always endangered eyesight had deteriorated; depressed, obese, cranky, and inconsolable, she had herself gone blind. Helen came under the care of her secretary, Polly Thomson, a Scotswoman who was both possessively loyal and dryly unliterary: the scenes she spelled into Helen's hand never matched Annie's quicksilver evocations.

But even as she mourned the loss of her teacher, Helen flourished. Annie was dead; only the near-at-hand are indispensable. With the assistance of

Nella Henney, Annie Sullivan's biographer, she continued to publish journals and memoirs. She undertook grueling visits to Japan, India, Israel, Europe, Australia, everywhere championing the blind, the deaf, the dispossessed. She was indefatigable until her very last years, and died in 1968 weeks before her eighty-eighth birthday.

Yet the story of her life is not the good she did, the panegyrics she inspired, or the disputes (genuine or counterfeit? victim or victimizer?) that stormed around her. The most persuasive story of Helen Keller's life is what she said it was: "I observe, I feel, I think, I imagine."

She was an artist. She imagined.

"Blindness has no limiting effect on mental vision. My intellectual horizon is infinitely wide," she was impelled to argue again and again. "The universe it encircles is immeasurable." And like any writer making imagination's mysterious claims before the material-minded, she had cause enough to cry out, "Oh, the supercilious doubters!"

But it was not herself alone she was shielding from these skirmishes: she was a warrior in a wide and thorny conflict. Helen Keller, if we are presumptuous enough to reduce her so, can be taken to be a laboratory for empirical demonstration. Do we know only what we see, or do we see what we somehow already know? Are we more than the sum of our senses? Does a picture—whatever strikes the retina—engender thought, or does thought create the picture? Can there be subjectivity without an object to glance off from? Metaphysicians and other theorists have their differing notions, to which the ungraspable organism that is Helen Keller is a retort. She is not an advocate for one side or the other in the ancient debate concerning the nature of the real. She is not a philosophical or neurological or therapeutic topic. She stands for enigma, and against obtuseness; there lurks in her still the angry child who demanded to be understood, yet could not be deciphered. She refutes those who cannot perceive, or do not care to value, what is hidden from sensation.

Against whom does she rage, whom does she refute? The mockers of her generation and ours. The psychiatrist Bruno Bettelheim, for instance. "By pretending to have a full life," he warned in a 1990 essay, "by pretending that through touch she knew what a piece of sculpture, what flowers, what trees were like, that through the words of others she knew what the sky or clouds looked like, by pretending that she could hear music by feeling the vibrations of musical instruments," she fooled the world into thinking the "terribly handicapped are not suffering deeply every moment of their lives." Pretender, trickster: this is what the notion of therapy makes of "the words of others," which we more commonly term experience; heritage; literature. At best the therapist pities, at worst he sees delusion. Perhaps Helen Keller did suffer deeply. Then all the more honor to the flashing embossments of the artist's mask. Oddly, practitioners of psychology—whom one would least expect to be literalists—have been quickest to blame her for imposture. Let them blame Keats, too, for his delusionary "Heard melodies are sweet, but those unheard are sweeter," and for his phantom theme of negative capability, the poet's oarless casting about for the hallucinatory shadows of desire.

Helen Keller's lot, it turns out, was not unique. "We work in the dark," Henry James affirmed, on behalf of his own art, and so did she. It was the same dark. She knew her Wordsworth: "Visionary power/Attends the motions of the viewless winds/Embodied in the mystery of word:/ There, darkness makes abode." She fought the debunkers who, for the sake of a spurious honesty, would denude her of landscape and return her to the marble cell. She fought the iron pragmatists who meant to disinherit her, and everyone, of poetry. She fought the tin ears who took imagining to be mendacity. Her legacy, after all, is an epistemological marker of sorts: proof of the real existence of the mind's eye.

In one respect, though, she was incontrovertibly as fraudulent as the cynics charged. She had always been photographed in profile: this hid her disfigured left eye. In maturity she had both eyes surgically removed and replaced with glass—an expedient known only to those closest to her. Everywhere she went, her sparkling blue prosthetic eyes were admired for their living beauty and humane depth.

Gary Panter

Nightmare Studio

Born December 1, 1950, in Durant, Oklahoma, Gary Panter is considered by many to be the "king of the ratty line" and "not so much punk as he is cyberpunk" (Mike Kelley). Panter told the *New York Times* that his cartoons are like "Picasso meets 'Yellow Submarine.'" Panter has been everything from an underground cartoonist to an interior designer to an Internet animator (his *Pink Donkey and the Fly* series can be seen online at Cartoon Network's Web site). His breakthrough work *Jimbo* (1970s, first published in L.A. punk-paper *Slash*, later in *RAW* magazine) starred a postnuclear punk-rock protagonist and was influenced in equal measure, says Panter, by "the '60s underground comix movement, Japanese monster movies, cheap commercial packaging, the work of Marvel Comics artist Jack Kirby, Mothers of Invention house artist Cal Schenkel, and the writing of cult science fiction author Philip K. Dick."

Panter is the recipient of three Emmy awards for his work as head set designer for the popular TV program *Pee-Wee's Playhouse*. Despite his day job as set designer, Panter also found the time to publish two graphic novels (*Dal Tokyo* and *Cola Madness,* both 1983), album covers for Frank Zappa and other rockers, and countless commercial art for magazines such as *Time, Rolling Stone, Entertainment Weekly,* and the *New Yorker*. When asked to describe the art of being a graphic novelist, he replied, "It's like digging in a coal mine in a way because you are digging in the dark then finally you see a little light so you keep hitting it with your pickaxe until you break through. It was very hard, very draining and very fun."

Gary Panter's Web site, complete with blog, is garypanter.com.

"Nightmare Studio," from *McSweeney's 13,* is a brief semipsychotic glimpse into dream state. Its form has much in common with the lyric essay.

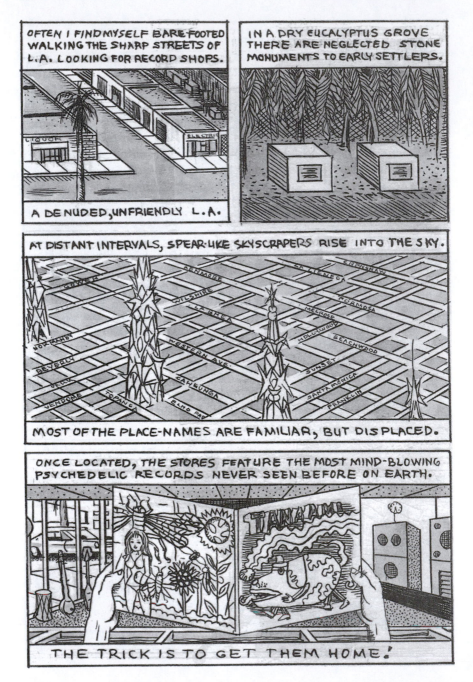

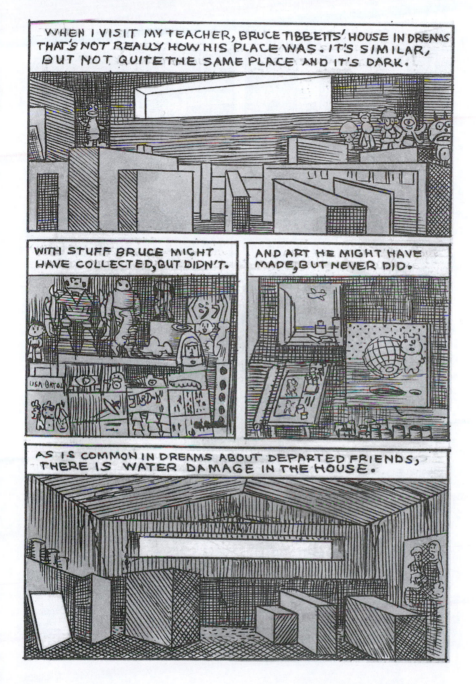

Leila Philip

Green Tea

Leila Philip is the author of the memoir and travelogue *The Road Through Miyama* (1989), for which she received the Martha Albrand Citation for Nonfiction in 1990; a work of journalism, *Hidden Dialogue: A Discussion Between Women in Japan and the United States* (1993); and a memoir, *A Family Place: A Hudson Valley Farm, Three Centuries, Five Wars, One Family* (2001). Her writing has been anthologized in a number of books, among them *Maiden Voyages: Writings of Women Travelers* (1993), *Writing Down the River* (1997), *Family Travels* (1999), *Japan: True Stories of Life on the Road* (1999), and *A Woman's Passion for Travel* (1999). Her writing has been recognized by numerous awards including fellowships from the National Foundation for the Arts, the National Endowment for the Humanities, the Radcliffe Research and Study Center, and the American Association of University Women.

She received an AB from Princeton University in 1986 as well as a fifth-year degree in East Asian studies. During her studies at Princeton she spent a summer at Middlebury's Intensive Language Program in Japanese. In 1990 she received an MFA in fiction from Columbia University. In 1992, she was awarded a Bunting Fellowship in creative writing at the Radcliffe Research and Study Center and attended classes at Harvard.

Philip lived in New York City until the age of fifteen, when her family moved to the Hudson Valley in order to save their family farm. After high school, she took a year off and worked on the *Hudson Valley Chronicle*, a small newspaper published in Hudson, New York. She wrote features articles, delivered newspapers, and eventually, edited and wrote entire sections of the paper. Then she went west, first to City Lights Bookstore in San Francisco, then on to Oregon, where she worked on a sheep ranch near Coos Bay. When the lambing season was over, Philip joined a tree-planting cooperative based in Roseburg. Throughout college she spent summers in Oregon, working as a Cheetah ranger. After studying Japanese and medieval Japanese literature at Princeton, she headed to Japan, where she apprenticed to a master potter in Southern Kyushu. That experience was the subject of her first book, *The Road Through Miyama*. She has worked as an interpreter (Japanese) and guide (Japan) for the Smithsonian Institution and the New York Japan Society.

Leila Philip has taught writing and literature at Princeton, Columbia, Emerson College, Colgate, Vassar, and Ohio University. She has taught in summer writing conferences including Breadloaf and the Chenango Writers' Conference. In 2004 she joined the English department at the College of the Holy Cross, where she has been the acting director of the Program in Creative Writing and teaches creative writing and literature. Philip lives in Woodstock, Connecticut, with her husband and son, one dog, two cats, two lizards, and a large, unruly garden.

What follows is taken from *The Road Through Miyama*.

May; month of camellia and bloom
azure sky and bamboo breeze
rustle of fern, tea harvest

Suzuki-san, in a wide straw hat, bends down over the narrow black tar road, cracked and twisted where thick bamboo shoots push toward April light. Beside him, on her knees, is his wife in her faded blue bonnet. On either side frail bamboo poles hold the living grove back, away from the road. New shoots will grow twelve inches a day, ten, twenty feet in two weeks, pushing through gardens, roads, walkways, anything in their way.

Armed with short-handled sickles and blades, the old couple attacks the irreverent plants in a silent fury. *Whack. Rip. Whack.* Splinters of bamboo shoot fly from their tools. I stand in the warm sun and watch.

"*Ohayō gozaimasu.*"

"*Ohayō gozaimasu.*"

"Need some help?" I ask casually, in Kagoshima ben. For the first time both heads rise. Okusan lifts the rim of her blue bonnet to get a better look. "Ah . . . *hora* . . . Ri-ra-san!" she exclaims, sitting back on her heels and smiling. "*Yōka, yōka.* It's okay." She wipes her brow with the back of a gloved hand before resuming her work. Her husband, who has looked up only once during our exchange, continues his furious reaping. I step forward to pass by, but Okusan looks back up, her eyes bright. "Where are you going?" she asks suddenly.

"Oh, just a little way, over there."

"Over there?"

"Yes, that way."

"Ahh, I see, a walk," she says slowly, nodding her head.

"Yes, a walk, I guess," I answer vaguely, pointing ahead to no place in particular. After months in Miyama I have come to realize that not all questions require answers. It is not that I mind telling her where I am going, but by tomorrow the news would be spread across the village. She laughs and waves me on, then bends back over the road, her small blade hooking neatly around a stiff brown shoot. *Whack. Rip. Whack.*

I walk on, scuffling through the bits and pieces of twig and scattered bamboo. On either side of the road amid the tall spires of adult growth a few new shoots poke through the bracken and broken fern. Some are already chest-high, others still barely visible spikes, their tips protected by thick layers of husk. They butt through the ground with the insistence of goats. Soon they will lose their rough brown coverings and shoot up higher, faster, green now and, tasting the light, unstoppable. It is a continuous spring battle: bamboo versus Miyama villagers.

Last week, one lone spindly shoot burst through the dirt floor in the workshop and Nagayoshi-san put a flower pot around the base and left it. When guests came he told them it was his new houseplant. He cut off the new shoots to keep it low and bushy, like a bonsai. It kept on growing.

He cut some more; it grew some more. Finally he took a sharp blade to the shoot; cutting it down took an hour.

Yet because of this weedlike growth, *take* is a ceaseless resource. In January when everything was cleaned for the New Year, we placed fresh bamboo poles across the outside faucet area as racks for glazing. My new measuring tools, like all others in the workshop and many of Nagayoshi-san's brushes, are made from the green wood. Bamboo shoots, known as *takenoko*—"bamboo child"—are edible. Stewed with tōfu, white radish, thick *kombu* seaweed and carrots, they become the standard winter stew called *oden.* Sweetened bamboo shoots appear at breakfast alongside bowls of miso soup, at lunch with scoops of steaming white rice. For dinner we devour the thick yellow slices like steak with bamboo chopsticks.

The giving and receiving of takenoko is a spring ritual, predictable as the cherry-blossom viewing in late March, or the daily exchange of information about volcanic ash. With a gentle bow, Suzuki-san's wife comes over with three or four long shoots every morning. Nagayoshi-san brings them in when he picks up the morning paper. Reiko looks at them warily. Preparation is a long process of boiling in rice-rinsing water to extract the bitterness, then flavoring with soy sauce and sweet rice wine. On Saturdays when I go to Kagoshima City to teach my English classes, Reiko hands me a bagful for my students; the boiled yellow meat is a country delicacy for city people. When I gave some to my ink painting (*sumie*) teacher, a tall, elegant woman who always wears dark red lipstick and a formal silk kimono, her husband was so pleased that he gave me a gift in return— a plastic wall clock in the shape of Sakurajima. On the back I made out the words "Compliments of Kagoshima Chamber of Commerce." My sumie teacher and her husband, who are quite wealthy, often give me small presents: a pink change purse from Kyoto, a miniature copy of a Japanese doll, a sake cup from Okinawa, an old silver fan. Even though they are clearly unwanted *omiyage* that someone had once given them, etiquette requires that I reciprocate somehow. I would stop along the way to the next class and buy some overpriced but beautifully wrapped rice-and-bean sweets. Once started, this cycle of gift-giving has no end and my pile of omiyage has grown. When Reiko discovered that I was buying a gift each week, she was shocked and insisted that I stop spending my own money. From then on she prepared something for me to take, usually a small assortment of sweets—leftovers from the boxes of teatime cakes pottery guests had brought.

> "Once started, this cycle of gift-giving has no end and my pile of omiyage has grown."

Yesterday on the way home from town I passed Yamanaka-san from the Sataro workshop, to whom I gave the volcano-shaped clock. She promptly ran into her house and emerged with a bag of freshly dug takenoko. I gave the shoots to Reiko. She glared. Reiko gave them to customers, who

were delighted, "*Natsukashii!*" they cried—"How nostalgic!"—and told
stories of their mothers in the country who used to boil them every
spring. In the evening Suzuki-san's wife with a soft bow brought more.

"*Itte irasshai*—go and come back," she calls when I reach the end of the
lane. "*Itte kimasu*—I go and come," I answer, as expected, and continue
on. The sounds of their energetic reaping fade and the bamboo grove
ends, intersecting with open light and, to the left, a wide, freshly tilled
and planted tobacco field. To the right on the corner is the single-story
weathered-board home of Shigenobu-san. Like many Miyama *obāsan*, she
lives alone. Her husband, once a famed shiromon carver, died two years
ago, and all eight of their children left Miyama for jobs in major cities. It
is a point of pride to Shigenobu-san that her children were educated, and
have not become potters or farmers. One son, a schoolteacher in nearby
Ibusuki, visits sometimes, but the others live too far away to return more
often than on an occasional New Year's or at *obon,* the August festival of
the dead. Shigenobu-san has lived to see the Depression, the war, postwar
inflation, Japan's economic success, and now, in her early eighties, she says
she doesn't mind living alone. "*Jiyū ga dekiru,*" she will say. "I can do
what I want." Her house is dark and dusty. Dirty dishes fill the sink, and
piles of papers lie everywhere. Only the boxes of fruit and other foods
that her children send each month are piled neatly in one corner.

The other day I passed her house and, noticing that the sliding front
doors were open, stepped in to say hello. Shigenobu-san sat waiting quietly on the raised entrance. She wore a long skirt as if on her way to town,
but no shirt at all.

"Hello?" I said tentatively. She looked up with a wan smile.

"Oh, hello, I'm waiting for the mailman. Shall I make some tea?"

"Oh, no, not at all, sorry to trouble you," I said quickly, edging back
out the door. It was once a common sight to see rural women, particularly obāsan, working in the fields bare-chested. But, like mixed bathing
at the public baths, it has since been deemed "improper." A loud voice
suddenly sounded from the entrance. In the doorway stood a neighboring
obāsan, dressed for work in the fields.

"Well, well, what's this?" she said, stepping in. Walking over to
Shigenobu-san she reached out and gave her a poke, then whispered
something in Kagoshima ben that made them both break out laughing.
"Oh, I am forgetful," said Shigenobu-san with a giggle, and slowly
reached behind for a shirt.

To pass the time Shigenobu-san watches TV, visits with friends, reads
the paper every day and putters in her garden. For a while she played
gateball with the group of old people who meet every morning on the
community exercise field, but she says she found it boring and quit. When
she first met me on the road in front of her house she immediately invited
me in for tea, and I go to see her sometimes. Each of my visits she faith-
fully records in the small green notebook that is her diary.

She has other rituals of her own invention. Before we sit down for tea, which is usually cups of instant hot chocolate with three teaspoons of white sugar, she carefully pries open the package of whatever teatime sweets I have brought, and then carries one over to the *butsudan*—the Buddhist altar. Kneeling down before the gilded altar, she pushes aside the fruit, cakes and other offerings, and places the sweet down in front of a framed photograph of her late husband. Almost every Miyama home has similar dark-framed photographs of the late family elders next to the butsudan; many have pictures of the Emperor as well.

"*Otō-chan . . . Amerika no musume ga mata kiyashta yo.* Daddy dear . . . that girl from America has come to visit again," she calls in a mix of local dialect and standard Japanese, then goes on to describe the weather, the gift of cakes that I have brought, and what she has done that day. At first I was alarmed. Whom was she talking to? Was this some prayer I wasn't supposed to hear? Should I leave? Was she perhaps senile? But I got used to these one-way conversations. Her direct manner of prayer-talk mirrored the way I had seen many villagers address the kami-sama at the village shrine. While ancestor worship is a declining concern for the younger generation, in Kagoshima many beliefs persist. In the August festival of obon, when the spirits of the dead are said to return, the usually crowded local beaches are not full, as it is believed that the returning spirits travel inland from the sea.

One early morning on the way back down from the shrine I met Shigenobu-san slowly climbing up the hill to her husband's grave. Carrying a tin bucket, two long-stemmed yellow chrysanthemums and a single-serving bottle of *shōchū*, she made her way slowly up the maze of gray markers lining the hillside. When I waved hello, she shouted for me to come down. "Shall we go together?" she said, handing me the bucket and taking my arm. Months before, a Tokyo anthropologist who had done fieldwork on Miyama had given me some cryptic advice. "If you want to learn about the old Miyama," he had said, "go to the graves—and listen." I had made it a habit to pass through the crowded cemetery on my morning loop through the village.

Scattered amid waist-high grass and thickets of low bamboo, the gravestones keep company with a colony of black pots. Squat wide-mouthed jars hold flowers and water; small cups hold shōchū and sake. By the grave of the famed kuromon potter Tanaka-san, two leaning urns mark his skill. In a thicket just below, Korean-style grave markers lie buried in bamboo and lichen. In the 1870's, when discrimination against Koreans flared, villagers tried to hide their origins, discarding the roofed Korean-style tombstones for upright Japanese markers. Often I saw Miyama obāsan tending the graves; when they left, flowers, cigarettes, cups of liquor and dishes of rice, salt and water filled the hillside. But no one had ever invited me to come along.

Following Shigenobu-san that day, I climbed back up the hillside. When we reached a rectangular gray marker on a stone base, she promptly knelt down, clapped her hands twice, and began to murmur. She told her husband about the yellow chrysanthemums and jar of shōchū she had brought, about my coming to help, the latest news in the village. Holding the tin bucket, I waited awkwardly at a distance, gazing down over the village.

When she was done, she clapped her hands twice and slowly rose. "Now, the cleaning," she said matter-of-factly, and motioned for me to draw water from a nearby tap. While I poured buckets of water on the stone marker, washing away a thin layer of volcanic ash, Shigenobu-san poured out the shōchū and placed the flowers in two waiting black jugs. Before leaving, we lit two sticks of incense and placed them in the small blue bowl full of sand in front of the grave.

"Do you always bring shōchū and flowers?" I asked on the way down.

"Why, of course," she answered in surprise. "Don't you tend your graves in America?"

"Well, yes . . . but not quite the same way. Flowers, of course, but people don't usually leave liquor."

"Well, if I didn't, he'd be lonely," she said matter-of-factly. "And Otō-chan . . ." Her voice trailed off and she smiled fondly—"he did like to drink."

April gives way to May, bamboo gives way to tea. May is the month of *shincha*, the first tea. Every spring Yamanaka-san, who works six days a week, from eight to five, at the Sataro workshop, takes two weeks off from her job to help with the tea harvest. For generations her family has run the only tea-drying business in Miyama. Yamanaka-san's house is in the old style, with a mongamae entrance and a once ornate formal garden denoting old village wealth, but she insists that her family is of Japanese, not Korean, descent. Three times a year the long shed behind her home transforms into a tea-processing factory, but the first crop, the shincha, is considered the most delicious.

Tea was first cultivated in Japan with seeds brought from China in the late eighth century. Prior to the Edo period (1600–1868) it was a beverage known only to the ruling classes. Today, teatime in country villages such as Miyama is ten o'clock sharp in the morning and three in the afternoon. Cups of caffeine-rich green tea also appear at breakfast, lunch and dinner. Squat green rows of tea bushes line yards and gardens, and on the hillcrest below the shrine, narrow hedges of pruned tea stretch as straight and long as racetracks.

Once harvesting begins, the tea leaves must be immediately dried and processed. The factory will run twenty-four hours a day as long as villagers continue to bring the freshly picked leaves to the entrance. First they are weighed, then carefully separated into net bags and labeled by grower. The grades range from the expensive powdered *matcha* for the tea ceremony down to the coarse *bancha* for daily use. All Miyama villagers grow bancha, but each swears by the taste of his or her particular leaves. The tea is sent through a series of churning gas-heated drums for drying, then through cutters and brushlike tea rollers, all connected by a network of belts and gears. It enters the conveyer belt looking like a giraffe's green picnic, and emerges at the other end cut, dried and rolled into tiny balls that resemble freeze-dried vegetables.

Last month after morning services at the shrine the Shintō priest climbed into the back of a waiting blue Toyota truck, one hand still holding his conical black plastic priest's hat. The truck roared off, the priest's white robes flowing jauntily behind him, and stopped at the other end of the fields. From his perch the priest scattered rice and blessings over a waiting tea combine. He waved his wand of white paper over the new machine, read a prayer, and clapped solemnly. The farmer was elated.

> "Drinking tea has many meanings, according to context."

In Kagoshima City one can buy green tea ice cream, Sno-cones, jelly, rolls and bread. Green tea is listed along with coffee and Coke at the McDonald's—popularly known as "Makkudonarudo." The Dunkin' Donuts store, popular among high school girls for its stylish "hatto pinku" decor, serves green tea and green tea doughnuts.

Drinking tea has many meanings, according to context. Accepting the tea offered by clerks in kimono shops means that you have come to buy. Eating the accompanying sweet signals clerks to wrap up everything you have seen. At the workshop, serving tea in Nagayoshi ware is good advertising. Pottery guests who have just come to look usually don't stay for tea. Those that intend to buy often accept only after several refusals and then apologies for all the trouble they have caused. When he is not rushing to entertain customers, a "Let's have tea" from Nagayoshi-san means that he simply wants a break or has something to discuss.

Nowhere is the drinking of tea more ritualized or important, however, than in the tea ceremony. A year ago last February I was invited to Chin Jukan's annual *ochakai*, tea ceremony gathering. The event was a plum blossom viewing: tickets, costing over fifty U.S. dollars, and including a set lunch by a caterer who specialized in tea ceremony cooking, were by invitation only. But the day of the event I put on my newest blue jeans, a clean shirt and a pair of white socks and asked at the gate if I could enter. I had meant just to take a look, but Chin Jukan's wife appeared and invited me to attend the ceremony and accompanying meal. I eagerly accepted.

In the sixteenth and seventeenth centuries, the principles of simplicity, poverty and humility came to characterize the Way of Tea. Governed by the aesthetic ideals of *wabi* and *sabi*, meaning a refined poverty, the teahouse is built of natural materials and left undecorated. Likewise, all jewelry and ornamentation must be left outside. The tea utensils, including the bowls, are of simple and quiet design. The tea host and guests wear white cloven-toed socks, *tabi*, to symbolize cleanliness and purity. In his essays on the tea ceremony, Okakuro Kakuzo writes: "Teaism is a cult founded on the adoration of the beautiful among the sordid facts of everyday existence."

But looking around at the invited guests that day, many of whom were tea ceremony teachers and their students, I saw little that was everyday or Zen. The workshop grounds swirled with women in silk kimonos of colors as vivid and surprising as the hues of tropical fish, accompanied by men in dark brown kimonos or dark business suits. In the quiet teahouse, with its stark white-paper-covered sliding doors, rush-covered mats and dark brown wooden beams, the colors seemed brighter still.

Most teahouses have low entrances through which one must, according to ritual, crawl to enter, and seat only three or four people. But Chin Jukan's spacious room seated ten guests that day. When everyone was assembled and silently sitting *seiza* around the perimeter, the ceremony began. With a soft thump, the white sliding door was pushed back to reveal the kneeling figure of Chin Jukan's wife in a brilliant burgundy silk kimono. Beside her, carefully placed on a black lacquer tray, were the utensils and the main teabowl, an antique shiromon piece whose white rounded sides were decorated with delicate motifs of gilded branches and flowering plum. She bowed low, and ten heads responded. Placing the tray inside, she propelled her still-kneeling figure into the room by pressing down and pulling with her knuckles. After closing the door behind her she stood up carefully, back straight, hands gently pressing into the red folds of cloth just above her knees.

I sat transfixed; in the small room, her tall, graceful figure seemed to float. The iron kettle, resting on its sunken bed of coals, softly hissed. The next hour passed in a series of stylized rites for receiving and drinking the bowls of frothy whipped green tea. After the hostess had prepared a bowl of whipped green tea for the guest of honor, individual bowls of tea, prepared behind the screens, were brought out and served to the rest of us. When everyone had finished his or her tea and the accompanying sweet, and each bowl had been carefully viewed, Chin Jukan's wife slowly cleaned the main teabowl by rinsing it with hot water from the kettle. Then came the closing ritual. The head guest, a frail older man in a brown kimono, asked a series of formalized questions about the ceremony and the tea utensils used.

"From where comes the tea container?" (From Satsuma. Twelfth-generation Chin Jukan.)

"Who made the tea scoop?" (The abbot of Daitokuji.)

Layers and layers of rules concerning etiquette and style and speech shaped each movement of the ceremony. Halfway through, my ankles had begun to burn from sitting seiza, and by the end I could barely sit still. By the time we ducked our heads and crawled back out into the sun, I was exhausted.

Afterwards, I made my way through the crowds of guests to sit under a flowering plum tree beside the small pool of fat orange carp. The gliding fish, the shimmering reflections of "sleeping dragon" plum blossoms restored my sense of what a tea ceremony should be. After a few minutes I was joined by the elderly tea ceremony teacher from whom I had taken a few tea lessons. She was delighted to see that I was finally seeing a "real tea." But after having met a ballerina from Kagoshima City, a man who owned an island in Okinawa, dozens of housewives and their tea ceremony teachers, and so many local businessmen, I felt I had been to a cocktail party. Guests rushed in and out of the showroom with bags of pottery, proclaiming the prices of their purchases like bargain hunters. The tea ceremony itself had a Zen-like concentration and grace, but the rest of the event, I realized, was a Jukan promotion.

I began to understand Nagayoshi-san's ambivalence toward this traditional art. Like all potters, he made tea ceremony ware; customers expected him to, and tea ware, priced higher than the other pottery, brought in necessary income. But he viewed it differently from the large ornamental plates that he spent hours designing and glazing. The few teabowls that he did make were not even displayed in the showroom, but kept in a separate cabinet in the house.

One night he and Reiko had a disagreement about the price of Nagayoshi teabowls. Nagayoshi-san had a habit of undercharging customers, which confused the finances and infuriated Reiko, who kept the workshop books. *Chawan* in particular had to be marked high, Reiko insisted, otherwise no one would buy them. Nagayoshi-san sat silent. The next morning I found pieces of smashed pottery scattered by the kitchen entrance, where a teabowl had been flung out the back door.

Yet it is Chanoyu—the Way of Tea—that underlies Japan's historic passion for ceramics. Yanagi Sōetsu wrote: "Tea taught people to look at and handle utilitarian objects more carefully than they had before, and it inspired in them a deeper interest and a greater respect for those objects." It had been the dream of fine teabowls that first inspired the Shimazu lords to found and sponsor Satsuma pottery. Centuries later, the making of tea ceremony ware is still a Japanese potter's bread and butter.

Jonathan Rauch

Caring for Your Introvert

Jonathan Rauch, a senior writer and columnist for *National Journal* magazine in Washington and a correspondent for the *Atlantic Monthly*, is the author of several books and many articles on public policy, culture, and economics. His latest book is *Gay Marriage: Why It Is Good for Gays, Good for Straights, and Good for America*, published in 2004. Of this book, a *Washington Post* reviewer said, "Thoughtful and convincingly argued. . . . Rauch's impressive book is as enthusiastic an encomium to marriage as anyone, gay or straight, could write." His other books include *Government's End: Why Washington Stopped Working* (1999), *Kindly Inquisitors: The New Attacks on Free Thought* (1993), and *The Outnation: A Search for the Soul of Japan* (1992). Among the many publications for which he has written are the *New Republic, Reason, Harper's, Fortune, U.S. News & World Report,* the *New York Times,* the *Wall Street Journal,* the *Washington Post,* the *Los Angeles Times, Slate,* and the *Chronicle of Higher Education.* Although much of his writing has been on public policy, he has also written on topics as widely varied as adultery, agriculture, economics, height discrimination, biological rhythms, and animal rights.

Rauch was born and raised in Phoenix, Arizona, and graduated in 1982 from Yale University. He went on to become a reporter for the *Winston-Salem Journal* in North Carolina before moving to Washington in 1984. From 1984 to 1989 he covered fiscal and economic policy for *National Journal.* In 1990 he spent six months in Japan as a fellow of the Japan Society Leadership Program, and in 1996 he was awarded the Premio Napoli alla Stampa Estera for his coverage in the *Economist* of the European Parliament. His essays have been reprinted in the *Best Magazine Writing 2005* and the *Best American Science and Nature Writing 2004.* He has appeared as a guest on many television and radio programs.

"Caring for Your Introvert," first published in the *Atlantic Monthly*, is a fairly unusual piece for Rauch, as it is not overtly political. The piece has gained something of an underground following, receiving an unusually high number of hits on the *Atlantic* Web site, and being republished in *Best American Essays 2005.*

Do you know someone who needs hours alone every day? Who loves quiet conversations about feelings or ideas, and can give a dynamite presentation to a big audience, but seems awkward in groups and maladroit at small talk? Who has to be dragged to parties and then needs the rest of the day to recuperate? Who growls or scowls or grunts or winces when accosted with pleasantries by people who are just trying to be nice?

If so, do you tell this person he is "too serious," or ask if he is okay? Regard him as aloof, arrogant, rude? Redouble your efforts to draw him out?

If you answered yes to these questions, chances are that you have an introvert on your hands—and that you aren't caring for him properly. Science has learned a good deal in recent years about the habits and requirements of introverts. It has even learned, by means of brain scans, that introverts process information differently from other people (I am not making this up). If you are behind the curve on this important matter, be reassured that you are not alone. Introverts may be common, but they are also among the most misunderstood and aggrieved groups in America, possibly the world.

I know. My name is Jonathan, and I am an introvert.

Oh, for years I denied it. After all, I have good social skills. I am not morose or misanthropic. Usually. I am far from shy. I love long conversations that explore intimate thoughts or passionate interests. But at last I have self-identified and come out to my friends and colleagues. In doing so, I have found myself liberated from any number of damaging misconceptions and stereotypes. Now I am here to tell you what you need to know in order to respond sensitively and supportively to your own introverted family members, friends, and colleagues. Remember, someone you know, respect, and interact with every day is an introvert, and you are probably driving this person nuts. It pays to learn the warning signs.

What is introversion? In its modern sense, the concept goes back to the 1920s and the psychologist Carl Jung. Today it is a mainstay of personality tests, including the widely used Myers-Briggs Type Indicator. Introverts are not necessarily shy. Shy people are anxious or frightened or self-excoriating in social settings; introverts generally are not. Introverts are also not misanthropic, though some of us do go along with Sartre as far as to say "Hell is other people at breakfast." Rather, introverts are people who find other people tiring.

Extroverts are energized by people, and wilt or fade when alone. They often seem bored by themselves, in both senses of the expression. Leave an extrovert alone for two minutes and he will reach for his cell phone. In contrast, after an hour or two of being socially "on," we introverts need to turn off and recharge. My own formula is roughly two hours alone for every hour of socializing. This isn't antisocial. It isn't a sign of depression. It does not call for medication. For introverts, to be alone with our thoughts is as restorative as sleeping, as nourishing as eating. Our motto: "I'm OK, you're OK—in small doses."

How many people are introverts? I performed exhaustive research on this question, in the form of a quick Google search. The answer: about 25 percent. Or: just under half. Or—my favorite—"a minority in the regular population but a majority in the gifted population."

Are introverts misunderstood? Wildly. That, it appears, is our lot in life. "It is very difficult for an extrovert to understand an introvert," write the education experts Jill D. Burruss and Lisa Kaenzig. (They are also the source of the

"*Are introverts misunderstood?* Wildly. That, it appears, is our lot in life."

quotation in the previous paragraph.) Extroverts are easy for introverts to understand, because extroverts spend so much of their time working out who they are in voluble, and frequently inescapable, interaction with other people. They are as inscrutable as puppy dogs. But the street does not run both ways. Extroverts have little or no grasp of introversion. They assume that company, especially their own, is always welcome. They cannot imagine why someone would need to be alone; indeed, they often take umbrage at the suggestion. As often as I have tried to explain the matter to extroverts, I have never sensed that any of them really understood. They listen for a moment and then go back to barking and yipping.

Are introverts oppressed? I would have to say so. For one thing, extroverts are overrepresented in politics, a profession in which only the garrulous are really comfortable. Look at George W. Bush. Look at Bill Clinton. They seem to come fully to life only around other people. To think of the few introverts who did rise to the top in politics—Calvin Coolidge, Richard Nixon—is merely to drive home the point. With the possible exception of Ronald Reagan, whose fabled aloofness and privateness were probably signs of a deep introverted streak (many actors, I've read, are introverts, and many introverts, when socializing, feel like actors), introverts are not considered "naturals" in politics.

Extroverts therefore dominate public life. This is a pity. If we introverts ran the world, it would no doubt be a calmer, saner, more peaceful sort of place. As Coolidge is supposed to have said, "Don't you know that four-fifths of all our troubles in this life would disappear if we would just sit down and keep still?" (He is also supposed to have said, "If you don't say anything, you won't be called on to repeat it." The only thing a true introvert dislikes more than talking about himself is repeating himself.)

With their endless appetite for talk and attention, extroverts also dominate social life, so they tend to set expectations. In our extrovertist society, being outgoing is considered normal and therefore desirable, a mark of happiness, confidence, leadership. Extroverts are seen as bighearted, vibrant, warm, empathic. "People person" is a compliment. Introverts are described with words like "guarded," "loner," "reserved," "taciturn," "self-contained," "private"—narrow, ungenerous words, words that suggest emotional parsimony and smallness of personality. Female introverts, I suspect, must suffer especially. In certain circles, particularly in the Midwest, a man can still sometimes get away with being what they used to call a strong and silent type; introverted women, lacking that alternative, are even more likely than men to be perceived as timid, withdrawn, haughty.

Are introverts arrogant? Hardly. I suppose this common misconception has to do with our being more intelligent, more reflective, more independent, more level-headed, more refined, and more sensitive than extroverts. Also, it is probably due to our lack of small talk, a lack that extroverts often mistake for disdain. We tend to think before talking, whereas extroverts tend to think *by* talking, which is why their meetings never last less than six hours. "Introverts," writes a perceptive fellow named Thomas P. Crouser, in an online review of a recent book called *Why Should Extroverts Make All the Money?* (I'm not making *that* up, either), "are driven to distraction by the semi-internal dialogue extroverts tend to conduct. Introverts don't outwardly complain, instead roll their eyes and silently curse the darkness." Just so.

The worst of it is that extroverts have no idea of the torment they put us through. Sometimes, as we gasp for air amid the fog of their 98-percent-content-free talk, we wonder if extroverts even bother to listen to themselves. Still, we endure stoically, because the etiquette books—written, no doubt, by extroverts—regard declining to banter as rude and gaps in conversation as awkward. We can only dream that someday, when our condition is more widely understood, when perhaps an Introverts' Rights movement has blossomed and borne fruit, it will not be impolite to say "I'm an introvert. You are a wonderful person and I like you. But now please shush."

How can I let the introvert in my life know that I support him and respect his choice? First, recognize that it's not a choice. It's not a lifestyle. It's an *orientation*. Second, when you see an introvert lost in thought, don't say "What's the matter?" or "Are you all right?" Third, don't say anything else, either.

Joe Sacco

From *Palestine*

Joe Sacco was born in Malta in 1960 and lives in Portland, Oregon. His illustrated comics on the Balkan war crime trials in The Hague, Netherlands (*Safe Area Gorazde*, 1998) and the Israeli-Palestinian conflict (*Palestine*, 1993) have helped to redefine the nature of international journalism. Sacco received his BA in journalism at the University of Oregon in 1981 but soon became frustrated and disenfranchised with traditional journalism, where he couldn't find "a job writing very hard-hitting, interesting pieces that would really make some sort of difference." After a brief stint working on the National Notary Association's annual journal (which he found "exceedingly, exceedingly boring") he returned to Malta, journalistic hopes temporarily forgotten. "I sort of decided to forget it and just go the other route, which was basically to take my hobby, which has been cartooning, and see if I could make a living out of that."

He worked thereafter as a freelance writer, first publishing local guide-books and then syndicating a series of Maltese romance comics called *Imħabba Vera* (*True Love*). He later returned to the United States, where he published comics in a number of presses. Sacco tired of being rooted to one spot, and returned to his passion for globe-trotting. During his travels, he completed his first autobiographical work, *Yahoo* (six issues, 1988–92), and collected research for *Palestine*.

In *Palestine* Sacco uses methods of personal journalism to describe his encounters with Palestinians and Israelis. The collection was first serialized as a comic book from 1993 to 2001, then published in several collections, the first of which won the 1996 American Book Award. "You see extremes of humanity in places like Palestine and Bosnia," Sacco said in a 2004 interview with *L.A. Weekly*. "You see enormously good people who'll give you the shirt off their backs despite the fact that they have nothing, and you see incredible cruelty. Mostly what you see is innocent people being crushed beneath the wheels of history." Sacco's recent publications include comics based on war crimes in Iraq.

Interview with Joe Sacco, p. 665

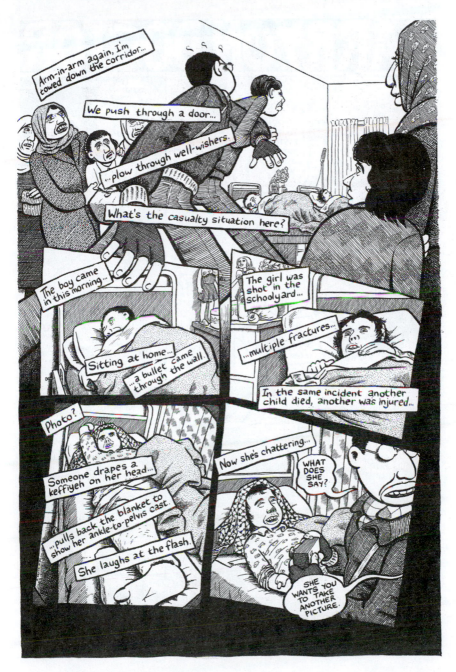

Interview with Joe Sacco

BECKY BRADWAY: What compelled you to travel to Palestine and tell this story?

JOE SACCO: When I began to understand the story of the Palestinians, it hit me in the gut. For the longest time I didn't pay close attention to news from the Middle East, and what I had "received" from osmosis was that "Palestinians" and "terrorists" were to be mentioned in the same sentence, if not in the same breath. I began to play closer attention to the Palestinian question around the time Israel bombed and then invaded Beirut in the early 1980s. And after the killings at Sabra and Shatila, I began to untangle the muddle the media had made of the issue in my mind. Eventually, I was quite upset at how poorly American journalists had framed the Palestinian reality for me— perhaps doubly so because I had studied journalism myself and expected better things from those to whom "objective" is a holy word. At some point I started my cartooning career, but I never lost interest in the Israeli-Palestinian conflict, and when I had the means I decided I would go and take a look for myself.

BB: Your drawings of yourself serve to establish a very particular character/ narrator in this book. Is there any particular effect you were going for in the way you designed yourself?

JS: Well, first of all, my drawn character in the panels reminds the reader that this is one person's perspective on the issue. It is the drawn equivalent of the pronoun "I." My work isn't objective, and that's the visual tip-off. But this useful device wasn't particularly thought out when I embarked on my journalistic work. Simply, like many cartoonists, I used to draw autobiographical stories, so when I decided to do a series of comics about my trip to the Palestinian Territories, my "character" transferred over. Yes, it is not a particularly visually defined character in relationship to others I draw, and some people have told me that helps them put themselves in my shoes. All the better, but that wasn't planned out either.

BB: Your piece takes no prisoners. Did you see this book as an argument or statement? Ideally, what kind of change would you want this book to effect?

JS: Let's be clear, I went to Palestine with the conviction that Palestinians had been historically wronged. What was important to me, however, was to keep my eyes and ears open and report honestly—as opposed to "objectively." In other words, if Palestinians said something that I knew would sound harsh or ugly to an American ear, that wouldn't keep me from reporting it. No one is an angel, and we certainly cannot expect history's victims to fit into that category. I don't think of my book as an argument or a statement so much as presenting a reality as lived by a dispossessed and sometimes bitter people. I don't know what change I'm trying to effect except to provide a greater feeling for the humanity of a people who have been pushed into a desperate corner.

Leslie Marmon Silko

Uncle Tony's Goat

Leslie Marmon Silko is a novelist, essayist, and poet. Her work often concerns the struggles of Native American and mixed-race people; she is Laguna Pueblo, Mexican American, and European American. She was raised on the edge of the reservation, both literally and figuratively. She was taught the traditions of the Pueblo people by the women in her family, but was simultaneously excluded from the ritual and social activities of the tribe. Her work melds mythological, historical, and highly realistic contemporary concerns. She received the MacArthur Foundation "Genius" Grant in 1981.

Silko was educated at Catholic school in Albuquerque, and went on to receive a BA from the University of New Mexico in 1969. Her life and work are set in New Mexico.

Her novel *Ceremony* (1977) received considerable praise. A *Boston Globe* reviewer said the book "is very deliberately a ceremony in itself—demanding but confident and beautifully written." Novelist Sherman Alexie called it the "greatest novel in Native American literature. It is one of the greatest novels of any time and place. I have read this book so many times that I probably have it memorized. I teach it and I learn from it and I am continually in awe of its power, beauty, rage, vision, and violence."

After writing *Ceremony*, Silko spent ten years on her powerful, controversial book *The Almanac of the Dead* (1991). Her most recent novel is *Garden in the Dunes* (1999). Throughout her career, she has written poetry, nonfiction, and short fiction; some of these pieces are collected in the anthology *Storyteller* (1981). It is from this book that we have taken her essay "Uncle Tony's Goat." While our selection takes the form of a memoir, her essays often are eloquent arguments against what she perceives as the wrongful acquisition of Native American identity by other writers, or the lack of social conscience by writers who are identified as Native American. Some of these are included in her collection of nonfiction, *Yellow Woman and a Beauty of the Spirit: Essays on Native American Life Today* (1996).

We had a hard time finding the right kind of string to use. We knew we needed gut to string our bows the way the men did, but we were little kids and we didn't know how to get any. So Kenny went to his house and brought back a ball of white cotton string that his mother used to string red chili with. It was thick and soft and it didn't make very good bowstring. As soon as we got the bows made we sat down again on the sand bank above the stream and started skinning willow twigs for arrows. It was past noon, and the tall willows behind us made cool shade. There were lots of little minnows that day, flashing in the shallow water, swimming back and forth wildly like they weren't sure if they really wanted to go up or down the stream; it was a day for minnows that we were always hoping for—we could have filled our rusty coffee cans and old pickle jars full. But this was the first time for making bows and arrows, and the minnows weren't much different from the sand or the rocks now. The secret is the arrows. The ones we made were crooked, and when we shot them they didn't go straight—they flew around in arcs and curves; so we crawled through the leaves and branches, deep into the willow groves, looking for the best, the straightest willow branches. But even after we skinned the sticky wet bark from them and whittled the knobs off, they still weren't straight. Finally we went ahead and made notches at the end of each arrow to hook in the bowstring, and we started practicing, thinking maybe we could learn to shoot the crooked arrows straight.

> "We were going up to the church to shoot at the cats old Sister Julian kept outside the cloister."

We left the river each of us with a handful of damp, yellow arrows and our fresh-skinned willow bows. We walked slowly and shot arrows at bushes, big rocks, and the juniper tree that grows by Pino's sheep pen. They were working better just like we had figured; they still didn't fly straight, but now we could compensate for that by the way we aimed them. We were going up to the church to shoot at the cats old Sister Julian kept outside the cloister. We didn't want to hurt anything, just to have new kinds of things to shoot at.

But before we got to the church we went past the grassy hill where my uncle Tony's goats were grazing. A few of them were lying down chewing their cud peacefully, and they didn't seem to notice us. The billy goat was lying down, but he was watching us closely like he already knew about little kids. His yellow goat eyes didn't blink, and he stared with a wide, hostile look. The grazing goats made good deer for our bows. We shot all our arrows at the nanny goats and their kids; they skipped away from the careening arrows and never lost the rhythm of their greedy chewing as they continued to nibble the weeds and grass on the hillside. The billy goat was lying there watching us and taking us into his memory. As we ran down the road toward the church and Sister Julian's cats, I looked back, and my uncle Tony's billy goat was still watching me.

My uncle and my father were sitting on the bench outside the house when we walked by. It was September now, and the farming was almost over, except for bringing home the melons and a few pumpkins. They were mending ropes and bridles and feeling the afternoon sun. We held our bows and arrows out in front of us so they could see them. My father smiled and kept braiding the strips of leather in his hand, but my uncle Tony put down the bridle and pieces of scrap leather he was working on and looked at each of us kids slowly. He was old, getting some white hair—he was my mother's oldest brother, the one that scolded us when we told lies or broke things.

"You'd better not be shooting at things," he said, "only at rocks or trees. Something will get hurt. Maybe even one of you."

We all nodded in agreement and tried to hold the bows and arrows less conspicuously down at our sides; when he turned back to his work we hurried away before he took the bows away from us like he did the time we made the slingshot. He caught us shooting rocks at an old wrecked car; its windows were all busted out anyway, but he took the slingshot away. I always wondered what he did with it and with the knives we made ourselves out of tin cans. When I was much older I asked my mother, "What did he ever do with those knives and slingshots he took away from us?" She was kneading bread on the kitchen table at the time and was probably busy thinking about the fire in the oven outside. "I don't know," she said; "you ought to ask him yourself." But I never did. I thought about it lots of times, but I never did. It would have been like getting caught all over again.

The goats were valuable. We got milk and meat from them. My uncle was careful to see that all the goats were treated properly; the worst scolding my older sister ever got was when my mother caught her and some of her friends chasing the newborn kids. My mother kept saying over and over again, "It's a good thing I saw you; what if your uncle had seen you?" and even though we kids were very young then, we understood very well what she meant.

The billy goat never forgot the bows and arrows, even after the bows had cracked and split and the crooked, whittled arrows were all lost. This goat was big and black and important to my uncle Tony because he'd paid a lot to get him and because he wasn't an ordinary goat. Uncle Tony had bought him from a white man, and then he'd hauled him in the back of the pickup all the way from Quemado. And my uncle was the only person who could touch this goat. If a stranger or one of us kids got too near him, the mane on the billy goat's neck would stand on end and the goat would rear up on his hind legs and dance forward trying to reach the person with his long, spiral horns. This billy goat smelled bad, and none of us cared if we couldn't pet him. But my uncle took good care of this goat. The goat would let Uncle Tony brush him with the horse brush and scratch him around the base of his horns. Uncle Tony talked to the billy goat—in the morning when he unpenned the goats and in the evening when he gave them their hay and closed the gate for the night. I never paid too much attention to what he said to the billy goat; usually it was something like "Get up, big goat! You've slept long enough," or "Move over, big goat, and let the others have something to eat." And I think Uncle Tony was proud of the way the billy goat mounted the nannies, powerful and erect with the great black testicles swinging in rhythm between his hind legs.

We all had chores to do around home. My sister helped out around the house mostly, and I was supposed to carry water from the hydrant and bring in kindling. I helped my father look after the horses and pigs, and Uncle Tony milked the goats and fed them. One morning near the end of September I was out feeding the pigs their table scraps and pig mash; I'd given the pigs their food, and I was watching them squeal and snap at each other as they crowded into the feed trough. Behind me I could hear the milk squirting into the eight-pound lard pail that Uncle Tony used for milking.

When he finished milking he noticed me standing there; he motioned toward the goats still inside the pen. "Run the rest of them out," he said as he untied the two milk goats and carried the milk to the house.

I was seven years old, and I understood that everyone, including my uncle, expected me to handle more chores; so I hurried over to the goat pen and swung the tall wire gate open. The does and kids came prancing out. They trotted daintily past the pigpen and scattered out, intent on finding leaves and grass to eat. It wasn't until then I noticed that the billy goat hadn't come out of the little wooden shed inside the goat pen. I stood outside the pen and tried to look inside the wooden shelter, but it was still early and the morning sun left the inside of the shelter in deep shadow. I stood there for a while, hoping that he would come out by himself, but I realized that he'd recognized me and that he wouldn't come out. I understood right away what was happening and my fear of him was in my bowels and down my neck; I was shaking.

Finally my uncle came out of the house; it was time for breakfast. "What's wrong?" he called out from the door.

"The billy goat won't come out," I yelled back, hoping he would look disgusted and come do it himself.

"Get in there and get him out," he said as he went back into the house.

I looked around quickly for a stick or broom handle, or even a big rock, but I couldn't find anything. I walked into the pen slowly, concentrating on the darkness beyond the shed door; I circled to the back of the shed and kicked at the boards, hoping to make the billy goat run out. I put my eye up to a crack between the boards, and I could see he was standing up now and that his yellow eyes were on mine.

My mother was yelling at me to hurry up, and Uncle Tony was watching. I stepped around into the low doorway, and the goat charged toward me, feet first. I had dirt in my mouth and up my nose and there was blood running past my eye; my head ached. Uncle Tony carried me to the house; his face was stiff with anger, and I remembered what he'd always told us about animals; they won't bother you unless you bother them first. I didn't start to cry until my mother hugged me close and wiped my face with a damp wash rag. It was only a little cut above my eyebrow, and she sent me to school anyway with a Band-Aid on my forehead.

Uncle Tony locked the billy goat in the pen. He didn't say what he was going to do with the goat, but when he left with my father to haul firewood, he made sure the gate to the pen was wired tightly shut. He looked at the goat quietly and with sadness; he said something to the goat, but the yellow eyes stared past him.

"What's he going to do with the goat?" I asked my mother before I went to catch the school bus.

"He ought to get rid of it," she said. "We can't have that goat knocking people down for no good reason."

I didn't feel good at school. The teacher sent me to the nurse's office and the nurse made me lie down. Whenever I closed my eyes I could see the goat and my uncle, and I felt a stiffness in my throat and chest. I got off the school bus slowly, so the other kids would go ahead without me. I walked slowly and wished I could be away from home for a while. I could go over to Grandma's house, but she would ask me if my mother knew where I was and I would have to say no, and she would make me go home first to ask. So I walked very slowly, because I didn't want to see the black goat's hide hanging over the corral fence.

When I got to the house I didn't see a goat hide or the goat, but Uncle Tony was on his horse and my mother was standing beside the horse holding a canteen and a flour sack bundle tied with brown string. I was frightened at what this meant. My uncle looked down at me from the saddle.

"The goat ran away," he said. "Jumped out of the pen somehow. I saw him just as he went over the hill beyond the river. He stopped at the top of the hill and he looked back this way."

Uncle Tony nodded at my mother and me and then he left; we watched his old roan gelding splash across the stream and labor up the steep path beyond the river. Then they were over the top of the hill and gone.

"The trail just gets higher and steeper."

Uncle Tony was gone for three days. He came home early on the morning of the fourth day, before we had eaten breakfast or fed the animals. He was glad to be home, he said, because he was getting too old for such long rides. He called me over and looked closely at the cut above my eye. It had scabbed over good, and I wasn't wearing a Band-Aid any more; he examined it very carefully before he let me go. He stirred some sugar into his coffee.

"That goddamn goat," he said. "I followed him for three days. He was headed south, going straight to Quemado. I never could catch up to him." My uncle shook his head. "The first time I saw him he was already in the piñon forest, halfway into the mountains already. I could see him most of the time, off in the distance a mile or two. He would stop sometimes and look back." Uncle Tony paused and drank some more coffee. "I stopped at night. I had to. He stopped too, and in the morning we would start out again. The trail just gets higher and steeper. Yesterday morning there was frost on top of the blanket when I woke up and we were in the big pines and red oak leaves. I couldn't see him any more because the forest is too thick. So I turned around." Tony finished the cup of coffee. "He's probably in Quemado by now."

I looked at him again, standing there by the door, ready to go milk the nanny goats.

"There wasn't ever a goat like that one," he said, "but if that's the way he's going to act, O.K. then. That damn goat got pissed off too easy anyway."

He smiled at me and his voice was strong and happy when he said this.

Sharon Solwitz

Abracadabra

Sharon Solwitz has been awarded numerous literary prizes, including a Pushcart, the Tara Fellowship in Short Fiction (from the Heekin Foundation), the Katherine Anne Porter Fiction Prize, the Nelson Algren Prize (three times), the Hemingway Days Festival Prize, as well as arts council fellowships. Her collection of stories, *Blood and Milk* (1997), won the Carl Sandburg Prize and the adult fiction award from the Society of Midland Authors, and was runner up for the National Jewish Book Award. Her short fiction has been published in numerous magazines including *Ploughshares,* the *Chicago Tribune, Tikkun,* and *Mademoiselle.*

Of *Blood and Milk*, the *New York Times Book Review* said, "A flair for dark comedy and the ability to turn on a dime are prized qualities for these unpredictable characters; time and again, their intrepid investigations lead them into uncharted territory where bizarre dramatic action seems to be the only possible move. Solwitz's fine-toothed examinations of complex emotional states are dead on." A novel, *Bloody Mary*, was published in 2003.

Sharon Solwitz is an associate professor of English at Purdue University in West Lafayette, Indiana, where she teaches fiction writing. She lives in Chicago with her husband, poet Barry Silesky, and son Seth. Our selection, Solwitz's only published essay, is an intense examination of the death of Jesse, one of her twin sons. It first appeared in the 2003 anthology *In the Middle of the Middle West: Literacy Nonfiction from the Heartland.*

For Jesse (February 10, 1987–January 31, 2001)

Once upon a time a woman gave birth to twin sons.

They had enough fingers and toes, and sweet-smelling bald heads and, eventually, wide, toothless grins, and she loved them.

Thirteen years passed, then one got sick. In the year that followed he was sick and better, then very sick, then a little better.

He died.

His mother, however, remained alive.

Those are the high points. Interesting (maybe), but not searing, not devastating. It's what I can write, that or aanhhh! James Joyce wrote a cat's cry not meow but mrrgniaouw, satisfying in its phonetic precision. Arrnyanghh?

Perhaps it needs back story.

The boys came in her forty-first year, after five of doctor-assisted trying. Pregnant, she sometimes referred to herself (mostly ironically) as biblical Sarah, Judaism's first first lady, blessed with child when she was (almost) too old to conceive. Like Sarah, she was hospitable. Her Hebrew

*name was (really) Sarah. She called the boys, among other things, angels,
devils, and little wild men. She called them her miracle babies.*

These words, general and distant from me, come easily to mind. But
other words clump together down somewhere, caught as in some internal
oil spill, slimy-billed, gasping for air, feathers stuck to emaciated wing-
bones. A few bedraggled words break loose. *Aaaaanrg!*

I once wrote an essay about turning life into fiction. One's own life. Pit
your enraged self (for example) against your obsequious self. It strikes me
now as frighteningly obtuse. Writing one's secrets and fears? Dare to do it! In
service of literature and one's psyche! Yeah, right, I say now to my relentlessly perky younger self, to whom the worst that ever happened was walking
in on her husband screwing another woman. Now I scream at her (not my ex-
husband's lover but my earlier self): That was nothing!!

How do you write about a hole in the world, a loss that renders
everything you still might have, see, feel, pointless or at least continually, repetitively painful? Yes, transformation is necessary, of dire
experience into something by means of which life becomes more than
a series of increasingly dire losses. But can writing transform? Will it
make me feel better?

Dialogue Between Two Halves of a Brain

X: I can't think straight. I want to die. It's like I'm already dead.

Y: Oh, shut up. By its nature, self is in bondage to death. Find a purpose apart from your desire to "feel better." Write for teeming humanity,
in which every household has suffered loss. *Om mani padme hum.*

Lost in the sea of bad feeling, X will try to follow the advice of the more
rational Y. Will the swimmer make it to shore? Will the swim be beautiful?

In my grad school days a fellow student, excellent poet, had a baby
with a problem who died at six weeks. The woman dropped out of the
program, went on to have another baby but, from what I've heard, couldn't
write another poem. Now, maybe she wasn't supposed to write poems;
maybe the world is happily free of her poetry, and she is happy in law or
medical school learning how to save physical lives and make money to
boot. But maybe, dissecting her cadaver, she looks into the abdominal
cavity and stumbles into the empty place in her that words might fill
nourishingly. Can words nourish? Can they replace, redeem?

I write to know, and so that you can know. Oh, lapsed M.F.A.; oh,
exile from the kingdom of poetry, in your pea-green scrubs following
chick-like after the attending physician, this essay—attempt at essay—
is for you.

Advice

Describe your state of mind. Make it concrete, an object to look at, a
piece of writing by, about, someone else.

Then you can step back from it, take in something new.

My mind is sludge; undifferentiated. No feelings, thoughts. No images even, of friends, family. I'm sorry, Seth, my other son. Remaining son. Twin, untwinned. Now his face comes, fleshy (he fattened up while Jesse shrank). It means nothing to me.

But I can breathe, am breathing. Hear my voice talking to people. I speak, therefore I am. Downstairs during shiva I sat on a low stool, liking the lowness, the non-necessity of making sense, of squeezing back the hands that squeezed mine. People's legs passed, clothed in fabric, I saw from my stool. Thinking: I like this stool—Bubby's mahogany footstool, salvaged by my mother from her mother's estate. I like this vantage point, reflecting exactly my sense of my state in the world. From now on, to dinner with friends, I'll bring my stool, and show, at table, the top half of my face. I'll walk to class with my stool under my arm. Teach from a low stool. No reason anyone should listen to me in that abject station, but I don't mind not being listened to. Let me stay here in this abased, overlooked place.

Then a thought, and it's bad. Hold still, stiff, for what's coming. His last breath. I heard it. In bed beside him I was listening to him breathe, fast and shallow (as he'd been breathing the past three days), and I was breathing in time with him, *in unison*, silently instructing him how to breathe better. He took a long, deep breath. A pause, maybe fifteen seconds. I held my own breath, open, alert that quarter of a minute for a squeeze of maybe hope, the thought of healing; from now on he'll start breathing normally again. Remembering the monitors over his hospital bed, the rise and fall of his respiration, varyingly sized troughs and crests, shallow, erratic, and me willing them into mountain peaks, an even row of crags, the breaths of someone who doesn't have to labor at it, who can climb a mountain on the fuel of his calm deep breaths. And voila!—not even a miracle, the normal expected—the boy up and out of the hospital, back to school, talking to friends on the phone, all things eternally possible . . . Another breath now. I taste it in my mouth, work to extend it in my mind. Another long pause. I wait, breathing shallowly, so as not to miss the next sound, however frail.

At some point I stopped waiting. For a reason I don't know even now, nine months later, since I am not an observant Jew, I rolled against him, breathed in his ear, *Shma yisrael adonai elohenu adonai echod. Hear O Israel the Lord our God, the Lord is one.* If the soul lives even ten seconds after death, he had to have heard me.

And now? Nine months later, the period of human gestation. I have cried. I have had sex. I have eaten in restaurants. Talked with friends. Taught classes. Played bridge. Petted my cat. Cut my fingernails. I've taken Seth to the doctor, to the orthodontist, and to Air Wair for new boots. I've had fights with my husband Barry and made up with him (sort of). But how I am? Adjectives galumph about: Depressed? Lost? And nouns: ache, anguish, agony. Piercing wound? The sound of his name twisting a place just above my belly button? Sentences resist completion. Jess. Jesse?

Advice

Think about Jesse, then. What do you remember?

I remember how he looked in his Johnny Jump-Up. He was less than a year, and I have no pictures of him in the spring-driven harness, but I remember his grinning mouth and how quickly he learned to bounce. He couldn't walk yet, but he could bend his knees, then straighten, sending himself high into the air, euphoric in charge of his own pleasure.

I remember how he'd nurse, frantic, seeking his rhythm, hands flailing, then finding my face, my mouth. Sucking evenly now, fingers in my mouth, calm with the full sensory load. A few years later, playing catch with a tennis ball, he'd daydream and miss. When we added a second ball to the game, he hardly ever missed.

His first written word, his name, on a piece of construction paper brought home from pre-kindergarten: ESSJE.

His first recital piece, "The Wild Swans," from the John Thompson book. Lots of triplets. He learned to play quickly and with flash, with dynamics—in part, I think, to best brother Seth.

Karate. He'd daydream or start a conversation and have to apologize to the class. He liked the loud, wild boys, cohorts under the flag of anarchy. He loved to laugh, to talk out of turn, to fall in a heap on the floor.

Table manners. The kindergarten teacher said that some of the other children were offended. That he was "inappropriate."

My father offered him twenty dollars for an essay on table manners. He was nine or ten. He wrote a remarkable essay, detailing the table rules, discussing their purpose, their possible origin. On his third grade statewide writing assessment test (IGAP) he got a 26, perfect score, highest in the school. And still ate with his hands, from the box, the serving plate, roaming the house dropping crumbs.

He couldn't sit still in a chair. Drove his grandparents crazy. "Put your feet on the floor. Why do you keep turning?"

He and Seth walking together along the sidewalk, bumping into each other, not as a dominance game but as an unconscious joining, a return to their junction in utero. In a room they'd gravitate toward each other till they were leaning on one another, a proximity that most other pairs would have found irksome. As if, for nourishment, the bodies needed physical contact.

Walking, he'd bump into me; he'd walk leaning against me. If I was seated, he'd sink into my lap as if my lap were a chair continually offered him.

He signed a mother's day card, Jesse "the Bomb" Silesky.

He told his widowed grandma, "If you smile nicely, you'll find a man to be your husband."

A girl's birthday party. He walked in a little shy, and she called out, "Chase me!" His face, changing from uncertainty to joy.

Some kids on the bus told him he smiled too much. He felt bad. But it was hard for him to stop smiling. If he'd lived, he'd have worked, at least for a while in junior high, to turn himself as cool as boy society required. I'd have watched aching from afar, hoping that he'd find the part of himself that was unassailable. Hoping he'd learn to love the self that loved the world to the point of self-negation, and wanted to be loved equally back.

Stretched out on the living room couch where he spent most of the last three weeks, he told my good friend, who was reading to him, "I love you, Joyce." He thought further, smiled: "I love all my Mom's girlfriends."

That same period Seth said to him, "God, don't you just hate this," referring to his sedentary state, or maybe the ongoing tedium of the illness (not, I think, to future terrors). And Jesse, on morphine but awake, alert, shrugging: "It's not so bad."

He used to be afraid of death. At times, age eight or nine, he'd curl up on the couch in the den, under a blanket, TV off. He wasn't afraid to talk about being afraid. He was easy to comfort. I told him, yes, he would die, everyone died, but it wouldn't be soon. He was young, his years stretching out and out.

A couple of years later, I asked him if he was still afraid of death, and he said no. He figured that without death, life had no meaning. Really? Where did that idea come from? Him smiling, knowing it was a cool thing.

I think of the woman lucky enough to marry him, the joy of her awareness of the depth of his love for her, a capacity burgeoning the last year of his life. His fascination with her mind, his eagerness to romp with her on the playground of ideas. Nothing in the mind verboten. He said he wasn't sure that Hitler was a sinner. If Hitler believed that Jews were demons or robots, then for Hitler killing them was like killing bad guys. That's what Jesse said. When Hitler learned that Jews were human, he probably "felt so sorry."

His last night I lay beside him in bed reading *When Bad Things Happen to Good People*. The theory didn't soothe me, but I was drawn by the author's personal tragedy, his son dying slowly from age three on up. I read about the country of the afflicted, a place I was determined to avoid. When Jesse made his awful fast gasps (sleeping? is that sleeping?), I thought of the acupuncturist I'd found for him, scheduled for ten the next morning. Ten was not far away.

Better describe his handwriting. On his old homework, turned in and marked *100% but write more clearly*. His letters were small, open in odd places, bouncing off the lines. He made honor roll his last semester, no checks for behavior. No irritated comment: He has trouble staying *on task*. The grades came, A after A after A. Jesse is an outstanding student. A pleasure to have in class. He was working at home then with the teacher mandated by the Chicago Board of Ed for homebound kids. He said with a smile of rue, "They think I'm great when I'm not there."

This Is Not Making Me Happy

Or sad in a good way. I'm sad in a scared and empty way, and haven't you heard enough? Aren't you (you must be) tired of this? I am, in a way that hurts the back of my neck.

Advice

Forget what I said before. Write for yourself, not for other people.

But I fear madness without my audience, my readers, however imaginary.

Hey, anyone out there who's lost, who feels lost, who feels what I feel?

Anyone out there?

I'm the babbler on the subway, lips moving at my reflection in the dark glass. I've lost my boy, anyone seen him?

It's not Jesse lost, it's me, lost without him. I was one of four, the one female in the family photo, my hand on a boy's shoulders, beside Barry behind boy number two. Four seats filled at the restaurant four-top. A carful: two in front, two in back. Four playing Cranium, hearts. We never got to bridge.

Three is stable, but barely.

For stability we build things, plant things, fill photo albums, arrange objects on shelves.

The last day at Camp Simcha, a weekend retreat for bereaved Jewish parents, we planted bushes for our loved ones. Tamped down the dirt. Watered.

There's a lilac bush in the garden outside of Newberry Math and Science Academy that will soon have a plaque with his name. There was a service, the gift of a quilt. Some girls cried. A song played: "I will remember you."

On his bookcase—along with the books he read, one he didn't get to. I bought it for him, read a few pages, hoping he'd pick it up himself— *The Amber Spyglass* by Philip Pullman. The last month he listened to books on tape, went to sleep to *Harry Potter*.

More on his bookcase: Chess trophies. An unwieldy purple-glazed ceramic bowl. Comic books in plastic sheaths. A magnetic toy from the hospital. These things are horrible to me now in their stillness, their refusal to give way to more adult mementos.

Most terrible: Our private "pieta" of his stuffed animals, Teddy—a knit rabbit, premier comfort icon, hero of the "teddy" stories. Teddy lies in the arms of Tigger, gift from his kind and hope-inducing doctor.

Is there a worthy monument? I think of the Vietnam Memorial, winding through its cleft in the earth.

I ordered his photo inset on his "memorial stone" at the cemetery, imagining people gathering round weeping. Even strangers. Even if they're not weeping for him but for a loss of their own. How can anyone help but weep for his luminous face, beaming in the enameled photo over those horrible dates (write it) 1987–2001. People stop, murmur to each other, "Beautiful. Sweet. And he died so young."

Other people's grief for Jesse, my link to them and the world.

Thus pain suddenly lifts. Mind irresponsible, footloose, slipping out from under its burdens. But, no sooner am I situated on the brink of pleasure or just the relief of surcease of pain, than it's back again. Tethered to me like a dog on a short leash, winding around me in tightening circles. Pulls up to the house and leans on the horn. We have a date, babe, did you think I'd forget?

Advice

Keep your date. Embrace what comes, even pain.

Jesse's Hair: A History

Newborn, it's fuzz on my lips. Smells of milk and something sweet, like flowers. (Love the present tense.) Seth's too.

At sixteen months, silky blond curls, color of new pine. Cut it myself. A snippet resides in an envelope labeled First Haircut May '88, J.A.S. I have one for Seth, too, identical.

Ages five, six, darkening. Earth brown, thick and straight, a shag rug, hard in your hand. Sturdy like his body, limbs, mind. He plays soccer, gets knocked around, never cries. First barber cut age seven or eight, for $8 (kids' special) at The Hair Cuttery. He chooses a style from the barbershop catalogue, adult section. The result is nothing like the picture, shaved close to the sides of his head. His head looks scrubbed, face too open and vulnerable. He looks in the mirror, shrugs. On to the next venture.

First round of chemo, Topo-cyclo, two weeks. Hair intact the first week. We think, He's lucky. One of the lucky ones. It starts to fall but leaves a thin layer, lank and fine, pale brown all over his head. I touch gently, so as not to dislodge.

Round two: Adriamycin, in hospital, forty-eight-hour drip. He's bald unto the eyebrows and eyelashes. Even the nose hairs are gone. Nose continually runs. I love his bare scalp, warm to my cheek and lips. Alive and warm.

Remission: in time for his bar mitzvah, June 27, 2000. Hairs sprout, hard prickles all over his scalp. Seth's is long and thick, enough hair for two.

Late summer, an inch of new hair, curly. He looks like a little Jewish boy. At Camp Simcha, two weeks with Hassids and Jewish cancer kids, he learns to love Torah and believe in the Jewish God. He will keep Kosher, place money in the Tsedakah box. His hair is strong and wiry on his scalp; you can grab, yank it. An observant Jew, he won't die.

For school he wants blue hair; a friend (Franco?) dyes it for him. His hair fits with the hair of the other smart eighth grade dissidents: Franco's Mohawk, Nick's crayon red, the gelled lavender peaks all over Seth's head. Jess is sensitive to looks from adults on the street, but bears it (he says) for the school camaraderie. Noticing how style bands you with one group and alienates you from others.

Recurrence, late October. Largest tumor is golfball-sized, operable. Chemo first. Doctors reassure us: Chemo will be light, killing cancer but not hair cells. But doctors are wrong. In three weeks the hair begins to fall. I pat his head. Hair sticks to my hand like cat hair.

Can I quit now?

His last good day. I type with my eyes closed, fingers keyboard punching—he went with Avi and Seth to Dave'n Busters, though he was already peeing blood. No more curly blue hair. He wore a derby hat I bought him for Chanukah. He looked like a Mafia accountant, small, shrewd, bright-eyed. Still animated, interested in his life, going to school, and out after school. At Dave'n Busters they played laser tag, and Jess so tired he could barely move, but he trained that fatigue into focus and got his man, every man, his score twice as high as the next closest. But the next game he lost, got wiped out by his laser-armed enemies, and the day after he was in the hospital with hemoglobin 7, half what it should have been, a wonder he could speak, let alone stand and shoot.

Oh, Jesse

I want other people to miss him, to be affected, hurt, overwhelmed by the loss of him. Nick cries in his room, Meesouk's grades have gone down, my friend Sheryl has upped her Zoloft. Good. Good, good, good.

Advice

You sound angry. You can write your anger.

I Hate

Grocery shopping, the process of selection that I used to love even in Jesse's last days when I thought flax oil or raw organic garlic or taro root ground up and mixed with ginger would start the long process of restoring his health.

I hate buying clothes, remembering the pleasure of buying him something that in his new thin state would look good on him.

I hate airports, remembering the last ride we took, Jesse in a wheelchair scared of a new pain in his chest, and me trying to hide how scared I was. Mom, is a tumor growing in my heart? Your heart, Jess, is loud and strong. On the plane we sat next to each other holding hands and agreed not ever to cry in each other's presence but always to be happy.

I hate Florida, my parents' house on the fifth hole of the golf course that I used to love because of how alive and well we all were there— every year before this last year—radiant in the warm, flowery air and the possibility of fun. The boys learning golf, at sunset hitting balls across the empty fairway. Scowling at bad shots. Ignoring well-meant advice: Keep your head down. Beaming at Grandpa's rare and moderate compliments. Pleased at something well hit, scourging each other with looks of triumph. I'm a better golfer.

I hate other people's young children, especially boys running down aisles at Wrigley Field or skateboarding down Clark Street. I hate mothers with two boys. Remembering driving back in the night after an evening at Sara's house, the boys wanting mother comfort in the back seat, and me glad to oblige, sitting between them with a head on either shoulder, the smell of those two thick beautiful heads of hair, and the feeling of being blanketed, of swimming in boy love.

I hate waking up, feeling something wrong and not knowing; then knowing. Passing the temple. Getting mail from the temple. Getting mail, usually a credit card offer, addressed to Jesse Silesky. His bank statement: quarterly earnings from his bar mitzvah money, $88.27. Finding old medical supplies: a needleless syringe or the red top to a syringe swept out from under the fridge. A prescription bottle for Diflucan, anti-fungal agent, 50 mg., (1) refill, never filled.

And what he said in the hospital as the nurse came in to irrigate his bleeding bladder: "Here's someone with another useless, pain-causing procedure."

I'd fight God if I believed in God. During a "bereavement weekend" at Camp Simcha, a feisty woman in my group said that she and He or She were going to have "a little chat" when she got to heaven. An Orthodox feminist. But my enemy is random chance, a guerillero, a spirit. Shrugs when you ask a question; dissolves when you raise your fist.

I hate the little box of memory. Contents depleting, fading. Or circling—coming back and back, a tightening, strangling rope around you.

Advice

Write what you can't remember.

I Can't Remember

The play of expressions on his face, the sound of his voice. High, low? He's disappearing into his face in his photographs, tapes of his Torah portion, his piano recital (*Für Elise*). Oh, this is frightening. Wanda leaps onto the desk, lands silently, displacing nothing, sdfg,.l; walks across the keyboard. m,;p Down, girl. Wanda was Jesse's cat. Who's the cutest kitty in the world? Jesse said that. Or was it Seth? Sometimes I say it.

Is this enough? It's excruciating, memories fading even as I write them into words that don't call up the boy at all but just the fact of his absence. Alive in me only in the sear of each eroding image, mangy ravens cawing nevermore.

Advice

I'll bet there are things you're afraid to remember. That you don't want to remember.

I don't want to remember that a kid spat on him in pre-school. I'd just walked him in, a little late, stayed to watch him "integrate." He'd run smiling to the jungle gym on which the kid was perched. The teacher made the boy sit down at an empty table. He had an older brother, she tried to explain, who bullied him. I tried not to show her or Jesse how angry I was. And hurt. Hurt, even though Jesse's hurt was mostly surprise, and vanished as he climbed onto the jungle gym.

I don't want to remember Jake. He and Jesse were wrestling, and he bit Jesse's ear. Made it bleed. I still hate Jake, asshole Jake, not for the biting but for the fact that his mother wouldn't let him play with Jesse after that, as if Jesse had incited the violence.

I don't want to remember his voice the last three days of his life, high and breathy, not like him. But it didn't quit. Gallant soul, hardly the breath to speak, and talking, talking, opinions on politics; oh, what did he say that impressed the rabbi and cantor? I sat next to him in bed, facing the visitors and their delight and amusement, their relief at him so sharp and feisty. (He'd rebuked his surgeon for having voted for George Bush.) Don't give flowers in honor of Jesse, or money or cards; just tell me what you remember he said. It makes me ache and feel good at the same time, more root to this plant that will never bloom again, but what a plant! His unpredictable, earnest, witty, joyous, outraged, hurt, scared, terrified, loving, honest, searching ideas and feelings and declarations: "Mother, you're golden inside. Mother, I don't want to die because I don't want to be reincarnated in another family." (Looking me in the eye) "I don't want to have another mother." The afternoon I stopped making him eat mashed-up cloves of garlic (then what can I do? how can I make him well?) he kissed me. "Mom, you're being the good mother again." I still ground up taro root, mixed it with ginger as a poultice for his swollen belly. Sorry, Jess. I know it itches.

I don't want to remember the color of his urine in the tube that led from his bladder to a removable bag, hues from pale pink to bright blood red. Sometimes, between the clots, the liquid was pure golden yellow. A sign of hope, from which hope could be derived, wrung (yield continually lessening). I don't want to remember dumping the bag, rinsing it, red to pale pink to water clear. Or the words of the resident (discountable on account of his inexperience), "He'll be wearing a bag for the rest of his life." The two implications of which—neither do I want to remember.

His last morning he woke up with yellow eyes. I called the doctor. He's been jaundiced for a while. We've noticed that. Oh. Does that mean it's okay? Afraid to ask.

His leg, one of his legs, one only, was swollen. Raise it up, said the doctor. It's already raised. He's lying on the couch. Should I raise it higher? I rubbed his feet, both of them, not looking at his one meaty-looking thigh, massaging in the hospital hand lotion, the new pink squeeze bottle that came with each hospital stay.

His last night, in bed upstairs, he called down to me—"Mom?!" I ran up, led him to the bathroom. He'd pooped in his pants and Yay! Who cares! He'd been constipated. Now his stomach was flatter, his pain less. (Still weak, though. Still talking high and thin, breathing fast and shallow.) I said, "Jess, the pain is gone from your face. You must be feeling better. This is what we've been waiting for. This is the beginning of healing." Me feeling the very slight loosening that might become, if it lasted, relief. And tomorrow the acupuncturist . . . We hadn't tried acupuncture. And he (hoarse but himself), "Don't overdo it, Mom." That his second last speech, ever. His last, interrupting my flow of crazed murmurings, "Jesse the best and sweetest boy that I'll love forever, darling amazing personthing . . ."

"Shhh." He put his arms around me. How can he get well with arms like that? Not looking at his arms. "Good night, Mom."

I don't want to remember . . . But there's nothing I don't want to remember, or feel—not even the pain of the biggest loss, the knowing that what I know now of him is all I'll ever know. I won't see him falling in love, to be dazzled, hurt, and dazzled again. I won't see him furious, tender, amused at the antics of his children. Would he have worked to serve the world or give himself joy, or both? Would he have developed his precocious intimacy with the life of the spirit into something to sit in the shade of? How can I take in that I won't know this—witness, even tend a little—the beauty and wonder of his becoming? His absence, an unredeemable, unfillable hole in things.

Magic

As a child I wanted a doll with shiny red hair and eyes that opened and closed, and instead of asking, since the gift-giving holidays were over, I tried to obtain it through magic. At that point in my life, the wall between life and imagination was full of holes, and I, not fully but almost, believed that if I pictured something hard enough, it could materialize. So I called to mind, sharply, for a good span of time, both the doll and the exact place where the doll would be—on the floor in the den between a certain armchair and our television set. I was at school then, early afternoon. To further ensure the desired outcome, I performed an uncharacteristic and daring act, rising from my desk and circling it three times, unusual for me, normally shy and rule-abiding. (God knows what the teacher thought, if she saw me.) But I came home from school, my heart pounding with hope, and ran to the place where my new doll was supposed to be . . .

And I know, as sure as my eyes are tearing up again (yet again), that I'm writing to make the same magic. To conjure the object of my desiring. If I can sing like Orpheus, I'll get permission to retrieve him from the land of the dead.

I'm not afraid. Abracadabra. Open sesame. I want him back in my house, in his room, at the table eating food I've cooked, fighting with his brother, talking on the phone, drawing his teddy pictures, doing his homework or not doing it, even playing video games, which I discouraged, or upstairs asleep behind the protective wall of his stuffed animals. I can almost see him on the futon in his room, I'm looking in on him, kneeling to kiss his cheek, or maybe just standing there, breathing the air of his sleeping . . .

And feel an absence bigger than the empty place at the table. Get me to a nunnery. Or med school, where I can maybe learn enough to be part of something that might accomplish someday the magic that failed for us. Because—didn't I know before I started?—writing is always about loss, is always a failure, an attempt that must fail, to bring back what can't be brought back. This attempt to memorialize Jesse only points to a double loss. Says Jacques Derrida, "Language, unable to recreate the world, only points to its absence." Abracadabra? If words can't raise the dead, if they can't restore what—if goodness or justice had any sway in the scheme of things—would never have been lost, what's the point of them?

Transformation?

At Camp Simcha the rabbi told us grieving parents to seek, in our grieving, a way to turn loss into something else. He didn't say what else. He did not mention "meaning"; I liked him for that. I think of Mother Jones, who lost her husband and children to yellow fever, then four years later her possessions to the Chicago fire; who spent the rest of her hundred-year life fighting for labor and child welfare.

We are fields cut down to be sown again.

I will not be sown! Acid hot, rocky and dry, I shrivel any seeds that flutter down here. I am so angry that words combust as they mount to my lips. Jesse, where are you? Jesse, do you hear me?! (I'm screaming) Jesse (he was always absent-minded, selectively deaf, upstairs reading or playing Quake), get down here this, this minute!!

Beyond Memoir

A couple of weeks after he died, I dreamed about him. I'd been going to bed in hopes of a dream. Friends had mentioned clear sharp dreams of departed loved ones that were almost "visits." I wanted a visit. In my dream Jess was standing on a sunlit path alongside a house. A white house, nice house. He was smiling at me, a little uncertainly, but smiling. His hair had just started to grow back in little prickly dots all over his skull; the beginning, the return, again, of life. I walked toward him slowly, as if he were a half-wild animal, and stood before him. I didn't touch him. I was afraid he'd disappear. We stood facing each other, beaming at each other, with clear though tentative joy in each other's presence. And I wanted to say something encouraging, health-affirming, like "You look so well, honey," or "Your hair looks really great." But I was afraid to speak, as if something in my words or tone would destroy the frail magic of his presence.

Now I'm back where I started from. I stand before his image, straining, clawing for words, my link to other human beings and myself and sanity. But the words that come lack the essential unpredictability of Jesse, the shimmer that surrounded him that was in part his potential, the becoming he was in the process of. I'm locked in a room with no windows. I'm lost in the shadowy caverns of memory.

Advice

Why limit your writing to what you think actually happened? Embellish. Invent, lie, write fiction. A story that centers on Barry, whom you fault (still fault) for his self-indulgent optimism. Or give Barry's traits to the mother of the sick child; it's she who overlooks the problem's seriousness.

Or you can mimic the voice of your sister in Cleveland, who seems to have it all together but who you know is jealous of you; wouldn't that be fun? In invention lies shimmer!

You can even pretend to be Jesse.

"Untitled"

A soccer morning, cool and sunny. Seth is in the back seat with you, wanting to see your Game Boy. He lost his own and he'll probably lose yours, just put it down somewhere and leave it, or take it apart, or chew on it, leaving teeth marks. "No way, José!"

"You're not even playing it."

"So?" You put the Game Boy under your butt.

He kicks you. You feel it through your shin guards. "Quit that!"

"Quit what?"

He does it again. You know better than to kick back. He'll shriek, and Dad will blame both of you. But the terror Seth can conjure in you— Seth your twin, your second self—like how you feel in the middle of an escape dream in which your legs are weakening, too weak to keep running—has no outlet but violence. You bend your arm, jab in his direction, hard and sharp.

Even before your elbow bone hit flesh, you knew it was a mistake. Frozen, you watch blood gush from his nose. (You were aiming for his ribs; how did his face get in the way?) Blood drips from his chin onto his shirt. He shrieks, "He just killed me!"

"Shut up," you whisper, and hand him the game. He throws it on the floor.

"I'll give you my allowance."

He smears blood onto his hand, wipes it on your soccer shirt.

"Don't," you cry, glad for the retaliation. "Cut it out, Seth!" The shirt is dark blue. The blood hardly shows. But you yell at your brother, for Dad to hear.

Dad drives faster, then pulls to a stop at a gas station. You think, by the stiff back of his neck, that he's going to grab you and Seth by your opposite ears: "Do you want me to knock both of your heads together?" A lame threat, but creepy. But he surprises you. He hands Seth a tissue and lets you climb in front. You and not Seth!

In front, though, in this comfortable seat that leans back, it's not as good as you expected. There's Seth behind you, kicking the back of your seat. You like sitting beside Dad, and you like your small victory over Seth, but Seth hates it; his hate burns the back of your neck. You turn, hoping that by the time your mouth opens you'll have words to fix things a little. He gives you the finger.

You watch the road. And then you remember: After the game you're going to the doctor. You won't be getting a shot, Dad said, but there are things Dad doesn't know; you've noticed that. You think of Mom, two hours away where she's just started teaching. For a second you wish she were here, though she's lots more nervous than Dad and sometimes makes you nervous. She came to your practice yesterday, and you ran at the ball and completely missed, and kids laughed and the coach said, "Earth to Jesse," which she had to have heard. Back home she made you walk up and down the sidewalk to see if something was wrong with your legs. But nothing was wrong with your legs. It's a little hard to breathe, maybe, but maybe not, maybe that's how breathing is. You don't see the point of this doctor appointment except to make Mom feel better. You close your eyes, recline against the seat back. In your mind kids are running around the soccer field in a million pointless directions, kicking balls, bumping into each other, falling down, and you far off away somewhere. It's a new perspective. A little scary.

I wrote this on the computer with my eyes closed, to get it down without experiencing it, like placing an aspirin tablet on the back of one's tongue. Could barely skim it for typos. But I think I see where it might go.

> "I wrote this on the computer with my eyes closed, to get it down without experiencing it."

His last December in Florida, when Bubby yelled at Seth for driving the golf cart into the mailbox, Jesse shed tears for his brother. Jesse, so weak he was in and out of a wheelchair, accosted me, weeping. "Seth feels so bad." At the funeral, Jesse's cousin, who plans to become a rabbi, spoke of the progress of Jesse's soul, that tormented but weirdly blessed final year, Jesse's gentleness and wisdom and humor and courage, "all of that on top of the wildness and wholeness of being and of personality and of spirit. . . ."

Jesse doesn't need to be a sage to make him merit remembrance. But illness was a fire that seemed to purify him. Can I look out from his brightening eyes? What can be seen?

Wanda's back on my lap with her ever polite retraction of claws. You're a sweet cat, Wanda, but I can't type with you here. I lift her to the ground. She jumps back up, and settles in the same place. Purrs aggressively. It buzzes my skin. Alive, alive-o.

So dim the lights. Bring up the background music, *Für Elise*, his last recital piece, played quick and competent, and him afterward suspicious of his teacher's praise combating his own shame at his two or three goofs. His face, screwed with self-disgust but eager to eat her cookies, laugh at someone, preparing to be happy again.

His beautiful, sad, smiling face.

Rory Stewart

The Missionary Dance

Rory Stewart is the author of two books of creative nonfiction: *The Places in Between* (2004), about his experiences from 2000 to 2002 walking six thousand miles on foot alone across Afghanistan, Pakistan, India, and Nepal; and *The Prince of the Marshes* (2006), about his service as deputy governor in the Marsh Arab region of Iraq in 2003. His work is both deeply personal and politically aware. A *New York Times* reviewer said that Stewart "writes with a mystic's appreciation of the natural world, a novelist's sense of character and a comedian's sense of timing."

Stewart, who speaks Farsi, Indonesian, Urdu, and Nepali, was born in Hong Kong and grew up in Malaysia. He served briefly as an officer in the British Army, studied at Oxford, and then joined the British diplomatic service. He worked in the British Embassy in Indonesia and, in the wake of the Kosovo campaign, as the British representative in Montenegro. In 2003, he became the coalition deputy governor of Maysan and Dhi Qar, two provinces in the Marsh Arab region of Southern Iraq. His government service provided him the opportunity to get to know the Iraqi people, as he, like others, realized the futility and damage of imposing outside rule. In 2004, he was awarded the Order of the British Empire and became a Fellow of the Carr Centre at Harvard University. He now lives in Kabul, Afghanistan, where he is the chief executive of the Turquoise Mountain Foundation, which is investing in the regeneration of the historic commercial center of Kabul, providing basic services, saving historic buildings, and constructing a new bazaar and galleries for traditional craft businesses.

The selection we have chosen is from *The Places in Between*.

As I turned away from the domes an old man rode up on a white horse decorated with a finely woven saddlecloth colored with soft vegetable dyes. The horse was bony and lame and he rode it timidly. He looked as though he was wearing not a turban but a barber's basin on his head.

"I," he said, "am Khalife Seyyed Agha, son of Haji Khalife Seyyed Ahmed, direct heir and descendant of Hazrat Maulana Sultan Maududi, the saint of Chist who died in 1132. My ancestor is buried beneath that dome. I am the lord of all the land that you can see."

"So you are the head of the Chistiyah dervishes?"

"I am but there are no dervishes living here anymore. Can you draw a picture of my horse?"

"I'll try." It was cold in the snow and my hands were stiff, but my drawing looked like a horse. A younger man joined us and stood silently watching.

"Can I keep your drawing?" asked the old man.

"Okay." I ripped it out of my notebook and gave it to him.

"I like your sunglasses. Can I try them on?"

I handed them over and he hung them on his long nose. "Excellent. Can I keep them?"

"No, I'm sorry, I need them. I am walking through the snows of Bamiyan—I need them for the glare."

"Please."

"I am sorry."

"Just the sunglasses . . ."

"I'm sorry."

"A pity; I might have offered you hospitality." The patriarch turned and rode off. The Chistiyah dervishes were once famous for refusing gifts.

The young man laughed. "He is nothing now. His ancestors were great Chistiyah teachers, men of mystical power and great lords. There are no Chistiyah here today. He was too scared to fight the Russians, too scared to fight the Northern Alliance, too scared to fight the Taliban. He has done nothing in twenty-four years; I had almost forgotten that he existed. He is lucky that we haven't taken all his land."

Only hints remained of why this local Sufi sect (called Chistiyah because they came from Chist) had been one of the four most powerful dervish orders in the world. Surviving descriptions suggest they had a great deal in common with other mystics, even non-Muslim mystics. They repeated sacred phrases and used rosaries like Hindus, Buddhists, and Christians, who may have encountered Sufis during the Crusades. Their saints talked of being able to see the ultimate oneness of God and they drowned details of religious doctrine in a transcendental fervor, seemingly intoxicated with an almost erotic love of the deity.

But they also differed from other mystics in very particular ways. It was not just that one of their saints, Baba Farid, prayed suspended by his feet for forty days, or that, with the distinguished exception of Amir Khosrow, the Chistiyah wrote little poetry. Nor was it their theological views on *walaya* (the spiritual authority of the Prophet) and *welaya* (divine love). Nor was it that they carried a toothbrush attached to their turban and wore four-cornered conical hats. What made the Chistiyah most famous was their music. Whereas some dervishes achieved mystical union by praying and others by walking or whirling, the Chistiyah did so by playing instruments and dancing.

The Ghorids brought their local sect with them when they invaded India, adding some legitimacy to a military action presented as a jihad. They may have built the domes to honor this association. But Juzjani, who chronicled the Ghorid dynasty, suggests that the dervishes were not acceptable to all Muslims. As a judge, he presided over a complaint made about a ceremony called Sama, in which the Chistiyah brought on religious ecstasy by dancing and playing music. Juzjani found in favor of the Chistiyah saint,[1] who died in ecstasy during one of these performances a little later. A Chistiyah saint[2] born in the thirteenth century records that these Sama sessions lasted throughout the night. They were led by male singers reciting Persian poetry and accompanied by drums, timbales, and tambourines, but not string or wooden instruments because these "blocked the taste and pain of the mystic." Hindus were allowed to attend and everyone was encouraged to dance and sing. Later descriptions showed how disturbing these practices must have been to the orthodox.

The disciple of this saint[3] stressed that the visitation of the unseen in the Sama dance ceremony should be considered a form of lovemaking. Sama must happen at night, not in a mosque but in a closed hall, perfumed with sandalwood. Garments may be torn or thrown off in ecstasy. The dancing could overcome you as a feeling of uncontrollable agitation, it could develop into a feeling of total harmony, or it could be assimilated by conforming to the other dancers:

> "Once again I was looking at evidence of a very different society and a very different Islam from what existed on the same site today."

> The Sufi may go round in circles in ecstasy, leap about, beat the ground in his place with his feet or lift his hands over his head, twisting them together and rotating them before bringing them down again.

The lavish domes make clear that the Ghorids had a particular affection for this dancing sect.[4] It was a relationship they advertised by placing the domes so visibly at the entrance to their lands and engraving them with long passages from the Koran. Was this their answer to the Arabs and Seljuks who had mocked the obscure province of Ghor as one of the last pagan enclaves in the Persian world? Once again I was looking at evidence of a very different society and a very different Islam from what existed on the same site today.

The police chief at Chist had a generator, a VCR, and a black-and-white television. Twenty of us gathered to watch filmed dancing. He handed me

[1]Qutb-al-Din Baktiar Kaki.

[2]Nezam Al-Din Aulia.

[3]Gisuderaz.

[4]Not much, however, is known about their relationship. I found a myth in India of how a great Chistiyah saint walked through Multan and Lahore in the late twelfth century and, reaching Ajmer, appeared to the Ghorid prince in a dream saying, "Arise, the land of India is yearning to kiss your feet and the crown and throne await you there," encouraging the Ghorid to conquer all of India. Muinuddin Chisti Sanjari went from Multan (which they conquered in 1175) to Lahore (1186) and then to Ajmer (where they held their decisive battle in 1193). The saint's march into India seemed to pass through the cities the Ghorids conquered and in the order in which they conquered them. It suggested at least that the military conquerors supported the work of missionaries and then were in turn encouraged by the missionaries. The conquest was a jihad, a holy war, and both warriors and saints were required.

the cassette sleeve, which showed a girl in a red sequined minidress with thigh-high boots. But when he switched on the video, the star was an overweight middle-aged woman in a puffy ballgown dancing in a tent in Peshawar. To the delight of rows of Afghan men seated on the floor, she had released her hair and bared her forearms. The film was shot in the dark by a man with unsteady hands, but he had captured most of her scowls. She danced by hopping stiffly up and down with her hands on her hips. Disappointed perhaps with her sloppy footwork, the cameraman zoomed in on her enormous breasts, which lurched from side to side as they filled the frame.

"Was there dancing here before?" I asked.

"Not in Chist, but we used to have it in Herat and Kabul when the king was in power," replied the police chief. "There was less with Najib because of the war. The Mujahidin stopped it completely."

"The Taliban?"

"No. Ismail Khan and the Northern Alliance stopped it as well. It is forbidden in Islam."

"Do you like dancing?"

"Me?" said the police chief. "I like it very much." Everyone laughed.

I sat down and wrote a long letter to my parents, in case I was killed. In the past sixteen months I had bribed, flattered, pried, bullied, begged, and wheedled in order to continue my walk. I was more of a tramp than a mystic, but as I wrote I felt at peace. I described to my parents the moments on the way that seemed to have a deep, unified relation to my past. I wondered if walking was not a form of dancing.

I was happy then and I slept well.

Sheryl St. Germain

Nigger: Notes from a New Orleans Daughter

Sheryl St. Germain is a prolific author of creative nonfiction and poetry whose work often examines questions of place and self. *Swamp Songs: The Making of an Unruly Woman*, a memoir about growing up in New Orleans, was published in 2003. She has written many books of poetry; her *New and Selected Poems* will be published by Autumn House Press in 2008. Her awards include fellowships from the National Endowment of the Arts and the National Endowment for the Humanities. She currently directs the MFA creative writing program at Chatham College in Pittsburgh, where she teaches poetry and creative nonfiction.

Of *Swamp Songs*, *Publishers Weekly* wrote: "St. Germain's passionate commitment to place is the lens through which she conveys the specialness of growing up in the Louisiana swampland, where Christmas celebrations, amusement parks, meals and even fishing are as ordained by the landscape as hurricanes . . . and Mardi Gras. St. Germain succeeds in simultaneously offering a sensitive memoir and an homage to Louisiana's swamps, the people who dwell near them and New Orleans."

Although St. Germain now lives in Pennsylvania, Hurricane Katrina has turned her eye again to her childhood home. The piece we've included is from St. Germain's forthcoming *Navigating Disaster*, a collection of essays exploring the flooding of New Orleans from the highly personal perspective of a daughter of that city. The essay was first published in the *Iowa Review*.

Interview with Sheryl St. Germain, p. 696.

> I saw cotton and I saw black
> Tall white mansions and little shacks.
> Southern man when will you pay them back?
> —*Neil Young, "Southern Man"*

I have been asked to write something about race and New Orleans, the assumption being that I know something about race and New Orleans since I was born and raised in that city. It is, I think, a somewhat false assumption, but one I have faced often since I moved away from Louisiana as an adult and found myself living in the rural Midwest. The farther south you are, the common wisdom goes, the more racist you are, and now look at all these photographs and images from Katrina. Doesn't it prove what everyone always suspected, that New Orleans is the worst of the worst?

No matter that the abstract for my Iowa house reproduces twice (once when the home was sold in the 1930s and again in the 1940s), the original owner's apparently legal directive that no black buy or live in the home. No matter that the city council in Galesburg, Illinois, where I lived for several years, voted down about eight years ago—unanimously and without discussion—a resolution that would have made it illegal to discriminate against renters because of their sexual preferences; no matter that my neighbors in Illinois stopped speaking to me when I openly dated a black man; no matter that the Illinois policeman who helped the kids in my son's school cross the street confided in me one day about how unhappy he was regarding the *niggers* who had moved in down the street; in the minds of the general public, and even some of my colleagues at the non-southern universities and colleges where I have taught, race is primarily a southern problem.

The southern rock band Lynyrd Skynyrd famously responded to Canadian Neil Young's accusations of racism in his "Southern Man" with a song of their own, "Sweet Home Alabama": "Well, I hope Neil Young will remember/a southern man don't need him around anyhow." Their critique was for his sweeping generalization; Young's song seems to suggest that all southerners are racist. Both songs have become popular emblems of either side of the race dispute, and have an eerie personal connection for me as well. Neil Young, the liberal intellectual's singer songwriter, was a favorite of mine, and Lynyrd Skynyrd, the working class, whiskey-drinking group, was my brother André's favorite band.

André died unexpectedly a few weeks before Katrina hit. Like many New Orleans working class men of his generation—he was born in 1964—he died conflicted about issues of race. My brother was clearly prejudiced against blacks; my mother called him racist and fought with him bitterly about his views, but the man who cried most at my brother's funeral, the man André paid well to work for him for ten years in the small body shop he owned, the man who was one of his favorite drinking companions, was a black man.

Things are not always what they seem, and often are more complicated than they seem. It turns out Neil Young was a big Skynyrd fan. Skynyrd's lead singer Ronnie Van Zant wore a Neil Young shirt on stage during the last two years of his life and supposedly was wearing one when he died. Van Zant grew up in Shantytown, a ghetto on the west side of Jacksonville, one of the few parts of town that wasn't segregated. In response to charges of racism in the band's lyrics, he said "We're southern rebels, but more than that, we know the difference between right and wrong."

* * *

I was born and raised a white woman in a city that is almost seventy percent black. The black culture had a profound influence on me. Mostly food and music, but food and music are religions in New Orleans, and are still twin gods of my sky. I grew up with a mother who loved music, especially music with soul, so my spiritual teachers were Mahalia Jackson, Sydney Bechet, Louis Armstrong, Irma Thomas, Clarence Gatemouth Brown and Professor Longhair, among others. The gumbo we ate every Sunday is unimaginable without the African contributions of okra and cayenne; indeed the word *gumbo* comes from *gombo*, the African word for okra. I learned, from the listening, watching and cooking I did as a young woman a certain *way* of being in the world, a way that respected things sensual, a way that was unafraid of speaking or singing sorrow, a way that saw a certain kind of cooking or singing as a way to transcendence. And I have brought all of what I learned from the listening of New Orleans blues, jazz and gospel and the making of gumbos and jambalayas and red beans and rice to the making of poems and essays. I am what I am, for better or worse, as a writer, at least partly because of what I learned from the black culture of New Orleans.

> "I am what I am, for better or worse, as a writer, at least partly because of what I learned from the black culture of New Orleans."

Louis Armstrong famously signed his letters "red beans and ricely yours," and the smell of red beans cooking still brings to mind his gravelly voice, the sound of sloppy jazz and the sense of triumph over adversity. Red beans and rice was the poor man's dish, and poor we were. My mother cooked beans and rice, spiced with cayenne and seasoned with salt pork, several times a week. About twenty years ago, when I was a budding poet, I sent a poem to Rita Dove for a journal she was editing. The poem, called "Mother's Red Beans and Rice," was written around my mother's inventive ways of cooking red beans during a time when money was scarce, and involved her putting not only onions, green pepper and salt pork in with the beans, but also her blood, her sorrow at the troubled marriage she had made, and her lost desire for the man she never married.

"We're filled up for that journal," Rita Dove wrote back, "but I'm also an editor for *Callaloo.* Would you allow me to publish your poem there?"

I knew *Callaloo* published only writers of color. Maybe they'd changed the rules, I thought. Maybe *Callaloo* was now accepting work from whites. It was a fine journal.

"Great," I wrote back. "Go ahead."

Two weeks later she wrote back again (these were the days before email) to say she had a delicate question to ask. She had assumed I was black. Was I?

My heart sunk. I was still a young poet lusting for publication.

"No," I wrote back. "I'm not black."

The letter I wrote her was a long one in which I elaborated on the importance of New Orleans' black culture to me. I went on at length about music and food and such. She published the poem in *Tri Quarterly.*

What I didn't tell her in my long letter was that I also came from a family of racists. I didn't tell her that of my entire extended family only my mother was not racist. I didn't tell her that my father, who was manager of a New Orleans bowling alley, had forced a black couple to leave in the early sixties when they tried to enter. Or that my younger sister, who had witnessed this drama, had saved it as a treasured memory of our father as a hero. I didn't tell her about my Catholic aunt who prayed the rosary every day but complained about the *niggers around the block.* I didn't tell her about my deaf-mute Cajun grandparents who thought it amusing to name their black cat *nigger.* I didn't tell her that I had learned, from these grandparents, their sign for *nigger.* It was very like the sign we had learned for *dirty*—you crook your index finger and drag it underneath your nose. I didn't tell her, because it hadn't happened yet, that everyone in the family outside of my mother and myself would vote for David Duke when he ran for governor. I didn't tell her that my family, whose roots go back two hundred years in Louisiana, had owned a working plantation, and slaves. I didn't tell her that while doing genealogical research I had found an inscription on a tombstone stating that no black person might be buried in that ground, and I didn't tell her about the hatred that sometimes shaped my people.

I come from a working class family. Neither my father nor my mother went to college. My father was an alcoholic who died of cirrhosis. There are many other drunks, addicts, and criminals in my family. I am a memoirist, and had no trouble writing about the drunks and criminals when I wrote my memoir *Swamp Songs,* about growing up in New Orleans. But race was another matter. It seemed such a huge thing, and I didn't know how to introduce it into the familial story of self-destruction and salvation I wanted to tell without having it dominate the whole thing.

When my great uncle agreed to be interviewed by me a few years ago for *Swamp Songs,* we spent a wonderful day talking. My uncle is an amateur singer with a rich and velvety voice, though it has become somewhat thinned with age. He sang *Too-Ra-Loo-Ra-Loo-Ra* for me, told me stories about the Korean war that made me cry, and stories about my mother as a girl that made me laugh. But after six hours of taping, he started in with the *niggers and the jews* and how they had "ruined" New Orleans. I immediately stopped taping, and excused myself to go to the bathroom. I sat in the bathroom, looking at the walls, knowing I could not write the story I had wanted to write.

I never listened to the tape and I never wrote about any of the stories my great uncle told me. I would have to figure out how to write a family story that included race some other time, I told myself.

It's difficult for me to talk about race specifically with respect to Katrina because there was so much personal family grief and tragedy surrounding the hurricane: the unexpected death of a brother, the destruction of my brother's home as well as that of two of my uncles, including the elderly uncle who sang *Too-Ra-Loo-Ra-Loo-Ra*, the displacement of my mother for a month, and the damage to her home.

I went home to New Orleans after Katrina and just before Rita to help my mother. I learned to use a chainsaw to cut up the fallen trees, helped put a tarp up on her roof, and moved the black bags filled with rotting food to the front yard where the city would pick them up some weeks later. I saw and smelled with my own eyes and nose the devastation.

In the evenings my mother and I watched, over and over, the images that were still being shown of the mostly black families trapped on the tops of houses; we watched the torture that seemed to go on forever of the poor families who could not afford to evacuate and had to suffer the slow response of the government. It was at once surreal and familiar, like the times when I was much younger and we used to watch scary movies together late at night, only this time I was not comforted, as I had been as a child, by my mother's presence and by the sense that all the scary stuff would go away when we turned off the television.

We watched, we witnessed, we took it in.

When I was first born my family was poor, and we lived on the edge of the ninth ward in New Orleans, the area that suffered deeply from the floods of Katrina. A few years ago, when I was writing the memoir, I wanted to go with my mother to see the house where we used to live.

"Oh Sheryl," she said, "that neighborhood is all black now," as if that settled the question. This from a woman I would not consider a racist. This from a woman who had said to me, when I was seeing a black man, "He will always be welcome in my home. I don't know what your brother will think, but I will welcome him."

I could have challenged my mother on her comment about the neighborhood, but instead I went by myself. The truth is my mother is old, New Orleans has a murder rate that is one of the highest in the nation, and my mother knows that these areas are not safe ones for women of any color to travel alone. My mother is not so unlike many other white New Orleanians who love their city and are well-meaning, but who are sometimes at odds with themselves about the question of race. We are not all racists, but my mother's generation of working class whites were mostly raised by racists, and they had to find their own way out of that jungle. Sometimes, having had no meaningful mentorship, they stumble, sometimes they get lost, but they often find the way again.

My mother is proud of being from New Orleans; she owns a fantastic collection of New Orleans books and music—mostly black musicians—and she goes to Mardi Gras, the Jazz Fest and indeed most of the festivals celebrating the culture every year, and has for the last seventy-five years. She has a sometimes irritating pride in the city. I can see now that not only is she in mourning for our birth city, but that she has had something stripped away in her by having had to witness this festering wound at the heart of a city she loves so much, this wound that houses the culture of the city, its blues and jazz and spicy food, its colorful personality. She can't say, as she did so many years ago, oh Sheryl, it's all black, let's not go, because it's there, every day, in the papers and on the television for everyone to see.

My mother didn't much like it when I wrote about the criminals and alcoholics in our family, and she is as shaken now seeing the city's hypocrisy exposed in such a public way. I don't wish my mother, who is old and frail, to suffer, but I am of the opinion that truth is a good thing, no matter how much it hurts. What about the children, she asked when I published my memoir. Indeed, what about the children? Don't we owe our children the truth?

New Orleans has always been a city of extremes, beginning with its location at the very end of the Mississippi, the very bottom of the bottom of the United States. It is already losing almost thirty square miles of land a year due to environmental degradation, so it's not an exaggeration to say it's falling off the edges of the country. Its people have always seemed larger than life, their appetites for food, drink, music, sex and fun, not to mention drugs, violence and murder genuinely spectacular. The drama and devastation of Hurricane Katrina is so surrealistically, unbelievably extreme, however, that it seems to me to have crossed some line, and to have rendered New Orleans and their inhabitants, almost, as freaks in a freak show.

> "We are all New Orleanians."

The reason we like to go to freak shows is because there is such a clear differentiation between the freaks and us. If *they* are the freaks, *we* are not. We need to resist the temptation to see New Orleans and New Orleanians as freakish. We need to see that there is much of the heart and soul of our country that resides in this city, and that it is, in some ways, a microcosm for what goes on in the rest of our country.

We are all New Orleanians. We are all racists to some extent, we are all responsible for the housing conditions in New Orleans, and we are *all* responsible for the slow response of our government to the floods. We elected the government that led the response.

✳ ✳ ✳

When I left my mother after Rita, she said goodbye to me with tears in her eyes, and stuttered out something I never thought I would ever hear her say, indeed it seemed as if she was speaking another language, one she hardly knew.

"I think, maybe, Sheryl," she said, "I mean I don't think, those poor people, they've lost everything, I can't complain. . . ."

She looked around at her ruined living room, carpet ripped up, the books swollen with water, the moldy furniture, the boarded up windows.

"I think I might have to move away from New Orleans. I don't think I can take another hurricane." She gave me a hug and pushed me out the door, as if she didn't want me to think about what she had said too much.

I hope my mother doesn't move. I hope everyone who has left—and some estimates put that, at this writing, at eighty percent of the city—returns. I hope that we find some way of looking bravely and responsibly at this situation we have caused, and that we find some way of not being blinded by the sight of the gaping wounds and flaws of this laboring beast of a city.

At my brother's funeral my entire family was in mourning and still in a bit of shock; preceded in death by my father and another brother, André was the third of the men in our immediate family to have died a young and unexpected death. My sister and I had no father and now we had no more brothers. We had no way of knowing the gods were not finished with us, that Katrina would pay us a visit in a few weeks.

Andy, my brother's black employee and friend, was the first to arrive at the funeral, and the last to leave. He was the only black present, and seemed mostly lost in his own sorrow, crumpled off to the side, sobbing, during most of the service. It was my sister, my racist sister, who, seeing his grief, walked up to him and held and kissed him for what seemed like a long time, holding his face, looking into his eyes. I was too far away to hear what they were saying, but I could see they were both crying.

Andy wasn't invited afterwards for gumbo, beer and a ritual playing of André's favorite Lynyrd Skynyrd songs.

Interview with Sheryl St. Germain

BECKY BRADWAY: Could you discuss any particular difficulties involved in interpreting a widely covered "news event" (Hurricane Katrina and its effects) from your own point of view?

SHERYL ST. GERMAIN: In the case of Katrina, visual imagery dominated the news coverage, and in particular, the same visual images, shown over and over again, skewed what the actual story was in New Orleans. When I sat down to write my family's story, I knew, first of all, that I wanted the writing to do something that the visual images could not. It's one thing to get information and images from the television; it's quite another to tell a story such that the reader takes a particular meaning and value away from that story. I knew that I didn't want to tell the "big" story because the media had done a pretty good job getting the big story out. I wanted to focus on the personal, the actual experience of my family. And I wanted to tell the story in an intimate way so that the reader felt the story. Big stories covered in the news sometimes lose the ability to move us because the television screen objectifies and renders abstract even the most moving stories by the fact that the screen compartmentalizes and protects us from intimacy with the people who are most affected by the catastrophe. Good writing does the opposite: it cultivates a sense of intimacy with the writer.

Unless you're writing journalism, you can't write about the big news event, but you can focus on something small that gets you deeper into the event. For example, instead of the loss of the city of New Orleans, I might write about the way my mother was worried about losing my brother's ashes, which were stored in her house as the water rose during the levee breaks of Katrina, or about her wedding rings, a box of letters from her dead mother, books she loved more than anything in the world, all with the potential to be destroyed by the rising water.

In short, the main thing is to tell your own story and to focus on the small things that are meaningful to you. In telling your own story as truthfully as you can, and by focusing on the objects that have meaning for you, you will effectively bring the reader into the larger context that the media may have already covered, but your narrative may be the one the reader remembers because you have not just given them facts, but a story.

BB: It's rather controversial for a white person to write about race at this time. How did you think through your approach in portraying this politically sensitive topic?

SSG: As I mention in the essay, I had *not* written about race in my memoir, and it bothered me. On some level I knew that I was going to have to address the topic of racism at some point, but I just didn't know how to do it in the context of a larger narrative. Members of my family are not just racists; some of them are loving fathers and mothers, and sometimes they belie their own racism, as my sister does in this piece. I felt that the issue was more complicated than we sometimes allow for, and I felt a bit cowardly for not having addressed it before. I had also learned through years of living in the rural Midwest where hardly anyone ever talks about race, that white or black, you don't get anywhere if you never talk about it. Just because Midwesterners where I used to live didn't talk about it doesn't mean it didn't exist there—far from it. I also felt that I needed to speak up for all the times others in my family did not. I think there are lots of white people writing about race these days and thinking more deeply, not only about what it might mean to be black in America, but what it means to be white. Whatever color we are, we need to be able to speak frankly about what needs to be said, and in important matters such as race we should not censor ourselves, especially if we feel our stories have something worthwhile to communicate to others.

BB: Did you have any qualms about using this title? How do you tend to come upon your titles, generally?

SSG: I was concerned about the title, but I wanted to be upfront about what kind of material the reader was going to find in the essay. Often when people are talking about matters of race, they tiptoe around words like the one I use for the title. This was a word I grew up with, it was a word I hated, but one that I heard all the time, and it seemed to me important to say the word. Using the word in the title clues the reader in, I hope, to the frank voice they will hear in the essay.

I don't usually title an essay until I've finished a good draft of it, and then I usually go through several different working titles as I revise the essay and find out what it's really about. When I start an essay I have a feeling about what I want to do, but it's not until I find the title that I really know how to make the final revisions on an essay. The early working titles are usually much broader and descriptive than the final titles. I try to end up with a title that goes beyond the merely descriptive; I want titles that are dynamic and that interact with the story in some way. I want to seduce the reader with the title, but I don't want to mislead the reader. The title has to provoke and excite the reader to read the essay, but it also has to live up to itself. The title has to deserve the essay, and the essay has to deserve the title.

And, finally, the last thing I want a title to do is to tell too much: "How I feel about race and New Orleans" is not only a boring title, but it leaves nothing to the imagination. A title needs to have a tiny bit of mystery.

BB: Did you experience any particular challenges when you were casting your family members as characters in the piece?

SSG: It's never easy to write about family because it's hard to capture the full spirit of a real person in a short piece. So it's a translation of a person that rarely fully satisfies, because you know what's not there. It's also difficult because no matter how you write about someone else, it's always your story about them, not theirs, and they are often not happy about how you portrayed them, even if you believe you've portrayed them in a positive light. I try to only tell stories that involve my family that have something to offer a reader. If I know that a family member may be hurt by what I have written, I have to be willing to accept the consequences for my words, and I had better be sure that the hurt I may have caused them is offset by what the piece might offer readers.

Craig Thompson

From *Blankets*

Craig Ringwalt Thompson was born in 1975 on the outskirts of Traverse City, Michigan, and raised in "a homogenous farming community in central Wisconsin." His interest in comic books developed later than most ("I loved comics as a kid, but I don't know if I necessarily loved them any more than all the other crap I was into"); it wasn't until his first years of college with the publications of Mike Allred's *Madman* and Jeff Smith's *Bone* that he began to seriously consider the comics medium as a future career. "A friend invited me to do a comic strip for the college newspaper, and as I tried that out, I just kind of fell in love with [comics], suddenly," said Thompson in a 2004 interview with Karin Kross. "It filled all my needs—I was able to draw cartoons, to tell a story; but I also had total control, and I wasn't just a cog in some machine somewhere."

His first graphic novella, *Good-Bye, Chunky Rice* (1999), tells the story of the diminutive turtle Chunky Rice who leaves his home and best friend (a tricycle-riding mouse by the name of Dandel) in search of something never quite specified. It is simply his time to move on, and so he does, and this idea of "leaving the nest" for the bigger, unsafe outside world is echoed in Thompson's life itself. He later went on to publish the mini-comics *"Bible Doodles"* (2000) and *"Doot Doot Garden"* (2001). His work-in-progress, *Habibi*, tackles Islamic mythology and Arabic themes. When asked why he was trepidatious about dealing with the material in *Habibi*, Thompson replied, "It's more so the sensitivity of, well, what right do I have to play with this material? Obviously when you're doing autobio, nobody can give you grief for that, because it's your own story. But I had a lot of trepidation with *Blankets,* too—would it come off as egocentric and not accessible, and kind of pathetic. I liked having the challenge."

Blankets is a graphic memoir centered around Thompson's childhood in an Evangelical Christian family, his first love, and his early adulthood. The novel grew out of a simple idea: to describe what it feels like to sleep next to someone for the first time. It swept several national book awards the year following its publication, winning three Harvey awards (*Best Artist*, *Best Graphic Album of Original Work* and *Best Cartoonist*), two Eisner awards (*Best Graphic Album* and *Best Writer/Artist*), and two Ignatz awards (*Outstanding Artist* and *Outstanding Graphic Novel or Collection*). It was also banned from the Marshall (Missouri) Public Library from October 11, 2006, to March 14, 2007, when the library's board of trustees voted to return it to the library's shelves.

Our selection from *Blankets* comes near the end of the book, after Craig has fallen in love, left the faith, experienced rejection, and begun to find his path.

uh....

What about the A.C.T.s?

Why?

Why?! For college! You can't get into any college if you don't get passing marks on those tests.

I'm taking the A.C.T. for the third time this Saturday.

College is our ticket out of this town.

GRADUALLY, HE'D REALIZE WHAT HE'D KNOWN AS A HUMAN WAS MERELY THE SHADOW OF A STATUE OF A HUMAN.

I've so many PRESSURES--with the divorce, and taking care of Sarah and Laura, and still crossing my fingers that I'll graduate; and a long distance relationship is just one more RESPONSIBILITY.

WHAT AN EVEN GREATER SHOCK IT WOULD BE TO BRING THE PRISONER OUT OF THE CAVE AND INTO THE SUN-LIGHT. THE INITIAL EFFECT WOULD BE BLINDING.

So ... you're saying?

And slowly the snow began to melt.

First, doing a number on childrens' constructions;

Then retreating to the foundations of barns and other buildings.

Mangy grass poked through the receding snow.

Patches of white were swallowed up in the till of the fields.

New shapes emerged.

Areas of the forest became INACCESSIBLE now that the snow no longer weighed down the weeds and brier.

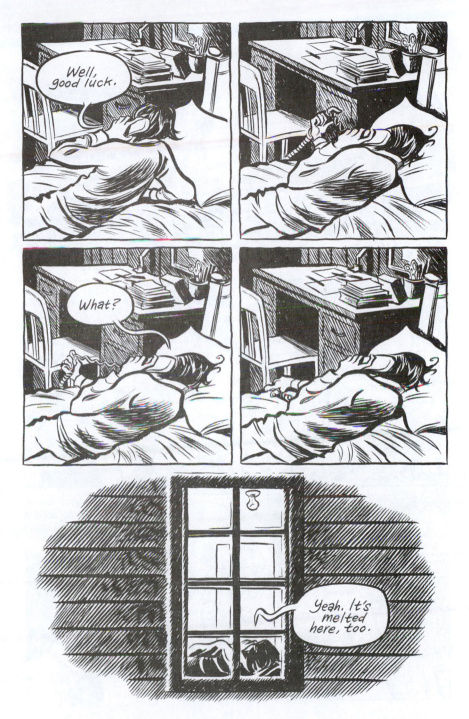

Touré

What's Inside You, Brother?

Touré has written three books: *The Portable Promised Land* (2003), a collection of short stories; *Soul City* (2004), a magical realist novel about life in an African American Utopia; and *Never Drank the Kool-Aid* (2006), a collection of his writing from *Rolling Stone,* the *New Yorker,* the *New York Times,* the *Village Voice,* the *Believer, Playboy, Tennis Magazine,* and others, published between 1994 and 2005.

In 1992 Touré dropped out of college and became an intern at *Rolling Stone*. He was fired after a few months "for being a terrible intern" (he says), but weeks later was asked to write record reviews and then feature stories. His first feature was about Run-DMC. Since 1997 he has been a contributing editor at *Rolling Stone,* where he has written cover stories about Alicia Keys, 50 Cent, Eminem, Beyonce, DMX, Lauryn Hill, and Jay-Z. He has often evoked the participatory journalism of Tom Wolfe and George Plimpton, for example, in pieces depicting the author playing high-stakes poker with Jay-Z, two-on-two basketball with Prince, one-on-one basketball with Wynton Marsalis, tennis with Jennifer Capriati, or writing illegal graffiti with known graffiti artists.

In 1996, "upset that a feature story he'd written for the *New Yorker* was rejected," he enrolled in the graduate school for creative writing at Columbia University to learn more about nonfiction. He took a fiction writing class and his career took a turn when he "wrote a story about a black saxophonist in Harlem named Sugar Lips Shinehot who loses the ability to see white people." His second story, called "A Hot Time at the Church of Kentucky Fried Souls and the Spectacular Final Sunday Sermon of the Right Revren Daddy Love," won an award from *Zoetrope: All Story,* and Touré embarked on a fiction career.

In 2004 he became CNN's first pop culture correspondent, covering the Oscars and the Grammys and doing a recurring segment on American Morning called "90 Second Pop." In 2005 he left CNN and became a correspondent for Black Entertainment Television (BET).

The piece we've included here was published in Touré's book *Never Drank the Kool-Aid* and was included in *Best American Essays 1999*. It's the most experimental nonfiction of Touré's that we've run across.

You ache with the need to convince yourself that you do exist in the real world, that you're a part of all the sound and anguish, and you strike out with your fists, you curse and you swear to make them recognize you.
—*Ralph Ellison,* Invisible Man

From outside the circle of spandexed actresses jumping rope, their ponytails bouncing politely, Body & Soul appears to be a boxing gym rated G. But push through the circle, past the portly, middle-age lawyers slugging through leg lunges and past the dumpy jewelry designers, wearing rouge, giggling as they slap at the speed bag. Keep pushing into the heart of the circle, toward the sound of taut leather pap-papping against bone, toward the odor of violence, and, as often as not, you'll find two men sparring, their fists stuffed into blue or red or black Everlast gloves, T-shirts matted down by hot perspiration, heavy breaths shushed through mouthpieces, moving quick and staccato and with tangible tinges of fear as they bob and weave and flick and fake, searching for a taste of another man's blood.

Sometimes Touré will be in the heart of the circle, maybe sparring with Jack, hands up, headgear laced tight, lungs heavy, ribs stinging after Jack backs him into a corner and slices a sharp left uppercut through Touré's elbows into the soft, very top section of his stomach. Then, for Touré, time stops. He loses control of his body, feels briefly suspended in air, his thoughts seemingly hollered to him from far away. Life is never faster than in the ring, except when you're reeling from a razing punch. Then, life is never slower. Sometimes Touré will be in the heart of the circle sparring, but I don't know why: he's not very good.

> "Being a lousy fighter is far different from sucking at, say, tennis."

I've known Touré a long, long time—you could say we grew up together. He's just over five feet ten inches and about one hundred sixty pounds. That's one inch taller and a few pounds lighter than the legendary middleweight Marvelous Marvin Hagler. Touré, however, has neither long arms to throw punches from a distance, which minimizes vulnerability, nor massive strength to chop a man down with a few shots. He has the stamina to stay fresh through five and occasionally six rounds, yet after four years of boxing he still lacks the weapons to put a boxer in real danger, and that puts him in danger. Being a lousy fighter is far different from sucking at, say, tennis. So, if he's not good, why does he continue climbing into the ring? I went to the gym to find out.

"Three men walkin down the deck of a luxury liner," says Carlos, the owner of Body & Soul. He is a yellow-skinned Black man and a chiseled Atlas who always gives his clients good boxing advice and a good laugh. "Italian guy, Jewish guy, Black guy." He begins giggling. "Italian guy pulls out a long cigar," he says and begins walking stiff and tough like Rocky. "He whips out his lighter, lights the cigar, puts it in his pocket, and keeps walking. Jewish guy wants to be as big as him, so he takes out a slightly longer cigar, grabs out his matchbook, and strikes the match on the book. It won't light."

"*Oy vay!*" a Jewish woman interjects dramatically.

"So the Jewish guy strikes the match on the deck. It lights. He puts the match in the ashtray and keeps steppin. Now the Black guy . . ."

"*Aww shit,*" you say.

". . . The Black guy want to be as big as them—you know how niggas are," he says, and everyone cracks up. "So he takes out the longest cigar and a match and goes to strike it on the matchbook. Won't light. Tries it on the deck. No dice. So finally, he strikes it *on the seat of his pants*. The match lights! He lights the cigar, tosses the match overboard. But when the match goes overboard, the luxury liner is passing an oil slick. The match hits the oil and the boat blows up." He pauses and smiles like the Kool-Aid man. "What's the moral of the story?"

Everyone grins expectantly.

"If a nigga scratch his ass he'll set the world on fire!"

You and Carlos laugh hard, doubling over together.

Nigga scratch his ass he'll set the world on fire, you say to yourself. How ridiculous. More of the silly Black chauvinist—negrovinist?—joking that we waste time with instead of thinking of ways to get ahead. Black is more often lit on fire by the world! How stupid to think that by doing something as crude as scratching your ass you could grab the world's attention, shake it up, maybe even blacken it. That just by being your Black self, you could make the world ours.

As Carlos's audience for the joke disperses, he pulls you close to put on your headgear in the same way that your parents once pulled you close to zip up your snowsuit. Your hands stuffed into large gloves in preparation for combat, you are immobilized, unable to do anything for yourself—not hold a cup of water, not scratch your ass—anything but throw punches. Carlos squeezes the thick leather pillow past your temples, down around your ears, and pulls tight the laces under your chin. The padding bites down on your forehead, your temples, your cheeks. You look into the mirror. Your head and face are buried so deeply in padding you can't tell yourself apart from another head wrapped up in headgear. You can't recognize your face.

The buzzer rings, launching the three-minute round, and you turn to the heavy bag, a large sack of leather and padding that hangs from the ceiling like a giant kielbasa. You approach the bag as you would another fighter, working your rhythms and combinations and strength, sinking in your hooks and jabs and crosses. You begin hitting slowly, paying close attention to each stinging shot, moving in slow, sharp rhythms like an old Leadbelly guitar-and-harmonica blues, each punch slapping the bag and sounding like a dog-eared, mud-splattered, ripped-apart boot stomping the floorboards of a little Alabama juke joint where they chased away the blues with the blues, sung in a key so deep whites thought they could hear it, but Negroes knew only they could. Because slaying the blues was a never-ending gig halted only for one thing, and that was radio dispatches of a Joe Louis bout. That cured the blues in a hurry, hearing the Brown Bomber slaying one or another white boy by fighting so slowly he looked like sepia-toned stop motion, his body stiff and slow like a cobra, hypnotizing his man, until the precise moment for the perfect punch. Then, lightning: a left-right would explode from Louis, and quick as a thunderclap his man would be sprawled on the ground below him, that's right, an Italian or a German with his spine on the canvas as thousands listened on, Louis having done what Negroes dreamed of doing but hardly dared think. Then Louis, the grandson of Booker T. Washington, the grandfather of Colin Powell, humbly retreated to his corner, his face wooden and emotionless, his aura as unthreatening as only the highest of the high-yellows could manage.

So you go on hitting the bag and talking to yourself in body English, the dialect of Joe Louis, talking with a near Tommish lilt as you slink slowly around the bag, but not quite Tommish because after a few racially quiet sentences you slash a few quick, deadly words and leave your opponent counting the sheep on the ceiling. You speak to yourself in the most necessary Black English in America, that of the humble assimilationist, and you move around the bag, trying to hypnotize your opponent, then lashing two, three rocket shots at him, and imagine yourself, like the Brown Bomber, lighting the world on fire, quietly.

The bell ring-ring-rings. The round is over. Fighters wander from their bags over toward Carlos, in the center of the room. Jack, a gruesome-looking, thirty-year-old white dentist, bumps into you, feigning an accident. "Touré! I didn't even see you!" he lies with a laugh. "I can't recognize you without my jab in your face."

People crack up. During breaks the fighting doesn't stop, it just turns oral—a crude variant on the verbal fisticuffs called the dozens takes its place. But instead of attacking your poverty, or your mama, it's your boxing or your looks. The one who makes everyone laugh loudest wins. And as with the dozens, sometimes it hurts, but when it's done by your own, to strengthen you for the onslaught from without, you know that a beatdown is really a buildup and you just keep on. "What's the point in us fighting?" you ask, looking at Jack's flattened nose and honeycombed skin. "That face cain't get ruined no worse." More laughs. This round is a tie.

The bell comes again and you head back to the heavy bag for three minutes more of fervor. You attack the bag savagely now, punching harder with all of the strength in your arms and all the evil in your hands, making the bag suck hard and send back flat, dull beats like the cold, thick drumbeats of raw, gutbucket southern soul, maybe Otis Redding, and now you are speaking Sonny Liston.

This is the body English of the back alley, the backroom, the back corner of the prison's back cell, where Liston, serious criminal, Mob enforcer, learned to box and became a straight-ahead, raw and rugged, black as blue, bruiser nigga. The grandson of Nat Turner, the grandfather of Mike Tyson. The scion and hero of every bully who ever lived. This is not the English of the street, no, too much bustling energy and zooming hustler's pace, no, this is the English of the street *corner*. Home of the long-faced, too-silent, thin-tie, black-black nigguhs who work only at night, who don't read *Ebony*, who have a look that could make death turn around. Liston knocked his man out and strolled over to a neutral corner with a glower that took the whole stadium right back to some alley that ain't seen the sun in decades off some long-forgotten street at the end of the world.

You're slamming your hands into the bag, but you're in that same alley, scrapping as you're sidestepping ancient garbage and streams of green water and body parts without bodies, as a single long-broken street lamp looks on, saying nothing. Liston lit the world on fire as the most hated man on the planet, and now here you come fighting ugly, banging the bag, banging like a ram, talking that crude, foul, dirty Liston-ese.

"Hey, Touré!" Jack screams from across the gym as the buzzer ending the second round begins to sound. "What's goin on inside that voodoo-do up on your head?"

The gym goes into hysterics. "Get out my face," you shoot back, "you melanin-*challenged* mothafucka." People double over. This round to you.

Before the third round starts, you stop moving long enough to get your heart back and your head together. This round you're going to put it all together. When the bell sounds you're a flurry of movement and flow, dancing out, then stepping in, weaving your head through the air and sliding in to land two, three, four, five quick punches and then out, dancing and bobbing, then three, four, five more quick shots to the bag on which you play a hot staccato tempo borrowed from high-pace jazz, from the sheets of sound of Coltrane. And now you're talking Muhammad Ali, the smooth-flowing, fan-dazzling, rhythm poet, the melding of Louis Armstrong and Malcolm X and Michael Jackson and the zip-bam-boom, the speed, swagger, swish, rope-a-dope jungle rumbler, Manila thriller, who turned the ring into an artist's studio, the canvas his own beautiful body.

Now, in front of the bag is a true African-American, a cool synthesis, not merely assimilating, not merely rebelling, but blending like jazz, melding what is gorgeous and grotesque about Africa and America. It's a body English that's the high-tech version of that spoken by Brer Rabbit, the Negro folktale trickster and blues-trained hero whose liquid mind and body could find a way past any so-called insurmountable force on any so-rumored impossible mission without the force even knowin he been there and gone. It's a body English filled with signifying, which means you say bad and mean good or you say bad and mean bad. And either way everyone who's supposed to know always know and know without anyone having to explain because everyone who's supposed to know know about signifying even if they don't know the word.

But you know all that, so you fire through the round in constant, unstoppable motion, lighting the entire universe on glorious, ecstatic, religious-fervor fire with your Ali-ese, and of Black, and of beauty. And then, as punches rain from deep within your heart onto the bag, you see that Carlos was right, a Black man can light the world on fire, wake it up, change it up, blacken it up, by something as crude and simple and natural as scratching his ass, that is, simply by being himself.

The round ends and Jack comes rushing over. You two are about to spar a few rounds, and he is teasing you now with a half-speed flurry of pantomimed jabs and hooks. Everyone looks on. "He's attacking me!" you call out in mock horror. "I sense a bias crime! Is there a lawyer in the house?" Again, laughter carries the day, but then the laughter carries you back, back to the laughter of the playground, back to the beginning of your fight career.

On the playground you sat alone, the only Black face as far as you could see on the playground of that century-and-a-half-old New England prep school. Matthew came over. He never liked you. He was brown-skinned with curly black hair, and Mom always whispered that he had to be part Black, but he never claimed it, never even admitted to being adopted. He saw you sitting alone in the playground and said, "Hey, Touré, why don't you come over and play?" You don't mean it. "If you get dirty, no one will know." Then he began to laugh.

You sprang at him in a frenzy, flinging tiny fists into his face, one after another without aim or direction, punch after punch flowing overhand and sloppy at his head and face and shoulders. Tears flying as easily as arms, finding room on your cheeks amid the hot sweat breaking into the brisk New England cold, you didn't feel his tiny fists jolting back at you, didn't hear the delighted screams of other children—*Fight! Fight!*—didn't hear the teacher Miss Farrah running to break it up after a few seconds that seemed like a year spent roaring at each other with tiny fists. You weren't even certain who you were as you rolled about in a gale of blows until you crawled inside yourself and found a serenity inside your embattled self, a peace beneath your warring skin, because you were fighting back and that made you certain that you could light the world on fire because there was a fire lit inside of you.

The Body & Soul buzzer screamed. Touré snapped back to attention as Jack came toward him, beginning their first round of sparring. Right away, Jack stepped close and stung Touré with a left jab to his nose, then another and another. Touré backed up and slipped a jab that landed on Jack's nose, pushing his head back sharply, then another jab that Jack blocked. Touré was much better fighting from the outside than the inside. The outside is when there's a few feet between fighters. They stand a polite distance away from each other, moving on their toes, occasionally jabbing or blocking and always looking for openings. When the boxers are outside, relatively speaking, there's a gentlemanly calm and leisurely pace about the fight. Inside, the fighters are just inches away from each other and it's point-blank range for both men and it's at once sexy and dangerous. Over and over again Touré tried to get inside, and finally Jack made him pay for coming into the wrong neighborhood. Touré stepped close to Jack and tried a quick left hook. Then a hard right uppercut caught Touré in the ribs. Jack saw him coming and pulled his trigger faster.

In the locker room of Body & Soul I caught up with Touré. Since we've known each other so long, I felt I could be completely honest. I was wrong.

"Why do you keep boxing?"

"I can't stop," he said without looking up.

"You mean, you won't stop."

"No. I can't. I love it."

"You get in the ring and get knocked down. Aren't you worried about—"

"Yo, man, a punch in the face ain't but a thing."

"Are you trying to take physical punishment to absolve your middle-class-based guilt and be literally banged into the gang of proletarian Blacks who live to give and take lumps every day and . . ."

Then he lunged at me. He swung at me with force and fury, and I fell hard on the ground. I saw my blood then, and for a fleeting second I felt a jolt of adrenaline. I was hot with anger and humiliation, but I was also not at all self-conscious and still wonderfully aware, as wide open as the sky. I was in pain and ecstasy. And from somewhere deep inside, I laughed loud and hard.

He stood over me and roared down, "I don't need to hear yo shit, man. I've sparred a few times. *I beat myself up all the time.*" He paused, then spoke with a soft intensity. "See, before my Moms sent me off to first grade she said, 'You have to be twice as good as those little white kids.' And that shit was real. But not here. In that ring all you got is two gloves and your head. That's a real . . . what's the word . . ."

"Meritocracy?"

"Boxocracy? Fightocracy? Whatever. I can do whatever I want and be whoever I want to be. All fighters live until the day they die. That's not a thing all men can say. But while he's alive, a fighter lives."

Then I looked away and my mind floated back and I saw myself in college, junior year, at a party. As things broke up, a group of juniors stood talking, fifteen or so others within easy earshot. A small argument began, quickly turned hot. Then, finally, The Whisper was stated—The Whisper that had begun my freshman year when I arrived on campus and, after a decade-plus in a white prep school, I didn't join the Black community but pledged a white fraternity and vacationed with white boys and dated white girls. I was branded a traitor then, a Black Judas, and The Whisper started, followed me sophomore year, when I consciously and conspicuously turned away from my white friends to party and protest with Black students. It chased me into junior year, when I moved into the Black house and became a campus political figure. And that night, as things broke up, The Whisper stepped from the shadows. "Touré, *you ain't Black.*"

And I said nothing. I stood in the middle of a circle of my Black classmates and heard the silence screaming in my ears and saw my chance to answer The Whisper, and I said nothing. I just turned slowly and walked away. I went to bed and promised myself never to tell the story of that night, not even to myself. I locked the memory away, closed my eyes. But the memory seeped out and kept me awake. And worse than the public humiliation was my nonanswer: I had taken the knockdown sitting down.

The memory obsessively replayed again and again, as I crossed the quad, ate lunch, sat bored in class, furtively took sex, sometimes adding something I should have done—a witty retort, a tough reply, a physical attack—sometimes not. And it germinated in me and festered and burned and with time turned inventively malignant, burning new each time, a tumor inside my personal history, throbbing, reaching out around the corners of my mind, grabbing toward my self-image, threatening my internal balance. Then, realizing the power of my conscience, my sense of regret, the fire inside me began burning hotter.

"No matter what," Touré said, looking directly at me, "I've got to fight, always fight, even in the face of sure defeat, because no one can hurt me as badly as I can."

I knew exactly what he meant. And he bent down and helped me up.

C. Tyler

Sub Zero

C. Tyler is a comic book artist/writer whose autobiographical stories reflect her struggles as an artist, worker, wife, and mother. She holds a BFA from Middle Tennessee State University and an MFA from Syracuse University. Cartoonist Chris Ware refers to her as "one of the true greats of the original Underground Comix generation." She has two solo works, *The Job Thing* (1993) and *Late Bloomer* (2005), both published by Fantagraphics of Seattle. Studs Terkel called *The Job Thing* "a beaut!" Cartoonist R. Crumb describes her work as having "the extremely rare quality of genuine, authentic heart." Currently, Tyler is working on a story about her father and World War II. Her Web site is www .bloomerland.com.

The piece we've included here is excerpted from *Late Bloomer*. It's a memoir about her experiences as a substitute teacher.

Interview with C. Tyler, p. 738.

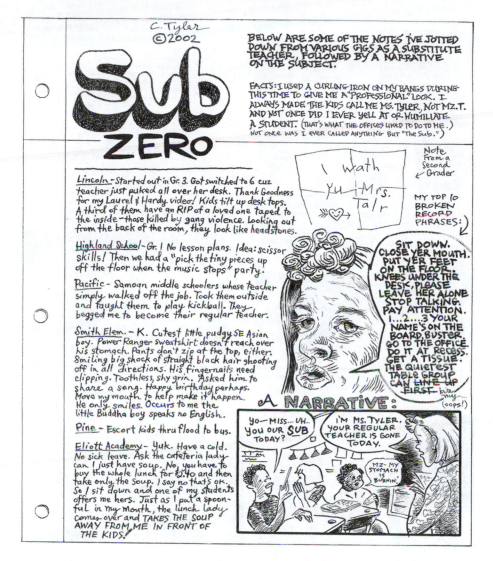

SUB ZERO

C. Tyler © 2002

BELOW ARE SOME OF THE NOTES I'VE JOTTED DOWN FROM VARIOUS GIGS AS A SUBSTITUTE TEACHER, FOLLOWED BY A NARRATIVE ON THE SUBJECT.

FACTS: I USED A CURLING IRON ON MY BANGS DURING THIS TIME TO GIVE ME A "PROFESSIONAL" LOOK. I ALWAYS MADE THE KIDS CALL ME MS. TYLER, NOT MZ.T. AND NOT ONCE DID I EVER YELL AT OR HUMILIATE A STUDENT. (THAT'S WHAT THE OFFICES LIKED TO DO TO ME.) NOT ONCE WAS I EVER CALLED ANYTHING BUT "The Sub."

Note from a Second Grader

I Wath YU Mrs. Talr

MY TOP 10 BROKEN RECORD PHRASES:

SIT DOWN. CLOSE YER MOUTH. PUT YER FEET ON THE FLOOR. KNEES UNDER THE DESK, PLEASE. LEAVE HER ALONE. STOP TALKING. PAY ATTENTION. 1...2...3 YOUR NAME'S ON THE BOARD BUSTER. GO TO THE OFFICE. DO IT AT RECESS. GET A TISSUE. THE QUIETEST TABLE GROUP CAN LINE UP FIRST - bite my... (oops!)

Lincoln - Started out in Gr. 3. Got switched to 6 cuz teacher just puked all over her desk. Thank Goodness for my Laurel & Hardy video! Kids tilt up desk tops. A third of them have an RIP of a loved one taped to the inside - those killed by gang violence. Looking out from the back of the room, they look like headstones.

Highland School - Gr. 1 No lesson plans. Idea: scissor skills! Then we had a "pick the tiny pieces up off the floor when the music stops" party.

Pacific - Samoan middle schoolers whose teacher simply walked off the job. Took them outside and taught them to play kickball. They begged me to become their regular teacher.

Smith Elem. - K. Cutest little pudgy SE Asian boy. Power Ranger sweatshirt doesn't reach over his stomach. Pants don't zip at the top, either. Smiling big shock of straight black hair shooting off in all directions. His fingernails need clipping. Toothless, shy grin. Asked him to share a song. Happy birthday perhaps. Move my mouth to help make it happen. He only smiles. Occurs to me the little Buddha boy speaks no English.

Pine - Escort kids thru flood to bus.

Eliott Academy - Yuk. Have a cold. No sick leave. Ask the cafeteria lady can I just have soup. No, you have to buy the whole lunch for $2.40 and then take only the soup. I say no that's ok. So I sit down and one of my students offers me hers. Just as I put a spoonful in my mouth, the lunch lady comes over and TAKES THE SOUP AWAY FROM ME IN FRONT OF THE KIDS!

A NARRATIVE:

Yo - MISS... UH. YOU OUR SUB TODAY?

I'M MS. TYLER. YOUR REGULAR TEACHER IS GONE TODAY.

MZ - MY STOMACH IS BURNIN'

Good morning. Welcome to yet another totally new situation. Take the challenge or leave. That's the lesson plan I follow.

Dear Sub, Math books are on the shelves under the windows. Pass out as soon as they come in.

I JUST MIGHT

Students like to test me by turning into little monsters, so behavior control is paramount. But I've learned what works.

BUT WE ALREADY *DID* CHAPTER 6.

SHUT UP, DARRELL. WE DID NOT.

DID TOO, BITCH...

ASSHOLE.

OOOH

FIGHT

HEY— WANNA LOSE YOUR RECESS!

πalkin' & chalkin' has been a very effective mode of self-protection from the little thugs, I mean sweethearts at War Zone Elementary.

GRR

SO THE CRABBY OLD NEIGHBOR CHOSE NEW YEAR'S EVE TO POISON MY POOCH— JAMAL, SIT DOWN OR I'LL HAVE TO STOP.

A 9MM WOULD TAKE CARE OF HIS ASS.

HMPH

Everyday, a new school, new staff, 36 brand new names to memorize in 5 minutes or less! This alone can be an education.

HERE GOES:

PENAMETH ARAKOUNTENIK? SORRY. JENNERY NGUYEN? IS THAT RIGHT? KIM SAECHAOU? SAY- CHOW, OK. CORNING MAISSAETA?...

TONGA

VIET NAM

L.A.

RUSSIA

LAOS

MEXICO

Thailand

Cambodia

HMONG

Phillipines

However, the lost recess threat coming from an unfamiliar white lady doesn't work at all with gang-member students. Time to entertain!

Latrina Nathanette de Andre

YOU KNOW HIM...

4+4= 44

OOH- DAT IS TIGHT

SHE DA BOMB

At the end of the day, I give thanks for my ability to draw, erase the protracted masterpiece, and get the hell out of there, $85 richer.

WHEW. I SURVIVED! NOW IF I CAN JUST MAKE IT OUT OF THE PARKING LOT ALIVE.

THANK YOU, JAMAL, FOR STAYING SEATED THOSE LAST 10 MINUTES.

JERK

NO PROBLEM MISS... UH, MISS WHATEVVA YO NAME IS.

Once, I was assigned to a school for "gifted" kids. I heard it was no problem to work there because the students were self-motivated.

Everything was going great. But during the afternoon recess break, the school Secretary came forward with a SHOCKER!

The Principal was at some conference and the lead teacher was also out, so it was up to me to serve as the instant psychologist.

This 6th grader was completely distraught, embroiled in a crisis that had been kept hidden from the regular teacher.

It was early heartbreak stuff, y' know. Seemed at first a bit petty. But then, she outlined the sad saga in complete sentences.

Twelve year olds! Stop it already! Shouldn't they be cuddling cute, fuzzy animals at a slumber party?

Panel 1: MCKENZIE SCHOOL. I BET CARI'S THE MOST POPULAR GIRL IN THE CLASS. I WOULDA *DIED* FOR HER GOOD LOOKS AT THAT AGE.

Panel 2: ARE YOU AWARE THAT CARI DAVIDSON JUST CAME TO THE OFFICE SAYING SHE WANTED TO KILL HERSELF? I'M JUST THE TYPIST. I DON'T KNOW WHAT TO DO. WATCH MY KIDS A SEC.

Panel 3: CHILD, I BARELY KNOW YOU, BUT YOUR PAIN IS SHOUTING AND *WE* ARE GONNA TALK ABOUT IT. I just wanna die let me die I feel so bad!

Panel 4: SO LET ME GET THIS STRAIGHT. YOUR EX-BEST FRIEND— IS ANGRY AT YOU— BECAUSE YOUR EX-BOYFRIEND BROKE UP WITH HER— AND SHE THINKS YOU TOLD HIM LIES ABOUT HER— SO HE'D BREAK UP WITH HER AND LIKE YOU AGAIN. RIGHT? yeah

Panel 5: TIARRA TOLD ME THAT SHE SAID THE SUBS ARE NOBODYS AND WON'T DO NOTHIN'. SO SHE GOT ALI AND ALL THEM TOGETHER... AND THEY LOCKED ME IN THE BATHROOM AND HIT ME WITH STICKS! !?

Panel 6: FUCKIN' BRA/NIAC PLEASE STOP IT YOU FUCK WI' ME LIKE THAT UH-GIN AND I'LL KILL YOU. NO

The first chance I had, I went back to Hopkins to analyze the incident with the class and with the regular teacher present.

I AM VERY DISAPPOINTED. WE WILL READ MS. TYLER HER CIVIL RIGHTS LIKE DR. KING TAUGHT US.

I'M SORRY ABOUT WHAT HAPPENED, MARA

I'M SORRY, TOO

free happiness. We have the right to a safe learning environment or dignity respect etc.

Two months later, I was reassigned to that same school, looking forward to seeing them. Imagine this playground greeting:

MIZ UH... YOU HEAR 'BOUT MARA?

SHE DEAD!

SHE HUNG HO-SEF

(NO ONE TOLD ME!)

A few kind words of small comfort, I offered what I could.

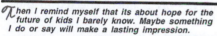

Beautiful children

my heart is broken, too.

I'm so sorry

...not your fault

trying to soothe

she had a mental illness?

I have brought so much to the job over the years and each day it's like back to sub zero. Sometimes I feel like what's the use.

NO ONE THOUGHT TO CALL ME.

'SCUSE ME. YOU'RE MS. GLADSTONE'S SUB, RIGHT? WELL, I CAN'T SEE PAYING YOU TO SIT HERE AND WRITE IN YOUR JOURNAL DURING HER FREE PERIOD. I'D LIKE YOU TO STUFF A FEW ENVELOPES DOWN IN THE BREAK ROOM. AND THEN THERE'S SOME ESSAYS TO GRADE FROM THE MID-SEMESTER TESTS. SO GRAB A RED PEN IF YOU WOULD.

OK?

Then I remind myself that its about hope for the future of kids I barely know. Maybe something I do or say will make a lasting impression.

MOM, THIS IS THE SUB WHO CALLED YOU.

SHE'S DOING SO MUCH BETTER. I REALLY APPRECIATE WHAT YOU DID.

HOW YA DOIN', CARI!

GEE THANKS.

When I least expect it.

HEY! ITS JAMAL AT THE MALL. WHUT UP, DUDE?

Sale

I'M HERE BUYIN' A NICE PENCIL 'CUZ I WANNA GROW UP AND DRAW LIKE YOU MIZ TY-LAH!

Class Dismissed!

Interview with C. Tyler

BECKY BRADWAY: This piece ("Sub Zero") has quite a lot of text for a graphic nonfiction work. Did you write the text before you did the illustrations?

C. TYLER: I had the idea and then I wrote it out. It's funny that you say that there's quite a lot of text, when in fact, I tried to use an economy of words.

BB: Why did you put this together as a graphic memoir rather than as a traditional (nonillustrated) essay?

CT: Essay? Yikes, the word "essay" puts me into a flop sweat! I love to write but I don't consider myself a writer. I see myself as an artist first—an artist who tells stories. I use writing to build the framework of the story, which is then completed through the image-making process.

BB: Your narrator isn't exactly a teenager, yet we think of graphic novels as appealing mostly to the young. Have you found that your readership extends beyond those who we usually think of as graphic novel fans?

CT: I came from the narrative tradition born in the Underground Comix movement. That genre appealed to the young in its heyday. But our loyal fans have grown up, as we have—as is now reflected in our subject matter.

BB: Have you ever heard from any of your readers?

CT: Yes, I do get praising fan mail, which I love. But mostly, I work in a void and don't know who's reading the work.

BB: More and more people seem to be reading graphic novels. To what do you attribute this?

CT: I don't know. I don't read them. I don't have time. I'm too busy writing and drawing my own longer, more complicated stories. But I'm glad to see the numbers increase and I would love for my readership to grow because of this boon.

BB: I get the impression that writing and art have not provided you with a lucrative or standard career.

CT: That is correct. "And it's getting scarier as I get older," spouted the Pioneer while trudging onward, across the amber fields of grain.

BB: You've subbed, raised kids, tried to work your graphic novel/memoir writing into your life. The schools are packed with students studying creative writing now. What would you say to someone who wants to be a writer or artist?

CT: If you're going to do it, do it with all of your heart. It's a dream-wave you'll be riding, but never call it that. Call it your life.

Luis Alberto Urrea

From *Across the Wire*

Luis Alberto Urrea, 2005 Pulitzer Prize finalist for nonfiction and member of the Latino Literature Hall of Fame, is a prolific writer who uses his dual-culture life experiences to explore themes of love, loss, and triumph. Though best known for his nonfiction—his 1999 memoir *Nobody's Son: Notes from an American Life* won the American Book Award—Urrea has also earned numerous awards and accolades for his poetry and fiction. *The Devil's Highway*, his 2004 nonfiction account of a group of Mexican immigrants lost in the Arizona desert, won the 2004 Lannan Literary Award and was a finalist for the Pulitzer Prize and the Pacific Rim Kiriyama Prize. A national bestseller, *The Devil's Highway* was named a best book of the year by the *Los Angeles Times*, the *Miami Herald*, the *Chicago Tribune*, the *Kansas City Star,* and many other publications. His most recent book, *The Hummingbird's Daughter* (2005), is a historical novel. A graphic novel, *Mr. Mendoza's Paintbrush,* illustrated by Christopher Cardinale, is forthcoming.

Urrea attended the University of California at San Diego, earning an undergraduate degree in writing, and did his graduate studies at the University of Colorado–Boulder. After serving as a relief worker in Tijuana and a film extra and columnist-editor-cartoonist for several publications, Urrea moved to Boston where he taught expository writing and fiction workshops at Harvard. He has also taught at Massachusetts Bay Community College and the University of Colorado and he was the writer in residence at the University of Louisiana–Lafayette. He is currently living with his family in Chicago, where he teaches at the University of Illinois–Chicago.

The excerpt we are including here is from *Across the Wire* (1993), his first book. The piece comes from Urrea's experience as a religious worker among those who live in trash heaps along the Mexican and American border.

Trash

One of the most beautiful views of San Diego is from the summit of a small hill in Tijuana's municipal garbage dump. People live on that hill, picking through the trash with long poles that end in hooks made of bent nails. They scavenge for bottles, tin, aluminum, cloth; for cast-out beds, wood, furniture. Sometimes they find meat that is not too rotten to be cooked.

This view-spot is where the city drops off its dead animals—dogs, cats, sometimes goats, horses. They are piled in heaps six feet high and torched. In that stinking blue haze, amid nightmarish sculptures of charred ribs and carbonized tails, the garbage-pickers can watch the buildings of San Diego gleam gold on the blue coastline. The city looks cool in the summer

739

when heat cracks the ground and flies drill into their noses. And in the winter, when windchill drops night temperatures into the low thirties, when the cold makes their lips bleed, and rain turns the hill into a gray pudding of ash and mud, and babies are wrapped in plastic trash bags for warmth, San Diego glows like a big electric dream. And every night on that burnt hill, these people watch.

In or near every Mexican border town, you will find trash dumps. Some of the bigger cities have more than one "official" dump, and there are countless smaller, unlicensed places piled with garbage. Some of the official dumps are quite large, and some, like the one outside Tecate, are small and well hidden. People live in almost every one of them.

> "This was where the untouchables of this society of untouchables slept, among the pigs awaiting slaughter."

Each *dompe* has its own culture, as distinct as the people living there. (*Dompe* is border-speak, a word in neither Spanish nor English. It is an attempt to put a North American word or concept— "dump"—into a Mexican context. Thus, "junkyard" becomes *yonke* and "muffler" becomes *mofle*.) Each of these *dompes* has its own pecking order. Certain people are "in." Some families become power brokers due to their relationships to the missionaries who invariably show up, bearing bags of old clothes and vanloads of food. Some *dompes* even have "mayors"; some have hired goons, paid off by shady syndicates, to keep the trash-pickers in line. It's a kind of illegal serfdom, where the poor must pay a ransom to the rich to pick trash to survive.

Then there are those who are so far "out" that the mind reels. In the Tijuana *dompe*, the outcasts were located along the western edge of the settlement in shacks and lean-tos, in an area known as "the pig village." This was where the untouchables of this society of untouchables slept, among the pigs awaiting slaughter.

I knew them all: the Serranos, the Cheese Lady, Pacha, Jesusita.

A Woman Called Little Jesus

It was raining. It had been raining for weeks, and the weather was unremittingly cold. The early-morning van-loadings were glum; all spring and summer and even into the fall, more volunteers than we'd known what to do with joined us for the weekly trips into Mexico. One day, we had over a hundred eager American kids loaded into buses ready to go forth and change the world. Now, though, as the late-winter/early-spring rain came, the group dwindled. Sometimes we were reduced to a small core of old-timers, six to ten at most.

When we pulled into the dump, the vans slid almost sideways in the viscous, slick mud. Windchill turned the air icy; there was no smoke to speak of that day, and the dogs were mostly hiding. Women awaiting food were lined up, covering their heads with plastic sheets. Even in this wind and wet they joked and laughed. This feature of the Mexican personality is often the cause of much misunderstanding—that if Mexicans are so cheer-ful, then they certainly couldn't be hungry or ill. It leads to the myth of the quaint and jovial peasant with a lusty, Zorba-like love affair with life. Like the myth of the lazy Mexican, sleeping his life away, it's a lie.

Perhaps the women laughed because they were simply relieved to be getting food. Perhaps they were embarrassed—Mexicans are often shamed by accepting help of any kind. When embarrassed or ashamed, they often overcompensate, becoming boisterous, seemingly carefree. Or maybe the poor don't feel the compunction to play the humble and quiet role we assign them in our minds.

As I climbed out of the van, Doña Araceli, the Cheese Lady, bustled over to me. We called her the Cheese Lady because she had taken to com-ing to the dump with globs of drippy white goat cheese wrapped in cloth. She sold it to the locals, and she always pressed a lump of it into my hands as a gift. Nobody in the crew had the guts to taste it. We'd pass the cheese around for a couple of hours, then unload it at an orphanage or a *barrio* in Tijuana.

Doña Araceli was extremely agitated. She had discovered a new family— a married couple, several children, including toddlers, and one daughter with an infant—and they had no house to stay in. They were very poor, she said, and in dire need of help.

One of our projects over the years was to build homes and churches for the poor. An associate of ours named Aubrey devised an ingeniously simple construction plan. He collected garage doors from houses being torn down or renovated; these doors, hammered to a simple wooden frame, made handy walls. Depending on how many doors were available, the new house could be as long or as wide as the builders chose. With saws and donated windows, Aubrey could modify the place and make it quite fancy. The roofs were either more garage doors, plywood, or two-by-six planks covered with plastic sheeting that was either carpet-tacked or stapled into place. Old carpets and plastic sheets were transformed into a quick floor. Once a month, we had a *dompe* workday: truckloads of youths armed with tools came in and began hammering, and in a matter of hours, they created a new building.

Doña Araceli wanted us to build this family a house right away. She said the mother was waiting to meet me. The woman's name was Jesusita. Little Jesus.

Jesusita shook my hand and called me "*Hermano*"—"Brother."

This is not a common Mexican greeting; it is used among Protestants as a shorthand for "fellow Christian." A "real" Mexican would never resort to such Protestant language (though it is a habit for Mexicans to call each other "*'mano*," which is short for "brother" but actually takes the place of "pal" or "dude." Mexican linguistics are a delicate and confusing art: *mano* also means "hand"). The poor, however, deal with missionaries and soon learn to use the more religious term freely. It is often a manipulative thing. They are hoping you will assume they are "*Hallelujahs*," too, and give them more goods than the rest. Consequently, Jesusita's "*Hermano*" didn't move me. I paid it no heed.

What really caught my eye instead was her face. She was small, a round woman with gray hair and the kind of face that retains a hint of young beauty under layers of pain and comfortless years. Her eyes, nestled in laugh lines, were a light, nut-brown color. She smiled easily. She wound her hair in twin braids and pinned it to the top of her head, framing her face. She made me feel happy, absurdly pleased, as though she were a long-lost aunt who had appeared with a plate of cookies.

Over the next year, as we got to be friends, she lavished me with bear hugs. Her head fit easily beneath my chin. On the day I met her, though, she cried.

"*Hermano*," she said, "*vinimos desde el sur, y no tenemos casa.*" (We came from the south, and we don't have a house.) "*Somos muchos, todos mis hijos, un nietito, y mi señor.*" (There are many of us, all my children, a little grandson, and my husband.)

"Help her, Luis!" cried Doña Araceli.

Jesusita's full name was María de Jesús. Mary of Jesus.

Requests for help were a constant; they were the rule. That Jesusita needed assistance didn't make her special, but something about her involved me right away. I suppose it is the thing we conveniently call "chemistry." Still, Jesusita was one face in a river of hundreds.

Everyone needed help. For example, there was the family recently arrived from near Guadalajara. They had no clothes except what they were wearing, and the children were so infected with scabies that their skin looked like old chewing gum. Scabies is a mange caused by a burrowing mite, a louse, that tunnels through your flesh, leaving eggs under your skin. You scratch and scratch, but can never quite get to the itch—the mites move in you at night. They like crotches and armpits. Scabies victims claw themselves raw. The kids didn't understand what was wrong with them. They all slept together, and the mites could easily move from body to body. Their beds were full of these mites; their clothes and underwear were also infested. When we tried to explain what was causing their itch, they looked at us with disbelief and laughed.

The family was living in a shack on a hillside across the highway from the dump. It could be reached only after a long and confusing drive through crooked alleys and ridgetop dirt paths. Lean-tos thrown together by junkies and winos surrounded their shack. You could smell the booze and urine coming through the slats. There was a small goat tied to a stake in the dirt, and no lights brightened the neighborhood save for small fires and the occasional flashlight. The men's voices were thick; they cursed and broke glass in the dark. In the shack hid Socorro, the thirteen-year-old daughter. The men wanted her. They'd come out after dark and storm the house, trying to break through the doors and walls to get to her. When I went up there one night, waving my flashlight in the dust clouds, I could hear them outside Socorro's door, howling.

Clearly, the Guadalajarans needed a new house. Everywhere we turned, someone needed a new house. Jesusita's family would have to wait for theirs, though we committed to giving them assistance wherever it was possible. I told Jesusita to wait for us in her place down the hill, and we'd be down as soon as we could. She cried again and put her arms around me. "*Gracias, Luis,*" she said. "*Gracias, Hermano Luis.*"

Fear

This is a record of a small event that happened on a typical spring day near the pig village.

I was unloading one of the vans—the huge Dodge we called "the White Elephant." Some of my friends were standing around the van with me— Doña Araceli, a Mixtec woman named Juanita, and a little girl named Negra. I noticed a woman standing in the distance, among the trash piles. I didn't recognize her. None of the dump people seemed to know her, either. We watched her lurch back and forth, spitting and waving her arms. She would occasionally glare at me, start toward me, then stop after a few steps and curse. Her face looked like a rubber mask: white creases and a red-slash mouth.

"Is she drunk?" said Juanita. I said something, no doubt a joke, and leaned into the van. I worked the box I was looking for free by shoving one of the heavy bags of beans out of the way. When I turned around, the woman was standing right beside me, staring into my face. She snarled.

I stumbled back from her. Her hair stood straight off her scalp as though she were taking a heavy charge of electricity through her feet. She was wheezing.

One of the women said, "She's crazy, *Hermano.*"

"Fuck you," she snapped. Her voice was deep, like a man's voice. "*Vete a la chingada.*"

She leaned toward me. "We know you," she said. "We know who you are. We know what you're doing."

I laughed nervously. "What?" I said.

"You'll pay for this."

I put down my box. "I don't understand," I said.

She began to rasp obscenities in her man's voice. "We *know* you. We'll get you."

She spun around and jerked away from us, very fast. She stumbled over rocks in the road, but kept moving, shouting all the time, "*¡Vas a ver!* You'll see! We'll get you. We'll stop you."

She paused in front of Pacha's house at the top of the hill, gesturing at me and yelling her strange threats. The hair at the back of my neck began to rise.

"Is she drunk?" Juanita repeated.

The woman threw her head back and screamed.

Pacha

Pacha had startling eyes. They had a kind of gold-green edge; they had yellow flecks, like the eyes of a cat. They slanted up the slightest bit. If she'd lived anywhere but the Tijuana garbage dump, her eyes would have seemed like a movie star's.

She lived with a thin, dark man named José. He called himself her husband, though he was not the father of her children. His face was craggy and his teeth long, hidden by a thick black mustache. When he talked to you, he'd bob his head and grin. When either of them laughed, they'd cover their mouths with their hands. They were pagans when they came north, of full Indian blood, and not used to church services or ministers. Their marriage ceremony was more personal and private—José moved into Pacha's bed. He became her mate, and he remained faithful to her. It was a simple agreement, as firm as a wolf's.

José liked Jesus very much. When Pastor Von and his workers visited his house, José always asked Von to pray for him. We put our arms around each other and Von prayed and I translated and José kept saying, "Thank you, Jesus, for listening to me." He cried.

Pacha wouldn't come to the vans to get food. She said it embarrassed her to be begging and fighting with all those other women. I made it a habit to save her out a box of goods, and after the crowds dissipated a bit, I would take it up to her.

Her home was on a slope that swept down into the dump; hers was a long, meandering shack with a low roof and uneven walls. The entire house was at an angle. José designed it this way so that the rain, when it came, would flow through the house, under their bed, and down the hill. He was very proud of his ingenuity: he had built one of the dump's best-engineered houses. Those who built below him, on flatland or in hollows, found themselves in puddles of mud all winter.

Their floor was a conglomeration of carpet pieces and stray linoleum squares. José and Pacha pressed them into wet soil. The exterior walls were board. The interior walls were cardboard, with an occasional bit of wood—fruit crates, barrel slats. They sealed the gaps with plastic sheeting.

They did have one luxury: a bed. It was quite odd to look through a door and see a big bed with an iron bedframe and headboard. Often a bed was the only thing people in the dumps owned that was worth anything. Except for televisions.

You'd see little black and white TV sets scattered through the dump. There was no electricity, but there were wrecked cars in the *yonkes* in the valleys. The men took the car batteries and hooked the TV sets to them. Sometimes the TVs were balanced on huge oil cans—rusted Pemex, Opec barrels—which, when filled with paper and dung or twigs, served as stoves.

Pacha didn't have a television, but she did have oil barrels: she cooked in one of them. The other she used to store water. It was full of mosquito larvae wiggling like tiny fish. Its water was the color of blood.

Pacha's eldest daughter offered to pay me to smuggle her across the border. She was pregnant—her husband had gone across the wire and never come back. She watched for him on a neighbor's television. I told her I couldn't do it.

On New Year's morning, she had her baby in the free clinic in Tijuana. The nurse took the infant and dunked it in a tub of icy water. It had a heart attack and died. It was a girl.

Pacha got pregnant next. Her belly stuck out far and hard, like a basketball, from her small body. When we arrived at the dump, she stood in front of her house with José, pointed at me and laughed. They laughed a lot. She was furious with me if I didn't come up the hill right away to see her kids.

José had hurt his back. He could barely stand, much less work, and the days were hard for Pacha and her kids. They all had to take the trash-picking poles and work the mounds, supporting José, who would give out after a few hours.

When I took them the food, I'd pat that huge stomach and shout, "What are you doing in there!" They would laugh, and she would scold me for waking him up. It was José's first child with her, the seal of their marriage.

One day, when we drove over the hill, a crowd was there, milling. It was hot—the flies had hatched, and were forming clouds that swept out of the trash like black dust devils. The rain had been over for months, and the deep heat was on. I glanced at Pacha's house—nobody in front. Then I saw an old pickup truck coming up the hill. José was in the back with a group of men. They held cloudy bottles by the necks.

I waved at him, but he just looked at me as the truck went by, no emotion at all on his face.

As we were unloading the vans, one of Pacha's girls came to me and put her hand on my arm. "Luis," she said, quietly. "Mama's baby died."

I stared at her.

"Don José just took him away in the truck. His head was too big. He was all black."

I asked her if it had been born here.

She shook her head. "Free clinic," she said.

She stood calmly, watching me. "Mama needs you," she said.

I didn't want to go up there.

It was a terrible charade: Pacha was blushing and overly polite, as though caught in an embarrassment. I was pleasant, as though we were having tea and crumpets at the Ritz. Everything felt brittle, ready to shatter. She wore baggy green stretch pants and stood holding a salvaged aluminum kitchen chair.

"Poor José," she said, looking off. It was very dark in the house, and it smelled of smoke. "Poor José. It hurt him so much."

That look as he drove past, drunk: where was Jesus now?

"The baby wouldn't come out," she said. She looked at her feet. "The doctor got up under my *chi-chis* and pushed on him after I tried for a few hours."

"He sat on your abdomen?"

She nodded. "*Sí.* They got up on my chest and shoved on me. And then the doctor had to get down there and pull me open because the baby was black and we were both dying." She swayed. I jumped up and took her arm, trying to get her into the chair. "It hurts," she said. She smiled. "It's hard to sit." I got her down. "They stuck iron inside me. They pulled him out with tools, and I'm scared because I'm fat down there. I'm still all fat." She couldn't look at me; she bowed her head. "It's hard and swollen and I can't touch it."

I told her not to move and ran down the hill to get Dave, a medical student who was working with us. He grabbed a flashlight and followed me up.

Pacha repeated her story; I translated.

He said, "Tell her to pull the pants tight against her crotch so I can see the swelling."

She did it. He bent close. It looked like she had grown a set of testicles. He whistled.

"Think it's a hernia?" he asked.

"I don't know. Could be." Many of the women in the dump get hernias that are never treated—I knew one woman who had one for fifteen years until she asked one of us to look at it.

Dave said, "Tell her I have to feel it."

I told Pacha. She just looked at me. Brown eyes flecked with gold. "Anything you say." She nodded.

"Is she all right?" Dave asked.

"Yeah."

He handled her very tenderly; she winced, sucked air. "Feels bad," he said.

She kept her eyes on my face.

"We have to get her pants off, buddy."

"Wonderful, Dave."

"Culturally?" he asked.

"A disaster."

One of my aunts, when she was pregnant, was attended to by a male obstetrician. My uncle ordered him to stand outside a closed door—his nurse looked at my aunt and called out the details to him. My uncle hovered nearby to make sure there would be no outrage against her womanhood.

Dave stood there for a moment. "Too bad. We have to look."

"Pacha," I said. "The, ah, doctor needs to see it."

She nodded. She took her children outside and told them not to come back for a while. I held her hand and helped her into the bed.

José had designed a little paper alcove for the bed. Pictures of musicians, movie stars, and saints were pasted to the walls. A ragged curtain hung beside the bed for privacy.

"He was too big," she said, stretching out. "Too fat."

She worked the pants down around her hips. A strip of dirty elastic—perhaps torn out of an old girdle—was wrapped around her fallen belly to hold it up. She unwrapped herself. Her navel hung out like a fat thumb.

She undid some safety pins that held her underpants together. They were blue, lightly stained. A smell rose of warm bread and vinegar. Dave sat beside her. She stared into my eyes.

I looked away. I was embarrassed and nervous.

Dave handed me the flashlight and said, "Here. Illuminate it for me."

> "The sky was black and brown—they were burning dogs at the end of the dump. It smelled like Hell."

Her right side was thick and grotesque. The right labium was red. Bits of lint stuck to her. Every time he touched her, Pacha gasped.

"Blood," he said. "Tell her it's blood. No hernia." He smiled at her.

I translated.

She smiled a little bit, more with her eyes than her lips.

We put her to bed for several days—no more trash-picking. She needed to let the blood reabsorb. Dave gave her a battery of vitamins, some aspirin, put her on lots of fluids.

"*Ay, Luis,*" she said.

I stepped out of her home. The sky was black and brown—they were burning dogs at the end of the dump. It smelled like Hell. I took a deep breath and walked away.

Coffee

It was finally time to go down and see Jesusita.

We climbed into the four-wheel-drive Blazer and drove down the slippery hill. The dirt road was already so deep in mud that the truck couldn't make it. We had to abandon it and slog down. In places, the mud went higher than my knees.

Jesusita and some of her brood waited for us at the bottom of the hill. They led us to what seemed to be—for the dump, anyway—an especially luxurious house. It was a small American-style place with stucco walls and what appeared to be a real roof. It even had a porch. We were a little suspicious at first. The Cheese Lady had made such a fuss about this? Our opinions changed when we got inside. Half of the interior walls had fallen in, with the back walls sagging and open to the wind. The floor was raw, uncovered cement, and the whole house was awash in one or two inches of water. Only two areas remained recognizable as rooms. In what had clearly been a living room, on a sheet of plastic, were piled all of Jesusita's possessions—clothes, bundles—forming a small dry island. The family slept on this pile. The other room was a kitchen.

They had dragged the empty shell of a stove from the dump. A linoleum-and-aluminum table stood in the kitchen, too, with four unmatched chairs. On the counter, a few coffee cups, a pan, and the meager food supplies we had given Jesusita. Her husband arrived, took off his straw *vaquero* hat, shook our hands, and very formally and graciously invited us to sit and have a cup of coffee with him. He was an iron-backed man, not tall, but erect and strong; his hands were thick and solid as oak burls. He wore old cowboy boots and faded jeans and a white pearl-snap shirt. We learned that he was a horse-breaker from the interior of Mexico, a real cowboy who took pride in his talents.

Jesusita said, "He is the best horse-tamer in our region."

He shushed her—he never liked too much talk of home. His tightly curled hair was tinged gray and white. A small peppery mustache sketched itself across his upper lip. He referred to each of us as "*usted*," the formal "you," and it was clear that he expected the same respect. The most lasting impression we took with us was one of dignity and pride.

Their children were remarkably attractive—several girls and two little boys. One of the girls, perhaps fifteen, had a baby. All their hair was shiny and black, and the girls wore it pulled back in loose ponytails.

Jesusita put wads of newspaper in the hollow stove and lit them. She heated water in the battered pan, and she made Nescafé instant coffee with it. It was clearly the last of their coffee, and she served it in four cups. We men sat at the table. Jesusita and the kids stood around us, watching us drink.

It was a lovely moment. The weak coffee, the formal and serious cowboy, the children, and Jesusita, hovering over us. She broke a small loaf of sweet bread into pieces and made us eat.

It was also a fearsome moment—the water was surely polluted, runoff from the miasma above. A great deal of disease infested the area from the constant flooding and the scattered bodies of dead animals. To refuse their hospitality would have been the ultimate insult, yet to eat and drink put us at risk. Von had the grim set in his lips that said, *Here we go again*, and with a glance at us, he took a sip. We drank. "*¡Ah!*" we exulted. "*¡Delicioso!*" Jesusita beamed. The cowboy nodded gravely, dipped his bit of sweet bread in his cup, and toasted us with it. Outside, the cold rain hammered down. Inside, we all shivered. We could find no way to get warm.

The Serranos

I first met the Serrano family on a Thursday. Halloween was coming. Several women told me there was a very dirty new family living out at the far end of the pig village. The children were sick, they said, and the mother—who was about to have a baby—was dying.

I walked out there, to where the Serranos had thrown together a small compound of stray boards and bedsprings. The roof was low—about three feet high—and I had to bend over to get inside. The only room of the house was a combination bedroom and kitchen. Its floor was dirt, and the room was dark and smoky. The smoke came from a little cook fire in the far corner, dangerously near the wooden wall. Some papers and a couple of pots rested on a cardboard mat in the dirt next to the fire. In the other three corners, pallets of rag and paper lay in the dirt: the beds.

Two boys and a little girl squatted in the dark. When they saw me, they started laughing. I said, "Come out here."

The little girl had an unusual name—Cervella (Ser-VEY-yah).

"Where's your father?" I asked.

The eldest boy shrugged.

They all giggled.

"Where's your mother?"

"*Cagando.*" (Shitting.) "She does it all the time."

They all nodded.

"All day," Cervella said.

Her face was covered in smudges, but under the dirt I could see dense scabs, dark as steak. I couldn't figure out what they were; they looked like a combination of scabies and impetigo.

"What is this?" I asked, putting my finger on her cheek. She shrugged. I took her arm, turned the elbow out; there they were again. When I touched the edge of a scab, pale orange blood leaked out. "Does it hurt?"

Shrug. "Itches." Giggle.

They all looked past me. I turned around. Mrs. Serrano had appeared in a patch of tall weeds. She scared me to death.

She was a zombie, right out of an old Boris Karloff movie. Her skin was sallow and had the texture of hide, all criss-crossed with tiny X's in the thick flesh. Her eyes were black, but overlaid with a dullness that looked like a layer of dust—I wanted to wipe them off with my fingertips. Her mood was so flattened that it seemed agreeable and mindless; on her mouth, a loose-lipped grin and a constant exhalation of dank air. When she stood next to me, I could feel her fever radiating.

She was very pregnant.

"Are you Mrs. Serrano?" I asked.

"Serrano?" she said.

Pause.

"Where is your husband, Mrs. Serrano?"

Pause.

She moved a hand in the direction of the dump.

"What's wrong with your daughter?"

She smiled slowly, looking at the ground. "My daughter? There is something wrong with her." She laughed in slow motion.

I was baffled.

I put my hand on her forehead; it was dry as a skull, burning.

"I have dysentery," she said.

Someone coughed behind me. Mr. Serrano had arrived to see who was bothering his family. He was a hearty man with a hat and a drooping mustache. He gripped my hand and pumped it.

"Good to meet you!"

I told him his wife was seriously ill.

"I know it," he said. "Watch this." He grabbed her arm and pinched up a section of her skin. When he let it go, it stayed elevated, like clay, or a pinch of Silly Putty. A sign of severe dehydration. They call it "tenting."

"*Está toda seca*," he said. (She's all dry.)

"The baby?" I asked.

She laughed.

"Touch it," Mr. Serrano said.

I put my hand on her stomach. It was hard.

I brought them supplies from the vans: water, a quart of vitamin D milk, a pound of rice, a pound of beans, a large can of tuna, a large can of peaches, a large can of fruit cocktail, one dozen flour tortillas, corn, a can of Veg-All mixed vegetables, bread, a fresh chicken, and doughnuts for the kids. I told Mr. Serrano to keep her in bed and to pour fluids down her, and I'd be back the next day with Dave and a *gringo* doctor.

They both laughed. He kept rubbing his hand over his face, up to the hat, down over the chin.

The next day, when Dave and I returned with the doctor, Mrs. Serrano was sitting in the sun on a broken kitchen chair.

"I'm back," I said. "Remember I told you I'd come back?"

She didn't respond.

The doctor crouched before her and felt her stomach. He pulled up her lids, felt her brow, and took her pulse. He shook out his thermometer and put it in her mouth. She submitted to everything.

"Tell her I need a stool sample. Tell her I need to see some stool."

I told her. She got up and motioned for us to follow her. She led us to the south wall of the shack—the outside of the kitchen wall. The single sheet of plywood was also the wall of the pigpen. And she had been leaning against it to go; bloody ropes and spatters of feces were all over the wall. We were standing in it. Dave cracked, "There's nothing like really getting into your work!" Our can of tuna simmered about six inches away from this mess.

"Doesn't she know anything about hygiene?" the doctor asked.

I translated.

"What is it?" she asked.

The doctor handed me a paper cup.

"Sample," he said.

He gave her Lomotil to stop the diarrhea. We gave her several jugs of Gatorade, more jugs of water, and some clothes.

Mr. Serrano, who had stood in the background during all this, came up to me and said, "Don't leave us a prescription."

I told him not to worry—we'd pay for it.

"No," he said. "We can't read. We won't know what we're getting." The doctor had given him a bottle of antibiotics, and Mr. Serrano held it up to me and said, "And you'd better tell me what this says, too, eh?"

Whatever Mrs. Serrano had, it was cured within a week or two because of one donated hour and some pale capsules the doctor prescribed. Within days, her eyes brightened, her skin turned tender, and her fever vanished. They moved the pigs away from the wall and went out into the weeds beside the dump to relieve themselves. In time, she had a healthy baby.

The Curandera's Curse

The Serranos' accents were peculiar, and I couldn't place them. After I had gotten to know him better, I asked Mr. Serrano. He said they'd come from *el sur* (the south).

We had been trying to treat Cervella's skin, but nothing worked. There were short periods of remission when the skin cleared, then the lumps returned. The scabs soon followed. I stood looking at her arms.

"We have a little Maya in us," Mr. Serrano said. The day was bright. We were beside his low front door.

"You know, *Hermano*," he continued, "you won't cure Cervella."

"Why not?"

"It's black magic."

In Mr. Serrano's homeland, near Yucatán, there lived a witch named Erlinda. She often worked as a *curandera* (healer woman), working her spells to help those who paid for medical attention—the area possessed few doctors, no public clinics, and certainly no hospitals. One way Erlinda healed people was to roll a raw egg on their bodies, over the afflicted area. She then broke the eggs into bowls—if the stuff inside had turned black, then the disease had been "sucked out."

Erlinda was embroiled in an unexplained feud with one of Mr. Serrano's kin. He did not know what started the fight, but he was not personally involved. One day, she appeared at his door, demanding money—568 pesos. Serrano didn't have it, and he told her so. She would not leave and became abusive, threatening him and his family. He physically ejected her from his plot of land, and she stood outside his little wood fence and put a curse on him.

That week, Cervella's aunt—Mrs. Serrano's sister—went into a swoon and died. They took her to a clinic in her last hours, but she never revived. The Serranos were terrified, unwilling to even leave their compound.

Then Cervella fell ill. It began with a fever, and the fever rose until she became delirious. She soon fell into a coma. Mr. Serrano bundled her up and carried her to the regional Red Cross station, but they couldn't break her fever. They kept her overnight.

Mr. Serrano, not knowing what else to do, went out to his land to work. In one corner, he found a small pyramid of stones. He took it apart and discovered a bundle of Cervella's clothes knotted up inside it. He rushed to the clinic, carried Cervella out, and took her to a missionary house in the jungle. There, he told me, they prayed over her, and she awoke.

It is possible that Mr. Serrano was telling me a whopper. However, he was crying as he told it.

"I swear to you, Luis," he said, "she woke up. And the fever?" He brushed his hands before his chest, as though flicking dust into the wind. "Gone."

The Serranos so feared Erlinda after this that they fled north, running until they ran out of country to run through. The last time I saw her, Cervella's arms were still lumpy, scabbed over, oozing blood.

Dompe workday, December: Steve Mierau and I were going to shacks in the pig village, visiting the families there. The crew was in the lower dump, hammering new houses together. We were alone. Mierau was a slim prairie liberal from Nebraska who had fallen into Mexico as if into a dream. Somehow, he had the misfortune of being promoted to second-in-command. He lived in a garage next to Von's trailer when he wasn't in Mexico.

Since we weren't expected, we were free of the usual crowds of hungry people. We could take in cartons of food to each family. The Serranos were at home, and as we walked out there, we heard a commotion. Mr. Serrano was hollering and laughing, running in circles with a broom. The boys were charging around his feet, whooping, and Cervella was shrieking and clapping her hands.

"What's this?" Steve said.

"Get him! Get him!" Cervella shouted.

Then I saw the rat.

It was a big dump rat, trapped between all of them, running in panicked circles. Everywhere it turned, a Serrano waited. Mr. Serrano repeatedly smashed the broom across its back. He finally cracked its spine, and it fell over, scrabbling in the dust. They all laughed.

The oldest boy knelt behind the rat. They crowded in.

Mr. Serrano said, "Good boy. Do it!"

The kid reached into his back pocket and withdrew a pair of wire cutters. He held the rat down with one hand and fitted the cutters over its snout. He began to cut its head off, centimeter by centimeter.

Steve and I backed away. Before we knew it, we were running for the van.

Corpses

Spring finally came, and the drive to Jesusita's house became more easy as the hills dried out. Her husband had not been able to find work, she said, but they had covered the biggest gaps in the walls, and they had settled into the house with a certain amount of comfort. Jesusita's husband was seldom there. "He's looking for a place with horses," she'd say.

He was the topic of gossip. Some people said he was a horse thief. This wasn't any big deal, especially in the dump. A boy who lived in the pig village had a pony that he'd stolen from one of the small ranches on the outskirts of Tijuana. He used the pony to rustle cattle from the same ranches.

He fed his two brothers this way—their parents had disappeared—and he was quite proud of his outlaw status. He was thirteen when he started.

Something else about Jesusita's husband caused them all to talk. Crime wasn't it—crime would have made him something of a celebrity. Perhaps it was that stoic silence of his. His self-possession seemed arrogant, perhaps, and Mexicans hate an arrogant man.

They said he'd been involved in a major crime down south and had turned evidence against his accomplices. The rumors said he'd fled north with his family to escape reprisals—both from the criminals and the cops. Now that he was known to the police in the region, he'd be hounded continually, forced to set people up for arrest or worse . . . even innocent people.

Jesusita, on the other hand, seemed genuinely popular. She took part in the dump's church services, attended every event and Bible study. (They had their own church, and their own itinerant preacher.) She and Doña Araceli enjoyed a cordial relationship, and every time we came over the hill into the dump, the two of them barreled into me and lifted me off the ground. It became a regular practice for us to give her a ride down the canyon at the end of the day. The little boys would charge out from the house and play tag with me. One of them delighted in being captured and held upside down. They had gotten some pigs, and I was always ready to heap lavish praise on such fine hogs.

But one day, Jesusita told me she had to leave the house. They'd been fixing it up, planting some corn and expanding the little pigpen in the back. She insisted someone was making threats. We didn't believe her.

The next week, she directed us to the home of an old woman in the valley across from her house. Jesusita told me the woman owned the house and had threatened to harm her family if they didn't leave. Von and I went to the woman's house and talked to her. There was no problem, she insisted. They could stay. I was confused. Was Jesusita lying?

As we left, Jesusita held me hard and cried. "I'm afraid," she said. I would never see her again.

From the condition and location of the corpses, police pieced together this scenario: Jesusita and her husband were led up a canyon several miles from the dump (or taken by car to an abandoned stretch of road—I couldn't get clear details). At least two men accompanied them, and a small boy, possibly Jesusita's son—the same one who loved to be chased around the yard. The boy escaped. According to the testimony of the children, the men had appeared at the door and had seemed friendly. They told the family that there was a great deal of free lumber at a certain site. They said they knew of the family's troubles, and they wanted to offer their help. Jesusita and her husband went with them. They took the boy for extra help, thinking there would be a heavy load to carry.

Jesusita's husband was held by the arms, and a sawed-off shotgun was notched under his nose and fired. It blew his head to pieces, leaving only the back of his skull, with the ears attached.

This must have happened very quickly. Apparently, the shooter had his shotgun under a coat.

Jesusita and the boy ran. The child hid himself. The gunmen went after her. She was not fast—her legs were short, too short to carry her out of range. They shot her in the spine, knocking her facedown in the dirt. They must have taken their time reloading, because she managed to crawl a short distance, bleeding heavily. The shooter walked up to her, put the shotgun to the back of her head, and fired.

"Apparently, the shooter had his shotgun under a coat."

The next day, a note was stuck to the door of the house. It said: IF YOU ARE NOT GONE BY TOMORROW WE WILL COME AND KILL EACH ONE OF YOU.

The children scattered. They were gone when I got there, and they left no word about where they could be found.

Through the grapevine, I was told that if I was really interested in the shooting, one of the men would sell me the shotgun. It was going for forty dollars.

David Foster Wallace

Consider the Lobster

David Foster Wallace's fiction books include *The Broom of the System* (1987), *The Girl with Curious Hair* (1989), *Infinite Jest* (1996), *Brief Interviews with Hideous Men* (1999), and *Oblivion* (2004). His nonfiction includes two collections: *A Supposedly Fun Thing I'll Never Do Again* (1997) and *Consider the Lobster* (2005), and the book-length narrative *Everything and More* (2003).

A reviewer for the *Guardian* said that Wallace is "a sublimely funny writer, both ha-ha and peculiar. . . . A contemporary American master working at the extreme edge of the radar." In the *New York Times Book Review*, Laura Miller wrote of his essays, "Mr. Wallace's distinctive and infectious style, an acrobatic cart-wheeling between high intellectual discourse and vernacular insouciance, makes him tremendously entertaining to read, whatever his subject." Of his book *Consider the Lobster*, a *New York Times* reviewer said, "If some American writers have a carefully hedged relation with actuality, or prefer an evasive irony over passionate engagement, this has at least something to do with their membership, in these days of generous publishing advances, fellowships and grants, in their country's most privileged classes. Wallace is clearly an exception. Certainly, few of his young peers have spoken as eloquently and feelingly as he has about the hard tasks of the moral imagination that contemporary American life imposes on them."

Wallace was raised in Champaign-Urbana, Illinois, where he was a prodigious thinker and junior tennis player. He double-majored in English and philosophy at Amherst College and later received his MFA from the University of Arizona. He then taught at Illinois State University for several years. While at ISU he continued working on his hefty novel *Infinite Jest*, which was published to much notice in 1996. Not long after, he was awarded a MacArthur Foundation grant. In 2002 he took a position as an endowed professor of creative writing and English at Pomona College in California, where he taught until his death in 2008.

"Consider the Lobster" was first published in *Gourmet* magazine.

Interview with David Foster Wallace, p. 770.

The enormous, pungent, and extremely well-marketed Maine Lobster Festival is held every late July in the state's midcoast region, meaning the western side of Penobscot Bay, the nerve stem of Maine's lobster industry. What's called the midcoast runs from Owl's Head and Thomaston in the south to Belfast in the north. (Actually, it might extend all the way up to Bucksport, but we were never able to get farther north than Belfast on Route 1, whose summer traffic is, as you can imagine, unimaginable.) The region's two main communities are Camden, with its very old money and yachty harbor and five-star restaurants and phenomenal B&Bs, and Rockland, a serious old fishing town that hosts the festival every summer in historic Harbor Park, right along the water.[1]

Tourism and lobster are the midcoast region's two main industries, and they're both warm-weather enterprises, and the Maine Lobster Festival represents less an intersection of the industries than a deliberate collision, joyful and lucrative and loud. The assigned subject of this *Gourmet* article is the 56th Annual MLF, 30 July–3 August 2003, whose official theme this year was "Lighthouses, Laughter, and Lobster." Total paid attendance was over 100,000, due partly to a national CNN spot in June during which a senior editor of *Food & Wine* magazine hailed the MLF as one of the best food-themed galas in the world. 2003 festival highlights: concerts by Lee Ann Womack and Orleans, annual Maine Sea Goddess beauty pageant, Saturday's big parade, Sunday's William G. Atwood Memorial Crate Race, annual Amateur Cooking Competition, carnival rides and midway attractions and food booths, and the MLF's Main Eating Tent, where something over 25,000 pounds of fresh-caught Maine lobster is consumed after preparation in the World's Largest Lobster Cooker near the grounds' north entrance. Also available are lobster rolls, lobster turnovers, lobster sauté, Down East lobster salad, lobster bisque, lobster ravioli, and deep-fried lobster dumplings. Lobster thermidor is obtainable at a sit-down restaurant called the Black Pearl on Harbor Park's northwest wharf. A large all-pine booth sponsored by the Maine Lobster Promotion Council has free pamphlets with recipes, eating tips, and Lobster Fun Facts. The winner of Friday's Amateur Cooking Competition prepares Saffron Lobster Ramekins, the recipe for which is now available for public downloading at www .mainelobsterfestival.com. There are lobster T-shirts and lobster bobblehead dolls and inflatable lobster pool toys and clamp-on lobster hats with big scarlet claws that wobble on springs. Your assigned correspondent saw it all, accompanied by one girlfriend and both his own parents—one of which parents was actually born and raised in Maine, albeit in the extreme northern inland part, which is potato country and a world away from the touristic midcoast.[2]

For practical purposes, everyone knows what a lobster is. As usual, though, there's much more to know than most of us care about—it's all a matter of what your interests are. Taxonomically speaking, a lobster is a marine crustacean of the family Homaridae, characterized by five pairs of jointed legs, the first pair terminating in large pincerish claws used for

---

[1] There's a comprehensive native apothegm: "Camden by the sea, Rockland by the smell."

[2] N.B. All personally connected parties have made it clear from the start that they do not want to be talked about in this article.

subduing prey. Like many other species of benthic carnivore, lobsters are both hunters and scavengers. They have stalked eyes, gills on their legs, and antennae. There are a dozen or so different kinds worldwide, of which the relevant species here is the Maine lobster, *Homarus americanus*. The name "lobster" comes from the Old English *loppestre*, which is thought to be a corrupt form of the Latin word for locust combined with the Old English *loppe*, which meant spider.

> "The point is that lobsters are basically giant sea insects."

Moreover, a crustacean is an aquatic arthropod of the class Crustacea, which comprises crabs, shrimp, barnacles, lobsters, and freshwater crayfish. All this is right there in the encyclopedia. And arthropods are members of the phylum Arthropoda, which phylum covers insects, spiders, crustaceans, and centipedes/millipedes, all of whose main commonality, besides the absence of a centralized brain-spine assembly, is a chitinous exoskeleton composed of segments, to which appendages are articulated in pairs.

The point is that lobsters are basically giant sea insects.[3] Like most arthropods, they date from the Jurassic period, biologically so much older than mammalia that they might as well be from another planet. And they are—particularly in their natural brown-green state, brandishing their claws like weapons and with thick antennae awhip—not nice to look at. And it's true that they are garbagemen of the sea, eaters of dead stuff,[4] although they'll also eat some live shellfish, certain kinds of injured fish, and sometimes one another.

But they are themselves good eating. Or so we think now. Up until sometime in the 1800s, though, lobster was literally low-class food, eaten only by the poor and institutionalized. Even in the harsh penal environment of early America, some colonies had laws against feeding lobsters to inmates more than once a week because it was thought to be cruel and unusual, like making people eat rats. One reason for their low status was how plentiful lobsters were in old New England. "Unbelievable abundance" is how one source describes the situation, including accounts of Plymouth Pilgrims wading out and capturing all they wanted by hand, and of early Boston's seashore being littered with lobsters after hard storms—these latter were treated as a smelly nuisance and ground up for fertilizer. There is also the fact that premodern lobster was cooked dead and then preserved, usually packed in salt or crude hermetic containers. Maine's earliest lobster industry was based around a dozen such seaside canneries in the 1840s, from which lobster was shipped as far away as California, in demand only because it was cheap and high in protein, basically chewable fuel.

Now, of course, lobster is posh, a delicacy, only a step or two down from caviar. The meat is richer and more substantial than most fish, its

[3]Midcoasters' native term for a lobster is, in fact, "bug," as in "Come around on Sunday and we'll cook up some bugs."

[4]Factoid: Lobster traps are usually baited with dead herring.

taste subtle compared to the marine-gaminess of mussels and clams. In the US pop-food imagination, lobster is now the seafood analog to steak, with which it's so often twinned as Surf 'n' Turf on the really expensive part of the chain steakhouse menu.

In fact, one obvious project of the MLF, and of its omnipresently sponsorial Maine Lobster Promotion Council, is to counter the idea that lobster is unusually luxe or unhealthy or expensive, suitable only for effete palates or the occasional blow-the-diet treat. It is emphasized over and over in presentations and pamphlets at the festival that lobster meat has fewer calories, less cholesterol, and less saturated fat than chicken.[5] And in the Main Eating Tent, you can get a "quarter" (industry shorthand for a 1¼-pound lobster), a four-ounce cup of melted butter, a bag of chips, and a soft roll w/ butter-pat for around $12.00, which is only slightly more expensive than supper at McDonald's.

Be apprised, though, that the Maine Lobster Festival's democratization of lobster comes with all the massed inconvenience and aesthetic compromise of real democracy. See, for example, the aforementioned Main Eating Tent, for which there is a constant Disneyland-grade queue, and which turns out to be a square quarter mile of awning-shaded cafeteria lines and rows of long institutional tables at which friend and stranger alike sit cheek by jowl, cracking and chewing and dribbling. It's hot, and the sagged roof traps the steam and the smells, which latter are strong and only partly food-related. It is also loud, and a good percentage of the total noise is masticatory. The suppers come in styrofoam trays, and the soft drinks are iceless and flat, and the coffee is convenience-store coffee in more styrofoam, and the utensils are plastic (there are none of the special long skinny forks for pushing out the tail meat, though a few savvy diners bring their own). Nor do they give you near enough napkins considering how messy lobster is to eat, especially when you're squeezed onto benches alongside children of various ages and vastly different levels of fine-motor development—not to mention the people who've somehow smuggled in their own beer in enormous aisle-blocking coolers, or who all of a sudden produce their own plastic tablecloths and spread them over large portions of tables to try to reserve them (the tables) for their own little groups. And so on. Any one example is no more than a petty inconvenience, of course, but the MLF turns out to be full of irksome little downers like this—see for instance the Main Stage's headliner shows, where it turns out that you have to pay $20 extra for a folding chair if you want to sit down; or the North Tent's mad scramble for the Nyquil-cup-sized samples of finalists' entries handed out after the Cooking Competition; or the much-touted Maine Sea Goddess pageant finals, which turn out to be excruciatingly long and to consist mainly of endless thanks and tributes to local sponsors. Let's not even talk about the grossly inadequate Port-A-San facilities or the

---

[5]Of course, the common practice of dipping the lobster meat in melted butter torpedoes all these happy fat-specs, which none of the council's promotional stuff ever mentions, any more than potato industry PR talks about sour cream and bacon bits.

fact that there's nowhere to wash your hands before or after eating. What the Maine Lobster Festival really is is a midlevel county fair with a culinary hook, and in this respect it's not unlike Tidewater crab festivals, Midwest corn festivals, Texas chili festivals, etc., and shares with these venues the core paradox of all teeming commercial demotic events: It's not for everyone.[6] Nothing against the euphoric senior editor of *Food & Wine*, but I'd be surprised if she'd ever actually been here in Harbor Park, amid crowds of people slapping canal-zone mosquitoes as they eat deep-fried Twinkies and watch Professor Paddywhack, on six-foot stilts in a raincoat with plastic lobsters protruding from all directions on springs, terrify their children.

Lobster is essentially a summer food. This is because we now prefer our lobsters fresh, which means they have to be recently caught, which for both tactical and economic reasons takes place at depths less than 25 fathoms. Lobsters tend to be hungriest and most active (i.e., most trappable) at summer water temperatures of 45–50 degrees. In the autumn, most Maine lobsters migrate out into deeper water, either for warmth or to avoid the heavy waves that pound New England's coast all winter. Some burrow into the bottom. They might hibernate; nobody's sure. Summer is also lobsters' molting season—specifically early- to mid-July. Chitinous arthropods grow

---

[6]In truth, there's a great deal to be said about the differences between working-class Rockland and the heavily populist flavor of its festival versus comfortable and elitist Camden with its expensive view and shops given entirely over to $200 sweaters and great rows of Victorian homes converted to upscale B&Bs. And about these differences as two sides of the great coin that is US tourism. Very little of which will be said here, except to amplify the above-mentioned paradox and to reveal your assigned correspondent's own preferences. I confess that I have never understood why so many people's idea of a fun vacation is to don flip-flops and sunglasses and crawl through maddening traffic to loud, hot, crowded tourist venues in order to sample a "local flavor" that is by definition ruined by the presence of tourists. This may (as my festival companions keep pointing out) all be a matter of personality and hardwired taste; the fact that I do not like tourist venues means that I'll never understand their appeal and so am probably not the one to talk about it (the supposed appeal). But, since this FN will almost surely not survive magazine-editing anyway, here goes:

As I see it, it probably really is good for the soul to be a tourist, even if it's only once in a while. Not good for the soul in a refreshing or enlivening way, though, but rather in a grim, steely-eyed, let's-look-honestly-at-the-facts-and-find-some-way-to-deal-with-them way. My personal experience has not been that traveling around the country is broadening or relaxing, or that radical changes in place and context have a salutary effect, but rather that intranational tourism is radically constricting, and humbling in the hardest way—hostile to my fantasy of being a true individual, of living somehow outside and above it all. (Coming up is the part that my companions find especially unhappy and repellent, a sure way to spoil the fun of vacation travel:) To be a mass tourist, for me, is to become a pure late-date American: alien, ignorant, greedy for something you cannot ever have, disappointed in a way you can never admit. It is to spoil, by way of sheer ontology, the very unspoiledness you are there to experience. It is to impose yourself on places that in all non-economic ways would be better, realer, without you. It is, in lines and gridlock and transaction after transaction, to confront a dimension of yourself that is as inescapable as it is painful: As a tourist, you become economically significant but existentially loathsome, an insect on a dead thing.

by molting, rather the way people have to buy bigger clothes as they age and gain weight. Since lobsters can live to be over 100, they can also get to be quite large, as in 30 pounds or more—though truly senior lobsters are rare now because New England's waters are so heavily trapped.[7] Anyway, hence the culinary distinction between hard- and soft-shell lobsters, the latter sometimes a.k.a. shedders. A soft-shell lobster is one that has recently molted. In midcoast restaurants, the summer menu often offers both kinds, with shedders being slightly cheaper even though they're easier to dismantle and the meat is allegedly sweeter. The reason for the discount is that a molting lobster uses a layer of seawater for insulation while its new shell is hardening, so there's slightly less actual meat when you crack open a shedder, plus a redolent gout of water that gets all over everything and can sometimes jet out lemonlike and catch a tablemate right in the eye. If it's winter or you're buying lobster someplace far from New England, on the other hand, you can almost bet that the lobster is a hard-shell, which for obvious reasons travel better.

As an à la carte entrée, lobster can be baked, broiled, steamed, grilled, sautéed, stir-fried, or microwaved. The most common method, though, is boiling. If you're someone who enjoys having lobster at home, this is probably the way you do it, since boiling is so easy. You need a large kettle w/ cover, which you fill about half full with water (the standard advice is that you want 2.5 quarts of water per lobster). Seawater is optimal, or you can add two tbsp salt per quart from the tap. It also helps to know how much your lobsters weigh. You get the water boiling, put in the lobsters one at a time, cover the kettle, and bring it back up to a boil. Then you bank the heat and let the kettle simmer—ten minutes for the first pound of lobster, then three minutes for each pound after that. (This is assuming you've got hard-shell lobsters, which, again, if you don't live between Boston and Halifax is probably what you've got. For shedders, you're supposed to subtract three minutes from the total.) The reason the kettle's lobsters turn scarlet is that boiling somehow suppresses every pigment in their chitin but one. If you want an easy test of whether the lobsters are done, you try pulling on one of their antennae—if it comes out of the head with minimal effort, you're ready to eat.

A detail so obvious that most recipes don't even bother to mention it is that each lobster is supposed to be alive when you put it in the kettle. This is part of lobster's modern appeal—it's the freshest food there is. There's no decomposition between harvesting and eating. And not only do lobsters require no cleaning or dressing or plucking, they're relatively easy for vendors to keep alive. They come up alive in the traps, are placed in containers of seawater, and can—so long as the water's aerated and the animals' claws are pegged or banded to keep them from tearing one another up under the

---

[7]Datum: In a good year, the US industry produces around 80,000,000 pounds of lobster, and Maine accounts for more than half that total.

stresses of captivity[8]—survive right up until they're boiled. Most of us have been in supermarkets or restaurants that feature tanks of live lobsters, from which you can pick out your supper while it watches you point. And part of the overall spectacle of the Maine Lobster Festival is that you can see actual lobstermen's vessels docking at the wharves along the northeast grounds and unloading fresh-caught product, which is transferred by hand or cart 150 yards to the great clear tanks stacked up around the festival's cooker—which is, as mentioned, billed as the World's Largest Lobster Cooker and can process over 100 lobsters at a time for the Main Eating Tent.

So then here is a question that's all but unavoidable at the World's Largest Lobster Cooker, and may arise in kitchens across the US: Is it all right to boil a sentient creature alive just for our gustatory pleasure? A related set of concerns: Is the previous question irksomely PC or sentimental? What does "all right" even mean in this context? Is the whole thing just a matter of personal choice?

As you may or may not know, a certain well-known group called People for the Ethical Treatment of Animals thinks that the morality of lobster-boiling is not just a matter of individual conscience. In fact, one of the very first things we hear about the MLF . . . well, to set the scene: We're coming in by cab from the almost indescribably odd and rustic Knox County Airport[9] very late on the night before the festival opens, sharing the cab with a wealthy political consultant who lives on Vinalhaven Island in the bay half the year (he's headed for the island ferry in Rockland). The consultant and cabdriver are responding to informal journalistic probes about how people who live in the midcoast region actually view the MLF, as in is the festival just a big-dollar tourist thing or is it something local residents look forward to attending, take genuine civic pride in, etc. The cabdriver (who's in his seventies, one of apparently a whole platoon of retirees the cab company puts on to help with the summer rush, and wears a US-flag lapel pin, and drives in what can only be called a very *deliberate* way) assures us that locals do endorse and enjoy the MLF, although he himself hasn't gone in years, and now come to think of it no one he and his wife know has, either.

[8]N.B. Similar reasoning underlies the practice of what's termed "debeaking" broiler chickens and brood hens in modern factory farms. Maximum commercial efficiency requires that enormous poultry populations be confined in unnaturally close quarters, under which conditions many birds go crazy and peck one another to death. As a purely observational side-note, be apprised that debeaking is usually an automated process and that the chickens receive no anesthetic. It's not clear to me whether most *Gourmet* readers know about debeaking, or about related practices like dehorning cattle in commercial feed lots, cropping swine's tails in factory hog farms to keep psychotically bored neighbors from chewing them off, and so forth. It so happens that your assigned correspondent knew almost nothing about standard meat-industry operations before starting work on this article.

[9]The terminal used to be somebody's house, for example, and the lost-luggage-reporting room was clearly once a pantry.

However, the demilocal consultant's been to recent festivals a couple times (one gets the impression it was at his wife's behest), of which his most vivid impression was that "you have to line up for an ungodly long time to get your lobsters, and meanwhile there are all these ex–flower children coming up and down along the line handing out pamphlets that say the lobsters die in terrible pain and you shouldn't eat them."

And it turns out that the post-hippies of the consultant's recollection were activists from PETA. There were no PETA people in obvious view at the 2003 MLF,[10] but they've been conspicuous at many of the recent festivals. Since at least the mid-1990s, articles in everything from the *Camden Herald* to the *New York Times* have described PETA urging boycotts of the Maine Lobster Festival, often deploying celebrity spokesmen like Mary Tyler Moore for open letters and ads saying stuff like "Lobsters are extraordinarily sensitive" and "To me, eating a lobster is out of the question." More concrete is the oral testimony of Dick, our florid and extremely gregarious rental-car liaison,[11] to the effect that PETA's been around so much during recent years that a kind of brittlely tolerant homeostasis now obtains between the activists and the festival's locals, e.g.: "We had some incidents a couple years ago. One lady took most of her clothes off and painted herself like a lobster, almost got herself arrested. But for the most part they're let alone. [Rapid series of small ambiguous laughs, which with Dick happens a lot.] They do their thing and we do our thing."

This whole interchange takes place on Route 1, 30 July, during a four-mile, 50-minute ride from the airport[12] to the dealership to sign car-rental

---

[10]It turned out that one Mr. William R. Rivas-Rivas, a high-ranking PETA official out of the group's Virginia headquarters, was indeed there this year, albeit solo, working the festival's main and side entrances on Saturday, 2 August, handing out pamphlets and adhesive stickers emblazoned with "Being Boiled Hurts," which is the tagline in most of PETA's published material about lobsters. I learned that he'd been there only later, when speaking with Mr. Rivas-Rivas on the phone. I'm not sure how we missed seeing him *in situ* at the festival, and I can't see much to do except apologize for the oversight—although it's also true that Saturday was the day of the big MLF parade through Rockland, which basic journalistic responsibility seemed to require going to (and which, with all due respect, meant that Saturday was maybe not the best day for PETA to work the Harbor Park grounds, especially if it was going to be just one person for one day, since a lot of diehard MLF partisans were off-site watching the parade (which, again with no offense intended, was in truth kind of cheesy and boring, consisting mostly of slow homemade floats and various midcoast people waving at one another, and with an extremely annoying man dressed as Blackbeard ranging up and down the length of the crowd saying "Arrr" over and over and brandishing a plastic sword at people, etc.; plus it rained)).

[11]By profession, Dick is actually a car salesman; the midcoast region's National Car Rental franchise operates out of a Chevy dealership in Thomaston.

[12]The short version regarding why we were back at the airport after already arriving the previous night involves lost luggage and a miscommunication about where and what the midcoast's National franchise was—Dick came out personally to the airport and got us, out of no evident motive but kindness. (He also talked nonstop the entire way, with a very distinctive speaking style that can be described only as manically laconic; the truth is that I now know more about this man than I do about some members of my own family.)

papers. Several irreproducible segues down the road from the PETA anec-dotes, Dick—whose son-in-law happens to be a professional lobsterman and one of the Main Eating Tent's regular suppliers—explains what he and his family feel is the crucial mitigating factor in the whole morality-of-boiling-lobsters-alive issue: "There's a part of the brain in people and ani-mals that lets us feel pain, and lobsters' brains don't have this part."

Besides the fact that it's incorrect in about nine different ways, the main reason Dick's statement is interesting is that its thesis is more or less echoed by the festival's own pronouncement on lobsters and pain, which is part of a Test Your Lobster IQ quiz that appears in the 2003 MLF pro-gram courtesy of the Maine Lobster Promotion Council:

> The nervous system of a lobster is very simple, and is in fact most similar to the nervous system of the grasshopper. It is decentralized with no brain. There is no cerebral cortex, which in humans is the area of the brain that gives the experience of pain.

Though it sounds more sophisticated, a lot of the neurology in this latter claim is still either false or fuzzy. The human cerebral cortex is the brain-part that deals with higher faculties like reason, metaphysical self-awareness, lan-guage, etc. Pain reception is known to be part of a much older and more primitive system of nociceptors and prostaglandins that are managed by the brain stem and thalamus.[13] On the other hand, it is true that the cerebral cortex is involved in what's variously called suffering, distress, or the emotional experience of pain—i.e., experiencing painful stimuli as un-pleasant, very unpleasant, unbearable, and so on.

Before we go any further, let's acknowledge that the questions of whether and how different kinds of animals feel pain, and of whether and why it might be justifiable to inflict pain on them in order to eat them, turn out to be extremely complex and difficult. And comparative neuro-anatomy is only part of the problem. Since pain is a totally subjective men-tal experience, we do not have direct access to anyone or anything's pain but our own; and even just the principles by which we can infer that other human beings experience pain and have a legitimate interest in not feeling pain involve hard-core philosophy—metaphysics, epistemology, value the-ory, ethics. The fact that even the most highly evolved nonhuman mam-mals can't use language to communicate with us about their subjective mental experience is only the first layer of additional complication in trying to extend our reasoning about pain and morality to animals. And every-thing gets progressively more abstract and convolved as we move farther and farther out from the higher-type mammals into cattle and swine and

---

[13]To elaborate by way of example: The common experience of accidentally touching a hot stove and yanking your hand back before you're even aware that anything's going on is explained by the fact that many of the processes by which we detect and avoid painful stimuli do not involve the cortex. In the case of the hand and stove, the brain is bypassed altogether; all the important neurochemical action takes place in the spine.

dogs and cats and rodents, and then birds and fish, and finally inverte-brates like lobsters.

The more important point here, though, is that the whole animal-cruelty-and-eating issue is not just complex, it's also uncomfortable. It is, at any rate, uncomfortable for me, and for just about everyone I know who enjoys a variety of foods and yet does not want to see herself as cruel or unfeeling. As far as I can tell, my own main way of dealing with this conflict has been to avoid thinking about the whole unpleasant thing. I should add that it appears to me unlikely that many readers of *Gourmet* wish to think about it, either, or to be queried about the morality of their eating habits in the pages of a culinary monthly. Since, however, the assigned subject of this article is what it was like to attend the 2003 MLF, and thus to spend several days in the midst of a great mass of Americans all eating lobster, and thus to be more or less impelled to think hard about lobster and the experience of buying and eating lobster, it turns out that there is no honest way to avoid certain moral questions.

There are several reasons for this. For one thing, it's not just that lobsters get boiled alive, it's that you do it yourself—or at least it's done specifically for you, on-site.[14] As mentioned, the World's Largest Lobster Cooker, which is highlighted as an attraction in the festival's program, is right out there on the MLF's north grounds for everyone to see. Try to imagine a Nebraska Beef Festival[15] at which part of the festivities is watch-ing trucks pull up and the live cattle get driven down the ramp and slaugh-tered right there on the World's Largest Killing Floor or something—there's no way.

The intimacy of the whole thing is maximized at home, which of course is where most lobster gets prepared and eaten (although note already the semiconscious euphemism "prepared," which in the case of lobsters really means killing them right there in our kitchens). The basic scenario is that we

---

[14]Morality-wise, let's concede that this cuts both ways. Lobster-eating is at least not abetted by the system of corporate factory farms that produces most beef, pork, and chicken. Because, if nothing else, of the way they're marketed and packaged for sale, we eat these latter meats without having to consider that they were once conscious, sentient creatures to whom horrible things were done. (N.B. "Horrible" here meaning really, really horrible. Write off to PETA or peta.org for their free "Meet Your Meat" video, narrated by Mr. Alec Baldwin, if you want to see just about everything meat-related you don't want to see or think about. (N.B.$_2$ Not that PETA's any sort of font of unspun truth. Like many partisans in complex moral disputes, the PETA people are fanatics, and a lot of their rhetoric seems simplistic and self-righteous. But this particular video, replete with actual factory-farm and corporate-slaughterhouse footage, is both credible and traumatizing.))

[15]Is it significant that "lobster," "fish," and "chicken" are our culture's words for both the animal and the meat, whereas most mammals seem to require euphemisms like "beef" and "pork" that help us separate the meat we eat from the living creature the meat once was? Is this evidence that some kind of deep unease about eating higher animals is endemic enough to show up in English usage, but that the unease diminishes as we move out of the mammalian order? (And is "lamb"/"lamb" the counterexample that sinks the whole theory, or are there special, biblico-historical reasons for that equivalence?)

come in from the store and make our little preparations like getting the kettle filled and boiling, and then we lift the lobsters out of the bag or whatever retail container they came home in . . . whereupon some uncomfortable things start to happen. However stuporous a lobster is from the trip home, for instance, it tends to come alarmingly to life when placed in boiling water. If you're tilting it from a container into the steaming kettle, the lobster will sometimes try to cling to the container's sides or even to hook its claws over the kettle's rim like a person trying to keep from going over the edge of a roof. And worse is when the lobster's fully immersed. Even if you cover the kettle and turn away, you can usually hear the cover rattling and clanking as the lobster tries to push it off. Or the creature's claws scraping the sides of the kettle as it thrashes around. The lobster, in other words, behaves very much as you or I would behave if we were plunged into boiling water (with the obvious exception of screaming[16]). A blunter way to say this is that the lobster acts as if it's in terrible pain, causing some cooks to leave the kitchen altogether and to take one of those little lightweight plastic oven-timers with them into another room and wait until the whole process is over.

There happen to be two main criteria that most ethicists agree on for determining whether a living creature has the capacity to suffer and so has genuine interests that it may or may not be our moral duty to consider.[17] One is how much of the neurological hardware required for pain-experience the animal comes equipped with—nociceptors, prostaglandins, neuronal opioid receptors, etc. The other criterion is whether the animal demonstrates behavior associated with pain. And it takes a lot of intellectual gymnastics and behaviorist hairsplitting not to see struggling, thrashing, and lid-clattering as just such pain-behavior. According to marine zoologists, it usually takes lobsters between 35 and 45 seconds to die in boiling water. (No source I could find talks about how long it takes them to die in superheated steam; one rather hopes it's faster.)

There are, of course, other ways to kill your lobster on-site and so achieve maximum freshness. Some cooks' practice is to drive a sharp heavy

---

[16]There's a relevant populist myth about the high-pitched whistling sound that sometimes issues from a pot of boiling lobster. The sound is really vented steam from the layer of seawater between the lobster's flesh and its carapace (this is why shedders whistle more than hard-shells), but the pop version has it that the sound is the lobster's rabbit-like death-scream. Lobsters communicate via pheromones in their urine and don't have anything close to the vocal equipment for screaming, but the myth's very persistent—which might, once again, point to a low-level cultural unease about the boiling thing.

[17]"Interests" basically means strong and legitimate preferences, which obviously require some degree of consciousness, responsiveness to stimuli, etc. See, for instance, the utilitarian philosopher Peter Singer, whose 1974 *Animal Liberation* is more or less the bible of the modern animal-rights movement:

> It would be nonsense to say that it was not in the interests of a stone to be kicked along the road by a schoolboy. A stone does not have interests because it cannot suffer. Nothing that we can do to it could possibly make any difference to its welfare. A mouse, on the other hand, does have an interest in not being kicked along the road, because it will suffer if it is.

knife point-first into a spot just above the midpoint between the lobster's eyestalks (more or less where the Third Eye is in human foreheads). This is alleged either to kill the lobster instantly or to render it insensate, and is said at least to eliminate some of the cowardice involved in throwing a creature into boiling water and then fleeing the room. As far as I can tell from talking to proponents of the knife-in-head method, the idea is that it's more violent but ultimately more merciful, plus that a willingness to exert personal agency and accept responsibility for stabbing the lobster's head honors the lobster somehow and entitles one to eat it (there's often a vague sort of Native American spirituality-of-the-hunt flavor to pro-knife arguments). But the problem with the knife method is basic biology: Lobsters' nervous systems operate off not one but several ganglia, a.k.a. nerve bundles, which are sort of wired in series and distributed all along the lobster's underside, from stem to stern. And disabling only the frontal ganglion does not normally result in quick death or unconsciousness.

Another alternative is to put the lobster in cold saltwater and then very slowly bring it up to a full boil. Cooks who advocate this method are going on the analogy to a frog, which can supposedly be kept from jumping out of a boiling pot by heating the water incrementally. In order to save a lot of research-summarizing, I'll simply assure you that the analogy between frogs and lobsters turns out not to hold—plus, if the kettle's water isn't aerated seawater, the immersed lobster suffers from slow suffocation, although usually not decisive enough suffocation to keep it from still thrashing and clattering when the water gets hot enough to kill it. In fact, lobsters boiled incrementally often display a whole bonus set of gruesome, convulsionlike reactions that you don't see in regular boiling.

Ultimately, the only certain virtues of the home-lobotomy and slow-heating methods are comparative, because there are even worse/crueler ways people prepare lobster. Time-thrifty cooks sometimes microwave them alive (usually after poking several vent-holes in the carapace, which is a precaution most shellfish-microwavers learn about the hard way). Live dismemberment, on the other hand, is big in Europe—some chefs cut the lobster in half before cooking; others like to tear off the claws and tail and toss only these parts into the pot.

And there's more unhappy news respecting suffering-criterion number one. Lobsters don't have much in the way of eyesight or hearing, but they do have an exquisite tactile sense, one facilitated by hundreds of thousands of tiny hairs that protrude through their carapace. "Thus it is," in the words of T. M. Prudden's industry classic *About Lobster*, "that although encased in what seems a solid, impenetrable armor, the lobster can receive stimuli and impressions from without as readily as if it possessed a soft and delicate skin." And lobsters do have nociceptors,[18] as well as invertebrate

---

[18]This is the neurological term for special pain-receptors that are "sensitive to potentially damaging extremes of temperature, to mechanical forces, and to chemical substances which are released when body tissues are damaged."

versions of the prostaglandins and major neurotransmitters via which our own brains register pain.

Lobsters do not, on the other hand, appear to have the equipment for making or absorbing natural opioids like endorphins and enkephalins, which are what more advanced nervous systems use to try to handle intense pain. From this fact, though, one could conclude either that lobsters are maybe even *more* vulnerable to pain, since they lack mammalian nervous systems' built-in analgesia, or, instead, that the absence of natural opioids implies an absence of the really intense pain-sensations that natural opioids are designed to mitigate. I for one can detect a marked upswing in mood as I contemplate this latter possibility. It could be that their lack of endorphin/enkephalin hardware means that lobsters' raw subjective experience of pain is so radically different from mammals' that it may not even deserve the term "pain." Perhaps lobsters are more like those frontal-lobotomy patients one reads about who report experiencing pain in a totally different way than you and I. These patients evidently do feel physical pain, neurologically speaking, but don't dislike it—though neither do they like it; it's more that they feel it but don't feel anything *about* it—the point being that the pain is not distressing to them or something they want to get away from. Maybe lobsters, who are also without frontal lobes, are detached from the neurological-registration-of-injury-or-hazard we call pain in just the same way. There is, after all, a difference between (1) pain as a purely neurological event, and (2) actual suffering, which seems crucially to involve an emotional component, an awareness of pain as unpleasant, as something to fear/dislike/want to avoid.

Still, after all the abstract intellection, there remain the facts of the frantically clanking lid, the pathetic clinging to the edge of the pot. Standing at the stove, it is hard to deny in any meaningful way that this is a living creature experiencing pain and wishing to avoid/escape the painful experience. To my lay mind, the lobster's behavior in the kettle appears to be the expression of a *preference;* and it may well be that an ability to form preferences is the decisive criterion for real suffering.[19] The logic of this (preference → suffering) relation may be easiest to see in the negative case. If you cut certain kinds of worms in half, the halves will often keep crawling around and going about their vermiform business as if nothing had happened. When we assert, based on their post-op behavior, that these worms appear not to be suffering, what we're really saying is that there's no sign the worms know anything bad has happened or would *prefer* not to have gotten cut in half.

Lobsters, though, are known to exhibit preferences. Experiments have shown that they can detect changes of only a degree or two in water temperature; one reason for their complex migratory cycles (which can

---

[19]"Preference" is maybe roughly synonymous with "interests," but it is a better term for our purposes because it's less abstractly philosophical—"preference" seems more personal, and it's the whole idea of a living creature's personal experience that's at issue.

often cover 100-plus miles a year) is to pursue the temperatures they like best.[20] And, as mentioned, they're bottom-dwellers and do not like bright light—if a tank of food-lobsters is out in the sunlight or a store's fluorescence, the lobsters will always congregate in whatever part is darkest. Fairly solitary in the ocean, they also clearly dislike the crowding that's part of their captivity in tanks, since (as also mentioned) one reason why lobsters' claws are banded on capture is to keep them from attacking one another under the stress of close-quarter storage.

In any event, at the MLF, standing by the bubbling tanks outside the World's Largest Lobster Cooker, watching the fresh-caught lobsters pile over one another, wave their hobbled claws impotently, huddle in the rear corners, or scrabble frantically back from the glass as you approach, it is difficult not to sense that they're unhappy, or frightened, even if it's some rudimentary version of these feelings . . . and, again, why does rudimentariness even enter into it? Why is a primitive, inarticulate form of suffering less urgent or uncomfortable for the person who's helping to inflict it by paying for the food it results in? I'm not trying to give you a PETA-like screed here—at least I don't think so. I'm trying, rather, to work out and articulate some of the troubling questions that arise amid all the laughter and saltation and community pride of the Maine Lobster Festival. The truth is that if you, the festival attendee, permit yourself to think that lobsters can suffer and would rather not, the MLF begins to take on the aspect of something like a Roman circus or medieval torture-fest.

Does that comparison seem a bit much? If so, exactly why? Or what about this one: Is it possible that future generations will regard our present agribusiness and eating practices in much the same way we now view Nero's entertainments or Mengele's experiments? My own initial reaction

---

[20]Of course, the most common sort of counterargument here would begin by objecting that "like best" is really just a metaphor, and a misleadingly anthropomorphic one at that. The counterarguer would posit that the lobster seeks to maintain a certain optimal ambient temperature out of nothing but unconscious instinct (with a similar explanation for the low-light affinities upcoming in the main text). The thrust of such a counterargument will be that the lobster's thrashings and clankings in the kettle express not unpreferred pain but involuntary reflexes, like your leg shooting out when the doctor hits your knee. Be advised that there are professional scientists, including many researchers who use animals in experiments, who hold to the view that nonhuman creatures have no real feelings at all, merely "behaviors." Be further advised that this view has a long history that goes all the way back to Descartes, although its modern support comes mostly from behaviorist psychology.

To these what-looks-like-pain-is-really-just-reflexes counterarguments, however, there happen to be all sorts of scientific and pro–animal rights counter-counterarguments. And then further attempted rebuttals and redirects, and so on. Suffice it to say that both the scientific and the philosophical arguments on either side of the animal-suffering issue are involved, abstruse, technical, often informed by self-interest or ideology, and in the end so totally inconclusive that as a practical matter, in the kitchen or restaurant, it all still seems to come down to individual conscience, going with (no pun) your gut.

is that such a comparison is hysterical, extreme—and yet the reason it seems extreme to me appears to be that I believe animals are less morally important than human beings;[21] and when it comes to defending such a belief, even to myself, I have to acknowledge that (a) I have an obvious selfish interest in this belief, since I like to eat certain kinds of animals and want to be able to keep doing it, and (b) I haven't succeeded in working out any sort of personal ethical system in which the belief is truly defensible instead of just selfishly convenient.

> "Do you think much about the (possible) moral status and (probable) suffering of the animals involved?"

Given this article's venue and my own lack of culinary sophistication, I'm curious about whether the reader can identify with any of these reactions and acknowledgments and discomforts. I'm also concerned not to come off as shrill or preachy when what I really am is more like confused. For those *Gourmet* readers who enjoy well-prepared and -presented meals involving beef, veal, lamb, pork, chicken, lobster, etc.: Do you think much about the (possible) moral status and (probable) suffering of the animals involved? If you do, what ethical convictions have you worked out that permit you not just to eat but to savor and enjoy flesh-based viands (since of course refined *enjoyment,* rather than mere ingestion, is the whole point of gastronomy)? If, on the other hand, you'll have no truck with confusions or convictions and regard stuff like the previous paragraph as just so much fatuous navel-gazing, what makes it feel truly okay, inside, to just dismiss the whole thing out of hand? That is, is your refusal to think about any of this the product of actual thought, or is it just that you don't want to think about it? And if the latter, then why not? Do you ever think, even idly, about the possible reasons for your reluctance to think about it? I am not trying to bait anyone here—I'm genuinely curious. After all, isn't being extra aware and attentive and thoughtful about one's food and its overall context part of what distinguishes a real gourmet? Or is all the gourmet's extra attention and sensibility just supposed to be sensuous? Is it really all just a matter of taste and presentation?

These last few queries, though, while sincere, obviously involve much larger and more abstract questions about the connections (if any) between aesthetics and morality—about what the adjective in a phrase like "The Magazine of Good Living" is really supposed to mean—and these questions lead straightaway into such deep and treacherous waters that it's probably best to stop the public discussion right here. There are limits to what even interested persons can ask of each other.

---

[21]Meaning *a lot* less important, apparently, since the moral comparison here is not the value of one human's life vs. the value of one animal's life, but rather the value of one animal's life vs. the value of one human's taste for a particular kind of protein. Even the most diehard carniphile will acknowledge that it's possible to live and eat well without consuming animals.

Interview with David Foster Wallace

BECKY BRADWAY: When your early work was published, the use of footnotes in a creative piece was fairly unusual. Now there are many
writers doing the same, using numerical footnotes, text boxes, etc.
Does this piss you off? (There are plenty of ways to rephrase this
question in a way that might address blatant imitation, the dodging
of cohesive writing by those writing undeveloped pieces, the ADD
effect of media, the inability of readers to focus on a long narrative,
etc. Feel free to revise and address in any way that you see fit.)

DAVID FOSTER WALLACE: I'm going to have to confess ignorance right away,
I can see. I'm not sure who these writers are or what work you're
referring to. (The truth is that most of the stuff I've been reading for
the last couple years has been work-related; I'm not much up on
what's happening in the Lit Scene right now.) In the abstract, if there
really are 'many writers doing the same, using numerical FNs, text
boxes, etc.' it pisses me off not a whit. This is partly because I obviously didn't invent and don't own things like footnotes. To mention
just the writers who spring right to mind, V. Nabokov, M. Puig, and
J. G. Ballard all used FNs in some of their fiction. And to very different effect. And that's another part of the non-pissedness: Diffractors
like footnotes, interpolations, or offset boxes can be put to all sorts
of different uses, narratively speaking. I've used different sorts of
diffractors for different purposes in different pieces for at least the
last ten years (though not so much in 'early work'). If other writers
are using them, it's doubtless for their own purposes . . . plus maybe
because they've seen that they're a good way of setting up or drama-
tizing a certain kind of doubling, or self-consciousness, or disassoci-
ation, or hypercircuitedness (kind of like the little kid who stutters
because his head is exploding and he can't get it all out fast enough),
or something. They're certainly not the only way, though—nor is
doubling or diffracting the only to which FNs can be put.

BB: Why lobster? (Or, less frivolously, how do you decide what makes
a subject or idea worthy of your personal energy?)

DFW: Another unsexy confession. I normally wouldn't have taken the
Gourmet assignment at all. They wanted an experiential (or 'atmos-
pheric') piece on the Maine Lobster Festival. I'd already done three or
four such pieces and didn't really burn to do any more. But Maine is
(a) where my mom's from; and (b) where my folks would be visiting
upstate; and (c) the magazine offered to fly both me and my then-
girlfriend (now spouse) out for the thing; and (d) my parents offered
to come down to the MLF and meet us; and (e) it was a chance to
introduce my then-girlfriend to my folks, which I was keen to do
because (f) I was even then starting to plot how to get her to marry
me, and my parents are extremely charming and convivial and make
for attractive in-law material. I know that none of this is what you

were interested in hearing about when you asked Qu. 2, but it's the truth. And then the Festival turned out to be—as I believe I tried to state in some maximally tactful way in the article—unbelievably dull and cheesy, such that really describing it would have consisted in making that point (MLF = dull & cheesy) over and over. But on the second or third day, one of the drivers mentioned PETA and a past controversy over the ethics and neurology of eating lobster, and—as my now-spouse alleges—my eyes lit up and I began rubbing my hands together, even as she pointed out that *Gourmet* was not apt to be keen on a piece about the dubious morality of an upscale entree. And so on. . . . In some ways, the whole thing became a nightmare, because the more I read and learned (and the more materials I got from PETA), the more upset I got; and really the hardest or most energy-intensive thing about doing that piece was trying to maintain some kind of measured, pseudo-objective, there-are-really-two-sides-to-this-whole-highly-complex-debate persona and tone. In fact, I early on became 100% convinced of the basic immorality of not just lobster-boiling but (especially) of factory farming, the details of which I'd been ignorant of before I stumbled into this whole area via PETA and P. Singer, etc. It's all totally messed with my life and the way I eat—there are now things I simply cannot eat, physically; they won't go down.

BB: Why should writers conduct research? How do you know where to start and when to stop?

DFW: The answer to the first clause seems self-evident w/r/t nonfiction. In writing fiction, you have to know enough that you can sound authoritative enough about whatever world & people you're writing about that the reader isn't distracted by suspicions of implausibility and/or cheesiness. The issue comes up a lot with undergrad writing students, who have to be told that if they want to do a believable story about, say, lawyers, they have to research enough about lawyers and law firms that the plot and dialogue sound halfway convincing. The second clause of your question is the really tricky one. It's tricky because there's a whole other good answer to the first clause: Because it's fun. It's fun to dip into unfamiliar disciplines and professions and hobbies and preoccupations, and to try to learn just enough about them so that you (and/or your narrator/characters) can seem believable about them. It's maybe a little like acting—or actually more like the game of trying to convince the person sitting next to you on an airplane that you're a NASA telemetrist, or a corporate color consultant, or the former personal assistant to Andy Garcia. What's tricky is just what you're asking: how much is enough? You can drown in research. I've done it. I'm arguably doing it now; I'm an immense bore on two or three subjects that no one I know is interested in. But this is just how I proceed, I guess—I get excited, or scared, research too much, write too much, get caught up in details that aren't inaccurate but are dull/irrelevant; and then so the last several drafts of anything are always full of drastic cutting, and I always realize that I've spent way more hours on research and fine-detailing than I needed to, which is frustrating, and I get jealous of people like R. Powers and W. T. Vollmann and J. Scott who seem able to do marvelous research and expertise-simulation without drowning or wasting time and thus write two or three times as many books as I do—really good ones. But, then, whatever; people just do what they can't help doing. It's a really good question, though, Becky, that second clause.

BB: What is the difference between fiction and nonfiction? Or: what can you do in nonfiction that you can't do in fiction?

DFW: I have the feeling that whole scholarly tomes have been written on this question, and that any sort of answer I came up with could immediately be shot down or shown to be puerile by an expert in the field. But I think it has to do with some weird, complex, and largely unspoken contract with the reader. Both genres promise truth of some sort, but since nonfiction promises something close to literal truth (i.e., "This really happened," or at least "This really is the way it seemed to me to happen"), the disbelief that fiction is classically required to seduce the reader into suspending is more or less *a priori* dropped or suspended by the nonfiction-reader from the outset. This, as far as I can see, is the reason why texts come with genre labels right there on the cover: the "A Novel" or "Stories" or "A Memoir" more or less let the reader know what the terms of the contract are before p. 1 even starts. The reader's pre-suspension of disbelief gives nonfiction a particular kind of power, but it also seems to encumber the nonfiction with a kind of moral obligation fiction doesn't have. If a piece of fiction is markedly implausible or "untrue" in some way, the reader feels a certain bored distaste, or maybe disappointment. If a piece of nonfiction, though, turns out to be "untrue," the reader feels pissed, betrayed, lied to in some personal way. (See, e.g., the whole swivet over that James Frey memoir's having turned out to be false or embellished.) It's all very strange, and the precise terms of the quote-unquote contract that different genres entail are probably next to impossible to spell out abstractly . . . but we seem all to feel them. Or at least I seem to.

BB: The whole question of whether creative nonfiction must be literally true continues to come up again and again and again. I know your opinion on this matter, and you probably know mine—but would you be willing to discuss the extent to which a nonfiction writer must lie?

DFW: Again, I can give you only an intuitive, laymanish answer to what is probably a whole hot complex question in contemporary rhetoric. The "truth" that nonfiction promises a reader is probably best represented by some continuum having to do with the quality of good faith, a.k.a. honor. Everyone knows that it's highly unlikely that Orwell really did or could clearly remember the condemned man stepping reflexively around that puddle in such detail for "A Hanging." Nor does any serious person believe that Frank Conroy, Toby Wolff, Mary Karr, et al. really can and do remember childhood incidents, conversations, or even angles of sunlight with the precision and accuracy that their memoirs represent. Human memory just doesn't work that way. We all know this on some level . . . just as we know that a reporter for *The Nation* and one for the *Washington Times* are going to represent elements of a George W. Bush policy speech very differently. But there appears to be some sort of point on the continuum that nonfiction is pledged not to cross. No one seriously doubts that Orwell believed that he saw and later remembered that guy's avoidance of the puddle . . . that is, no one doubts that he was remembering and writing in good faith. Nor do we doubt that good memoirists are doing their best to remember and recount stuff as it seems to them (in memory) to have been. That is, good memoirists haven't exceeded that point at which we feel they're no longer showing good faith. Frey exceeded that point; the guy who wrote *Sleepers* and turned out to have made some stuff up for lurid effect exceeded the point. A journalist who misrepresents a speech, or skews quotations or facts in order to lend credence to a political argument or to advance a certain agenda . . . this is bad faith. But these are clear cases. I remember that we all noodled a lot in class, at ISU, about whether embellishing, or restructuring, or fabricating just a little bit was OK . . . especially if the exaggeration or falsehood actually enhanced the dramatic power or overall thematic "truth" of a piece of nonfiction. What did we decide? I don't remember what we decided (since my memory of ten-year-old seminars is no clearer or sharper than anyone else's), if anything. But we all knew, and know, know that any embellishment is dangerous, and that a writer's justifying embellishment via claiming that it actually enhances overall "truth" is exceedingly dangerous, since the claim is structurally identical to all Ends Justify Means rationalizations. Some part of nonfiction's special contract with the reader specifically concerns means, not just ends, and also concerns the writer's motives . . . and maybe the ultimate honesty that good nonfiction entails, and promises, is the writer's honesty with herself.

(PS Did that answer make any sense at all?)

BB: What is your opinion of the B-52s' song "Rock Lobster"?
DFW: The B-52s give me the creeps and always have.
:-) :-)
:-) :-) :-) :-)

S. L. Wisenberg
Holocaust Girls/Lemon

S. L. Wisenberg—Sandi to those who know her—has published two collections of prose: *The Sweetheart Is In* (2001, short stories), and *Holocaust Girls: History, Memory, & Other Obsessions* (2002, essays). A memoir based upon her Weblog *Cancer Bitch* (cancerbitch.blogspot.com) will be published by University of Iowa Press. Following college, Wisenberg worked as a reporter for the *Miami Herald* and has published prose and poetry in the *New Yorker, Ploughshares, Tikkun, New England Review, Michigan Quarterly Review,* and in several anthologies. She is the creative nonfiction editor of *Another Chicago Magazine* and codirector of Northwestern's MA in creative writing program. She has received fellowships from the Illinois Arts Council, Fine Arts Work Center in Provincetown, and the National Endowment for the Humanities.

Wisenberg supplied the following biographical sketch: "I am a third-generation native Texan on my mother's side. I was a substitute portrait artist at an amusement park, Astro World. Despite the worst grades of my life senior year in college, I was accepted into the Iowa Writers' Workshop at the University of Iowa. Nobody was talking about 'creative nonfiction' back in those days. I think I was accepted because I submitted a short story written in the second person, and this was before Jay McInerney used it in *Bright Lights, Big City*. I studied fiction, worked for newspapers, wrote fiction, did journalism, and so on and so forth. I also have written book reviews, though I don't have the right kind of mind that makes it easy to write them. I spent three wonderful summers teaching journalism cherubs at Northwestern. I spent three other wonderful summers getting educated by Uncle Sam in the National Endowment for the Humanities' summer seminars. I have taught at Northwestern, DePaul, School of the Art Institute of Chicago, Ragdale, and Roosevelt. I've published graphic art in the *Chicago Tribune* and Crain's *Chicago Business*."

"Holocaust Girls/Lemon" is a short lyrical piece from Wisenberg's essay collection *Holocaust Girls*.

Interview with S. L. Wisenberg, p. 777.

We are the Holocaust Girls
The Holocaust Girls, the Holocaust Girls
We are the Holocaust Girls,
We like to dig in the dark.

to the tune of "Lullaby League and
Lollypop Guild" from The Wizard of Oz

1.

You don't have to be Jewish to be a Holocaust Girl. But it helps. It helps to have been born in the U.S.A. to parents born here, without accents. But it's not necessary. And you don't have to be a girl, either. What matters most is that you must love suffering. You have to pick at wounds, must be encumbered by what you consider an affliction. You have to see your pain as a dark hole you could fall into. You practice falling into the darkness. You immerse yourself in descriptions of horror. You stand in the library aisle in the World War II–Europe section and thumb through familiar pages. You stare at the photographs of the skeletons, compositions you've memorized. You watch your tears make little dents, like tiny upturned rose petals, on the pages.

> "What matters most is that you must love suffering."

2.

Sometimes, what you have to do is jump.

In Lvov, Poland, which was also known as Lemberg, and which became L'viv, Ukraine, the Jews were trapped with no place to go. It was 1943, the time of daily roundups and shootings. *Aktions*. The Jews of the town were cornered. There was no escape, only the possibility of hiding, disappearing. A number of daring, desperate souls stepped down into the sewers and lived there. Eleven of them survived, among the rats and slime and damp, without sun, for fourteen months. They paid jewelry and gold and devalued zlotys to the sewer workers who found them and kept them alive. When the Germans retreated, when the Russians reclaimed the city, the Jews emerged from the sewer. They were pale as larvae. Covered in filth, backs hunched. Dripping. Their pupils had shrunk, too small to hold daylight. Everything looked blood red to them, or black and white. A crowd formed and stared at them; they seemed like cavemen. The group found its way to an empty apartment, climbed the stairs. The young mother among them, Paulina Chiger, took her two children to a window and opened it. "Breathe the air," she told them; they breathed, looking down at the street through a blood-red haze. "Breathe deeply the fresh air."

The Aryan side of Warsaw, it has been said, looked the same as it always had except there were no Jews. The ghetto revolt began in April 1943. In early May, before the ghetto burned completely, after particularly wrenching battles, a Jewish resistance fighter named Tuvia Borzykowski, along with seven of his comrades, slipped down to the sewers to pass to the Aryan side. It was dangerous; all day the Germans had been sending gas and grenades into the sewers. After walking and crawling underground for several hours, the eight men saw a huge light. It could only be Germans looking for Jews. Borzykowski and his friends froze, resigned to discovery and death.

But instead: two friends and a sewer worker, looking for survivors of the revolt. They carried candy and lemons. Borzykowski took a lemon. "It was the first fresh food we had tasted in months," he remembered. He bit into the lemon, ate it, peel and all.

That is what the Holocaust Girls yearn for—to want and appreciate something as intently, as specifically, as that whole lemon, to love the air and sun as much as the family crouched fourteen months in the sewers of Lvov.

They want to greet lovers with that lemon, night after night. They want to see the dark hunger, the preternatural need. They want to *be* that lemon, consumed by one survivor after the other.

That they can't explain this to anyone is part of their tragedy.

3.

The Holocaust Girls want to haunt people, from far away, from another childhood. They want everyone to know they have unreachable souls. They want people to understand that their beings can't be easily grasped or understood, the way it's hard to make the link between the half-century-old photo of prisoners in a bunk, the face of young Elie Wiesel circled, and the glossy photo of the now–Nobel Laureate. It's hard to make the cognitive leap from the one stick among other sticks to the American man in a suit, wearing matching socks, silk or otherwise tie, shoes with names, perhaps (wing tips, oxfords), his hair cut professionally—in short, civilized. In short, named.

4.

Whenever the Holocaust Girls have a task to do, when they're standing in the 15-items-or-fewer line at the supermarket, and the other customers are looking at *People* or turning the pages of the *Weekly World News*, the Girls are looking deep into the darkness of Liz Taylor's newsprint eyes, they're imagining roll call, when prisoners in the camps lined up— 15 degrees, wooden clogs, thin filthy clothing, empty stomachs—standing hour upon hour. They're wondering if they would have collapsed. They're wondering if they would have formed alliances with strangers with similarly shaven heads, if anyone would have loved them hard enough or loved life fiercely enough to have saved them crusts of bread and slipped them filched potatoes. "Do you have a preferred card?" asks the young cashier at the Jewel, and the person in front of the Holocaust Girl hands over her card. The Girl waits, sighing, while the cashier summons an older employee to ring up the six-pack of beer. The Girl always finds it odd that teenagers aren't allowed to push the register buttons for liquor, but the Girl feels strangely reassured in the shelter of letter-of-the-law rules. A few minutes later she's trudging down the street, one plastic bag dangling from each arm, on her way home. Home, home, says the Holocaust Girl under her breath. She knows how lucky she is to have always had a home, keys, heat. She looks at her wooden floors and doesn't allow herself to wish for a big rug, Oriental, magenta with a golden mandala-like design, flamboyantly fringed, deep pile. *Comfort*, it would sing to her, *comfort*.

Interview with S. L. Wisenberg

BECKY BRADWAY: Sandi, can you talk about the specific challenges of writing a short, compressed piece such as this one?

S. L. WISENBERG: I think I naturally write compressed. This piece began as part of a novel that has been in progress for a very long time. Then I decided to add other pieces that seemed to fit.

BB: Regarding point of view: In this piece, you shift from "you" and "they" and the label "Holocaust Girl." Although each implies something distinct, they also seem to be variations on using the personal "I." (They imply the "I," even if they are not "I.") What did each of these usages mean to you? Why and how did you decide to write the piece in this way?

SLW: I think I was trying to keep some distance, to universalize the experience, also to speak to the reader. So the "you" is both an address to the reader and to myself.

BB: Do you consider this to be a lyric essay? If not, how would you categorize it (if you had to)?

SLW: I would say lyric or researched essay.

BB: Can you talk about the process of doing the research for *Holocaust Girls*?

SLW: It was in pieces. I happened to think of the *Wizard of Oz* song while I was walking down the dark sidewalks of Lake Forest, Illinois, during a residency at Ragdale. It just came to me. Then I researched to find out the exact name of the song. I'd read a book called "In the Sewers of Lvov: A Heroic Story of Survival from the Holocaust" by Robert Marshall, and the scene of them emerging stuck with me. I'd also read "Memoirs of a Warsaw Ghetto Fighter" by Kazik (Simha Rotem), and the image of him in the sewers stuck with me also. So I keep things in my head and then bring them out when I need them in my work.

BB: You hold degrees in both journalism and creative writing. What do you see as the benefits and drawbacks of each path of study, particularly as this applies to the writing of creative nonfiction?

SLW: Journalism forces you out into the world. I never would have understood zoning or property taxes without being a journalist. By that I mean I learned in my twenties how the world works, the material, nonacademic world. I'm also not a very friendly person, and journalism forced me to talk to people. Other people with a gift of gab wouldn't need the excuse of an interview to talk to people. Journalism also forces you out of yourself. (I realize I've used the word "force" three times. I think this proves that journalism has always been hard for me.) The problem with studying journalism is that you are learning a formula. You are learning to write clearly and concisely. You are not encouraged to develop your own voice. I did learn about voice, though, when I was at the *Miami Herald*. I also learned about structure. In journalism school I learned that you could get any information quickly, and that you have to understand something in order to explain it. That belief has helped me. I've interviewed people for my creative nonfiction. I might be more adept at research than I would have been had I not studied journalism. And I'm less intimidated; I was taught you could master a subject quickly, and so I believed I could.

I have an MFA in fiction writing. I hadn't heard of creative nonfiction when I was applying to grad schools in fall 1980. When I got to Iowa, I learned there was an MA in creative nonfiction (it may have been called something else; it's since become an MFA) down the hall. I learned a few terms from a friend who was in that program. My sense was that the people in that program were learning about writing more methodically than we were in the fiction workshops. Our learning was more laissez-faire. We took workshops and forms classes, though the forms classes were very loose. They were in actuality discussions of Professor X's favorite books. It's taken me a long time to learn about structure and other technical aspects of creative writing. Mostly I go by feel and ear. I've learned a lot about form from teaching.

Karen Tei Yamashita

June: Circle K Recipes

Karen Tei Yamashita is a Japanese American writer from California. She was a student at Carleton College in Minnesota, and spent junior high in Japan as an exchange student. She then lived for nine years in Brazil, where she met her husband. This location is the setting for her first two novels, *Through the Arc of the Rain Forest*, published in 1990 and awarded the American Book Award and the Janet Heidinger Kafka Award, and *Brazil-Maru*, named by the *Village Voice* as one of the twenty-five best books of 1992. Yamashita also received a Rockefeller Playwright-in-Residence Fellowship at East West Players in Los Angeles for her play *Omen: An American Kabuki*. Her third novel, *Tropic of Orange,* is set in Los Angeles. Published in 1997, it was a finalist for the Paterson Fiction Prize. A fourth book, *Circle K Cycles*, is based on her research of the Brazilian community in Japan and was published in 2001 by Coffee House Press. She is an associate professor of literature and creative writing at the University of California, Santa Cruz.

In *Asian Week*, Roy Osamu Kamada wrote of *Circle K Cycles*: "Karen Tei Yamashita blurs the boundaries of genre, ethnicity, and national identity. . . . Taking license with form as well as content, Yamashita's new book mixes text with visual collage, essay with story, and explores the evolution of the transnational, postcolonial, migrant global Asian. She represents the Pacific Rim in the 21st century: imagined and caught in a continuous mobius strip of transformation and perpetually subjected to the transnational forces of global capitalism. The characters in her stories and essays are the children of the Japanese diaspora come home to be confronted by economic and cultural displacements that force them to question who they are and where they come from."

We have included Yamashita's representation for the month of June, from *Circle K Cycles*.

Interview with Karen Tei Yamashita, p. 785.

GOHAN

Wash rice until the water runs clear. For each cup of rice, add a cup of water. Place in rice cooker, and push the button.

ARROZ

Rinse rice and drain. Sauté chopped garlic, onion, and salt in oil. Add rice and sauté. Add water. For each cup of rice, add about 2 cups of water. Bring to a boil. Lower heat and cover until tender. (If you live in Japan, dump the sautéed rice into the rice cooker, add water, and push the button.)

One day, at a restaurant that specializes in tofu, I heard the people at the next table ordering *raisu*. "*Raisu, hitotsu*."[1] I thought I had misunderstood, but after I could read the katakana on menus, I got it. That you can order rice at a Japanese restaurant seems obvious, but that it's called "rice" is one of those things in Japan that has a reason you can only guess. My guess is that the word *kome* means rice, the grain; and the word *gohan* also means rice, but refers to food generally as well. There's no word for just an extra bowl of rice. So, *raisu*. But, in the old days, if you were eating food (*gohan*), you were eating rice (*gohan*).

My grandfather came from the small village of Naegi, which has been incorporated into the larger city of Nakatsugawa, in Gifu Prefecture. His family apparently owned enough land to parcel a portion out to tenants who paid in rice. In those days, rice was legal tender. A large storehouse used to stand where the family turned that rice into sake. My father once speculated that the fall of his family may have come about from *drinking* that legal tender. Recently, the family who now owns and farms the land in Naegi sent us a large sack of rice produced on that very land, *Naegi no okome*. I washed and cooked several cups of it very carefully, and we all ate it, trying to taste each grain. It was an odd little ritual, like eating your ancestors. Or eating legal tender.

I was born in the year of the rabbit. On evenings with a full moon, I look up to find the outline of a rabbit pounding rice into the giant omochi that is, they say, the moon. When I was a child, my grandmother stuck a few grains of rice to the lobes of my ears. I always thought my ears were too big, but she said they were good luck; if you can stick rice to your lobes, you'll be rich. *Kanemochi*.[2] The sticky rice knows. Legal tender here.

In Japan, rice must be sticky and polished white. One eats the purity of it. It doesn't matter if its nutrition is negligible. You can rarely find any other sort of rice, or grain for that matter. No brown rice. No barley. No cracked wheat. No cornmeal. No long grain. A Brazilian woman explained the difference between the short and long grains: "Japanese rice: *Juntos venceremos!* / Together we will succeed! Brazilian rice: *Sozinho, consigo!* / I can do it myself!"

And heaven forbid that the Japanese should eat the long-grain rice of Thailand.

Everyone can tell you how Thai rice was introduced into the Japanese market only to be given a bad rep and thrown away by the tons. They complained: It had a funny smell. Someone found a piece of insect in it. It wasn't sticky. It was cheap. It was just a food staple from a poor country. In that sense, it wasn't rice. It wasn't legal tender. Who's eating it now? Probably the Brazilians.

✳ ✳ ✳

[1] one bowl of rice [All notes are the author's]

[2] to have money

It's the rainy season in Japan. Water fills the rice paddies across the country-side. Houses, mini-marts, and factories encroach upon the planted land, replacing the fields gradually, but nothing yet replaces the reign of rice. It's rare in some parts of the country to see gardens of vegetables or fruits. And rarer still are corn, beans, cover crops, or other grains. From the looks of the supermarket offerings, variety and quantity are sacrificed for an almost cloned perfection in the produce. For example, every eggplant looks like every other eggplant. The same goes for cucumbers, tomatoes, onions, potatoes, apples, oranges, melons, etc. Someone produced the incredible statistic that Japan throws away imperfect vegetables and fruits in quantities that equal the weight of the total production of rice each year. You pay for this statistic:

> "Although food (gohan) is rice (gohan), obviously rice is not really food."

```
1 tomato = $1.00
1 apple = $1.00
1 head of lettuce = $2.00
¼ head of nappa cabbage = $1.50
20 lbs rice = $40.00
```

Although food (gohan) is rice (gohan), obviously rice is not really food. Certainly it is also sake, nuka, roof thatching, paper, glue, starch, matting, and, in the past, foot gear and raincoats. But beyond these by-products, its production, its purity, its mythic qualities, its value, define every other thing called food. Everything is measured against it. Legal tender. The stubbornness of rice. The persistence of rice. The gold standard was abolished years ago, but not the rice standard.

MISO-SHIRU

Bring a pot of water with dashi to boil. Add a scoop of miso paste, and chopped vegetables, seaweed, mushrooms, or tofu.

FEIJÃO

Separate the beans from any pebbles or insects. Wash and soak. Cook in pressure cooker until tender. In a separate pan, sauté onions, garlic, and salt in oil or fat. Smash a cup of the cooked beans into this mixture to make a thickening paste; then stir everything back into the cooked beans. Salt and pepper to taste.

Rice and beans. Arroz e feijão, Inseparable. For Brazilians, the only food that sustains. When the early Japanese immigrants to Brazil arrived on coffee plantations in the twenties, they received a ration of rice, beans, salt, coffee, and sugar. Sugar has always been plentiful in Brazil, and in those days the Japanese knew only to add it to the beans. After several weeks of the sweet stuff, the salty fare must have been a pleasant surprise. In any case, rice and beans became an accepted staple, the food that defines the people, the daily blessing, a *comida sagrada*. If *gohan* (and probably miso soup) is food to Japanese, *arroz e feijão* is gohan to Brazilians.

Thanks to this cultivation of the Brazilian palate, the first commercial ventures among Brazilians in Japan have been related to the making and sale of Brazilian food. What is it that the food of your homeland, of your mother's kitchen, will provide you? Why do we crave it so badly? Why do our tongues pull us home? Was mom's cooking really that good? When Japanese immigrants got to Brazil, they spent much of their years laboring to make vegetables, tofu, miso, and *shoyu*. Now, the *dekasegi* in Japan finance a lucrative network of imports from Brazil, New Zealand, Australia, and the Philippines to eat the stuff that pleases the literal mother tongue: *mandioca, Sonho de Valsa, Guaraná, pão de queijo, linguiça, goiabada, fubá, suco de maracujá.*

In the center of every enclave of Brazilian life in Japan, you find food. Sometimes it is a restaurant; sometimes a cantina and grocery store, or a karaoke bar. Sometimes it is a truck stocked with Brazilian goods making designated stops at the lodgings of factory workers in remote towns. Often it is the *obento/marmita* lady, the woman who delivers box lunches and dinners to factory workers.

The *obento* lady brings a box lunch with the always dependable *arroz e feijão*, a piece of meat, and a side of vegetables. The young Brazilian men say that the Japanese lunches don't "sustain." Rice and pickles don't cut it. They need food that sticks to their ribs. Some don't care for fish. In the first months of their arrival, they all lose weight quickly. The *obento* lady also brings news, gossip, and motherly advice. Often she's a walking social service; she'll give you information about health insurance, your visa, your driver's license. She's been here a while, started her own business, knows the ropes. Her cellphone rings constantly as she delivers her food. "Carlos, listen, you perforated your lungs once already. Forget the overtime for a while. Give it a rest. Do you hear me?" "Luís? I heard you moved to Toyota. Of course there's a friend of mine over there who makes obento. Do you want her telephone number?"

Arroz e feijão, the daily blessing, the tie that binds. Not just food—a social construct.

YAKI-NIKU

Arrange thin slices of filet mignon on a plate with a variety of cut vegetables, tofu, and mushroom. Cook at the table on a hot plate with a little oil. Serve with rice, beer, and sake.

BIFE À MILANESA

Pound slices of beef flat. Dip them in egg and bread crumbs and fry. Serve with rice and beans.

About seven years ago, a small butcher shop in the town of Yoro in Gifu put out a flyer offering imported meat from Australia at extraordinarily cheap prices. The flyer attracted several Brazilians who came to buy the meat and who also returned on the following Sunday, despite the fact that the offer was for one week only. The Brazilians peered past the counter and asked about some pieces of meat on the block. This was meat cut away from the fine rib eye or perhaps from the filet that Japanese customers expected to buy, but the Brazilians offered to take this unwanted meat. Every weekend, the Brazilians returned for more meat, for the side cuts and the tougher meats. Finally, the owner found herself too busy to handle these Brazilians and invited them into the shop to cut away the pieces they wanted: *picanha, coxão duro, coxão mole, ponta de agulha.*

In time, Brazilians came by the busloads, set up barbecue pits in the empty lot on the side of the shop, roasted meat, played music, sang, and danced. The owners covered the empty lot when it became cold and rainy, and the churrasco and the music continued. They gave up trying to sell fancy cuts of fine Hida and Kobe beef at 200 yen /$2.00 per 100 grams, and transformed the business to provide imported Australian meat cheaply for a more voracious clientele, for Brazilians whose families can be counted on to each buy as much as 10 kilos of meat—beef, chicken, pork, bacon, ham, and sausages—per week. Brazilian grocery items were added to the shop. The empty lot turned into a *churrascaria* restaurant complete with live music and karaoke. Finally it sponsored a soccer team and turned completely Brazilian. Now there are four other such shops in four other cities in Japan, and they also do a mail-order business, shipping meat directly to the homes of individuals in places as far away as Okinawa and Hokkaido. To fill all these orders, 100 tons of meat are shipped from Australia every month.

As for the owners, the husband is Japanese; the wife is Korean. It's one of those Creole situations: Korean Japanese buying Australian meat and selling it in Japan to Brazilians.

GYOZA

Fill gyoza wrappers with a mixture of ground pork and chopped vegetables. Arrange them on a pan, frying them all on one side in a small amount of oil. When browned, spill about a $\frac{1}{4}$ cup of water into the pan, lower heat, cover, and cook until tender.

PASTEL

Fill pastel wrappers with cheese, hearts of palm, tomatoes, or ground beef. Fry until crisp and golden.

I learned from my grandmother that after rice, everything else is *okazu*. At her house, lunch was always a bowl of rice and every jar of *tsukemono* (pickled vegetables), fermented beans, pickled fish, and salted squid she could bring out of the refrigerator. I imagine *okazu* is an old term, not used much in Japan today. The Hawaiians still use it; in Hilo, I tried a sushi they call *okazu-maki*. The Brazilians have a similar term: *mistura*. Everything after rice and beans is *mistura*. *Gyoza* is *okazu*. Pastel is *mistura*.

I don't know if anyone has ever done a study of the origins of the pastel in Brazil. I assume the Chinese brought fried wonton to Brazil and adapted it to Brazilian tastes. But it was the Japanese immigrants who became attached to its production, frying it behind stands at the *feiras,* or open marketplaces. In Brazil, fried wonton became much larger in size. Instead of a pork filling, there is cheese, hearts of palm, tomatoes, or ground beef. The dough is thicker; the secret in the recipe they say is pinga, that most potent of cane brandies. Now pastel is back in Asia, but it is back as *pastel.* It is not Chinese or Korean or even Japanese; it is Brazilian.

***

We recently visited the very traditional village of Shirakawa, where all the houses are 200 years old and have thatch roofs. Also special to this area is the mountain cooking, which includes fern sprouts, bamboo shoots, and mushrooms gathered from the mountainside. Curious, we visited a factory that packages these mountain veggies because we had heard that a Brazilian family worked there. As it turns out, all the materials for this local specialty are imported from China and Russia, and have been for the last twelve years. To use the local produce would be far too expensive. So there you have it: unknown to thousands of tourists who pass this way, the packages of mountain vegetables bought as *omiyage*[3] come from China and Russia and are made and packaged by Brazilians.

***

An Okinawan nutritionist in Yokohama opened a Brazilian restaurant because she noticed that the young Brazilians coming to work in Japan were all losing weight, all seemed to have difficulty eating Japanese food. She wondered about this and went to Brazil to learn to cook Brazilian dishes. Also, a Brazilian cook came to Japan to study Japanese cuisine, and now she is the chef at a Brazilian restaurant in Nagoya whose fine food attracts a clientele both Japanese and Brazilian. A Nikkei whose family traveled from Okinawa to Bolivia to Brazil to Yokohama recently opened her kitchen in Kawasaki, offering both Okinawan and Brazilian dishes. Everybody is making *okazu.* Everybody is making *mistura.*

CHAWANMUSHI

Beat eggs and a clear dashi soup together. Place pieces of chicken, gingko nuts, bamboo shoots, mushroom, and fish cake in ceramic cups. Pour egg-soup mixture on top. Steam over boiling water until set. Serve hot in cups.

PUDIM

Beat eggs, sweetened condensed milk, and cream in blender. Pour into a pan lined with sugar caramelized with cinnamon and cloves. Steam over boiling water until set. When cool, turn the pudim over onto a plate to serve.

[3]a gift, souvenir

Lately I have been using the *chawanmushi* cups to make Brazilian *pudim*. The last time I made pastel, I tried it with cheese and *omochi*. Using omochi in this way reminded me that some California company makes pizza *omochi*, garlic-cheese *omochi*, and raisin-cinnamon *omochi*. Another company specializes in jalapeño and smoked tofu. The other day we received a fancy box of chocolate-covered rice crackers. In Japan, McDonald's has a teriyaki-chicken burger, the pizzas all have corn on them, and curry rice comes with pickled ginger. A Hawaiian outfit sells popcorn mix that adds furikake[4] and rice crackers with the butter to the final product. I heard some Brazilian women have used the rice cooker to bake cakes. Nothing is sacred. Your tradition is someone else's originality. It's a big taste adventure. And then again, "*Raisu, hitotsu.*" *Gochisosamadeshita.*[5]

Interview with Karen Tei Yamashita

BECKY BRADWAY: The use of recipes works so nicely in your piece—they mark new sections, give us some useful information, and just look rather pretty in the Coffee House Press edition. At what point in the process of writing did you decide to use the recipes? Did you have any input in the way your book is designed?

KAREN TEI YAMASHITA: The creation of this piece was probably organic, matching experience to food and customs, comparing preparation, and thinking about how food travels as ingredient and dish. Perhaps the recipes serve as epigrams or food poems, open a path to the narrative that follows. While I provided the text and suggested some textual logistics, the book was designed by Linda Koutsky who created the look of the book. I sent her two large boxes, one of my personal photo albums and another filled with gathered research materials including maps, magazines, newspapers, pamphlets. Linda scanned and chose the images and their placement in the book. We did a bit of back and forth over the phone and via mail to make very slight adjustments. I think Linda, Coffee House Press, and I are very excited and pleased with the final result.

BB: This piece really seems a celebration of the blending of cultures. Do you see this blending of cultures and foods, and especially the movement of global foods into the commercial sphere, as entirely a good thing? Do you ever fear that the original culture will lose its distinctiveness, or will we always be able to carry the old home with us?

KTY: When people travel with their memories and sometimes only the seeds of the foods from their homelands, the food reproduced in a new home may never be exactly the same. This is true of everything we try to replant in a new place: shelters, language, rituals, family.

[4] a rice seasoning with seaweed flakes, sesame seeds, shaved bonito, etc.
[5] literally, I have received a feast. Spoken at the close of a meal to thank the host

We are always rearranging or re-creating our homes. As for food that travels as does a tourist or a wanderer to a new place, it will change simply because it is a stranger in a different context. The same food eaten with chopsticks or the fingers or metal utensils is not exactly the same food. This sort of traveling food is different perhaps from the invasive consumer globalization of Starbucks, Coca-Cola, or McDonald's. Still a cola taste connoisseur will tell you that that brown soda water has a different taste in different locations, and, as I say, in Japan, McDonald's offers a teriyaki burger.

BB: I loved the way that your piece looked closely at particular words, studying their various meaning and evolutions, integrating words from Brazil, Japan, and North America. How did you become so focused on individual words? How and when did you fall in love with the single word? Did you ever study linguistics or languages? To what extent did your awareness of language emerge from your multicultural background?

KTY: In this particular piece on food, I'm probably just trying to decipher the menus or the recipes, but perhaps you are referring to the essay on *saudades,* a word Brazilians say cannot be translated. I suppose I would be fascinated with other untranslatable words that require a longer narration to impart understanding to others. While you go digging around for the etymology of any word, you find a history and a past and a traveling, and I guess it's the same for food.

Acknowledgments

Steve Almond, from *Candyfreak*. © Steve Almond.

Margaret Atwood, "A Path Taken, with All the Certainty of Youth." © 2002 by The New York Times Co. Reprinted with permission.

Tara Bahrampour, "Persia on the Pacific." Copyright © Tara Bahrampour.

Kim Barnes, "The Ashes of August." All rights: Kim Barnes. "The Ashes of August" has previously appeared in the following publications: *The Georgia Review* (Summer 2000); *A Year in Place*, eds. W. Scott Olsen and Brett Lott (University of Utah, 2001); *Forged in Fire*: *Essays by Idaho Writers*, eds. Mary Clearman Blew and Phil Durker (University of Oklahoma, 2005).

Gabrielle Bell, from *Lucky*. Copyright © Gabrielle Bell.

Sven Birkerts, "Reflections of a Nonpolitical Man; or, Why I Can't in Good Conscience Write about Noam Chomsky." © Sven Birkerts.

Chester Brown, from *Louis Riel*. © Chester Brown, 2003.

Wanda Coleman, "The Evil Eye." From *Native in a Strange Land*: *Trials & Tremors*, copyright © 1996 by Wanda Coleman.

Frank Conroy, "A Yo-Yo Going Down, a Mad Squirrel Coming Up." Reprinted by permission of Donadio & Olson, Inc. Copyright 1967 by Frank Conroy.

Dennis Covington, from *Salvation on Sand Mountain*. Reprinted by permission of Da Capo Press, a member of Perseus Books Group.

Guy Delisle, from *Pyongyang*. Permission granted by Guy Delisle and L'Association (publisher).

Annie Dillard, "Total Eclipse." Pages 1–18 from *Teaching a Stone to Talk*: *Expeditions and Encounters* by Annie Dillard. Copyright © 1982 by Annie Dillard. Reprinted by permission of HarperCollins Publishers.

Debbie Drechsler, "The Dead of Winter." © Debbie Drechsler.

David James Duncan, "What Fundamentalists Need for Their Salvation." © 2006 by David James Duncan.

Gerald Early, "'I Only Like It Better When the Pain Comes': More Notes toward a Cultural Definition of Prizefighting." Used by permission.

Cynthia Ozick, "What Helen Keller Saw." From *The Din in the Head: Essays* by Cynthia Ozick. Reprinted by permission of the Houghton Mifflin Company. All rights reserved.

Gary Panter, "Nightmare Studio." © 2006 by Gary Panter.

Leila Philip, "Green Tea." *The Road Through Miyama* (Random House: 1989; Vintage: 1991, 1992). Copyright © Leila Stott Philip.

Jonathan Rauch, "Caring for Your Introvert." Copyright © 2003 by Jonathan Rauch. First published in *The Atlantic*, March 2003.

Joe Sacco, from *Palestine*. © Joe Sacco.

Leslie Marmon Silko, "Uncle Tony's Goat." Copyright © 1981 by Leslie Marmon Silko. Reprinted from *Storyteller* by Leslie Marmon Silko, published by Seaver Books, New York, New York.

Sharon Solwitz, "Abracadabra." © Sharon Solwitz.

Rory Stewart, "The Missionary Dance." From *The Places in Between*, copyright © 2004 by Rory Stewart, illustrations copyright © 2006 by Rory Stewart. Reproduced by permission of Harcourt, Inc.

Sheryl St. Germain, "*Nigger*: Notes from a New Orleans Daughter." © Sheryl St. Germain.

Craig Thompson, from *Blankets*. Reprinted with permission from Craig Thompson.

Touré, "What's Inside You, Brother?" © 2006 by Touré.

C. Tyler, "Sub Zero." © Carol Tyler.

Luis Alberto Urrea, from *Across the Wire*. Used by permission.

David Foster Wallace, "Consider the Lobster." From *Consider the Lobster* by David Foster Wallace. Copyright © 2005 by David Foster Wallace. By permission of Little, Brown and Co.

S. L. Wisenberg, "Holocaust Girls/Lemon." Reprinted from *Holocaust Girls: History, Memory, and Other Obsessions* by S. L. Wisenberg by permission of the University of Nebraska Press. © 2002 by the University of Nebraska Press.

Karen Tei Yamashita, "June: Circle K Recipes." From *Circle K Cycles*. Copyright © 2001 by Karen Tei Yamashita. Reprinted with the permission of Coffee House Press, Minneapolis, Minnesota, www.coffeehousepress.org.

Photo Credits

Page 157: © Stephen Sette-Ducati/Courtesy Steve Almond. 171: © Jennifer Graylock/AP Images. 174: © Karen Bahrampour/Courtesy Tara Bahrampour. 188: © Scott M. Barrie/Courtesy Brick House Literary Agents. 206: © Gabrielle Bell/Courtesy Drawn and Quarterly. 217: © Richard Howard/Courtesy Graywolf Press. 224: © Sam Javanrouh. 236: © Sophie Bassouls/Corbis. 241: © Charlie Niebergall/AP Images. 257: © Dave Martin/AP Images. 272: © Guy Delisle/Courtesy Drawn and Quarterly. 283: © Phyllis Rose/Courtesy HarperCollins. 295: Courtesy Debbie Drechsler. 303: © Rachel Cudmore/Courtesy David James Duncan. 320: Courtesy The Center for Humanities, Washington University in St. Louis. 342: © Christopher Felver/Corbis. 368: Courtesy HarperCollins. 379: © Bettina Strauss. 398: © Deborah Lopez. 403: © Stephen Gonzales/Courtesy Laurence Gonzales. 428: Courtesy Emily Hiestand. 442: © Steven E. Frischling/Corbis. 451: © Marion Ettlinger. 463: Courtesy Jennifer Kahn. 471: © Steven L. Hopp.

Index